**AAMC**

# MSAR® Online Access

Begin accessing comprehensive U.S. and
Canadian medical school and BS/MD profiles today!

Go to *www.aamc.org/msar* and click on
"Enter your Access Code", then follow the steps
to create your AAMC username and password.

---

**Your MSAR® Access Code**

# Hq3WqMfAeF

*Please note: your access code is case-sensitive.*

---

**Terms and Conditions for MSAR® Web Site Access**
Purchase of the MSAR® Guidebook entitles the purchaser to one year of
unlimited use from the date of activation for individual use. Access codes
are single use and cannot be re-activated or transferred to additional users.
Any access code not activated prior to April 1, 2012 or the publication of
the next edition of the MSAR® Guidebook, whichever occurs first, is subject
to expiration. Use of the MSAR® web site is subject to the Site Terms and
Conditions (see *www.aamc.org/msar* for details).

As a reminder, this means:
- you may not share your MSAR® site account access with anyone;

- you may not copy or share any text, data or passage of the MSAR site
  with anyone else; and

- you may not sell or distribute, in print or electronic form, any text,
  data or content from the MSAR® web site.

For Access Code questions, contact *memberservice@aamc.org*.

Association of
American Medical Colleges

# Timeline for Application/Admission

This should be considered a general guide for applicants. It is important that an applicant considering medical school consult with his or her pre-health advisor to devise a schedule that works for him or her.

**COLLEGE YEAR 1**

Fall semester
- Meet pre-health advisor and investigate pre-health advisory program
- As applicable, ensure that pre-health advisor receives course directors' evaluations
- Successfully complete first-semester required premedical coursework and other degree requirements

Spring semester
- Visit "Considering a Career in Medicine" Web site at *www.aamc.org/students*
- Identify summer employment/volunteer medically related opportunities
- Successfully complete second-semester required premedical coursework and other degree requirements
- Ensure that pre-health advisor receives course directors' evaluations

**SUMMER 1**
- Complete summer employment/volunteer medically related experience
- Attend summer school, if desired or necessary

**COLLEGE YEAR 2**

Fall semester
- Check in with pre-health advisor and participate in pre-health activities
- Investigate available volunteer/paid medically related clinical or research activities
- Successfully complete first-semester required premedical coursework and other degree requirements
- Ensure that pre-health advisor receives course directors' evaluations

Spring semester
- Check in with pre-health advisor and participate in pre-health activities
- Participate in volunteer/paid medically related clinical or research activities
- Identify summer employment/volunteer medically related opportunities
- Successfully complete second-semester required premedical coursework and other degree requirements
- Ensure that pre-health advisor receives course directors' evaluations

**SUMMER 2**
- Complete summer employment/volunteer medically related experience
- Participate in a summer health careers program, if available
- Attend summer school, if desired or necessary

**COLLEGE YEAR 3**

Fall semester
- Check in with pre-health advisor and participate in pre-health activities
- Continue participation in volunteer/paid medically related activities
- Investigate:
  — Medical education options in MSAR® and *www.aamc.org/medicalschools*
  — Medical College Admission Test (MCAT®) Web site *www.aamc.org/mcat*
  — Information about the Medical College Admission Test (MCAT®) and American Medical College Application Service (AMCAS®) fee assistance on the AAMC Fee Assistance Program Web site *www.aamc.org/fap*, as appropriate
  — AAMC's "Applying to Medical School" Web site *www.aamc.org/students/applying/start.htm*
  — As applicable, information for students from groups underrepresented in medicine on the AAMC Minorities in Medicine Web site *www.aamc.org/students/minorities/start.htm*
- Begin preparation and register for desired MCAT® administration; visit MCAT® web site *www.aamc.org/mcat* for available test date options
- Successfully complete first-semester required premedical coursework and other degree requirements
- Ensure that pre-health advisor receives course directors' evaluations

*...continued on next page*

| | |
|---|---|
| **COLLEGE YEAR 3** (continued) | **Spring semester** |

**COLLEGE YEAR 3** (continued)

**Spring semester**
- Consult regularly with pre-health advisor regarding:
  — Schedule for completion of school-specific requirements for advisor/committee evaluation
  — Advice about medical education options
- Continue participation in volunteer/paid medically related activities
- Prepare for and take desired MCAT® administration; visit MCAT® web site *www.aamc.org/mcat* for available test date options
- Continue review of medical education options
- Take desired MCAT® administration. Registration opens for summer MCAT® administrations
- Investigate information about medical school application services:
  — the American Medical College Application Service (AMCAS®) on the AMCAS® Web site *www.aamc.org/amcas*
  — the Texas Medical and Dental Schools Application Service (TMDSAS) on the TMDSAS Web site *www.utsystem.edu/tmdsas/*
  — the Ontario Medical School Application Service (OMSAS) on the OMSAS Web site *www.ouac.on.ca/*
  — the American Association of Colleges of Osteopathic Medicine Application Service (AACOMAS) on the AACOMAS Web site *https://aacomas.aacom.org/*
- Investigate as applicable, the AAMC Curriculum Directory Web site *http://services.aamc.org/currdir* for information about medical school curricula and joint, dual, and combined-degree programs
- Successfully complete second-semester required premedical coursework and other degree requirements
- Ensure that pre-health advisor receives course directors' evaluations

**SUMMER 3**
- Participate in a summer health careers program, if available
- Complete AMCAS® application
- Take desired MCAT® administration
- Attend summer school, if desired or necessary
- Become familiar with:
  — AAMC Recommendations for Medical School Applicants document *www.aamc.org/students/applying/policies*
  — AAMC Recommendations for Medical School Admission Officers document *www.aamc.org/students/applying/policies*

**COLLEGE YEAR 4**

**Fall semester**
- Complete supplementary application materials for schools applied to
- Consult regularly with pre-health advisor regarding:
  — Completion of school-specific requirements for advisor/committee evaluation
  — Status of application/admission process at medical schools applied to
- Continue participation in volunteer/paid medically related activities
- Interview at medical schools
- Continue review of medical education options
- Investigate financial aid planning process
- Successfully complete first-semester elective science and non-science coursework and other degree requirements
- Ensure that pre-health advisor receives course directors' evaluations

**Spring semester**
- Make interim and final decisions about medical school choice
- Immediately notify medical schools which you will not be attending
- Ensure that all IRS forms are submitted as early as possible for financial aid consideration
- Successfully complete second-semester elective science and non-science coursework and other degree requirements
- Graduate

**SUMMER 4**
- Prepare for medical school enrollment: purchase books and equipment and make appropriate living arrangements
- Relax and prepare for medical school
- Attend orientation programs and matriculate at medical school

# Medical School Admission Requirements (MSAR®)

*The Most Authoritative Guide to U.S. and Canadian Medical Schools*

## *Featuring Newly Accredited Medical Schools*

Florida Atlantic University Charles E. Schmidt College of Medicine
Hofstra North Shore—LIJ School of Medicine at Hofstra University
Oakland University William Beaumont School of Medicine
Virginia Tech Carilion School of Medicine

Association of
American Medical Colleges

# Medical School Admission Requirements, 2012–2013, United States and Canada

**AAMC Staff**

*MSAR® Guide Program Staff*
**Tami Levin,**
Senior Web and Technology Specialist
Academic Affairs

**Kim Reed,**
Web and MSAR®Content Specialist
Academic Affairs

**Deborah Finkel,**
Senior Writer, Communications

**Douglas Ortiz,**
Director, Creative Services

*Content Specialist*
**Henry M. Sondheimer, M.D.,**
Senior Director,
Student Affairs and Programs
Academic Affairs

*Consultants*
**Kelly Begatto,**
Program Director, AMCAS
Mission Support

**Geoffrey Reddin,**
Database Specialist
Mission Support

**Gwen Garrison, Ph.D.,**
Director, Student and Applicant Studies
Mission Support

**Lily May Johnson,**
Manager, Constituent Diversity Services
Office of the Executive Vice President

**Jack Krakower, Ph.D.,**
Senior Director, Med School Financial and
Administrative Affairs
Mission Support

**Jodi Lubetsky, Ph.D.,**
Manager, Science Policy
Scientific Affairs

**David A. Matthew, Ph.D.,**
Senior Research Analyst,
Student and Applicant Studies
Mission Support

**H. Collins Mikesell,**
Senior Research Analyst,
Student and Applicant Studies
Mission Support

**Karen Mitchell,**
Senior Director,
Admissions Testing Services
Mission Support

**Nancy-Pat Weaver,**
Senior Education Debt Management
Specialist
Academic Affairs

**Shelley Yerman,**
Senior Specialist, Student Financial Aid
Academic Affairs

**To order additional copies of this publication, please contact:**

Association of American Medical Colleges
Publications Department
2450 N Street, NW
Washington, DC 20037
Phone: 202-828-0416
Fax: 202-828-1123
E-mail: *publications@aamc.org*
Web *site: www.aamc.org/publications*

Price: $25.00, plus shipping (single copy).
Includes access for 12 months to the
MSAR® website (www.aamc.org/msar).

978-1-57754-097-7

Printed in the United States of America
Revised annually; new edition available in
early spring.

## Group on Student Affairs (GSA) Steering Committee, 2010–2011

**Chair**
Maureen Garrity, Ph.D.
Associate Dean for Student Affairs
University of Colorado
School of Medicine

**Chair Elect**
Patricia A. Barrier, M.D., M.P.H.
Associate Dean for Student Affairs
Mayo Medical School

**Vice Chair**
W. Scott Schroth, M.D., M.P.H.
Associate Dean for Academic Affairs
George Washington University
School of Medicine and Health Sciences

**Immediate Past Chair**
Michael G. Kavan, Ph.D.
Associate Dean for Student Affairs
Creighton University
School of Medicine

**Previous Past Chair**
Molly Osborne, M.D., Ph.D
Associate Dean for Student Affairs
Oregon Health & Science University
School of Medicine

**Chair, Central Region**
Anita Pokorny, M.Ed.
Director, Career Development & Advising
Northeastern Ohio Universities
College of Medicine

**Chair, Southern Region**
Robert L. Hernandez
Senior Associate Dean for
Medical Student Administration
University of Miami
Leonard M. Miller School of Medicine

**Chair, Northeast Region**
Kathleen A. Reeves, M.D.
Associate Dean for Student Affairs
Temple University
School of Medicine

**Chair, Western Region**
Gabriel Garcia, M.D.
Associate Dean for Admissions
Stanford University
School of Medicine

**Chair, Committee on Admissions**
Steven Case, Ph.D., M.S.
Associate Dean for Admissions
University of Mississippi
School of Medicine

**Chair, Committee on Diversity Affairs**
Karen A. Lewis, M.D.
Assistant Vice President for Enrollment
Management Student Services
Meharry Medical College

**Chair, Committee on Student Affairs**
Marc J. Kahn, M.D., M.B.A
Senior Associate Dean for Admissions and
Student Affairs
Tulane University
School of Medicine

**Chair Committee on Student Financial Assistance**
Robert D. Coughlin
Director of Financial Aid
Harvard Medical School

**Chair, Committee on Student Records**
Chris Meiers, Ph.D.
Assistant Dean of Students Registrar
University of Kansas
School of Medicine

**Council of Deans Liaison**
Steven L. Berk, M.D.
Vice President for Medical Affairs and
Dean, School of Medicine
Texas Tech University Health Sciences Center
School of Medicine

**Chair-Elect, Organization of Student Representatives**
Joe Thomas
Student
University of Kentucky
College of Medicine

**National Association of Advisors for the Health Professions Liaison**
Lori Provost
Director of Health Professions
Muhlenberg College

## Association of American Medical Colleges

The Association of American Medical Colleges (AAMC) has as its purpose the advancement of medical education and the nation's health. In pursuing this purpose, the Association works with many national and international organizations, institutions, and individuals interested in strengthening the quality of medical education at all levels, searching for biomedical knowledge, and applying these tools to providing effective health care.

As an educational association representing members with similar purposes, the primary role of the AAMC is to assist those members by providing services at the national level that will facilitate the accomplishment of their missions. Such activities include collecting data and conducting studies on issues of major concern, evaluating the quality of educational programs through the accreditation process, providing consultation and technical assistance to institutions as needs are identified, synthesizing the opinions of an informed membership for consideration at the national level, and improving communication among those concerned with medical education and the nation's health. Other activities of the Association reflect the expressed concerns and priorities of the officers and governing bodies.

The Association of American Medical Colleges is a not-for-profit association representing all 134 accredited U.S. and 17 accredited Canadian medical schools; nearly 400 major teaching hospitals and health systems, including 68 Department of Veterans Affairs medical centers; and nearly 90 academic and scientific societies. Through these institutions and organizations, the AAMC represents 125,000 faculty members, 70,000 medical students, and 104,000 resident physicians.

In addition to the activities listed above, the AAMC is responsible for the Medical College Admission Test (MCAT®) and the American Medical College Application Service (AMCAS®) and provides detailed admissions information to the medical schools and to undergraduate premedical advisors.

## Important Notice

The information in this book is based on the most recent data provided by member medical schools prior to publication at the request of the Association of American Medical Colleges (AAMC).

This material has been edited and in some instances condensed to meet space limitations. In compiling this edition, the AAMC made every reasonable effort to assure the accuracy and timeliness of the information, and, except where noted, the information was updated as of January 2011. All information contained herein, however, especially figures on tuition and expenses, is subject to change and is non-binding for medical schools listed or the AAMC. All medical schools listed in this edition, as with other educational institutions, are also subject to federal and state laws prohibiting discrimination on the basis of race, color, religion, sex, age, handicap, or national origin. Such laws include Title VI of the Civil Rights Act of 1964, Title IX of the Education Amendments of 1972, Section 504 of the Rehabilitation Act of 1973, the Americans with Disabilities Act, and the Age Discrimination Act of 1975, as amended. For the most current and complete information regarding costs, official policies, procedures, and other matters, individual schools should be contacted.

In applying to U.S. or Canadian medical schools, applicants need not go through any commercial agencies. The AAMC does not endorse any organization or entity that purports to assist applicants to achieve admission to medical school other than undergraduate pre-medical advisors and medical school admissions officers.

All URLs in this book can be found at *www.aamc.org/msar.*

## AAMC Commitment to Diversity

Diversity within medical education and the physician workforce is essential to the health of the nation. The benefits of diversity in medicine will continue to increase as the nation ages, becomes more diverse along many dimensions, and experiences inequities in health care. The AAMC's commitment to diversity in medicine and biomedical research spans more than three decades and is demonstrated by ongoing leadership and engagement in activities that promote diversity through programs, advocacy, and research. This commitment has been reaffirmed in the publication Learn, Serve, Lead: The Mission, Vision, and Strategic Priorities of the AAMC, which states that the AAMC's mission is to serve and lead the academic medicine community to improve the health of all. To support its mission, AAMC's vision and that of its members is, in part, to establish "...a healthy nation and world in which... [t]he nation's medical students, biomedical graduate students, residents, fellows, faculty, and the health care workforce are diverse and culturally competent...." As a result, leading efforts to increase diversity in medicine is among the AAMC's nine strategic priorities.

To achieve this end, the AAMC works with its members to:

- advance diversity in academic medicine and biomedical research that fully embraces the diversity of the nation;

- generate and coordinate research, collect evidence, and disseminate studies pertinent to diversity in academic medicine and biomedical research;

- lead policy and advocacy efforts for diversity in academic medicine and biomedical research;

- direct pipeline programs and services across the education continuum to increase diversity in academic medicine and biomedical research;

- communicate the relationship of diversity in medicine and biomedical research to ameliorating disparities in health and health access outcomes; and

- supply resources and guidance to educators seeking to maximize the benefits of diversity across the medical education continuum.

# Contents

# List of Tables and Charts

## Chapter 14
## U.S. Medical Schools

# Chapter 15
# Canadian Medical Schools

Maybe it was the great feeling you had from volunteering, or the profound concern stirred by a family member's illness that made you first think seriously about becoming a doctor. Or, perhaps it was the thrill you experienced solving a complex research problem that inspired you to dream about finding the next "big cure." Whatever reason led you to consider a career in medicine, you have come to the right place: the Medical School Admissions Requirements (MSAR®).

Published annually by the AAMC (Association of American Medical Colleges)—the national association representing all 134 accredited U.S. and 17 accredited Canadian medical schools—the MSAR® is the only medical school application guide authorized by medical schools themselves. This comprehensive resource will tell you about each school's focus, mission, and curriculum, as well as its entrance requirements and selection factors. It also will explain how, increasingly, medical schools are taking a holistic approach to admissions decisions by evaluating candidates' experiences and personal attributes in addition to their academic credentials and metrics such as the MCAT®.

Here, you will find details about financial aid and costs, and see the degree of diversity represented by 2010–11 matriculants. And, in what I think is one of the MSAR's best features, you will see that diversity reflected in the number of accepted applicants at each school who took certain premed courses, performed community service, or worked in research or other medically related positions. In other words, you will read about students who, only a few years ago, went through the same decision-making process you are undertaking now.

We have made a special effort to further "demystify" the medical school application and acceptance process. For example, the book provides a more detailed description of the American Medical College Application Service® (which you will use to apply to medical school) and includes a new chapter on choosing the right school for you. We also have drawn from a wealth of data gathered by the AAMC and other sources to provide a more in-depth profile of today's medical students. Examples range from at what age these students decided to become a doctor, to the specialties they considered at the time of matriculation, to the ways they prepared for medical school.

Should you decide to apply to medical school, I think you will find it is an extraordinary time to be a doctor. You will be entering medicine at a time when the country needs your services most, given predicted physician shortages in coming years, and when national attention is focused like never before on the need to improve health care delivery. It is also a time when our profession is undergoing an exciting period of transformative change, with clinical care becoming increasingly patient-centered and team-based, biomedical research more technically sophisticated and collaborative, and medical education itself evolving into a continuum of lifelong learning.

Whatever career you decide to pursue, please accept my best wishes for success. And, if being a doctor is the path you choose, please know that the AAMC stands ready to help you. It would be a special pleasure for me if—during your education and training—our paths should cross and we have the opportunity to meet.

*Darrell G. Kirch*

Darrell G. Kirch, M.D.
President and CEO, Association of American Medical Colleges

Dear Medical School Applicant,

Congratulations on your decision to pursue a career in medicine! In so doing, you've committed yourself to a challenging and exciting profession. In becoming a physician, you will learn the skills necessary to become a healer, an advocate, a lifelong learner, and a leader in your community, as you work to improve the health and well-being of your patients.

The process of applying to medical school is daunting. Learning how to navigate this time-consuming, expensive, and difficult process can be extremely frustrating. To help demystify the process and guide you through the steps necessary to successfully complete the application process, the Association of American Medical Colleges (AAMC) has created this book to help you along the way. The Medical School Admission Requirements (MSAR®) guide will provide you with the most up-to-date information about U.S. and Canadian medical schools so that you can make a well-informed decision about how and where to pursue your medical studies.

Don't forget that there is no one path to becoming a physician. Medical schools around the country are interested in applicants with a diverse set of experiences and backgrounds. If your goal is to become a doctor, stay focused, become as informed as possible about the process, and stick with it. The rewards are great.

As Chair of the AAMC Organization of Student Representatives (OSR), and on behalf of the 75,000 medical students and 106,000 resident physicians, we look forward to welcoming you into the profession as a future colleague. It's an exciting time for the health care industry with promise of reform and innovation. We hope you will join us as we commit ourselves to learn, serve and lead, while working towards improving the health of all.

David Friedlander
Third Year Medical Student
Vanderbilt University School of Medicine
2010-2011 Chair, AAMC Organization of Student Representatives

# Chapter 1:

## So… You Want to Be a Doctor

*Maybe it was the day you won first place in your 7th grade science fair. Maybe it was the time your family physician made a lifesaving call during your little brother's illness. Maybe it was the summer you volunteered with a health care program in an underdeveloped country.*

*At some point, you just knew. You wanted to be a doctor.*

*But, as you also undoubtedly know, you now face a major step in the journey: getting into medical school. It involves everything from completing your undergraduate preparation to taking the MCAT® exam…from selecting appropriate schools to navigating the application process…from arranging for financing to performing well on the interview. Big challenges do indeed lie ahead.*

*But so too does the ultimate reward: a career in medicine.*

### An Exciting and Gratifying Career

It's something that many of you knew from an early age. In fact, a recent AAMC survey shows that almost half of all entering medical students had decided upon a medical career before they even set foot in undergraduate school—and one in five had made the decision before they even started high school.

And small wonder. Nowhere else can you find a career that offers as many opportunities to make a real difference in the lives of thousands of people.

You'll have job security, of course, knowing that your services will always be in demand. You'll earn an excellent living. You'll never experience the tedium of a nine-to-five desk job.

There's so much more than that, of course. As a doctor, you're likely to see new life come into the world, or provide comfort to those about to leave it. Or maybe you'll choose to help build the future of medicine by educating the next generation of physicians. Perhaps you'll dedicate yourself to discovering new cures for diseases that devastate millions of people and their families.

Whichever direction you follow, you will—either directly or indirectly—reduce or eliminate people's pain and suffering, improve their quality of life, and, in general, provide invaluable service to your local community or the country as a whole.

How many careers can even come close?

---

**When Did You Decide to Study Medicine?**

Most of you knew early on that you wanted to be a doctor. According to an AAMC survey, half of all entering medical students made their decision to study medicine before they even started college:

- 20% before high school
- 29% during high school or before college
- 24% during first two years of college
- 11% during junior year of college
- 4% during senior year of college
- 10% after receiving bachelor's degree
- 2% after receiving advanced degree

*Source: AAMC's 2010 Matriculating Student Questionnaire (MSQ)*

## Dozens of Options from Which to Choose

The fact that you have so many options is yet another benefit of a career in medicine. From clinical practice to biomedical research, from public health to medical education—the choices are almost limitless. Beyond that, you'll also enjoy the flexibility that a medical career provides. If your interests change with time and experience, medicine—because of its emphasis on lifelong learning—will provide you with ample opportunity to refine your skills and reorient your practice. A number of possible career options are listed below:

- The satisfaction of long-term patient relationships is one attraction of **family medicine or internal medicine**, where the bulk of time is spent in direct contact with patients. Physicians in this area—which comes under the umbrella term of "primary care"—often care for entire families and enjoy the challenge that comes from treating a diverse population with varied backgrounds and conditions.

- Other physicians may prefer to pursue detailed knowledge about the intricacies of a single organ or system, such as that required of **cardiologists, ophthalmologists, dermatologists, and endocrinologists**.

- Interested in **scientific exploration** and the desire to **break new ground in medical knowledge**? Physicians with these traits are found in the nation's private and public laboratories and research institutions.

- Those with a commitment to social justice and an interest in fulfilling the health care needs of the underserved and disadvantaged can meet those challenges in **urban and rural clinics, in public health, or as medical missionaries**.

- Careers in **general surgery** often suit those with a desire to see immediate results of their interventions. **Plastic and reconstructive surgery** draws others with artistic skills and aesthetic interests.

- Those interested in mind-body interactions and the emotional lives of their patients might find a home in **neurology or psychiatry**.

- The fast pace of medicine draw some to work as **emergency physicians or trauma surgeons**.

- Others motivated in the interest of national defense may use their skills as **flight surgeons or in military medicine**.

- The **economic and public policy aspects of health care** guide some physicians to think-tanks and health-related organizations, as well as to serve in the legislative and executive branches of government.

- For those fascinated by the issues facing groups of patients with age-defined illnesses and problems—from the risks of infancy and early childhood to the challenges of older life—fulfillment can come in careers as **pediatricians and geriatricians**.

- Assisting patients in overcoming complex fertility and gestational problems is the hallmark of the specialists in **reproductive endocrinology and obstetrics and gynecology**.

- Those dedicated to reducing the incidence of birth defects and inherited diseases might find their calling in the field of **medical genetics**.

- The detection, prevention, and eradication of injury and disease draw people to the fields of **preventive medicine and epidemiology**.

Clearly, the possibilities in medicine are almost endless. No matter what your personal interests, skills, or needs may be, medicine encourages you to find your niche.

## How to Decide Which Path Is "Best"

Which path is right for you? With the ever-changing world of medicine and a myriad of options and practice settings, figuring out where you belong as a physician can be one of the hardest decisions of your career.

Fortunately, you won't have to make this determination alone.

That's because medical schools realize how daunting this decision can be—and the critical role they play in helping you make it. They therefore have a program in place to help you assess your personal values and interests, identify specialty options, determine personal "fit," and make a well-informed choice about your career path. This program, called Careers in Medicine® (CiM) was developed by the Association of American Medical Colleges (AAMC) in collaboration with its 134 member medical schools, consists of four phases (described on next page) to guide you through the decision-making process.

The Careers in Medicine program is completely free of charge to students attending AAMC-member medical schools. For more information, go to *www.aamc.com/careersinmedicine*.

## What About the Future?

As long as we're looking ahead, let's look way ahead. Five years. Ten years. Fifteen years. What will medicine look like then?

### Career Intentions: Academic v. Clinical?

A relatively small—but not insignificant—percentage of matriculants plan to work in academia, and a larger percentage are undecided. Students' career intentions at the time they enter medical school are shown below.

| | |
|---|---|
| **Full-time academic faculty** (teaching and research) | **10.3%** |
| **Full-time clinical practice** | **60.4%** |
| **Other** | **8.5%** |
| **Undecided** | **20.8%** |

Source: AAMC's 2010 Matriculating Student Questionnaire (MSQ)

### Specialties Entering Students Are Considering

Entering medical students have a definite preference for the medical practice areas they plan to enter after graduation. The following list shows the percent of students who are considering the specialties listed below.

| Specialty | Percent |
|---|---|
| Internal Medicine | 17.7 |
| Pediatrics | 13.7 |
| Orthopedic Surgery | 8.7 |
| Emergency Medicine | 8.5 |
| Family practice | 7.9 |
| Obstetrics and Gynecology | 4.9 |
| Neurology | 4.4 |
| Radiology | 3.3 |
| Dermatology | 3.0 |
| Anesthesiology | 3.0 |
| Ophthalmology | 2.5 |

Source: AAMC's 2010 Matriculating Student Questionnaire (MSQ)

### Recent Advances and Future Trends

One thing is for certain. This is not your father's (or mother's*) medical career. Take a look back just a single generation, and you'll discover an abundance of fields that weren't even in the embryonic stage 25 years ago.

- An obvious example made its entrance in the early 1980s. Back then, a new—and fatal—illness was taking hold that nobody could identify. Now, though, it has a well-known name—**AIDS**—and infectious disease is currently a large medical subspecialty. As a result, significant advances have been made in extending the lives of those infected with **HIV**.

- Other advances are more recent. **Minimally invasive** surgery, in which surgeons carry out precise procedures with the assistance of a robot, is becoming increasingly more popular. It is currently used for a variety of surgeries, including those involving the lungs, esophagus, prostate, uterus, and kidneys. Through robotic-assisted surgery, patients are likely to benefit from smaller incisions, lower risk of complications, shorter hospital stays, less pain, and a speedier recovery.

---

* In the 1976–77 academic year, women comprised just 24.7 percent of all medical school matriculants. Compare that to 2009–10, the latest year for which data are available, in which they made up almost half—or 47.9 percent—of the entering class. Source: AAMC Data Book.

- What about the exciting advances in personalized medicine? A nonexistent career path for the previous generation, the technology in this field allows physicians to identify mutated genes and alert patients of their predisposition to a specific disease. (The next step—to actually treat disease with genes—is on the horizon. See section below.)

- Then there are more established fields that have evolved to take on new parameters. Take radiology, for example, which is no longer about just reading an X-ray. The radiologist can now do the actual surgery as part of a new field called **interventional radiology**.

Even more exciting, though, is what lies ahead. Genetics therapy. Portable medical records. Distance surgery. Focused medication. And more.

- Right now, physicians can diagnose predisposition to certain illnesses by identifying mutated genes. Currently in the research and development stage is the next step—**gene therapy**—in which physicians will actually replace defective genes by giving patients copies of the correct gene (which, in turn, "overtakes" the mutant gene). Early tests have been especially favorable for cystic fibrosis, in which the correct CFTR gene is transported via a harmless virus or liposome.

- Similarly, research is underway in the field of **pharmogenetics**—in which a patient's treatment is tailored according to the specific genetic code in question. For example, if a patient's genes fit a certain type of cancer code, the physician will prescribe the "matching" pharmaceutical that has been developed to destroy them—and will know, rather than hope, that the treatment is likely to work. Most forms of focused medication care involve oncology, but studies are progressing in areas of cardiology, diabetes, psychiatric disorders, and more.

- Also in development is **focused preventive care**, which, using genetic diagnosis, identifies to a very specific degree how likely a patient is to develop a certain disease or condition—and then usurps that development before it has a chance to begin.

- Other advances will be administrative in nature: The days of hunting down medical records may come to an end. One possibility being explored is a **portable medical records system**, or a national online database of individual health records. Everyone will carry a smart card (or have a microchip inserted under his or her skin!), allowing physicians to access medical records. The benefit? Errors are reduced; files can no longer be lost; delays are minimized; and the experience of having repeated—i.e., unnecessary—tests is eliminated.

- And what about the robotics-assisted surgery we mentioned earlier? It provides the foundation for the next step forward—that of **distance surgery**. One day, surgeons will operate via a computerized system that will be located hundreds, even thousands, of miles away from patients. This, of course, opens up a "world" of possibilities and opportunities, in which specialists in one country can perform surgery on patients located in another.

| New Trends in the Past 25 Years | New Trends on the Horizon |
|---|---|
| Interventional Radiology | Genetics Therapy |
| Virtual Surgery | Focused Preventive Medicine |
| HIV Specialty | Pharmogenetics |
| Genetics Diagnosis | Portable Medical Records |
| | Distance Surgery |

## Workforce Issues

Above all, know this: Whatever specialty you choose, your services as a physician will be needed—a need that will only increase as the years move forward.

According to the AAMC's Center for Workforce Studies, there will be 45,000 too few primary care physicians – and a shortage of 46,000 surgeons and medical specialists – in the next decade. The passage of health care reform, while setting in motion long-overdue efforts to insure an additional 32 million Americans, will increase the need for doctors and exacerbate a physician shortage driven by the rapid expansion of the number of Americans over age 65. Our doctors are getting older, too. Nearly one-third of all physicians will retire in the next decade just as more Americans need care. Continued demand for physicians and other medical professionals is obvious.

The graph below illustrates the growing physician shortages between now and 2020. Still, the shortage will be experienced unevenly, and some areas will feel the effect more strongly than others. With that in mind, you may wish to consider the trends as you think about the direction you'd like your career to take.

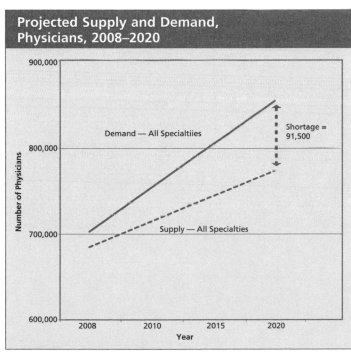

**Projected Supply and Demand, Physicians, 2008–2020**

Source: AAMC Center for Workforce Studies, 2010.

- *Primary Care:* Although the nation is facing an overall shortage of physicians, many are particularly concerned about the growing deficit of primary care doctors. To encourage more U.S. medical school graduates to pursue a career in primary care, the government is exploring ways to more fairly value primary care efforts and lessen administrative burdens associated with general medicine. You might want to explore the rewards these specialty offer, including the satisfaction that comes from the delivery of comprehensive care and the continuity of patient relationships.

- *Underserved Areas:* In addition, the impact of this shortage is expected to be greatest on underserved areas—the urban and rural areas where health care is already scarce. If you choose to serve in a community designated as a Health Professional Shortage Area, you may be able to take advantage of a federal program—the National Health Services Corps—that offers scholarships and loan repayment. *(Learn more about this program in Chapter 11, How to Finance Your Medical Education.)*

## A More Collaborative Approach

As Congress explores various scenarios as it moves toward instituting health care reform, one thing is all but certain: Given the projected shortage of physicians, we'll need to develop new models of health care delivery that make better and more efficient use of all health care professionals—not just doctors. That means you can expect to work within a more collaborative, "shared" environment, in which a team of health care providers—including physician's assistants and nurse practitioners, for example—work more in tandem. Exactly how that will play out is still in the development stages, but the idea is to create a more efficient system, increase patient satisfaction, and, ultimately, improve health outcomes.

*This collaborative approach to health care delivery is instilled beginning in the early years of medical education. Read more about the use of small group discussions, problem-based learning, and other educational models in Chapter 3, From Here to There: The Medical Education Process.*

## The Immediate Steps that Lie Ahead

That's the long-range future, or at least what we anticipate it is likely to entail. Right now, though, you're undoubtedly more fixated on the short term—getting into medical school.

So what's the process like? What lies ahead?

First, let's be candid. Getting into medical school isn't easy. (But it's definitely doable, a fact to which the more than 76,000 students currently there can testify!) You'll need to prepare for and do well on the MCAT® exam, select appropriate schools to which to apply, complete the application process, write a personal statement, gather letters of recommendation, and make it through the interview. And then you'll need to wait (…and wait… and wait) for notices of acceptance and make your final decision. On the other hand, if you're not accepted, you will need to evaluate options and determine a course of action.

All this we review in the following chapters.

But first, there are many steps you can take while still in college to make yourself a more attractive candidate to admissions committees. From taking the necessary courses, to working effectively with your pre-health advisor, to participating in extracurricular and volunteer activities that demonstrate your true interest in medicine, there's much you can do.

In the next chapter, we take a look at your undergraduate preparation.

## Countdown to Medical School

The **Timeline for Application and Admission**, included as a tear sheet at the front of this guide, outlines in detail the steps you should take at various stages during your undergraduate years. Major components include:

- Taking the MCAT® exam
- Selecting schools to which to apply
- Investigating medical school application services
- Completing the application process
- Learning about the financial aid system
- Applying for financial aid, if necessary
- Preparing a personal statement
- Participating in interviews
- Waiting for notification(s) of acceptance
- Making a final acceptance decision

# Chapter 2:

## Building a Strong Foundation: Your Undergraduate Years

*Your voyage to the M.D. degree begins well before you set foot on a medical school campus. In reality, it starts during your undergraduate years—a time during which you'll build a foundation that will not only make you a strong candidate to medical school, but ultimately an effective physician, as well.*

### Some Ways Students Prepare for Medical School

College students take advantage of a wide variety of programs to prepare for a career in medicine or science. The following shows the percentage of students who participated in:

| Program | Percent |
| --- | --- |
| Volunteered or worked in the health care field | 92.8 |
| MCAT® preparation course | 65.3 |
| Laboratory research apprenticeship | 57.8 |
| Summer academic enrichment | 12.4 |
| Post-baccalaureate program to complete premedical requirements | 8.4 |
| Post-baccalaureate program to strengthen academic skills | 5.9 |

*Source: AAMC's 2010 Matriculating Student Questionnaire (MSQ)*

*As a college student planning to pursue the study of medicine, you have much to accomplish. You'll need to master general academic skills, select a major and fulfill its requirements, complete all necessary premedical courses, and, ideally, pursue advanced coursework in areas of special interest. But there's more to your undergraduate years than intellectual development alone. You'll also want to participate in a variety of extracurricular activities, and cultivate the personal traits expected of a physician.*

*And finally, you'll want to seek out someone to advise you. Although there are a number of people who can be invaluable—a professor, a current medical student, a physician, your parents—you'll certainly want to establish a relationship with a pre-health advisor.*

*These areas combined—academic preparation, the nurturing of desirable personal attributes, participation in extracurricular activities, and appropriate guidance—will help ready you for entry to medical school.*

### Academic Preparation

Much of your preparation for medical school comes in the form of academic groundwork and development, which encompasses your major field of study, the mastery of specific scientific principles, and advanced coursework. Let's take a look at each of these a bit further.

## Choice of Major

Unbeknownst to many college students, there is no such thing as the "best" major for those bound for medical school. **In fact, no medical school requires a specific major of its applicants.** That's because admissions committee members know that students develop the essential skills of acquiring and synthesizing information through a wide variety of academic disciplines and therefore should be free to select whichever majors they find interesting and challenging.

### Undergraduate Major: Difference in MCAT® Scores?

**The Official Guide to the MCAT Exam®**, available for purchase at *www.aamc.org/officialmcatguide*, includes a chart that provides the median MCAT® scores of applicants by undergraduate major. There you will see that the total median score for humanities majors, biology majors, and social sciences majors were 29.6, 28.1 and 28.5, respectively. This attests to the fact that students from any major, as long as they have the basic science preparation, are equally prepared for acceptance to medical school.

*Source: Official Guide to the MCAT Exam®, 2010*

Even so, many premedical students choose to major in a scientific discipline. If that's the direction you're heading, and you're doing so because you are fascinated by science and believe that such a major will be the foundation for a variety of career options, great. If you're doing so because you believe it will enhance your chances for admission, think again. Admissions committee welcome students whose intellectual curiosity leads them to a wide variety of disciplines.

And no…you won't necessarily be at a disadvantage if you choose to major in English, for example, rather than biology. Using just one measure, those of MCAT® scores, you may be surprised to learn that there is very little difference in median total scores among those who major in the humanities, social sciences, and biological sciences. (See box, left.)

## Scientific Preparation

Still, medical schools recognize the importance of a strong foundation in the natural sciences—biology, chemistry, and physics—and mathematics, and most schools have established minimum course requirements for admission. These courses usually represent about one-third of the credit hours needed for degree completion (hence, leaving room for applicants to pursue a broad spectrum of college majors, as mentioned on the left). In particular, medical schools expect that their entering students will have mastered basic scientific principles by successfully completing one academic year (two semesters or three quarters) of biology and physics and one academic year each of general chemistry and organic chemistry, and including adequate laboratory experiences.

While only a few medical schools require applicants to complete a specific course in mathematics, all schools appreciate that mathematical competence provides a strong foundation for understanding basic sciences. A working knowledge of statistics helps students fully grasp medical literature, and familiarity with computers is valuable, as well. Many medical schools therefore recommend coursework in mathematics, statistics, and computer science in addition to the science courses named above. The table on the next page gives an overview of the most common courses required by medical schools.

### AP and CLEP Courses

Students intending to apply college credit earned through **Advanced Placement (AP) and College Level Examination Placement (CLEP)** to meet premedical requirements should be aware that some medical schools have requirements involving the use of such credit. Please review the Web sites and publications of the medical schools in which you're interested for information.

## Subjects Required by U.S. Medical Schools, 2010–2011 Entering Class

Finally, for those of you reading this in the early years of college (or even in high school), we'd like to draw your attention to the fact that some medical schools may one day define their prerequisites by competencies—rather than courses. This comes about because, as a study undertaken by the Howard Hughes Medical Institute (HHMI) and the AAMC points out, the scientific knowledge medical schools seek in their applicants can be obtained in a variety of courses as opposed to specific ones. (In other words, a student might be able to master chemistry principles in a zoology class.) The box on the next page provides additional information.

## Table 2-A

Subjects Required by 10 or More U.S. Medical Schools

| Required Subject | # of Schools |
|---|---|
| Biochemistry | 15 |
| Biology | 92 |
| Biology/Zoology | 37 |
| Calculus | 20 |
| College Mathematics | 32 |
| English | 85 |
| Humanities | 15 |
| Inorganic (General) Chemistry | 122 |
| Organic Chemistry | 124 |
| Physics | 122 |

*N = 134. For premedical coursework required by the specific medical schools in which you are interested, please see the school entries later in this guide.*

## Advanced Coursework

You should also know that upper-level science coursework is not typically required by medical schools. That said, your success in advanced courses is often a way to demonstrate science proficiencies and strengthen your preparation for medical school. Still, taking additional science courses that duplicate basic science content of the first two years of medical school is not recommended.

In fact, practicing physicians often suggest that premedical students take advantage of what might be their final opportunity for study in non-science areas (such as music, art, history, and literature) they find of interest. Beyond that, medical schools encourage honors courses, independent study, and research work by premedical students. Activities such as these demonstrate in-depth scholarly exploration and the presence of lifelong learning skills that are essential to a career in the medicine.

## Into the Future: Competency-Based Prerequisites

The study undertaken by the HHMI and the AAMC recommends a shift in focus from requiring specific courses to requiring specific competencies and outlines the competencies that entering medical students should demonstrate. In brief, these include:

- both the knowledge of and ability to apply basic principles of mathematics and statistics, physics, chemistry, biochemistry, and biology to human health and disease;
- the ability to demonstrate observational and analytical skills; and
- the ability to apply those skills and principles to biological situations.

You may download a copy of this report, free-of-charge, at *www.aamc.org/scientificfoundations*.

## Personal Attributes

As we mentioned in this chapter's introduction, academic and scientific accomplishments alone are not sufficient for a student's entry into medical school. While intellectual capacity is obviously important to success as a physician, so too are other attributes—those that portend the ability to develop and maintain effective relationships with patients, work collaboratively with other team members, act ethically and compassionately, and in many other ways master the "art" of medicine.

An AAMC publication entitled *Learning Objectives for Medical Student Education: Guidelines for Medical Schools* describes the personal attributes required of a physician. While making note of the fact that graduating medical students must, of course, be knowledgeable about medicine and skillful in its application, the publication also emphasizes how vital it is for students to:

- Make ethical decisions;
- Act with compassion, respect, honesty, and integrity;
- Work collaboratively with team members;
- Advocate on behalf of one's patients;
- Be sensitive to potential conflicts of interest;
- Be able to recognize one's own limits;
- Be dedicated to continuously improving one's knowledge and abilities;
- Appreciate the complex nonbiological determinants of poor health;

- Be aware of community and public health issues;

- Be able to identify risk factors for disease;

- Be committed to early identification and treatment of diseases;

- Accept responsibility for making scientifically based medical decisions; and

- Be willing to advocate for the care of the underserved.

A number of these traits are developed not only in medical school, but also may be nurtured throughout the college years, as well (and, as you will see in Chapter 7, are among the attributes that admissions officers seek when deciding whom to admit to their programs). You will have an abundance of opportunities to foster many of these qualities through your interactions with friends, classmates, and faculty…in the classroom, dining hall, and dorm…on sports teams, in school clubs, and during summer or part-time jobs.

## Extracurricular Activities Related to Medicine

Your undergraduate years offer wonderful opportunities to become involved in a wide range of extracurricular activities, and certainly at least a few of them should involve the medical field. Experience in a health care setting; caring for an ill or elderly family member; participating in basic or clinical research efforts; working as an emergency medical technician; "shadowing" a physician; providing support to people in a rape crisis center, emergency room, or social service agency—these types of activities are recommended to those considering a career in medicine.

These pursuits provide you with the chance to learn more about the medical profession—and yourself. You will, for example, be able to:

- Explore different interests,

- Test out your natural inclinations to one or more endeavors,

- Come to better understand the nature of medical practice and the daily demands placed upon physicians,

- Assess your ability to communicate and empathize with people from different backgrounds and cultures, and

- Evaluate your willingness to put others' needs before your own.

### Dutifulness and Altruism

In the publication referenced on the previous page, the AAMC categorizes these varied traits as they relate to **dutifulness** and **altruism**. Those interested in exploring these concepts further can download the publication, free-of-charge.

*Go to www.aamc.org/msop to read more.*

While this self-analysis can help you decide if a career in medicine is an appropriate choice for you, your involvement with clinical or research activities might help admissions committees determine where your interests lie and demonstrate to them that you have explored various aspects of the medical field. We say *might*, though—rather than *will*—because admissions committees evaluate your experiences using at least three different criteria, and a greater value is assigned to certain types of pursuits than others.

Specifically, admissions committees look at the length of time you've invested, the depth of the experience, and lessons learned—in relation to any particular activity—so that a day-long blood drive or one-time-only shadowing experience is less enlightening than semester or year-long commitments. By the same token, active participation in an activity is viewed as more instructive than a passive one (such as observation). Most important, though, admissions committees want to know what students learned from their experiences, and you should therefore be prepared to address these kinds of questions about your community, clinical, or research experiences in your application materials (which we will discuss in Chapter 6).

### Be Wary of the Checklist Approach

Do **not** approach your extracurricular activities with the idea of "checking off" a wide range and number of pursuits in order to impress the admissions committee. Three or four in-depth experiences from which you gained valuable lessons are far more significant—and telling—to admissions officers than dozens of short-term involvements.

## Pre-Health Advisors

Fortunately, you're not on your own when it comes to preparing for medical school. You have a valuable resource to which you can turn—a resource very likely available right on your college campus.

We speak of your pre-health advisor.

Depending on the individual school, pre-health advisors function on either a full- or part-time basis, and may be faculty members (often in the science department), staff members in the office of an academic dean or in the career center, directors of an advising office for pre-professional students, or a physician in part-time practice. Advisors belong to organizations such as the National Association of Advisors for the Health Professions (NAAHP, *www.naahp.org*) that assist them in their work—and help them to help you.

## Services Provided

The support provided by pre-health advisors varies according to a number of factors. Generally speaking, though, services fall into five categories:

- **Academics.** Advisors are well informed about premedical coursework on their campuses and about developing suitable academic programs for premedical students. They collaborate with campus academic staff in designing study, reading skill, and test preparation workshops, and in offering tutoring programs, as well as inform their students of regional and national programs likely to be of interest.

- **Clinical and research experiences.** In working with advisory groups composed of college and medical school teaching and research faculty and community clinicians, advisors help identify part-time jobs, volunteer positions, and opportunities for independent study credit in local laboratories and offices.

- **Advising and support.** Advisors help students pursue realistic goals and maximize their potential, both meeting with them individually and providing group opportunities for students to meet with one another. Advisors often establish peer advising and mentoring programs, and are particularly sensitive to the needs of students who are members of a group currently underrepresented in medicine or are the first in their family to attend college.

- **Assistance to student organizations.** Advisors coordinate the activities of local and national organizations that serve premed students by planning programs, identifying funding sources, and arranging for campus visits from admissions and financial aid officers.

- **Sharing resources.** Well aware of the need by students for timely and pertinent information, advisors disseminate publications and other resources from relevant organizations, including the AAMC and the NAAHP. In addition, advisors provide computer access to Web-based content on health careers programs and educational financing; distribute information about local regional, national, and international research and service opportunities; and stock a library of publications related to medical school and medical education.

Please contact your school's advisor to discuss the availability of these services.

## The Pre-Health Committee Letter of Recommendation

There's another vital service that pre-health advisors offer their students (and often their alumni) that we haven't yet mentioned: the pre-health committee letter of recommendation.

This is usually a composite letter written on behalf of a medical school applicant by the college or university's pre-health committee. It presents an overview of the student's academic strengths, exposures to health care and medical research environments, contributions to the campus and community, and personal attributes such as maturity and altruism. In addition, the letter may address any extenuating circumstances that may have resulted in deficits in the student's performance during a course or semester, provide perspective on challenges the student may have encountered, and explain school-specific courses and programs in which the student has participated.

Some undergraduate institutions do not provide composite letters of recommendation but instead collect individual letters throughout the student's enrollment. Then, at the appropriate time, they distribute the letters to the medical schools where the student has applied.

---

### Pre-Health Advisors: A Wide Range of Guidance

There are many instances in which a pre-health advisor may assist you. These include helping you:

- Identify courses that satisfy premedical requirements;
- Determine a sequence for completing those courses;
- Find tutorial assistance, if needed;
- Plan academic schedules to accommodate both premedical coursework and other educational objectives, such as a study program abroad, a dual major, or a senior honors thesis;
- Locate volunteer or paid clinical and research experience;
- Strengthen your medical school application;
- Prepare for interviews and standardized tests;
- Arrange for letters of evaluation and recommendation; and
- Determine the most appropriate career paths based on individual strengths, values, and life goals.

---

## Special Programs

Finally, we'd like to draw your attention to the following two programs that may be of interest (depending on where you fall in the education process):

- **Combined Baccalaureate/M.D. Programs**
  If you're reading this book during the latter stages of high school, you might want to explore a combined B.S./M.D. program, offered at about a quarter of U.S. medical schools. Graduates of these programs, which range in length from six to nine years, receive both a bachelor's degree from the undergraduate institution and an M.D. from the medical school. For more details and a list of participating schools, please see Chapter 12.

- **Post-Baccalaureate Programs**
  Perhaps, though, you're at a different stage along the educational continuum and have already graduated from college. If your major was something other than science, it's quite possible that you'll need to pursue additional coursework before applying to medical school. Post-baccalaureate programs, offered at colleges and universities across the country and ranging from formal one- or two-year programs to information part-time programs, allow those with a college degree to strengthen their knowledge in the sciences or complete certain required premedical courses. A searchable database of these programs can be found at *http://services.aamc.org/postbac*.

---

### Finding a Pre-Health Advisor through the NAAHP

If you can't identify the pre-health advisor on your campus, contact the NAAHP for help. If your school does not have an advisor, you may make use of the services of volunteer advisors at other institutions, as listed on the NAAHP Web site. In addition, the NAAHP offers publications to help student prepare for medical school that may be of interest, as well.

Contact the NAAHP at:
National Association of Advisors for the Health Professions
P.O. Box 1518, Champaign, IL 61824-1518
T (217) 355-0063    F (217) 355-1287
*www.naahp.org*

# Chapter 3:

## From Here to There:
## The Medical Education Process

*What lies on the journey between the day you grasp your college diploma, shake the dean's hand, and flash a broad smile for your family and friends—and the day you're licensed as a fully certified physician? What steps must you successfully navigate before you are deemed a competent doctor, ready to function independently in your chosen field?*

*You probably already know the answer: Four demanding years of medical school, a residency program lasting anywhere from three to eight years (or more, on occasion), and passing scores on the three USLME step exams administered at various stages along the way.*

*But that's only the short version. There's more to the discussion than that—much more. How has the medical education process changed in recent years— both in terms of teaching methods and the topics you'll be taught? Which technological innovations are being used to train students? How does medical education today differ from that of a generation ago?*

*We take a look at these questions, and others, in the material that follows.*

**Undergraduate Medical Education**

▼

**Graduate Medical Education (Residency)**

▼

**Licensure and Certification**

▼

**Continuing Medical Education**

### Undergraduate Medical Education:
### An Overview of the Medical School Years

At the core, all U.S. and Canadian medical schools have the same purpose—to educate their students in both the art and science of medicine, provide them with clinical experience, and, ultimately, prepare them to enter a three- to eight-year-long residency program (otherwise referred to as "graduate medical education"). That is why every school follows the same basic program—requiring students to acquire a basic foundation in the medical sciences, apply this knowledge to diseases and treatments, and master clinical skills through a series of "rotations."

That doesn't mean that a medical school...is a medical school... is a medical school. Far from it. Each school establishes its own curriculum and course format, so that, for example, a particular class required by one institution is an elective course in another. Even when medical schools seem to require identical courses, the content within them may differ, so that the some of the material covered in immunology in one school, for instance, is presented in pathology in another. (The sequence in which courses are taken—and the very method by which the content is taught—may differ, as well.) Beyond that, the processes by which students are graded also vary from school to school, with some institutions following a pass/fail system, others an honors/pass/fail system, and still others a letter grading system.

But we're not saying that "anything goes," either, when it comes to medical schools. To the contrary, they must meet very exacting standards to earn (and maintain) accreditation, as established by the **Liaison Committee on Medical Education** (LCME). The LCME, cosponsored by the AAMC and the American Medical Association, is the authority that accredits programs of medical schools that grant the M.D. degree in the United States, and reviews and approves curricula, organization, and student performance.

Beyond that required by the standards of accreditation, there are other strong parallels among medical schools. Speaking in very simplistic terms—and recognizing there is significant overlap between what has traditionally been referred to as "pre-clinical" and "clinical" years (see box below)—the general structure of the overall programs follow a similar path: Students concentrate their efforts on the scientific underpinnings of medicine during the first two years, and on applying and refining that knowledge during a series of rotations during the second two years.

Let's take a look...

## Building a Foundation of Knowledge

In almost all cases, you'll begin your medical school studies by learning how the human body is supposed to work—both in terms of structure and function. The focus will then shift to abnormal conditions and diseases, methods of diagnosis, and treatment options. We follow with a brief summary.

- *Normal Structure and Function*
  How does the healthy body work? That's what you'll be studying right out of the starting gate, and your courses will be many—and varied. Typically, your "basic" classes will include gross and microscopic anatomy, physiology, biochemistry, behavioral sciences, and neurology.

- *Abnormalities, Diagnostics, and Treatment*
  After you've learned what "healthy" looks like (and acts like), the focus of your coursework will shift—again, both in terms of structure and function. You'll study the full range of diseases and atypical conditions, methods by

*Accreditation by the LCME is required for schools to receive federal grants and to participate in federal loan programs. In addition, eligibility of U.S. students to take the United States Medical Licensing Exam (USMLE)—a discussion of which appears on page 22—requires LCME accreditation of their school. All medical schools listed in this guide are accredited by the LCME.*

which diagnoses are made, and therapeutic principles and treatments. It is at this stage that you'll have classes in immunology, pathology, and pharmacology.

- *Other Topics*
  You'll also be exposed to a wide variety of other topics, too. These will range from nutrition, to medical ethics, to genetics…from laboratory medicine, to substance abuse, to geriatrics. Health care delivery systems. Human values. Research. Preventive medicine. Human sexuality. Community health. The fact is that the subjects taught at medical schools are as varied, and potentially as numerous, as are the institutions themselves.

And that's just part of the picture. There's much more to "building a foundation" than simply (or not so simply!) mastering the scientific basis of medicine. During this period of your medical education, you will also learn the basics of interviewing and obtaining historical data from patients, conducting physical exams, interpreting laboratory findings, and considering diagnostic treatment and alternatives—in effect, readying yourself for the clinical rotations that follow in the latter half of medical school.

Finally, keep in mind that it's not all science—or even application of science (such as that required to interpret lab results and figure out a course of treatment). Medical schools recognize that physicians practice in a social environment—one in which effective team-building, collaborative, and communications skills are necessary. As a result, the very way in which students learn, and are taught, has evolved in recent years. *We discuss this in more depth in the section on the next page—the "Changing Face of Medical Education."*

---

### What A Typical Curriculum* May Include

**Year 1 – Normal structure and function**
Biochemistry, cell biology, medical genetics, gross anatomy, structure and function of human organs, behavioral science, and neuroscience

**Year 2 – Abnormal structure and function**
Abnormalities of structure and function, disease, microbiology, immunology, pathology, and pharmacology

**Years 3 and 4 – Clinical clerkships**
**Generalist core:** family and community medicine, general and ambulatory care, internal medicine, obstetrics and gynecology, pediatrics, surgery, and research

**Other requirements:** neurology, psychiatry, subspecialty segments (anesthesia, dermatology, urology, radiology, etc.), emergency room and intensive care experiences, and electives

*The curriculum outlined above is a representation only— and not inclusive of all courses/clerkships.*

---

### Acquiring "Hands-On" Experience through Clerkships

A major component of your undergraduate medical education, typically occurring in the third and fourth years, will be a series of required clinical clerkships or "rotations." These clerkships usually last from four to 12 weeks each, and provide students with first-hand experience in working with both patients and their families, and in both inpatient and outpatient settings.

While the pattern, length, and number of rotations differ from school to school, core clinical training usually includes clerkships in internal medicine, family medicine, obstetrics/gynecology, pediatrics, psychiatry, and surgery. Beyond that, and depending on your specific school's requirements, your program may also include clerkships in primary care and neurology, for example, or require participation in a community or rural program.

- *What You'll Do*
  During a clerkship, you'll be assigned to an outpatient clinic or inpatient hospital unit where you will assume responsibility for "working-up" a number of patients each week—collecting relevant data and information from them—and presenting findings to a faculty member. Beyond that, you'll participate in the ongoing care of patients, either during hospitalizations or through the course of outpatient treatment, and, when appropriate, interact not only with the patients themselves, but with their families, as well.

- *And What You'll Learn*
  There's no substitute, as you know, for "hands-on" experience—and plenty of it. During the course of your clerkships, you'll learn to apply basic science knowledge and clinical skills in diagnosing and treating patients' illnesses and injuries and will become adept interacting with patients (and their families) as you provide information, answer questions, and prepare them for the likely outcome. At the same time, you'll become effective working with all members of the health care team, whether at the bedside, during inpatient team discussions ("rounds"), or in case-based lectures and small-group discussions.

### Electives

Medical schools, just like colleges, each have their own requirements—the courses and clerkships you must take to graduate. That's a given.

But, also just like college, you'll enjoy an opportunity to explore special interests by way of electives. Offered in basic, behavioral, and clinical sciences, as well as in basic and clinical research, electives are usually available during your final year of medical school (although you might be able to take them at other times). They may be completed on your own campus, at other medical schools through a "visiting student program," through federal and state agencies, in international settings, and service organizations.

## The Changing Face of Medical Education

Some of you may have heard of Abraham Flexner, who wrote a groundbreaking report on medical education 100 years ago. Although the basics of his 1910 model have survived to the present day—mainly, a four-year program affiliated with a university*—he never intended his model to serve for more than a generation. He knew, after all, that he could not predict the future.

Time has certainly proven him correct.

There is no way that Flexner could have anticipated the shifting demographics, technological advances, and evolving teaching techniques of the late 20th century and the first decade of the 21st century. You, on the other hand, will experience first-hand the reforms taking place in medical education—both in terms of what you'll learn, and how you'll learn it. Your courses may range from cultural diversity to health care financing, and you'll benefit from educational developments such as computer-aided instruction, virtual patients, and human patient simulation. It's an exciting (albeit very challenging!) time to be a medical student.

### Medical School Activities on Elective/Volunteer Basis

The range of activities in which medical students participate is broad. The following are among the most popular:

| Activity | % Participating |
| --- | --- |
| Experience related to cultural awareness/competence | 67.0 |
| Learned proper use of interpreter when needed | 69.3 |
| Experience related to health care disparities | 65.5 |
| Research project with faculty member | 64.2 |
| Provided health education (e.g., HIV education, Breast cancer awareness, smoking cessation) | 57.2 |
| Field experience in community health (e.g., rape hotline, adult/child protective services, family violence program) | 44.8 |
| Educating elementary, high school, or college students about health care careers | 43.2 |

*Source: AAMC's 2010 Graduation Questionnaire (GQ)*

### Changing Demographics = Changing Education

The U.S. population over age 65 is expected to be almost 70 million by 2030—accounting for one in every five Americans. Demographics such as that, together with advanced technologies, scientific discoveries, and evolving teaching techniques, all contribute to significant changes in medical education.

*Source: Population Projections of the United States by Age, Sex, Race, and Hispanic Origin: 1995 to 2050, U.S. Bureau of the Census*

### What You'll Learn

You're going to have to wield a scalpel in anatomy class early on in medical school, just as students in your parents' and grandparents' generations did 30 and 60 years ago. Certain things stay the same. That type of effort aside, though, there are many significant changes in medical education content, and schools are continually revising their curricula to reflect advances in science, breakthroughs in medicine, and changes in society. For example:

- Consider the demographic shift we'll experience as the baby boomers age. By 2030, the population of those over age 65 is expected to have doubled, and physicians will spend an increasing amount of time treating age-related problems such as Alzheimer's, heart failure, pulmonary disease, and bone disorders. As a result, most medical schools now include courses on geriatrics, palliative care, pain management, and complementary medicine, and other similar age-based material, in their curricula.

- Issues such as health literacy, nutrition, drug abuse, and family violence are important components of medical education. Because many of these and other health problems are related to culture and lifestyle, medical schools haves increasingly focused efforts on areas such as disease prevention, health promotion, and cultural diversity.

- Medical schools are placing an increasingly important emphasis on helping their students develop effective communications, allowing them to interact successfully with a diverse group of patients. Rather than being "left to chance," you'll be directly taught to assess family, lifestyle, and socioeconomic factors that may influence your patients' behavior, or affect their care.

Then, of course, there are the advancements in science and medicine themselves. (As researchers make breakthroughs in genetics diagnoses and treatments, for instance, that new knowledge is incorporated into the medical school program.)

*At the time of Flexner's report, many medical schools were small trade schools unaffiliated with a university, and a degree was awarded after only two years of study.

There are also expanded courses on medical ethics, examining some of the dilemmas physicians may face amid the advent of new technology; classes on financial decision making, in which students are taught to weigh the likely costs and benefits of various treatments; and sessions on evidence-based medicine and patient quality, providing students with the informational and tools they will need to deliver the best possible care.

*The topics described here are only an overview of some possibilities. The specific courses you'll take as a medical student will vary depending on the school.*

### And How You'll Learn It

Do you have an image of sitting in a large lecture hall, surrounded by hundreds of your peers? While you'll certainly experience that aspect of medical school, that method of teaching is being replaced (to a significant degree) by other techniques. Here are a few of the most widespread methods:

- The traditional lecture-based approach is increasingly giving way to student-centered, small-group instruction—similar to the "case study" teaching method so popular in both law and business schools. In your case, you're likely to be assigned to small groups of students—overseen by a faculty member—in which you will focus on specific clinical problems. The aim here is to instill medical knowledge and skill as well as help you build the communications and collaboration skills you'll need as a resident, and, ultimately, as a fully licensed physician.

- Fast-moving technological advances have certainly affected the medical school education program. You'll probably use a computerized patient mannequin (or "whole body simulator") to apply the basic sciences you've mastered to a clinical context and refine your diagnostic skills. These simulators, which are easily customized to replicate a wide range of situations, are currently part of the curriculum in most medical schools.

- Another way medical schools employ new technology is with computer-aided instruction and "virtual" patients. Here, you'll apply newfound knowledge and skills via interactive Web-based (or software) programs that simulate complex cases.

*To learn more about the specific teaching methods of the medical school(s) in which you are interested, please see the applicable school listing in the latter portion of this guide.*

### Examples of "New" Topics in Medical Education

Of 126 medical schools surveyed, the following topics were required at the vast majority of institutions:

| Topic area | # of Medical Schools Requiring Topic |
|---|---|
| Cultural Diversity | 125 |
| Substance Abuse | 125 |
| Communication Skills | 124 |
| Preventive/Health Maintenance | 124 |
| Medical Genetics | 121 |
| Family/Domestic Violence | 121 |
| Culturally-Related Health Behaviors | 121 |
| Pain Management | 120 |
| Counseling for Health Risk Reduction | 120 |
| Health Care Systems | 119 |
| Alternative/Complementary Medicine | 113 |
| Health Care Financing | 111 |

*Source: 2008 LCME Part II Annual Medical School Questionnaire*

## Choosing a Specialty and Applying for Residency

Required courses. Clerkships. Electives. There's a lot occupying your time and energy as you advance through medical school. Along with all that, you undoubtedly will give a lot of thought about the career path you'd like to pursue, exploring various options and researching different possibilities.

It is during your final year, though, that some real decisions must be made. It is at this stage that you'll choose a specialty and begin applying to residency programs (the portion of your education that follows graduation from medical school). These training programs are described below, but for now…how will you make your selection, and how will you get in?

## Types of Educational Technologies

Most medical schools use a combination of the following technologies in their educational programs:

**Computer-aided instruction**
- Enables visualizing complex processes
- Allows independent exploration
- Offers easy access
- Relatively low cost

**Virtual patients**
- Covers multiple aspects of a clinical encounter
- Offers easy access
- Readily customized

**Human Patient Simulation**
- Offers active experience
- Engages emotional and sensory learning
- Fosters critical thought and communication

*Source: AAMC Handbook*

## Choosing a Specialty

You really should begin exploring specialty options in your second year of medical school, and there's much to think about. You'll want to consider the nature of the work, training and residency requirements, lifestyle and salary factors, characteristics of physicians in the specialty, issues facing professionals in that particular field, and, of course, your own interests, values, and skills.

Where to begin your explorations? You will, of course, seek out the guidance of your advisor as you investigate your options, and your school will likely offer various workshops and presentations to help you with your decision. In addition, and as we mentioned in the first chapter of this guide, you will probably have access to the **Careers in Medicine** (CiM) program sponsored by the Association of American Medical Colleges (AAMC). This largely Web-based program—which is available free-of-charge to students attending AAMC-member medical schools—contains detailed information and interactive tools to help you work through the specialty choice process. Included in this program are:

- specialty descriptions;
- residency and training requirements;
- Match data;

- workforce statistics;
- compensation; and
- links to more than 1,000 specialty associations, journals, and publications.

*Registration is required for access to the CiM program. For more, go to www.aamc.org/careersinmedicine.*

### Getting In

Once you've decided on a specialty, there's more to it than simply shooting off an e-mail to the director of a residency program and letting him or her know of your interest (as we're sure you already suspect). Rather, you must compete for a slot. Much like the application process to medical school, you'll complete an application, craft a personal statement, submit letters of recommendation, and go through interviews. This undertaking is usually facilitated through an application service such as the AAMC's **Electronic Residency Application Service** (ERAS®), which transmits all related documentation via the Internet.

Applying is just the half of it, though, you've also got to be accepted by (or "matched" with) a residency program. This pairing comes about through the **National Resident Matching Program** (NRMP®) by which students' preferences for specific residency programs are compared with the preferences of residency program directors for specific applicants. The matching process occurs on a specific day every March—more familiarly known as **"Match Day"**—and is met with a great deal of anticipation as 16,000 medical school seniors learn where they will spend the next several years of their training.*

## Graduate Medical Education (GME): The Residency Program

Once you've graduated from medical school, you can claim title to that hard-earned M.D. (or D.O., for graduates of osteopathic schools). But although much of the work is done—and people now call you "doctor"—the journey is far from over. In actuality, you're a "doctor-in-training," and your next phase is that of graduate medical education. The residency program awaits.

We won't get into the details of postgraduate work here, as we imagine that right now you're more interested in getting into medical school—and that you plan to worry about your residency program later. In a nutshell, though, the primary purpose of these programs is to provide medical school graduates (such as you, one day) with the skills and knowledge

---

*These 16,000 students are the graduates of medical schools that grant the M.D. In addition, 15,000 graduates of osteopathic (those granting the D.O.), Canadian, and international medical schools also compete for residency program assignments through the NRMP. To learn more about ERAS and NRMP, go to www.aamc.org/eras and www.nrmp.org.*

they need to become competent, independent physicians. Ranging in length from three to eight years, and sometimes more, their completion is necessary for board certification.

Because of their very nature, residency programs are conducted primarily in clinical settings—hospitals, outpatient clinics, community health centers, and physicians' offices, for example—and require residents (or "house officers" as they're sometimes known) to participate fully in patient diagnoses and treatment. When your time comes, you'll work under the supervision of physician faculty as you develop experience in your chosen specialty, become proficient with both common and uncommon illnesses and conditions, attend conferences, teach less experienced colleagues, and, in general, adjust to the demands of medical practice.

## Inter-professional Education

When it comes to caring for patients, remember…you're not in this alone.

Rather, the delivery of medical care is a "team-based" effort that often includes not only doctors, but nurses, pharmacists, physical therapists, and other health care providers, as well. Because of that, it's absolutely vital that practitioners from all disciplines become familiar with one another's roles, perspectives, and even language and communication styles in order to be able to collaborate effectively and efficiently.

And medical educators want to help you develop that knowledge and ability. Your medical education therefore is likely to involve some form of "inter-professional education" in which you will share learning resources, work as a unit, or participate in other activities that encourage interaction among various categories of health care providers. In such a way, you—and they—will become more adept and successful working as a team, and, ultimately, be able to deliver a higher quality of care to patients.

Finally, just as medical schools vary, so too do residency programs. Depending on the area you choose to pursue, you might complete a preliminary year of broad clinical training before focusing on the specialty, as is common in anesthesiology, dermatology, psychiatry, and radiology. In other areas, such as family medicine and pediatrics, you'll enter the specialty track directly. (Your medical school advisor, and programs such as Careers in Medicine®, will present you with full information as you approach this stage of your medical education.)

Residency will be a demanding time, no doubt, but rewarding as well. Many physicians look back on their residency years as ones providing invaluable lessons that they carry with them to this day.

### U.S. Residents by Specialty

|  |  |
|---|---|
| Allergy/Immunology | 294 |
| Anesthesiology | 5,322 |
| Colon/Rectal Surgery | 73 |
| Dermatology | 1,080 |
| Emergency Medicine | 4,922 |
| Family Medicine | 9,391 |
| Internal Medicine | 22,292* |
| Medical Genetics | 84 |
| Neurological Surgery | 1,096 |
| Neurology | 1,825 |
| Nuclear Medicine | 152 |
| OB/GYN | 4,842 |
| Ophthalmology | 1,266 |
| Orthopedic Surgery | 3,371 |
| Otolaryngology | 1,406 |
| Pain Medicine | 244 |
| Pathology | 2,358 |
| Pediatrics | 8,124 |
| Physical Medicine/Rehab | 1,211 |
| Plastic Surgery | 372 |
| Preventive Medicine | 262 |
| Psychiatry | 4,745 |
| Radiation Oncology | 608 |
| Radiology, Diagnostic | 4,486 |
| Sleep Medicine | 100 |
| Surgery, General | 7,661 |
| Thoracic Surgery | 223 |
| Urology | 1,039 |

Source: AAMC Data Book, 2011, for the 2009–10 academic year

*Breaking it down further, the most popular subspecialties in internal medicine (by number of residents) include cardio-vascular disease (2,429); gastroenterology (1,302); hematology and oncology (1,412); and pulmonary disease and critical care medicine (1,273).

Note: The standards surrounding residency programs—including educational experiences, duty hours, evaluations, and safety—are established and enforced by the Accreditation Council of Graduate Medical Education (ACGME). You can learn more about the ACGME and its requirements at www.acgme.org.

## Examples of Training Requirements for Specialty Board Certification

| Specialty | Years Required |
|---|---|
| Anesthesiology | 4 |
| Emergency Medicine | 3 |
| Family Practice | 3 |
| Internal Medicine | 3 |
| OB/GYN | 4 |
| Pathology | 4 |
| Pediatrics | 3 |
| Psychiatry | 4 |
| Radiology | 5 |
| Surgery | 5 |
| Surgical subspecialties | 6 or 7 |

*Source: 2008 LCME Part II Annual Medical School Questionnaire*

## Licensure and Certification: Ready to Function Independently

There's something else you'll need to do before you can be licensed as a physician: You've got to meet the standards of the **National Board of Medical Examiners** (NBME) and the **Federation of State Medical Boards** (FSMB). Together, these two bodies cosponsor the United States Medical Licensing Examination (USMLE), a three-step exam given at various stages of the medical education process.

So, along with documenting that you've completed the necessary educational and training programs for your specialty, you must also get passing scores on the USMLE. It is administered in stages as follows:

- **Step 1:** Usually taken at the end of your second year of medical school, Step 1 tests whether you understand and can apply sciences basic to the practice of medicine. Its focus is on principles and systems of health, disease, and methods of therapy.

- **Step 2:** Many medical schools require you to take (and pass!) Step 2 prior to graduation. It's actually two tests in one—the first evaluating your clinical knowledge (CK) and the second your clinical skills (CS). Basically, Step 2 assesses your ability to provide patient care *under supervision.*

- **Step 3:** After you've completed the first year of your residency program, you're eligible for Step 3—the concluding test that determines your readiness to apply your medical knowledge and clinical skills *without supervision*, with an emphasis on patient management in ambulatory settings.

It is the final assessment of your ability to assume independent responsibility for delivering medical care.

Upon completion of the appropriate educational and training programs, and achievement on the USMLE, you've done it. You are ready to apply for licensure in any of the 50 states, 10 provinces, 3 territories or the District of Columbia.

But…there's one additional step: certification. While it's not required for medical practice—as is licensure from a state or provincial medical board—certification in a specialty is strongly encouraged. Physicians apply voluntarily for this additional credential, which is granted by the **American Board of Medical Specialties** (ABMS) and involves a comprehensive examination. (Those who have satisfied all ABMS requirements are certified and are known as "diplomates" of the specialty board.) More than 75 percent of licensed physicians in the United States have been certified by one of the specialty boards, and interest remains high among the current cohort of new doctors. Almost 9 in 10 medical school graduates plan to become certified in a medical specialty.

## Continuing Medical Education: The Practice of Lifelong Learning

Finally, medical education is a lifelong process, providing you with the opportunity to learn new skills and stay current with exciting and innovative developments.

The fast pace of change in medicine makes continuing education essential, and most states require participation in accredited continuing medical education (CME) activities. Physicians therefore participate in CME programs throughout their careers, ensuring they stay up-to-date with the rapid advancements in their specialties and maintain their clinical competence. Offered by medical schools, teaching hospitals, and professional organizations, these CME programs are reviewed by the **Accreditation Council for Continuing Medical Education** (ACCME) to ensure that high standards are achieved and upheld.

Continuing medical education reflects a commitment to lifelong learning that is a hallmark of the medical profession. For those of you interested in what your CME efforts will entail, go to *www. accme.org.*

## Plans for Certification in a Specialty

When asked if they planned to become certified in a specialty, medical school graduates answered:

| | |
|---|---|
| Yes | 84.7% |
| No | 5.0% |
| Undecided | 10.3% |

*Source: AAMC's 20010 Graduation Questionnaire (GQ)*

# Chapter 4:

## All About the MCAT® Exam

*One of our MCAT® staffers overheard a couple of college seniors commiserating with one another about the test that loomed so ominously in their futures. After about 20 minutes of nonstop talk about various review courses, prep books, and practice options, one student stopped mid-sentence, looked at the other, and asked with a mix of exasperation and fear, "Why do they DO this to us?" The other student shook her head and shrugged in empathy, but we know the answer:*

*Because the MCAT® exam does its job.*

> ### MCAT® Essentials: A Must-Read!
>
> To be sure that you get the most complete and up-to-date information about the MCAT® exam, it is crucial that you read **MCAT® Essentials** (posted online at *www.aamc.org/mcat*) prior to registration.

### The Role of the Exam

Simply put, the MCAT® exam helps admissions officers identify which students are likely to succeed in medical school. It does that by spotting those students who not only have a basic knowledge of science—which provides the foundation necessary in the early years of medical school—but also those with strong critical thinking and written communications skills.

One can argue that college grades do essentially the same thing. But because an "A" in one school is not necessarily equivalent to an "A" in another, admissions officers do not have a "standard measure" against which to evaluate students. The MCAT® exam fills that void.

> ### Your MCAT® Score: One of Many Selection Factors
>
> It's important to recognize that admissions officers consider MCAT® results in concert with many other selection factors—including those related to your experience and personal attributes—when making their decisions. See Chapter 7 to learn more about the various ways in which admissions officers evaluate medical school applicants.

It's no surprise, then, that when admissions officers look at MCAT® scores in conjunction with grades—as opposed to grades alone—their ability to predict who will be successful in medical school increases by as much as 50 percent (using first- and second-year medical school grades as a benchmark). As a result, virtually every medical school in the United States, and many in Canada, requires applicants to submit recent MCAT® scores.

### How the Exam Is Structured

It's a pretty sure bet that you're no stranger to the concept of standardized testing. Starting in elementary school, and continuing on through your college admission exam (be it the SAT™ or ACT®), you've had lots of experience with multiple-choice and essay questions taken in a controlled, timed environment.

## Exam Structure

| Specialty | # of Qs | Time |
|---|---|---|
| Physical Sciences | 52 | 70 minutes |
| Verbal Reasoning | 40 | 60 minutes |
| Writing Sample | 2 | 60 minutes |
| Biological Sciences | 52 | 70 minutes |

*There are optional breaks of 10 minutes each between sections.*

The MCAT® exam follows the same basic format. In this case, it's a computer-based test that lasts just over five hours and consists of three multiple-choice sections—that of Physical Sciences, Biological Sciences, and Verbal Reasoning—and a writing assessment. Let's take a closer look:

- **Physical Sciences (PS)**
  The PS section covers general chemistry and physics via a total of 52 questions—39 of which are based on passages, as well as 13 "free-standing," independent questions. For this section, you will be tested on your capacity to interpret data presented in graphs and tables, your knowledge of basic physical sciences concepts and principles, and your ability to solve problems using that knowledge as a foundation.

- **Verbal Reasoning (VR)**
  The VR section evaluates your ability to understand, evaluate, and apply information and arguments presented in writing. The test consists of seven passages, each of which is about 600 words long, taken from the humanities, social sciences, and natural sciences. Each passage-based set consists of five to seven questions that assess your ability to extrapolate information from the accompanying passage. In total, there are 40 questions in this section.

- **Writing Sample (WS)**
  Consisting of two 30-minute essays, the WS assesses your skill in developing ideas cohesively and logically, and writing clearly and accurately. Your general assignment will be to craft a response to a "prompt"—or statement—that discusses a topic of general interest in areas such as business, politics, or history (as examples). Topics do not pertain to the technical content of biology, chemistry, physics, or math, or to religious or other emotionally charged issues.

- **Biological Sciences (BS)**
  The format of the BS section, which covers biology and organic chemistry, is identical to that of the PS section. It too has 52 questions, 39 passage-based and 13 independent. Like the PS section, it also tests your problem-solving ability and scientific knowledge (but in this instance based on biological sciences).

There's another reason for the wide range of content you'll find covered on the MCAT® exam. Medical school faculty hope to encourage undergraduates with broad educational backgrounds to consider careers in medicine, and, on the flip side, they want to persuade premed majors to explore a wide variety of courses outside of the natural sciences. That explains why the exam tests for such diverse abilities, and why everyone has an equal crack at achieving a high score (assuming they've mastered the entry-level science courses tested on the exam).

## MCAT® Scores

There are five scores associated with the MCAT® exam, one for each of the four sections, and a "composite" (or total) score that presents the results in the aggregate. The following is a quick overview:

- Each of the three multiple-choice sections (PS, VR, and BS) is scored individually from a low of 1 to a high of 15.

- The WS is scored on an alphabetic scale, from a low of J to a high of T.

- In addition to the four scores above, you will also receive a score representing the total of your three multiple-choice sections together with your writing score. If, for example, you received a 9-10-11 and P, your total score would be reported as 30P.

*If you'd like to learn more about the scoring process itself, including how scores are "equated" across test forms and the myth of the "curve," you'll find a full discussion included in The Official Guide to the MCAT® Exam, available for purchase online: www.aamc.org/officialmcatguide.*

### Putting Your Scores in Context

**Comparing Your Score to Other Applicants and Acceptees, in General**
For more information about how your score compares to others (and how likely you are to be accepted to any medical school based on your score and other selection factors), see Chapter 10 on Applicant and Acceptee Data or *www.aamc.org/facts*.

**Comparing Your Score to Those Accepted by a Specific Medical School**
You're likely to want to know even more—namely, how your scores compare to those accepted by the specific medical school(s) in which you're interested. For that information, view individual school profiles on the MSAR® website: *www.aamc.org/msar*.

## Preparing for the Exam

There's no real mystery when it comes to preparing for the MCAT® exam. Although there are a number of ways to get ready—poring over various review guides, studying your class notes, rereading your textbooks, and/or taking a commercial prep course—it all comes down to the same three steps:

1. *Master the content.* You should complete the usual premedical biology, general and organic chemistry, and physics coursework before you take the MCAT® exam. (You can learn more about the specific subject matter covered on the exam by reviewing the topic outlines posted on the MCAT® web site.)

2. *Become familiar with the exam.* You'll also want to get comfortable with the passage-based testing format, prepare with "real" questions (i.e., ones that appeared on previous MCAT® exams), gain insights as to why specific answers are correct, and become familiar with the pitfalls that sometimes trip up examinees.

3. *Practice effectively.* Finally, you've got to practice as effectively as possible. You'll want to create your own mock testing environment—one that mimics the operational exam—and focus much of your effort on your weak spots. The AAMC's official practice tests (see box at right) can provide that opportunity.

As always, we recommend you speak to your advisor for further guidance in preparing for the exam.

## Test Dates, Registration, and Fees

The MCAT® exam is administered more than two dozen times each year from January through September. (Specific dates are listed on the **MCAT® Exam Schedule**, posted on the MCAT® Web site at *www.aamc.org/mcat*.) While the AAMC selects exam dates to ensure that scores are available to meet most medical school application deadlines, we recommend that you check the specific scheduling requirements of the school(s) of your choice, provided in the "school pages" of this guide. Once you've determined the date you prefer, you can find the registration schedule for that particular exam session on the **MCAT® Registration Deadline & Score Release Schedule**, also posted online.

After you have read the MCAT® Essentials (*www.aamc.org/mcat*), you can register for the exam—a process available online through the MCAT® web site. There will be a fee of $235 for each exam you take, a payment that covers both the cost of the test itself as well as distribution of your scores. If you register late, make changes to your registration, and/or test at an international site, there will be additional charges.

As a general rule, you should plan on taking the MCAT® exam 12 to 18 months prior to your expected entry into medical school—but not before you've completed basic coursework in general biology, inorganic chemistry, organic chemistry, and general physics. Many medical schools prefer that applicants take the MCAT® exam in the spring because of the short time between the availability of late summer scores and school application deadlines. (Taking the exam in the spring also allows time for students to retake the test later in the summer, if necessary). For more guidance, please see your pre-health advisor.

## Testing with Accommodations

The AAMC supports the policies of the federal government and will provide accommodations to students whose disabilities—or other conditions—necessitate an adjustment to the test or testing environment, pending review and approval by the MCAT® Office of Accommodated Testing Services. Information about the process by which accommodations are requested (and the documentation that must accompany the request) is available at *www.aamc.org/mcat*.

### MCAT® Preparation Resources

**Computer-aided instruction.**
The Official MCAT® Web Site. Your first stop should be the MCAT® Web site (*www.aamc.org/mcat*) where you will find a wealth of information. Included there, and available free of charge, are such materials as the MCAT® Essentials (required reading), a "Preparing for the Exam" section, and Preparation FAQs.

**The Official Guide to the MCAT® Exam.**
You can get even more detailed information from this affordable 400-page guidebook (*www.aamc.org/officialmcatguide*), which includes more than 100 practice questions taken from real exams, tips to arrive at the correct answer, thoroughly explained solutions, step-by-step registration instructions, and extensive data on both applicants and acceptees.

**Official Practice Tests from the AAMC.**
Also available are eight practice tests—updated versions of retired exams—that include solutions for each item, automated scoring and diagnostics, customizable feedback, and test assistance features such as the ability to highlight and search the passage text. **One of the practice tests is available free-of-charge at *www.e-mcat.com*.**

## Score Reporting

The time between the date of your exam and the day you find out how you did can seem like an eternity. In reality, though, scores will be reported through the MCAT® program's computerized Testing History Report System (THx) approximately 30 days after each exam. Through this program, located at *www.aamc. org/mcat*, you can check your scores and print your own official score report.

Of course, you're not the only one who's interested in finding out how you did. The medical schools to which you've applied (or will apply) want to know, as well. How then do admissions committees learn of their applicants' scores?

- *Automatic Score Release to AMCAS:*
  The good news is that, in most cases, it's all automatic—and no action is required on your part. The American Medical College Application Service, or AMCAS® (see box at right), automatically releases your scores via the THx for all scores that date from April 2003 (which is probably your situation). For those of you who have scores prior to April 2003, you can use the THx system to make selected scores part of your current AMCAS® application.

- *Score Release to Non-AMCAS® Schools:* For the 2011 entering classes, all but 9 of the 134 U.S. medical schools are part of the AMCAS® program. In the event you're applying to a non-AMCAS® institution, you can use the THx system to select those recipients.

*The various options and procedures available through the THx system are explained in detail when you log into the system.*

### What's AMCAS®?

AMCAS® is a nonprofit, centralized application processing service in which most U.S. medical schools take part, and the process by which you will manage your application (to participating institutions). Through this system, scores are submitted to each school you've designated. For more information, please see Chapter 6, in which we discuss the AMCAS® application process in detail.

## Retaking the Exam

If you're not happy with your performance on the MCAT® exam, you have the option to take it again. But it's a tough decision. Many medical schools average the scores from all tests taken—or consider only the last take—so that if you do worse the second time around, you may have actually weakened your position.

There are times when a retake is well worth considering. Perhaps you discovered that your coursework or study didn't cover the topics as thoroughly as you needed. Or there's a large discrepancy between your grade in a subject and your score on a particular section. Or maybe you simply didn't feel well the day of the exam. In all these cases, your pre-health advisor may be of great help, and we recommend you discuss the issue with him or her.

If you decide to retake the exam, please bear in mind that it may be taken a maximum of three times during each calendar year. Registration procedures for retaking the exam are identical to those for initial testing.

*The MCAT® exam is administered and scored by the MCAT® Program Office at the direction of the AAMC. Information about the exam's content, organization, scoring system, accommodations process, and more, is available at www.aamc.org/mcat.*

### Preparing for a Retake

When matriculating medical students were asked for the major reason their scores improved upon a retake (if their scores improved), here's what they said:

**Preparation Method**

Changing my study habits ...................................................39.1

Taking online MCAT® practice exam ...................................25.3

Taking an MCAT® preparation course ...............................12.6

Taking additional coursework ...............................................7.4

Getting advice from advisor/mentor......................................1.1

Private tutoring.......................................................................1.9

*Source: AAMC's 2010 Matriculating Student Questionnaire (MSQ)*

# Chapter 5:

## Choosing the School That's Right for You

*No doubt you have many questions about the medical school application process. What forms will I need to complete? What are the logistics involved? What type of supporting documentation must I get? What's the timing of it all? How much will it cost me?*

*We address all that in the next chapter. For now, though, you've got an even bigger question to consider, and that's because the initial stage of the application process isn't really a "how" at all. It's a "where." You first need to figure out to which school (or schools) you should apply. It's a question that is answered by looking not only at various medical schools, but at yourself, as well.*

*Because you're not searching merely for a school you can "get into." You're searching for a match.*

### The Overall Mission of the School

If you've seen one medical school…you've seen one medical school.

That's the standard way of saying that medical schools differ from one another. And many of these differences are pretty obvious. Some schools are located in the East; some in the West. Some are private; others, public. Some have a large entering class; others, small. And, as we explained in Chapter 3, medical schools vary in the content of their courses, in the way they teach, and even in the way they grade students.

These are all factors you'll want to consider as you narrow your selection, and we touch upon them in the pages that follow. But the differences go even deeper, and at a very core level: Medical schools have diverse missions and priorities. Because of those distinctions, what's significant to one school may be of only moderate importance to another, and these goals naturally carry into the selection process.

To figure out where to apply, then, requires that you become aware not only of the differences among schools, but that you also analyze yourself—your skills, experiences, career goals, and so forth—to identify the most appropriate matches. Take, for instance, an institution that places a strong emphasis on primary care. Is that the career path you intend to follow? If so, and especially if you can demonstrate your interest through extensive experience related to that area, you become a more attractive candidate on that basis alone.

That's one example. Other schools may be actively seeking students from specific geographic or rural areas. Others may be looking for students with a high potential for a research career. Still others may want to increase the number of doctors who plan to practice in their states (this last goal is often found among public institutions). The differing missions among schools will be reflected in their admissions policies and standards.

If you need help with this self-analysis, think back to the various experiences you've had over the years. The ones you found especially rewarding or inspirational are likely to correlate to a specific area of interest, and, by extension, a career goal.

- Did you volunteer two summers for a clinic in a **rural, underserved area**? Perhaps that's the direction you'd like your career to take, and, if so, you'll want to seek out medical schools that place a high priority on that area.

- Were the part-time jobs you had with a research firm particularly gratifying? If you'd like to pursue **a research career**, look for schools that have a strong reputation in that area or are known for graduating a large percentage of medical students going into research careers.

- There are also other ways that speak to your interests and career goals. Did you spend your junior year tutoring freshmen and sophomores in entry-level biology or chemistry? Perhaps you'd like to join a **medical school faculty** and educate the next generation of physicians. If so, look for a medical school with a relatively large percentage of their graduates in teaching positions.

Once again, keep in mind that this is a two-way street. While you're looking for a match, so are the schools. Your experiences will provide good insights for the admissions officers and help them determine if your interests and their missions are congruent.

## The Educational Program

As you weigh your decision, you'll also want to consider the differences among the educational programs themselves. We touch on a few of these below.

- There's very likely going to be a relationship between a school's mission and its **curriculum**. You'll therefore be able to further gauge whether a particular institution's objectives and your interests align by analyzing course requirements and electives programs. A medical school with a mission to graduate more primary care doctors may, for example, have a track that provides for additional training in that area. A school that emphasizes research might have their students devote an extended period of time to scholarly pursuits.

- As you do your research, also consider what **teaching methods** you find most effective. Do you tend to do well with self-directed or participatory learning exercises, or do you do better with the more traditional, lecture-based style of learning? While most medical schools use an educational model that combines various methods, there will be a difference as to precisely how this mix has been adapted. You'll want to explore the degree to which you're likely to find small group discussions and problem-based learning exercises (as examples) versus a traditional teaching approach. A good starting point for your exploration is a school's Web site, as well as the AAMC's curriculum directory.

- There are key differences as to **grading intervals** (or systems). Some institutions use a pass/fail system; others an honors/pass/fail system; and still others use letter grades. Some students have definite preferences, and if you're one of them, you may wish to consider a school's grading system as you narrow your selection.

There are many other factors connected with the educational program that you might want to think about. How will you be evaluated? At what point must students pass the first two steps of the United States Medical Licensing Examination (USMLE) before advancing in their education? What level of academic support is available? Is there a mentor system, for instance? What about support services or organizations for cultural and other minorities—are they available? Questions such as these will undoubtedly enter into your final decision as you deliberate between offers, and you may wish to consider them now.

### "How Do My Grades and MCAT® Scores Factor In?"

Don't choose schools based solely on where you think your grades and MCAT® scores will be accepted. While there's no question that your educational record is important and that admissions officers seek candidates who are likely to succeed academically in their programs, it's important to realize that **academics alone do not predict who will become an effective physician, and admissions officers know that all too well**.

The very fact that there are so many instances in which a "high scoring" applicant does not receive an acceptance to medical school—and in which an applicant with lower-than-average grades and scores does—tells you that admissions officers must be looking at other factors.

Admissions officers are taking a more "holistic" approach to evaluating their applicants, a method we discuss thoroughly in Chapter 7. Through this practice, admissions officers assess their candidates more broadly, looking not only at their "metrics" (GPA and MCAT® scores) but at their experiences and personal attributes, as well.

You can read about the holistic approach to admissions in Chapter 7, "The Admissions Decision."

### Attending Medical School in Your "Home" State

State residents enrolled in state-supported medical schools pay lower tuition than nonresidents. In addition to that, though, in-state residents are often given preference for admission (compared to out-of-state residents) for at least some of their places because the school receives state government support. You therefore may want to give strong consideration to the public institution in your state as you decide where to apply.

And many students do just that. Nationally, 62 percent of 2010 matriculants attended schools in their home states.

### State Residency Requirements

Requirements are established by state legislatures and are usually available from school officials or the school's (or state's) Web site. We encourage you to clarify your official residency status before applying.

## Public or Private?

You also may be deliberating between public and private institutions. If you're considering a public medical school in your state of residence, one aspect of this decision, as we just mentioned, is likely to be cost. (If you're from out of state, the cost differential between a public institution and a private school virtually disappears. See chart in Chapter 11.) But don't automatically assume, even if you are interested in a state school near your home, that the private route will be more expensive under all circumstances. Some private institutions, for example, may have large endowments that allow them to provide significant scholarship aid to qualifying students and thus lower the "effective" tuition rate, permitting those students to graduate with less educational debt than they would have generated if they had attended a public medical school in their "home" state.

But cost is only one consideration. Another element to be aware of when investigating the differences between private and public institutions is the school's mission—and how it might relate to your own aspirations and interests. Although all medical schools—public or private—have different missions, certain public institutions may have specific goals related to their state, such as increasing the supply of physicians there. (If the school is in your home state and you'd like to remain there after graduation, that will be a factor from both your perspective and the school's.) Other public institutions were founded by state legislators with an emphasis on the needs of a particular patient population—such as elder, rural, or underserved groups—which should enter into your evaluation if that objective corresponds to your own.

### International Students

There are only a small number of international students—those who are not U.S. citizens or permitted to reside permanently in this country—at U.S. medical schools. If you hope to be among this group, know that private medical schools are more likely to accept international students than public schools, and that most medical schools require completion of premedical coursework at a U.S. college or university.

## Additional Factors to Consider

There are many other factors that may be important to you as you search for a good "match." Some of these include:

- **Location**

  Besides the impact of state residency on the costs of a public medical school, there are other aspects to the issue of location and how it factors into your decision where to apply. Perhaps you simply prefer a specific geographic region. Do you, for example, want to be close to family and friends? Do you prefer a warmer (or cooler) climate? Are you a fan of the East coast…or the South…or the West? These factors play to your comfort level, and are all valid considerations. Beyond that, though, location can also relate to your career goals, as well as to a school's mission. If you hope to specialize in geriatrics, for example, a medical school located in an area with a higher-than-average proportion of older adults may be able to provide you with the experience you seek.

  That's looking at it from your perspective. Consider, for a moment, the school's perspective. In some cases, a school may be seeking students from particular geographic regions in order to bolster its diversity, and you'll want to consider the impact—if any—that your own state residence might have on your application to medical schools in other areas.

- **Size and Demographics**

  The size and demographics of the medical school—both in terms of its student body as well as its faculty—may be a consideration for you, as well. The school entries in this guide include data on the prior year's entering class, including the number of students by gender as well as by (self-reported) race and ethnicity.

- **Costs**

  Medical education doesn't come cheap, and the expenses associated with particular institutions will no doubt be a factor in your decision. At this stage, though, you won't know what your actual costs will be (or the degree of assistance you will get) until a school sends you a financial aid package in conjunction with its offer. Still, in looking through the school entries, you can get a general idea as to the relative expenses of various institutions, and you will probably keep that in mind as you narrow your selection.

## Special Regional Opportunities

Finally, you should be aware that some states without a public medical school participate in special interstate and regional agreements to provide their residents with access to a medical education. Currently, there are six interstate agreements, listed below:

- The Delaware Institute of Medical Education and Research
  *http://dhss.delaware.gov/dhss/dhcc/dimer.html*
  1-302-577-3240, 1-800-292-7934

- The Finance Authority of Maine's Access to Medical Education Program
  *www.famemaine.com/files/Pages/education/students_and_families/Medical_Education.aspx*
  1-800-228-3734

- University of Utah School of Medicine Idaho Contract
  *http://medicine.utah.edu/admissions/begin/residency.htm*
  1-208-282-2475, residency@sa.utah.edu

- The Western Interstate Commission for Higher Education
  *www.wiche.edu/SEP/PSEP/cert-off.asp*
  1-303-541-0200

- The WWAMI (Washington, Wyoming, Alaska, Montana, and Idaho) Program
  *http://uwmedicine.washington.edu/Education/WWAMI/Pages/Medical-School.aspx*

You can learn more about each of these regional opportunities by visiting their Web sites or calling their program offices.

---

### The Importance of Additional Factors

Just because we call them "additional" doesn't lessen their importance. Below is the percentage to which matriculating students felt specific factors were either a positive or very positive factor in choosing the medical school they now attend:

| | |
|---|---|
| Geographic location of school | 80.0% |
| Faculty mentorship | 72.1% |
| Diversity of the student body | 57.1% |
| Financial costs of attending | 54.2% |
| Diversity of the faculty | 47.4% |

*Source: AAMC's 2010 Matriculating Student Questionnaire (MSQ)*

# Chapter 6:

## Applying to Medical School

*Ahh…the signs of spring. The robins chirp, the dandelions bloom, and thousands of students embark on the annual application process to medical school. This year, one of those students is likely to be you.*

*The big question is how to proceed.*

### The Responsibilities of the Medical School Applicant

It is vital that you be aware of the responsibilities you have as an applicant to medical school. These are reviewed at length at the end of this chapter, but we'd like to list a few of the most critical below:

- Meet all deadlines
- Complete the AMCAS® application accurately
- Know the admission requirements at each school
- Promptly notify AMCAS® of any change in contact information
- Respond promptly to interview invitations
- File for financial aid as soon as possible
- Withdraw from the schools you will not attend

*Please see "AAMC Recommendations for Medical School and M.D.-Ph.D. Candidates" on page 37 for detail.*

*Now that you've identified the schools that seem right for you, you're ready to tackle the steps in applying to them. In this chapter, we'll review the AAMC's American Medical College Application Service (AMCAS®), provide an overview of the application and admissions cycle, talk about your personal statement and letters of recommendation, and give you information about application costs and other specifics.*

### American Medical College Application Service (AMCAS®)

You very likely may have heard about AMCAS® from your pre-health advisor, career counselor, or even your classmates. In a nutshell, AMCAS® is a Web-based application processing service offered by the AAMC and utilized by almost every medical school in the country. (For schools that do not participate in AMCAS®, see box on page 33.) This service does not screen applicants, but rather provides admissions officers with an abundance of information they can use to make preliminary assessments.

This service has benefits to applicants, as well. The most obvious one is that AMCAS® allows students to apply to as many medical schools as they want with a single application (although many schools require a "secondary application," a topic we will discuss later in this chapter). Beyond that, it provides applicants with a single point of transmission for official transcripts, letters of recommendation, and other supporting documentation.

Even if you're not yet ready to begin the application process, you might want to go to *www.aamc.org/amcas* for a preview. There, you'll find links to key steps involved in starting an application, including an application timeline, tips, and checklists useful in completing the application, answers to frequently asked questions, and a comprehensive instruction booklet.

## Sections of the AMCAS® Application

The AMCAS® application consists of nine basic sections. It might sound like a lot, but remember…you don't have to complete it all in one sitting. (You can save your work and return to your application as many times as you wish until you've finished it.) We thought we'd give you an overview of what to expect:

1. **Identifying Information.** This section asks you to enter your name, identification numbers, birth information, and sex.

2. **Schools Attended.** Here, you'll enter high school and college information. Once this section (and the identifying section above) is completed, you will be able to download a "transcript request form" from AMCAS®.

3. **Biographic Information.** You'll use this section to enter basic information about citizenship, legal residence, languages spoken, and other biographic information.

4. **Course Work.** You'll next enter grades and credits for every course that you have enrolled in at any U.S., U.S. territorial, or Canadian postsecondary institution. (It is important that you provide information for all courses.)

5. **Work/Activities.** Here, you'll enter any work and extracurricular activities, awards, honors, or publications that you would like to bring to the attention of the medical school(s). Up to 15 experiences may be listed.

6. **Letters of Evaluation.** You will use this section to provide information about letters of evaluation that will be submitted to schools on your behalf. (We cover this step in a bit more detail later in this chapter.)

7. **Medical Schools.** In this section, you will designate the medical schools to which you want to submit an application. In addition to that, you will have an opportunity to designate which letters of recommendation you wish to submit to specific schools.

8. **Personal Statement.** Here, you will compose a personal essay. (We discuss this step more thoroughly later in this chapter, as well.)

9. **Standardized Tests.** And finally…your MCAT® scores. In this section, you'll review your MCAT® scores and enter any additional test information such as GRE scores. Please note: MCAT® scores earned in 2003 or later will automatically be released to AMCAS®, and no further action will be required on your part.

Bear in mind that the above is a brief overview of the AMCAS® application. We suggest you read the instruction book, available online, and explore the various resources on the general AMCAS® site at *www.aamc.org/amcas*.

### AMCAS® Registration

If you have previously registered for the MCAT® exam, the Fee Assistance Program, or other AAMC services, you have already selected an AAMC username and password and received an AAMC ID. **Please use this same access information to enter the AMCAS® application site.** If, on the other hand, you have not registered for an AAMC service, you will need to complete the AMCAS® registration form, select a username and password, and be assigned an AAMC ID. Go to *www.aamc.org/amcas* whenever you're ready to begin the process.

### Transcript Requests via AMCAS®

In addition to completing your AMCAS® application, you must request that an official transcript be forwarded to AMCAS® by the registrar of every postsecondary school you've attended. Here again, AMCAS® facilitates the application process by providing a "transcript request form." This includes junior college, community college, trade school, or other professional school—regardless of whether credit was earned—within the United States, Canada, or U.S. territories. (This requirement also applies to any college courses you took in high school.) For regular applicants, all official transcripts must be received no later than two weeks following the deadline date for application materials. Please refer to the AMCAS® online instruction booklet or help text for detailed information about official transcript requirements.

### Limited Changes After Submission

You'll want to check your work carefully before you hit "submit." That's because you're limited in what changes you can make to your application following submission. More specifically, you can make changes to your contact information (such as addresses) and add additional schools or letters of recommendation. Other than these few exceptions, your application will be submitted to schools exactly as you have completed it.

### To How Many Schools Do Students Apply

For the 2011 AMCAS® application cycle, students applied to an average of 14 schools.

*Source: AMCAS® Data*

## Application Processing and Verification

Once AMCAS® has received the service fee and official transcripts from each postsecondary school at which you've been registered, AMCAS® verifies the accuracy of your academic record by comparing the information you entered on the application to that contained in your transcripts. Once processing has been completed, AMCAS® makes the application available to all medical schools you designated and distributes MCAT® scores. (As mentioned earlier, MCAT® scores from 2003 and later are automatically included; those from years prior to 2003 are provided to medical schools only if the applicant has released those scores to AMCAS®.)

## The Application and Admissions Cycle

Now that you have an idea as to what the AMCAS® process involves, you're likely wondering when it all takes place. Generally speaking, the AMCAS® application process opens to students in early May of each year, and participating schools begin receiving applicant data in late June.

Also generally speaking, the deadlines for receipt of primary applications to medical schools that participate in AMCAS® are from mid-October to mid-December. (See page 35 for information on secondary applications.) Speaking in specifics, though, there is no one application timetable, as each school establishes its own deadlines for receipt of required materials. You can find the dates in medical schools' bulletins and Web sites and in the school listings in this guide. It is critical, of course, that you are aware of and adhere to all deadlines.

That's probably obvious.

What is less obvious, though, is that medical schools vary not only in terms of their application deadlines, but also in the timing by which they make their admissions decisions. Most schools use a system of "rolling admissions," selecting students for interviews (and sending out acceptance letters!) as the applications are received, rather than waiting until a specific cut-off date before beginning their decision process. In these instances, schools are likely to have offered admission to some students while others have yet to be interviewed—meaning that you run the risk that a medical school you're interested in fills all slots for its entering class before you've even had a turn at bat!

(You can find out if a medical school uses a rolling admissions system by checking its Web site.) That's why, when it comes to applying to medical school…the sooner, the better.

As far as interviews go, admissions committees usually meet with candidates from fall through spring, with most interviews held during the winter months. (We discuss this part of the admissions cycle in Chapter 7.) By March 30, medical schools will—by collective agreement—issue a number of acceptances at least equal to the size of their first-year entering class.

## Personal Statements and Letters of Recommendation

As you'll learn when you get to Chapter 7, admissions officers want to know more about you than just where you went to college, what courses you took and what grades you got, and how you scored on the MCAT® exam. They want to know who you are at a more personal level. That's why an essay and letters of recommendation are integral components of your application to medical school and part of the AMCAS® process. We briefly describe both of these on the following page.

### Your Personal Statement

Every applicant is required to submit a Personal Comments essay of up to 5,300 characters (or approximately one page) in length. This is your opportunity to distinguish yourself from the others and provide admissions officers with insights as to why you are interested in medicine—and why you would be a dedicated and effective physician.

You should know that many admissions committees place significant weight on this section, so you should take the time and effort to craft an organized, well-written, and compelling statement. Some questions you may want to consider while formulating your essay are:

- Why have you selected the field of medicine?

- What motivates you to learn more about medicine? Were there any special hardships, challenges, or obstacles that may have influenced your decision?

- Or, were there any special hardships or challenges that you overcame in general?

- What do you want medical schools to know about you that hasn't been disclosed in another section of the application? Are there, for example, any significant fluctuations in your academic record that are not explained elsewhere?

- Why are you unique? What sets you apart from the pack?

As you begin to carve out your essay, keep in mind that in order to be unique, you must be specific. Rather than write, for example, that *"challenges in my childhood led me to consider medicine at an early age,"* write that *"the summer I turned eight my 11-year-old sister was diagnosed with Diabetes Type I, and I witnessed first-hand the compassion and understanding with which the doctor dealt with my parents. It was during those first few difficult months that I decided I wanted to be a physician."*

In addition to being specific, you will want to ensure that your essay is persuasive (and interesting!), follows a logical and orderly flow, and relates to your reasons for choosing medicine and/or why you believe you will be successful in medical school and as a physician. Beyond that, of course, your writing must adhere to correct grammar and be free of typographical errors and misspellings.

### Letters of Recommendation or Evaluation

Medical schools have various requirements regarding letters of recommendation or evaluation, but they all require them in one form or another. If your college has a pre-health advisor, for example, medical schools will probably require a letter from him or her (or from the pre-med committee, if your school has one) as well as a letter of evaluation from at least one faculty member. In instances where there is no pre-health advisor, many medical schools may ask for additional letters from faculty—often specifying that at least one comes from a science professor. Still, other medical schools do not specify from where the letters come, welcome additional letters beyond those that are required, and/or limit the number they will accept. In all cases, you should review the Web sites of the medical schools in which you are interested to learn of their specific requirements.

In general, though—and as you would expect—medical schools want references from those who are in a position to judge your ability to be successful in medical school. While these individuals are largely in the academic arena, primarily pre-health advisors and science professors, those outside the "college gates" may also be helpful. If the medical school you are considering invites additional letters, you might want to ask your current supervisor, particularly if the position is medically related.

In all cases, letters should be from those who know you well and will speak enthusiastically about your abilities, dedication, and unique traits. Beyond that, though, make sure to seek out those whose opinions will be highly valued. (Admissions committees, for example, are not likely to value the input of your teaching assistant. On the other hand, they will weigh heavily the thoughts of the chair of the biology department who taught your "honors" biology class.) In short, seek out letters from those who know you well…can speak highly of you…and count in the eyes of the admissions committee!

## Secondary Applications

Your "primary" application is that associated with AMCAS®. In addition, though, about half of all medical schools require school-specific, or "secondary," applications. That's because, while the primary application provides admissions officers with much of the information they need, by its very nature a universal application—such as AMCAS®—cannot be "all things to all people" and address issues specific to individual schools. Many institutions therefore require a secondary application that will be used to assess students' reasons for applying to that particular school. (Medical schools will notify you if such an application is needed.) Secondary applications may call for additional letters of recommendation, supplementary writing samples, and/or updated transcripts. Go to the Web sites of the medical schools in which you are interested to learn more.

## Costs of Applying

Finally, and as you probably know, there are fees associated with applying to medical school. These costs fall into four general categories, which we summarize below.

### Primary Application

For the 2012 entering class, the fee was $160 for the first school and $32 for each additional school. (Remember, too, that there are several schools that do not use AMCAS® and that you may incur a different fee in those instances.)

### Secondary Application

Fees for secondary applications typically range from $25 to $100.

### College Service Fees

There is usually a small fee for transmittal of your transcript from your college registrar and occasionally a fee for transmittal of letters of recommendation.

### MCAT® Exam Fees

Although technically not an "application" fee, the costs associated with the MCAT® exam are a necessary component of the overall process. Registration for the MCAT® exam is $235 and covers the cost of the exam as well as distribution of your scores. In addition, you may incur fees for late registration, changes to your registration, or testing at international test sites. You can read more about the MCAT® exam in Chapter 4 and at the MCAT® web site (*www.aamc.org/mcat*).

Go to *www.aamc.org/firstfacts* for more information on the costs of applying.

## Criminal Background Check

The AAMC has initiated a national background check service through which Certiphi Screening, Inc. (a Vertical Screen® Company) will obtain a background report on all accepted applicants to participating medical schools. This service benefits both medical schools and applicants alike, filling the needs of schools to obtain criminal background checks, while, at the same time, preventing applicants from paying additional fees to each medical school to which they are accepted. For more information, please go to *www.aamc.org/students/applying/ amcas/faqs/63230/faq_background.html*.

You should be aware that participating medical schools may continue to require applicants to undergo a separate national background check process, if required to do so by their own institutional regulations or by applicable state law.

## Fee Assistance Program

The AAMC's Fee Assistance Program (FAP), available to individuals with financial limitations,* assists MCAT® examinees and AMCAS® applicants by reducing the associated costs. FAP recipients receive:

- Waiver of the application fee for submitting the completed AMCAS® application to a maximum of 14 medical schools. (Applicants paid $32 for each school beyond the 14 free applications.)

- Reduction of the MCAT® registration fee from $235 to $85.

- One complimentary copy of the *Official Guide to the MCAT Exam®* and access to the *Medical School Admissions Requirements (MSAR®)* website.

Go to *www.aamc.org/fap* for details on this program.

*FAP eligibility decisions are tied directly to the U.S. Department of Health and Human Services' poverty-level guidelines. For the 2011 calendar year, applicants whose total family income is 300 percent or less of the poverty level for their family size are eligible for fee assistance.*

## Special Note About Deferred Entry

In recent years, most medical schools have developed delayed matriculation policies to allow their accepted applicants to defer entry without giving up their medical school places. Deferrals are only granted after acceptance. These programs usually require that the applicant submit a written request, and some schools may also ask for a report at the end of the deferral period. Delays of matriculation are usually granted for one year, although some schools may occasionally defer for longer periods of time. Some institutions may require delayed matriculants to sign an agreement to not apply to other medical schools in the interim, while others permit application to other schools. Interested applicants should seek specific information from schools where they applied.

## AAMC Recommendations for Medical School and M.D.-Ph.D. Candidates

To help ensure that all M.D. and M.D.-Ph.D. candidates are provided timely notification of the outcome of their application and timely access to available first-year positions, and that schools and programs are protected from having unfilled positions in their entering classes, the Association of American Medical Colleges has distributed the following recommendations. They are provided for the information of prospective students, their advisors, and personnel at the medical schools and programs to which they apply. The AAMC recommends that:

1. Each applicant be familiar with, understand, and comply with the application, acceptance, and admission procedures at each school or program to which the applicant has applied, as well as with these Recommendations.

2. Each applicant provide accurate and truthful information in all aspects of the application, acceptance, and admission processes for each school or program to which the applicant has applied.

3. Each applicant submit all application documents (e.g., primary and secondary application forms, transcript[s], letters of evaluation/recommendation, fees) to each school in a timely manner and no later than the school's or program's published deadline date.

4. Each applicant promptly notify all relevant medical school application services and all medical schools or programs with independent application processes of any change, permanent or temporary, in contact information (e.g., mailing address, telephone number, e-mail address).

5. Any applicant who will be unavailable for an extended period of time (e.g., during foreign travel, vacation, holidays) during the application/admission process:

   a. Provide instructions regarding his or her application and the authority to respond to offers of acceptance to a parent or other responsible individual in the applicant's absence.

   b. Inform all schools or programs at which the applicant remains under consideration of this individual's name and contact information.

6. Each applicant respond promptly to a school's or program's invitation for interview. Any applicant who cannot appear for a previously scheduled interview should notify the school or program immediately of the cancellation of the appointment in the manner requested by the school or program.

7. Each applicant in need of financial aid initiate, as early as possible, the steps necessary to determine eligibility, including the early filing of appropriate need analysis forms and the encouragement of parents, when necessary, to file required income tax forms.

8. In fairness to other applicants, when an applicant has made a decision, prior to May 15, April 30 for M.D.-Ph.D. applicants, not to attend a medical school or program that has made an offer of acceptance, the applicant promptly withdraw his or her application from that (those) other school(s) or program(s) by written correspondence delivered by regular or electronic methods.

9. By May 15 of the matriculation year (April 15 for schools whose first day of class is on or before July 30), April 30 for M.D.-Ph.D. programs, each applicant who has received an offer of acceptance from more than one school or program choose the specific school or program at which the applicant prefers to enroll and withdraw his or her application, by written correspondence delivered by regular or electronic methods, from all other schools or programs from which acceptance offers have been received. (See additional explanation in box below.)

10. Immediately upon enrollment in, or initiation of an orientation program immediately prior to enrollment at, a U.S. or Canadian school or program, each applicant withdraw his or her application from consideration at all other schools or programs at which he or she remains under consideration.

*Approved: Council of Deans Administrative Board, February 17, 2009*

# Chapter 7:

## The Admissions Decision

*Your heart pounds as you tear open the envelope or click on the e-mail. Will the answer be yea—or nay?*

*So much seems to come down to this moment. The years of college study and extracurricular activities, the MCAT® exam and application process, the campus tours and interviews—all culminate as you learn whether the admissions committee at the medical school(s) of your choice has offered you a slot in its entering class.*

*You know how you chose to which schools to apply. How do schools choose which applicants to accept?*

---

### AAMC Recommends a Holistic Approach...

In its *Handbook for Admissions Officers*, the AAMC clearly states that admissions committees have a responsibility to **"Create the process that identifies applicants whose personal characteristics, level of educational achievement, and professional and career goals conform to those of the institution and who are most likely to contribute to and benefit from the school's learning climate."**

*Source: AAMC Handbook for Admissions Officers*

---

### The Holistic Approach to Medical School Admissions

Holistic. What does that mean, and how does it enter into the admissions decision?

The term comes from the Greek word holos—meaning all, entire, or total—and it's far from a new idea. In fact, Aristotle himself is credited with having recognized that "the whole is greater than the sum of its parts" in his philosophical work Metaphysics more than two millennia ago. Fast forward 2,000 years and you'll find that medical school admissions committees are making use of this very concept.

How so? In brief, admissions officers carefully review a multitude of criteria—rather than emphasize just one or two facets—in order to gain an appreciation of the "whole" person. Take, for example, the erroneous belief among many applicants that admissions officers weigh high GPAs and MCAT® scores above all else. While these metrics are important components of the admissions decision, they are only one part of the overall package. That explains why there are so many instances in which a high-scoring student with a near-perfect GPA does not get into medical school, and why many of those with scores and grades below the average do.

Obviously, something more than metrics alone enters into the admissions decision.

In fact, according to a survey of medical schools conducted by the AAMC, the #1 factor that determines your acceptance to medical school is…the interview. It all ties back to the fact that schools have different missions, and that it is during the interview that admissions officers can really get a sense of who you are and how well your interests and aspirations align with their own goals and purpose. If that sounds familiar, it should. It's the flip side to the analysis you did while you were searching for the "right" schools, analyzing the goals and philosophies of individual schools to determine where you would best fit. Now, it's the medical school's turn to do the same thing from its perspective.

## Experiences

Your experiences convey a lot about your interests, your capabilities, and your knowledge. As a result, medical schools take a hard look at what you've done—and where you've been—up to this stage in your life. It helps them gauge not only how likely you are to be successful in their programs, but to what degree you will support their mission and contribute as a physician.

We mentioned in the chapter on undergraduate preparation how important your extracurricular activities may be to an admissions committee, and we don't mean just those clubs and organizations within your college. We mean outside of school, as well. Your experience—particularly that related to medical or clinical work—is an important component of your appeal as a candidate to medical school.

Beyond that, the degree to which you contributed in these activities is vital, too. (See box below.) Medicals schools value a demonstration of true commitment, so if you have been an officer of an organization or a long-term member, for example, you'll want to make that clear to the admissions committee.

**Depth...not Breadth!**

As we mentioned in Chapter 2, a series of short-term involvements (volunteering a day here, spending an afternoon there, and so forth) does not really convey a true interest in the area, and this underlying motivation is actually transparent to admissions officers. Rather, admissions officers are looking for deep, committed participation in areas that are truly of importance to you. Only then are they able to gain some insights as to your real interests and judge how well your goals and their missions align.

Here again, the mission of each school will play a large part in how it evaluates your experiences. Institutions with a stated goal of increasing the number of physicians practicing in underserved areas will look with great interest on the summer you spent volunteering in a clinic in a rural location or inner city. In general, though, medical schools especially value community or volunteer experience related to the medical or clinical field.

### Concept of "Distance Traveled"

There's another element we'd like to draw to your attention. We mention in the box below that admissions officers are likely to place significance on any obstacles or hardships you've overcome to get to this point in your education. This is a concept known as "distance traveled," and medical schools view life challenges you've faced and conquered as admirable experience—and indicative of some very positive traits.

## Attributes

Admissions committees want to know if you have what it takes to become a good doctor. You've got to have the ability to master the science and medicine behind it all, of course, but you also must have some key personal attributes.

**Examples of Experiences Likely to Be Important to Admissions Committees**

- Serving as the primary caregiver for an ill family member
- Special obstacles or hardships overcome
- Employment history (if medically related)
- Research experience
- Experience in a health care setting
- Membership in community-based or volunteer organizations

*Source: Roadmap to Diversity: Integrating Holistic Review into Medical School Admissions Processes, AAMC 2010*

Are you empathetic? Do you have integrity? Can you communicate effectively? Traits such as these are necessary to develop into an effective physician, and admissions committees will use a number of means to determine if you possess them. While your experiences can help demonstrate your appeal in these areas (volunteering for three consecutive summers at a medical clinic certainly conveys dedication, for instance), admissions committees will look to your personal statement, letters of recommendation, and interview(s) to gauge whether you have the desired qualities.

## Examples of Attributes Likely to Be Important to Admissions Committees

- Adaptability
- Critical thinking
- Integrity
- Logical reasoning
- Oral communication skills
- Personal maturity
- Reliability
- Self-discipline
- Work habits
- Compassion
- Cultural competence
- Intellectual curiosity
- Motivation for medicine
- Persistence
- Professionalism
- Resilience
- Teamwork

*Source: Survey conducted by the AAMC's Medical College Admission Test staff, 2008*

Medical schools analyze a broad range of attributes, including those related to the applicant's skills and abilities, personal and professional characteristics, and demographic factors. Examples follow.

- **Skills and abilities** could include active listing, critical thinking, and multilingual ability

- **Personal and professional characteristics** could include resilience, intellectual curiosity, and empathy

- **Demographic factors** could include socioeconomic status, race, and gender

We've listed many of the attributes that admissions committees consider in evaluating their application. In addition to these general qualities, though, remember that medical schools give weight to specific characteristics in alignment with their missions. Examples could include research experience and potential, commitment to caring for the underserved, volunteer and community service experience, and knowledge about health care delivery systems.

## Metrics

Admissions committees also need to determine (of course!) if you have the academic skills and knowledge necessary to successfully complete the medical school program. To a large extent, committee members will look to your academic record and MCAT® scores to answer those questions. Taken together, these two measures provide objective information about your knowledge and ability (compared to other applicants).

## Academic History

Your academic history helps admission committees establish whether your study skills, persistence, course of study, and grades predict success in (their) medical school. Committee members are able to make this determination, to a significant degree, by reviewing your college transcript. More specifically, committee members consider:

- Grades earned in each course and laboratory

- Number of credit hours carried in each academic period

- Distribution of coursework among the biological, physical, and social sciences and the humanities

- Need for remediation of unsatisfactory academic work

- Number of incomplete grades and course withdrawals

- Number of years taken to complete the degree program

## MCAT® Scores

The ability of admission committees to predict success is heightened when they add MCAT® scores into the mix. That's because, as you probably already know, there can be significant differences in grading scales and standards from college to college, and MCAT® scores provide admissions officers with a standardized measure by which to compare applicants. In fact, the ability of admissions officers to predict who will be successful in their programs increases by as much as 50 percent (gauging by first- and second-year medical school grades) when they look at MCAT® scores in conjunction with undergraduate GPAs as opposed to grades alone.

As a result, the better your grades and higher your scores, the more likely you are to be accepted. It is important to remember, though, that there is still a wide range of MCAT® scores and GPAs found among accepted applicants, and that scores and grades are used in conjunction with other factors as discussed earlier in this chapter.

## Making the Evaluation

Admission committees gauge all three of these areas— experience, attributes, and metrics—in several ways.

First, areas connected with the application process speak to your experience and attributes. Your personal statement, as mentioned in Chapter 6, provides the opportunity for you to tell committee members of your extracurricular activities, "distance traveled" (if applicable; see page 40), volunteer efforts, and medical-related work experience—and, by inference, the personal attributes that go along with that. A role as the officer in a school club conveys leadership skills. Working in a medical clinic summer after summer demonstrates motivation for medicine. A long history of volunteering with fundraisers for cancer research certainly suggests teamwork and compassion.

## What Do Committee Members Generally Prefer?

Although each medical school establishes its own criteria, schools usually prefer applicants who balanced science and humanities coursework, carried respectable course loads, and, generally speaking, earned 3.0–4.0 grades (on a 4.0 scale).

See Chapter 10 for information on the range of GPA averages of all applicants for the 2010 entering class. Or, for the range of GPAs of accepted applicants to a particular medical school, see that institution's entry in the school listings section of this guide.

Your letters of recommendation, also described in Chapter 6, attest to your personal attributes, as well. You'll certainly want your professors and advisor (and other evaluators) to address your persistence, strong work habits, and self-discipline. (The faculty and administrative staff at your undergraduate school will know how to craft a letter, but for others, you might want to suggest a few key concepts.)

Then there are the metrics. As you know, your academic record is part of your AMCAS® application and includes both your college transcript(s) and MCAT® scores. From there, committee members can determine whether you have the grades, range of coursework, and foundation of knowledge they seek in their successful applicants.

## Wondering Where YOUR Metrics Place You?

You can gain some insights by reviewing the chart on page 60, which shows what percentage of applicants were accepted to medical school based on combinations of specific grades and scores. In addition, the individual school entries in this guide include the range of MCAT® scores generally deemed acceptable for admission, along with the median overall GPA and science GPA of their accepted students.

## The Interview Is Key

And then…there is the interview.

If you've been invited to an interview, you've made it through the preliminary trials by virtue of an impressive personal statement, an appealing background of experiences, strong letters of recommendation, and a superior academic history. But now, you've really got to "shine." Medical schools usually interview three, four, even five times as many applicants as their class size, and that is why the interview is likely to be the #1 determining factor at this phase in the assessment as to whether or not you receive an acceptance.

The very fact that interviews are given at all, by the way, is a significant distinction of medical schools, since some professional schools do not necessarily require them. This alone attests to the degree to which admissions officers seek—and medical schools value—qualities and characteristics such as empathy, self-awareness, communications ability, and interpersonal skills that can best be judged in a direct interview situation. You can take a number of steps to ensure you're prepared for it:

- *Know the Basics*
  Whether it's for a new job or for a slot in a medical school's entering class, certain similarities exist in all interviewing situations. A good start would be to pick up one of any of the dozens of books on interviewing skills and familiarize yourself with the basics.

- *Know What Type of Interview to Expect*
  It will also be helpful to be ready for any number of different interview formats. At some schools, interviews are held with individual admission committee members; at others, group interviews are the norm. In addition, while most interviews are typically held on the medical school campus, some schools have designated interviewers in different geographic regions to minimize time and expense for applicants. (Information about a school's interview policies and procedures is usually provided to applicants in the initial stages of the selection process.)

- *Be Comfortable with Different Interviewing Styles*
  You've probably had some experience interviewing for summer and part-time jobs (and possibly for your undergraduate school), so it won't surprise you that interviewers have their own styles and follow different formats. Some follow a structured design, asking questions from a predetermined list and assigning numeric scores to each answer. Others prefer a more free-flowing arrangement and provide the applicant with a greater degree of open input. Still others fall somewhat in the middle. Again, be ready for any approach.

- *Do Your Research*

  Investigate the school thoroughly by reviewing its entry in this guidebook, its Web site, the information packet sent to you, and any articles you can get your hands on. (Hint: Do an Internet search.) You'll want to impress your interviewer with not only your potential for success but also your interest in his or her specific institution. You can demonstrate these qualities through the answers to the interviewer's questions as well as by the questions you ask (see box below).

- *Practice*

  Since most admission committee members are experienced interviewers who want to learn about the "real" person, you should be forthright and open in your meeting and not try to "game" the interviewer. If you're apprehensive about the process, find a trusted advisor or friend with whom you can conduct mock interviews to help build your confidence.

Remember, the interview provides applicants with opportunities to discuss their personal histories and motivation for a medical career and to draw attention to any aspects of their application that merit emphasis or explanation. Make certain you present yourself in the best possible light by preparing thoroughly for your meeting.

# Know Your Interview Rights and Responsibilities

Although interviewers are instructed by admissions officers and guided by federal statutes on what are unfair or discriminatory pre-admission inquiries, there may be an occasion when an interviewer asks an inappropriate question. (See examples in box at right.)

You have the right not to answer what you sense is an inappropriate question. If such a question is asked, try to relax and provide a thoughtful and articulate response (two essential characteristics of a good physician). You may also respectfully decline to answer the question and explain that you were advised not to answer questions that you sensed were inappropriate.

You have the responsibility to report being asked an inappropriate question to help prevent further occurrences. Medical schools have the responsibility to establish procedures that enable applicants to report such incidents in a confidential manner. Medical schools should inform applicants of these procedures prior to interviews and assure them that reporting an incident will not bias the applicant's evaluation.

If a medical school did not inform you of its procedure and an incident occurs, use these guidelines. If possible, report in confidence the interviewer's name and the interview question(s) that was asked to an admissions officer during the interview day. Otherwise, e-mail this informaton to an admisisons officer within 24 hours of the interview noting the date and time of the incident. Furthermore, you have the right to ask if another interview is deemed necessary to ensure an unbiased evaluation of your application to that medical school.

Some interviewers use the interview to assess how well you function under stress and may purposely ask challenging questions to observe how you respond under pressure. How you communicate will be a critical part of the encounter; however, this does not give an interviewer the right to ask you inappropriate questions in their attempt to challenge you during the interview.

---

**Examples of inappropriate questions:**

- What is your race, ethnicity, religion, sexual orientation, political affiliation, marital status, opinion on abortion and/or euthanasia, income, value of your home, credit score, etc.?
- Are you planning on having children during medical school?
- Do you have any disabilities?
- Will you require special accommodations?
- Have you ever been arrested?
- Have you ever done drugs?
- How old are you?

---

**Sample response to an inappropriate questions:**

Q. *What are your plans for expanding your family during medical school?*

A. Can you please clarify your question? I want to make sure that I'm providing information that is most relevant to my candidacy.

Q. *Have you ever done drugs?*

A. I am uncomfortable discussing my medical history and possible use of prescription medications during this interview.

# Chapter 8:

## Building Toward Greater Diversity

*Why is diversity in medical education important?*

*The very process of education itself is enhanced when the student body includes those from varying cultures and backgrounds—and research bears it out. Over the past 40 years, many studies on undergraduate campuses have attested to the value of diversity in the classroom and the overall school environment. It generates a wealth of ideas, helps students challenge their assumptions, and broadens their perspectives. Diversity in group settings has even been linked to greater cognitive results, ultimately leading to better learning outcomes.\**

### Benefits of Diversity Extend Beyond Education*

Increased diversity brings with it benefits that extend beyond the classroom. For example, a greater degree of diversity:

- **Increases access to health care.**
  Research has shown that diversity in the physician workforce contributes to increased access to health care.

- **Accelerates advances in research.**
  Diversity among clinician-scientists has been linked to an increase in research dedicated to diseases that disproportionately affect racial and ethnic minorities.

*It is for all these reasons that the AAMC strives to increase diversity among medical school applicants and therefore offers students a wide range of programs and resources to help meet that goal. Similarly, medical schools themselves almost always have programs—and staff—to ensure that all candidates to their institutions have an equal opportunity for admittance. We review these resources in the pages that follow.*

### The Diversity of Diversity, and Where We Now Stand

But first…what exactly do we mean by "diversity"?

When you mention the word, diversity, many people automatically think in terms of race and ethnicity. And while it is certainly true that it is important to attract more racial and ethnic minority populations to medicine, the concept of diversity is much more expansive. The AAMC recognizes that diversity encompasses a variety of factors that also include gender, socio-economic status, disability, age, sexual orientation, religious affiliation, and other personal characteristics.

So, what's our current situation? Let's look at it from a few different perspectives.

*\*See list of suggested readings and resources at the end of this chapter to learn more about diversity in educational settings.*

- First, consider race and ethnicity. While diversity extends beyond this particular measure, as just mentioned, it nevertheless remains a critical component. With that in mind, you can see from the chart below that racial ethnic minority groups are underrepresented in medicine. The data show, for example, that only 7.2 percent of matriculating students are black or African American, 8.2 percent are Hispanic or Latino, and 1 percent are American Indian or Alaska Native.

- **What about family income?** This is another area of great imbalance—and inequity. Parental income of students entering medical school skews heavily to the upper range, with median income of $100,000. (That's almost double the estimated U.S. median family income of $62,000 reported by the U.S. Census Bureau.) Looking at it from another angle, we see that almost one in six students come from homes in which their parents earn $250,000 or more a year.

- Let's look at the situation from yet a third perspective— **gender**. On the surface, it appears that male and female applicants are fairly equal in number, but there are instances where that is not the case. You'll see, for example, from the chart below left, that there is a relative shortage of male applicants within the black or African American demographic. Within this specific group, males comprise barely one-third of those who apply to medical school.

## Low-Income Households Are Underrepresented...

**Parental Income of Entering Medical Students, 2010**

| Income | Percent |
| --- | --- |
| Less than $10,000 | 2.6 |
| $10,000 - $19,999 | 2.4 |
| $20,000 - $29,999 | 3.4 |
| $30,000 - $39,999 | 4.5 |
| $40,000 - $49,999 | 4.2 |
| $50,000 - $74,999 | 12.8 |
| $75,000 - $99,999 | 11.3 |
| $100,000 - $249,999 | 42.8 |
| $250,000 - $499,999 | 13.1 |
| $500,000 or more | 3.0 |
| Median income of parents | $110,000 |

*Source: AAMC's 2010 Matriculating Student Questionnaire (MSQ)*

*These examples barely scratch the surface when it comes to the issue of diversity, but they should be sufficient to demonstrate our point.*

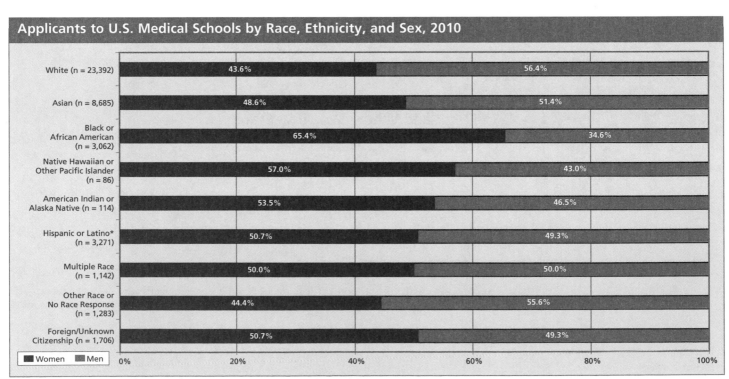

## Applicants to U.S. Medical Schools by Race, Ethnicity, and Sex, 2010

| | Women | Men |
| --- | --- | --- |
| White (n = 23,392) | 43.6% | 56.4% |
| Asian (n = 8,685) | 48.6% | 51.4% |
| Black or African American (n = 3,062) | 65.4% | 34.6% |
| Native Hawaiian or Other Pacific Islander (n = 86) | 57.0% | 43.0% |
| American Indian or Alaska Native (n = 114) | 53.5% | 46.5% |
| Hispanic or Latino* (n = 3,271) | 50.7% | 49.3% |
| Multiple Race (n = 1,142) | 50.0% | 50.0% |
| Other Race or No Race Response (n = 1,283) | 44.4% | 55.6% |
| Foreign/Unknown Citizenship (n = 1,706) | 50.7% | 49.3% |

*Note: Since 2002, following U.S. federal guidelines, AMCAS® has asked applicants who are U.S. citizens or Permanent Residents to self-identify using two separate questions: the first question ("Ethnicity") asks applicants whether they are "Spanish/Hispanic/Latino/Latina" or "Not Spanish/Hispanic/Latino/Latina"; the second question ("Race") asks applicants to self-identify using non-Hispanic or Latino race categories, and applicants are asked to "check all that apply." The ethnicity category and several race categories permit further self-identification by sub-categories. Prior to 2002, AMCAS® applicants were not able to select more than one race. One applicants in 2010, who declined to report gender, is excluded here.*
*Source: AAMC: Data Warehouse: Applicant Matriculant File as of October 15, 2010.*

## AAMC Programs and Resources

With the benefits that diversity offers, it's no wonder that the AAMC is strongly committed to improving the situation. To that end, the AAMC's Diversity Policy and Programs is engaged in a number of programs and initiatives to help increase diversity and open the campus gates to capable and promising students from a broad range of backgrounds. (It's important to note that while these programs are open to all, they are sensitive to the challenges and needs of those from groups underrepresented in medicine.) Examples of these initiatives are described below.

### Career Fairs and Enrichment Programs

Medical schools throughout the country provide all sorts of programs and resources designed to recruit students and prepare them for medical education. Some of these programs are held during the school year; others in the summer. Some are designed for high school students; others, for college students; and still others, for those who have completed undergraduate study. The AAMC is affiliated with two such programs:

- *Minority Student Medical Career Awareness Workshops and Recruitment Fair*
  This event, held each fall at the AAMC's annual meeting, is a wonderful opportunity for high school and college students to explore medical careers. Representatives from all 133 AAMC-member medical schools are invited, and students have the chance to talk with them about preparing for medical school, enrichment programs, admission policies and procedures, financial aid, and more. There are interactive medical and health activities, as well, and workshops are also sponsored for family

members. You can find out the date and location of the next annual fair at *www.aamc.org/careerfair*.

- *Summer Medical and Dental Education Program (SMDEP)*
  The Summer Medical and Dental Education Program is a free six-week summer academic enrichment program for college freshmen and sophomores interested in careers in medicine or dentistry. Components of the program include science and mathematics-based courses, learning and study skills seminars, career development activities, clinical experiences, and a financial planning workshop. Funded by the Robert Wood Johnson Foundation and offered at 12 U.S. medical and 9 dental schools across the nation, the program includes tuition, housing, and meals. For additional information, visit *www.smdep.org*, or call toll-free at 1-866-58SMDEP.

### AspiringDocs.org

The AAMC has developed a campaign designed to encourage students who aspire to medical school by providing a broad range of information and support. The centerpiece of the campaign is a rich Web site at *www.aspiringdocs.org* that allows "aspiring doctors" to get the information they need to prepare for application to medical school. Through a variety of online features, such as Ask the Experts, Hot Topics, and Inspiring Stories, and podcasts, students are provided with easy-to-understand information about applying to medical school and financing a medical education.

### Other AAMC Resources

And that's just the start. The AAMC also offers a wide variety of publications, online tools, and other information in the "Minorities in Medicine" section of the AAMC's Web site at www.aamc.org/students/minorities and the AAMC's Diversity Web site at www.aamc.org/diversity. Among the resources you will find there are:

- **Medical Students with Disabilities: Resources to Enhance Accessibility**
This recently published guide book informs users about current resources available to medical schools as they accept and matriculate a growing number of medical students with a wide range of disabilities. Specifically there is an emphasis in this publication on the assistive technologies available for medical students. You can order a copy of this guide book at https://services.aamc.org/publications/index.cfm.

- **Enrichment programs online**
This site includes a free database to help undergraduate students locate summer enrichment programs on medical school campuses. You can search by school, state, region, area of focus, and length of program. Go to www.services.aamc.org/summerprograms to explore programs of interest.

*For information about the AAMC's definition of those "underrepresented in medicine," go to www.aamc.org/urm.*

- **Medical Minority Applicant Registry**
Students applying to medical school who identify themselves as members of groups that are underrepresented in medicine, or who are economically or educationally disadvantaged, can register for Med-MAR at the time they take the MCAT® exam. This web-based program circulates basic biographical information and MCAT® scores of registered examinees to all U.S. medical schools, thereby providing institutions with opportunities to enhance their diversity efforts. Go to www.aamc.org/students/minorities/resources/medmar for more information.

- **Medical School Career Fairs and Events Calendar**
With this online calendar, students can search for recruitment events at schools in their state or within a specific date range. Information is available at www.aamc.org/calendar/careerfairs.

- **Fee Assistance Program (FAP)**
The AAMC is pleased to offer its Fee Assistance Program to students whose financial limitations would otherwise prevent them from taking the MCAT® exam or applying to medical school. Details about the FAP can be found at www.aamc.org/fap and in Chapter 6 of this book.

- **Data about Applicants, Matriculants, and Graduates**
The AAMC also collects and presents detailed data about medical students from an array of racial and ethnic groups, most of which are available online free-of-charge on the AAMC Web site (and a good deal of which is included in this guide). Several resources likely to be of interest are highlighted below.

— AAMC information about recent matriculant data for each medical school is presented in this chapter in Table 8-A, Matriculants by *Medical School and Race and Ethnicity*, 2010.

— Chapter 10 includes a table showing the self-reported racial and ethnic identification of medical school applicants and accepted applicants for the 2010 entering class.

— A large collection of data about medical school applicants, matriculants, and graduates are available on the AAMC Web site at www.aamc.org/facts.

— The AAMC publication, *Diversity in Medical Education, Facts & Figures* 2008, provides race and ethnicity data on medical school applicants, accepted applicants, matriculants, enrollment, graduates, and faculty. You can access the full text without charge at www.aamc.org/students/minorities.

— Data on medical school faculty, including information by race and ethnicity, can be found at www.aamc.org/data/facultyroster/reports.

## School Programs and Resources

It's not just the AAMC that's interested in the issue of diversity. As you would expect, colleges and medical schools are also committed to making medical education accessible to all individuals—and you'll certainly want to take advantage of these resources as well. Among them are:

- **Pre-medical school programs at undergraduate colleges**
Pre-health advisors have an abundance of pertinent information at their fingertips. Not only can they help you with the application process and refer you to appropriate contacts, they also know about programs that students from underrepresented groups and disadvantaged backgrounds are likely to find useful. If your college has a pre-health advisor (and the majority of them do), make sure you take advantage of this valuable resource. Learn more about pre-health advisors at www.naahp.org.

- **Medical School Web sites**
You'll also want to explore the medical school Web sites for information on their diversity programs and resources. Go to www.aamc.org/medicalschools for a listing of all U.S. and Canadian M.D.-granting medical schools and links to their Web sites.

- *Medical school diversity affairs representatives*
  Another invaluable resource will be the medical school diversity affairs representatives. These individuals are dedicated to increasing diversity among medical schools at their institutions and are an excellent source of information for applicants (or potential applicants). You can get the name of the diversity affairs contacts at any U.S. medical school through a searchable database (see box at right) provided by the AAMC.

- *Financial assistance for medical school*
  Don't let the cost of medical school deter you from your dreams. As you'll learn in Chapter 11 of this publication, more than four-fifths of medical students across the country receive some form of financial assistance. Medical schools—both public and private—work hard to offer a variety of financial aid plans to ensure that capable students are not denied access to their institutions as a result of financial limitations. In addition to discussing possibilities for assistance with the financial aid officer at the medical schools that interest you, you should familiarize yourself with general information about financing a medical education by reading the relevant material in this book, reviewing the wealth of information about loans (and other programs) at *www.aamc.org/students/financing*, and learning about scholarships at *www.aamc.org/students/minorities/scholarships.htm*.

- *Programs at medical schools*
  Once you've enrolled in medical school, you'll find that a variety of academic and personal support programs are available to you. These programs assist students from various backgrounds to successfully complete their medical studies, with the ultimate goal of increasing diversity among physicians entering careers in patient care, teaching, and research, and of eliminating racial and ethnic disparities in health care. The staff members at each medical school who are responsible for these programs are identified in the school-by-school entries in Chapters 14 and 15 of this publication.

### Directory of Diversity Affairs Representatives

The Directory of Diversity Affairs Representatives is a searchable database of diversity affairs representatives at all U.S. medical schools. It is searchable by name, location, and institution, and is available at *www.aamc.org/coda*.

### For those who wish to explore the benefits of diversity, may we suggest the following readings:

Antonio AL, Chang MJ, Hakuta K, Kenny DA, Levin S, Milem JF. *Effects of racial diversity on complex thinking in college students.* Psychological Science. 2004:15;507-10.

Astin AW. *What matters in college? Four critical years revisited.* San Francisco, CA:Jossey-Bass, 1993.

Gurin P. *The compelling need for diversity in higher education: Expert testimony in Gratz*, et al. v. Bollinger, et al. Michigan J of Race & Law. 1999:5; 363–425.

Nemeth CJ, Wachtler J. *Creative problem solving as a result of majority vs. minority influence.* European J of Social Psychology, 1983:13; 45–55.

Saha S; Guiton G; Wimmers PF.; Wilkerson L. *Student Body Racial and Ethnic Composition and Diversity-Related Outcomes in US Medical Schools.* Journal of the American Medical Association, JAMA, 2008. 300: 1135–1145.

Smith DG & Associates. *Diversity works: The emerging picture of how students benefit.* Washington, DC: Association of American Colleges and Universities, 1997.

Smith DG; *Diversity's Promise for Higher Education: Making It Work.* Baltimore, MD; The Johns Hopkins University Press, 2009.

### No Advisor? Contact the NAAHP for Help

If your institution does not have a pre-health advisor, you can contact the National Association of Advisors for the Health Professions (NAAHP). There, you will find a list of NAAHP members who have volunteered to help students without access to a pre-health advisor. Learn more about what pre-health advisors do and how to locate one at *www.naahp.org/advisors.htm*.

# Table 8-A:

## Matriculants by Medical School and Race and Ethnicity 2010*

| | Matriculants 2010 | Mexican American | Cuban | Puerto Rican | Other Hispanic or Latino | Total Hispanic or Latino | Chinese | Asian Indian | Pakistani | Filipino | Japanese | Korean | Vietnamese | Other Asian | Total Asian | Native American | Black | Native Hawaiian /OPI | White | Unduplicated |
|---|---|---|---|---|---|---|---|---|---|---|---|---|---|---|---|---|---|---|---|---|
| AL | Alabama | 1 | 0 | 1 | 2 | 4 | 6 | 13 | 1 | 1 | 0 | 1 | 3 | 3 | 24 | 1 | 11 | 0 | 140 | 176 |
| | South Alabama | 0 | 0 | 0 | 2 | 2 | 2 | 2 | 0 | 1 | 0 | 2 | 0 | 3 | 6 | 1 | 6 | 0 | 61 | 74 |
| AR | Arkansas | 3 | 0 | 0 | 5 | 8 | 8 | 4 | 2 | 0 | 2 | 0 | 2 | 3 | 20 | 2 | 5 | 1 | 137 | 168 |
| AZ | Arizona | 10 | 0 | 0 | 4 | 14 | 13 | 13 | 2 | 0 | 2 | 1 | 4 | 6 | 39 | 0 | 5 | 1 | 113 | 163 |
| CA | Loma Linda | 6 | 1 | 1 | 8 | 15 | 6 | 11 | 2 | 6 | 2 | 19 | 3 | 6 | 44 | 0 | 8 | 1 | 91 | 165 |
| | Southern Cal-Keck | 13 | 0 | 1 | 5 | 17 | 15 | 8 | 1 | 4 | 7 | 4 | 1 | 10 | 47 | 2 | 9 | 1 | 110 | 172 |
| | Stanford | 4 | 0 | 0 | 4 | 8 | 13 | 8 | 1 | 1 | 2 | 4 | 4 | 4 | 34 | 2 | 7 | 1 | 35 | 86 |
| | UC Berkeley/SF Joint Prog | 1 | 0 | 0 | 1 | 2 | 2 | 0 | 0 | 1 | 1 | 0 | 0 | 1 | 5 | 0 | 1 | 0 | 10 | 16 |
| | UC Davis | 10 | 0 | 0 | 4 | 14 | 13 | 3 | 0 | 2 | 1 | 3 | 5 | 1 | 30 | 1 | 10 | 1 | 48 | 96 |
| | UC Irvine | 8 | 0 | 0 | 5 | 13 | 11 | 8 | 1 | 4 | 0 | 1 | 11 | 6 | 40 | 1 | 3 | 2 | 55 | 104 |
| | UC San Diego | 13 | 0 | 0 | 2 | 15 | 25 | 8 | 3 | 2 | 3 | 6 | 5 | 3 | 46 | 1 | 5 | 0 | 61 | 125 |
| | UC San Francisco | 18 | 0 | 1 | 2 | 21 | 22 | 7 | 3 | 2 | 2 | 3 | 4 | 8 | 49 | 2 | 17 | 2 | 72 | 149 |
| | UCLA Drew | 2 | 0 | 0 | 2 | 4 | 2 | 1 | 0 | 1 | 0 | 1 | 1 | 0 | 5 | 1 | 9 | 1 | 3 | 24 |
| | UCLA-Geffen | 22 | 1 | 0 | 3 | 25 | 28 | 10 | 2 | 0 | 6 | 6 | 11 | 13 | 70 | 1 | 9 | 0 | 69 | 163 |
| CO | Colorado | 9 | 0 | 1 | 8 | 18 | 5 | 6 | 0 | 1 | 2 | 0 | 4 | 0 | 19 | 4 | 6 | 1 | 131 | 160 |
| CT | Connecticut | 0 | 1 | 4 | 6 | 10 | 9 | 8 | 1 | 0 | 0 | 0 | 0 | 0 | 19 | 0 | 8 | 0 | 59 | 89 |
| | Yale | 3 | 1 | 0 | 5 | 9 | 20 | 6 | 0 | 0 | 0 | 4 | 0 | 1 | 31 | 0 | 2 | 0 | 54 | 100 |
| DC | George Washington | 0 | 2 | 2 | 3 | 7 | 7 | 30 | 4 | 3 | 2 | 3 | 5 | 5 | 54 | 0 | 16 | 1 | 99 | 177 |
| | Georgetown | 1 | 1 | 1 | 5 | 6 | 13 | 7 | 1 | 5 | 1 | 5 | 1 | 2 | 34 | 2 | 12 | 0 | 137 | 196 |
| | Howard | 1 | 0 | 4 | 6 | 11 | 2 | 4 | 2 | 0 | 0 | 0 | 5 | 2 | 14 | 1 | 68 | 1 | 16 | 110 |
| FL | Central Florida | 0 | 1 | 4 | 5 | 10 | 3 | 4 | 1 | 1 | 0 | 0 | 2 | 1 | 12 | 1 | 4 | 1 | 40 | 60 |
| | FIU-Wertheim | 2 | 12 | 0 | 7 | 19 | 1 | 1 | 0 | 0 | 0 | 0 | 1 | 1 | 4 | 0 | 5 | 0 | 29 | 43 |
| | Florida | 3 | 2 | 1 | 5 | 10 | 8 | 5 | 4 | 0 | 0 | 3 | 3 | 3 | 26 | 3 | 16 | 2 | 82 | 131 |
| | Florida State | 3 | 1 | 3 | 8 | 19 | 3 | 10 | 2 | 1 | 0 | 0 | 7 | 3 | 26 | 0 | 9 | 0 | 84 | 120 |
| | Miami-Miller | 0 | 9 | 4 | 8 | 20 | 8 | 16 | 4 | 2 | 1 | 1 | 1 | 5 | 35 | 1 | 8 | 1 | 99 | 149 |
| | South Florida | 4 | 5 | 3 | 8 | 16 | 7 | 16 | 2 | 2 | 0 | 1 | 2 | 1 | 30 | 2 | 10 | 0 | 73 | 120 |
| GA | Emory | 1 | 0 | 0 | 2 | 3 | 9 | 6 | 0 | 1 | 1 | 3 | 0 | 5 | 24 | 0 | 11 | 0 | 100 | 135 |
| | MC Georgia | 2 | 0 | 1 | 3 | 6 | 12 | 31 | 4 | 2 | 0 | 6 | 5 | 7 | 67 | 0 | 21 | 0 | 140 | 230 |
| | Mercer | 0 | 0 | 0 | 2 | 2 | 2 | 7 | 0 | 1 | 0 | 2 | 2 | 0 | 14 | 0 | 4 | 0 | 79 | 101 |
| | Morehouse | 0 | 0 | 0 | 3 | 3 | 1 | 0 | 2 | 0 | 0 | 0 | 0 | 3 | 6 | 0 | 47 | 0 | 7 | 57 |
| HI | Hawaii-Burns | 0 | 0 | 1 | 1 | 2 | 18 | 1 | 0 | 8 | 18 | 8 | 3 | 5 | 49 | 1 | 0 | 8 | 23 | 64 |
| IA | Iowa-Carver | 5 | 0 | 0 | 0 | 5 | 4 | 4 | 0 | 1 | 2 | 2 | 2 | 2 | 16 | 3 | 8 | 0 | 124 | 149 |
| IL | Chicago Med-Franklin | 0 | 0 | 0 | 1 | 1 | 16 | 19 | 6 | 5 | 0 | 7 | 4 | 8 | 59 | 1 | 6 | 1 | 101 | 190 |
| | Chicago-Pritzker | 3 | 0 | 0 | 3 | 4 | 9 | 5 | 1 | 0 | 1 | 2 | 0 | 0 | 18 | 1 | 13 | 0 | 50 | 88 |
| | Illinois | 21 | 6 | 4 | 18 | 45 | 29 | 42 | 5 | 3 | 1 | 11 | 1 | 6 | 94 | 3 | 32 | 0 | 165 | 322 |
| | Loyola-Stritch | 7 | 1 | 3 | 4 | 14 | 2 | 2 | 1 | 2 | 7 | 2 | 0 | 5 | 12 | 3 | 8 | 0 | 127 | 150 |
| | Northwestern-Feinberg | 6 | 1 | 3 | 6 | 16 | 16 | 15 | 4 | 1 | 0 | 2 | 0 | 3 | 43 | 3 | 9 | 0 | 96 | 170 |
| | Rush | 4 | 2 | 0 | 10 | 15 | 8 | 16 | 1 | 1 | 1 | 0 | 1 | 3 | 29 | 1 | 8 | 0 | 91 | 136 |
| | Southern Illinois | 0 | 1 | 0 | 2 | 3 | 2 | 4 | 0 | 1 | 0 | 0 | 2 | 1 | 10 | 0 | 7 | 0 | 55 | 72 |
| IN | Indiana | 9 | 0 | 3 | 3 | 15 | 11 | 24 | 3 | 3 | 3 | 1 | 3 | 4 | 50 | 9 | 24 | 1 | 239 | 322 |
| KS | Kansas | 4 | 0 | 0 | 3 | 7 | 6 | 4 | 1 | 0 | 1 | 1 | 5 | 1 | 19 | 1 | 10 | 0 | 144 | 176 |
| KY | Kentucky | 0 | 1 | 0 | 1 | 2 | 3 | 2 | 0 | 0 | 1 | 1 | 1 | 0 | 7 | 0 | 5 | 1 | 92 | 113 |
| | Louisville | 2 | 1 | 0 | 3 | 5 | 3 | 10 | 0 | 0 | 0 | 2 | 1 | 1 | 17 | 0 | 13 | 0 | 124 | 160 |
| LA | LSU New Orleans | 1 | 2 | 0 | 6 | 9 | 2 | 7 | 3 | 0 | 1 | 2 | 10 | 3 | 26 | 1 | 17 | 0 | 148 | 192 |
| | LSU Shreveport | 0 | 0 | 0 | 2 | 2 | 2 | 6 | 1 | 0 | 0 | 1 | 1 | 0 | 13 | 1 | 4 | 0 | 101 | 118 |
| | Tulane | 0 | 1 | 1 | 4 | 5 | 20 | 9 | 1 | 4 | 3 | 4 | 5 | 4 | 47 | 2 | 3 | 1 | 127 | 187 |

Source: AAMC: Data Warehouse: Applicant Matriculant File as of 10/19/2010. *Hispanic Ethnicities are alone or in combination with some other Hispanic Ethnicity and include any Race. Ethnicity Counts include U.S. Citizens and Permanent Residents only. Race Counts include U.S. Citizens and Permanent Residents only, are alone or in combination with some other Race, and include both Hispanic and Non-Hispanic Ethnicity. The total represents an unduplicated count and also includes matriculants for whom we have no race data or who are foreign.

# Table 8-A:

## Matriculants by Medical School and Race and Ethnicity 2010* (continued)

| | Matriculants 2010 | Mexican American | Cuban | Puerto Rican | Other Hispanic or Latino | Total Hispanic or Latino | Chinese | Asian Indian | Pakistani | Filipino | Japanese | Korean | Vietnamese | Other Asian | Total Asian | Native American | Black | Native Hawaiian /OPI | White | Unduplicated |
|---|---|---|---|---|---|---|---|---|---|---|---|---|---|---|---|---|---|---|---|---|
| MA | Boston | 3 | 2 | 1 | 13 | 18 | 21 | 22 | 0 | 0 | 1 | 9 | 4 | 7 | 62 | 1 | 14 | 1 | 86 | 178 |
| | Harvard | 8 | 1 | 4 | 5 | 18 | 15 | 14 | 3 | 1 | 2 | 13 | 5 | 3 | 52 | 1 | 14 | 1 | 86 | 165 |
| | Massachusetts | 0 | 0 | 3 | 2 | 5 | 10 | 8 | 0 | 0 | 1 | 3 | 3 | 3 | 27 | 2 | 5 | 0 | 95 | 125 |
| | Tufts | 5 | 4 | 1 | 9 | 17 | 9 | 18 | 1 | 3 | 0 | 8 | 2 | 5 | 45 | 0 | 9 | 0 | 133 | 200 |
| MD | Johns Hopkins | 0 | 2 | 1 | 6 | 9 | 17 | 8 | 1 | 1 | 3 | 7 | 2 | 6 | 40 | 1 | 9 | 1 | 67 | 120 |
| | Maryland | 0 | 0 | 1 | 4 | 5 | 13 | 14 | 3 | 1 | 2 | 2 | 2 | 2 | 38 | 0 | 9 | 0 | 109 | 160 |
| | Uniformed Services-Hebert | 6 | 1 | 1 | 1 | 8 | 7 | 4 | 0 | 5 | 3 | 12 | 5 | 2 | 36 | 4 | 1 | 2 | 130 | 169 |
| MI | Michigan | 4 | 0 | 0 | 2 | 6 | 20 | 16 | 0 | 0 | 0 | 3 | 2 | 3 | 44 | 3 | 12 | 0 | 101 | 170 |
| | Michigan State | 6 | 1 | 2 | 5 | 12 | 10 | 9 | 1 | 3 | 0 | 2 | 1 | 3 | 28 | 3 | 13 | 0 | 146 | 200 |
| | Wayne State | 0 | 1 | 0 | 1 | 2 | 15 | 24 | 6 | 7 | 2 | 5 | 1 | 7 | 64 | 2 | 16 | 0 | 191 | 290 |
| MN | Mayo | 0 | 0 | 0 | 1 | 1 | 3 | 3 | 0 | 1 | 1 | 1 | 0 | 1 | 10 | 1 | 4 | 0 | 33 | 51 |
| | Minnesota | 2 | 2 | 0 | 5 | 9 | 5 | 4 | 0 | 0 | 1 | 3 | 5 | 6 | 23 | 8 | 4 | 1 | 177 | 229 |
| MO | Missouri Columbia | 1 | 0 | 0 | 2 | 3 | 2 | 5 | 1 | 0 | 0 | 1 | 1 | 4 | 13 | 2 | 1 | 0 | 86 | 104 |
| | Missouri Kansas City | 0 | 0 | 0 | 4 | 4 | 1 | 1 | 0 | 0 | 0 | 1 | 0 | 48 | 51 | 0 | 9 | 0 | 27 | 101 |
| | St Louis | 0 | 1 | 0 | 0 | 1 | 15 | 19 | 1 | 3 | 1 | 5 | 7 | 1 | 54 | 0 | 10 | 0 | 96 | 177 |
| | Washington U St Louis | 2 | 0 | 2 | 1 | 5 | 18 | 9 | 2 | 0 | 0 | 3 | 0 | 3 | 35 | 1 | 8 | 0 | 71 | 121 |
| MS | Mississippi | 0 | 0 | 0 | 2 | 2 | 0 | 4 | 0 | 0 | 0 | 0 | 1 | 0 | 5 | 1 | 13 | 1 | 113 | 135 |
| NC | Duke | 2 | 0 | 5 | 3 | 9 | 18 | 4 | 1 | 0 | 2 | 3 | 1 | 2 | 31 | 1 | 9 | 0 | 55 | 100 |
| | East Carolina-Brody | 1 | 0 | 0 | 2 | 3 | 0 | 6 | 1 | 1 | 0 | 1 | 0 | 1 | 10 | 3 | 10 | 0 | 53 | 78 |
| | North Carolina | 0 | 2 | 0 | 4 | 6 | 3 | 6 | 3 | 0 | 1 | 2 | 2 | 1 | 23 | 1 | 18 | 0 | 113 | 160 |
| | Wake Forest | 2 | 1 | 1 | 7 | 9 | 3 | 4 | 0 | 0 | 1 | 3 | 0 | 0 | 11 | 1 | 12 | 0 | 98 | 120 |
| ND | North Dakota | 0 | 0 | 0 | 0 | 0 | 0 | 1 | 0 | 0 | 1 | 0 | 0 | 0 | 2 | 7 | 0 | 0 | 55 | 62 |
| NE | Creighton | 2 | 0 | 2 | 0 | 6 | 4 | 4 | 0 | 1 | 1 | 0 | 2 | 3 | 18 | 3 | 5 | 0 | 126 | 150 |
| | Nebraska | 2 | 1 | 0 | 0 | 3 | 2 | 6 | 2 | 0 | 0 | 0 | 0 | 3 | 11 | 1 | 3 | 0 | 109 | 127 |
| NH | Dartmouth | 1 | 1 | 1 | 3 | 6 | 6 | 3 | 0 | 1 | 1 | 3 | 2 | 4 | 24 | 0 | 3 | 0 | 49 | 90 |
| NJ | UMDNJ New Jersey | 0 | 3 | 7 | 10 | 20 | 14 | 41 | 4 | 5 | 0 | 12 | 1 | 3 | 77 | 0 | 19 | 1 | 67 | 178 |
| | UMDNJ-RW Johnson | 0 | 0 | 1 | 3 | 4 | 8 | 17 | 4 | 2 | 0 | 5 | 1 | 6 | 43 | 0 | 12 | 0 | 56 | 113 |
| NM | New Mexico | 20 | 2 | 0 | 11 | 33 | 3 | 3 | 0 | 1 | 0 | 0 | 0 | 0 | 7 | 4 | 3 | 2 | 63 | 94 |
| NV | Nevada | 1 | 1 | 0 | 0 | 2 | 4 | 3 | 1 | 4 | 2 | 1 | 3 | 3 | 17 | 1 | 0 | 0 | 45 | 62 |
| NY | Albany | 0 | 0 | 0 | 1 | 1 | 16 | 20 | 2 | 3 | 0 | 5 | 4 | 6 | 50 | 0 | 7 | 0 | 72 | 137 |
| | Buffalo | 1 | 0 | 1 | 0 | 2 | 20 | 11 | 2 | 3 | 1 | 4 | 3 | 6 | 47 | 2 | 4 | 1 | 89 | 144 |
| | Columbia | 2 | 3 | 5 | 7 | 15 | 10 | 8 | 0 | 2 | 0 | 4 | 2 | 4 | 28 | 0 | 19 | 0 | 99 | 166 |
| | Cornell-Weill | 1 | 2 | 2 | 8 | 12 | 11 | 5 | 2 | 0 | 1 | 4 | 0 | 1 | 24 | 1 | 9 | 1 | 59 | 101 |
| | Einstein | 1 | 2 | 4 | 9 | 14 | 18 | 9 | 2 | 1 | 1 | 4 | 4 | 6 | 42 | 1 | 14 | 0 | 112 | 183 |
| | Mount Sinai | 2 | 0 | 4 | 10 | 14 | 17 | 8 | 2 | 3 | 1 | 0 | 1 | 1 | 28 | 2 | 12 | 0 | 82 | 141 |
| | New York Medical | 7 | 1 | 3 | 6 | 16 | 13 | 17 | 1 | 3 | 4 | 6 | 4 | 6 | 49 | 0 | 16 | 0 | 115 | 194 |
| | New York University | 2 | 1 | 2 | 11 | 16 | 24 | 14 | 1 | 2 | 2 | 7 | 2 | 2 | 48 | 1 | 3 | 1 | 99 | 162 |
| | Rochester | 1 | 0 | 0 | 2 | 3 | 6 | 1 | 3 | 1 | 0 | 0 | 0 | 4 | 17 | 0 | 12 | 0 | 75 | 104 |
| | SUNY Downstate | 1 | 2 | 1 | 8 | 12 | 24 | 20 | 3 | 5 | 0 | 5 | 0 | 7 | 64 | 0 | 20 | 0 | 92 | 183 |
| | SUNY Upstate | 6 | 0 | 0 | 6 | 12 | 8 | 9 | 0 | 2 | 1 | 1 | 1 | 4 | 25 | 1 | 20 | 1 | 94 | 161 |
| | Stony Brook | 0 | 1 | 0 | 5 | 5 | 22 | 11 | 2 | 0 | 2 | 7 | 2 | 4 | 48 | 0 | 7 | 0 | 61 | 124 |
| OH | Case Western | 4 | 3 | 2 | 2 | 11 | 26 | 17 | 1 | 0 | 2 | 9 | 0 | 6 | 61 | 2 | 10 | 1 | 114 | 199 |
| | Cincinnati | 2 | 1 | 2 | 2 | 5 | 10 | 20 | 2 | 2 | 2 | 5 | 4 | 5 | 45 | 1 | 15 | 0 | 107 | 170 |
| | Northeastern Ohio | 0 | 0 | 2 | 4 | 5 | 4 | 27 | 3 | 0 | 0 | 2 | 0 | 4 | 41 | 2 | 0 | 0 | 73 | 114 |
| | Ohio State | 4 | 2 | 2 | 7 | 15 | 16 | 16 | 1 | 1 | 1 | 3 | 1 | 5 | 43 | 1 | 18 | 0 | 149 | 220 |
| | Toledo | 2 | 1 | 1 | 0 | 4 | 10 | 12 | 4 | 1 | 0 | 1 | 0 | 4 | 31 | 0 | 10 | 0 | 125 | 175 |
| | Wright State-Boonshoft | 0 | 0 | 0 | 0 | 0 | 2 | 8 | 1 | 0 | 0 | 0 | 1 | 1 | 15 | 0 | 3 | 0 | 78 | 101 |
| OK | Oklahoma | 1 | 0 | 0 | 0 | 1 | 3 | 5 | 2 | 0 | 1 | 3 | 6 | 5 | 25 | 11 | 1 | 0 | 133 | 165 |
| OR | Oregon | 0 | 0 | 0 | 0 | 0 | 10 | 1 | 4 | 1 | 3 | 3 | 2 | 2 | 19 | 2 | 1 | 1 | 100 | 124 |

Source: AAMC: Data Warehouse: Applicant Matriculant File as of 10/19/2010. *Hispanic Ethnicities are alone or in combination with some other Hispanic Ethnicity and include any Race. Ethnicity Counts include U.S. Citizens and Permanent Residents only. Race Counts include U.S. Citizens and Permanent Residents only, are alone or in combination with some other Race, and include both Hispanic and Non-Hispanic Ethnicity. The total represents an unduplicated count and also includes matriculants for whom we have no race data or who are foreign.

# Table 8-A:

## Matriculants by Medical School and Race and Ethnicity 2010* (continued)

| | Matriculants 2010 | Mexican American | Cuban | Puerto Rican | Other Hispanic or Latino | Total Hispanic or Latino | Chinese | Asian Indian | Pakistani | Filipino | Japanese | Korean | Vietnamese | Other Asian | Total Asian | Native American | Black | Native Hawaiian /OPI | White | Unduplicated |
|---|---|---|---|---|---|---|---|---|---|---|---|---|---|---|---|---|---|---|---|---|
| PA | Commonwealth | 2 | 0 | 0 | 0 | 2 | 1 | 7 | 0 | 0 | 1 | 1 | 0 | 3 | 13 | 1 | 2 | 0 | 49 | 65 |
| | Drexel | 1 | 2 | 1 | 7 | 10 | 22 | 55 | 2 | 1 | 2 | 6 | 3 | 6 | 95 | 1 | 13 | 2 | 137 | 260 |
| | Jefferson | 2 | 1 | 1 | 6 | 10 | 18 | 27 | 3 | 1 | 1 | 5 | 6 | 5 | 62 | 0 | 3 | 1 | 182 | 260 |
| | Penn State | 1 | 0 | 0 | 1 | 2 | 7 | 10 | 1 | 2 | 1 | 2 | 2 | 1 | 26 | 0 | 7 | 0 | 104 | 145 |
| | Pennsylvania | 0 | 2 | 2 | 14 | 17 | 17 | 7 | 1 | 2 | 2 | 4 | 0 | 4 | 34 | 2 | 23 | 0 | 101 | 162 |
| | Pittsburgh | 1 | 2 | 2 | 6 | 10 | 17 | 22 | 1 | 2 | 3 | 6 | 0 | 1 | 50 | 0 | 9 | 0 | 84 | 148 |
| | Temple | 2 | 4 | 3 | 12 | 19 | 13 | 17 | 3 | 2 | 3 | 7 | 1 | 3 | 47 | 0 | 16 | 0 | 114 | 178 |
| PR | Caribe | 0 | 3 | 56 | 7 | 62 | 0 | 0 | 0 | 0 | 0 | 0 | 0 | 0 | 1 | 1 | 4 | 0 | 48 | 65 |
| | Ponce | 0 | 3 | 56 | 7 | 64 | 0 | 1 | 0 | 0 | 0 | 0 | 0 | 0 | 1 | 0 | 10 | 0 | 45 | 66 |
| | Puerto Rico | 0 | 0 | 106 | 2 | 108 | 0 | 0 | 0 | 0 | 0 | 0 | 0 | 0 | 0 | 0 | 11 | 0 | 73 | 110 |
| | San Juan Bautista | 2 | 3 | 47 | 6 | 56 | 1 | 1 | 0 | 0 | 1 | 0 | 0 | 1 | 2 | 1 | 3 | 1 | 45 | 65 |
| RI | Brown-Alpert | 4 | 0 | 5 | 5 | 13 | 13 | 9 | 1 | 1 | 3 | 1 | 6 | 1 | 34 | 1 | 9 | 0 | 39 | 97 |
| SC | MU South Carolina | 1 | 0 | 0 | 2 | 3 | 5 | 10 | 1 | 0 | 0 | 0 | 1 | 0 | 4 | 2 | 21 | 0 | 119 | 165 |
| | South Carolina | 1 | 1 | 0 | 2 | 4 | 1 | 6 | 0 | 0 | 1 | 0 | 1 | 1 | 10 | 0 | 4 | 0 | 75 | 90 |
| SD | South Dakota-Sanford | 0 | 0 | 0 | 0 | 0 | 1 | 0 | 0 | 0 | 0 | 0 | 0 | 0 | 1 | 1 | 1 | 0 | 50 | 54 |
| TN | East Tennessee-Quillen | 0 | 1 | 0 | 0 | 1 | 2 | 6 | 1 | 0 | 1 | 1 | 0 | 0 | 11 | 2 | 1 | 0 | 60 | 71 |
| | Meharry | 1 | 2 | 1 | 1 | 4 | 4 | 4 | 1 | 1 | 0 | 1 | 0 | 0 | 10 | 3 | 86 | 0 | 10 | 105 |
| | Tennessee | 2 | 0 | 0 | 6 | 8 | 7 | 8 | 1 | 0 | 0 | 0 | 2 | 1 | 21 | 3 | 17 | 0 | 121 | 165 |
| | Vanderbilt | 5 | 3 | 1 | 4 | 11 | 9 | 9 | 0 | 0 | 2 | 1 | 5 | 0 | 24 | 1 | 9 | 1 | 61 | 105 |
| TX | Baylor | 12 | 2 | 0 | 12 | 26 | 19 | 22 | 6 | 2 | 1 | 5 | 7 | 6 | 66 | 2 | 8 | 0 | 109 | 185 |
| | Texas A & M | 4 | 0 | 0 | 13 | 17 | 3 | 15 | 4 | 1 | 0 | 4 | 6 | 13 | 44 | 1 | 7 | 1 | 93 | 150 |
| | Texas Tech | 1 | 0 | 1 | 4 | 6 | 5 | 9 | 3 | 2 | 0 | 3 | 2 | 10 | 33 | 6 | 10 | 1 | 97 | 144 |
| | Texas Tech-Foster | 1 | 0 | 0 | 4 | 5 | 4 | 2 | 2 | 0 | 1 | 2 | 2 | 5 | 17 | 0 | 0 | 1 | 40 | 60 |
| | UT Galveston | 12 | 1 | 1 | 41 | 54 | 11 | 12 | 3 | 2 | 1 | 2 | 5 | 17 | 51 | 1 | 22 | 1 | 142 | 229 |
| | UT HSC San Antonio | 9 | 0 | 1 | 32 | 42 | 11 | 9 | 1 | 3 | 0 | 1 | 6 | 14 | 43 | 0 | 8 | 0 | 162 | 220 |
| | UT Houston | 6 | 2 | 0 | 13 | 17 | 12 | 14 | 4 | 4 | 3 | 0 | 0 | 6 | 55 | 2 | 11 | 0 | 149 | 230 |
| | UT Southwestern | 13 | 0 | 0 | 16 | 28 | 32 | 33 | 2 | 2 | 2 | 2 | 6 | 4 | 91 | 0 | 17 | 0 | 117 | 230 |
| UT | Utah | 1 | 0 | 0 | 3 | 4 | 1 | 4 | 2 | 3 | 0 | 1 | 3 | 2 | 15 | 1 | 2 | 0 | 61 | 82 |
| VA | Eastern Virginia | 0 | 0 | 5 | 3 | 6 | 5 | 14 | 2 | 0 | 0 | 6 | 3 | 6 | 34 | 0 | 7 | 0 | 74 | 118 |
| | Virginia | 0 | 6 | 2 | 7 | 15 | 12 | 14 | 1 | 2 | 0 | 9 | 2 | 1 | 40 | 2 | 9 | 0 | 94 | 153 |
| | Virginia Commonwealth | 2 | 2 | 0 | 4 | 8 | 18 | 19 | 2 | 3 | 1 | 7 | 7 | 7 | 59 | 0 | 21 | 0 | 115 | 200 |
| | Virginia Tech Carilion | 0 | 0 | 0 | 0 | 0 | 2 | 2 | 0 | 0 | 0 | 1 | 0 | 1 | 5 | 2 | 0 | 0 | 36 | 42 |
| VT | Vermont | 2 | 0 | 0 | 7 | 8 | 13 | 8 | 1 | 2 | 2 | 1 | 2 | 2 | 29 | 0 | 3 | 1 | 78 | 111 |
| WA | U Washington | 12 | 0 | 1 | 4 | 17 | 15 | 5 | 1 | 2 | 2 | 2 | 6 | 5 | 38 | 9 | 3 | 1 | 170 | 216 |
| WI | MC Wisconsin | 3 | 0 | 1 | 1 | 5 | 20 | 8 | 1 | 4 | 4 | 3 | 6 | 5 | 48 | 4 | 7 | 1 | 149 | 204 |
| | Wisconsin | 1 | 1 | 2 | 0 | 4 | 8 | 7 | 0 | 0 | 0 | 0 | 6 | 3 | 26 | 3 | 7 | 1 | 139 | 171 |
| WV | Marshall-Edwards | 1 | 0 | 0 | 2 | 3 | 2 | 5 | 2 | 0 | 0 | 0 | 0 | 0 | 9 | 1 | 0 | 0 | 60 | 75 |
| | West Virginia | 0 | 0 | 0 | 1 | 1 | 2 | 5 | 2 | 3 | 1 | 0 | 0 | 1 | 14 | 2 | 0 | 1 | 91 | 104 |
| | **Totals** | 412 | 142 | 405 | 647 | 1,539 | 1,280 | 1,343 | 185 | 186 | 156 | 434 | 295 | 526 | 4,214 | 191 | 1,350 | 61 | 12,098 | 18,665 |

Source: AAMC: Data Warehouse: Applicant Matriculant File as of 10/19/2010. *Hispanic Ethnicities are alone or in combination with some other Hispanic Ethnicity and include any Race. Ethnicity Counts include U.S. Citizens and Permanent Residents only. Race Counts include U.S. Citizens and Permanent Residents only, are alone or in combination with some other Race, and include both Hispanic and Non-Hispanic Ethnicity. The total represents an unduplicated count and also includes matriculants for whom we have no race data or who are foreign.

# Chapter 9:

## Be in the Know: AAMC Recommendations for Medical School Admission Officers

*This chapter is a little different from the ones that have come before it—and the ones that will come after it. That's because it does not talk to you about the application process, or about financing your medical education, or about the MCAT® exam.*

*In fact, it doesn't contain any information directed specifically at you at all.*

*What follows are a set of recommendations for medical school application, acceptance, and admission procedures that all 134 of our members have agreed to follow. We share them with you here because it is important you be aware of these procedures as they relate to your own application, ensuring that these processes are timely and fair for all concerned.*

### These recommendations correspond directly to the AAMC Recommendations for Applicants in Chapter 6

### The AAMC recommends that:

1. Each school:
   a. Publish annually, amend publicly, and adhere to its application, acceptance, and admission procedures.
   b. Utilizing an application service, abide by all conditions of its participation agreement with that application service.

2. Each school:
   a. Between August 1 and March 15, notify the AAMC Section for Medical School Application Services of all admission actions within four weeks of those actions being taken.
   b. Between March 16 and the first day of class, notify the AAMC Section for Medical School Application Services of all admission actions within seven days of those actions being taken.

3. Each school notify all applicants—other than Combined College/M.D., Early Decision Program (EDP), and deferred matriculation applicants—of acceptance to medical school only after October 15 of each admission cycle. It may be appropriate to communicate notifications of decisions other than acceptance to medical school to applicants prior to October 15.

continued...

4. By March 30 of the matriculation year, March 15 for M.D.-Ph.D. programs, each school or program have issued a number of offers of acceptance at least equal to the expected number of students in its first-year entering class and have reported those acceptance actions to the AAMC Section for Medical School Application Services.

5. Prior to May 15 of the matriculation year (April 15 for schools whose first day of class is on or before July 30), April 30 for M.D.-Ph.D. programs, each school or program permit ALL applicants (except for EDP applicants)— including those to whom merit or other special scholarships have been awarded:

   a. A minimum two-week time period for their response to the acceptance offer.

   b. To hold acceptance offers from any other schools or programs without penalty.

6. After May 15 of the matriculation year (April 15 for schools whose first day of class is on or before July 30), April 30 for M.D.-Ph.D. programs, each school or program implement school-specific procedures for accepted applicants who, without adequate explanation, continue to hold one or more places at other schools or programs. These procedures:

   a. May require applicants to:

      i. Respond to acceptance offers in less than two weeks.

      ii. Submit a statement of intent, a deposit, or both.

   b. Should recognize the problems of applicants with multiple acceptance offers, applicants who have not yet received an acceptance offer, and applicants who have not yet been informed about financial aid opportunities at schools to which they have been accepted.

   c. Should permit accepted applicants to remain on other schools' or programs' waiting lists and to withdraw if they later receive an acceptance offer from a preferred school or program.

7. Each school's acceptance deposit not exceed $100 and (except for EDP applicants) be refundable until May 15, April 30 for M.D.-Ph.D. applicants. If the applicant enrolls at the school, the school is encouraged to credit the deposit toward tuition.

8. After June 1, May 15 for M.D.-Ph.D. programs, any school that plans to make an acceptance offer to an applicant already known to have been accepted by another school or program for that entering class ensure that the other school or program is advised of this offer at the time that the offer is made. This notification should be made immediately by telephone and promptly thereafter by written correspondence delivered by regular or electronic methods. Schools and programs should communicate fully with each other with respect to anticipated late roster changes in order to minimize inter-school miscommunication and misunderstanding, as well as the possibility of unintended vacant positions in a school's first-year entering class.

9. No school make an acceptance offer, either verbal or written, to any individual who has enrolled in, or begun an orientation program immediately prior to enrollment at, a U.S. or Canadian school. Enrollment is defined as being officially matriculated as a member of the school's first-year class.

10. Each school treats all letters of recommendation submitted in support of an application as confidential, except in those states with applicable laws to the contrary. The contents of a letter of recommendation should not be revealed to an applicant at any time.

*Approved: AAMC Council of Deans Administrative Board, February 17, 2009*

# Chapter 10:

## Applicant and Acceptee Data

*Up until this point, we've touched upon a wide range of topics related to acceptance to medical school—including undergraduate preparation, the MCAT® exam, choosing a school, the application process, and the factors that enter into the admissions decision. We now turn to two additional questions that are likely at the very top of your mind:*

*Who applies to medical school…and who gets in?*

*We realize, of course, that the question you're really asking is "based on my numbers, will I get in?" We can't tell you. What we can do, however, is provide you with data related to last year's applicants—both those who were accepted and those who were not—so that you can determine your relative standing on a variety of admissions-related factors. Together with the school-specific data in Chapter 14 and your advisor's help, this information will enable you to make appropriate decisions related to your application to medical school. Extensive information about medical school applicants and matriculants can also be found at www. aamc.org/facts.*

### A Quick Look at the 2010 Entering Class

- In 2009–10, 42,742 people applied to the 2010 entering class at all M.D.-granting medical schools in the United States.

- By the fall of 2010, 19,641 applicants had been offered an acceptance to at least one medical school, and 18,665 accepted applicants had matriculated.

These accepted applicants possessed a broad range of MCAT® scores and undergraduate grade point averages, and a wide variety of personal characteristics and life experiences. Both male and female applicants were distributed across numerous racial and ethnic groups. A small number applied through the Early Decision Program, but the majority used the regular application process. A small number of accepted applicants chose not to matriculate in 2010.

This chapter contains graphic representations of relevant data for the entire applicant pool, as well as for accepted and nonaccepted applicants, for the 2010 entering class. All data presented in this chapter are accurate as of October 19, 2010*. In the following charts:

• "All applicants" refers to all applicants to the 2010 entering class

• "Accepted applicants" refers to those applicants accepted to at least one medical school

• "Not accepted applicants" refers to those applicants not accepted to any medical school

In the following pages, we provide data related to performance on the MCAT, undergraduate grade point average, MCAT® and undergraduate GPA combined, undergraduate major, gender, age, type of application, and race and ethnicity.

*\*Source: AAMC DataWarehouse; Applicant Matriculant File*

## Chart 10-A

MCAT® Verbal Reasoning Score Distribution, Year 2010 Applicants

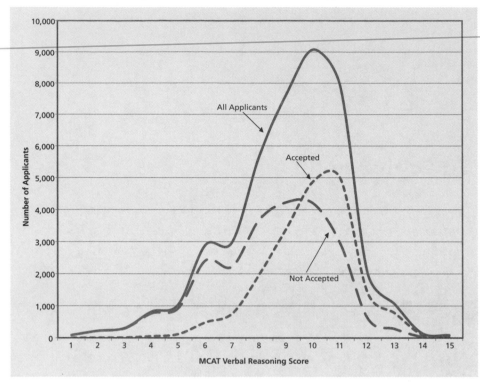

Source: AAMC Data Warehouse: Applicant Matriculant File

As of October 19, 2010

*The new medical schools accredited in 2010 will enroll their first matriculants in 2011.

## Performance on the MCAT

Charts 10-A—10-E present information about the performance of applicants on the MCAT®:

- **Chart 10-A** shows that applicants achieved Verbal Reasoning (VR) scores at each score from 1 to 15; the largest number achieved a VR score of 10. Accepted applicants' scores ranged from 1 to 15, although very few had VR scores below 5 (just under 70). At a VR score of 10, the number of accepted applicants exceeded the number not accepted.

- **Chart 10-B** shows that applicants achieved Physical Sciences (PS) scores at each score from 2 to 15; the largest number achieved a PS score of 10. Accepted applicants' scores ranged from 3 to 15; fewer than 90 accepted applicants achieved a score of 5 or below. Accepted applicants exceeded not accepted applicants at a PS score of 10.

## Chart 10-B

Physical Sciences Score Distribution, Year 2010 Applicants

Source: AAMC Data Warehouse: Applicant Matriculant File

As of October 19, 2010

- **Chart 10-C** shows that applicants achieved Writing Sample (WS) scores at each score from J to T; the largest number achieved a WS score of Q. Accepted applicants' scores ranged from J to T; the number with scores of K and below was about 130. Accepted applicants exceeded not accepted applicants at a score of Q.

- **Chart 10-D** shows that applicants achieved Biological Sciences (BS) scores at each score from 1 to 15; the largest number achieved a BS score of 10. Accepted applicants' scores ranged from 3 to 15; about 25 scored 5 or below. Accepted applicants exceeded not accepted applicants at a score of 11.

## Chart 10-C

MCAT® Writing Sample Score Distribution, Year 2010 Applicants

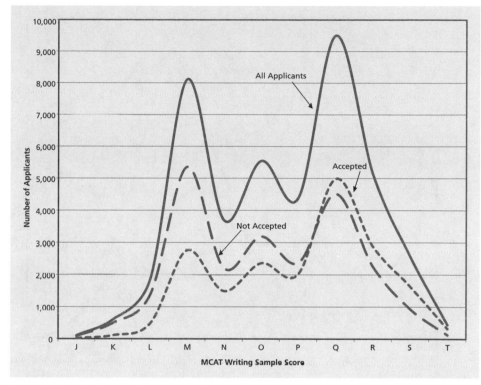

Source: AAMC Data Warehouse: Applicant Matriculant File

*As of October 19, 2010*

## Chart 10-D

MCAT® Biological Sciences Score Distribution, Year 2010 Applicants

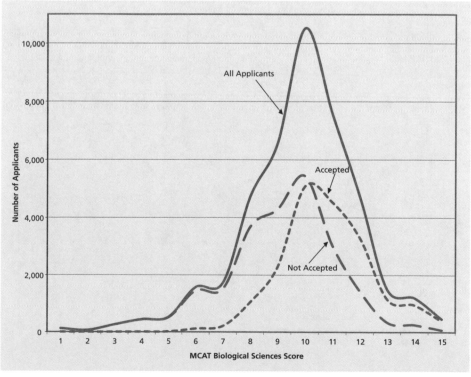

Source: AAMC Data Warehouse: Applicant Matriculant File

*As of October 19, 2010*

## Chart 10-E

MCAT® Total Numeric Score Distribution, Year 2010 Applicants

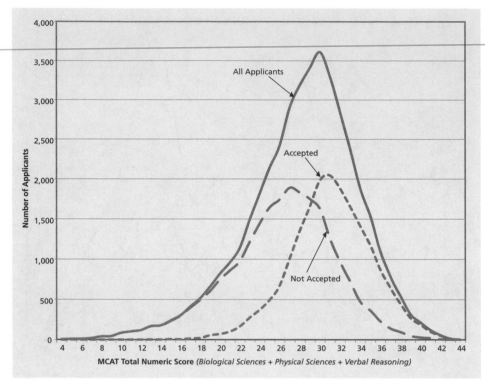

All Applicants

Accepted

Not Accepted

*Source: AAMC Data Warehouse: Applicant Matriculant File*

*As of October 19, 2010*

## Chart 10-F

Science GPA Distribution, Year 2010 Applicants

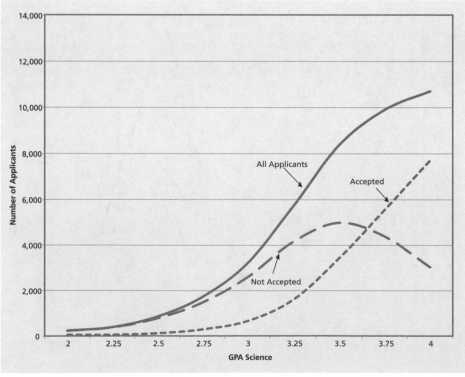

All Applicants

Accepted

Not Accepted

*Source: AAMC Data Warehouse: Applicant Matriculant File*

*As of October 19, 2010*

- **Chart 10-E**—which shows total scores on the numerically scored sections of Verbal Reasoning, Physical Sciences, and Biological Sciences—reveals that applicants achieved total scores from 4 to 44; the largest number achieved a total score of 30. Accepted applicants achieved total scores from 13 to 44; the number of accepted applicants with total scores of 17 and below (an average of almost 6 on each section) was about 30. Accepted applicants exceeded not accepted applicants at a total score of 30.

No score on a single MCAT® section and no total MCAT® score "guarantees" admission to medical school. Charts 10-A, 10-B, and 10-D reveal that, while applicants with VR, PS, and BS scores of 10 and above had a higher probability of being accepted to medical school, a significant number of applicants with such scores were not accepted. The same holds true for the Writing Sample section; a score of Q and above is a likely, though not definite, barometer for acceptance. Finally, Chart 10-E shows that a substantial number of applicants with total MCAT® scores of 29 and above were not accepted. These findings reveal the importance of factors other than MCAT® performance— including undergraduate academic performance and a variety of personal characteristics and experiential variables—in the medical student selection process.

## Undergraduate Grade Point Average (GPA)

**Charts 10-F—10-H** present information about the undergraduate academic performance of applicants:

- **Chart 10-F:** undergraduate science GPA (biology, chemistry, physics, and mathematics)

- **Chart 10-G:** undergraduate non-science GPA

- **Chart 10-H:** undergraduate total GPA

## Chart 10-G

Non-Science GPA Distribution, Year 2010 Applicants

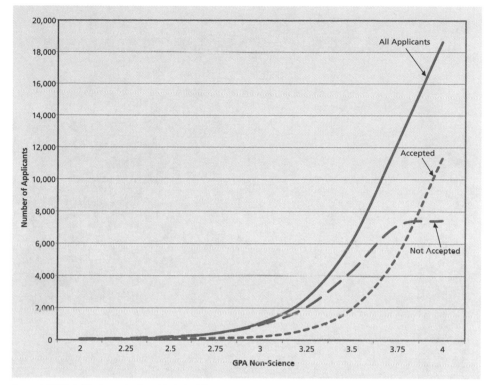

Source: AAMC Data Warehouse: Applicant Matriculant File

*As of October 19, 2010*

**Chart 10-F** shows that the undergraduate science GPAs of all applicants were on a continuum from 2.0 to 4.0, on a 4.0 scale; most were between 3.75 and 4.0. Accepted applicants also had undergraduate science GPAs across the entire range, but few had GPAs of 2.50 or below (just under 100). The undergraduate science GPA at which accepted applicants exceeded those not accepted was between 3.50 and 3.75.

**Chart 10-G** shows applicants' undergraduate non-science GPAs along the continuum from 2.0 to 4.0, with most between 3.75 and 4.0. Accepted applicants' undergraduate non-science GPAs also ranged from 2.0 to 4.0, but only about 90 had a GPA of 2.75 or below. At 3.75 to 4.0, accepted applicants exceeded not accepted applicants.

As shown in **Chart 10-H**, all applicants had total undergraduate GPAs from 2.0 to 4.0, and most were in the range of 3.50 to 3.75. Accepted applicants' total undergraduate GPAs ranged from 2.0 to 4.0, but only about 100 possessed undergraduate total GPAs of 2.75 or below. Accepted applicants exceeded not accepted applicants at an undergraduate total GPA of between 3.50 and 3.75.

As is the case with MCAT® data, GPA data in **Charts 10-F–10-H** show that no undergraduate GPA assures admission to medical school. While applicants with undergraduate science, nonscience, and total GPAs in the range of 3.50 to 3.75, 3.75 to 4.0, and 3.50 to 3.75, respectively, were more likely to be accepted to medical school, a significant number of such applicants were not accepted. Again, these findings underscore the importance of a wide variety of personal characteristics and experiential variables in the medical student selection process.

## Chart 10-H

Total GPA Distribution, Year 2010 Applicants

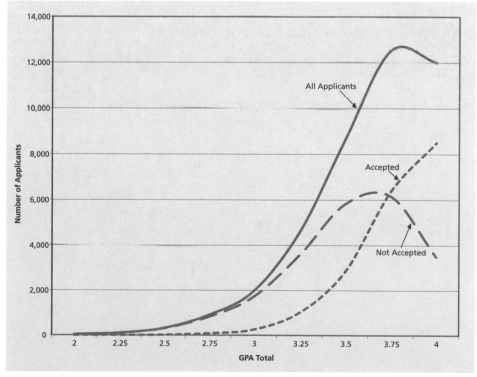

Source: AAMC Data Warehouse: Applicant Matriculant File

*As of October 19, 2010*

# Chart 10-I

MCAT® and Undergraduate GPA Combined

| GPA Total | MCAT Total | | | | | | | | | |
|---|---|---|---|---|---|---|---|---|---|---|
| | 5-14 | 15-17 | 18-20 | 21-23 | 24-26 | 27-29 | 30-32 | 33-35 | 36-38 | 39-45 |
| **3.80-4.00** | 4% | 6% | 18% | 25% | 42% | 67% | 82% | 86% | 90% | 92% |
| Acceptees | 3 | 11 | 88 | 330 | 1,370 | 3,915 | 5,975 | 4,884 | 2,894 | 1,128 |
| Applicants | 69 | 181 | 485 | 1,301 | 3,282 | 5,818 | 7,258 | 5,678 | 3,225 | 1,233 |
| **3.60-3.79** | 1% | 4% | 12% | 18% | 29% | 52% | 72% | 80% | 85% | 86% |
| Acceptees | 1 | 14 | 122 | 409 | 1,313 | 3,753 | 5,485 | 3,702 | 1,636 | 359 |
| Applicants | 180 | 351 | 989 | 2,217 | 4,490 | 7,283 | 7,610 | 4,625 | 1,925 | 420 |
| **3.40-3.59** | 2% | 3% | 10% | 17% | 23% | 36% | 56% | 67% | 73% | 80% |
| Acceptees | 6 | 13 | 120 | 440 | 1,060 | 2,417 | 3,540 | 2,127 | 852 | 174 |
| Applicants | 298 | 488 | 1,184 | 2,534 | 4,522 | 6,657 | 6,376 | 3,176 | 1,172 | 219 |
| **3.20-3.39** | 1% | 2% | 8% | 13% | 18% | 26% | 39% | 51% | 61% | 62% |
| Acceptees | 2 | 11 | 87 | 280 | 597 | 1,109 | 1,490 | 904 | 324 | 58 |
| Applicants | 391 | 534 | 1,120 | 2,084 | 3,324 | 4,282 | 3,850 | 1,762 | 530 | 93 |
| **3.00-3.19** | 1% | 3% | 6% | 11% | 16% | 23% | 30% | 42% | 42% | 44% |
| Acceptees | 3 | 18 | 58 | 168 | 326 | 566 | 522 | 339 | 100 | 19 |
| Applicants | 440 | 546 | 921 | 1,479 | 2,026 | 2,417 | 1,758 | 817 | 236 | 43 |
| **2.80-2.99** | -- | 1% | 5% | 11% | 15% | 16% | 24% | 33% | 28% | 57% |
| Acceptees | 0 | 4 | 31 | 94 | 156 | 166 | 177 | 93 | 25 | 8 |
| Applicants | 383 | 389 | 616 | 838 | 1,049 | 1,038 | 744 | 281 | 90 | 14 |
| **2.60-2.79** | -- | 1% | 5% | 7% | 11% | 15% | 18% | 21% | 17% | 8% |
| Acceptees | 0 | 2 | 20 | 35 | 56 | 67 | 53 | 29 | 6 | 1 |
| Applicants | 329 | 225 | 386 | 475 | 520 | 450 | 294 | 141 | 36 | 12 |
| **2.40-2.59** | -- | -- | 2% | 3% | 8% | 10% | 15% | 26% | 18% | -- |
| Acceptees | 0 | 0 | 3 | 7 | 18 | 18 | 19 | 15 | 3 | 0 |
| Applicants | 217 | 140 | 178 | 222 | 216 | 175 | 124 | 57 | 17 | 1 |
| **2.20-2.39** | -- | -- | 2% | 5% | 7% | 5% | 6% | 11% | 25% | -- |
| Acceptees | 0 | 0 | 2 | 4 | 6 | 3 | 2 | 2 | 1 | 0 |
| Applicants | 147 | 79 | 99 | 85 | 82 | 58 | 33 | 18 | 4 | 0 |
| **2.00-2.19** | -- | 2% | -- | 4% | 4% | -- | 8% | 100% | -- | -- |
| Acceptees | 0 | 1 | 0 | 1 | 1 | 0 | 1 | 2 | 0 | 0 |
| Applicants | 77 | 43 | 32 | 27 | 24 | 23 | 12 | 2 | 0 | 1 |
| **1.47-1.99** | -- | -- | -- | -- | 13% | -- | -- | -- | -- | -- |
| Acceptees | 0 | 0 | 0 | 0 | 1 | 0 | 0 | 0 | 0 | 0 |
| Applicants | 35 | 20 | 14 | 11 | 8 | 7 | 4 | 2 | 0 | 0 |

Percent Accepted = ■ 25% – 49%  ■ 50% – 74%  ■ 75% – 100%

Source: AAMC Data Warehouse: Applicant Matriculant File

As of October 19, 2010

Note: – – Signifies cells with fewer than 10 applicants

## MCAT® and Undergraduate GPA

**Chart 10-I** combines MCAT® scores and undergraduate GPA for all applicants to medical school from 2008 to 2010. The data may not reflect your particular circumstances. As a result, we recommend that you go to *www.aamc. org/facts* to see acceptance rates for particular demographic groups. Note that these results are presented without regard to any of the other selection factors.

## Chart 10-J

Undergraduate Major Distribution, All Applicants, 2006–2010

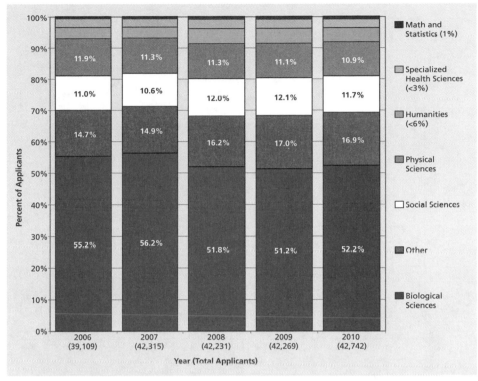

Source: AAMC Data Warehouse: Applicant Matriculant File

As of October 19, 2010

Chart 10-J presents information about the undergraduate majors of all medical school applicants to the 2006–2010 entering classes. Over the past five years, more than half of all applicants reported undergraduate biological science majors, while the remainder reported a variety of majors, including the humanities, mathematics and statistics, physical sciences, social sciences, other health sciences, and a broad "other" category. The proportion of these majors has remained relatively constant over time, despite annual fluctuations in the applicant pool.

Chart 10-K presents similar information about the undergraduate majors of applicants accepted to the 2006–2010 entering classes. Comparisons of the majors of the total applicant pool with those of accepted applicants reveal acceptance rates, for various science-related majors, ranging from 36.2 percent for applicants with specialized health science majors, to 44.8 percent for biological science majors, to 50.0 percent for physical science majors, the highest rate of acceptance for science-related majors.

## Chart 10-K

Undergraduate Major Distribution, Accepted Applicants, 2006–2010

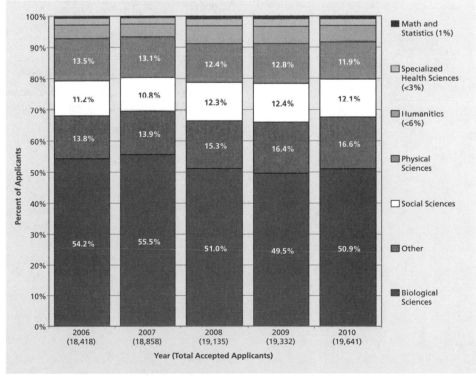

Source: AAMC Data Warehouse: Applicant Matriculant File

As of October 19, 2010

# Chart 10-L

Applicants by Gender and Acceptance Status, 1992-2010

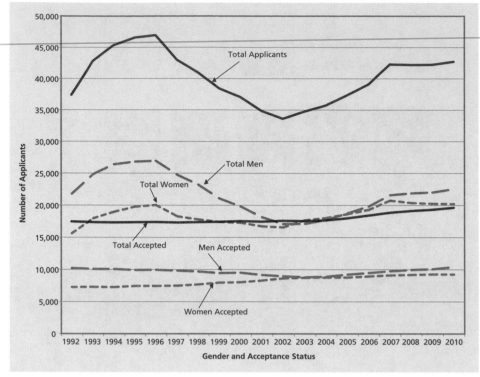

Source: AAMC Data Warehouse: Applicant Matriculant File

*As of October 19, 2010*

## Gender

**Chart 10-L** presents information about the number and gender of the entire applicant pool and of accepted applicants for the 1992–2010 entering classes. The largest annual applicant pool during the past 20 years was for the 1996 entering class; since that year, the pool gradually declined until 2003, when there was a slight increase (3.5 percent) in applicants. The applicant pool increased again by 2.7 percent in 2004, by 4.6 percent in 2005, by another 4.6 percent in 2006, and by 8.2 percent in 2007. In 2008 and 2009, the applicant pool held relatively steady, with a slight decrease of 0.2 percent from 2007 to 2008 and a slight increase of 0.1 percent from 2008 to 2009. In 2010, the applicant pool increased 1.1 percent. The number of male applicants to the 2010 entering class increased by about

520 from the number of male applicants to the previous year's entering class, but that number was still smaller than it had been for any other entering class from 1993 through 1998. The number of female applicants to the 2010 class decreased by about 45 over the number of female applicants to the previous year's entering class, the year 2007 being the largest number of female applicants on record. While the number of accepted applicants remained fairly constant for 10 years, it has started to increase in recent years, from a low of 17,312 in 1997 to a high of 19,641 in 2010. The number of accepted male applicants has fluctuated from a low of 8,810 in 2003 to a high of 10,404 in 2010. The number of accepted female applicants has increased, with small fluctuations, from a low of 7,255 in the 1994 entering class to a high of 9,264 in 2009 and is 9,237 in 2010. The significant gaps between male and female applicants for the 1992 entering class (6,166) and the 1993 entering class (6,892) have disappeared; 553 and 301 more women than men applied to the 2003 and 2004 entering classes, respectively. In 2005, only 121 more men than women applied. In 2010, 2,327 more men than women applied to medical school. During the same time span, the gaps between accepted male and accepted female applicants also dropped. Accepted male applicants outnumbered accepted female applicants by 2,951 for the 1992 entering class, but only by 1,167 for the 2010 entering class. The national ratio of male to female applicants was 49.2: 50.8 percent for the 2003 entering class, the first time that the number of female applicants was greater than the number of male applicants to medical school. For the 2004 entering class, this trend continued, with a ratio of male to female applicants of 49.6 : 50.4. For the 2005 entering class, there were once again more male than female applicants, with a ratio of male to female applicants of 50.2 : 49.8. This trend continued in 2010, with a ratio of male to female applicants of 52.7 : 47.3.

## Age

**Chart 10-M** shows that the age distribution for all applicants to the 2010 entering class was broad, with 12 applicants under the age of 19 at the time of anticipated matriculation, and 74 applicants aged 48 and over. The largest contingent of applicants, 38,805, was between 21 and 28 at the time of anticipated matriculation; the rest of the applicant pool were either under 21 (501) or over 28 (3,435) at the time of anticipated matriculation. Chart 10-M illustrates a similar finding for accepted applicants. Accepted applicants for the 2010 entering class were between 17 and 57 years of age at the time of expected matriculation.

## Applicant and Accepted Applicant Experiences

**Chart 10-N** presents information regarding the volunteer, paid, and lab experiences of applicants and accepted applicants to the 2010 entering class. The chart clearly shows the steady increase in both applicants and accepted applicants reporting volunteer medical, community service, and research experience since 2002:

- 82% of accepted applicants reported medical/clinical community service/volunteer clinical experience, an increase of about 9% since 2002

- 78% of applicants reported medical/clinical community service/volunteer clinical experience, an increase of about 8% since 2002

- 77% of accepted applicants reported research/lab experience, an increase of about 10% since 2002

- 70% of applicants reported research/lab experience, an increase of about 11% since 2002

- 68% of accepted applicants reported non-medical/non-clinical community service/volunteer clinical experience, an increase of about 5% since 2002

- 65% of applicants reported non-medical/non-clinical community

### Chart 10-M

Age Distribution, Year 2010 Applicants

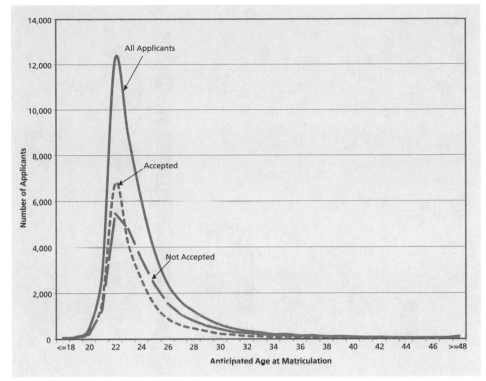

Source: AAMC Data Warehouse: Applicant Matriculant File    As of October 19, 2010

### Chart 10-N

Percentage of Applicants and Accepted Applicants Reporting Selected Experiences

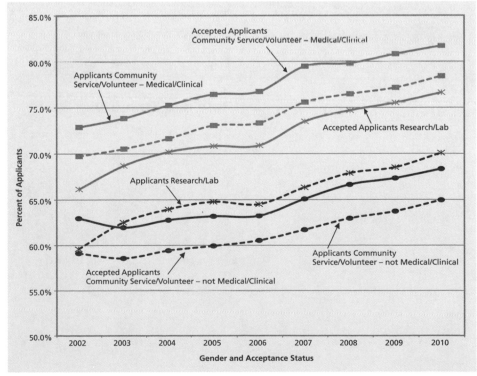

Source: AAMC Data Warehouse: Applicant Matriculant File    As of October 19, 2010

## Chart 10-O

Distribution of Self-Reported Ethnicity and Race: All Applicants, 2006–2010

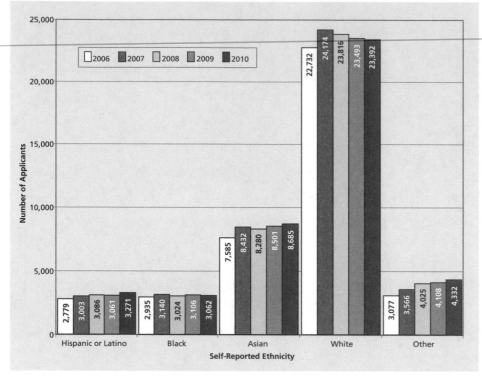

Source: AAMC Data Warehouse: Applicant Matriculant File

As of October 15, 2010

\* "Hispanic or Latino Ethnicity" includes all Races; Applicants' Self-Report of only "Black" OR "Asian" OR "White" Race is counted in "Black", "Asian", or "White"; Applicants' Self-Report of Multiple Races is counted in "Other"

service/volunteer clinical experience, an increased of about 6% since 2002

The rising trend in reported experiences among applicants and accepted applicants is expected to continue in the coming years.

## Race and Ethnicity

**Chart 10-O** shows applicant self-reported race and ethnicity data for all applicants to the 2006 through 2010 entering classes. The following changes occurred in the self-reported racial and ethnic make-up of the applicant pool from 2009 to 2010:

- The number of self-described white applicants in 2009 was 23,493; the number of white applicants in 2010 was 23,392, a decrease of 0.4 percent.

- The number of self-described Asian applicants in 2009 was 8,501; the number of Asian applicants in 2010 was 8,685, an increase of 2.2 percent.

- The number of self-described black applicants in 2009 was 3,106; the number of black applicants in 2010 was 3,062, a decrease of 1.4 percent.

- The number of self-described Hispanic applicants in 2009 was 3,061; the number of Hispanic applicants in 2010 was 3,271, an increase of 6.9 percent.

- The number of applicants in 2009 whose self-description of their race or ethnicity was in some other category was 4,108; the number of applicants in this cohort in 2010 was 4,332, an increase of 5.5 percent from 2009.

Simultaneously, the following changes occurred among those applicants accepted to the 2009 and 2010 entering classes:

- The number of self-described white accepted applicants in 2009 was 11,236; the number of white accepted applicants in 2010 was 11,199, a decrease of 0.3 percent.

- The number of self-described Asian accepted applicants in 2009 was 3,868; the number of accepted Asian applicants in 2010 was 3,948, an increase of 2.1 percent.

- The number of self-described black accepted applicants in 2009 was 1,186; the number of accepted black applicants in 2010 was 1,226, an increase of 3.4 percent.

- The number of self-described Hispanic accepted applicants in 2009 was 1,469; the number of Hispanic accepted applicants in 2010 was 1,611, and increase of 9.7 percent.

- The number of accepted applicants in 2009 whose self-description of their race or ethnicity was in some other category was 1,573; the number of accepted applicants in this cohort in 2010 was 1,657, an increase of 5.3 percent from 2009.

Additional information of interest to applicants from groups under-represented in medicine is available in Chapter 8.

# Chapter 11:

## Financing Your Medical Education

*The very thought of medical school undoubtedly conjures up feelings of excitement and anticipation. You're about to embark on the journey to a medical degree, a road filled with new discoveries, challenging professors, and wide-open opportunities.*

*But on the other hand, you've got to figure out how to pay for it.*

*There's no doubt that medical school is an expensive undertaking, and you'll soon face a myriad of expenses. Beyond the tuition itself, you'll also have fees, books, equipment, living expenses, medical insurance, and transportation to consider.*

*Fortunately, there's help. In this chapter, we review the various ways you can finance your medical education—from grants and scholarships, to federal student loans with attractive terms, to service commitment programs that provide financial support—as well as the resources available to help you through the process.*

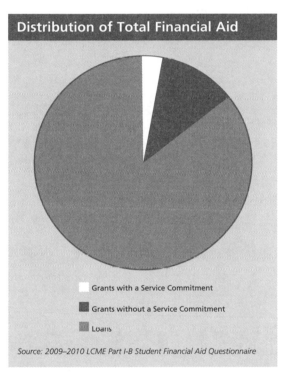

**Distribution of Total Financial Aid**

- Grants with a Service Commitment
- Grants without a Service Commitment
- Loans

*Source: 2009–2010 LCME Part I-B Student Financial Aid Questionnaire*

### Building a Strong Financial Plan

You'll need to develop a strategy to cover the significant costs associated with your education. Tuition and fees top the list, of course, but you'll also need to buy books and equipment, purchase insurance, cover the costs of transportation, and, quite likely, pay for housing and food.

When you look at the figures in the table on the following page, we understand how the financial challenges that face you might seem overwhelming. Annual tuition and fees at state medical schools in 2010–2011 average approximately $25,000 for state residents and $48,000 for nonresidents; at private schools, the averages were $42,000 for residents and $43,000 for nonresidents.

But don't let these numbers discourage you. There's help available—and lots of it.

And you certainly won't be the only one taking advantage of that assistance. According to recent surveys conducted by the AAMC, 84.3 percent of newly graduated M.D.'s have medical school education loans, while 58.3 percent reported receiving some degree of help through scholarships, stipends, and/or grants (which you don't have to repay). So, it can be done, and it is…by tens of thousands of medical students, every single year.

But first… you'll need a plan.

## Table 11-A

Tuition, Fees and Health Insurance for 2010–2011
First-Year Students in U.S. Medical Schools* (in Dollars)

### Private Schools

| Student Category | Range | Median | Average |
|---|---|---|---|
| Resident | $18,176 – $56,199 | $46,899 | $44,591 |
| Nonresident | $23,881 – $57,457 | $45,893 | $47,459 |

### Public Schools

| Student Category | Range | Median | Average |
|---|---|---|---|
| Resident | $11,978 – $40,684 | $28,365 | $27,005 |
| Nonresident | $21,234– $78,888 | $49,495 | $48,710 |

*Analysis excludes Massachusetts, Mercer, and Mississippi. These schools do not accept nonresident medical students, and therefore, they do not report nonresident tuition and fees. Public medical schools excludes Uniformed Services University of Health Sciences which does not charge tuition or student fees.*

*Source: 2010–11 AAMC Tuition and Student Fees Questionnaire*

And by "plan," we mean more than simply learning about the assistance available to you and securing the necessary financing. Before you can get to that admittedly vital step, it's important that you understand—and adhere to—the basic principles of successful money management. With that in mind, the two basic recommendations that follow should help you build a strong financial foundation.

## Overview: The Financial "Basics"

### 1. Live Within Your Means

Let's face it. Money will be tight during your medical school years, and a realistic budget will be critical to your financial well-being. A well-crafted plan will help you maintain better control of your spending, ensure you cover your essential expenses before making an optional purchase, and prepare for an unexpected expense by building an emergency fund.

The steps involved in creating a budget are actually quite simple. You just add up your monthly income, determine your monthly expenses, and calculate the difference. One helpful tip is to categorize your expenses as either "fixed" (ones that stay the same each month, such as rent and insurance premiums) and "variable" expenses (such as groceries and clothing).

From that point, you can identify areas in which you can scale back (if necessary) to assure that your income and outgo remain in balance. Obvious cost-savings steps include sharing housing costs with a roommate, buying generic products rather than brand names, preparing more of your meals at home, and taking public transportation or carpooling when possible.

Need a hand? Check out the interactive budget worksheet available from the AAMC's FIRST program (see box on next page) at *www.aamc.org/download/78858/data/ budgetworksheet.pdf.*

### 2. Manage Your Debt Wisely

Given the costs of medical school, it's understandable that the vast majority of medical students borrow money to fund their education—and graduate with an average medical school debt of $150,000. And although the ability to manage debt wisely is important regardless of one's situation, it becomes even more critical for you—a prospective medical student—when you consider the degree to which you're likely to rely on loans to help pay for your education.

- Your first step is to be fully cognizant of the amount you plan to borrow and be comfortable that your future income will allow you to cover your debt payments.

- You will, of course, need to learn about, apply for, and secure the most cost-effective financing available.

- You'll need to understand your responsibilities as a borrower. Your primary obligation is, of course, know what loans you hold (and from which lender), the amount of each, and the repayment schedule, but beyond that, you must keep lenders notified of any changes in your name, contact information, or enrollment status.

### Get Your Financial House in Order

Before you apply for student loans, make sure your "financial house" is in order by:

- Creating a budget
- Paying down debt to the extent possible
- Making sure you are current on all outstanding credit obligations

*Students with a history of credit problems may not qualify for the loans that are based on credit, whether federal or private.*

- You must maintain accurate records, including promissory notes (your legal promise to pay back the loans), copies of application forms, and any related disclosure statements.

*\* The entries in school and combined undergraduate program pages provide information about individual schools' tuition and fee schedules and other financial data.*

- You need to build and maintain a good credit score by meeting your financial obligations. In doing so, you'll strengthen your ability to qualify for and obtain attractive interest rates for credit-based loans, land a job, or even rent an apartment. For more information, go to *www.aamc.org/ download/78864/data/creditscore.pdf.*

*Fortunately, you have an abundance of resources to assist you through this process—including that provided by your pre-health advisor, the pages that follow in this very book, and the FIRST program (see box below) offered by the AAMC.*

---

### FIRST for Medical Education

**FIRST** *for Medical Education* is an AAMC program that provides a wide range of **F**inancial **I**nformation, **R**esources, **S**ervices, and **T**ools to help medical school applicants and students make smart decisions about students loans, effectively manage their education debt, and expand their financial literacy.

Please see *www.aamc.org/first* for more information.

---

## Types of Financial Aid

Now we're ready for specifics. How will you pay for medical school?

First, we'd like to remind you that you're not on your own here. While the ultimate financial responsibility for your medical education rests with you and your family, there are many resources and tools available to help. The financial aid office at the medical school to which you've been accepted will assist you, of course, but you'll also want to talk to your pre-health advisor and familiarize yourself with the informational "fact sheets" you'll find on the AAMC FIRST Web site.

That said, there are two* general types of financial aid available to medical students: loans and grants or scholarships. We discuss both of these funding sources next.

---

### You Can Help Your Credit Score By...

- Paying your bills on time
- Having no more than three credit cards
- Keeping balances less than 50% of the assigned credit limit
- Checking your credit report for errors at *www. annualcreditreport.com*

---

## Loans

Most of your funding will come from loans—which, in the case of federal loans, are a form of financial aid. Fortunately, there are a variety of loan programs available to help you finance your education. Within this category, there are both subsidized and unsubsidized loans, each of which is described briefly below.

- *Subsidized Loans (Based on Financial Need)*
  Subsidized loans carry no interest cost to borrowers during the time they are in school, in grace (a period following graduation during which no payments are due), or in deferment (a temporary suspension of payments granted to qualifying borrowers). It is only during the active period of repayment that these loans incur any interest.

- *Unsubsidized Loans (Not Based on Financial Need)*
  Unsubsidized loans, on the other hand, accrue interest from the date they are disbursed. While borrowers are not required to pay interest that is accruing on unsubsidized loans while they are in school, in grace, or in deferment, any unpaid accrued interest on these loans will be capitalized (adding to the loan principal) and must be repaid.

---

### Available Sources of Financing Include...

**Grants, Scholarships and Loan Repayment Programs**
- Service Commitment Programs
- Scholarships for Disadvantaged Students
- Loan Repayment/Forgiveness Programs

**Loans**
- Stafford Loans
- Grad PLUS Loans
- Federal Perkins Loans
- Primary Care Loans
- Loans for Disadvantaged Students

Information on these programs is provided on the following pages and in the table on page 69.

---

In both cases, however—subsidized or unsubsidized—interest charges and repayment options for federal loans are quite attractive, and students are advised to apply for these loans before considering private options. The table on the next page provides specific information about four popular federal student loan programs.

Finally, we want to say a word about the amount of the debt itself. We know it sounds like a lot—and it is. Bear in mind,

---

*Federal work-study programs are a third type of financial aid. Most medical students, however, are unable to supplement their funds with employment due to educational demands.*

though, that your income as a physician is likely to be excellent. (Starting salaries for doctors in family practice, for example, are projected to average $165,000 by 2012,* with many other specialties averaging even higher.) An investment in medical education is likely to be returned to you many times over.

## Students With Medical School Loans

Nearly 85.45 percent of graduating medical students owe money on medical school education loans, with an average debt of $140,622.

*Source: 2009–10 LCME Student Financial Aid Questionnaire*

### Grants and Scholarships

Naturally, when it comes to financing your medical education, the most desirable way is through "free" money—sometimes referred to as "gift aid"—which you don't have to repay.

While grants and scholarships are likely to cover only a portion of your overall educational costs, it's worth noting that many students get some degree of funding from these sources. The source of gift aid can be the federal government, the state government, and/or your medical school itself. Your medical school financial aid office is the best source of information as to which grants and scholarships may be available to you.

## The Financial Aid Application Process

Because the specific process by which you'll apply for financial aid varies by medical school, you'll need to check with the financial aid office for exact instructions. Still, regardless of the medical school, there's an overall process which every prospective student should take. We review these steps below.

- **Step 1: Complete the FAFSA**
  Complete and submit the FAFSA form in January—preferably after you've filed your income taxes—filling in both the student and parent** information. The resulting Institutional Student Information Report (ISIR) is sent to your school and determines your financial need. Remember to list your medical school's federal ID code to ensure the results of your FAFSA are sent to your medical school's financial aid office.

- **Step 2: Investigate Sources of Aid**
  Contact the financial aid office at your medical school to investigate sources of institutional aid as well as to learn about various student loan programs in detail. (You'll need to complete a separate application from the FAFSA when applying for a student loan.)

- **Step 3: Apply Early**
  Complete and return applications as soon as possible. In many cases, programs have limited funds and students who apply early have a better chance of receiving aid. You'd hate to miss out on an offer of financial aid simply because you were late in submitting applications.

- **Step 4: Receive and Reply to the Award Letter**
  Once your FAFSA results are received and processed by your medical school's financial aid office, you'll receive an award letter indicating the types and amounts of financial aid for which you qualify—along with directions for accepting or declining the aid.

## Make Sure You Are "Credit Ready"

Some medical schools require a credit history as part of the financial aid application and require that the applicant resolve any credit problems before the process gets underway. Many medical schools will grant a delay of matriculation to an accepted applicant who must address credit problems. Applicants are advised to contact financial aid offices at medical schools of interest to them to discuss financial aid eligibility and, if necessary, resolve any outstanding credit problems.

*The table on the next page outlines the parameters of four major federal loan programs—Primary Care Loans, Federal Perkins Loans, Federal Stafford Loans, and Graduate PLUS loans. For eligibility and other information, we suggest you talk with the financial aid office at the medical school you plan to attend.*

---

*From AAMC's The Economics of Becoming a Doctor (www.aamc.org/video/first/mdeconomics.htm). For other compensation studies, see www.aamc.org/download/48732/data/compensation.pdf.*

**Although the FAFSA does not ask for parental information for students working toward a graduate degree, many medical schools require that information for purposes of awarding institutional aid (funds given by the school itself).*

## Federal Loan Programs for Students

| Characteristic | Primary Care Loan | Federal Perkins | Federal Subsidized/ Unsubsidized Stafford | Graduate PLUS Loan |
|---|---|---|---|---|
| Lender | Medical school financial aid office on behalf of the Department of HHS | Medical school financial aid office on behalf of the federal government | The federal government | The federal government |
| Based on Need | Note[1] | Yes | Subsidized–Yes Unsubsidized–No | No |
| Citizenship Requirement | U.S. citizen, U.S. national, U.S. permanent resident, or asylum status | U.S. citizen, U.S. national, U.S. permanent resident, or asylum status | U.S. citizen, U.S. national, U.S. permanent resident, or asylum status | U.S. citizen, U.S. national, U.S. permanent resident, or asylum status |
| Borrowing Limits | Up to cost of attendance (Third- and fourth-year students may receive additional funds to repay previous educational loans received while attending medical school)[2] | $6,000/year $40,000 aggregate undergraduate and graduate | $40,500 including subsidized Stafford $8,500, annual maximum; $224,000 including $65,000 subsidized Stafford, cumulative maximum, for premed and medical borrowing[2] | Annual cost of attendance minus other financial aid |
| Interest Rate | Note[3] | 5% | For loans first disbursed since July 1, 2006, 6.8% for life of loan | 7.9% from the federal government for life of loan |
| Borrower is responsible for interest during: | | | | |
| • School | No | No | Subsidized: No Unsubsidized: Yes | Yes |
| • Deferments | No | No | Subsidized: No Unsubsidized: Yes | Yes |
| • Grace Period | No | No | Subsidized: No Unsubsidized: Yes | n/a |
| Grace Period | 1 year after graduation | 9 months after graduation | 6 months after graduation | None |
| Deferments | During school and primary care residency (check your promissory note or ask your financial aid officer) | During school and other deferment periods based on eligibility (check your promissory note or ask your financial aid office) | During school and other deferment periods based on eligibility (check your promissory note or ask your financial aid office) | Minimum: $50/month; level, graduated, income-sensitive, income-based, and extended repayment options available; eligible for loan consolidation |
| Repayment Requirements | Minimum: $40/month; 10 to 25 years to repay; Not eligible for loan consolidation | Minimum: $40/month, including interest; maximum 10 years to repay; eligible for loan consolidation | Minimum: $50/month; level, graduated, income-contingent, income-based, and extended repayment options available; eligible for loan consolidation | Minimum: $50/month; level, graduated, income-contingent, income-based, and extended repayment options available; eligible for loan consolidation |
| Prepayment Penalties | None | | | |
| Allowable Cancellations | Death or total and permanent disability | | | |

1 Yes; in addition, borrower must agree upon signing loan agreement to enter and complete a primary care residency and practice in a primary care field, which together must be a total of 10 years in length or until the loan is repaid in full, whichever occurs first. Parent financial information is required for consideration for dependent students.
2 Both annual and aggregate maximums are subject to change, pending congressional action.
3 Five percent; however, rate is recomputed at 7% from the date of noncompliance should borrower fail to meet primary care requirements (for primary care loans made on or after March 23, 2010).

## How Medical Schools Determine Eligibility for Financial Aid

Medical schools are well aware that their programs are expensive, and that most students will need at least some degree of financial aid. Financial aid offices will determine the amount of aid for which you are eligible by answering the following three questions:

1.  **How much does it cost?**
    For purposes of determining financial need, the cost of medical education is comprised of three components: tuition and fees; books, supplies, and equipment; and living expenses. The total dollar amount of these three –which varies not only by school but also by the specific year in school—is frequently referred to as the COA ("cost of attendance") or the "student financial aid budget."

    **The COA for each medical school is included in that institution's entry in Chapters 14 and 15 of this book.**

2.  **What are your resources?**
    The next area to be considered is the degree to which you can contribute to the overall costs (see "the financial aid philosophy" box on next page). This amount, called the "Expected Family Contribution (EFC)," is determined through a need-analysis formula to ensure that all students are treated equitably. Both income and assets are considered.

A word about the "family" in the EFC: Even though you are considered to be independent for purposes of federal loans, some institutions require financial information about parents or other family members to determine eligibility for institutional grants, scholarships, and school-based loans. School officials use this information to assess ability—rather than willingness—to pay, thus helping ensure that certain types of aid are awarded to students with the greatest need.

3.  **What additional resources are needed?**
    Finally, the financial aid office will subtract your EFC from the institution's total cost of attendance. The remainder determines how much need-based financial assistance you will require for the upcoming academic year.

The medical school will then send you an "award letter," detailing the amount and type of financial aid it can provide. You will then be asked to accept or decline the offer—or a portion of it—and return the letter to the school. (The amount of financial aid an institution offers is an important factor in choosing which school to attend. See Chapter 5 for additional information and guidance on making your selection.)

## Service Commitment and Loan Forgiveness Programs

Were you aware of ways to minimize or almost negate your debt? Either may be possible through a service commitment or loan forgiveness program.

Service commitment programs provide financial assistance to enrolled medical students in return for services after completion of medical training. (Most programs require one year of service for each year of funding, and sometimes offer monthly stipends in addition to payments for educational expenses.) The other possibility—a loan forgiveness program—cancels a portion of a borrower's student loan debt, assuming eligibility requirements are met, while he or she is working in a qualifying public service job. Students must apply for these competitive programs, examples of which are described below.

- The U.S. Army, Navy, and Air Force have programs that offer full support to students enrolled in civilian medical schools in exchange for service in the branch that provided the funding. On the civilian side, the federal government provides both service commitment and loan repayment benefits to medical students interested in pursuing careers in primary care for the underserved.

## The Financial Aid Philosophy

The philosophy of financial aid is that a student and his or her family bear primary responsibility of paying educational expenses to the extent possible. That is why eligibility for financial aid is determined by comparing the cost of attendance to a student's available resources.

- State programs are frequently available to students and graduates in return for a commitment to serve in the state's areas of need.
- The College Cost Reduction and Access Act of 2007 passed by Congress brings you yet another possible means of loan repayment assistance—a program that forgives some federal student loans under certain circumstances.

*For additional details on service commitment and loan forgiveness, please see the AAMC's First Fact sheets (listed in the "Repayment" section) at www.aamc.org/firstfacts.*

## General Eligibility Criteria

Financial aid programs usually require that the applicant or student is:

- A U.S. citizen, a permanent resident, or permitted to reside indefinitely in the U.S. by the U.S. Citizenship and Immigration Services.
- Making satisfactory academic progress
- In compliance with Selective Service registration requirements

## A Word About Repayment

There are, no doubt, a number of benefits to the federal student loans—whether subsidized or unsubsidized. You don't have to begin repaying the loan until after medical school and residency. There are often interest rate deductions for electronic payment and/or making your payments on time.

And…there is an array of options available to you when it comes time to repaying your loans. Beyond standard repayment, which involves a fixed payment that remains the same during the repayment period, you may choose a graduated repayment schedule, in which your payments are smaller in the early years and increase in the later years, an income-sensitive (or income-contingent) program, in which payments are based on the borrower's income and other data, or even an income-based repayment plan that caps loans payments at a particular percentage of income.

*Your financial aid office will provide you with complete information as the time nears for repayment as part of your "Exit Counseling" program. For those of you interested in learning more now, please check out the First Fact sheets on loan repayment choices at www. aamc.org/firstfacts.*

## Service Commitment and Loan Forgiveness Programs

Learn more about these programs at the applicable web site(s) listed below:

**Army:** *www.goarmy.com/amedd/hpsp.html*

**Navy:** *www.navy.com/careers/healthcare/physicians/*

**Air Force:** *www.airforce.com/opportunities/healthcare/ education*

**Federal Government:** *www.nhsc.hrsa.gov/index.htm*

**State Programs:** *www.aamc.org/stloan*

**Public Service Programs:** *www.studentaid.ed.gov/ students/attachments/siteresources/LoanForgivenessv4.pdf*

# A Final Word About
# Financing Your Medical Education

This chapter is intended to provide you with an overview of the types of available financial aid, student loans, the financial aid process, and how eligibility for aid is determined. Please bear in mind that once you have been accepted to medical school, you will work closely with that institution's financial aid office(s) to determine the requirements for and specifics of your own education financing plan.

## Education Tax Credits and Deductions

Do you know that the IRS can help you put some of the cost of medical school back in your pocket? It does so through (a) a student loan interest deduction of up to $2,500 for qualified individuals, and (b) the Lifetime Learning Tax Credit of up to $2,000 for eligible borrowers

**Want to learn more? Read an overview of these programs—and learn the difference between a tax deduction and a tax credit!—by clicking on "Education Tax Credits" at** *www.aamc.org/firstfacts*.

# Chapter 12:

## Information on Combined Undergraduate/ M.D. Programs

*About one-quarter of U.S. medical schools offer combined college/M.D. programs for graduating high school students. These programs range in length from six to nine years. The first two to four years of the curriculum consist of undergraduate courses, including required premedical courses; the remaining years are devoted to the medical school curriculum. Graduates receive both a bachelor's degree from the undergraduate institution and an M.D. degree from the medical school.*

### The purposes of these programs vary by institution:

- to permit highly qualified students to plan and complete a broad liberal arts education before initiating their medical studies

- to attract highly capable students to the sponsoring medical school

- to enhance diversity in the educational environment

- to reduce the total number of years required to complete the M.D. degree

- to educate physicians likely to practice in particular geographic areas or to work with medically underserved populations

- to reduce the costs of a medical education

- to prepare physician-scientists and future leaders in health policy.

Potential applicants should familiarize themselves with the mission and goals statement of each combined degree program in which they have an interest to ensure a match between their educational and professional goals and those of the program.

These programs typically represent relationships between a medical school and one or more undergraduate colleges located in the same geographic region. They are sometimes part of the same university system, or they can be independent institutions.

Admission is open to highly qualified, mature high school students who are committed to a future career in medicine. State-supported schools generally admit few out-of-state applicants to their combined college/M.D. programs; private schools tend to have greater flexibility regarding state of residency.

While academic requirements vary among the schools sponsoring these programs, they typically include biology, chemistry, physics, English, mathematics, and social science courses. Calculus and foreign-language courses are also frequently required; a computer science course is sometimes recommended. Admission to the medical curriculum may occur immediately or after a student completes a prescribed number of semesters with a minimum grade point average (GPA). In some programs, students are not required to take the MCAT®; in other programs, a minimum MCAT® score must be attained for progression through the program.

Progressing through the program from the undergraduate to the medical curriculum is usually contingent on a student's achieving specific criteria in terms of standardized test scores and GPAs and meeting the school's expectations regarding personal and professional behavior.

High school students interested in a combined undergraduate/M.D. program should consult their high school guidance counselor to ensure that they are enrolled in a challenging college preparatory curriculum, one that incorporates the specific courses required for admission to the program. The program descriptions that follow were compiled from responses to a survey sent to all medical schools sponsoring programs of interest to high school students. For additional information, contact each school directly.

## The following abbreviations are used in the school entries in this chapter:

**ACT**
American College Testing Program

**AP**
Advanced Placement

**BCPM**
Biology, Chemistry, Physics, and Mathematics

**CEEB**
College Entrance Examination Board

**FAFSA**
Free Application for Federal Student Aid

**GPA**
Grade Point Average

**MCAT**
Medical College Admission Test

**SAT**
Scholastic Aptitude Test

**USMLE**
United States Medical Licensing Examination

# List of Medical Schools Offering Combined Undergraduate/M.D. Programs by State, 2012–13

**Alabama**
University of Alabama School of Medicine

University of South Alabama College of Medicine

**California**
University of California, San Diego, School of Medicine

University of Southern California College of Letters, Arts, and Sciences and Keck School of Medicine

**Connecticut**
University of Connecticut and University of Connecticut School of Medicine

**District of Columbia**
The George Washington University School of Medicine and Health Sciences and The Columbian School of Arts and Sciences

Howard University College of Medicine

**Florida**
University of Florida College of Medicine
University of Miami

**Illinois**
Northwestern University Feinberg School of Medicine

University of Illinois at Chicago College of Medicine

**Massachusetts**
Boston University School of Medicine

**Missouri**
Saint Louis University School of Medicine

University of Missouri—Kansas City School of Medicine

**New Jersey**

Rutgers University and Drexel University College of Medicine

Rutgers University and UMDNJ—New Jersey Medical School

Rutgers University and UMDNJ—Robert Wood Johnson Medical School

University of Medicine and Dentistry of New Jersey—New Jersey Medical School

**New Mexico**

University of New Mexico School of Medicine

**New York**

Brooklyn College and SUNY Downstate Medical Center

Hobart and William Smith Colleges/SUNY Upstate Medical University

Rensselaer Polytechnic Institute and Albany Medical College

St. Bonaventure University/The George Washington University School of Medicine and Health Sciences

Siena College and Albany Medical College

Sophie Davis School of Biomedical Education at the City College of New York

Stony Brook University and Stony Brook University School of Medicine

Union College and Albany Medical College

University of Rochester School of Medicine and Dentistry

**Ohio**

Case Western Reserve University School of Medicine

Northeastern Ohio Universities College of Medicine

University of Cincinnati College of Medicine

**Pennsylvania**

Drexel University and Drexel University College of Medicine

Lehigh University and Drexel University College of Medicine

Pennsylvania State University and Jefferson Medical College

Temple University School of Medicine

Villanova University and Drexel University College of Medicine

Wilkes University/SUNY-Upstate Medical University

**Rhode Island**

Warren Alpert Medical School of Brown University

**Tennessee**

Fisk University and Meharry Medical College

**Texas**

Rice University and Baylor College of Medicine

University of Texas School of Medicine at San Antonio

**Virginia**

Eastern Virginia Medical School

Virginia Commonwealth University School of Medicine

## List of Medical Schools Offering Combined Undergraduate/M.D. Programs by Number of Years, 2012–13

**6 Years**

University of Missouri—Kansas City School of Medicine

**6–7 Years**

University of Miami

Northeastern Ohio Universities College of Medicine

Pennsylvania State University and Jefferson Medical College

## 7 Years

The George Washington University School of Medicine and Health Sciences and The Columbian School of Arts and Sciences

University of Florida College of Medicine

Northwestern University Feinberg School of Medicine

University of Illinois at Chicago College of Medicine

Boston University School of Medicine (8-year option available)

University of Medicine and Dentistry of New Jersey—New Jersey Medical School

Rensselaer Polytechnic Institute and Albany Medical College

Sophie Davis School of Biomedical Education/City College of New York

Drexel University and Drexel University College of Medicine

Lehigh University and Drexel University College of Medicine

Villanova University and Drexel University College of Medicine

Fisk University and Meharry Medical College

University of Texas School of Medicine at San Antonio

## 8 Years

University of Alabama School of Medicine

University of South Alabama College of Medicine

University of California, San Diego School of Medicine

University of Southern California College of Letters, Arts, and Sciences and Keck School of Medicine

University of Connecticut and University of Connecticut School of Medicine

Howard University College of Medicine

University of New Mexico School of Medicine Combined BA/MD Degree Program

Saint Louis University School of Medicine

Rutgers University and Drexel University College of Medicine

Rutgers University and UMDNJ—New Jersey Medical School

Rutgers University and University of Medicine and Dentistry of New Jersey—Robert Wood Johnson Medical School

Brooklyn College and SUNY Downstate Medical Center

Hobart and William Smith Colleges/SUNY Upstate Medical University

St. Bonaventure University/The George Washington University School of Medicine and Health Sciences

Siena College and Albany Medical College

Stony Brook and Stony Brook University School of Medicine

Union College and Albany Medical College

University of Rochester School of Medicine and Dentistry

Case Western Reserve University School of Medicine

University of Cincinnati College of Medicine

Temple University School of Medicine

Wilkes University/SUNY-Upstate Medical University

Warren Alpert Medical School of Brown University

Rice University and Baylor College of Medicine

Eastern Virginia Medical School

Virginia Commonwealth University School of Medicine

## 9 Years

University of Cincinnati College of Medicine
(College of Engineering—undergraduate)

# University of Alabama School of Medicine

Birmingham, Alabama

**Address inquiries to:** Amelia Johnson, Program Administrator, UAB Honors Academy, University of Alabama at Birmingham HUC 272, 1530 3rd Avenue, South, Birmingham Alabama 35294-1150

**T** 205 996 9842   **F** 205 996 9838  •  www.uab.edu/emsap  •  honorsacademy@uab.edu

## Purpose

The UAB Early Medical School Acceptance Program (EMSAP) is designed to give exceptional high school graduates an opportunity to take advantage of the best resources of the undergraduate and medical programs through a mentored relationship with medical school faculty. A medical school professor advises students from high school graduation until the second year of the medical program, establishing a unique relationship. This is not an accelerated program, rather a program to allow gifted students to explore a broad range of educational, research and community service opportunities beyond the typical Premedical experiences.

## Requirements for Entrance

Students are selected in their senior year of high school. Both residents and non-residents of Alabama are eligible to apply to the program. Applicants must submit the following documents: (1) a UAB application; (2) a completed EMSAP application; (3) two letters of recommendation from high school administrators, counselors, or teachers describing their suitability for a career in medicine; (4) a brief essay incorporating information about themselves and their career objectives and expectations for contributing to society; and (5) a resume listing their academic achievements, honors received, activities, employment, health-related experience, etc. Applicants must meet the requirements for freshman admission to the university and be admitted to the University by the EMSAP application deadline, December 15, 2011. Students who wish to be considered for merit scholarships should postmark the undergraduate application and all supporting credentials (official transcript and official ACT and/or SAT scores) by December 1 of the senior year in high school.

## Selection Factors

Required high school courses include: four years of English, four years of mathematics, one year of chemistry or physics, and one year of biology. Minimum GPA: 3.5 overall GPA (on a 4.0 scale). Test scores: at least 30 ACT or a minimum 1340 SAT (critical reading + math). Selected applicants are invited for a required interview.

## Curriculum

This eight-year program leads to a baccalaureate degree awarded by the University of Alabama at Birmingham (UAB), and to the M.D. degree granted by the University of Alabama School of Medicine. Students must meet the regular undergraduate course requirements for the University of Alabama at Birmingham, complete two required EMSAP (Early Medical School Acceptance Program) seminars and live on campus during their first two years. Applicants may apply to one of three other Honors programs in the Honors Academy. The deadline to apply for both programs is December 15. In order to matriculate to the medical school phase of the program, students must: (1) take the MCAT® and receive a minimal total score of 28; (2) maintain an overall GPA of 3.6 and a math and science GPA of 3.5; (3) receive their baccalaureate

degree; and (4) meet all requirements and conditions to remain in good standing for their acceptance into the University of Alabama School of Medicine. After the second year of medical school, students must pass the USMLE Step 1 in order to be promoted and graduate. Passing the USMLE Step 2 Clinical Knowledge (CK) examination and sitting for the Step 2 Clinical Skills (CS) examination are required in order to graduate from the medical school. Passing an Observed Structured Clinical Examination (OSCE) is also required for graduation from medical school.

## Expenses

| | Resident Tuition and Fees | Non-resident Tuition and Fees |
|---|---|---|
| Undergraduate | $5,806 | $13,198 |
| U.S. Medical School | $21,873 | $59,783 |

## Financial Aid

For the undergraduate degree, UAB awards comprehensive federal, state, institutional, and private financial aid on the basis of merit, financial need, or both. Each year, the university offers more than 1,500 scholarships, including approximately $1.5 million in merit-based awards. Applicants are automatically considered for all academic scholarships when accepted to the university. As academic scholarships are awarded on a first come-first served basis, applicants are encouraged to apply no later than December 1 (prior to EMSAP application deadline) of the senior year of high school. Scholarships for medical school are awarded by the SOM, which awards a limited number of scholarships each year.

---

### Application and Acceptance Policies

**Filing of application—**
**Earliest date:** September 1, 2011
**Latest date:** December 15, 2011

**Application fee:** $30   **Fee waiver available:** Yes

**Acceptance notice—**
**Earliest date:** Mid-February 2012
**Latest date:** Late February 2012

**Applicant's response to acceptance offer—**
**Latest date:** May 1, 2012

**Deposit to hold place in class:** No

**Starting date:** Mid-August 2012

### Information on 2010–2011 Entering Class

| Number of | In-State | Out-of-State | Total |
|---|---|---|---|
| Applicants | 89 | 112 | 201 |
| Applicants Interviewed | 19 | 10 | 29 |
| New Entrants | 4 | 6 | 10 |
| **Total number of students enrolled in program:** 38 | | | |

---

# University of South Alabama College of Medicine
Mobile, Alabama

**Address inquiries to:** Jay Hunt, Assistant Director of Admissons, Office of Admissions
University of South Alabama, Meisler Hall, 2500, Mobile Alabama  36688-0022

**T** 251 460 6141    **F** 251 460 7876 • www.southalabama.edu/com/ • jayhunt@usouthal.edu

## Purpose
Candidates selected for the program will receive early acceptance from the University of South Alabama and its College of Medicine. Students participating in the program are expected to enter the University of South Alabama College of Medicine in the fall after completion of the baccalaureate degree.

## Requirements for Entrance
Students in the senior year of high school or recently graduated individuals who have not yet entered college are eligible to apply for the program. Both residents and non-residents of Alabama may apply.

## Selection Factors
Candidates must have a minimum high school GPA of 3.5, as computed by the University of South Alabama, and must present a minimum enhanced composite ACT score of 30 (or comparable SAT score). Candidates must also have demonstrated evidence of leadership qualities, community service, communication skills, and motivation for the study of medicine.

## Curriculum
The curriculum will include core requirements for the selected baccalaureate program and prerequisites for matriculation in medical school. Students in the program must maintain a minimum overall GPA of 3.5 and a minimum GPA of 3.4 in the sciences (biology, chemistry, physics) and mathematics. All required courses must be taken at the University of South Alabama unless otherwise approved in advance by the student's undergraduate program director and the Director of Admissions for the College of Medicine. Students will be required to participate in CP-200 (Career Planning; Clinical Observation) for a minimum of four quarters. Students will be given the opportunity to participate in a special summer premedical clerkship. These activities will be planned to give participants a broad exposure to medical education. Students will be required to take the MCAT® for admission to the College of Medicine and will be required to achieve a composite score of 27. A formal assessment, including an interview, will be conducted after the student has completed 96 quarter hours of academic work. At this time, students' academic performance and continued interest in a medical career will be assessed.

## Expenses

| | Resident Tuition and Fees | Non-resident Tuition and Fees |
|---|---|---|
| Undergraduate | $ 6,500 | $ 13,000 |
| U.S. Medical School | $ 22,328 | $ 43,153 |

## Financial Aid
Information can be obtained from the Office of Financial Aid, Meisler Hall, Room 1200, University of South Alabama, Mobile, Alabama 36688-0002; by phone at (251) 460-6231; or on the school Web site at *www.finaid2.usouthal.edu*.

## Application and Acceptance Policies

**Filing of application—**
**Earliest date:** December 15, 2011
**Latest date:** June 11, 2012

**Application fee:** Yes, $35    **Fee waiver available:** No

**Acceptance notice —**
**Earliest date:** March 15, 2012
**Latest date:** Until program is filled

**Applicant's response to acceptance offer—**
**Maximum time:** Two weeks

**Deposit to hold place in class:** No
**Deposit — Resident:** n/a
**Deposit refundable:** n/a    **Refundable by:** n/a

**Starting date:** August 2012

### Information on 2010–2011 Entering Class

| Number of | In-State | Out-of-State | Total |
|---|---|---|---|
| Applicants | 78 | 50 | 128 |
| Applicants Interviewed | 31 | 14 | 45 |
| New Entrants | 11 | 4 | 15 |
| **Total number of students enrolled in program:** 60 | | | |

# University of California, San Diego School of Medicine

La Jolla, California

**Address inquiries to:** Yvonne Coleman, Director of Medical Scholars Program, University of California, San Diego, School of Medicine, Office of Admissions, 0621, 9500 Gilman Drive, La Jolla, California 92093-0621

**T** 858 534 3880 **F** 858 534 5282 • http://meded.ucsd.edu/groups/med-scholars/ somadmissions@ucsd.edu

## Purpose

The Medical Scholars Program was established to encourage the recruitment of unusually talented high school students, who would then be attracted to both the University of California, San Diego, (UCSD) undergraduate and medical schools, and to promote the goal of increasing diversity on both campuses.

## Requirements for Entrance

Students are selected for this program during their senior year of high school. The program is open to California residents only. Applicants must meet course requirements for UCSD undergraduate admission. They must take either the SAT or ACT and achieve a minimum score of 2250 on the SAT or 34 on the ACT.

## Selection Factors

To be eligible for consideration, applicants must have a minimum high school GPA of 4.0 and 2250 on the SAT or 34 on the ACT. The average high school grade-point average for the 2010 entering class was 4.26. Applicants must also demonstrate strong extracurricular involvement, particularly in community service and leadership. Letters of recommendation and an essay are additional considerations. An interview is required. The MCAT® is not required.

## Curriculum

This program leads to a baccalaureate degree granted by the University of California, San Diego, and to the M.D. degree granted by the UCSD School of Medicine. It takes eight years to fulfill the requirements for both degrees. The specific course requirements for the baccalaureate degree include a minimum of 6 quarters in either humanities or social sciences and 15 quarters in the natural and physical sciences. Students must take Step 1 of the USMLE after the second year of medical school. Passing Steps 1 and 2 of the USMLE is required in order to be promoted and to graduate.

## Expenses

| | Resident Tuition and Fees | Non-resident Tuition and Fees |
|---|---|---|
| Undergraduate | $12,176 | $35,055 |
| U.S. Medical School | $28,345 | $40,590 |

## Financial Aid

Sources of financial aid include scholarships, grants, loans, and work-study. Additional information is available from the undergraduate financial aid office: Building 201, University Center, La Jolla, California 92093-0013, or at *http://ucsd.edu/prospective-students/finances/financial-aid.html*.

### Application and Acceptance Policies

**Filing of application—**
**Earliest date:** February 13, 2012
**Latest date:** March 12, 2012

**Application fee:** No    **Fee waiver available:** n/a

**Acceptance notice —**
**Earliest date:** April 17, 2012
**Latest date:** April 30, 2012

**Applicant's response to acceptance offer—**
**Maximum time:** One week after acceptance

**Deposit to hold place in class:** No
**Deposit — Resident:** n/a
**Deposit refundable:** n/a    **Refundable by:** n/a

**Starting date:** September 2012

### Information on 2010–2011 Entering Class

| Number of | In-State | Out-of-State | Total |
|---|---|---|---|
| Applicants | 468 | n/a | 468 |
| Applicants Interviewed | 28 | n/a | 28 |
| New Entrants | 12 | n/a | 12 |
| **Total number of students enrolled in program:** 42 | | | |

# University of Southern California
# College of Letters, Arts, & Sciences and Keck School of Medicine
Los Angeles California

**Address inquiries to:**   Karen Rowan-Badger, Director of Admission, Office of Admission, College of Letters, Arts, and Sciences
University of Southern California, Los Angeles California  90089-0152

**T**  (213) 740-5930   **F**  (213) 740-1338  •  www.usc.edu/schools/college/admission/baccalaureatemd/
admission@college.usc.edu

## Purpose
The goal of this program is to encourage bright and motivated students to expand the breadth of their education through a diverse liberal arts education. Students accepted into this program have the opportunity to study a wide variety of disciplines beyond the course of the standard premedical curriculum. It is the hope of the university to graduate physicians who are educated in medical science, the arts, and the humanities.

## Requirements for Entrance
Students are selected for this program in the senior year of high school. Both residents and non-residents of California and international students are eligible to apply. Although there are no specific high school course requirements, applicants are required to take either the SAT or ACT.

## Selection Factors
Academic factors considered include grades and standardized test scores. Participation in extracurricular activities and demonstrated leadership and community service are valued. Students who enrolled in 2009 had a mean high school GPA of 4.36 (weighted) and a mean SAT score of 2220. An interview is required and is granted by invitation following careful evaluation of an applicant's file.

## Curriculum
This program leads to a baccalaureate degree awarded by the University of Southern California, and to the M.D. degree granted by the University of Southern California Keck School of Medicine. This is not an accelerated program; all students must complete four years of undergraduate education and four years of medical school. Students must complete requirements for the bachelor's degree and may pursue any major offered in the university that is compatible with the requirements of the program. There are specific requirements for the bachelor's degree, which include the humanities and social, natural, and physical sciences. Advancement to the medical school phase of the program is based on acceptable academic performance and MCAT® scores as defined by the program. The MCAT® is required and must be taken by the spring of the junior year. Students must take USMLE Steps 1 and 2, and pass Step 1 of the USMLE in order to graduate from the School of Medicine.

## Expenses

| | Resident Tuition and Fees | Non-resident Tuition and Fees |
|---|---|---|
| Undergraduate | $43,998 | $43,998 |
| U.S. Medical School | $47,072 | $47,072 |

## Financial Aid
Sources of aid include scholarships, grants, work-study programs, and loans. For additional information, contact the Office of Financial Aid, University of Southern California, Los Angeles, California 90089-0912; call (213) 740-1111; or visit *www.usc.edu/admission/fa/*.

### Application and Acceptance Policies

**Filing of application—**
**Earliest date:** August 1, 2011
**Latest date:** December 1, 2011

**Application fee:** $65    **Fee waiver available:** Yes

**Acceptance notice —**
**Earliest date:** April 1, 2012
**Latest date:** April 1, 2012

**Applicant's response to acceptance offer—**
**Maximum time:** One month

**Deposit to hold place in class:** Yes
**Deposit — Resident:** $300
**Deposit refundable:** No    **Refundable by:** n/a

**Starting date:** August 2012

### Information on 2010–2011 Entering Class

| Number of | In-State | Out-of-State | Total |
|---|---|---|---|
| Applicants | 500 | 274 | 774 |
| Applicants Interviewed | 63 | 40 | 103 |
| New Entrants | 16 | 6 | 22 |
| **Total number of students enrolled in program:** 104 | | | |

# University of Connecticut and University of Connecticut School of Medicine

Storrs, Connecticut

**Address inquiries to:** Office of Undergraduate Admissions, Special Programs in Medicine & Dental Medicine
University of Connecticut, 2131 Hillside Road, U-88, Storrs, Connecticut 06269-3088

**T** 860 486 3137 **F** 860 486 1476 • http://medicine.uchc.edu/prospective/admissions/babs_md.html

## Purpose

This prestigious program offers gifted and talented high school students, who are focused on a career in medicine, the opportunity to combine a broad-based liberal arts program with a medical education. Its purpose is to provide select students with a unique educational experience focusing on both professional and personal development. This program links four years of undergraduate preparation with four years of medical education, resulting in dual degrees: a B.A. or B.S. degree and the M.D. degree.

## Requirements for Entrance

Students are selected for this program during the senior year of high school. Both residents and non-residents of Connecticut are eligible to apply. Applicants must take either the SAT I or ACT.

## Selection Factors

To be considered for this program, the student should have the following: a high school class ranking in the top five percent; an overall high school grade-point average of 3.5 (4.0 scale); an SAT combined score of 1300 or an ACT composite score of 30; a completed regular undergraduate admission application and a supplemental application for the program in medicine by the January 1 postmark deadline; and, an interview at the School of Medicine. In addition, recommendations from teachers/advisors, as well as evidence of maturity, extracurricular activities, and a commitment to the health profession, are considered. To matriculate in the School of Medicine upon completion of undergraduate preparation, the student must meet additional criteria that include: maintaining a college 3.6 cumulative grade-point average (4.0 scale); obtaining an MCAT® score of 30+ with section scores of 8 or greater; participation in clinical, research, and community service activities; and favorable interviews during the senior undergraduate year.

## Curriculum

Students must complete requirements for a baccalaureate degree from the University of Connecticut. Requirements include courses in the humanities and social sciences. The curriculum typically takes eight years to complete: Years 1 through 4 in the liberal arts and sciences and Years 5 through 8 in the School of Medicine. The MCAT® is required for admission to the medical school phase of the program. Students are required to pass Step 1 and Step 2 of the USMLE in order to graduate.

## Expenses

| | Resident Tuition and Fees | Non-resident Tuition and Fees |
|---|---|---|
| Undergraduate | $7,632 | $23,232 |
| U.S. Medical School | $28,435 | $52,632 |

## Financial Aid

All enrolled candidates will be automatically considered for merit scholarships. A full range of financial aid options based on student financial need is available, as well. Candidates for need-based aid must submit the Free Application for Federal Student Aid (FAFSA) by March 1. For more information about student aid programs, contact the University of Connecticut's Office of Student Financial Aid Services at (860) 486-2819; write to U-4116, Storrs, Connecticut 06269; or visit the UConn homepage at *www.uconn.edu*.

### Application and Acceptance Policies

**Filing of application—**
**Earliest date:** September 1, 2011
**Latest date:** January 1, 2012

**Application fee:** $70   **Fee waiver available:** Yes

**Acceptance notice —**
**Earliest date:** March 1, 2012
**Latest date:** Until class is full

**Applicant's response to acceptance offer—**
**Maximum time:** May 1, 2012

**Deposit to hold place in class:** Yes
**Deposit — Resident:** $150
**Deposit refundable:** No   **Refundable by:** n/a

**Starting date:** August 2012

### Information on 2010–2011 Entering Class

| Number of | In-State | Out-of-State | Total |
|---|---|---|---|
| Applicants | 93 | 139 | 232 |
| Applicants Interviewed | 26 | 16 | 42 |
| New Entrants | 12 | 3 | 15 |
| **Total number of students enrolled in program: 56** | | | |

# George Washington University School of Medicine and The Columbian College of Arts and Sciences

Washington, District of Columbia

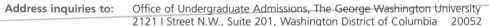

**Address inquiries to:** Office of Undergraduate Admissions, The George Washington University
2121 I Street N.W., Suite 201, Washington District of Columbia    20052

**T** 202 994 6040 • www.gwu.edu/apply/undergraduateadmissions/learningatgw/acceleratedprograms/bamdprogram
gwadm@gwu.edu

## Purpose

A joint program of The George Washington (GW) University Columbian College of Arts and Sciences and the School of Medicine and Health Sciences, the seven-year B.A.-M.D. program is designed for the high school senior who exhibits academic excellence, leadership in activities, and community service and healthcare experience, and who has confirmed the goal to become a physician. The purpose of the program is to encourage a liberal arts focus in preparation for medical school. Students typically choose majors in a wide variety of fields ranging from economics and psychology to religion and biology.

## Requirements for Entrance

Students are selected in their senior year of high school. Applicants must be a U.S. citizen, U.S. permanent resident, or Canadian citizen in order to apply. Applicants are expected to complete the SAT or ACT, as well as the SAT Subject Tests in Mathematics, Science, and English. Competitive SAT scores for the program are (equivalent) 2100 and above.

## Selection Factors

Academic factors considered in selecting applicants include the strength of the academic program, grades in high school, class rank, and standardized test scores. In addition to academic factors, extracurricular and health-related activities, community service, essays, and letters of recommendation are reviewed. Competitive applicants are those who rank in the top ten percent of their high school class, have shown leadership ability through participation in extracurricular activities, have demonstrated interest in the medical field through experience, and have taken advantage of advanced course offerings. An interview is required and is by invitation only.

## Curriculum

A special faculty committee reviews each student's progress throughout the program annually. To continue each year in the program, students must maintain a minimum of a "B" in courses required for admission to the medical school and an overall 3.6 average. Students do not take the MCAT. Students participate in seminars of interest and are involved in community service and health care experiences throughout the undergraduate portion of the curriculum. The review committee will make a final recommendation concerning promotion to the medical school curriculum at the end of the third year. In the fourth year, students enroll in the School of Medicine and Health Sciences and begin their formal medical training. The baccalaureate degree is received

before entrance to the M.D. program. The integration of clinical skills begins in the first and second years of medical school, as students spend time with physicians, learning the art and skill of patient interviewing and physical diagnosis. The sixth and seventh years are devoted to developing clinical expertise in a wide variety of hospitals in the D.C. metropolitan area. At the end of the seventh year, students are awarded the M.D. degree.

## Expenses

| | Resident Tuition and Fees | Non-resident Tuition and Fees |
|---|---|---|
| Undergraduate | $44,145 | $44,145 |
| U.S. Medical School | $49,062 | $49,062 |

## Financial Aid

Information may be obtained from The George Washington University, Office of Student Financial Assistance, 2121 "I" Street, N.W., #310, Washington, D.C. 20052. The Office of Student Financial Assistance may be reached by phone at 1- 800-222-6242.

### Application and Acceptance Policies

**Filing of application—**
**Earliest date:** September 1, 2011
**Latest date:** December 1, 2011

**Application fee:** $70    **Fee waiver available:** Yes

**Acceptance notice —**
**Earliest date:** April 2012
**Latest date:** April 2012

**Applicant's response to acceptance offer—**
**Maximum time:** May 1, 2012

**Deposit to hold place in class:** Yes
**Deposit — Resident:** $800
**Deposit refundable:** No    **Refundable by:** n/a

**Starting date:** August 2012

### Information on 2010–2011 Entering Class

| Number of | In-State | Out-of-State | Total |
|---|---|---|---|
| Applicants | 0 | 700 | 700 |
| Applicants Interviewed | 0 | 50 | 50 |
| New Entrants | 0 | 10 | 10 |
| **Total number of students enrolled in program:** 105 | | | |

# Howard University College of Medicine
Washington, District of Columbia

**Address inquiries to:** Julie Chang Andrist, M.Ed., Associate Director/Preprofessional Advisor, Center for Preprofessional Education
College of Arts and Science, 2225 Georgia Avenue, N.W., Room 518,
Howard University, Washington District of Columbia  20059

**T** 202 238 2363  **F** 202 588 9828 • www.coas.howard.edu/preprofessionaleducation/
preprofessional@howard.edu

## Purpose
The goal of this combined-degree program is to encourage talented undergraduate students to choose medicine as a career and to retain these excellent students in the Howard University College of Medicine.

## Requirements for Entrance
Students can be selected for this program during the senior year of high school or during the first year of college. There are no state residence requirements. Applicants are expected to have completed the following courses by the time they graduate from high school: at least two years of a foreign language; at least one year each of biology, chemistry, and physics; two years of mathematics; and four years of English, including literature. They must take either the SAT or the ACT Assessment.

## Selection Factors
The academic factors considered in offering admission to an applicant are rank in high school class, GPA, and test scores. Applicants are expected to be in the top five percent of their high school class. In the 2010-2011 entering class, the average GPA was 3.7, and the average SAT combined score was 2250. ACT Assessment cumulative scores ranged from 30. Personal qualities considered are: superior writing skills, maturity, positive self-confidence, realistic self-appraisal, a realistic assessment of the medical profession, good leadership skills, and sustained demonstration of service to people who are less fortunate. An interview is required.

## Curriculum
his program leads to a bachelor's degree awarded by the College of Arts and Sciences at Howard University and to the M.D. degree granted by the Howard University College of Medicine. Students must complete work for a baccalaureate degree. They are expected to complete at least 40 semester hours of humanities and social sciences courses to fulfill general education requirements and at least 46 semester hours of natural and physical sciences courses. Students meet with the director (the advisor) of the Center for Preprofessional Education to design a curriculum tailored to their individual needs. The specific course selection must have the advisor's approval. Students are encouraged to select a major of personal interest. The curricula for both degrees are completed in six years. In the first two years, the curriculum focuses on work toward the bachelor's degree and premedical requirements, and in the last four years the focus is on studies related to medicine. Students in this program must take the MCAT® in April of the second year.

The results of the MCAT, the GPA, the demonstration of a high level of maturity, and a strong commitment to service in areas where there is a shortage of health professionals are factors in gaining admission to the medical school phase of the combined degree program. Students are also expected to take Steps 1 and 2 of the USMLE while at Howard University College of Medicine; they must pass these examinations prior to promotion and graduation.

## Expenses

| | Resident Tuition and Fees | Non-resident Tuition and Fees |
|---|---|---|
| Undergraduate | $ 18,121 | $ 18,121 |
| U.S. Medical School | $ 39,606 | $ 39,606 |

## Financial Aid
Information can be obtained from The Office of Financial Aid, Scholarships and Student Employment at Room 205, Johnson Administration Building, 2400 6th Street, N.W., Washington, D.C. 20059. Contact Information: Telephone (202) 806-2820, Fax (202) 806-2818, *https://www.howard.edu/financialaid/contacts/*

### Application and Acceptance Policies

**Filing of application—**
**Earliest date:** March 1, 2012
**Latest date:** March 1, 2012

**Application fee:** Yes, $45   **Fee waiver available:** No

**Acceptance notice —**
**Earliest date:** Varies
**Latest date:** Varies

**Applicant's response to acceptance offer—**
**Maximum time:** June 15, 2012

**Deposit to hold place in class:** Yes
**Deposit — Resident:** $300
**Deposit refundable:** No   **Refundable by:** n/a

**Starting date:** August 2012

### Information on 2010–2011 Entering Class

| Number of | In-State | Out-of-State | Total |
|---|---|---|---|
| Applicants | 22 | 73 | 95 |
| Applicants Interviewed | 8 | 20 | 28 |
| New Entrants | 2 | 10 | 12 |
| **Total number of students enrolled in program: 12** | | | |

# University of Florida College of Medicine
Gainesville, Florida

**Address inquiries to:** Leila Amiri, Director of Admissions, Medical Selection Committee, University of Florida College of Medicine, P.O. Box 100216, Gainesville Florida 32610

**T** 352 273 7990   **F** 352 392 1307  •  http://jhmp.med.ufl.edu  •  med-admissions@ufl.edu

## Purpose
The Junior Honors Medical Program is an accelerated pathway to medical school for undergraduate students who have decided on a career in the medical profession and who have demonstrated superior scholastic ability and personal development during their first two academic years of college enrollment.

## Requirements for Entrance
Students are selected for this program during their second year of college enrollment. Admission is open to all possible candidates who are United States citizens or permanent residents, with preference given to Florida residents. By the end of the second year of undergraduate work in a university setting, applicants must have completed the following courses: Biology — 8 semester hours (12 quarter hours); Calculus — 4 semester hours (6 quarter hours); General Chemistry — 8 semester hours (12 quarter hours); Organic Chemistry — 8 semester hours (12 quarter hours); One additional 3000 (or higher) level math or science course. Applicants must have a GPA of at least 3.7 in these prerequisite courses (not overall GPA). The following courses may be completed in the junior year: General Physics I & II (both with labs) and Biochemistry.

## Selection Factors
The academic factors considered in offering admission to an applicant include two years of college classroom enrollment, competitive SAT or ACT scores, competitive GPA, and completion of prerequisite courses. Consistent health care experience and community service as well as involvement in research prior to application is considered positively. The MCAT® is currently not required. Selected applicants are invited for a required interview held in April. Applicants are not informed of acceptance decisions until grades for the Spring semester are posted and an official transcript is received in the UF COM Admissions Office, usually in May.

## Curriculum
The Junior Honors Medical Program (JHMP) is a seven year baccalaureate/MD program. All courses in the first two baccalaureate years are completed in the various undergraduate colleges in the majors that prospective students have declared. During their third baccaluareate year accepted students complete any remaining requirements for the Liberal Arts and Sciences or Agricultural and Life Sciences, as well as College of Medicine classes. This includes required courses in Cell Biology, Pharmacology and Translational Neuroscience, and electives in Health Care Economics and Humanities & Clinical Care, all with College of Medicine faculty. JHMP students must also complete an Honors Research Thesis prior to entering medical school. The bachelor's degree is awarded after the fourth year of college enrollment, which is concurrently the first year of medical school. The most frequent major for the baccalaureate degree is the B.S. in Interdisciplinary Biological and Medical Sciences through the College of Liberal Arts and Sciences. Some students choose Nutrition as a major through the College of Agricultural and Life Sciences. In years 4 through 7, all courses are in Medicine, and the College of Medicine awards the Doctor of Medicine degree.

## Expenses

| | Resident Tuition and Fees | Non-resident Tuition and Fees |
|---|---|---|
| Undergraduate | $5,020 | $25,160 |
| U.S. Medical School | $30,755 | $59,995 |

## Financial Aid
There is a full service Financial Aid Office within the UF College of Medicine. Scholarships and low interest loans are available to all students who show need.

---

### Application and Acceptance Policies

**Filing of application—**
**Earliest date:** January 13, 2012
**Latest date:** January 27, 2012

**Application fee:** No   **Fee waiver available:** n/a

**Acceptance notice —**
**Earliest date:** May 11, 2012
**Latest date:** May 12, 2012

**Applicant's response to acceptance offer—**
**Maximum time:** Two weeks

**Deposit to hold place in class:** No
**Deposit — Resident:** n/a
**Deposit refundable:** n/a   **Refundable by:** n/a

**Starting date:** August 2012

### Information on 2010–2011 Entering Class

| Number of | In-State | Out-of-State | Total |
|---|---|---|---|
| Applicants | 69 | 5 | 74 |
| Applicants Interviewed | 24 | 1 | 25 |
| New Entrants | 12 | 0 | 12 |
| **Total number of students enrolled in program: 50** | | | |

---

# University of Miami Honors Program
Coral Gables, Florida

**FL**

**Address inquiries to:** Megan Ann Stamm, Assistant Director of Admission
Office of Admissions, University of Miami, P.O. Box 248025, Coral Gables Florida 33124

**T** 305 284 4323 • http://www6.miami.edu/UMH/CDA/UMH_Main/0,1770,2613-1;14415-3,00.html
webrequest.admission@miami.edu

## Purpose
The Honors Program in Medicine (HPM) offers exceptionally motivated and talented high school students, who have reached a mature and independent decision to study medicine, an opportunity to earn the B.S. and M.D. degrees in seven or eight years.

## Requirements for Entrance
Applicants must be U.S. citizens or permanent residents. Both residents and non-residents of Florida are considered for admission. Applicants must be in their last year of high school at the time of application. Applicants must have a minimum combined score of 1400 on the SAT (Math and Verbal) or a composite score of 32 on the ACT, an unweighted GPA of at least 3.75, and take the SAT II Subject Tests in Mathematics, and one science (a minimum score of 600 is required in each). All applicants must have completed eight semesters of mathematics and English and two semesters each of biology and chemistry by the time of graduation from high school.

## Selection Factors
Academic factors taken into account include scores on standardized tests, the quality of the high school curriculum (including the number and nature of Advanced Placement courses and/or International Baccalaureate coursework), and the amount of university-level work already completed. Of equal importance to academic achievements are personal factors such as maturity of thought and action, common sense, empathy, interpersonal skills, appropriate freedom from parental influence, and social cognizance. Most important, the applicant must have made a practical decision to study medicine based on self-initiated patient-contact experiences.

## Curriculum
The first three years are spent on the Coral Gables campus taking required science and humanities courses and focusing almost exclusively on work related to the bachelor's degree. The undergraduate portion of the curriculum may be extended to four years if the student is in good academic standing and has established a clear plan of academic and personal growth. All HPM students must have a 3.7 science GPA and a 3.7 cumulative GPA and an MCAT® composite score of 30 to be promoted to the School of Medicine after three or four years. All students must develop a continuous history of involvement at the undergraduate level in a variety of experiences that must include patient contact, and some combination of research, campus or community

service, study abroad, or employment, consistent with a sincere desire to study and practice medicine. HPM students will attend medical school at the medical campus in Miami. Students receive their clinical training at Jackson Memorial Hospital, University of Miami Hospital and the Miami Veterans Administration Hospital and several other hospitals affiliated with the Miller School of Medicine.

## Expenses

| | Resident Tuition and Fees | Non-resident Tuition and Fees |
|---|---|---|
| Undergraduate | $34,834 | $34,834 |
| U.S. Medical School | $30,113 | $39,319 |

## Financial Aid
Scholarships, work-study, loans, and state tuition grants are sources of financial assistance. Information on undergraduate financial aid is available from the Office of Admissions on the Coral Gables campus.

### Application and Acceptance Policies

**Filing of application—**
**Earliest date:** October 1, 2011
**Latest date:** November 1, 2011

**Application fee:** $55     **Fee waiver available:** Yes

**Acceptance notice —**
**Earliest date:** April 1, 2012
**Latest date:** April 1, 2012

**Applicant's response to acceptance offer—**
**Maximum time:** May 1, 2012

**Deposit to hold place in class:** Yes
**Deposit — Resident:** $300
**Deposit refundable:** No     **Refundable by:** n/a

**Starting date:** August 2012

### Information on 2010–2011 Entering Class

| Number of | In-State | Out-of-State | Total |
|---|---|---|---|
| Applicants | 84 | 143 | 227 |
| Applicants Interviewed | 27 | 59 | 86 |
| New Entrants | 9 | 5 | 14 |
| **Total number of students enrolled in program: 51** | | | |

# Northwestern University Feinberg School of Medicine

Evanston, Illinois

**Address inquiries to:** Dr. Marianne Green, Associate Dean for Medical Education, Office of Undergraduate Admission
Northwestern University, 1801 Hinman Avenue, Evanston Illinois 60204-3060

**T** 312 503 8915  **F** 312 503 0840 • www.feinberg.northwestern.edu/AWOME/hpme/index.html
hpme@northwestern.edu

## Purpose

The Honors Program in Medical Education (HPME), one of the oldest in the nation, offers a unique opportunity for gifted and highly motivated students who seek careers in medicine or medical science. The HPME provides a broad, flexible and challenging undergraduate education free from many of the pressures related to gaining acceptance to medical school. Students are encouraged to explore focused areas of concentration during their undergraduate years that may prepare them personally and professionally for their careers in medicine. Students spend their undergraduate years on the Evanston Campus; the medical school curriculum is conducted at the Feinberg School of Medicine Chicago Campus.

## Requirements for Entrance

Students are selected during their senior year of high school. Residents and non-residents of Illinois are eligible to apply. Applicants must meet the following high school course requirements: 8 semesters of English; 8 semesters of Mathematics- including differential and integral calculus; 2 semesters of Chemistry; 2 semesters of Physics; 2 semesters of Biology; and 4 semesters of a foreign language. Students must take the SAT Reasoning Test or the ACT Assessment with Writing, plus the SAT Subject Tests in Mathematics Level 2 and Chemistry.

## Selection Factors

Class rank, grades in high school, and scores on college entrance tests are all taken into consideration. Average test scores for the 2009-2010 entering class were: SAT Critical Reading, 752; SAT Mathematics, 781; SAT Writing 758; Subject Tests - Chemistry, 763; Mathematics II, 779; ACT plus Writing, 33. Motivation for a career in medicine, concern for others, maturity, team work and leadership are also considered. An interview is required.

## Curriculum

The degrees offered are a baccalaureate degree (B.A., B.S. in medicine, B.S. in biomedical engineering, or B.S. in communication) and the M.D., all from Northwestern University. Students must complete requirements for a baccalaureate degree in addition to the required science courses (inorganic & organic chemistry, calculus-based physics, biological science sequence). The majority of students in the Feinberg College of Arts & Science major in biological sciences but have many other options within the college. Students in the McCormick School of Engineering & Applied Sciences major in biomedical engineering and take the basic & advanced engineering courses, in addition to non-science courses. The program in the School of Communication includes special courses in communication

sciences and disorders. The curriculum usually takes seven or eight years to complete, and students are encouraged to develop a unique curricular path. The MCAT® is not required. Students must take Steps 1 and 2 of the USMLE and record passing grades in order to graduate from the medical school.

## Expenses

| | Resident Tuition and Fees | Non-resident Tuition and Fees |
|---|---|---|
| Undergraduate | $39,840 | $39,840 |
| U.S. Medical School | $44,993 | $44,993 |

## Financial Aid

Sources of aid include Northwestern University and federal, state, and private programs. Undergraduate applicants can receive more information from the Office of Admission and Financial Aid: *http://ug-finaid.northwestern.edu/* or phone (847) 491-7271. Information about medical school financial aid can be obtained from Financial Aid Professional Schools: *http://chicagofinancialaid.northwestern.edu/*.

---

### Application and Acceptance Policies

**Filing of application—**
**Earliest date:** Students must request an application by December 1, 2011 by visiting *http://request.ugadm.northwestern.edu/*
**Latest date:** January 2, 2012

**Application fee:** Yes, $65     **Fee waiver available:** Yes

**Acceptance notice —**
**Earliest date:** April 2, 2012
**Latest date:** n/a

**Applicant's response to acceptance offer—**
**Maximum time:** May 1, 2012

**Deposit to hold place in class:** Yes
**Deposit — Resident:** $400
**Deposit refundable:** No     **Refundable by:** n/a

**Starting date:** September 15, 2012

### Information on 2010–2011 Entering Class

| Number of | In-State | Out-of-State | Total |
|---|---|---|---|
| Applicants | 94 | 514 | 608 |
| Applicants Interviewed | n/r | n/r | n/r |
| New Entrants | 2 | 19 | 21 |
| **Total number of students enrolled in program: 68** | | | |

---

# University of Illinois at Chicago College of Medicine

Chicago, Illinois

**Address inquiries to:** Josephine Volpe, Assistant Director,
University of Illinois at Chicago, Academic Affairs/Special Scholarship Programs
2506 University Hall, M/C 115, 601 S. Morgan Street, Chicago, Illinois 60607

**T** 312 355 2477 **F** 312 355 1233 • www.uic.edu/depts/oaa/spec_prog/gppa/ • gppauic@uic.edu

## Purpose

The Guaranteed Professional Program Admissions (GPPA) initiative is a combined effort of the University of Illinois at Chicago (UIC) Honors College on the undergraduate campus and the College of Medicine. This program is offered only to high school seniors from Illinois. The GPPA guarantees incoming freshmen a seat in the College of Medicine at one of the four locations provided they qualify upon completion of their undergraduate studies at UIC.

## Requirements for Entrance

This program is limited to Illinois residents. Students are selected for this program during the senior year of high school. There are no specific high school course requirements.

## Selection Factors

The academic factors considered are rank in high school class, grade-point average, and test scores. Applicants must be in the top 15 percent of their high school class. Applicants must have a minimum ACT composite score of 28, or its SAT equivalent score. In addition to academic factors, extracurricular health-related activities and letters of recommendations are required. All applicants are invited for a required interview with the Honors College. A selected number of applicants are invited to return for a second interview with the College of Medicine.

## Curriculum

The GPPA-Medicine program is designed to be completed in four years of undergraduate education at the University of Illinois at Chicago (UIC). Students are free to choose any of UIC's majors in eight undergraduate colleges. Throughout their undergraduate education, students participate in a number of required seminars and courses that will introduce them to various aspects of the medical profession. The final course is the Independent Study Seminar, which is a "capstone" project and presentation. Students must maintain at least a 3.5 cumulative grade-point average throughout their undergraduate education. During the year proceeding expected entry into medical school, students must take the Medical College Admissions Test (MCAT). Students must earn a MCAT® score of at least the mean of the matriculating students into the College of Medicine in the year prior to expected entry, with no score below 9 in any segment of the exam. Students successfully completing the GPPA requirements are guaranteed a seat in one of the four

University of Illinois College of Medicine campuses. However, students are not required to attend the University of Illinois College of Medicine. Once enrolled in the College of Medicine, students in the program are bound by the policies in force at the time of their matriculation.

## Expenses

| | Resident Tuition and Fees | Non-resident Tuition and Fees |
|---|---|---|
| Undergraduate | $12,864 | n/a |
| U.S. Medical School | $35,032 | $71,412 |

## Financial Aid

Please visit *www.uic.edu*.

---

### Application and Acceptance Policies

**Filing of application—**
**Earliest date:** September 15, 2011
**Latest date:** December 1, 2011

**Application fee:** $0    **Fee waiver available:** Yes

**Acceptance notice —**
**Earliest date:** April 1, 2012
**Latest date:** April 1, 2012

**Applicant's response to acceptance offer—**
**Maximum time:** May 1, 2012

**Deposit to hold place in class:** No
**Deposit — Resident:** n/a
**Deposit refundable:** n/a    **Refundable by:** n/a

**Starting date:** August 2012

### Information on 2010–2011 Entering Class

| Number of | In-State | Out-of-State | Total |
|---|---|---|---|
| Applicants | 400 | n/a | 400 |
| Applicants Interviewed | 60 | n/a | 60 |
| New Entrants | 30 | n/a | 30 |
| **Total number of students enrolled in program:** 90 | | | |

# Boston University School of Medicine

Boston, Massachusetts

**Address inquiries to:**  Boston University, Office of Undergraduate Admissions
121 Bay State Road, Boston Massachusetts   02215

**T** 617 353 2300   **F** 617 353 9695  •  www.bu.edu/bulletins/und/item14.html  •  admissions@bu.edu

## Purpose

This combined degree program, one of the oldest in the nation, provides an undergraduate premedical preparation that also emphasizes the humanities and social sciences and affords a quality medical education even though the overall period of study is shortened.

## Requirements for Entrance

Students are selected for the program at Boston University during the senior year of high school (or after high school if they have not been enrolled in any other degree-granting program). There are no state residence requirements. Students who are completing their high school graduation requirements in three years are not eligible for this program. Applicants are expected to have completed the following courses by the time they graduate from high school: four years each of English and mathematics (one year of calculus is required); three years each of social sciences and a foreign language; and one year each of biology, chemistry (AP chemistry is strongly recommended), and physics. Applicants must take the SAT or the ACT with Writing. They must take SAT Subject Tests in Mathematics Level 2 and Chemistry. An SAT Subject Test in a foreign language is recommended.

## Selection Factors

The academic factors taken into account in offering admission to an applicant include the following: the high school GPA, the SAT or the ACT with Writing score, scores on the SAT Subject Tests, rank in high school class, and the nature of the applicant's high school curriculum. In the 2010–2011 entering class, the average high school GPA was an unweighted 3.9 on a 4.0 scale, and rank in class was in the top one percent. The average combined Critical Reading and Math SAT score was 1523. The average SAT Writing score was 765. SAT Subject Test scores in Chemistry averaged 762. SAT Subject Tests in Mathematics Level 2 averaged 785. Personal characteristics sought in applicants are compassion, integrity, maturity, motivation, and an understanding of a career in medicine. An interview with College of Arts and Sciences and School of Medicine faculty is required.

## Curriculum

This program leads to a baccalaureate degree granted by the College of Arts and Sciences at Boston University and to the M.D. degree awarded by Boston University School of Medicine. Students complete work for the baccalaureate degree in three years with a major in medical science and a minor concentration in a College of Arts and Sciences approved minor. Students must also satisfy the course distribution and language requirements of the college. Requirements for this degree include nine one-semester courses in the natural and physical sciences and two one-semester courses in the humanities, mathematics and computer science, and social sciences. The program is seven years in length, with an eight-year option. Students must meet GPA and MCAT® requirements of the program. They are also required to take Step 1 of the USMLE during the medical school portion of the program. Taking Step 2 of the USMLE is strongly recommended.

## Expenses

| | Resident Tuition and Fees | Non-resident Tuition and Fees |
|---|---|---|
| Undergraduate | $39,864 | $39,864 |
| U.S. Medical School | $48,716 | $48,716 |

## Financial Aid

The usual sources of financial aid are available to students during the undergraduate portion of this program. Once in the medical school, students can qualify for need-based, low-interest, and government-sponsored loans. More information about aid can be obtained from the Office of Financial Assistance, Boston University, 881 Commonwealth Avenue, Boston, Massachusetts 02215, or by phone (617) 353-2965.

### Application and Acceptance Policies

**Filing of application—**
**Earliest date:** September 1, 2011
**Latest date:** December 1, 2011

**Application fee:** $75   **Fee waiver available:** Yes

**Acceptance notice —**
**Earliest date:** April 1, 2012
**Latest date:** April 15, 2012

**Applicant's response to acceptance offer—**
**Maximum time:** May 1, 2012

**Deposit to hold place in class:** Yes
**Deposit — Resident:** $650
**Deposit refundable:** No   **Refundable by:** n/a

**Starting date:** September 2012

### Information on 2010–2011 Entering Class

| Number of | In-State | Out-of-State | Total |
|---|---|---|---|
| Applicants | 49 | 495 | 544 |
| Applicants Interviewed | 5 | 90 | 95 |
| New Entrants | 3 | 19 | 22 |
| **Total number of students enrolled in program:** 70 | | | |

# Wayne State University School of Medicine
Detroit, Michigan

**Address inquiries to:**   Nancy Galster, Program Coordinator, Irvin D. Reid Honors College
Wayne State University, 2100 Undergraduate Library, Detroit Michigan  48202

**T**  313 577 8523   **F**  313 577 6425  •  www.honors.wayne.edu/medstart.php  •  honors@wayne.edu

## Purpose
The MedStart Program is intended to train medical innovators and creative thinkers. As undergraduates, students are treated as part of the medical community, with an emphasis on mentoring and research.

## Requirements for Entrance
Students are selected for this program during their senior year of high school. Applicants must be citizens or permanent residents of the United States or citizens of Canada. Although there are no specific high school course requirements, applicants are required to take the ACT or SAT.

## Selection Factors
To be considered for this program, applicants must have a minimum ACT score of 25 (or a 1710 on the SAT II) and a high school GPA of at least 3.5. Community service, team activities, leadership, extracurricular activities, and experience in health care are among the personal attributes and experiential factors sought in applicants. An interview is also required. Once admitted into the program, students are expected to maintain a 3.50 GPA in the sciences and overall during their undergraduate studies. For subsequent admission to Wayne State University School of Medicine, students in this program must complete all prerequisite courses, take the MCAT® (with a minimum total score of 27, and no less than a nine in any individual section), and submit an AMCAS® application.

## Curriculum
The program, eight years in duration, allows students to obtain a baccalaureate degree from Wayne State University and the M.D. degree from Wayne State University School of Medicine. During the four years of their undergraduate studies, 100 percent of their coursework will be related to the bachelor's degree. The coursework in the four years of medical school will be spent in achieving the medical degree. Students must meet university requirements for the Irvin D. Reid Honors College and degree completion. Throughout the eight-year baccalaureate-medical program, monthly seminars are held which are relevant to medical fields and topics in medicine. Students may apply for a ten-week paid clinical research experience in the summer following the junior undergraduate year.

## Expenses

| | Resident Tuition and Fees | Non-resident Tuition and Fees |
|---|---|---|
| Undergraduate | $9,587 | $20,482 |
| U.S. Medical School | $30,350 | $61,225 |

## Financial Aid
Information about financial aid can be obtained from the Office of Scholarships and Financial Aid, Welcome Center, P.O. Box 4230, Detroit, MI 48202; by telephone (313) 577-3378; or visit *www.financialaid.wayne.edu*.

### Application and Acceptance Policies

**Filing of application—**
**Earliest date:** November 1, 2011
**Latest date:** January 15, 2012

**Application fee:** $30   **Fee waiver available:** No

**Acceptance notice —**
**Earliest date:** April 1, 2012
**Latest date:** Varies

**Applicant's response to acceptance offer—**
**Maximum time:** May 1, 2012

**Deposit to hold place in class:** No
**Deposit — Resident:** n/a
**Deposit refundable:** n/a   **Refundable by:** n/a

**Starting date:** September, 2012

### Information on 2010–2011 Entering Class

| Number of | In-State | Out-of-State | Total |
|---|---|---|---|
| Applicants | 205 | 66 | 271 |
| Applicants Interviewed | 26 | 4 | 30 |
| New Entrants | 15 | 0 | 15 |

**Total number of students enrolled in program: 55**

# St Louis University School of Medicine
St. Louis, Missouri

**Address inquiries to:**   Dr. Monica Kempland, Ph.D., Director, Pre-Professional Health Studies
Pre-Professional Health Studies, Verhaegen Hall, Room 314, 3634 Lindell Blvd., St. Louis Missouri  63108-3302

**T** 314 977 2840  **F** 314 977 3660 • www.slu.edu/prehealth.xml • prehealth@slu.edu

## Purpose
This combined-degree program awards special recognition to exceptional first-year (freshmen) premedical students. It is intended to enhance the educational experience and reduce the stress associated with premedical-medical education.

## Requirements for Entrance
Students apply to this program when they apply to Saint Louis University for undergraduate admission. Both residents and non-residents of Missouri are eligible to apply to the program. Applicants are required to complete the following courses prior to graduation from high school: one year of biology, one year of chemistry, and three years of mathematics. In addition to meeting these requirements, applicants must take either the ACT (minimum score of 30) or SAT (minimum score of 1330).

## Selection Factors
Outstanding academic achievement in high school is a favorable factor in qualifying for the combined-degree program at Saint Louis University. Selected applicants usually rank in the top ten percent of their high school class. It is required that all candidates achieve a minimum ACT score of 30 or SAT score of 1330. An interview is not required. Students are required to take the MCAT® in April of the junior year (no minimum score required). MCAT® scores are not a factor for promotion or admission to the medical school phase of the program.

## Curriculum
This eight-year program leads to a baccalaureate degree awarded by Saint Louis University and to the M.D. degree granted by the Saint Louis University School of Medicine. Students have much flexibility in choosing a major and are encouraged to study in an area of their choice. During the first four years of the curriculum, students will spend 100 percent of their time in coursework related to the bachelor's degree, which includes 42 to 46 semester hours of natural and physical science, 3 to 4 semester hours of mathematics, and 12 semester hours of humanities. There are strict GPA requirements to remain in the program. The remaining four years focus on achieving the M.D. degree.

## Expenses

| | Resident Tuition and Fees | Non-resident Tuition and Fees |
|---|---|---|
| Undergraduate | $32,180 | $32,180 |
| U.S. Medical School | $46,185 | $46,185 |

## Financial Aid
Information can be obtained from the Office of Financial Aid/Scholarships, DuBourg Hall 121, Saint Louis University, 221 North Grand Boulevard, St. Louis, MO 63103.

### Application and Acceptance Policies

**Filing of application—**
**Earliest date:** October 1, 2011
**Latest date:** December 1, 2011

**Application fee:** No    **Fee waiver available:** n/a

**Acceptance notice —**
**Earliest date:** March 1, 2012
**Latest date:** n/a

**Applicant's response to acceptance offer—**
**Maximum time:** May 1, 2012

**Deposit to hold place in class:** Yes
**Deposit — Resident:** $200
**Deposit refundable:** No    **Refundable by:** n/a

**Starting date:** Mid-August 2012

### Information on 2010–2011 Entering Class

| Number of | In-State | Out-of-State | Total |
|---|---|---|---|
| Applicants | 121 | 430 | 551 |
| Applicants Interviewed | 0 | 0 | 0 |
| New Entrants | 30 | 101 | 131 |
| **Total number of students enrolled in program:** 312 | | | |

# University of Missouri-Kansas City School of Medicine

Kansas City Missouri

**Address inquiries to:** Alice Arredondo, Assistant Dean for Admissions and Recruitment
Council on Selection, University of Missouri – Kansas City School of Medicine
2411 Holmes, Kansas City Missouri 64108-2792

**T** 816 235 1870 **F** 816 235 6579 • www.med.umkc.edu • medicine@umkc.edu

## Purpose

The combined baccalaureate-M.D. degree program integrates the humanities, social sciences, basic sciences, and clinical medicine throughout the curriculum so that graduates will develop nine core competencies: effective communication; clinical skills; using basic science in medicine; diagnosis, management, continuing care and prevention; lifelong learning in medicine, basic sciences, the social sciences and humanities; self-awareness, self-care, personal growth and professional behavior; diversity and the social context of health care; moral reasoning and ethical judgment; problem solving skills. Students will receive clinical experience throughout all six years of the B.A./M.D. program to further encourage the development of these competencies.

## Requirements for Entrance

Designed for high school graduates who are entering college, both residents and non-residents of Missouri may apply. All applicants must meet the minimum academic standards for the College of Arts and Sciences at UMKC. An applicant's core high school curriculum must include: eight semesters of English; eight semesters of mathematics; six semesters of science, including two semesters of biology and two semesters of chemistry; six semesters of social studies; two semesters of fine arts; and four semesters of a foreign language. Applicants must also submit all required application materials in order to be considered for admission. This includes the UMKC application for admission, the School of Medicine supplemental application, standardized test score, high school transcript, an essay, list of high school activities and health experience, and a minimum of three references. The process for review is competitive, individualized, and holistic.

## Selection Factors

Cognitive and non-cognitive characteristics are utilized in holistically evaluating applications. Applicants' academic potential is evaluated by the strength of high school courses, core grade point average, and scores on the ACT/SAT. In the 2010-2011 entering class, the average test score was in the 98th percentile and the average GPA was 3.85. Non-cognitive characteristics, such as maturity, leadership, motivation for medicine, interpersonal skills, and compassion are assessed by the essay, high school activities, health experience, and references. After initial review, a number of applicants are invited for a required interview which is designed to also assess non-cognitive characteristics. Admission is competitive, and no one score or application component will guarantee an offer of admission.

## Curriculum

The six-year curriculum leads to a baccalaureate degree granted by the UMKC College of Arts and Sciences or the UMKC School of Biological Sciences and the doctor of medicine degree granted by the UMKC School of Medicine. Students must complete requirements for the bachelor's degree. Students have a choice of majors, but most select liberal arts, chemistry, biology or psychology. Course requirements for the bachelor's degree in liberal arts include 21 semester hours of humanities, 21 semester hours of social sciences, and 50 semester

hours of natural and physical sciences. During the first two years of the curriculum, students spend 75 percent of their time in coursework related to the bachelor's degree. Conversely, in the last four years, students spend a majority of their time in courses, clerkships, and electives related to the M.D. degree. Thus, the study of liberal arts, basic sciences, and clinical medicine is integrated throughout the entire curriculum. Students are assigned a faculty advisor (docent), and younger students are paired with older students in a mentoring relationship. During the last four years of the curriculum, students attend an outpatient clinic for a half-day each week. Students in this program do not take the MCAT. They must pass Steps 1 and 2 of the USMLE for graduation. An alternate path is available for extended study.

## Expenses

| | Resident Tuition and Fees | Non-resident Tuition and Fees |
|---|---|---|
| Undergraduate | n/a | n/a |
| U.S. Medical School | $30,150 | $57,619 |

## Financial Aid

The UMKC Student Financial Aid Office can assist with providing additional information regarding financial aid programs. The University participates in federal and state grant and loan programs, and need-based scholarships may also be available to students who qualify. For additional information related to costs and financial assistance, please contact: UMKC Student Financial Aid office, 5115 Oak Street, Kansas City, MO, 64110.

## Application and Acceptance Policies

**Filing of application—**
**Earliest date:** August 1, 2011   **Latest date:** November 1, 2011

**Application fee:** $35   **Fee waiver available:** Yes

**Acceptance notice —**
**Earliest date:** April 1, 2012   **Latest date:** Varies

**Applicant's response to acceptance offer—**
**Maximum time:** May 1, 2012

**Deposit to hold place in class:** Yes
**Deposit — Resident:** $100
**Deposit refundable:** Yes   **Refundable by:** May 15, 2012

**Starting date:** August 2012

### Information on 2010–2011 Entering Class

| Number of | In-State | Out-of-State | Total |
|---|---|---|---|
| Applicants | 256 | 500 | 756 |
| Applicants Interviewed | 115 | 125 | 240 |
| New Entrants | 59 | 39 | 98 |

**Total number of students enrolled in program:** 617

# University of Nevada School of Medicine

Reno, Nevada

**Address inquiries to:** Ann E. Diggins, MA, Program Director, BS-MD Accelerated Degree Program, University of Nevada School of Medicine, 2040 W. Charleston Boulevard, Suite 504, Las Vegas, Nevada 89102

**T** 702 671 6457  **F** 702 671 6414

http://www.medicine.nevada.edu/dept/asa/prospective_applicants/programs_bsmd.htm • bsmd@medicine.nevada.edu

## Purpose

The BS-MD program offers a seven year accelerated pathway to medical school for a small number of motivated, mature Nevada high school seniors focused on a career in medicine. Students accepted into this program will complete the first three years of the required undergraduate curriculum at the University of Nevada, Reno (UNR) or the University of Nevada Las Vegas (UNLV), then enter the University of Nevada School of Medicine.

## Requirements for Entrance

Applicants are selected for the program during their senior year of high school, must be US citizens or permanent residents of the US, and be Nevada residents. Non-US citizens must have a permanent resident visa and Nevada residency. In addition, applicants must attend a Nevada high school for a minimum of two years and graduate from a Nevada high school.

## Selection Factors

Academic factors taken into consideration for admissions into the accelerated degree program include SAT/ACT scores, high school GPA, and class placement. Applicants considering the program should be in the top 10% of their graduating high school class and hold an un-weighted GPA of a 3.7 or higher. An SAT combined Math/Critical Reading score of 1270 or greater or combined ACT score of 29 or greater are required for consideration. Other factors to be evaluated include extracurricular activities (i.e. athletics, music, clubs, community service, etc.), demonstrated leadership and maturity (i.e. community, school, or other activities), healthcare experiences, and work experience, if applicable. An interview is required and is by invitation only.

## Curriculum

The first three years of the curriculum include the core requirements for the selected baccalaureate degree in biology, biochemistry and molecular biology, or chemistry and prerequisites for matriculation in medical school. Students in the program must maintain a minimum overall college GPA of 3.5 and minimum science GPA of 3.5. Students will be required to take the MCAT® for admission to the School of Medicine and must achieve a composite score of 28 with no subscore lower than 7. Students participate in seminars and are involved in community service activities, clinical observational experiences, and research. The Academic Review and Promotion Committee will make a final recommendation concerning promotion to the School of Medicine.

The BS degree is granted by the undergraduate institution and the MD degree is granted by the University of Nevada School of Medicine. The BS degree is awarded after the fourth year of college enrollment, which is concurrently the first year of medical school. Upon entering the School of Medicine, students will follow the traditional path through their medical education and will be required to comply with the University of Nevada School of Medicine policies and procedures.

## Expenses

| | Resident Tuition and Fees | Non-resident Tuition and Fees |
|---|---|---|
| Undergraduate | $6,200 | n/a |
| U.S. Medical School | $15,711 | n/a |

## Financial Aid

All BS-MD applicants are encouraged to apply for any and all scholarships for which they are eligible. More information about financial aid at the University of Nevada, Reno or the University of Nevada Las Vegas can be found at *www.unr.edu/financial-aid/* and *http://finaid.unlv.edu/*.

---

### Application and Acceptance Policies

**Filing of application—**
**Earliest date:** December 15, 2011
**Latest date:** February 25, 2012

**Application fee:** No    **Fee waiver available:** n/a

**Acceptance notice —**
**Earliest date:** n/a
**Latest date:** April 15, 2012

**Applicant's response to acceptance offer—**
**Maximum time:** Two weeks

**Deposit to hold place in class:** No
**Deposit — Resident:** n/a
**Deposit refundable:** n/a    **Refundable by:** n/a

**Starting date:** August 22, 2012

### Information on 2010–2011 Entering Class

| Number of | In-State | Out-of-State | Total |
|---|---|---|---|
| Applicants | 38 | 1 | 39 |
| Applicants Interviewed | 28 | n/a | 28 |
| New Entrants | 12 | n/a | 12 |
| **Total number of students enrolled in program: 27** | | | |

# Rutgers University – New Brunswick and UMDNJ New Jersey Medical School

Piscataway, New Jersey

**NJ**

**Address inquiries to:**  Loretta Stepka, Program Coordinator, Rutgers, The State University of New Jersey, Bachelor/Medical Degree Program, Nelson Biological Laboratory, Room A207, 604 Allison Road, Piscataway, New Jersey 08854-8082

**T** 732 445 5667   **F** 732 445 6341  •  http://hpo.rutgers.ed  •  hpo@biology.rutgers.edu

## Purpose

Designed for high-achieving premedical students on the Rutgers-New Brunswick campus, the BA/MD program permits students to begin their medical education after their third year or at least 94 degree credits at Rutgers. Specially selected students will obtain bachelors and medical degrees in a seven-year program of study.

## Requirements for Entrance

The program is open to all students enrolled at Rutgers University — New Brunswick who are United States citizens or permanent residents of the United States. It is not directly associated with any one college within the Univeristy. Applicants must have completed a minimum of 40 credits, of which 30 credits must be at Rutgers, and they must have been in attendance at Rutgers a minimum of 1 year. Additionally, applicants must have a minimum cumulative GPA of 3.5.

## Selection Factors

The applicants must provide the Executive Committee with official high school and college transcripts. A minimum of five letters of recommendation from Rutgers University faculty must also be submitted. The academic and personal criteria to be evaluated are, in many ways, the same as those used to evaluate regular candidates for admission to medical school. Successful applicants should be those who have demonstrated interests that they have pursued in depth. The Executive Committee will take into account how the applicant has used his or her free time in the past. Because the program hopes to graduate broadly educated students who will assume leadership roles in medicine and their communities, the Executive Committee will look for evidence of positive peer recognition and leadership potential. In the 2010–2011 entering class, matriculants had achieved an average GPA of 3.67 at the end of the first two years of college. An interview is required. The MCAT® is required but it is not a determining factor in the acceptance or retention of the student.

## Curriculum

This program leads to the baccalaureate degree awarded by Rutgers University and to the M.D. degree granted by the University of Medicine and Dentistry of New Jersey-New Jersey Medical School. Students may choose either a seven-or eight-year program with year one being the first undergraduate year. Students will be admitted at the end of the spring term of year two and be formal members of the joint program beginning with year three. In the seven-year program students will spend one year at Rutgers University after admission to the program and prior to matriculation at NJMS. In the eight-year rpogram, students will spend two years at Rutgers after admission to the program and before moving to NJMS. Prior to leaving Rutgers, students must satisfy all college and major requirements, except for the 26 credits which they will receive from NJMS. Fifteen of the latter credits from NJMS will be applied towards a Biological Sciences major. The most popular major is Biological Sciences.

## Expenses

| | Resident Tuition and Fees | Non-resident Tuition and Fees |
|---|---|---|
| Undergraduate | $12,560 | $24,316 |
| U.S. Medical School | $32,013 | $50,722 |

## Financial Aid

Undergraduates should contact the Office of Financial Aid, Rutgers University, 620 George Street, New Brunswick, New Jersey 08901-7385; or visit the Web site at http://studentaid.rutgers.cdu. For NJMS, visit the Web site at www.umdnj.edu/studentfinancialaid.

---

### Application and Acceptance Policies

**Filing of application—**
**Earliest date:** April 1, 2012
**Latest date:** June 1, 2012

**Application fee:** No    **Fee waiver available:** n/a

**Acceptance notice —**
**Earliest date:** July 15, 2012
**Latest date:** n/a

**Applicant's response to acceptance offer—**
**Maximum time:** Two weeks

**Deposit to hold place in class:** No
**Deposit — Resident:** n/a
**Deposit refundable:** n/a    **Refundable by:** n/a

**Starting date:** August 1, 2012

### Information on 2010–2011 Entering Class

| Number of | In-State | Out-of-State | Total |
|---|---|---|---|
| Applicants | 6 | 1 | 7 |
| Applicants Interviewed | 6 | 1 | 7 |
| New Entrants | 5 | 0 | 5 |
| **Total number of students enrolled in program:** 5 | | | |

# Rutgers University and
# UMDNJ Robert Wood Johnson Medical School
Piscataway, New Jersey

**Address inquiries to:** Loretta Stepka, Program Coordinator
Rutgers, The State University of New Jersey, Bachelor/Medical Degree Program,
Nelson Biological Laboratory, Room A207, 604 Allison Road, Piscataway, New Jersey 08854-8082

**T** 732 445 5667  **F** 732 445 6341  •  http://hpo.rutgers.ed  •  hpo@biology.rutgers.edu

## Purpose
The program permits the early identification and admission of quality medical students. It also integrates medical studies with liberal arts study.

## Requirements for Entrance
This program is open to all students enrolled at Rutgers University. Students are selected for this program at the end of their sophomore year. Students must have a 3.50 overall GPA by the end of their third semester and sustain this GPA through the fourth semester at Rutgers University. Residents and non-residents of New Jersey are considered.

## Selection Factors
An applicant's high school and college transcripts and faculty recommendations are taken into account in offering admission. In the 2010–2011 entering class, matriculants had achieved an average GPA of 3.8 at the end of the first two years of college. They had average scores of 650 in the Critical Reading section, 720 on the Mathematics section and 710 on the Writing section. Maturity, motivation, and broad interests are personal characteristics sought in applicants. An interview is required. The MCAT® is not used.

## Curriculum
This program leads to the baccalaureate degree awarded by Rutgers University and to the M.D. degree granted by the University of Medicine and Dentistry of New Jersey-Robert Wood Johnson Medical School. Students must complete requirements for a baccalaureate degree. The most frequent majors for that degree are biological sciences, followed by Cell Biology and Neuroscience. The program is seven years in duration. The basic sciences and the liberal arts are studied together during a four-year period. While in medical school, students must take and pass Steps 1 and 2 of the USMLE.

## Expenses

| | Resident Tuition and Fees | Non-resident Tuition and Fees |
|---|---|---|
| Undergraduate | $12,560 | $24,316 |
| U.S. Medical School | $32,391 | $51,100 |

## Financial Aid
Undergraduates should contact the Office of Financial Aid, Rutgers University, 620 George Street, New Brunswick, New Jersey 08901-7385; call (732) 932-7057; or visit the Web site at *http://studentaid.rutgers.edu.*

## Application and Acceptance Policies

**Filing of application—**
**Earliest date:** April 1, 2012
**Latest date:** June 1, 2012

**Application fee:** No  **Fee waiver available:** n/a

**Acceptance notice —**
**Earliest date:** July 15, 2012
**Latest date:** n/a

**Applicant's response to acceptance offer—**
**Maximum time:** Two weeks

**Deposit to hold place in class:** No
**Deposit — Resident:** n/a
**Deposit refundable:** n/a  **Refundable by:** n/a

**Starting date:** August 1, 2012

### Information on 2010–2011 Entering Class

| Number of | In-State | Out-of-State | Total |
|---|---|---|---|
| Applicants | 22 | 0 | 22 |
| Applicants Interviewed | 17 | 0 | 17 |
| New Entrants | 5 | 0 | 5 |
| **Total number of students enrolled in program:** 12 | | | |

# Rutgers University and Drexel College of Medicine

Piscataway, New Jersey

**Address inquiries to:** Tracey Hasse, Administrative Assistant, Rutgers, The State University of New Jersey BA/MD Program
Nelson Biological Laboratory, Room A207, 604 Allison Road, Piscataway New Jersey 08854-8082

**T** 732 445-5667    **F** 732 446 6341  •  hpo@biology.rutgers.edu

## Purpose

The program is designed to attract highly motivated students of superior ability and accomplishments. The program permits the early identification of these students and their making of an early decision regarding admission to Drexel University College of Medicine (DUCOM).

## Requirements for Entrance

Qualified students who are in their fourth term (semester) at one of the Rutgers-New Brunswick undergraduate schools may apply for admission into the program. Applicants are required to have completed at least 40 college credits of which 30 credits are earned at Rutgers, and they must have been in attendance in Rutgers a minimum of one year. Students are required to have a minimum GPA of 3.5 by the end of their third semester and sustain this GPA through the fourth semester at Rutgers University. Applicants should have completed, or be in the process of completing by the end of their fourth semester, one semester of English, one semester of college-level Mathematics, two semesters of Biology with lab, two semesters of General Chemistry, General Chemistry lab, and two semesters of Organic Chemistry.

## Selection Factors

Applicants are screened on the basis of academic credentials, letters of recommendation, a personal statement, official high school and college transcripts and SAT scores. Selected applicants will be invited for two separate interviews; one with Rutgers University and one with Drexel University College of Medicine. The Rutgers/Drexel Review Committee will then make the final recommendation of students to be admitted to the DUCOM Admissions Committee. The DUCOM Admissions Committee makes the final decision on acceptance into the program.

## Curriculum

The program consists of four years at a Rutgers-New Brunswick/Piscataway undergraduate school followed by a four-year medical program. Students in the program are required to maintain a minimum cumulative GPA of 3.5 and a minimum cumulative GPA of 3.5 in all BCPM courses (all biological sciences, chemistry, physics and mathematics courses) with no individual grade of less than a "C" in any course. No repeated courses are allowed. The MCAT® must be taken no later than April 30 of the third year and students must receive in a single examination a minimum MCAT® score of "9" or better in the verbal section and "10's" in the physical and biological sciences section, or a total minimum score of 31 (with no individual sub-section score less than "8"), a letter score of "P" or higher on the MCAT® writing section. Students are not allowed to take the MCAT® more than three (3) times to achieve the required scores. In New Jersey, DUCOM is affiliated with

Saint Peter's University Hospital, and accepted BAMD students have the unique opportunity to conduct a required clinical and/or research project at Saint Peter's University Hospital for which they will earn two credits each for their last four (4) semesters at Rutgers. Furthermore, students will complete a preceptorship with staff physicians. The credits awarded will fulfill elective credits towards the Rutgers BA degree. Students cannot apply to any other medical school other than DUCOM and must matriculate into the College of Medicine in the year stipulated in their offer letter from the College of Medicine. Once matriculated, students take a minimum of one of DUCOM's clinical experiences at Saint Peter's University Hospital and, during their senior year, enroll in at least one clinical rotation experience at the hospital.

## Expenses

| | Resident Tuition and Fees | Non-resident Tuition and Fees |
|---|---|---|
| Undergraduate | $12,560 | $24,316 |
| U.S. Medical School | $46,985 | $46,985 |

## Financial Aid

Undergraduates should contact the Office of Financial Aid, Rutgers University, 620 George Street, New Brunswick, New Jersey 08901-7385, call (732) 932-7057; or visit the Website at *http://studentaid.rutgers.edu.* For DUCOM, visit the Website at *www.drexel.edu/financialaid/com_students.asp*

---

### Application and Acceptance Policies

**Filing of application—**
**Earliest date:** April 1, 2012
**Latest date:** May 25, 2012

**Application fee:** $75    **Fee waiver available:** No

**Acceptance notice —**
**Earliest date:** July 15, 2012
**Latest date:** n/a

**Applicant's response to acceptance offer—**
**Maximum time:** Two weeks

**Starting date:** August 1, 2012

### Information on 2010–2011 Entering Class

| Number of | In-State | Out-of-State | Total |
|---|---|---|---|
| Applicants | n/r | n/r | n/r |
| Applicants Interviewed | n/r | n/r | n/r |
| New Entrants | n/r | n/r | n/r |
| **Total number of students enrolled in program:** n/r | | | |

# University of Medicine and Dentistry of New Jersey and New Jersey Medical School

Newark, New Jersey

**Address inquiries to:** Director of Admissions, UMDNJ – New Jersey Medical School
P.O. Box 1709, Newark New Jersey    07101-1709

**T** 973 972 4631   **F** 973 973 7986   •   http://njms.umdnj.edu/admissions/prospective/programs_7_8_year.cfm
njmsadmiss@umdnj.edu

## Purpose

The New Jersey Medical School (NJMS) currently has baccalaureate/M.D. degree programs in collaboration with eight undergraduate institutions. The goal of these programs is to give highly qualified students the best opportunity to broaden their premedical preparation, while establishing their career path.

## Requirements for Entrance

Applicants must be high school seniors who are in the top ten percent of their class and have a combined SAT Critical Reading and Math test score of 1400. Please note that we only consider the Critical Reading and Math sections and not the Essay section of the SAT. Applicants must be either U.S. citizens or permanent residents of the U.S. The most qualified and dedicated applicants will receive the highest consideration.

## Selection Factors

Applicants are initially screened by the undergraduate school on the basis of academic credentials, letters of recommendation, and an essay. Those meeting the criteria are invited for an interview at the undergraduate school. The undergraduate schools then forward credentials of qualified applicants to NJMS for further review and consideration for an interview at NJMS. The application deadline to the undergraduate institution is January 3, 2012.

## Curriculum

The program consists of three years at an undergraduate school followed by a four-year medical program. Although not used to determine admission, the MCAT® must be taken prior to medical school matriculation. Promotion to the medical school is contingent upon achieving grades of "B" or better in all premedical courses and maintaining an overall grade point average of at least 3.5 each semester. The baccalaureate degree is awarded by the undergraduate institution upon completion of the first year of medical school. The M.D. degree is awarded by NJMS upon successful completion of all NJMS degree requirements. Students are required to pass Step 1 of the USMLE for promotion to the third year. Passing Step 2 of the USMLE is required for graduation. Eight programs are currently available: Caldwell College provides a well-rounded program that incorporates course work in the humanities, liberal arts and social behavioral sciences, as well as the premedical sciences. For additional information contact: *squinn@ caldwell.edu*. Drew University offers premedical preparation in all sciences and liberal arts subjects. For more information contact: *ksmall@ drew.edu*. Montclair State University offers premedical preparation in biology, chemistry, biochemistry, molecular biology, computer science, mathematics, psychology, and anthropology. For more information contact: *vegaq@mail.montclair.edu*. New Jersey Institute of Technology offers undergraduate study in the Honors Premedical Curriculum within the Engineering Science Program. For more information contact: *kristol@adm.njit.edu*. Rutgers University-Newark Campus offers

premedical preparation in the sciences. For more information contact: *nyeste@ugadm.rutgers.edu*. Stevens Institute of Technology offers premedical preparation in chemical biology. For more information contact: *mhadidi@stevens.edu*. The College of New Jersey offers preparation in biology, chemistry, history, philosophy, and psychology. For more information contact: *shevlin@tcnj.edu*. The Richard Stockton College of New Jersey offers preparation in chemistry, biology, physics, and liberal arts. For more information contact: *admissions@stockton. edu*. NJMS also offers Articulated Programs, which allow students in their second year of college to apply to matriculate at NJMS after completion of their third year of college through programs with: St. Peter's College (contact *lsciorra@spc.edu*), Rutgers University—Newark (contact *jmaiello@andromeda.rutgers.edu*) and Rutgers University—New Brunswick (contact *hpo@biology.rutgers.edu*).

## Expenses

| | Resident Tuition and Fees | Non-resident Tuition and Fees |
|---|---|---|
| Undergraduate | $25,218 | $39,461 |
| U.S. Medical School | $32,013 | $50,722 |

## Financial Aid

Financial aid packages for the undergraduate years are determined by the undergraduate schools.

---

### Application and Acceptance Policies

**Filing of application—**
**Earliest date:** Varies
**Latest date:** January 3, 2012

**Application fee:** No
**Fee waiver available:** n/a

**Acceptance notice —**
**Earliest date:** Varies
**Latest date:** April 14, 2012

**Applicant's response to acceptance offer—**
**Maximum time:** Varies by undergraduate school

**Starting date:** Varies

### Information on 2010–2011 Entering Class

| Number of | In-State | Out-of-State | Total |
|---|---|---|---|
| Applicants | 191 | 76 | 267 |
| Applicants Interviewed | 127 | 0 | 127 |
| New Entrants | 24 | 0 | 24 |
| **Total number of students enrolled in program:** 169 | | | |

# University of New Mexico School of Medicine
Albuquerque New Mexico

**Address inquiries to:** Dr. Robert Sapien, School of Medicine Director
1 University of New Mexico, MSC 09 5065, Albuquerque, New Mexico 87131-0001

**T** 505 925 4500  **F** 505 925 4004  •  http://hsc.unm.edu/som/combinedbamd/  •  combinedbamd@salud.unm.edu

## Purpose
The UNM Combined BA/MD Degree Program is designed to help address the physician shortage in New Mexico by assembling a class of diverse students committed to serving New Mexico communities with the greatest need.

## Requirements for Entrance
Application eligibility for the Combined BA/MD Degree Program requires that a student must be: 1. A New Mexico resident (at time of application) 2. A current New Mexico high school senior (high school seniors outside NM who are enrolled members of the Navajo Tribe and live in the Navajo Nation are also eligible) 3. Have an ACT math sub-score of 22 or better or a SAT math sub-score of 510 or better and 4. Have a personal commitment to pursue a medical career in New Mexico's rural or under-served areas.

## Selection Factors
The Combined BA/MD Degree Program considers all aspects of an applicant's background, experience and academic progress including: Academic excellence (ACT, GPA, honors courses, Advanced Placement courses), community connection and involvement, volunteer service, commitment to practice medicine in New Mexico, honors and awards, extracurricular activities, letters of recommendation, personal statement, and medically-related experience (where feasible/available). Applicants with a Math ACT subscore of a 22 or a Math SAT subscore of a 510 will automatically be invited for two individual interviews with members of the Admissions Committee.

## Curriculum
The UNM Combined BA/MD Degree Program is a two-step, dual-degree program. Students will first earn a baccalaureate degree through the College of Arts & Sciences (A&S) in a challenging four-year curriculum specifically designed to prepare them for medical school and ultimately to practice medicine in New Mexico. Upon successfully completing the undergraduate academic and eligibility requirements of the program, students will then enter the School of Medicine to complete their doctor of medicine (M.D.) degree. All BA/MD students have three options for their undergraduate major: 1. Arts and Sciences Major— The College of Arts and Sciences offers degrees in a variety of subjects that relate to humanity's cultural, social and scientific achievements. 2. Health Medicine and Human Values (HMHV):Health, Humanities, and Society Concentration— This option is designed for students who prefer a distributed liberal arts and sciences program of study. 3. Health Medicine and Human Values (HMHV): Biomedical Sciences Concentration— This option is designed for students who wish to pursue a rigorous program of study in the physical and natural sciences. Health Medicine and Human Values (HMHV)— the HMHV program offers students flexibility in choosing an undergraduate major while providing them a structured pre-medical core of special seminars focusing upon humanities, fine arts, and social/behavioral sciences studies in the context of health science and medicine. All three options include a suite of courses in the humanities, social sciences, mathematics, and physical and natural

sciences that prepare the student for medical school. The Community Health Practicum is a six hour required summer program designed to allow students to engage in experiential learning projects involved in community and clinical health.

## Expenses

| | Resident Tuition and Fees | Non-resident Tuition and Fees |
|---|---|---|
| Undergraduate | $5,506 | n/a |
| U.S. Medical School | $19,498 | n/a |

## Financial Aid
All UNM BA/MD students are required to apply for all UNM scholarships for which they are eligible and strongly encouraged to apply for external scholarships for which they are qualified. UNM BA/MD students are also required to fill out the Free Application for Federal Student Aid (FAFSA). The BA/MD Undergraduate Scholarship meets basic educational costs that are not covered by other scholarships. The amount of BA/MD scholarship awarded varies from student to student. Student loans and work-study awards are included in the award package and BA/MD scholarship will be adjusted accordingly. Awards are totaled for the academic year and cannot exceed UNM's cost of attendance. The BA/MD Program considers basic educational costs to include tuition, student fees, housing, meals, and books. Housing cost is based on Redondo apartment rates; meal plan is based on an average cost of available plans; book allowance is set at $460 per semester. Course fees over $108 per semester will be the student's responsibility. Any choices made by a student that produce extra cost, will be the student's responsibility. The BA/MD scholarship covers only undergraduate costs.

## Application and Acceptance Policies

**Filing of application—**
**Earliest date:** August 15, 2011
**Latest date:** November 15, 2011

**Application fee:** No   **Fee waiver available:** n/a

**Acceptance notice —**
**Earliest date:** March 1, 2012   **Latest date:** April 1, 2012

**Applicant's response to acceptance offer—**
**Maximum time:** May 1, 2012

**Deposit to hold place in class:** No

**Starting date:** August 20, 2012

### Information on 2010–2011 Entering Class

| Number of | In-State | Out-of-State | Total |
|---|---|---|---|
| Applicants | 233 | n/a | 233 |
| Applicants Interviewed | 189 | n/a | 189 |
| New Entrants | 28 | n/a | 28 |

**Total number of students enrolled in program:** 102

# Brooklyn College and SUNY-Downstate Medical Center

Brooklyn, New York

**Address inquiries to:** Steven B. Silbering, Ph.D., Director, B.A.-M.D. Program
2231 Boylan Hall, Brooklyn College, 2900 Bedford Avenue, Brooklyn, New York 11210-2889
**T** 718 951 4706 **F** 718 951 4559 • http://bamd.brooklyn.cuny.edu/bamdmain.html • silbering@brooklyn.cuny.edu

## Purpose

The undergraduate portion of this program is designed to expose students to a broad range of disciplines, which includes not only the sciences but the humanities and social sciences as well. The students then enter medical school better prepared to become skilled and knowledgeable physicians who are also sensitive to cultural differences and the emotional needs of their patient population.

## Requirements for Entrance

Students are selected in their senior year of high school. Admission is limited to residents of the states of New York, New Jersey and Connecticut, with preference given to New York State residents. Applicants are recommended to have at least a 90 percent CAA (College Admission Average, academic subjects only) and a combined score of at least 1200 on the Mathematics and Critical Reading sections of the SAT Reasoning Test.

## Selection Factors

The academic factors taken into account in offering admission to applicants include the high school GPA, SAT scores, New York State Regents Examination scores, and scores on Advanced Placement tests. In the 2008 entering class, most students had a high school average above 90, and the sum of the SAT Mathematics and Critical Reading scores was between 1300 and 1450. Non-academic factors include community service, participation in scientific research projects and other extracurricular activities. These should preferably be described in a separate resume. Maturity and motivation are qualities highly sought after among the applicants. An interview is required.

## Curriculum

This program leads to a baccalaureate degree from Brooklyn College and an MD degree from SUNY Downstate Medical Center College of Medicine. Students in the baccalaureate portion of the BA-MD program are encouraged to choose a non-science major; however, if a science major is chosen, the student must choose a non-science minor. While in Brooklyn College, BA-MD students must fulfill not only the requirements for the major and minor, but must also complete a liberal arts (Core) curriculum consisting of six lower-tier and two upper-tier core classes. Three of the lower-tier classes must be Honors sections. In addition, students must complete the pre-med requirement, which includes various biology, chemistry and physics courses. No student is permitted to remain in the BA-MD program if either the overall or science GPA's fall below 3.5 in any semester after the freshman year. However, a student can be reinstated if the GPA is raised to 3.5 during subsequent semesters. The MCAT® examination must be taken no later than the summer following the junior year. If a score on any of the three sections of the MCAT® examination is less than 9, the MCAT® must be repeated. Students are permitted to take the MCAT® three times in order to achieve a 9 on each section of the same examination. Aside from the academic requirements, undergraduate BA-MD students must complete 320 hours of a clinical internship during any of the summers except that following the senior year. Also, during each semester after the freshman year, BA-MD students must perform 60 hours of non-clinical community service. After four years at Brooklyn College, students matriculate into the four-year medical school program at SUNY Downstate.

## Expenses

| | Resident Tuition and Fees | Non-resident Tuition and Fees |
|---|---|---|
| Undergraduate | $4,600 | $12,450 |
| U.S. Medical School | $25,422 | $49,342 |

## Financial Aid

All students admitted to the BA-MD program are provided with a $4000 scholarship. If any student receives TAP financial aid, the amount of this aid is subtracted from the scholarship.

---

### Application and Acceptance Policies

**Filing of application—**
**Earliest date:** September 1, 2011
**Latest date:** December 31, 2011

**Application fee:** No    **Fee waiver available:** n/a

**Acceptance notice —**
**Earliest date:** March 15, 2012
**Latest date:** March 15, 2012

**Applicant's response to acceptance offer—**
**Maximum time:** May 1, 2012

**Deposit to hold place in class:** No
**Deposit — Resident:** n/a
**Deposit refundable:** n/a    **Refundable by:** n/a

**Starting date:** August 26, 2012

### Information on 2010–2011 Entering Class

| Number of | In-State | Out-of-State | Total |
|---|---|---|---|
| Applicants | 292 | 6 | 298 |
| Applicants Interviewed | 89 | 1 | 90 |
| New Entrants | 14 | 1 | 15 |
| **Total number of students enrolled in program:** 51 | | | |

# Hobart and William Smith Colleges/ SUNY Upstate Medical University

Geneva, New York

**Address inquiries to:**  Dr. Scott MacPhail, Pre-Health Advisor, Elizabeth Blackwell Medical Scholars Program, Hobart & William Smith Colleges Office of Admissions, 629 South Main Street, Geneva New York  14456

**T** 800 852 2256  **F** 315 781 3914 • www.hws.edu/admissions/adm_apply/firstyear.asp • admissions@hws.edu

## Purpose

The Elizabeth Blackwell Medical Scholars program is designed for exceptional high school seniors who wish to attend medical school. Applicants to this program must be from a rural community, a group underrepresented in medicine, or be a first generation college student.

## Requirements for Entrance

Students apply to the program in their senior year of high school. They must have a minimum SAT I score of 1250 (Mathematics and Critical Reading only) or a 28 ACT score and a high school grade point average of 90 or higher, as well as have demonstrated a commitment to a career in medicine. Students accepted into this program will complete their undergraduate degree at Hobart and William Smith Colleges and are guaranteed admission to Upstate Medical University's College of Medicine, pending all program standards are met.

## Selection Factors

This program is for high school students who are from rural areas, from groups underrepresented in medicine, or who are among the first generation in their families to attend college. The following factors are taken into consideration in assessing applicants for admission into this program: grades, rank in class, SAT (ACT) scores, and extracurricular activities. Selected applicants are invited for a required interview.

## Curriculum

This eight-year program leads to a baccalaureate degree awarded by Hobart and William Smith Colleges and to the medical degree awarded by SUNY Upstate Medical University. Students in this program will need to take the MCATs and receive a score of 30 or greater to secure admission to the medical school.

## Expenses

| | Resident Tuition and Fees | Non-resident Tuition and Fees |
|---|---|---|
| Undergraduate | $ 40,592 | $ 40,592 |
| U.S. Medical School | $ 26,190 | $ 50,110 |

## Financial Aid

Blackwell Scholars are awarded a full-tuition scholarship to attend Hobart and William Smith Colleges. To retain the full-tuition scholarship, awardees must maintain a GPA of at least 3.0 during each semester while at Hobart and William Smith Colleges. More information about financial aid at Hobart and William Smith Colleges can be found at: *www.hws.edu/admissions/fin_edu.aspx or www.upstate.edu/ prospective/tuition.php.*

---

### Application and Acceptance Policies

**Filing of application—**
**Earliest date:** August 2011
**Latest date:** January 15, 2012

**Application fee:** Yes, $45  **Fee waiver available:** yes

**Acceptance notice —**
**Earliest date:** Within two weeks of interview
**Latest date:** n/a

**Applicant's response to acceptance offer—**
**Maximum time:** Two weeks after offer is sent

**Deposit to hold place in class:** Yes
**Deposit — Resident:** $100
**Deposit refundable:** Yes
**Refundable by:** by May 15 of year of entry

**Starting date:** The fall following graduation from Hobart and William Smith Colleges

### Information on 2010–2011 Entering Class

| Number of | In-State | Out-of-State | Total |
|---|---|---|---|
| Applicants | 17 | 9 | 26 |
| Applicants Interviewed | 7 | 1 | 8 |
| New Entrants | 2 | 0 | 2 |
| **Total number of students enrolled in program:** 10 | | | |

# Rensselaer Polytechnic Institute and Albany Medical College

Troy, New York

**Address inquiries to:** Dean of Undergraduate Admissions, Rensselaer Polytechnic Institute
110 Eighth Street, Troy New York 12180-3590

**T** 518 276 6216    **F** 518 276 4072
www.rpi.edu/dept/admissions/resources/Physician-ScientistProgramAccelerated.pdf   •   admissions@rpi.edu

## Purpose

The Accelerated Physician-Scientist Program offers qualified individuals the opportunity to become physicians who are intensively trained in medical research. This innovative approach provides a well-rounded perspective that prepares future practitioners and physician-scientists to perform with confidence and care in a technologically changing environment.

## Requirements for Entrance

Students are selected for this program during the senior year of high school. Residents of New York, as well as non-residents of the state, are eligible to apply. Applicants are expected to have completed the following courses by the time they graduate from high school: four years of English; one year each of biology, chemistry, and physics; and four years of mathematics (through pre-calculus). They must take the SAT Reasoning Test and two SAT Subject Area Tests: one mathematics and one science. In lieu of these tests, American College Testing (ACT) Assessment program scores, including the Writing Test, may be submitted. All tests must be completed by the December testing date prior to the proposed September matriculation.

## Selection Factors

Academic factors considered in offering admission to an applicant include the quality and nature of coursework in high school, performance in those courses, rank in high school class, and test scores. The 2010-2011 entering class had an average score of 705 on the SAT Critical Reading, 727 on the SAT Mathematics, and 743 on the SAT Writing. Personal qualities sought in applicants are motivation, maturity, and intellectual capacity necessary to pursue the accelerated course of study. An interview is required.

## Curriculum

The program leads to a B.S. degree awarded by Rensselaer Polytechnic Institute and the M.D. degree granted by Albany Medical College (AMC). The curriculum for the B.S. and M.D. degrees usually requires seven years to complete. During the first three years of the program spent at Rensselaer, the curriculum involves 70 percent premedical science courses and 30 percent liberal arts courses. Students take 18 courses in the natural and physical sciences and 8 elective courses in the humanities and social sciences. The cornerstone of the program is a mentored research project. During the sixth semester, students split their time between Rensselaer and AMC and begin research that extends over the third and final year at Rensselaer and into the summer preceding the first year of medical school. The research continues throughout the freshman year at AMC and into the following summer. Training in making oral and written scientific presentations is also included. At the medical college, basic and clinical sciences are integrated into themes (primarily organ systems) stressing normal function in Year 1 and pathological processes in Year 2. There are also five longitudinal themes that are integrated throughout the curriculum:

clinical skills, ethical and health systems issues, evidence-based medicine, nutrition, and informatics. In every theme, student learning is focused on clinical presentations. Basic science seminars reinforce the importance of the basic sciences in Years 3 and 4. Emphasis is placed on primary care throughout the four years, with an increased emphasis on care in ambulatory settings in the clinical rotations of Year 3. Year 4 emphasizes specialty care in various required rotations. Additional electives are available in Year 4. Students admitted to the program are not required to take the MCAT® for admission to Albany Medical College. Students are expected to pass Steps 1 and 2 of the USMLE while at Albany Medical College.

## Expenses

| | Resident Tuition and Fees | Non-resident Tuition and Fees |
|---|---|---|
| Undergraduate | $54,035 | $54,035 |
| U.S. Medical School | $48,241 | $48,241 |

## Financial Aid

Sources of financial aid are restricted and include endowed scholarships based on need, merit scholarships, work-study, and student loans through federal and institutional programs. Applicants can receive more information by contacting the Financial Aid Office of Rensselaer Polytechnic Institute at (518) 276-6813 or Albany Medical College at (518) 262-5435.

---

### Application and Acceptance Policies

**Filing of application—**
**Earliest date:** September 1, 2011
**Latest date:** November 1, 2011

**Application fee:** $70
**Fee waiver available:** Yes

**Acceptance notice —**
**Earliest date:** March 2012    **Latest date:** Until class is full

**Applicant's response to acceptance offer—**
**Maximum time:** May 1, 2012

**Deposit to hold place in class:** Yes
**Deposit — Resident:** $500   **Deposit refundable:** No

**Starting date:** August 2012

### Information on 2010–2011 Entering Class

| Number of | In-State | Out-of-State | Total |
|---|---|---|---|
| Applicants | 128 | 395 | 523 |
| Applicants Interviewed | 22 | 42 | 64 |
| New Entrants | 7 | 7 | 14 |
| **Total number of students enrolled in program: 38** | | | |

# St. Bonaventure University and George Washington School of Medicine

St. Bonaventure, New York

**Address inquiries to:** Dr. Allen Knowles, III Director, Franciscan Health Care Professions Programs
St. Bonaventure University Biology Department
De La Roche Hall, Room 219, St. Bonaventure, New York 14778

**T** 716 375 2656 • www.sbu.edu • prehealth@sbu.edu; aknowles@sbu.edu

## Purpose

The joint program of St. Bonaventure University (SBU) and the George Washington University School of Medicine and Health Sciences in Washington, DC (GW), the eight-year program is designed for the high school senior who exhibits academic excellence, leadership in activities, and community service and healthcare experience, all of which have resulted in a passion for a career as a physician. The goal is to prepare the student with a strong background in the natural sciences in preparation for the rigors of medical school. SBU has opened its new science facilities that coordinate with the educational processes at GW.

## Requirements for Entrance

Students are selected in their senior year of high school. Applicants must be U.S. or Canadian citizens or Permanent Residents of the U.S. Applicants must complete the SAT (Verbal/Mathematics of at least 1300) or ACT (minimal score of 29), as well as the SAT Subject Test in Biology (preferably M).

## Selection Factors

Academic factors considered in selecting applicants include high school grades, class rank, and standardized test scores. In addition, extracurricular and health-related activities, community service, volunteerism, research, medical field exposure, personal essays, and letters of recommendation are reviewed. Rank must be in the top 10% of the class, with a GPA of greater than 90 percent. Qualities demonstrating leadership, interest in the medical field through experiences, and AP and Honors courses are considered.
An interview is required at SBU and GW and is by invitation only.

## Curriculum

The student's progress is reviewed on a regular basis. Students must maintain a minimum of a "B" in courses required for admission to the medical school and an overall 3.6 average. The recommended major is biology, with interests outside of the sciences being encouraged. Students do not take the MCAT. Students are required to remain active in community service, volunteer programs, research components, and internships established through SBU. Students attend presentations and interact with GW MD students on the Medical Center campus. At the end of four years, the student is granted the baccalaureate degree from SBU. In the first and second years at GW, the integration of clinical skills begins, as students spend time with physicians, developing patient interviewing skills, conducting physical examinations, and assisting in diagnosis. The third and fourth years at GW are used to develop clinical expertise in a variety of hospitals in the greater D.C. metropolitan area. Upon completion of all requirements, the M.D. degree is awarded by GW.

## Expenses

| | Resident Tuition and Fees | Non-resident Tuition and Fees |
|---|---|---|
| Undergraduate | $26,895 | $26,895 |
| U.S. Medical School | $49,062 | $49,062 |

## Financial Aid

For information on financial aid, fees, and expenses, please refer to the Web sites for each institution (*www.sbu.edu* and *www.gwumc.edu/smhs/fin-aid*) or contact the Financial Aid Offices.

---

### Application and Acceptance Policies

**Filing of application—**
**Earliest date:** September 1, 2011
**Latest date:** December 15, 2011

**Application fee:** $30    **Fee waiver available:** Yes

**Acceptance notice —**
**Earliest date:** March 15, 2012
**Latest date:** n/a

**Applicant's response to acceptance offer—**
**Maximum time:** May 1, 2012

**Deposit to hold place in class:** Yes
**Deposit — Resident:** $500
**Deposit refundable:** No    **Refundable by:** n/a

**Starting date:** Late August 2012

### Information on 2010–2011 Entering Class

| Number of | In-State | Out-of-State | Total |
|---|---|---|---|
| Applicants | 30 | 50 | 80 |
| Applicants Interviewed | 20 | 40 | 60 |
| New Entrants | 5 | 10 | 15 |
| **Total number of students enrolled in program:** 54 | | | |

# Siena College and Albany Medical College
Loudonville, New York

**Address inquiries to:**   Office of Admissions, Siena College, 515 Loudon Road, Loudonville, New York  12211-1462
**T** 518 783 2423 • www.siena.edu/amc • admit@siena.edu

## Purpose
The Science, Humanities and Medicine Program offers an eight-year continuum of education that has a special emphasis on the humanities and on community service to the medically underserved, while providing a sound understanding of both the natural and social sciences.

## Requirements for Entrance
Students are selected for this program during the senior year of high school. Both residents and non-residents of New York are eligible to apply. Candidates for admission to the Siena/Albany Medical College program must have completed: four years of laboratory science (including biology, chemistry, and physics) and four years of mathematics (including a minimum of pre-calculus [calculus preferred]). Typically, successful candidates will have enrolled in, or completed, advanced-level courses by the end of their senior year in high school. A well-rounded background and demonstrated leadership experience are also important. Of equal significance is the student's proven concern for others and for the community. Applicants must take either the SAT Reasoning Test or ACT Assessment, including the optional Writing test. Tests must be completed by the November testing date prior to the proposed September matriculation.

## Selection Factors
Academic factors considered in offering admission to an applicant include: required and elective courses taken, grades earned, class standing, SAT Reasoning Test or ACT scores, including the Writing test, honors received, letters of recommendation, and unique academic experiences. Of great importance to the admission committee are such factors as extracurricular activities, evidence of intellectual curiosity, and interest in the humanities and in the sciences. Students generally rank among the top ten percent of their high school class. The 2010-2011 entering class had an average score of 670 on the SAT Critical Reading section and 710 on the SAT Mathematics section. An interview is required.

## Curriculum
This program offers a coordinated eight-year curriculum of premedical and medical education. The undergraduate phase offers an equal distribution of science and non-science courses. Students graduate in four years with a bachelor of arts degree in biology with a minor in the humanities. The undergraduate phase of the program also includes a required summer of human service in a health-related agency, usually in an urban setting or developing nation. Passage from the undergraduate college to the medical school requires achievement of a 3.40 GPA and a continued interest in the human service dimension of the program. At the medical college, basic and clinical sciences are integrated into themes (primarily organ systems) stressing normal function in Year 1 and pathological processes in Year 2. There are also five longitudinal themes

integrated throughout the curriculum: clinical skills, ethical and health systems issues, evidence-based medicine, nutrition, and informatics. In every theme, student learning is focused on clinical presentations. The summer between the sophomore and junior years is dedicated to medically related volunteer service, usually in a rural or inner city clinic. Seminars reinforce the importance of the basic sciences in Years 3 and 4. Emphasis is placed on primary care throughout the four years, with an increased emphasis on care in ambulatory settings in Year 3 clinical rotations. Year 4 emphasizes specialty care in various required rotations. Additional electives are available in Year 4. Students admitted to the program are not required to take the MCAT® for admission to AMC. Students must pass Steps 1 and 2 of the USMLE while at AMC.

## Expenses

| | Resident Tuition and Fees | Non-resident Tuition and Fees |
|---|---|---|
| Undergraduate | $41,640 | $41,640 |
| U.S. Medical School | $48,241 | $48,241 |

## Financial Aid
Applicants can receive more information by contacting the Siena College Financial Aid Office at (518) 783-2427 or the Albany Medical College Financial Aid Office at (518) 262-5435.

### Application and Acceptance Policies

**Filing of application—**
**Earliest date:** September 1, 2011
**Latest date:** December 1, 2011

**Application fee:** $50
**Fee waiver available:** Yes

**Acceptance notice —**
**Earliest date:** March 2012
**Latest date:** Until class is full

**Applicant's response to acceptance offer—**
**Maximum time:** May 1, 2012

**Deposit to hold place in class:** Yes
**Deposit — Resident:** $350
**Deposit refundable:** No      **Refundable by:** n/a

**Starting date:** September 2012

### Information on 2010–2011 Entering Class

| Number of | In-State | Out-of-State | Total |
|---|---|---|---|
| Applicants | 247 | 149 | 396 |
| Applicants Interviewed | 27 | 19 | 46 |
| New Entrants | 7 | 7 | 14 |
| **Total number of students enrolled in program:** 57 | | | |

# Sophie Davis School of Biomedical Education and City University of New York

New York, New York

**Address inquiries to:** Mr. Chris Wanyonyi, Director of Admissions Sophie Davis School of Biomedical Education at the CCNY Office of Admissions, Harris Hall, 160 Convent Avenue, New York New York 10031

**T** 212 650 7718 **F** 212 650 7708 • http://med.cuny.edu • cwanyonyi@med.cuny.edu

## Purpose

The purposes of this combined-degree program are to train primary care physicians who will work in medically underserved urban areas, to increase the number of physicians from groups underrepresented in medicine, to intervene in the disparity of access to high quality pre-college science education, and to create a medical school pipeline.

## Requirements for Entrance

Students are selected for this program in the senior year of high school. Only residents of New York State are eligible to apply. Applicants are expected to have completed the following courses by the time they graduate from high school: two semesters each of chemistry and biology and six to eight semesters of mathematics. They must take the ACT Assessment and SAT tests.

## Selection Factors

Academic factors taken into account in offering admission to an applicant are: high school GPA, SAT I scores, ACT Assessment scores, and scores on the New York State Regents Examinations. In the 2010 entering class, high school grades averaged 95 and the sub-score on the Mathematics ACT Assessment averaged 28. The SAT Mathematics average was 675, and the SAT Verbal average was 675. Personal qualities sought in applicants include interest in people, concern for others, initiative, and leadership. An interview is required.

## Curriculum

This seven-year program leads to a baccalaureate degree granted by The City College of New York (CCNY) and to the M.D. degree awarded by one of five participating medical schools (Albany Medical College, New York Medical College, New York University, SUNY Brooklyn, or SUNY Stony Brook University). During the first five years of the program, students fulfill all requirements for the B.S. degree and study the preclinical portion of the medical school curriculum. After successfully completing the five-year sequence and passing Step 1 of the USMLE, students transfer to one of the participating medical schools for their final two years of clinical training. Students are expected to pass Step 1 of the USMLE to proceed to Years 3 and 4 of medical school. Additionally, students are expected to pass Step 2 of the USMLE to graduate. Students complete the core liberal arts curriculum of CCNY during the first two years. At this time, they also take courses emphasizing the importance of understanding cultural differences for good medical practice and, through community medicine courses, do field work at various community agencies, including many family practice clinics. The final years of the five-year sequence at CCNY include courses necessary in the first two years of medical school, including basic science courses and several community medicine courses. Students also benefit from counseling and academic support services.

## Expenses

| | Resident Tuition and Fees | Non-resident Tuition and Fees |
|---|---|---|
| Undergraduate | $4,830 | n/a |
| U.S. Medical School | n/a | n/a |

## Financial Aid

Pell grants, New York State Tuition Assistance Program Awards, and NYC Merit Awards are all sources of financial aid. The school generally awards several scholarships to incoming students, including the CCNY New Era Scholarship, the Bronx High School of Science/CCNY Scholarship, the Stuyvesant High School/CCNY Scholarship and the William R. Hearst Endowed Scholarship. Scholarships available later in the program include those from the Alan Seelig Memorial Fund, the Aranow Fund, the Mack Lipkin Broader Horizon Fellowship and the Sophie and Leonard Davis Scholarships. Applicants can contact the Financial Aid Office at (212) 650-5819.

---

### Application and Acceptance Policies

**Filing of application—**
**Earliest date:** September 2011
**Latest date:** January 8, 2012

**Application fee:** No    **Fee waiver available:** n/a

**Acceptance notice —**
**Earliest date:** March 25, 2012
**Latest date:** April 1, 2012

**Applicant's response to acceptance offer—**
**Maximum time:** May 1, 2012

**Deposit to hold place in class:** No
**Deposit — Resident:** n/a
**Deposit refundable:** n/a    **Refundable by:** n/a

**Starting date:** Late August 2012

### Information on 2010–2011 Entering Class

| Number of | In-State | Out-of-State | Total |
|---|---|---|---|
| Applicants | 864 | n/a | 864 |
| Applicants Interviewed | 247 | n/a | 247 |
| New Entrants | 64 | n/a | 64 |
| **Total number of students enrolled in program: 354** | | | |

# Stony Brook University and Stony Brook School of Medicine

Stony Brook, New York

**Address inquiries to:** Undergraduate Admissions, Honors Programs, 118 Administration Building
Stony Brook University, Stony Brook New York    11794-1901

T 631 632 6868   F 631 632 9898 • www.stonybrook.edu/ugadmissions/newhonors/scholarsmed.shtml
enroll@stonybrook.edu

## Purpose

The Scholars for Medicine Program offers conditional acceptance to the Stony Brook University School of Medicine to a select number of outstanding and highly motivated students through one of three programs: The Honors College, WISE (Women in Science and Engineering) and the Engineering Program of Stony Brook University. In addition to acquiring a solid background in the sciences, accepted students have access to a wide array of liberal arts courses through the university. Students also have access to medical school programs in research and a series of health-related seminars.

## Requirements for Entrance

Students are selected for this program only during the senior year of high school. There are no state residency requirements. No specific courses are required. Applicants must take the SAT. For non-U. S. citizens, documentation of permanent residency status will be required of accepted students prior to matriculation.

## Selection Factors

To be considered for this program, applicants must have a minimum SAT score of 1350 (Critical Reading and Mathematics) and an unweighted high school GPA of 95. The applicant's high school academic record, standardized test reports, essay, history of interests and activities, and required interview at the School of Medicine are factors taken into account in offering admission.

## Curriculum

This eight-year program leads to the baccalaureate and M.D. degrees granted by Stony Brook University. Students are expected to complete the requirements for any of the baccalaureate degrees awarded by the university as well as the requirements for either the Honors College, WISE Program or Engineering Program. Undergraduate work taken must include courses required by the School of Medicine, including one year each of biology, physics, inorganic chemistry, organic chemistry (all with lab), and English. No specific major is required for the premedical undergraduate phase. The program provides a seminar series of health-related lectures given by nationally and internationally recognized individuals in health care delivery. In addition, students have an opportunity to engage in cutting-edge research. Admission to the School of Medicine is contingent upon maintaining a minimum specified gpa during the first three undergraduate years. All scholars are required to take the MCAT® no later than September of their senior year in college and must attain a specified minimum MCAT® score. USMLE Steps 1 and 2 are required for promotion and graduation from the School of Medicine.

## Expenses

| | Resident Tuition and Fees | Non-resident Tuition and Fees |
|---|---|---|
| Undergraduate | $ 6,580 | $ 14,990 |
| U.S. Medical School | $ 26,159 | $ 50,079 |

## Financial Aid

Financial aid available to enrolled students includes federal Perkins loans, Equal Opportunity Program, federal work-study, federal Pell Grants, Federal Supplemental Educational Opportunity, NY State Tuition Assistance Program (TAP), and NY State Aid for Part-time Students. Applicants can receive more information by contacting the Office of Financial Aid and Student Employment at Stony Brook University at (631) 632-6840 or visiting the Web site at *www.stonybrook.edu/ ugadmissions/financial/costs.shtml*. Please contact the programs directly concerning scholarship opportunities.

## Application and Acceptance Policies

**Filing of application—**
**Earliest date:** August 15, 2011
**Latest date:** January 15, 2012

**Application fee:** No    **Fee waiver available:** n/a

**Acceptance notice —**
**Earliest date:** March 15, 2012
**Latest date:** April 1, 2012

**Applicant's response to acceptance offer—**
**Maximum time:** May 1, 2012

**Deposit to hold place in class:** Yes
**Deposit — Resident:** $100
**Deposit refundable:** Yes    **Refundable by:** n/a

**Starting date:** August 2012

### Information on 2010–2011 Entering Class

| Number of | In-State | Out-of-State | Total |
|---|---|---|---|
| Applicants | 662 | 197 | 859 |
| Applicants Interviewed | 15 | 9 | 24 |
| New Entrants | 4 | 3 | 7 |
| **Total number of students enrolled in program: 25** | | | |

# Union College and Albany Medical College

Schenectady, New York

**Address inquiries to:** Associate Dean of Admissions, Union College, Schenectady, New York  12308

**T**  518 388 6112  **F**  518 388 8034  •  www.medicine.union.edu/LIM  •  admissions@union.edu

## Purpose

The Leadership in Medicine Program is specifically designed for students who want to prepare for the challenge of medical leadership by taking advantage of additional educational opportunities as part of their undergraduate education. In addition to offering the standard coursework required for attaining the degrees of B.S., M.S. or M.B.A., and M.D., the integrated program focuses on three areas essential for future leaders in medicine: the economic and financial problems facing medicine, including health policy and health management; the increasing complexity of biomedical ethics; and the need to maintain a global perspective.

## Requirements for Entrance

Students are selected for this program during the senior year of high school. Residents of New York, as well as non-residents of the state, are eligible to apply. Applicants are expected to have completed a challenging curriculum in high school, which must include biology, chemistry, and physics. They must take either the ACT Assessment or the SAT Reasoning Test and two SAT Subject Area Tests (one mathematics and one science). Tests must be completed by the December testing date prior to the proposed September matriculation.

## Selection Factors

Academic factors considered in offering admission to an applicant include the quality and nature of coursework in high school, performance in those courses, rank in high school class, and standardized test scores. In the 2010–2011 entering class, the average score was 705 for SAT Critical Reading, 727 for SAT Mathematics, and 743 for SAT Writing. Personal qualities sought in applicants include motivation, maturity, and personal development. Interviews at Union College and Albany Medical College are required.

## Curriculum

This program leads to B.S. and M.S. or M.B.A. degrees awarded by Union College and the M.D. degree granted by Albany Medical College. At Union College, students take 30 courses (15 science and 15 non-science) and complete an interdepartmental major in the humanities or social sciences. A special bioethics program supplemented by a health services practicum, a term abroad, and a program in health care management at the Union College Graduate Management Institute are also integral parts of the educational experience. The curriculum for the B.S., M.S., or M.B.A. and M.D. degrees requires eight years to complete. At the medical college, basic and clinical sciences are integrated into themes (primarily organ systems) stressing normal function in Year 1 and pathological processes in Year 2. Five longitudinal themes are integrated throughout the curriculum: clinical skills, ethical and health

systems issues, evidence-based medicine, nutrition, and informatics. In every theme, student learning is focused on clinical presentations. Basic science seminars reinforce the importance of the basic sciences in Years 3 and 4. Emphasis is placed on primary care throughout the four years, with an increased emphasis on care in ambulatory settings in Year 3 clinical rotations. Year 4 emphasizes specialty care in various required rotations. Additional electives are available in Year 4. Students admitted to the program are not required to take the MCAT® for admission to Albany Medical College. Students are expected to pass Steps 1 and 2 of the USMLE while at Albany Medical College.

## Expenses

| | Resident Tuition and Fees | Non-resident Tuition and Fees |
|---|---|---|
| Undergraduate | $52,329 | $52,329 |
| U.S. Medical School | $48,241 | $48,241 |

## Financial Aid

Sources of financial aid include various programs based on need, student loans through federal and state assistance, work-study, and merit scholarships. For more information, contact the Financial Aid Office of Union College (518) 388-6123 or at Albany Medical College (518) 262-5435

---

### Application and Acceptance Policies

**Filing of application—**
**Earliest date:** September 1, 2011
**Latest date:** December 1, 2011

**Application fee:** $50    **Fee waiver available:** Yes

**Acceptance notice —**
**Earliest date:** March 2012
**Latest date:** Until class is full

**Applicant's response to acceptance offer—**
**Maximum time:** May 1, 2012

**Deposit to hold place in class:** Yes
**Deposit — Resident:** $600
**Deposit refundable:** No    **Refundable by:** n/a

**Starting date:** September 2012

### Information on 2010–2011 Entering Class

| Number of | In-State | Out-of-State | Total |
|---|---|---|---|
| Applicants | 162 | 207 | 369 |
| Applicants Interviewed | 42 | 51 | 93 |
| New Entrants | 8 | 6 | 14 |
| **Total number of students enrolled in program: 58** | | | |

# University of Rochester School of Medicine and Dentistry

Rochester, New York

**Address inquiries to:** Dr. Flavia Nobay, Rochester Early Medical Scholars Coordinator
University of Rochester, Undergraduate Admissions, Box 270251, Rochester New York 14627-0251

**T** 585 275 3221  **F** 585 461 4595 • http://enrollment.rochester.edu/admissions/learning/programs.shtm
admit@admissions.rochester.edu

## Purpose

The Rochester Early Medical Scholars Program (REMS) provides both acceptance to the University of Rochester College of Arts, Sciences, and Engineering and conditional acceptance to the School of Medicine and Dentistry to a group of exceptionally talented and motivated students. REMS highly encourages the utmost flexibility in degree programs, focuses on mentoring relationships with medical school staff, and promotes early exposure to the medical school curriculum through a series of lectures and seminars.

## Requirements for Entrance

Students are selected for this program during their senior year of high school from a large pool. A recommended high school curriculum includes at least three years of foreign language and social studies, four years each of English, mathematics, and science. A transcript that includes honors, AP and/or IB courses is strongly recommended. Applicants are expected to take the SAT or ACT Assessment. SAT Subject Tests are highly recommended, especially, Mathematics Level 1C or Mathematics Level 2C, and Biology or Chemistry.

## Selection Factors

Outstanding achievement in a challenging high school curriculum, character, interests, maturity, experience in health care or research settings, and motivation necessary for a career in medicine are required for consideration for entry into the REMS program. Fifty finalists will be invited to interview for REMS, and those interviews are required. In the 2009–2010 entering class, REMS students had an average SAT Verbal (Critical Reading) score of 712, an average Mathematics score of 723 and average Writing score of 722. In order to take their place in the first-year medical school class, REMS students must carry at least a 3.3 overall GPA and a 3.3 biology-chemistry-physics-math GPA by the end of the freshman year, a 3.4 for the sophomore year, and 3.5 thereafter by the time of undergraduate graduation. In order to matriculate into medical school, all students must have an overall GPA of 3.5 and a biology-chemistry-physics-math overall GPA of a 3.5. REMS students do not have to take the MCAT® examination.

## Curriculum

The eight-year program leads to a baccalaureate degree and the M.D. degree, both granted by the University of Rochester. Students must complete the baccalaureate degree in order to matriculate into medical school. The most popular major is biology, followed by chemistry, and health and society. However, an undergraduate science major is not required nor encouraged in order to matriculate into medical school. A Social Service project is also required in order to matriculate to the medical school, this project is highly individual. The University of Rochester School of Medicine and Dentistry's particularly innovative Double-Helix Curriculum (DHC) focuses on a fully integrated basic and clinical science curriculum across all four years of medical school. Students begin their clinical clerkships in January of their first year and

learn in an environment that fosters critical thinking, problem-solving and active learning in small group Problem-Based Learning sessions, lectures, laboratories and clinical skills workshops. See *www.urmc.rochester.edu/education/md/prospective-students/curriculum/* for details. As home of the "biopsychosocial model," Rochester values the art and science of medicine as a continuum, and fosters an educational model that is humanistic and patient-centered. REMS students also may apply for any of our combined degree programs; MD/PhD, MD/MBA, MD/MPH, MD/MS. A "Take 5" program, offering a tuition-free, fifth undergraduate year, is available to selected REMS students. Summer research programs and extensive international experiences are available at both the undergraduate and medical school levels.

## Expenses

| | Resident Tuition and Fees | Non-resident Tuition and Fees |
|---|---|---|
| Undergraduate | $40,282 | $40,282 |
| U.S. Medical School | $42,970 | $42,970 |

## Financial Aid

University of Rochester scholarships and loans, plus governmental loans, are available. For more information, write the Financial Aid Office, University of Rochester, Box 270261, Rochester, New York 14627-0261, or phone (585) 275-3226 or (800) 881-8234. Website: *http://enrollment.rochester.edu/financial*.

---

### Application and Acceptance Policies

**Filing of application—**
**Earliest date:** August 1, 2011
**Latest date:** December 1, 2011

**Application fee:** $30   **Fee waiver available:** Yes

**Acceptance notice —**
**Earliest date:** March 2012   **Latest date:** May 2012

**Applicant's response to acceptance offer—**
**Maximum time:** May 1, 2012

**Deposit to hold place in class:** Yes
**Deposit — Resident:** $600
**Deposit refundable:** No   **Refundable by:** n/a

**Starting date:** Early September 2012

### Information on 2010–2011 Entering Class

| Number of | In-State | Out-of-State | Total |
|---|---|---|---|
| Applicants | 280 | 429 | 709 |
| Applicants Interviewed | 10 | 32 | 42 |
| New Entrants | 2 | 5 | 7 |
| **Total number of students enrolled in program: 62** | | | |

# Case Western Reserve University School of Medicine
Cleveland, Ohio

**Address inquiries to:**  Christine DeSalvo Miller,  Associate Director
Office of Undergraduate Admission, Wolstein Hall
11318 Bellflower Road, Cleveland Ohio    44106-7055

**T**  216 368 4450  **F**  216 368 5111  •  http://admission.case.edu  •  admission@case.edu

## Purpose
This program is intended to provide college students with a greater sense of freedom and choice in the pursuit of a premedical baccalaureate degree.

## Requirements for Entrance
Students are selected for this program during the senior year of high school. Both residents and nonresidents of Ohio are considered for admission. Applicants are expected to have completed the following courses by the time they graduate from high school: one year each of biology, chemistry, and physics and four years of mathematics. They must take either the ACT Assessment with the Writing Test or the SAT Reasoning Test.

## Selection Factors
The applicant's high school academic record, standardized test reports, history of interests and activities, and a required interview are factors taken into account in offering admission. Evidence of strong interpersonal and leadership skills is also sought. While there is no minimum requirement for standardized test scores, in the Fall 2010 entering class, SAT scores ranged from approximately 680–800 on the Critical Reading section, 710–800 on the Math section, and 710–800 on the Writing section. The composite ACT score ranged from approximately 33–35.

## Curriculum
This eight-year program leads to the baccalaureate and M.D. degrees granted by Case Western Reserve University. Students are expected to complete the requirements for any of the baccalaureate degrees awarded by the colleges of the university. They are expected to satisfy all requirements of, and earn a baccalaureate prior to matriculating in, the School of Medicine. The work taken for the baccalaureate must include the studies specifically required of applicants by the School of Medicine, including one year of biology, two years of chemistry (including organic chemistry), one year of physics, one year of calculus, and first-year (freshman) seminar. One year of biochemistry is strongly recommended. No specific major concentration is required for the premedical undergraduate phase. To date, the majors most common majors been biology and biochemistry. Psychology, chemistry, and biomedical engineering are also popular majors. The first four years of the program are devoted to study for the baccalaureate and the last four years to the curriculum in medicine. Students in the medical phase are required to pass Step 1 of the USMLE for promotion within the program and to pass Step 2 of the USMLE in order to graduate. Video recorded lectures are offered for selected undergraduate courses to supplement the classroom work only; they do not replace traditional courses.

## Expenses

| | Resident Tuition and Fees | Non-resident Tuition and Fees |
| --- | --- | --- |
| Undergraduate | $37,300 | $37,300 |
| U.S. Medical School | $47,770 | $47,770 |

## Financial Aid
Sources of aid for the undergraduate phase include merit and need-based aid, college work-study, and university grants and scholarships. For information about aid, contact the Office of University Financial Aid at (216) 368-4530.

### Application and Acceptance Policies

**Filing of application—**
**Earliest date:** n/a
**Latest date:** December 1, 2011

**Application fee:** $35    **Fee waiver available:** Yes

**Acceptance notice —**
**Earliest date:** n/a
**Latest date:** Approximately April 1, 2012

**Applicant's response to acceptance offer—**
**Maximum time:** May 1, 2012

**Deposit to hold place in class:** Yes
**Deposit — Resident:** $500
**Deposit refundable:** No    **Refundable by:** n/a

**Starting date:** August 27, 2012

### Information on 2010–2011 Entering Class

| Number of | In-State | Out-of-State | Total |
| --- | --- | --- | --- |
| Applicants | 210 | 630 | 840 |
| Applicants Interviewed | 9 | 46 | 55 |
| New Entrants | 2 | 10 | 12 |
| **Total number of students enrolled in program: 25–35** | | | |

# Northeastern Ohio Universities College of Medicine

Rootstown, Ohio

**Address inquiries to:** Michelle Cassetty Collins, M.S.Ed., Executive Director, Enrollment Services
Northeastern Ohio Universities College of Medicine
4209 State Route 44, P.O. Box 95, Rootstown, Ohio 44272-0095

**T** 330 325 6270  **F** 330 325 8372  •  www.neoucom.edu/audience/applicants  •  admission@neoucom.edu

## Purpose

The mission of the Northeastern Ohio Universities College of Medicine (NEOUCOM) is to graduate qualified physicians oriented to the practice of medicine at the community level, with an emphasis on primary care (family medicine, internal medicine, pediatrics, and obstetrics-gynecology). NEOUCOM strives to improve the quality of health care in northeast Ohio. All graduates, regardless of specialty, are provided with a strong background in community and public health.

## Requirements for Entrance

Students are selected for the BS/MD program during their senior year of high school. During high school, applicants should pursue a college preparatory curriculum, including 4 years of math and science; and take either the ACT or SAT; and be citizens or permanent residents of the U.S. Strong preference given to in-state applicants.

## Selection Factors

Factors considered in admission include standardized test scores, high school overall and science/math GPAs, extracurricular involvement, medical exposure, coursework, and interview outcome. This past year, the mean high school unweighted GPA of matriculants was 3.87; average ACT test score was 31; average SAT was 1330 (verbal and math only). An interview is required and is offered by invitation only.

## Curriculum

Students accepted into the combined B.S./M.D. program pursue the baccalaureate degree at The University of Akron, Kent State University, or Youngstown State University. The accelerated B.S./M.D. program may be completed in six or seven years. The M.D. degree is granted by NEOUCOM. The integrated curriculum is offered in five steps during the four years of medical school. The four-year longitudinal curriculum includes the biomedical, behavioral, social, community and population health, clinical sciences, and humanities.

**Step 1:** Curriculum focuses on professionalism, doctor-patient relationships, clinical skills, human anatomy, biochemistry, molecular pathology, and genetics.

**Step 2:** Curriculum establishes physiological concepts in the body while introducing the medical impact of pathologies; includes anatomy, physiology, and chemistry of the nervous system; and integrates the microbiology, immunology, and pharmacology of infectious diseases.

**Step 3:** Curriculum is centered on organ systems pathophysiology.

**Step 4:** Curriculum is core clinical clerkships in family medicine, internal medicine, obstetrics/gynecology, pediatrics, psychiatry, and surgery, and a four-week exploratory experience. Step 5: Curriculum is clinical electives and Clinical Epilogue and Capstone, which focus on professionalism and social science disciplines, and provides vital skills needed as residents.

## Expenses

| | Resident Tuition and Fees | Non-resident Tuition and Fees |
|---|---|---|
| Undergraduate | varies | varies |
| U.S. Medical School | $31,483 | $60,955 |

## Financial Aid

Financial aid at the B.S. phase of the program is administered by the undergraduate universities. During medical school, students apply for aid by completing the FAFSA, the NEOUCOM financial aid application, and submitting copies of federal tax returns. A limited number of need-based grants are available, as well as other limited scholarship funds for disadvantaged students and students from groups underrepresented in medicine. Federal educational loans are a major part of the aid program. About 80 percent of enrolled students receive some form of financial aid. Financial need is not a factor in admission considerations.

---

### Application and Acceptance Policies

**Filing of application—**
**Earliest date:** August 1, 2011
**Latest date:** December 15, 2011

**Application fee:** $195
**Fee waiver available:** Yes

**Acceptance notice —**
**Earliest date:** December 18, 2012
**Latest date:** May 19, 2012

**Applicant's response to acceptance offer—**
**Maximum time:** May 1, 2012

**Deposit to hold place in class:** No
**Deposit — Resident:** n/a
**Deposit refundable:** n/a     **Refundable by:** n/a

**Starting date:** June 1, 2012

### Information on 2010–2011 Entering Class

| Number of | In-State | Out-of-State | Total |
|---|---|---|---|
| Applicants | 307 | 237 | 544 |
| Applicants Interviewed | 201 | 25 | 226 |
| New Entrants | 98 | 7 | 105 |
| **Total number of students enrolled in program: 241** | | | |

# University of Cincinnati College of Medicine
Cincinnati, Ohio

**Address inquiries to:** Nikki Bibler, M.Ed., Director, Student Affairs & Recruitment Programs
University of Cincinnati College of Medicine,
231 Albert Sabin Way, P.O. Box 670552, Cincinnati Ohio  45267-0552

**T**  513 558 5581  **F**  513 558 6259 • www.med.uc.edu/hs2md • hs2md@uc.edu

## Purpose
The University of Cincinnati College of Medicine's Connections Dual Admissions Program accepts high school seniors into our undergraduate college and into the College of Medicine. Once accepted into this special program, students will receive an outstanding education while preparing for medical school and developing the qualities and characteristics to become excellent physicians.

## Requirements for Entrance
Students are selected in their senior year of high school. Both residents and non-residents of Ohio are eligible to apply. Priority will be given to Ohio residents. Students must achieve a minimum composite ACT score of 29 or a minimum composite SAT score of 1300 in order to be considered for admissions.

## Selection Factors
In making admissions decisions, the College of Medicine works in conjunction with the University of Cincinnati undergraduate institution to review an applicant's academic record, standardized test performance, examples of leadership, interpersonal skills, and interest in and motivation for medicine. Mature and independent thinking students who have good decision-making and coping skills are very desirable. Only students who have applied to and been accepted by the undergraduate college will be considered for the Connections Dual Admissions Program. Thus, students are encouraged to apply first to the undergraduate institution and then complete the Connections Dual Admissions Application.

## Curriculum
The course of study consists of four years at the undergraduate college, followed by four years in the College of Medicine. Connections Dual Admissions Program students are required to satisfactorily fulfill graduation requirements at the undergraduate college. Students must earn a 3.4 cumulative GPA and a 3.45 BCPM GPA by the beginning of their final undergraduate year. At this time, they must also earn a composite score of 27 on the MCAT, with no less than a 9 in Biological Sciences and no less than an 8 in Verbal Reasoning or Physical Sciences. The student must pass Steps 1 and 2 of the USMLE in order to graduate from the College of Medicine. The USMLE Step 1 is administered at the completion of Year 2.

## Expenses

| | Resident Tuition and Fees | Non-resident Tuition and Fees |
| --- | --- | --- |
| Undergraduate | $13,420 | $32,784 |
| U.S. Medical School | $30,855 | $47,406 |

## Financial Aid
Opportunities for Financial Aid are made available by the University of Cincinnati undergraduate college.

---

### Application and Acceptance Policies

**Filing of application—**
**Earliest date:** October 1, 2011
**Latest date:** December 1, 2011

**Application fee:** $25    **Fee waiver available:** Yes

**Acceptance notice —**
**Earliest date:** April 1, 2012
**Latest date:** May 1, 2012

**Applicant's response to acceptance offer—**
**Maximum time:** May 1, 2012

**Deposit to hold place in class:** No
**Deposit — Resident:** n/a
**Deposit refundable:** n/a    **Refundable by:** n/a

**Starting date:** September 2012

### Information on 2010–2011 Entering Class

| Number of | In-State | Out-of-State | Total |
| --- | --- | --- | --- |
| Applicants | 87 | 75 | 162 |
| Applicants Interviewed | 15 | 7 | 22 |
| New Entrants | 8 | 2 | 10 |
| **Total number of students enrolled in program: 68** | | | |

# Drexel University and Drexel University College of Medicine
Philadelphia, Pennsylvania

**PA**

**Address inquiries to:**   Matthew Biester, Assistant Director
Drexel University, 3141 Chestnut Street, Philadelphia Pennsylvania 19104

**T** 215 895 2400   **F** 215 895 5939   •   http://www.drexel.edu/undergrad/apply/freshmen-instructions/bs-md/
enroll@drexel.edu

## Purpose
This combined-degree program provides outstanding high school seniors, who are highly motivated toward the medical profession, an opportunity to combine a strong liberal arts undergraduate program in a highly technological environment with a medical education in seven years.

## Requirements for Entrance
Students are selected for this program during their senior year of high school. Both residents and non-residents of Pennsylvania are eligible to apply. Students must be U.S citizen or Permanent Residents and graduate from a U.S. high school. Prior to graduating from high school, applicants are required to complete one semester of biology, one semester of chemistry, one semester of physics, four years of English, and four years of mathematics. They must take either the SAT or the ACT Assessment.

## Selection Factors
The academic factors taken into consideration for admission into the combined-degree program include SAT/ACT scores, high school GPA, and AP and honors courses. The average high school GPA for the 2009-2010 entering class was 3.9, with a mean score of 1483 on the Math and Critical Reasoning sections of the SAT and a 34 Composite on the ACT. Medically related volunteer activities, leadership qualities, and community service are among the personal attributes sought in applicants. An interview at the college of medicine is also required. Once admitted into the program, students are expected to maintain an overall GPA of 3.5 in undergraduate studies; complete all prerequisite courses; and receive no grade less than a C in any course. Additionally, applicants must receive, in a single examination, a minimum MCAT® score of "9" or better in the verbal section and "10's" or better in the physical or biological science section, or a total minimum score of 31 (with no individual subsection score less than an 8), and a letter score of "P" or higher in the MCAT® written section. Students apply through AMCAS® in the second year. The MCAT® is a factor in admittance and promotion to the medical school phase of the program.

## Curriculum
This seven-year program leads to a baccalaureate degree awarded by Drexel University and to the M.D. degree granted by the Drexel University College of Medicine. The most frequent major is biology, followed by chemistry. Students may also choose from a variety of humanities majors. During the first three years of the undergraduate phase, students spend 100 percent of their time in coursework related to the bachelor's degree, which includes 3 semester hours of natural and physical science.

## Expenses

|  | Resident Tuition and Fees | Non-resident Tuition and Fees |
|---|---|---|
| Undergraduate | $40,130 | $40,130 |
| U.S. Medical School | $46,985 | $46,985 |

## Financial Aid
All Students are automatically considered for academic scholarships when applying for admission. Students should complete the FAFSA form by March 1st to be considered for need based financial aid.

### Application and Acceptance Policies

**Filing of application—**
**Earliest date:** Rolling
**Latest date:** December 1, 2011

**Application fee:** $75     **Fee waiver available:** No

**Acceptance notice —**
**Earliest date:** March 31, 2012
**Latest date:** April 15, 2012

**Applicant's response to acceptance offer—**
**Maximum time:** May 1, 2012

**Deposit to hold place in class:** Yes
**Deposit — Resident:** $300
**Deposit refundable:** No     **Refundable by:** n/a

**Starting date:** September 19, 2012

### Information on 2010–2011 Entering Class

| Number of | In-State | Out-of-State | Total |
|---|---|---|---|
| Applicants | 534 | 2001 | 2535 |
| Applicants Interviewed | 20 | 139 | 159 |
| New Entrants | 6 | 24 | 30 |
| **Total number of students enrolled in program:** 75 | | | |

# Lehigh University and Drexel University College of Medicine

Bethlehem, Pennsylvania

**PA**

**Address inquiries to:**  Nneka M. Fritz, Assistant Director
Office of Admissions, Lehigh University, 27 Memorial Drive West, Bethlehem, Pennsylvania  18105

**T** 610 758 3100  **F**  610 758 4361  •  http://cas.lehigh.edu/casweb/content/default.aspx?pageid=129

## Purpose

This program is designed to give gifted high school students, who are highly motivated for a career in medicine, the opportunity to combine a liberal arts program with a medical education. The baccalaureate degree is awarded after Year 4 (the first year of medical school).

## Requirements for Entrance

Applicants are expected to take the SAT Reasoning Test. SAT Subject tests are highly recommended in Mathematics Level 1 or Mathematics Level 2 and Chemistry. Applicants must be U.S. citizens or permanent residents.

## Selection Factors

Generally, a combined SAT score of 1360 (or minimum 31 ACT), a class rank in the top 5 percent of the high school class, and a strong motivation for science are necessary for entrance into this program. Most recent matriculants had a high school GPA of 3.7, an SAT Verbal score of 720, and an SAT Mathematics score of 780. Maturity, stability, scholarship, flexibility, independence, and service to others are personal characteristics sought among applicants. An interview is required. Once admitted to the program, students are expected to maintain an overall grade point average of 3.5 or better and a science and math GPA of 3.5 or better with no grade less than a "C" in any courses. All program requirements must be completed at Lehigh University. Candidates are required to take the MCAT®. Scores of either 9 or better on the verbal section of the MCAT® and 10 or better on the science sections or a total minimum score of 31 (with no individual section score less than 8) are required.

## Curriculum

This program, seven years in duration, allows students to obtain a bachelor's degree from Lehigh University and the M.D. degree from Drexel University College of Medicine. The Lehigh bachelor's degree is awarded after completion of the first year of study at Drexel. Students have the flexibility to pursue additional coursework or study abroad during the undergraduate portion of the program. However, specific course requirements for the degree include two semesters of English, three semesters of mathematics, eight semesters of natural and physical sciences, three semesters each of humanities and social sciences, a first year seminar, a writing intensive, and four elective courses. All students must pass USMLE Steps 1 and 2 in order to graduate from the medical school.

## Expenses

| | Resident Tuition and Fees | Non-resident Tuition and Fees |
|---|---|---|
| Undergraduate | $50,300 | $50,300 |
| U.S. Medical School | $46,985 | $46,985 |

## Financial Aid

Institutional scholarships and loans are available, as well as federal loan programs and armed services scholarships. More financial aid information can be obtained from the Financial Aid Office, Lehigh University, 218 W. Packer Avenue, Bethlehem, Pennsylvania 18015.

### Application and Acceptance Policies

**Filing of application—**
**Earliest date:** September 1, 2011
**Latest date:** November 15, 2011

**Application fee:** $70   **Fee waiver available:** No

**Acceptance notice —**
**Earliest date:** April 1, 2012
**Latest date:** n/a

**Applicant's response to acceptance offer—**
**Maximum time:** May 1, 2012

**Deposit to hold place in class:** Yes
**Deposit:** $500
**Deposit refundable:** No   **Refundable by:** n/a

**Starting date:** August 2012

### Information on 2010–2011 Entering Class

| Number of | In-State | Out-of-State | Total |
|---|---|---|---|
| Applicants | 15 | 150 | 165 |
| Applicants Interviewed | 4 | 24 | 28 |
| New Entrants | 0 | 1 | 1 |
| **Total number of students enrolled in program:** 8 | | | |

# Pennsylvania State University and Jefferson Medical College

University Park, Pennsylvania

**Address inquiries to:** Director of Admissions, Undergraduate Admissions Office
Pennsylvania State University, 201 Shields Building, University Park, Pennsylvania 16802

**T** 814 865 5471  **F** 814 863 7590 • www.science.psu.edu/premedmed

## Purpose

This accelerated, B.S.-M.D. premedical-medical program, which began in 1963 and has graduated over 1000 students, is a cooperative effort between Pennsylvania State University, University Park, and Jefferson Medical College of Thomas Jefferson University in Philadelphia. Accepted students can select either a six- or seven-year schedule, which gives them either two years (with summers) or three years at Penn State before proceeding to four years at Jefferson Medical College. All students selecting the six-year option must begin their studies at the University Park campus in the summer session. Students selecting the seven-year option begin their studies at the University Park campus in the fall semester.

## Requirements for Entrance

Students are selected for this program only during the senior year of high school. Both residents and non-residents of Pennsylvania are considered for admission, but preference is given to qualified applicants from Pennsylvania. Applicants are expected to have completed the following courses by the time they graduate from high school: four units of English, 1 ½ units of algebra, one unit of plane geometry, one-half unit of trigonometry, three units of science, and five units of social studies, humanities, and/or the arts.

## Selection Factors

To be considered for this program, applicants must be in the top ten percent of their high school class and offer a minimum combined score of 2100 on the SAT I or ACT score of 32. In the 2010–2011 entering class, the average combined score on the SAT was 2250. Motivation, compassion, integrity, dedication, and performance in nonacademic areas are among the personal characteristics sought in applicants. An interview is required. Special attention is given to the student's progress during each semester while at Pennsylvania State University. Students must take a full course load and maintain a minimum GPA of 3.5 in both science and non-science courses. For subsequent admission to Jefferson Medical College, students in this combined-degree program must achieve an average score of 9 (average) or better on each section of the MCAT® prior plus a composite score of at least 30 prior to matriculation in medical school.

## Curriculum

This six-year program leads to a baccalaureate degree granted by Pennsylvania State University and to the M.D. degree awarded by Jefferson Medical College. Students begin this program in June immediately after high school graduation. They spend two full years on the Pennsylvania State, University Park, campus; they then proceed to Jefferson Medical College for the regular four-year curriculum. The B.S. degree from Pennsylvania State University is awarded after successful completion of the second year at Jefferson Medical College, and the M.D. degree is awarded after successful completion of the senior year at Jefferson Medical College. Students in the seven-year schedule spend three years at Pennsylvania State, but do not attend summer sessions. Their B.S. degree is awarded after Year 1 at Jefferson Medical College.

## Expenses

| | Resident Tuition and Fees | Non-resident Tuition and Fees |
|---|---|---|
| Undergraduate | $15,250 | $27,114 |
| U.S. Medical School | $46,628 | $46,628 |

## Financial Aid

At Penn State, scholarships, loans and grants are the sources of financial assistance available. For more information, write the Office of Financial Aid, Pennsylvania State University, University Park, Pennsylvania 16802; or call (814) 865-5471. At Jefferson Medical College, financial aid application materials are mailed in January of the year of medical school matriculation. Students are encouraged to contact the University Office of Student Financial Aid to discuss all financial aid matters.

## Application and Acceptance Policies

**Filing of application—**
**Earliest date:** September 1, 2011
**Latest date:** Novemer 30, 2011

**Application fee:** $50    **Fee waiver available:** Yes

**Acceptance notice —**
**Earliest date:** March 15, 2012   **Latest date:** March 30, 2012

**Applicant's response to acceptance offer—**
**Maximum time:** May 1, 2012

**Deposit to hold place in class:** Yes
**Deposit — Resident:** $300
**Deposit refundable:** No    **Refundable by:** n/a

**Starting date:** Late June 2012

### Information on 2010–2011 Entering Class

| Number of | In-State | Out-of-State | Total |
|---|---|---|---|
| Applicants | 69 | 389 | 458 |
| Applicants Interviewed | 7 | 83 | 90 |
| New Entrants | 5 | 19 | 24 |
| **Total number of students enrolled in program: 52** | | | |

# Temple University School of Medicine
Philadelphia, Pennsylvania

**Address inquiries to:**   Office of Admissions, Temple University School of Medicine, 3500 North Broad Street, Suite 124, Philadelphia Pennsylvania 19140

**T** 215 707 3656   **F** 215 707 6932  •  www.temple.edu/medicine/admissions/special_admissions.htm
medadmissions@temple.edu

## Purpose
The Medical Scholars Program, in conjunction with three undergraduate institutions in Pennsylvania, provides an opportunity for outstanding high school seniors to gain a provisional acceptance to Temple University School of Medicine at the same time that they are accepted into their undergraduate school.

## Requirements for Entrance
Students are selected for this program during their senior year of high school. Both residents and non-residents of Pennsylvania are eligible to apply. Although there are no specific high school course requirements, applicants are expected to have a substantial background in science and mathematics. AP coursework is viewed favorably, and students are required to take the SAT or ACT.

## Selection Factors
In conjunction with the School of Medicine, each undergraduate institution considers an applicant's GPA, standardized test performance, extracurricular activities (including leadership roles), and interpersonal skills in making admission decisions. Substantial maturity and strong motivation are among the important personal qualities considered by the Admissions Committee. The minimum SAT score required is 1350 in the combined Critical Reading and Mathematics sections, with no individual section less than 600 (including the Writing section). The minimum composite ACT score required is 31. Students are expected to be in the top one to five percent of their high school graduating class. Academic ability should be demonstrated across a wide variety of courses, including AP science coursework. Selected applicants are required to interview with a representative of the undergraduate institution and a medical school admissions officer. Contact the partnering undergraduate institutions directly to obtain additional information about the Medical Scholars Program: Duquesne University, (412) 396-6335; Washington and Jefferson College, *tklitz@washjeff. edu*; and Widener University, (610) 499-4030.

## Curriculum
Students in this combined-degree program will complete their baccalaureate degree at one of the three partnering universities listed above. The medical degree is granted by Temple University School of Medicine. Students may choose to be a science major, but are free to explore all available options as long as they complete the premedical science requirements. Matriculation to Temple University School of Medicine is conditional upon successful completion of all requirements

as outlined by each institution's agreement. Curricula are unique at each undergraduate institution. All students are required to complete the M.D. program without deviation from the standard curriculum, including passing USMLE Steps 1, 2CS (Clinical Skills), and 2CK (Clinical Knowledge).

## Expenses

| | Resident Tuition and Fees | Non-resident Tuition and Fees |
|---|---|---|
| Undergraduate | Varies | Varies |
| U.S. Medical School | $44,368 | $54,182 |

## Financial Aid
For information about financial aid, contact the Financial Aid Office of the specific partnering undergraduate institution listed above. Financial aid available to medical students includes grants, scholarships, and student loans. For additional information, visit the School of Medicine Web site at: *www.temple.edu/sfs/med/.*

---

### Application and Acceptance Policies

**Filing of application—**
**Earliest date:** Varies by program
**Latest date:** n/a

**Application fee:** No   **Fee waiver available:** n/a

**Acceptance notice —**
**Earliest date:** March 15, 2012
**Latest date:** April 15, 2012

**Applicant's response to acceptance offer—**
**Maximum time:** May 1, 2012

**Deposit to hold place in class:** No
**Deposit — Resident:** n/a
**Deposit refundable:** n/a
**Refundable by:** Deposit determined by undergraduate institution

**Starting date:** Varies by undergraduate program

### Information on 2010–2011 Entering Class

| Number of | In-State | Out-of-State | Total |
|---|---|---|---|
| Applicants | n/a | n/a | 23 |
| Applicants Interviewed | n/a | n/a | 15 |
| New Entrants | n/a | n/a | 7 |
| **Total number of students enrolled in program: 14** | | | |

# Villanova University and
# Drexel University College of Medicine
Villanova, Pennsylvania

**Address inquiries to:**   John D. Friede, Ph.D., Health Professions Advisor, Office of University Admission
Villanova University, 800 Lancaster Avenue, Villanova, Pennsylvania  19085

**T** 610 519 4833   **F** 610 519 8042  •  www.villanova.edu/artsci/healthprofessions/affiliates/medicine/index.htm
admission@villanova.edu

## Purpose
This combined-degree program provides outstanding high school seniors, who are highly motivated toward the medical profession, an opportunity to combine a strong liberal arts undergraduate program with a medical education in seven years.

## Requirements for Entrance
Students are selected for this program during the senior year of high school. Both residents and non-residents of Pennsylvania are eligible to apply. Applicants must take either the SAT I or ACT.

## Selection Factors
The academic factors taken into consideration for admission into the combined-degree program include: SAT scores, high school GPA and class rank, and letters of recommendation. The average high school GPA for the 2009–2010 entering class was 3.85, unweighted. Extracurricular activities and community service are among the personal attributes sought in applicants; exposure to medicine is expected. An interview is required. Once admitted into the program, students are expected to maintain an overall GPA of 3.50 and a science GPA of 3.50, and they are required to achieve scores of either a 9 on the Verbal Reasoning and a 10 on the Physical Sciences and Biological Sciences sections or a combined score of 31 or better (with no score less than 8 on any section of the MCAT). A P or greater on the Writing Sample is required.

## Curriculum
Students are required to complete a baccalaureate degree within the first year of medical school. The most frequent major is biology, followed by comprehensive science. This seven-year program leads to a baccalaureate degree awarded by Villanova University and to the M.D. degree granted by the Drexel University College of Medicine. During the undergraduate phase of the program, students will spend 100 percent of their time in coursework related to the bachelor's degree, which includes 41 semester hours of natural and physical science, six semester hours of mathematics, and 51 semester hours of humanities.

## Expenses

| | Resident Tuition and Fees | Non-resident Tuition and Fees |
| --- | --- | --- |
| Undergraduate | $39,900 | $39,900 |
| U.S. Medical School | $46,985 | $46,985 |

## Financial Aid
For information on financial aid, visit *www.villanova.edu/enroll/finaid* and *http://webcampus.drexelmed.edu/admissions/financialaid.asp.*

### Application and Acceptance Policies

**Filing of application—**
**Earliest date:** September 1, 2011
**Latest date:** November 1, 2011

**Application fee:** $75    **Fee waiver available:** Yes

**Acceptance notice —**
**Earliest date:** March 15, 2012
**Latest date:** March 30, 2012

**Applicant's response to acceptance offer—**
**Maximum time:** May 1, 2012

**Deposit to hold place in class:** Yes
**Deposit — Resident:** $700
**Deposit refundable:** No     **Refundable by:** n/a

**Starting date:** August 27, 2012

### Information on 2010–2011 Entering Class

| Number of | In-State | Out-of-State | Total |
| --- | --- | --- | --- |
| Applicants | 52 | 252 | 304 |
| Applicants Interviewed | 6 | 51 | 57 |
| New Entrants | 1 | 2 | 3 |

**Total number of students enrolled in program:** 18

# SUNY-Upstate Medical University and Wilkes University

Wilkes-Barre, Pennsylvania

**PA**

**Address inquiries to:** Eileen Sharp, Coordinator for Health Science Professional Programs
Wilkes University, 84 West South Street, Wilkes-Barre Pennsylvania 18766

**T** 570 408 4823 **F** 570 408 7812 • www.wilkes.edu/pages/102.asp • eileen.sharp@wilkes.edu

## Purpose

This cooperative program is motivated by the need for physicians interested in serving in rural and semi-rural health care delivery systems, as well as the interest of each institution in attracting students of superior ability and accomplishment.

## Requirements for Entrance

Students apply to the program in their senior year of high school; applicants must be New York State residents. Candidates for admission must have completed the following high school course requirements: four years each of mathematics, English, science, and social science. Applicants must take the ACT or SAT examination.

## Selection Factors

The following factors are taken into consideration in assessing the applicant for admission: grades, rank in class, SAT (ACT) scores, and extracurricular activities. Selected applicants are invited for a required interview.

## Curriculum

This eight-year program leads to a baccalaureate degree awarded by Wilkes University and to the M.D. degree granted by SUNY Upstate Medical University. The most frequent major for the baccalaureate degree is biology, followed by chemistry and biochemistry. The M.D. portion of the curriculum does not depart from the "traditional" design. Upstate accepts a special responsibility to provide physicians to New York's underserved rural communities. A student from a rural setting or one subsequently trained there is more likely to practice there. This B.S.-M.D. program attracts students from rural areas who are not likely to otherwise find their way to medical school. Upstate also provides many special opportunities during medical school (Rural Medicine Program, Clinical Campus) to train students in community and rural settings. Students in this program will need to take the MCATs and receive a score of 30 or greater to secure admission to the medical school. The USMLE Step 1 is required; it must be passed, prior to beginning clinical rotations, to be promoted and in order to graduate. Students must record a score on USMLE Step 2, but passing USMLE Step 2 is not a factor in graduation from the medical school.

## Expenses

| | Resident Tuition and Fees | Non-resident Tuition and Fees |
|---|---|---|
| Undergraduate | $27,178 | $27,178 |
| U.S. Medical School | $26,190 | $50,110 |

## Financial Aid

The sources of available financial aid are grants, scholarships, and student loans. For more information about financial aid, visit *http://www.wilkes.edu/pages/573.asp*, or contact the Financial Aid Office at SUNY Upstate Medical University by emailing *FinAid@upstate.edu*.

### Application and Acceptance Policies

**Filing of application—**
**Earliest date:** August 1, 2011
**Latest date:** November 15, 2011

**Application fee:** Yes, $40    **Fee waiver available:** Yes

**Acceptance notice —**
**Earliest date:** Within two weeks of medical school interview
**Latest date:** Two weeks after medical school interview

**Applicant's response to acceptance offer—**
**Maximum time:** Two weeks from receiving acceptance offer

**Deposit to hold place in class:** Yes
**Deposit — Resident:** $100
**Deposit refundable:** Yes
**Refundable by:** May 15th of the year of entry

**Starting date:** The fall following graduation from Wilkes

### Information on 2010–2011 Entering Class

| Number of | In-State | Out-of-State | Total |
|---|---|---|---|
| Applicants | 6 | n/a | 6 |
| Applicants Interviewed | 4 | n/a | 4 |
| New Entrants | 1 | n/a | 1 |
| **Total number of students enrolled in program: 5** | | | |

# Brown Medical School

Providence, Rhode Island

**Address inquiries to:** College Admission Office, Brown University
Box 1876, Providence Rhode Island   02912

**T** 401 863 2378 • http://med.brown.edu/plme • Admissions@Brown.edu

## Purpose

The Program in Liberal Medical Education (PLME) seeks to graduate physicians who are broadly and liberally educated and who will view medicine as a socially responsible human service profession. Designed as an eight-year program, the PLME combines liberal arts and professional education. Great flexibility is built into the program. Working with PLME advising deans who are physicians, each student develops an individualized educational plan consistent with his or her particular interests. The PLME is a primary route of admission to The Warren Alpert Medical School.

## Requirements for Entrance

Students are selected for the PLME in the senior year of high school. The Brown Admission Office recommends that applicants should have completed the following courses: four years of English, with significant emphasis on writing; three years of college preparatory mathematics; three years of a foreign language; two years of laboratory science above the freshman level; two years of history, including American history; at least one year of coursework in the arts; and at least one year of elective academic subjects. Prospective science or engineering majors should have taken physics, chemistry, and advanced mathematics. Applicants must take the SAT Reasoning Test and any two SAT Subject Tests (except for the SAT II Writing Test), or the ACT. (PLME applicants are encouraged to include a science SAT Subject Test.)

## Selection Factors

Students are selected on the basis of scholastic accomplishment and promise, intellectual curiosity, emotional maturity, character, motivation, sensitivity, caring, and particularly the degree to which they seem adapted to the special features of the program. In the 2010-2011 entering class, the average SAT Reasoning Test scores were 729 Critical Reading, 743 Math, and 743 Writing. Of the students whose schools rank, 88% were in the top five percent of their high school class. Although an interview is not "required," it is highly encouraged that applicants take advantage of the Brown Alumni Schools Committee (BASC) alumni interview program.

## Curriculum

The PLME leads to a baccalaureate degree and to the M.D. degree granted by The Warren Alpert Medical School. Students must complete a baccalaureate degree in the field of their choice. Each student's educational plan is highly individualized. The PLME combines the flexibility and opportunities of an undergraduate education at Brown University with effective preparation for participation in an equally innovative medical education program.

## Expenses

| | Resident Tuition and Fees | Non-resident Tuition and Fees |
|---|---|---|
| Undergraduate | $51,360 | $41,436 |
| U.S. Medical School | $43,838 | $43,838 |

## Financial Aid

For undergraduates in the first four years of the PLME, financial aid is awarded by the Financial Aid Office at Brown University as a package. Students are awarded monies via scholarships, work-study, and loans. During the last four years of the PLME, financial aid is administered by The Warren Alpert Medical School Office of Financial Aid. Both loans and scholarships are available, although loans are the most common form of assistance.

## Application and Acceptance Policies

**Filing of application—**
**Earliest date:** November 1, 2011
**Latest date:** January 1, 2012

**Application fee:** $75    **Fee waiver available:** Yes

**Acceptance notice —**
**Earliest date:** December 15, 2011
**Latest date:** Early April 2012

**Applicant's response to acceptance offer—**
**Maximum time:** May 1, 2012

**Deposit to hold place in class:** No
**Deposit — Resident:** n/a
**Deposit refundable:** n/a    **Refundable by:** n/a

**Starting date:** September 2012

### Information on 2010–2011 Entering Class

| Number of | In-State | Out-of-State | Total |
|---|---|---|---|
| Applicants | 32 | 1940 | 1972 |
| Applicants Interviewed | 0 | 0 | 0 |
| New Entrants | 2 | 55 | 57 |
| **Total number of students enrolled in program:** 210 | | | |

# Fisk University and Meharry Medical College

Nashville, Tennessee

**Address inquiries to:**   Keith Chandler,  Dean of Admissions
Office of Admissions, 1000 17th Avenue North, Nashville Tennessee   37208

**T**  615 329 8666   **F**  615 329 8774  •  www.mmc.edu  •  Kchandler@fisk.edu

## Purpose

The Joint Program in Biomedical Sciences is designed to address America's need to train bright young students from groups underrepresented in medicine who are dedicated to finding solutions to biomedical problems through research and who will be future health care providers.

## Requirements for Entrance

Students are selected early in their second semester of undergraduate coursework on the Fisk University campus. There are no specific high school course requirements. Applicants must have competitive scores on the ACT and/or the SAT. They must have completed at least one semester at Fisk University and have a GPA compatible with success in this accelerated program (See Selection criteria, below). Participants must submit an application with a personal statement which details their career goals and letters of recommendation from two college science or mathematics professors to the Office of Admissions.

## Selection Factors

The courses taken and grades earned at Fisk University, plus ACT and/or SAT scores, are considerations for eligibility for this program. Applicants must rank in the top 20 percent of their high school class. Students must maintain an undergraduate GPA of 3.50 in Fisk coursework. Students must take the MCAT® prior to admission and earn a minimum score of 24.

## Curriculum

The Joint Program in Biomedical Sciences, seven years in duration, allows students to obtain a baccalaureate degree from Fisk University and the M.D. degree from Meharry Medical College. Course requirements for the baccalaureate degree include 8 semesters of natural and physical sciences and 12 semesters each in the humanities and social sciences. Students are required to spend two summers in a structured academic enrichment program. Students must take Steps 1 and 2 of the USMLE during the medical school portion of the program. Passing these examinations is a factor in promotion and graduation from medical school. The most frequent major chosen by students is biology, followed by chemistry.

## Expenses

| | Resident Tuition and Fees | Non-resident Tuition and Fees |
|---|---|---|
| Undergraduate | $25,170 | $25,170 |
| U.S. Medical School | $38,894 | $38,894 |

## Financial Aid

Applicants and students can apply for institutional scholarships and grants, U.S. Department of Education Title IV Federal Student Aid (work-study and loans), U.S. Department of Health and Human Services Student Aid Programs (loans and scholarships), Southern Regional Education Board Grants, and Tennessee Black Conditional Grants. Meharry's Office of Student Financial Aid makes available most federal, regional, and state financial aid applications and brochures on numerous funding opportunities. Fisk University and local public libraries have publications on most sources of student financial aid.

---

### Application and Acceptance Policies

**Filing of application—**
**Earliest date:** September 15, 2011
**Latest date:** February 1, 2012

**Application fee:** n/a    **Fee waiver available:** n/a

**Acceptance notice —**
**Earliest date:** February 15, 2012
**Latest date:** March 15, 2012

**Applicant's response to acceptance offer—**
**Maximum time:** One week

**Deposit to hold place in class:** No
**Deposit — Resident:** n/a
**Deposit refundable:** n/a    **Refundable by:** n/a

**Starting date:** Retroactive second semester, undergraduate year one

### Information on 2010–2011 Entering Class

| Number of | In-State | Out-of-State | Total |
|---|---|---|---|
| Applications | 3 | 3 | 6 |
| Applicants Interviewed | 2 | 2 | 4 |
| New Entrants | 1 | 1 | 2 |
| **Total number of students enrolled in program:** 4 | | | |

# Rice University and Baylor College of Medicine
Houston, Texas

**Address inquiries to:** Rice University Office of Admissions – MS-17
P.O. Box 1892, Houston Texas 77251-1892

**T** 713 348 7423    **F** 713 348 5323  •  www.bcm.edu/medschool/baccmd.htm  •  admi@rice.edu

## Purpose
To promote the education of future physicians who are scientifically competent, compassionate, and socially conscious in order to apply insight from the extensive study of liberal arts and other disciplines to the study of modern medical science.

## Requirements for Entrance
Students are selected for this program during their senior year of high school. Both residents and non-residents of Texas are considered for admission. Applicants are expected to have had a varied and rigorous high school program with high academic achievement. They must take the SAT Reasoning Test or ACT, plus three SAT Subject tests.

## Selection Factors
The high school academic record, standardized test scores, course selection, extracurricular activities, and letters of recommendation are some of the factors taken into account in offering admission to an applicant. In the most recent entering class, students averaged above the top five percent in their high school class.

## Curriculum
This is not an accelerated program; all students are expected to complete four years of undergraduate education and four years of medical school. Students earn a baccalaureate degree from Rice University, and are awarded the M.D. degree by Baylor College of Medicine. Minimum course requirements for this program include at least two semesters each in the humanities and social sciences and eight semesters in the natural and physical sciences. The medical part of the curriculum devotes approximately 1 ½ years to the basic sciences with clinical experience, and 2 ½ years to clinical science with some basic science coursework. The MCAT® is not required for promotion or admission to the medical school. Students are required to take Step 1 of the USMLE in their second or third years. They are also required to take Step 2 of the USMLE, but passing these examinations is not a graduation requirement.

## Expenses

|  | Resident Tuition and Fees | Non-resident Tuition and Fees |
|---|---|---|
| Undergraduate | $33,771 | $33,771 |
| U.S. Medical School | $15,668 | $28,768 |

## Financial Aid
Sources of financial aid include academic, athletic, and need-based scholarships. Applicants can receive more information from the Rice University Admission Office, M.S. 17, 6100 Main Street, Houston, Texas 77035.

## Application and Acceptance Policies

**Filing of application—**
**Earliest date:** August 1, 2011
**Latest date:** December 1, 2011

**Application fee:** $70
**Fee waiver available:** Yes

**Acceptance notice —**
**Earliest date:** n/a
**Latest date:** Mid–April 2012

**Applicant's response to acceptance offer—**
**Maximum time:** May 1, 2012

**Deposit to hold place in class:** Yes
**Deposit — Resident:** $400
**Deposit refundable:** Yes      **Refundable by:** May 1, 2012

**Starting date:** August 2012

### Information on 2010–2011 Entering Class

| Number of | In-State | Out-of-State | Total |
|---|---|---|---|
| Applicants | 145 | 213 | 358 |
| Applicants Interviewed | 14 | 13 | 27 |
| New Entrants | 4 | 3 | 7 |
| **Total number of students enrolled in program:** 50 | | | |

# University of Texas School of Medicine at San Antonio

San Antonio, Texas

**Address inquiries to:** Belinda Gonzalez, Director of Admissions and Special Programs
University of Texas School of Medicine at San Antonio
7703 Floyd Curl Drive, Mail Code 7790, San Antonio, Texas 78229

**T** 210 567 6080 **F** 210 567 6962 • http://som.uthscsa.edu/admissions/index.asp
medadmissions@uthscsa.edu

## Purpose

In partnership with the University of Texas-Pan American this program offers the opportunity to achieve conditional acceptance to medical school as early as the junior year at UT Pan American. Participants are provided mentorship by medical school faculty and educational enrichment and clinical experiences in the Summer Premedical Academy. Frequent meetings with medical school faculty during the year provide encouragement and support toward matriculation into medical school. Acceptance to medical school after three years of undergraduate school is possible.

## Requirements for Entrance

Students are selected during their senior year of high school. The program is only open to residents of Texas who are citizens or permanent residents of the United States. While there are no specific high school course requirements, applicants are encouraged to complete courses in chemistry and biology and are required to take the SAT and/or ACT. Concurrent or AP coursework is encouraged.

## Selection Factors

Academic factors considered in selecting applicants include SAT/ACT scores and strength in science and mathematics coursework. In addition to an impressive academic portfolio, applicants must also demonstrate a sincere interest in medicine and present letters of recommendation from their high school counselors or teachers. An interview by members of the School of Medicine Admissions Committee is also required. Students are admitted to medical school based on a sliding scale of the ratio of MCAT® scores and science GPA, a successful interview with the Admissions Committee as well as a demonstrated continued commitment to study medicine.

## Curriculum

Students must maintain a science and overall GPA of 3.25 or better and are required to complete all medical school prerequisite coursework with a grade of "C" or better. Students also participate in six-week Summer Premedical Academies for which scholarships are provided. During each summer starting after their freshman year, students come to the medical school campus in San Antonio to participate in academic enrichment programs, as well as twice weekly clinical preceptorships. The program is designed to increase the students' academic preparedness for the next year's coursework and for an MCAT® review course during the summer between their junior and senior years. The clinical preceptorships are designed to increase students' awareness of issues in clinical medicine and to develop a clear understanding of performance expectations while in medical school.

## Expenses

| | Resident Tuition and Fees | Non-resident Tuition and Fees |
|---|---|---|
| Undergraduate | $11,898 | $26,361 |
| U.S. Medical School | $15,813 | $28,913 |

## Financial Aid

Financial aid, services and programs are not offered by the School of Medicine to undergraduate program participants.

---

### Application and Acceptance Policies

**Filing of application**
**Earliest date:** December 1, 2011
**Latest date:** February 1, 2012

**Application fee:** No    **Fee waiver available:** n/a

**Acceptance notice —**
**Earliest date:** April 1, 2012
**Latest date:** April 1, 2012

**Applicant's response to acceptance offer—**
**Maximum time:** Two weeks after acceptance

**Deposit to hold place in class:** No
**Deposit — Resident:** n/a
**Deposit refundable:** n/a    **Refundable by:** n/a

**Starting date:** May 20, 2012

### Information on 2010–2011 Entering Class

| Number of | In-State | Out-of-State | Total |
|---|---|---|---|
| Applicants | 24 | n/a | 24 |
| Applicants Interviewed | 14 | n/a | 14 |
| New Entrants | 4 | n/a | 4 |

**Total number of students enrolled in program: 20**

---

# Eastern Virginia Medical School
Norfolk, Virginia

**Address inquiries to:** Office of Admissions, Mail Code 3, Eastern Virginia Medical School
700 W. Olney Road, Norfolk Virginia 23507-1607

**T** 757 446 5812 **F** 757 446 5896 • www.evms.edu/md-programs/md-programs-home.html

## Purpose
Eastern Virginia Medical School currently has combined programs with twelve colleges and universities: Christopher Newport University, The College of William and Mary, Old Dominion University, Hampton University, Norfolk State University, Hampden-Sydney College, Randolph-Macon College, Saint Paul's College, Virginia Military Institute, Virginia State University, Virginia Union University and Virginia Wesleyan College. The purpose of these programs is to enlist outstanding undergraduate students into a track that provides great freedom and choice in the pursuit of a baccalaureate degree.

## Requirements for Entrance
Students are selected during their sophomore year of college. Both residents and non-residents of Virginia are eligible to apply. There are no specific high school course requirements, but students must take the SAT.

## Selection Factors
Applicants will be evaluated on their academic performance during their freshman year of college and the first semester of their sophomore year of college. An emphasis is placed on leadership skills and extra-curricular activities, including medical volunteering. Selected applicants are invited for an interview.

## Curriculum
The eight-year curriculum leads to a baccalaureate degree awarded by Christopher Newport University, Hampden-Sydney College, Hampton University, Norfolk State University, Old Dominion University, Randolph-Macon College, Saint Paul's College, The College of William and Mary, Virginia Military Institute, Virginia State University, Virginia Union University or Virginia Wesleyan College. The M.D. degree is granted by Eastern Virginia Medical School. Course requirements for the baccalaureate degree vary at each undergraduate institution. The most frequent major is biology. This early assurance program does, however, permit the student the opportunity for academic diversity. Students selected who have combined SAT scores greater than 1250 (math and verbal) will not be required to take the MCAT. Step 1 of the USMLE must be taken at the completion of the second year of medical school. Students must pass Steps 1 and 2 of the USMLE to complete the program and receive the M.D. degree.

## Expenses

| | Resident Tuition and Fees | Non-resident Tuition and Fees |
|---|---|---|
| Undergraduate | n/a | n/a |
| U.S. Medical School | $ 29,196 | $ 54,634 |

## Financial Aid
For information about financial aid during the undergraduate phase, contact the Office of Financial Aid at the undergraduate institutions identified. Ten programs are available: Christopher Newport University, Harold Grau, Ph.D. (757) 594-7946; The College of William and Mary, Beverley T. Sher, Ph.D. (757) 221-2852; Old Dominion University, Terri Mathews (757) 683-5201; Hampton University, Michael Druitt (757) 728-6757; Norfolk State University, Alicia McClain, Ph.D. (757) 823-8991; Hampden-Sydney College, H.O. Thurman, Ph.D. (434) 223-6177; Saint Paul's College, Sunday Adesuyi, Ph.D. (434) 848-6484; Randolph-Macon College, James Foster, Ph.D.( 804) 752-3783; Virginia Military Institute, Wade Bell, Ph.D.( 540) 464-7432; Virginia State University, Pamela Leigh-Mack, Ph.D., (804) 524-5285, Virginia Union University, Phillip W. Archer, Ph.D., (804) 257-5692 and Virginia Wesleyan College, Deirdre Gonsalves-Jackson, Ph.D., (757) 455-3265. For information about financial aid during the medical school phase, contact the Office of Financial Aid at Eastern Virginia Medical School at (757) 446-5804.

## Application and Acceptance Policies

**Filing of application—**
**Earliest date:** Varies    **Latest date:** n/a

**Application fee:** $35    **Fee waiver available:** No

**Acceptance notice —**
**Earliest date:** Varies    **Latest date:** Varies

**Applicant's response to acceptance offer—**
**Maximum time:** Varies

**Deposit to hold place in class:** Yes
**Deposit — Resident:** $100
**Deposit refundable:** Yes    **Refundable by:** May 15, 2012

**Starting date:** August 2012

### Information on 2010–2011 Entering Class

| Number of | In-State | Out-of-State | Total |
|---|---|---|---|
| Applicants | 18 | 8 | 26 |
| Applicants Interviewed | 14 | 7 | 21 |
| New Entrants | 12 | 1 | 13 |
| **Total number of students enrolled in program:** n/a | | | |

# Virginia Commonwealth University School of Medicine

Richmond, Virginia

**Address inquiries to:** Dr. Anne L. Chandler, Senior Associate Dean, The Honors College
Virginia Commonwealth University, P.O. Box 843010, Richmond Virginia 23284-3010

**T** 804 828 1803 **F** 804 827 1669 • https://www.pubapps.vcu.edu/honors/guaranteed/medicine/index.aspx
achandle@vcu.edu

## Purpose

The Guaranteed Admission Program of the Honors College offers academically capable, highly focused students an opportunity to pursue diverse, intellectually challenging programs of study. Students who successfully complete the Guaranteed Admission Program will be able to enter the medical school without the pressure of further competition. Close contact with the School of Medicine throughout the undergraduate program aids students in testing their career choice and in preparing for a lifelong commitment to learning in the profession.

## Requirements for Entrance

Students are selected during their senior year of high school, and there are no state residency restrictions. All candidates are considered. The specific minimum high school course requirements are as follows: four units in English; three units in mathematics (to include algebra I and either geometry or algebra II); two units in science (at least one a laboratory science); and three units of history or social sciences or government. Students are strongly encouraged to present at least two units in a modern or ancient foreign language. Also required are standardized test scores on the ACT or SAT. The ACT composite score must be at or above 29. The combined SAT1 score must be at or above 1910 and obtained in a single sitting, with no score below 530. An unweighted GPA of 3.5 (on a 4.0 scale) is also required.

## Selection Factors

Factors considered in offering admission to an applicant include: GPA, letters of reference, test scores, well-rounded and rigorous academic preparation, health care-related experience, and written and oral communication skills. The average GPA for students accepted for the 2010–2011 class was 3.86 (unweighted scale of 4.0), and the average SAT score was 2140. Selected applicants are invited for a required interview.

## Curriculum

Students are required to complete a baccalaureate degree. The most frequent major is biology; the next most frequent major is chemistry. The undergraduate degree is awarded by Virginia Commonwealth University. Specific course requirements vary, depending upon the major. During the medical school program, there is a longitudinal clinical experience (Foundations of Clinical Medicine) in a community primary care practice that meets weekly for both of the first two years. Students are required to take Step 1 of the USMLE at the end of their second year and must earn a minimum score of 188. They must also take USMLE Step 2 and pass with a minimum score of 189 in order to graduate. The doctor of medicine degree is also awarded by Virginia Commonwealth University. It takes eight years to fulfill the requirements for both degrees.

## Expenses

| | Resident Tuition and Fees | Non-resident Tuition and Fees |
|---|---|---|
| Undergraduate | $8,809 | $21,949 |
| U.S. Medical School | $29,185 | $43,648 |

## Financial Aid

There are several sources of financial aid available to students, including scholarships, loans, grants, and work-study. For more information, contact the Virginia Commonwealth University Financial Aid Office, P.O. Box 842506, Richmond, Virginia 23284-2506; (804) VCU-MONY.

## Application and Acceptance Policies

**Filing of application—**
**Earliest date:** September 1, 2011
**Latest date:** November 15, 2011

**Application fee:** $50    **Fee waiver available:** Yes

**Acceptance notice —**
**Earliest date:** April 1, 2012
**Latest date:** n/a

**Applicant's response to acceptance offer—**
**Maximum time:** May 1, 2012

**Deposit to hold place in class:** Yes
**Deposit — Resident:** $100
**Deposit refundable:** No    **Refundable by:** n/a

**Starting date:** August 2012

### Information on 2010–2011 Entering Class

| Number of | In-State | Out-of-State | Total |
|---|---|---|---|
| Applicants | 85 | 136 | 221 |
| Applicants Interviewed | 26 | 34 | 60 |
| New Entrants | 13 | 9 | 22 |
| **Total number of students enrolled in program: 95** | | | |

# Chapter 13:

## M.D. – Ph.D. Dual Degree Programs

*Most all medical students will ultimately become practicing clinicians. The specialties they select will differ, and so will the settings. But regardless of the variation, these students share one major similarity: They plan to devote themselves completely to the direct care and treatment of patients.*

*Perhaps you envision something different. You look forward to a future in which you help advance medical knowledge. In addition to—or maybe even in lieu of—clinical work, you want to develop innovative techniques and study new treatments. You want to engage in scientific research to promote health, solve medical problems, combat disease, and improve medical care. You want to bridge the gap between the laboratory and a patient's bedside.*

*You want a career in medical research.*

### The Education of a Physician-Scientist

Physician-scientists—those who are trained in both medicine and research—are greatly needed in today's world. There is a synergy that results when experimental and clinical thinking are joined, and that combination is found among those who have completed both M.D. and Ph.D. degrees. These individuals help translate the achievements of basic research into active clinical practice, and, in doing so, strengthen the link between medical knowledge and prevent, diagnose, and treat disease. If this is the path you prefer, you will enjoy a busy, challenging, and rewarding career.

#### Advantages of the M.D.-Ph.D. Dual Degree

One route to a career as a physician-scientist is enrollment in a combined M.D.-Ph.D. program. Although you can complete a Ph.D. program after receiving your M.D. degree, there are several advantages to pursuing joint M.D.-Ph.D. training:

- The greatest advantage of the dual-degree program is the integration of research and clinical training. This integrated approach may include seminars that cross departments and interactions with teams composed of both basic science and clinical investigators.

- In addition, you can save a significant amount of time. The combined program can be completed in a total of seven or eight years, compared to the nine or ten it would take to earn both degrees independently.

- Beyond that, M.D.-Ph.D. students enjoy opportunities for research and faculty mentoring frequently unavailable to M.D.-only students. As a result, these students are often able to enhance their mastery of the basic science background underlying patients' clinical problems, and, ultimately, use that information to develop improvements in diagnosis and treatment.

## Research Specialties

Just as with an Ph.D.-only career, students with a combined degree can pursue any one of many scientific specialties. Most students earn their Ph.D. degrees in biomedical laboratory disciplines such as biochemistry, biomedical engineering, biophysics, cell biology, genetics, immunology, microbiology, neuroscience, and pharmacology.

It is important to realize that not every research specialty is offered at every medical school, and that curricula can vary from institution to institution. In some schools, for example, M.D.-Ph.D. trainees also can complete their graduate work outside of laboratory disciplines in fields such as anthropology, computational biology, economics, health care policy, mathematics, physics, and sociology.

## Clinical Specialties

M.D.-Ph.D. students can also pursue any one of many clinical specialties. The clinical specialty choices of students graduating from M.D.-Ph.D. programs over the past five years indicate that the most common residencies were internal medicine, pathology, and pediatrics. Approximately 50% of all dual degree graduates chose these departments. Both Internal Medicine and Pediatrics offer board-certified Research Pathway Residency Programs for trainees who are interested in combining research and clinical training during their residency and fellowship program.

When compared to M.D.-only graduates, M.D.-Ph.D. graduates have been more likely to enter residencies in radiation oncology, child neurology, and pathology and are less likely to go into family medicine, emergency medicine, and obstetrics/gynecology. Additionally, the majority of dual-degree students enter residencies after graduation. The approximately five percent that do not enter residency usually go straight into a postdoctoral fellowship position.

## The Typical Program

Almost all U.S. and Canadian medical schools have M.D.-Ph.D. programs in one or more areas of specialization. Some are relatively small in size (one or two new students each year, with a dozen or so total students), while others are much larger (up to 25 new students annually and a total enrollment of around 190).

Although, as we mentioned, there are differences among programs, core elements are common to almost all. The typical program is completed in a total of seven to nine years and includes:

- Completion of the first two years of combined medical and graduate school coursework, followed by

- Three to five years of doctoral research, including the completion of a thesis project, and

- A return to medical school for core clinical training and electives during the final years of the medical curriculum.

At most schools, integrated approaches to graduate and medical education have been introduced throughout the curricula. In addition, most programs engage students in a wide range of other activities to enrich their training experience. The median time for completion of a M.D.-Ph.D. program is eight years.

## Application and Admission

Nearly all M.D.-Ph.D. programs participate in the AMCAS® application process described in Chapter 6.

If you choose to pursue the dual-degree program, you will designate yourself as a Combined M.D.-Ph.D. Training Applicant and complete two additional essays—one related to why you are interested in the joint training program, and the other describing your research experience. There are, however, specifics in the application process—and the prerequisites required for admission—that vary from school to school. (Some institutions, for example, require GRE scores.) For complete information, make certain to review the description of the dual-degree program at the Web site of each medical school in which you are interested.

### Factors Considered by the Admission Committee

Admission committee members will review the application material for the usual experiences, attributes, and metrics that are important for admission of students to M.D.-only programs (see Chapter 7). But because M.D.-Ph.D. applicants plan to become both physicians and scientists, committee members will also look for evidence of an applicant's passion and aptitude for research. They accomplish this largely through review of an applicant's statement of career goals and in letters of recommendation from faculty or researchers with whom the applicant has previously worked. In particular, committee members seek confirmation of:

- Relevant and substantive research experience during or after college;

- An appreciation for and understanding of the work of physician-scientists; and

- Intellectual drive, research ability, and perseverance.

If you hope to pursue the M.D.-Ph.D. joint degree, you will be expected to have clinical experience—be it through volunteer work, shadowing a physician-scientist, or specific training. Other experiences that admission committee members generally look favorably upon are similar to those of the M.D.-only candidate, such as leadership positions, community service activities, and teaching roles.

Finally, it's important to be aware that while significant weight is placed upon an applicant's interest and experience in research activities, he or she is also expected to demonstrate a degree of academic excellence similar to those accepted in the M.D.-only program. For students entering M.D.-Ph.D. programs in 2010, for example, the median GPA for students was 3.8 and total MCAT® scores was 35* as reported by the American Medical College Application Service (AMCAS).

*Keep in mind that the range of GPAs and MCAT® scores for accepted applicants is quite broad, and considered in conjunction with other selection factors.*

### Acceptance Policies

Just as application requirements vary from school to school, so too do their acceptance policies. Some institutions permit an applicant who is not accepted to the M.D.-Ph.D. dual degree program to pursue admission to the M.D.-only curriculum. Other medical schools will accept applications from M.D.-Ph.D. candidates only for both degree programs, and failure to gain admittance to one program precludes consideration from another. Since school policies differ, applicants should clarify these matters at each school prior to application, and let admission office staff know of their interest in pursuing an M.D.-only program (if that is the case) should they not be admitted to the dual-degree program.

## Financing M.D. – Ph.D. Programs

The sources of funding for M.D.-Ph.D. programs vary from school to school. Many schools offer full support for both the M.D. and Ph.D. components of their education, including tuition waivers, a stipend, and health insurance. At other institutions, varying degrees of support are available, sometimes only for the Ph.D. component of the program. Before you apply to an M.D.-Ph.D. dual-degree program, you should determine the level of financial assistance available.

A significant amount of funding comes from institutional sources and both individual and institutional grants. The latter includes the Medical Scientist Training Program (MSTP) sponsored by the National Institutes of Health (NIH), as well as other NIH grants. While you will undoubtedly want to review the list of medical schools participating in the MSTP (*www.nigms.nih.gov/Training/InstPredoc/PredocInst-MSTP.htm*), you will also want to contact the program officials at the institutions of interest and review their Web sites for full information.

Bear in mind that although most M.D.-Ph.D. programs offer support for their students, additional resources are available. Most take the form of competitive applications submitted by the trainee and their research mentor. These include fellowships from both private sources and a number of NIH institutes. You can review the list of these opportunities at *www.aamc.org/mdphd/fundingformdphd.pdf.*

## Medical Scientist Training Program (MSTP)

During the award period from July 1, 2010 through June 30, 2011, the NIH supported 40 M.D.-Ph.D. programs through the MSTP.

*For additional information and guidance about application to and enrollment in a combined M.D.-Ph.D. program, please visit the AAMC's Web site on the dual-degree program at www.aamc.org/mdphd or contact your pre-health advisor and the M.D.-Ph.D. program director at the medical schools of interest.*

*For additional information regarding clinical specialties, see:*

*Brass LF, Akabas MH, Burnley LD, Engman DM, Wiley CA, Andersen OS. Are MD-PhD programs meeting their goals? An analysis of career choices made by graduates of 24 M.D.-Ph.D. programs. Acad Med. 2010; 85(4):692-701.*

*Paik JC, Howard G, Lorenz RG. Postgraduate choices of graduates from medical scientist training programs, 2004-2008. JAMA. 2009; 302(12):1271-3.*

# Chapter 14:

## Information About U.S. Medical Schools
## Accredited by the LCME

*Information about individual U.S. medical schools is given in the following two-page entries for the 134 schools (130 in the 50 states, four in Puerto Rico) that will be considering applications for the summer 2012 entering class. The schools presented here are accredited as of February 2011 by the Liaison Committee on Medical Education (LCME), which is sponsored by the Association of American Medical Colleges (AAMC) and the American Medical Association (AMA).*

*Individual school entries are comprised of narrative, data and tabular information:*

### Narrative Information

- **Contact Information**—Admissions office staff, mail and e-mail addresses, phone and fax numbers, and Web site addresses for the medical school, admissions office, and financial aid office.

- **General Information**—Background and basic information about the medical school and its program.

- **Curricular Highlights**—Information about the medical education curriculum, educational philosophy and methodologies, and community service and research/thesis requirements.

- **Selection Factors**—Basic information regarding coursework, personal characteristics and experiences, and general requirements for applicants to be considered for acceptance and matriculation.

- **Information about Diversity Programs**—Information about the school's diversity initiatives and programs for students from groups underrepresented in medicine, as well as additional contact information.

- **Campus Information**—Information about total enrollment figures, campus setting, housing, special features, and satellite and/or regional campuses.

### Data and Tabular Information

- **Application Process and Requirements**
*Primary Application Service*—Notation of which type of application the school utilizes for primary applications (the American Medical College Application Service [AMCAS®], the Texas Medical and Dental School Application Service [TMDSAS], or a school-specific application) and information about the earliest and latest filing dates for the primary application.

*Secondary Application*—This section notes if a secondary application is required, to whom the secondary application is to be submitted, required fees, the potential availability of a fee waiver, and the earliest and latest filing dates for secondary application materials.

*Latest MCAT® Considered*—The most recent MCAT administration from which an MCAT score can be submitted in support of an application.

*Oldest MCAT® Considered*—The earliest MCAT administration from which an MCAT score can be submitted in support of an application.

*Early Decision Program*—This section notes if the school participates in an Early Decision Program (EDP), when EDP applicants are notified about acceptance decisions, and if the Early Decision Program is available only to state residents or to both state residents and nonresidents.

*Regular Acceptance Notice*—The earliest and latest dates on which acceptance notices are sent to applicants. These dates do not refer to those applicants who have applied to special programs.

*Applicant's Response to Acceptance Notice—Maximum Time*—The maximum period of time applicants are provided to respond to an acceptance offer.

*Requests for Deferred Entrance Considered*—Information about deferred entrance opportunities at the school.

*Deposit*—Information on the amount of the deposit required to hold a place in the next entering class, when the deposit is due, if the deposit is applied to tuition, if the deposit is refundable, and final date for requesting a deposit refund.

*Estimated Number of New Entrants*—The number of regular, EDP, and special program applicants expected to matriculate in the next year's entering class.

*Start Month/Year*—The anticipated starting date in 2012 for the program.

*Interview Format*—General information on how interviews are conducted and about the availability of regional interviews.

- **Other Programs**—Information regarding the availability of postbaccalaureate premedical, summer, and combined degree programs. Web sites and contact information are provided, as available.

- **First Year Class Data for 2010–11**—Data in this chart reflect verified applications, not initiated applications. The chart notes the number of applicants (in-state, out-of-state, international, and total) who applied, were interviewed, and the total number of matriculants from any application process in the school's 2010–2011 entering class.

- **Financial Information**—Cost of Attendance, Tuition and Fees, Other Expenses, and Health Insurance information is derived from the 2010–2011 AAMC Tuition and Student Fees Questionnaire. Regarding health insurance, "can be waived" means that this fee may be waived for any student with existing and comparable health insurance coverage (e.g., through a parent or a spouse).

Data about Percentage of Enrolled Students Receiving Financial Aid and For 2011, Total Indebtedness are derived from the 2009–2010 Liaison Committee on Medical Education (LCME) 1B Survey.

## Abbreviations

Listed below are the abbreviations used in the school entries in this chapter.

**AMCAS®**—American Medical College Application Service

**CACMS**—Committee on Accreditation of Canadian Medical Schools

**CLEP**—College-Level Examination Program

**EAP**—Early Assurance Program

**EDP**—Early Decision Program

**FAF**—Financial Aid Form

**FAFSA**—Free Application for Federal Student Aid

**FAP**—AAMC Fee Assistance Program

**GPA**—Grade Point Average

**LCME**—Liaison Committee on Medical Education

**LCME 1B**—Liaison Committee on Medical Education 1B Survey

**MCAT**—Medical College Admission Test

**NA**—Not Applicable

**NC**—Not Collected

**NR**—Not Reported

**TMDSAS**—Texas Medical and Dental School Application Service

**TSF**—Tuition and Student Fees Questionnaire

**USMLE**—United States Medical Licensing Examination

**WICHE**—Western Interstate Commission for Higher Education

**WWAMI**—WWAMI is an enduring partnership between the University of Washington School of Medicine and the states of Wyoming, Alaska, Montana, and Idaho. Its purpose is to provide access to publicly supported medical education across the five-state region. "WWAMI" is derived from the first letter of each of the five cooperating states.

# University of Alabama School of Medicine

## Birmingham, Alabama

Medical Student Services/Admissions
University of Alabama School of Medicine
VH 100, 1530 3rd Ave. S.
Birmingham, Alabama 35294-0019

**T** 205 934 2433   medschool@uab.edu

**Admissions:** www.medicine.uab.edu/admissions

## General Information

The School of Medicine was founded in Mobile in 1859 and has been located in Birmingham since 1945. The main campus is in Birmingham with branch campuses, created in 1969, in Huntsville and Tuscaloosa.

## Mission Statement

The School of Medicine is dedicated to the education of physicians and scientists in all of the disciplines of medicine and biomedical investigation for careers in practice, teaching, and research. Necessary to this educational mission are the provision of outstanding medical care and services and the enhancement of new knowledge through clinical and basic biomedical research.

## Curricular Highlights

**Community Service Requirement:** Optional.

**Research/Thesis Requirement:** Optional.

The four-year program emphasizes the fundamentals underlying clinical medical practice, with attention to the emotional, cultural, and social characteristics of patients and to the importance of adapting care to meet their needs. The Preclinical curriculum integrates basic and clinical sciences into organ system modules co-directed by basic scientists and clinicians. The objective of the curriculum is for students to learn basic sciences in a clinically relevant context, teaching them to think comprehensively about organ function and disease rather than to memorize mountains of facts. The first two years also provide training in medical professionalism, interviewing, and physical examination. The third and fourth years consist of required rotations and electives, with clinical experiences in both hospital and ambulatory settings. There are structured opportunities for research.

## Selection Factors

The Admissions Committee is committed to admitting those applicants who possess the intelligence, skills, attitudes, and other personal attributes to become excellent physicians and to meet the health care needs of the state of Alabama. Desirable attributes include: solid academic performance, effective communication and interpersonal skills, evidence of service to others, empathy, emotional maturity, personal resilience, honesty, leadership ability, sense of purpose, and experiences to promote an understanding of what it means to be a physician (shadowing). Particular attention is directed to individuals with commitment and ability to meet the school's missions including: meeting healthcare needs of Alabama's underserved populations (urban and rural), careers in biomedical research/academics and primary care. There is a special acceptance program for state residents committed to rural practice in Alabama. AP or CLEP coursework appearing on the AMCAS® application will be accepted to meet a premedical requirement, although further coursework in biology and chemistry are desirable and may be necessary to be a competitive applicant. To meet our English coursework requirement, we accept composition and literature courses or intensive interdisciplinary reading and writing courses that expand knowledge beyond science. Other requirements: minimal total MCAT of 24 on the most recent exam, minimum grade of "C" on all required coursework, and completion of 90 hours of undergraduate credit from an accredited US college or university. With rare exceptions, completion of an undergraduate degree is required; all work toward current degrees must be completed prior to matriculation to the medical school.

## Information About Diversity Programs

The University of Alabama School of Medicine (UASOM) has a fundamental commitment to the identification, recruitment, retention, and career advisement of minorities and students from underrepresented populations.

## Regional/Satellite Campuses

**Regional Campus Location(s):** Huntsville, AL, and Tuscaloosa, AL.

Both the Huntsville and Tuscaloosa campuses offer students opportunities for community-based education, as well as rotations in regional medical centers offering a full range of medical specialties. Both campuses have new clinical education facilities.

## Application Process and Requirements 2012–2013

**Primary application service:** AMCAS®
**Earliest filing date:** June 1, 2011
**Latest filing date:** November 1, 2011

**Secondary application required:** Yes
**Sent to:** Screened applicants
**URL:** Provided to invited applicants
**Fee:** Yes, $75   **Waiver available:** Yes
**Earliest filing date:** August 1, 2011
**Latest filing date:** November 15, 2011

**MCAT® required:** Yes
**Latest MCAT® considered:** September 2011
**Oldest MCAT® considered:** January 2009

**Early Decision Program:** School does have EDP
**Applicants notified:** October 1, 2011
**EDP available for:** In-State Applicants only

**Regular acceptance notice —**
**Earliest date:** October 15, 2011
**Latest date:** Until class is full
**Applicant's response to acceptance offer —**
**Maximum time:** Two weeks from receipt of Acceptance Letter

**Requests for deferred entrance considered:** Yes

**Deposit to hold place in class:** Yes
**Deposit — In-State Applicants:** $50  **Out-of-State Applicants:** $100   **Deposit due:** With acceptance offer
**Applied to tuition:** Yes  **Refundable:** Yes
**Refundable by:** May 15, 2012

**Estimated number of new entrants:** 176
**EDP:** 10, **Special Programs:** 55

**Start month/year:** July 2012

**Interview format:** Individual interviews are held only on most Thursdays, September through March. Regional interviews are not available. Video interviews are not available.

## Preparatory Programs

**Postbaccalaureate Program:** No

**Summer Program:** Yes, www.uasom.uab.edu/shep

**Rural Medical Programs:** Yes, http://medicine.uab.edu/education/prospectie/66902

**Summer Health Enrichment Program:** Yes, www.uasom.uab.edu/shep

## 2010–2011 First Year Class

|  | In-State | Out-of-State | International |
|---|---|---|---|
| Applications | 424 | 1,930 | 27 |
| Interviewed | 270 | 135 | 0 |
| Matriculated | 151 | 25 | 0 |

**Total Matriculants: 176**   **Total Enrollment: 747**

## Financial Information

|  | In-State | Out-of-State |
|---|---|---|
| Total Cost of Attendance | $42,628 | $80,538 |
| Tuition and Fees | $21,873 | $59,783 |
| Other (incl. living expenses) | $18,902 | $18,902 |
| Health Insurance (can be waived) | $1,853 | $1,853 |

**Average 2010 Graduate Indebtedness: $116,542**
**% of Enrolled Students Receiving Aid: 82%**

Source: 2009-2010 LCME I-B survey and 2010-2011 AAMC TSF questionnaire

# University of South Alabama College of Medicine

## Mobile, Alabama

Office of Admissions, MSB 241
University of South Alabama
College of Medicine
Mobile, Alabama 36688-0002
**T** 251 460 7176   mscott@usouthal.edu

**Admissions:** www.southalabama.edu/com/
admissions.shtml

### General Information

The College of Medicine of the University of South Alabama was approved by the Board of Trustees of the university in 1967; the Alabama state legislature passed a resolution authorizing the college on August 19, 1967. The college admitted a charter class in January 1973. The basic medical sciences are housed on the university campus. The University of South Alabama Medical Center, operating continuously since 1831, has provided clinical medical education for more than a century. It is the major physician-staffed emergency facility in South Alabama and has been named a Level I trauma center by the Alabama Committee on Trauma. Other clinical training facilities include the USA Children's and Women's Hospital, Infirmary West Hospital and the USA Mitchell Cancer Institute.

### Mission Statement

To prepare talented, highly qualified students to become physicians, providing them the opportunity to develop basic science and clinical skills that will carry them successfully through residency and their career in medicine.

### Curricular Highlights

**Community Service Requirement:** Optional.

**Research/Thesis Requirement:** Optional.

The first year is devoted to the basic sciences of anatomy, physiology, biochemistry, neuroanatomy, and embryology. Early introduction to clinical problems is also offered in courses through Clinical Correlation Conferences and Medical Practice and Society. The second year includes pathology, physical diagnosis, microbiology-immunology, pharmacology, and behavioral science. Public health/epidemiology and medical genetics round out the second-year curriculum. The third year has six clinical clerkships: medicine, surgery, pediatrics, psychiatry/neurology, obstetrics-gynecology, and family practice. The fourth year is composed of nine rotations of four weeks each. Students are required to select one rotation each in clinical neuroscience, surgical subspecialties, ambulatory care, primary care, subspecialty in medicine, pediatrics or obstetrics-gynecology, an acting internship, and an in-house elective. Three of the rotations may be used for approved extramural experiences. Letter grades are given until the fourth year, where a pass/fail/honors system is used.

### Selection Factors

The Committee on Admissions will consider candidates whose undergraduate grades and scores on the MCAT indicate that they can handle the rigorous curriculum of the College of Medicine. However, admission is based on more than scholastic achievement. Applicants will be considered on their potential to become conscientious and capable physicians. The University of South Alabama provides equal educational opportunities and is open to all qualified students without regard to race, creed, national origin, sex, or handicap with respect to all of its programs and activities. Because the college is state-supported, preference is given to Alabama residents. However, highly qualified out-of-state applicants are seriously considered. Disadvantaged, rural, and minority residents are strongly encouraged to apply. Fee waivers, based solely on economic need, are granted, when documented.

### Information about Diversity Programs

The school is committed to the enrollment and education of individuals from all disadvantaged groups. For information, contact Dr. Hattie M. Myles, Assistant Dean of Special Programs and Student Affairs.

### Regional/Satellite Campuses

Students do their hospital training in any one of four hospitals, depending on the rotation. The College of Medicine also has clinic-based training with preceptors in facilities located throughout Alabama.

---

## Application Process and Requirements 2012–2013

**Primary application service:** AMCAS®
**Earliest filing date:** June 1, 2011
**Latest filing date:** November 15, 2011

**Secondary application required:** Yes
**Sent to:** All applicants
**URL:** www.usouthal.edu
**Contact:** D. Mark Scott, (251) 460-7176,
mscott@usouthal.edu
**Fee:** Yes, $75  **Waiver available:** Yes
**Earliest filing date:** June 15, 2011
**Latest filing date:** December 31, 2011

**MCAT® required:** Yes
**Latest MCAT® considered:** September 2011
**Oldest MCAT® considered:** 2008

**Early Decision Program:** School does have EDP
**Applicants notified:** October 1, 2011
**EDP available for:** Both residents and non-residents

**Regular acceptance notice —**
**Earliest date:** October 15, 2011
**Latest date:** Until class is full
**Applicant's response to acceptance offer —**
**Maximum time:** Two weeks

**Requests for deferred entrance considered:** Yes

**Deposit to hold place in class:** Yes
**Deposit — In-State Applicants:** $50  **Out-of-State Applicants:** $100
**Deposit due:** With response to acceptance offer
**Applied to tuition:** Yes  **Refundable:** Yes
**Refundable by:** May 15, 2012

**Estimated number of new entrants:** 74
**EDP:** 15, **Special Programs:** 5

**Start month/year:** August 2012

**Interview format:** Students meet one-on-one with three interviewers. Regional interviews are not available. Video interviews are not available.

### Preparatory Programs

**Postbaccalaureate Program:** Yes, contact Dr. Cindy Stanfield, (251) 380-2686, cthursto@usouthal.edu

**Summer Program:** Yes, contact Dr. Hattie Myles, (251) 460-7313, hmyles@usouthal.edu

## 2010–2011 First Year Class

|              | In-State | Out-of-State | International |
|--------------|----------|--------------|--------------|
| Applications | 383      | 730          | 56           |
| Interviewed  | 178      | 40           | 0            |
| Matriculated | 59       | 15           | 0            |

**Total Matriculants: 74**     **Total Enrollment: 296**

## Financial Information

|                                      | In-State | Out-of-State |
|--------------------------------------|----------|--------------|
| Total Cost of Attendance             | $47,164  | $67,989      |
| Tuition and Fees                     | $22,328  | $43,153      |
| Other (incl. living expenses)        | $21,836  | $21,836      |
| Health Insurance (can be waived)     | $3,000   | $3,000       |

**Average 2010 Graduate Indebtedness: $128,508**
**% of Enrolled Students Receiving Aid: 92%**

*Source: 2009-2010 LCME I-B survey and 2010-2011 AAMC TSF questionnaire*

# University of Arizona College of Medicine

## Tucson, Arizona

Admissions – Tucson
P.O. Box 245075, Tucson, Arizona 85004
**T** 520 626 6214    medapp@email.arizona.edu

Admissions and Recruitment – Phoenix
550 E Van Buren Street, Phoenix, Arizona 85043
**T** 602 827 2005    phxmed@email.arizona.edu

**Admissions:** www.medicine.arizona.edu

## General Information

The University of Arizona College of Medicine provides education and training for the MD through two separate four-year campuses: Tucson and Phoenix. The Tucson campus enrolled its first class of medical students in 1967 and is located adjacent to the main UA campus. The Phoenix campus, located in downtown Phoenix started in 1992 as a clinical campus and became a four-year campus in 2006. Each campus offers dual-degree programs.

## Mission Statement

The Tucson and Phoenix campuses offer distinct, but related four-year educational programs leading to the M.D. degree. Both are designed for student achievement in the following six core competencies: (1) Medical Knowledge; (2) Patient Care; (3) Interpersonal and Communication skills; (4) Professionalism; (5) Practice-based Learning and Improvement; and (6) Systems-based Practice & Population Health.

## Curricular Highlights

**Community Service Requirement:** Optional. Extensive opportunities.

**Research/Thesis Requirement:** Required. Scholarly Project (Phoenix).

The educational track at each campus utilizes a similar core structure, while each also offers distinct elements. The first two years of curricula at each campus are structured in integrated blocks that focus on organs systems. The second two years consist of required clinical clerkships in key disciplines and significant time for elective work. Basic and clinical science are interwoven with threads: behavioral science and humanism, health and society, and interprofessional education. Both curricula emphasize active learning, guided independent learning, working in teams, and early clinical experience. Nearly all students take part in our robust co-curricular activities, including medical student research, rural health and service learning programs.

## Selection Factors

Each campus gives strong preference to residents of Arizona and Native Americans who reside on reservations contiguous with the State of Arizona. Highly qualified nonresident applicants will be considered for up to 25% of the student body. Many factors are considered when evaluating applicants, including the entire academic record, performance on the MCAT, personal statement, interviews, and letters of recommendation. Applicants are chosen who demonstrate, motivation, academic ability, integrity, maturity, altruism, communication skills, and leadership abilities. Clinical, research, and community service experiences are evidence to these attributes. Each campus strives to accept a student body representative of the diverse Arizona population and who are determined to best meet the medical needs of our state, country and global community.

## Information About Diversity Programs

Each campus believes in the educational benefits of a diverse student body, and provides ample opportunities and activities that enhance the educational experience.

## Regional/Satellite Campuses

**Regional Campus Location(s):** Phoenix, AZ.

Students in Phoenix not only can complete all four-years of medical education in the city, but they can also earn a Masters in Public Health and/or a Masters of Business Administration. In addition to the students who begin and finish medical education at the Phoenix campus, Phoenix also receives approximately 25% of the Tucson-originating medical student body each year to complete their clinical education. The fifth largest city in our nation, Phoenix bodes an impressive diverse patient population, from which our students are privileged to train and learn. The entering class of 2012 is increasing to 80 students, a substantial increase from the previous class size of 48. The medical program will have also celebrated the successful residency placement and graduation of the inaugural class of 24 students, who will each be in graduate medical education as first-year residents in Arizona and across the country.

## Application Process and Requirements 2012–2013

**Primary application service:** AMCAS®
**Earliest filing date:** June 1, 2011
**Latest filing date:** November 1, 2011

**Secondary application required:** Yes
**Sent to:** Campus-specific by invitation-only, separate application and $75 fee
**URL:** n/a
**Fee:** Yes, $75    **Waiver available:** Yes
**Earliest filing date:** July 1, 2011
**Latest filing date:** January 15, 2012

**MCAT® required:** Yes
**Latest MCAT® considered:** September 2011
**Oldest MCAT® considered:** 2008

**Early Decision Program:** School does not have EDP
**Applicants notified:** n/a
**EDP available for:** n/a

**Regular acceptance notice —**
**Earliest date:** October 2011
**Latest date:** Until class is full
**Applicant's response to acceptance offer —**
**Maximum time:** Two weeks

**Requests for deferred entrance considered:** Yes

**Deposit to hold place in class:** No
**Deposit — In-State Applicants:** n/a  **Out-of-State:** n/a
**Applicants:** n/a
**Deposit due:** n/a
**Applied to tuition:** n/a
**Deposit refundable:** n/a
**Refundable by:** n/a

**Estimated number of new entrants:** 195
**EDP:** n/a, **Special Programs:** n/a

**Start month/year:** July (Phoenix), August (Tucson) 2012

**Interview format:** Multiple Mini-Interview (Phoenix); One on-site (Tucson). Regional interviews are not available. Video interviews are not available.

## Preparatory Programs

**Postbaccalaureate Program:** No

**Summer Program:** No

## 2010–2011 First Year Class

|  | In-State | Out-of-State | International |
|---|---|---|---|
| Applications | 588 | 2,237 | 38 |
| Interviewed | 416 | 160 | 0 |
| Matriculated | 140 | 23 | 0 |

**Total Matriculants: 163**    **Total Enrollment: 630**

## Financial Information

|  | In-State | Out-of-State |
|---|---|---|
| Total Cost of Attendance | $47,424 | $64,958 |
| Tuition and Fees | $26,198 | $43,306 |
| Other (incl. living expenses) | $19,564 | $19,990 |
| Health Insurance (can be waived) | $1,662 | $1,662 |

**Average 2010 Graduate Indebtedness: $135,525**
**% of Enrolled Students Receiving Aid: 96%**

Source: 2009-2010 LCME I-B survey and 2010-2011 AAMC TSF questionnaire

# University of Arkansas College of Medicine

## Little Rock, Arkansas

Office of the Dean, University of Arkansas for
Medical Sciences College of Medicine
4301 West Markham Street, Slot 551
Little Rock, Arkansas 72205-7199

**T** 501 686 5354    southtomg@uams.edu

**Admissions:** www.uams.edu/com/applicants/

## General Information

In 1879, eight visionary physicians had the foresight to each invest $625 to secure a charter from the Arkansas Industrial University. On October 7, 1879 the medical school opened its doors to 22 eager students. From these humble beginnings grew the excellence and prestige now embodied in the College of Medicine. Today, the College of Medicine has over 1000 full-time and part-time faculty, over 600 residents, and over 600 medical students. UAMS is Arkansas' only institution of professional and graduate education devoted solely to the health and biological sciences. In fulfilling its educational mission, the College of Medicine, in conjunction with the UAMS Medical Center, provides the environment and opportunities for students and practitioners alike to learn and maintain the knowledge and skills required in the 21st century. Comprehensive services are delivered in an interdisciplinary environment to all Arkansans, regardless of their ability to pay. The school has completed a major expansion initiative: a replacement hospital, new student housing, new psychiatry center, an addition to both the Jones Eye Institute and the Outpatient Center, and a new affiliated state psychiatric hospital. The university's commitment is to facilitate discovery through applied research and to teach the best science and compassionate care to tomorrow's caregivers. As much as the school is proud of its past achievements, it believes that its best still lies ahead.

## Mission Statement

"In relentless pursuit of excellence, every day" summarizes the essence of the school's fourfold mission to teach, to heal, to search, and to serve.

## Curricular Highlights

**Community Service Requirement:** Optional.

**Research/Thesis Requirement:** Optional.

Along with the standard courses in anatomy, biochemistry, and physiology, the first year includes a program to introduce the student to clinical contacts and concepts. This is accomplished with formal lectures in medico-socioeconomic topics, small-group discussions, faculty-supervised interviews with patients, and the extensive use of standardized patients. The third year is a full 48 weeks with rotation through the major clinical services. This expanded clinical year provides substantial preparation for the predominantly elective fourth year, which consists of a minimum of 36 weeks to a maximum of 48 weeks of courses selected with the assistance of a faculty advisor. On- and off-campus electives are available to round out preparation for each student's career goals. Opportunities are provided for students to engage in research activities and to pursue graduate courses leading to the M.D./Ph.D. and M.D./M.P.H. degrees. The number of M.D./Ph.D. scholarships has increased significantly in recent years. Students are also provided with expanded opportunities through the M.D./M.B.A. and M.D./J.D. degree programs.

## Selection Factors

Selection is based on scholastic attainment, performance on the MCAT, personal interviews with members of the faculty, and recommendations, particularly evaluations by college pre-professional advisory committees. Applicants should also demonstrate time and effort devoted to volunteerism and community service. Selection is made without regard to race, sex, creed, national origin, age, or handicap. Unsuccessful applicants may reapply without prejudice. Non-Arkansas residents who have strong ties to Arkansas are encouraged to apply.

## Information About Diversity Programs

Students from groups underrepresented in medicine are encouraged to apply. The Office of Admissions and the Center for Diversity have developed an active recruitment and retention program. The five-week Summer Science Program offers an introduction to the medical school curriculum, along with reading and study skill enrichment sessions designed to strengthen students' mastery of these areas.

## Regional/Satellite Campuses

The College of Medicine has established a branch campus in Northwest Arkansas. All students will complete the first two years of training in Little Rock at the main campus. A minimum of 14 junior students will be assigned each year to complete their junior and senior years of medical school at the Northwest branch campus.

## Application Process and Requirements 2012–2013

**Primary application service:** AMCAS®
**Earliest filing date:** July 1, 2011
**Latest filing date:** November 1, 2011

**Secondary application required:** Yes
**Sent to:** All applicants
**URL:** www.uams.edu
**Contact:** Tom South, (501) 686-5354, SouthTomG@uams.edu
**Fee:** Yes, $100    **Waiver available:** Yes
**Earliest filing date:** July 1, 2011
**Latest filing date:** November 1, 2011

**MCAT® required:** Yes
**Latest MCAT® considered:** September 2011
**Oldest MCAT® considered:** April 2009

**Early Decision Program:** School does not have EDP
**Applicants notified:** n/a
**EDP available for:** n/a

**Regular acceptance notice —**
**Earliest date:** December 15, 2011
**Latest date:** Until class is full
**Applicant's response to acceptance offer —**
**Maximum time:** Two weeks

**Requests for deferred entrance considered:** Yes

**Deposit to hold place in class:** No
**Deposit — Resident:** n/a  **Non-resident:** n/a
**Deposit due:** n/a
**Applied to tuition:** n/a
**Deposit refundable:** n/a
**Refundable by:** n/a

**Estimated number of new entrants:** 174
**EDP:** n/a, special program: n/a

**Start month/year:** August 2012

**Interview format:** Blind team interviews on scheduled interview dates. Regional interviews are not available. Video interviews are not available.

### Preparatory Programs
**Postbaccalaureate Program:** No

**Summer Program:** No

## 2010–2011 First Year Class

|  | In-State | Out-of-State | International |
|---|---|---|---|
| Applications | 287 | 1,780 | 17 |
| Interviewed | 287 | 104 | 0 |
| Matriculated | 145 | 23 | 0 |

**Total Matriculants: 168**    **Total Enrollment: 625**

## Financial Information

|  | In-State | Out-of-State |
|---|---|---|
| Total Cost of Attendance | $38,226 | $56,206 |
| Tuition and Fees | $19,478 | $37,458 |
| Other (incl. living expenses) | $16,850 | $16,850 |
| Health Insurance (can be waived) | $1,898 | $1,898 |

**Average 2010 Graduate Indebtedness: $134,556**
**% of Enrolled Students Receiving Aid: 91%**

Source: 2009-2010 LCME I-B survey and 2010-2011 AAMC TSF questionnaire

# Keck School of Medicine of the University of Southern California

## Los Angeles, California

University of Southern California
Keck School of Medicine, Office of Admissions
1975 Zonal Avenue, KAM 100-C
Los Angeles, California 90089-9021

**T** 323 442 2552    medadmit@usc.edu

**Admissions:** www.usc.edu/schools/medicine/
education/admissions

### General Information

The Keck School of Medicine of the University of Southern California was established in 1885 as the region's first medical school. All Keck students train at the Los Angeles County+USC Medical Center, one of the largest medical teaching centers in the United States. Through affiliations with over a dozen other private and public hospitals, Keck students have a highly diverse clinical training experience.

### Mission Statement

The mission of the Keck School of Medicine is to improve the quality of life for individuals and society by promoting health, preventing and curing disease, advancing biomedical research, and educating tomorrow's physicians and scientists.

### Curricular Highlights

**Community Service Requirement:** Optional.

**Research/Thesis Requirement:** Optional.

Students are progressively involved with regular patient contact beginning the first week of medical school. An important feature in the curriculum is the Introduction to Clinical Medicine course. The doctor-patient relationship and interviewing are presented during the first year, and physical diagnosis and history-taking are taught in the second. Groups of six to seven students are led by a faculty member who serves as a clinical tutor for their first two years. The curriculum is designed to enhance students' understanding of the basic sciences and their relevance to clinical medicine. Curricular themes are guided by select Pathways and delivered in a case-centered format with the integration of small-group learning sessions, directed-independent study, and innovative instructional technologies. The first year of the Year I-II continuum begins with 18 weeks of Core Principles of Health and Disease, followed by 49 weeks of organ system review, ending with a 10-week Integrated Cases Study section. Each week of the academic year is composed of approximately 20 hours of lecture and small-group sessions, with an additional 20 hours of directed-independent study or Introduction to Clinical Medicine. Examinations in all systems throughout the first two years are graded pass/fail. Dean's Recognition is awarded on the basis of year-end comprehensive examinations and special projects. The final two years are designed as a continuum of two academic calendar years. Each student's program is individually designed to include 50 weeks of required clerkships, 16 weeks of selective clerkships, 16 weeks of elective clerkships, and required senior seminars. Grading for the final two years is on an honors, high pass, pass, and fail basis.

### Selection Factors

The Admissions Committee seriously considers candidates whose academic achievement and MCAT performance indicate the ability to satisfactorily complete the rigorous demands of the medical school curriculum. Also, the committee evaluates various non-academic factors, including personal motivations, evidence of qualities deemed desirable for the study and practice of medicine, significant achievements in extracurricular pursuits, research, and/or a demonstrated commitment to service and community.

### Information About Diversity Programs

The Office of Diversity at the Keck School of Medicine strives to recruit, enroll, and retain students of all socioeconomic, cultural, and ethnic backgrounds. For additional information and opportunities, please visit *www.usc.edu/schools/medicine/school/offices/diversity.html*.

### Regional/Satellite Campuses

Supervised by Keck School faculty, medical students play a key role in patient care in more than a dozen affiliated hospitals, including the adjacent LAC+USC Medical Center.

## Application Process and Requirements 2012–2013

**Primary application service:** AMCAS®
**Earliest filing date:** June 1, 2011
**Latest filing date:** November 1, 2011

**Secondary application required:** Yes
**Sent to:** All AMCAS-certified applicants
**URL:** http://keck.usc.edu
**Fee:** Yes, $90    **Waiver available:** Yes
**Earliest filing date:** July 1, 2011
**Latest filing date:** December 1, 2011

**MCAT® required:** Yes
**Latest MCAT® considered:** August 2011
**Oldest MCAT® considered:** August 2009

**Early Decision Program:** School does have EDP
**Applicants notified:** September 5, 2011
**EDP available for:** Both In-State and Out-of-State Applicants

**Regular acceptance notice —**
**Earliest date:** November 1, 2011
**Latest date:** Until class is full
**Applicant's response to acceptance offer —**
**Maximum time:** Ten days

**Requests for deferred entrance considered:** Yes

**Deposit to hold place in class:** Yes

**Deposit — In-State Applicants:** $100
**Out-of-State Applicants:** $100
**Deposit due:** Within ten days after notification of acceptance
**Applied to tuition:** Yes
**Deposit refundable:** No
**Refundable by:** n/a

**Estimated number of new entrants:** 180
**EDP:** 5, **Special Programs:** n/a

**Start month/year:** August 2012

Interview format: On-campus interviews only, closed-file. Regional interviews are not available. Video interviews are not available.

### Preparatory Programs

**Postbaccalaureate Program:** Yes,
http://chem.usc.edu/undergraduate/premed.html

**Summer Program:** No

## 2010–2011 First Year Class

|  | In-State | Out-of-State | International |
|---|---|---|---|
| Applications | 3,502 | 2,663 | 279 |
| Interviewed | 319 | 205 | 2 |
| Matriculated | 126 | 47 | 1 |

**Total Matriculants: 174**    **Total Enrollment: 681**

*Includes two M.D./D.D.S. matriculants*

## Financial Information

|  | In-State | Out-of-State |
|---|---|---|
| Total Cost of Attendance | $71,104 | $71,104 |
| Tuition and Fees | $47,072 | $47,072 |
| Other (incl. living expenses) | $22,992 | $22,992 |
| Health Insurance (can be waived) | $1,040 | $1,040 |

**Average 2010 Graduate Indebtedness: $186,099**
**% of Enrolled Students Receiving Aid: 91%**

*Source: 2009-2010 LCME I-B survey and 2010-2011 AAMC TSF questionnaire*

# Loma Linda University School of Medicine

## Loma Linda, California

Associate Dean for Admissions
Loma Linda University
School of Medicine
Loma Linda, California 92350
**T** 909 558 4467    admissions.sm@llu.edu
**Admissions:** www.llu.edu/medicine/admissions.page

## General Information

The School of Medicine was established in 1909. It consists of basic science facilities and the Loma Linda University Medical Center. Also used for clinical instruction are local, regional, county, community, and Veterans Affairs hospitals. The School of Medicine's objectives include providing the student with a solid foundation of medical knowledge, assisting the student to attain professional skills, motivating investigative curiosity, and instilling a desire to participate in the advancement of knowledge. The school seeks to foster the practical application of Christian principles through service to humanity.

## Mission Statement

The school's overriding purpose is the formation of Christian physicians, educated to serve as generalists or specialists and providing whole-person care to individuals, families, and communities.

## Curricular Highlights

**Community Service Requirement:** Optional.

**Research/Thesis Requirement:** Optional. Numerous opportunities available.

The School of Medicine seeks to prepare students who will be well grounded in the science and art of medicine. The first two years involve an organ systems-based approach to the study of the biomedical sciences, including their application to clinical medicine. The last two years provide clinical rotations in the major areas of medical practice. Elective time is available for additional experience in clinical or research areas. Qualified students interested in a career in academic medicine may earn an M.S. or Ph.D. degree along with the M.D. degree in a total of six to eight years. Student performance is evaluated by standard or scaled scores. The grading system is on a pass/fail basis.

## Selection Factors

The MCAT and a minimum of three years (90 semester hours or 135 quarter hours) of collegiate preparation in an accredited college or university in the U.S. or Canada are required. Preference is given to applicants who will have completed the baccalaureate degree prior to matriculation. No specific major is preferred. Demonstrated ability in the sciences is important. CLEP and pass/fail credits are not acceptable for required courses. Applicants are urged to take the MCAT by the spring of the application year. The Admissions Committee seeks candidates who have demonstrated the greatest potential for becoming capable physicians. A strong academic background is needed in preparation for medical studies. While special attention is given to performance in science courses, candidates should also have a solid foundation in the humanities, social sciences, and human behavior. The Admissions Committee seeks applicants who demonstrate problem-solving skills, critical judgment, and the ability to pursue independent study and thinking. For nonacademic qualifications, the committee looks for a commitment to medicine, sound judgment, a positive attitude, the ability to make decisions, participation in meaningful extracurricular activities, service orientation, emotional stability, and integrity. The School of Medicine is owned and operated by the Seventh-day Adventist Church. While, therefore, preference for admission is given to members of this church; it is a firm policy of the Admissions Committee to admit a number of applicants from other faith traditions who have demonstrated a strong commitment to Christian principles. No candidate is accepted on the basis of religious affiliation alone. The school does not discriminate on the basis of race, sex, age, or disability. After receipt of the AMCAS® application, each applicant is requested to submit a supplementary form and supply preprofessional faculty evaluations and/or personal letters of recommendation. Invitations for an interview are extended to selected applicants. Final selections are made by the Admissions Committee on the basis of overall scholastic record, personal qualities, promise of success as a physician, and commitment to the school's mission.

## Information About Diversity Programs

The School of Medicine encourages applications from persons from groups underrepresented in medicine. The Center for Health Disparities in the School of Medicine sponsors pipeline programs to increase the number of students from these groups.

## Application Process and Requirements 2012–2013

**Primary application service:** AMCAS®
**Earliest filing date:** June 1, 2011
**Latest filing date:** November 1, 2011

**Secondary application required:** Yes
**Sent to:** All applicants
**URL:** Made available upon receipt of verified AMCAS® application
**Fee:** Yes, $75  **Waiver available:** Yes
**Earliest filing date:** July 1, 2011
**Latest filing date:** November 15, 2011

**MCAT® required:** Yes
**Latest MCAT® considered:** September 2011
**Oldest MCAT® considered:** 2009

**Early Decision Program:** School does have EDP
**Applicants notified:** October 1, 2011
**EDP available for:** Both In-State and Out-of-State Applicants

**Regular acceptance notice —**
**Earliest date:** December 15, 2011
**Latest date:** Until class is full
**Applicant's response to acceptance offer —**
**Maximum time:** Thirty days

**Requests for deferred entrance considered:** Yes

**Deposit to hold place in class:** Yes
**Deposit — In-State Applicants:** $100  **Out-of-State Applicants:** $100
**Deposit due:** With acceptance offer
**Applied to tuition:** Yes
**Deposit refundable:** Yes
**Refundable by:** May 15, 2012

**Estimated number of new entrants:** 165
**EDP:** 10, **Special Programs:** n/a

**Start month/year:** August 2012

**Interview format:** On-campus interviews only. Regional interviews are not available. Video interviews are not available.

## Preparatory Programs

**Postbaccalaureate Program:** No

**Summer Program:** No

## 2010–2011 First Year Class

|  | In-State | Out-of-State | International |
|---|---|---|---|
| Applications | 2,093 | 2,581 | 303 |
| Interviewed | 168 | 174 | 33 |
| Matriculated | 79 | 71 | 15 |

**Total Matriculants: 165**     **Total Enrollment: 685**

## Financial Information

|  | In-State | Out-of-State |
|---|---|---|
| Total Cost of Attendance | $64,861 | $64,861 |
| Tuition and Fees | $41,876 | $41,876 |
| Other (incl. living expenses) | $21,313 | $21,313 |
| Health Insurance (cannot be waived) | $1,672 | $1,672 |

**Average 2010 Graduate Indebtedness: $165,869**
**% of Enrolled Students Receiving Aid: 90%**

Source: 2009-2010 LCME I-B survey and 2010-2011 AAMC TSF questionnaire

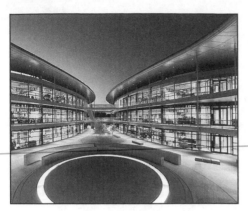

# Stanford University School of Medicine
## Stanford, California

Office of M.D. Admissions
Stanford University School of Medicine
251 Campus Drive, MSOB X301
Stanford, California 94305-5404

**T** 650 723 6861  mdadmissions@stanford.edu

**Admissions:** http://med.stanford.edu/md/
admissions

## General Information

The history of Stanford Medical School begins in 1858 with the founding in San Francisco by Dr. Elias Samuel Cooper of the first medical school on the Pacific Coast. In 1908, Stanford University adopted the Cooper Medical College in San Francisco as its medical school and moved it to the university campus in 1959. The Stanford School of Medicine is consistently ranked in the top ten of all research university medical centers in the country.

## Mission Statement

Stanford seeks to admit a diverse body of students who are interested in the intellectual substance of medicine and are committed to advancing the field of medicine, broadly defined (i.e. clinical medicine, biomedical sciences, health policy, medical education, and community health).

## Curricular Highlights

**Community Service Requirement:** Optional. Opportunities available and encouraged.

**Research/Thesis Requirement:** Required. Scholarly concentration is required.

Stanford is committed to ensuring that each graduate has fully explored his/her potential as a student and as a scholar. Key goals of the curriculum are the melding of 21st century laboratory and medical sciences, and helping each student build in-depth expertise in an area of personal interest through our Scholarly Concentrations program. All M.D. candidates must satisfactorily complete at least 13 quarters of academic work. Courses are graded pass/fail.

## Selection Factors

Applicants are selected based on their academic readiness, relevant life experiences, and personal qualities, taking into account their educational context. Stanford University admits qualified students of any race, color, national or ethnic origin, sex, age, disability, religion, sexual orientation, and gender identity to all the rights, privileges, programs, and activities generally accorded or made available to students at the University.

## Information About Diversity Programs

Stanford takes pride in its highly diverse and exceptionally qualified student body and is committed to increasing the representation of members of groups underrepresented in medicine. A year long program in Leadership in Health Disparities, sponsored by the Center of Excellence in Diversity in Medical Education, provides all Stanford medical students with the skills, attitudes and knowledge to address the social determinants of health and understand the urgency to provide access to high quality care to all communities.

## Regional/Satellite Campuses

Student rotations take place in the major clinical teaching facilities: Stanford Hospital (663 beds), Lucile Packard Children's Hospital (152 beds), Santa Clara County Valley Medical Center (791 beds), the Palo Alto Veterans Affairs Hospital (1,000 beds), and Kaiser Santa Clara Medical Center (327 beds).

## Application Process and Requirements 2012–2013

**Primary application service:** AMCAS®
**Earliest filing date:** June 1, 2011
**Latest filing date:** October 15, 2011

**Secondary application required:** Yes
**Sent to:** All applicants
**URL:** https://med.stanford.edu/aes/
**Fee:** Yes, $80  **Waiver available:** Yes
**Earliest filing date:** July 1, 2011
**Latest filing date:** November 15, 2011

**MCAT® required:** Yes
**Latest MCAT® considered:** August 2011
**Oldest MCAT® considered:** August 2008

**Early Decision Program:** School does not have EDP
**Applicants notified:** n/a
**EDP available for:** n/a

**Regular acceptance notice —**
**Earliest date:** November 2011
**Latest date:** Until class is full
**Applicant's response to acceptance offer —**
**Maximum time:** Two weeks

**Requests for deferred entrance considered:** Yes

**Deposit to hold place in class:** Yes
**Deposit — In-State Applicants:** $100
**Out-of-State Applicants:** $100
**Deposit due:** May 15, 2010
**Applied to tuition:** Yes
**Deposit refundable:** Yes
**Refundable by:** May 15, 2011

**Estimated number of new entrants:** 86
**EDP:** n/a, **Special Programs:** n/a

**Start month/year:** August 2012

**Interview format:** Multi mini interview. Regional interviews are not available. Video interviews are not available.

## Preparatory Programs

**Postbaccalaureate Program:** No

**Summer Program:** Yes, http://ssrp.stanford.edu/

## 2010–2011 First Year Class

|  | In-State | Out-of-State | International |
|---|---|---|---|
| Applications | 2,274 | 3,299 | 300 |
| Interviewed | 170 | 252 | 12 |
| Matriculated | 43 | 41 | 2 |

**Total Matriculants: 86**  **Total Enrollment: 456**

## Financial Information

|  | In-State | Out-of-State |
|---|---|---|
| Total Cost of Attendance | $74,114 | $74,114 |
| Tuition and Fees | $45,042 | $45,042 |
| Other (incl. living expenses) | $26,000 | $26,000 |
| Health Insurance (can be waived) | $3,072 | $3,072 |

**Average 2010 Graduate Indebtedness: $103,157**
**% of Enrolled Students Receiving Aid: 78%**

Source: 2009-2010 LCME I-B survey and 2010-2011 AAMC TSF questionnaire

# University of California, Davis, School of Medicine

## Sacramento, California

Office of Admissions
UC Davis School of Medicine
4610 X Street, Suite 1202
Sacramento California 95817

**T** 916 734 4800    medadmsinfo@ucdavis.edu

**Admissions:** www.ucdmc.ucdavis.edu/
mdprogram/admissions/

## General Information

With a state-of-the-art home on the Sacramento campus, the UC Davis School of medicine prides itself in offering a rich and diverse academic environment. The school grooms students for leadership roles in medicine, research, health policy, medical education and management/administration. Distinctions include: ranking in the top 50 schools for research and primary care, strong emphasis on interprofessional education with other Schools of Health (nursing, public health, informatics), and a five-year program for students interested in telecommunications-enhanced rural medicine. The school admitted its first class in 1968.

## Mission Statement

With a mantra of, "Learn. Discover. Share.", the school's educational mission is to create a supportive and collaborative environment which empowers students to develop skills, knowledge and attitudes to become tomorrow's leaders in patient care, public service, research and education. The mission of the larger UC Davis Health System is "discovering and sharing knowledge to advance health."

## Curricular Highlights

**Community Service Requirement:** Required. Required project in the third year Primary Care Clerkship.

**Research/Thesis Requirement:** Optional. Fourth year scholarly project is an option for credit toward graduation requirement.

UC Davis believes that acquiring and perfecting the skills needed to become a compassionate, culturally-competent and knowledgeable physician requires a combination of hands-on experiences, didactic instruction and problem-based challenges. With an emphasis on self-directed and small group learning, our curriculum is designed to encourage students to evaluate, think and formulate decisions to provide the highest level of patient care. Basic and clinical science courses are designed to illuminate situations that arise in the clinical setting as well as to spark interest in biomedical research, public health and other areas. A cutting edge Clinical Skills Center in our new medical education building maximizes technology's role in learning from standardized patients. Our students gain valuable experience through their leadership roles in the community, including through the provision of free health care to various underserved populations in the diverse Sacramento area. Our Rural Program in Medical Education (Rural-PRIME) has a 5-year curriculum contextualized to rural health, including training in public health and distance education via telemedicine.

## Selection Factors

Academic strengths in both physical/biological sciences and humanities are valued, as are experiences in both research and clinical care. We look for a broad array of life experiences which align with our institutional values of diversity, equality, community engagement and accessible healthcare.

## Information About Diversity Programs

Our curriculum's emphasis on cultural competency aligns well with our diverse medical student body, which reflects the diversity of California. The health system often hosts and/or sponsors local, state and regional meetings of medical student organizations including the Latino Medical Student Association and the Student National Medical Association. The UC Davis Health System's Office of Diversity is committed to fostering a supportive environment that maximizes the learning and working experiences for all medical students, residents, faculty and staff.

## Regional/Satellite Campuses

Most clinical rotations take place at the UC Davis Medical Center in Sacramento and other facilities in the UC Davis Health System. Others take place at Sacramento's Kaiser, Sutter and Methodist hospitals as well as David Grant Medical Center at Travis Air Force Base, the San Joaquin General Hospital in Stockton and the VA Hospital in Rancho Cordova. Students enrolled in Rural-PRIME have opportunities to rotate through our rural hospital network sites and some students gain credit at hospitals and clinics abroad.

## 2010–2011 First Year Class

|  | In-State | Out-of-State | International |
|---|---|---|---|
| Applications | 3,615 | 897 | 84 |
| Interviewed | 501 | 17 | 1 |
| Matriculated | 94 | 2 | 0 |

**Total Matriculants: 96**    **Total Enrollment: 434**

## Financial Information

|  | In-State | Out-of-State |
|---|---|---|
| Total Cost of Attendance | $53,912 | $66,157 |
| Tuition and Fees | $32,521 | $44,766 |
| Other (incl. living expenses) | $19,591 | $19,591 |
| Health Insurance (can be waived) | $1,800 | $1,800 |

**Average 2010 Graduate Indebtedness: $136,996**
**% of Enrolled Students Receiving Aid: 92%**

*Source: 2009-2010 LCME I-B survey and 2010-2011 AAMC TSF questionnaire*

# University of California, Irvine School of Medicine

Irvine, California

University of California, Irvine
School of Medicine
Office of Admissions and Outreach
836 Medical Sciences Court
Irvine, California 92697-4089

T 800 824 5388   medadmit@uci.edu

**Admissions:** www.meded.uci.edu/Admissions

## General Information

The UC Irvine School of Medicine's academic and clinical training facilities are located on the UC Irvine main campus, the UC Irvine Douglas Hospital in the City of Orange and its community clinics and affiliates. The School of Medicine has 650 full-time faculty and 1,500 voluntary members in 25 academic departments. Areas of research and clinical emphasis include: neurosciences, oncology, urology, cardiovascular and pulmonary diseases, infectious diseases, and stem cell research. Special programs within the medical school include MD/MBA and MD/PhD (MSTP) programs and the Program in Medical Education for the Latino Community (PRIME-LC) that incorporates a MD and Master's degree emphasizing Latino heath care issues.

## Mission Statement

The UC Irvine School of Medicine is dedicated to advancing the knowledge and practice of medicine for the benefit of society. This mission will be achieved through programs of excellence in education, research, clinical care, and service to the public.

## Curricular Highlights

**Community Service Requirement:** Optional.

**Research/Thesis Requirement:** Optional.

The curriculum has been designed to provide training in the technical skills necessary to be a competent physician and to foster the humanistic qualities essential to be a well-rounded, caring and compassionate clinician. In addition to the basic science courses in the first two years, substantial clinical material has been integrated into the curriculum through the Clinical Foundations series which spans the four years of medical school. In the first year, students work with standardized patients to develop interview and physical examination skills. These clinical skills are further strengthened in the second year through a community preceptorship program. In addition, clinically oriented courses are designed to complement the material covered in basic science courses. During the clinical years, students rotate through the core clinical services of internal medicine, family medicine, surgery, obstetrics and gynecology, psychiatry, pediatrics, emergency medicine, radiology and neurology. In addition, students assume advanced clinical responsibilities through intensive care unit experience and a sub internship. Clinical advisors guide students in the selection of 20 weeks of electives tailored to the students' career goals and educational needs.

## Selection Factors

The Admissions Committee screens for applicants whose academic records indicate that they will be able to handle the medical school curriculum. In addition to scholastic achievement, attributes deemed desirable in prospective students include leadership and participation in extracurricular activities, including exposure to clinical medicine, research, and community service. Consideration is given to applicants from disadvantaged backgrounds. Preference is given to applicants who are either U.S. citizens or Permanent Residents. The School of Medicine does not accept transfer students.

## Information About Diversity Programs

UC Irvine is a multicultural community composed of individuals from diverse backgrounds. The Office of Diversity and Community Engagement and the Office of Admissions and Outreach work together to encourage and support applicants from disadvantaged backgrounds. Post baccalaureate programs provide students from disadvantaged backgrounds the academic platform and support they may need to gain acceptance to medical school. In addition, workshops and conferences are held that are focused on increasing diversity in the Health Sciences.

## Regional/Satellite Campuses

Student rotations are divided between UC Irvine Douglas Hospital, Veterans Affairs Long Beach Healthcare System, Children's Hospital of Orange County (CHOC), Long Beach Memorial Medical Center, and several clinics in the Orange County area.

## Application Process and Requirements 2012–2013

**Primary application service:** AMCAS®
**Earliest filing date:** June 1, 2011
**Latest filing date:** November 1, 2011

**Secondary application required:** Yes
**Sent to:** Screened applicants
**URL:** n/a
**Fee:** Yes, $70   **Waiver available:** Yes
**Earliest filing date:** July 15, 2011
**Latest filing date:** January 2012

**MCAT® required:** Yes
**Latest MCAT® considered:** October 2011
**Oldest MCAT® considered:** June 2008

**Early Decision Program:** School does not have EDP
**Applicants notified:** n/a
**EDP available for:** n/a

**Regular acceptance notice —**
**Earliest date:** November 1, 2011
**Latest date:** Until class is full
**Applicant's response to acceptance offer —**
**Maximum time:** Two weeks
**Requests for deferred entrance considered:** Yes

**Deposit to hold place in class:** No
**Deposit — In-State Applicants:** n/a  **Out-of-State**
**Applicants:** n/a
**Deposit due:** n/a
**Applied to tuition:** n/a
**Deposit refundable:** n/a
**Refundable by:** n/a

**Estimated number of new entrants:** 104
**EDP:** n/a, **Special Programs:** 18

**Start month/year:** August 2012

**Interview format:** Selected applicants are interviewed by both a faculty member and a student. Regional interviews are not available. Video interviews are not available.

## Preparatory Programs

**Postbaccalaureate Program:** Yes,
Outreach@uci.edu, www.meded.uci.edu/Admissions/PostBac.html

**Summer Program:** No

## 2010–2011 First Year Class

|  | In-State | Out-of-State | International |
|---|---|---|---|
| Applications | 3870 | 921 | 53 |
| Interviewed | 483 | 23 | 0 |
| Matriculated | 100 | 4 | 0 |

**Total Matriculants: 104**   **Total Enrollment: 440**

## Financial Information

|  | In-State | Out-of-State |
|---|---|---|
| Total Cost of Attendance | $53,876 | $66,121 |
| Tuition and Fees | $28,604 | $40,849 |
| Other (incl. living expenses) | $22,928 | $22,928 |
| Health Insurance (can be waived) | $2,344 | $2,344 |

**Average 2010 Graduate Indebtedness: $120,151**
**% of Enrolled Students Receiving Aid: 89%**

Source: 2009-2010 LCME I-B survey and 2010-2011 AAMC TSF questionnaire

# University of California, Los Angeles
# David Geffen School of Medicine at UCLA

## Los Angeles, California

David Geffen School of Medicine at UCLA
Office of Admissions
10833 Le Conte Avenue
Los Angeles, California 90095-7035

**T** 310 825 6081  somadmiss@mednet.ucla.edu

**Admissions:** www.medstudent.ucla.edu/
prospective/

## General Information

The David Geffen School of Medicine at UCLA is on the UCLA campus. Ronald Reagan Medical Center, Mattel Children's, Neuropsychiatric Hospital, and Jules Stein Eye Institute are all located in the Westwood Campus. These institutions, together with the School of Dentistry, Nursing, and Public Health, are integral parts of the environment. Major affiliations include LA County Harbor and Olive View Medical Centers, Veterans Affairs Medical Centers West LA and Sepulveda, Cedars-Sinai Medical Center and Kaiser Permanente. The decision of which medical school to attend is extremely important. We provide applicants with critical information through website. Applicants may check their status on the Admission Web site. Students invited for interviews participate in student tours, meet faculty, students, staff, and members of the Admissions Committee.

## Mission Statement

The school seeks students who will be future leaders, have distinguished careers in clinical practice, teaching, research, and public service. The school strives to create an environment in which students prepare for a future where scientific knowledge, societal values and human needs are ever-changing.

## Curricular Highlights

**Community Service Requirement:** Optional. Student-run clinics are numerous; 80% do service.

**Research/Thesis Requirement:** Optional. Over 75% participate in research.

The first two years present a thorough grounding in the science basic to medicine. An integrated approach to basic & clinical sciences is enhanced through problem-based learning in small groups. Students are introduced to a holistic approach to patient care from the beginning through the nationally recognized Doctoring course. The first two years center on processes of disease, with emphasis on organ system-oriented instruction. The third year core clerkships encompass internal medicine, surgery, obstetrics and gynecology, pediatrics, psychiatry, family practice, radiology, and neurology. The senior year, through a set of Colleges, provide a unique mentoring and educational experience bringing together student and faculty with similar interests. Senior electives are designed to provide students with a foundation to develop and fulfill personal interests, broaden clinical knowledge, and provide an advantage in securing desired residencies. UCLA has a pass/fail grading system, allowing students to actively participate in school and student-organized activities. There are student run clinics at the Salvation Army Homeless Center, Mobile Clinic, Health Fairs, and activities teaching high school students preventive health, and work with the underserved. Student use summers for research, community work, and international work. The MSTP programs leads to M.D.–Ph.D. degrees for those interested in research. This program requires 3–5 additional years to the M.D. study. Stipends are provided for this program. The school also offers joint M.D.–M.B.A. and M.D.–M.P.H. programs chosen in the junior year. The program is designed for students interested in organization leadership roles. Our Drew program is for those interested in the underserved. Our UCR/UCLA Program is a cooperative venture with the University of California, Riverside. Students spend their first two years at UCR with the same curriculum as UCLA, followed by their final two clinical years at the UCLA School of Medicine.

## Selection Factors

Preference is given to those showing evidence of broad training and high achievement in college education and those who possess those traits of personality and character essential to the success in medicine and the provision of quality, professional and humane medical care. We look for through coursework, school activities, community service and research for evidence of maturity, intellect, scholarship, and service to their communities and to those who are underprivileged and disadvantaged, are culturally aware and are able to speak a second language, especially Spanish. Final selections are made on the basis of individual qualifications and not on the basis of race, ethnicity, sex, age, sexual orientation, national origin or disability.

## Information About Diversity Programs

We pride ourselves on the diversity of our student body. Multiple programs to celebrate our diversity are part of student life and are integral to the learning environment.

## Application Process and Requirements 2012–2013

**Primary application service:** AMCAS®
**Earliest filing date:** June 1, 2011
**Latest filing date:** November 1, 2011

**Secondary application required:** Yes
**Sent to:** Screened applicants
**URL:** Supplied after screening
**Fee:** Yes, $/0  **Waiver available:** Yes
**Earliest filing date:** n/a
**Latest filing date:** within 45 days of request

**MCAT® required:** Yes
**Latest MCAT® considered:** September 2011
**Oldest MCAT® considered:** 2009

**Early Decision Program:** School does not have EDP
**Applicants notified:** n/a
**EDP available for:** n/a

**Regular acceptance notice —**
**Earliest date:** December 15, 2011
**Latest date:** Until class is full
**Applicant's response to acceptance offer —**
**Maximum time:** Two weeks

**Requests for deferred entrance considered:** Yes

**Deposit to hold place in class:** No
**Deposit — In-State Applicants:** n/a  **Out-of-State**
**Applicants:** n/a
**Deposit due:** n/a
**Applied to tuition:** n/a
**Deposit refundable:** n/a
**Refundable by:** n/a

**Estimated number of new entrants:** 187
**EDP:** n/a, **Special Programs:** n/a

**Start month/year:** August 2012

**Interview format:** Multiple mini-interviews (MMI). Regional interviews are not available. Video interviews are not available.

## Preparatory Programs

**Postbaccalaureate Program:** Yes,
www.medstudent.ucla.edu/prospective

**Summer Program:** Yes, Elizabeth Yzquierdo
(310) 825-3575

## 2010–2011 First Year Class

|  | In-State | Out-of-State | International |
|---|---|---|---|
| Applications | 5,384 | 2,979 | 240 |
| Interviewed | 620 | 226 | 8 |
| Matriculated | 160 | 24 | 3 |

**Total Matriculants: 187**  **Total Enrollment: 739**

## Financial Information

|  | In-State | Out-of-State |
|---|---|---|
| Total Cost of Attendance | $56,394 | $68,639 |
| Tuition and Fees | $28,162 | $40,407 |
| Other (incl. living expenses) | $26,311 | $26,311 |
| Health Insurance (can be waived) | $1,921 | $1,921 |

**Average 2010 Graduate Indebtedness: $108,829**
**% of Enrolled Students Receiving Aid: 92%**

*Source: 2009-2010 LCME I-B survey and 2010-2011 AAMC TSF questionnaire*

# University of California, San Diego, School of Medicine

## La Jolla, California

Office of Admissions, 0621,
Medical Teaching Facility
UC San Diego School of Medicine
9500 Gilman Drive
La Jolla, California 92093-0621

**T** 858 534 3880   somadmissions@ucsd.edu

**Admissions:** http://meded.ucsd.edu/admissions

## General Information

Students at the University of California, San Diego (UCSD) benefit from a diverse faculty and access to a wide variety of research and clinical opportunities.

## Mission Statement

The overall objective of the medical school curriculum is to instill graduates with the knowledge, skills, and attributes that will lead to their becoming capable and compassionate physicians. Our educational philosophy is to give students an opportunity to go beyond the core curriculum and pursue electives and independent study that take full advantage of the resources available at UCSD and in the surrounding region, helping them to become expert clinicians and scientists who are aware of, and responsive to, community needs.

## Curricular Highlights

**Community Service Requirement:** Optional. Many community service activities are available.

**Research/Thesis Requirement:** Optional. Independent Study Project is required.

The goal of the medical curriculum and faculty-student interactions is to develop critical, objective, conscientious physicians prepared for changing conditions of medical practice and continuing self-education. The new integrated scientific curriculum utilizes a systems based approach to provide a solid foundation in the various scientific disciplines basic to medicine. Students are introduced to patient care in the outpatient setting from the beginning of their first year. The core curriculum of the last two years is composed of the major clinical specialties taught in hospital and out-patient settings, and relevant extended-care facilities. Elective opportunities are pursued during both the pre-clinical and clinical years. Several combined M.D.-Master's degree programs are available. A Program in Medical Education in Health Equity (PRIME-HEq) is entering its sixth year. The Medical Scientist Training Program provides the opportunity to earn both the M.D. and Ph.D. degrees over a seven to eight-year period of study. A Medical Scholars Program at UCSD (B.S.-M.D.) is available for outstanding California high school seniors planning careers in medicine. A second B.S.-M.D. program is available between UCSD School of Medicine and California Institute of Technology.

## Selection Factors

The Admissions Committee selects applicants who have demonstrated intelligence, maturity, integrity, and dedication to the ideal of service to society. The school is seeking a student body with a broad diversity of backgrounds and interests. The Admissions Committee seeks students with broad training and in-depth achievement in a particular area of knowledge, whether in the humanities, social sciences, or natural sciences. Other evaluation factors include evidence of meaningful involvement in extracurricular activities, performance on the MCAT, letters of recommendation, and personal interviews. The Admissions Committee interview evaluates the applicant's abilities and skills necessary to satisfy the non-academic or technical standards established by the faculty and the personal characteristics necessary to become an effective physician. Preference is afforded to California residents, and applicants who are U.S. citizens or permanent residents. The UCSD School of Medicine participates in the WICHE Professional Student Exchange Program. The School of Medicine does not accept transfer students.

## Information About Diversity Programs

The UCSD School of Medicine is committed to expanding the educational opportunities for applicants coming from disadvantaged educational or economic backgrounds. This institutional commitment is expressed through a pre-matriculation summer program, a conditional acceptance program, educational support programs, and financial aid assistance. The Office of Diversity and Community Partnerships supports innovative programs that enhance the academic, clinical, scholarly and advocacy skills of middle school, high school, community college, undergraduate, post-baccalaureate, graduate and medical students. More information on these programs is available at: *https://meded.ucsd.edu/asa/dcp/.*

## Regional/Satellite Campuses

Clinical rotations are conducted at the two UCSD Medical Centers, VA San Diego Healthcare System, Rady Children's Hospital, Scripps-Mercy Hospital, Balboa Naval Medical Center, and a variety of ambulatory care sites throughout San Diego.

## Application Process and Requirements 2012–2013

**Primary application service:** AMCAS®
**Earliest filing date:** June 1, 2011
**Latest filing date:** November 1, 2011

**Secondary application required:** Yes
**Sent to:** Screened applicants
**URL:** Supplied after screening
**Fee:** Yes, $80   **Waiver available:** Yes
**Earliest filing date:** July 1, 2011
**Latest filing date:** One month after receiving Secondary Application invitation

**MCAT® required:** Yes
**Latest MCAT® considered:** September 2011
**Oldest MCAT® considered:** January 2009

**Early Decision Program:** School does not have EDP
**Applicants notified:** n/a
**EDP available for:** n/a

**Regular acceptance notice —**
**Earliest date:** October 15, 2011
**Latest date:** Until class is full
**Applicant's response to acceptance offer —**
**Maximum time:** Two weeks

**Requests for deferred entrance considered:** Yes

**Deposit to hold place in class:** No
**Deposit — In-State Applicants:** n/a
**Out-of-State Applicants:** n/a
**Deposit due:** n/a   **Applied to tuition:** n/a
**Deposit refundable:** n/a   **Refundable by:** n/a

**Estimated number of new entrants:** 125
**EDP:** n/a, **Special Programs:** 18

**Start month/year:** August 2012

**Interview format:** Two one-hour open-file interviews. Regional interviews are not available. Video interviews are not available.

## Preparatory Programs

**Postbaccalaureate Program:** Yes,
http://meded.ucsd.edu/asa/dcp/postbac/,
Saundra Kirk, (858) 534-4171, sjkirk@ucsd.edu

**Summer Program:** Yes,
http://meded.ucsd.edu/ugme/oesssummer_program/,
Carrie Owen, (858) 534-1519, cnowen@ucsd.edu

## 2010–2011 First Year Class

|  | In-State | Out-of-State | International |
|---|---|---|---|
| Applications | 3,611 | 1,820 | 20 |
| Interviewed | 593 | 94 | 0 |
| Matriculated | 113 | 12 | 0 |

**Total Matriculants: 125**   **Total Enrollment: 505**

## Financial Information

|  | In-State | Out-of-State |
|---|---|---|
| Total Cost of Attendance | $50,666 | $62,911 |
| Tuition and Fees | $28,345 | $40,590 |
| Other (incl. living expenses) | $20,677 | $20,677 |
| Health Insurance (can be waived) | $1,644 | $1,644 |

**Average 2010 Graduate Indebtedness: $102,289**
**% of Enrolled Students Receiving Aid: 89%**

*Source: 2009-2010 LCME I-B survey and 2010-2011 AAMC TSF questionnaire*

# University of California, San Francisco, School of Medicine

## San Francisco, California

School of Medicine, Admissions
C-200, Box 0408
University of California, San Francisco
San Francisco, California 94143

**T** 415 476 4044 admissions@medsch.ucsf.edu

**Admissions:** http://medschool.ucsf.edu/admissions

### General Information

The UCSF School of Medicine is dedicated to excellence in education, research, and patient care. Woven throughout all of these pursuits is a strong commitment to public service. The UCSF School of Medicine earns its greatest distinction from the quality of its students and its outstanding faculty — including three Nobel laureates, 40 National Academy of Sciences members, 57 American Academy of Arts and Sciences members, 71 Institute of Medicine members, and 17 Howard Hughes Medical Institute investigators.

### Mission Statement

The UCSF School of Medicine strives to advance human health through a four-fold mission of education, research, patient care, and public service.

### Curricular Highlights

**Community Service Requirement:** Optional.

**Research/Thesis Requirement:** Optional.

The first two years consist of competency-based and integrated core instruction in the basic, behavioral, social, and clinical sciences; clinical experience is introduced within the first week of classes and clinical skills education continues throughout. Emphasis is placed on active, student-centered learning with plentiful small-group learning. In the third year, Clinical Core, immerses students in practice-based learning of clinical medicine. The fourth year, Advanced Studies, includes required subinternships, elective rotations, research, and specific fields of inquiry via the Pathways to Discovery program (*http://medschool.ucsf.edu/pathways/*) that prepares students for post-graduate training. For more detailed information, visit the School of Medicine Web site at *www.medschool.ucsf.edu/curriculum/overview/index.aspx*. The five-year PRIME-US program provides skills and support to medical students at UCSF and in the JMP with demonstrated interest in working with urban underserved communities (visit *http://medschool.ucsf.edu/PRIME/* for more information). The UCB-UCSF Joint Medical Program is a five-year MS/MD program with the first three years spent at UC Berkeley completing a case-based core medical curriculum, elective coursework and research in support of a health related MS. JMP students then transition to UCSF for their last two years of clinical work. For detailed information, please visit *http://jmp.berkeley.edu*.

### Selection Factors

UCSF students must have demonstrated the ability to perform at a very high level in their prior academic pursuits. Among the many applicants who meet this essential criterion, the school seeks to create a student community that is characterized by diversity in background, extra-curricular talents, academic interests, and career aspirations. There is no single mold that defines a UCSF student. UCSF wants some students who aspire to become terrific doctors, some who will become great scientists, some who will be leaders in health policy, and so on. The goal is to create the most stimulating and enjoyable possible environment in which to live and learn. For further details regarding the admissions process, please visit the School of Medicine's Web site at *www.medschool.ucsf.edu/admissions/apply/index.aspx*.

### Information About Diversity Programs

The School of Medicine welcomes applicants from all ethnic, economic, and cultural backgrounds without discrimination, and has a long-standing commitment to increasing the number of physicians who come from communities that are underserved and/or underrepresented in medicine. As a result, over the last 30 years, UCSF has had one of the highest minority enrollment and graduation rates of any continental U.S. medical school. The curriculum includes both coursework and practical opportunities focused on narrowing health care disparities.

### Regional/Satellite Campuses

**Regional Campus Location(s):** Fresno Center for Medical Education and Research.

Student rotations may be conducted at the UCSF Parnassus Campus, San Francisco General Hospital, UCSF/Mt Zion, SF VA Medical Center, and the UCSF Fresno Medical Education Program, as well as at several other Bay Area affiliated hospitals and clinics.

## Application Process and Requirements 2012–2013

**Primary application service:** AMCAS®
**Earliest filing date:** June 1, 2011
**Latest filing date:** October 15, 2011

**Secondary application required:** Yes
**Sent to:** Screened applicants after preliminary review
**URL:** n/a
**Contact:** UCSF School of Medicine Admissions (415) 476-4044, admissions@medsch.ucsf.edu
**Fee:** Yes, $60  **Waiver available:** Yes
**Earliest filing date:** August 2, 2011
**Latest filing date:** January 13, 2012

**MCAT® required:** Yes
**Latest MCAT® considered:** September 2011
**Oldest MCAT® considered:** September 2009

**Early Decision Program:** School does not have EDP
**Applicants notified:** n/a
**EDP available for:** n/a

**Regular acceptance notice —**
**Earliest date:** January 2012
**Latest date:** Until class is full
**Applicant's response to acceptance offer —**
**Maximum time:** Two weeks

**Requests for deferred entrance considered:** Yes
**Deposit to hold place in class:** No
**Deposit — In-State Applicants:** n/a
**Out-of-State Applicants:** n/a
**Deposit due:** n/a  **Applied to tuition:** n/a
**Deposit refundable:** n/a  **Refundable by:** n/a

**Estimated number of new entrants:** 165
**EDP:** n/a, **Special Programs:** n/a

**Start month/year:** June 2012 (UCB/UCSF Joint Medical Program); September 2012 (UCSF)

**Interview format:** Required to interview at UCSF, if invited. Two interviews, 40 minutes to one hour each. Regional interviews are not available. Video interviews are not available.

### Preparatory Programs

**Postbaccalaureate Program:** Yes, www.medschool.ucsf.edu/outreach

**Summer Program:** No

## 2010–2011 First Year Class

| | In-State | Out-of-State | International |
|---|---|---|---|
| Applications | 3,269 | 3,054 | 158 |
| Interviewed | 362 | 149 | 0 |
| Matriculated | 139 | 26 | 0 |

**Total Matriculants: 165**  **Total Enrollment: 631**

## Financial Information

| | In-State | Out-of-State |
|---|---|---|
| Total Cost of Attendance | $53,426 | $65,671 |
| Tuition and Fees | $28,005 | $40,250 |
| Other (incl. living expenses) | $22,952 | $22,952 |
| Health Insurance (can be waived) | $2,469 | $2,469 |

**Average 2010 Graduate Indebtedness: $112,202**
**% of Enrolled Students Receiving Aid: 89%**

*Source: 2009-2010 LCME I-B survey and 2010-2011 AAMC TSF questionnaire*

# University of Colorado School of Medicine

## Denver, Colorado

CO

Medical School Admissions
University of Colorado School of Medicine
Anschutz Medical Campus, Mail Stop 297
13001 East 17th Place
Aurora, Colorado 80045

T 303 724 8025   SOMadmin@uchsc.edu

**Admissions:** www.medschool.ucdenver.edu/
admissions

## General Information

The University of Colorado School of Medicine (UCSOM) is a part of the University of Colorado located in Denver and Aurora, Colorado. The Anshutz Medical Campus in Aurora includes the schools of dentistry, nursing, pharmacy, public health and the graduate school as well as the SOM. Clinical opportunities for medical students are located throughout the Denver metropolitan area and Colorado. The UCSOM is home to 2,483 full-time and 2,601 volunteer faculty. In addition to educating students and participating in research, the faculty assumes considerable responsibility for patient care. Student research opportunities and a variety of extracurricular activities are available. The UCSOM moved to the new 217-acre Anschutz Medical Campus in Aurora in January 2008.

## Mission Statement

The mission of the University of Colorado School of Medicine is to provide Colorado, the nation, and the world with programs of excellence in: Education – through the provision of educational programs to medical students, allied health students, graduate students and house staff, practicing health professionals, and the public at large; Research – through the development of new knowledge in the basic and clinical sciences, as well as in health policy and health care education; Clinical Care – through state-of-the-art clinical programs, which reflect the unique educational environment of the university, as well as the needs of the patients it serves; and Community Service – through sharing the School's expertise and knowledge to enhance the broader community, including our affiliated institutions, other health care professionals, alumni and other colleagues, and citizens of the state.

## Curricular Highlights

**Community Service Requirement:** Optional. Many community service electives are available.

**Research/Thesis Requirement:** Required. A scholarly project is required for graduation.

The curriculum is designed to provide the scientific and clinical background to prepare graduates for the practice of medicine. A systems-based curriculum was introduced in 2005. The Essentials block runs for 18 months. The core clinical year runs through April of year 3. The elective year allows students time to do sub-internships, critical care rotations and other courses essential to their career choices. A capstone presentation and course occurs in the spring of year 4. The Foundations of Doctoring curriculum begins after the first block of year one and continues through year 3. Standardized patients are widely used in Foundations.

## Selection Factors

Places are offered to the applicants who are most highly qualified in terms of intelligence, achievement, character, motivation, and maturity. Grades, MCAT scores, recommendations, and personal interviews are assessed. Humanistic qualities, indications of peer collaboration, and professionalism are characteristics of our students. Approximately 75 percent of the class is comprised of Colorado residents. Applicants from rural areas and from groups underrepresented in medicine are encouraged to apply. Wyoming and Montana (WICHE) applicants are treated as in-state. All undergraduate majors are considered acceptable. Excellent performance in the required science courses is essential. The medical school has an active Medical Scientist Training Program (MSTP) for those who wish to combine medical school with intensive laboratory research. The UCSOM does not discriminate on the basis of race, sex, creed, national origin, age, or disability. Financial status is not a factor in the selection of applicants.

## Information About Diversity Programs

The UCSOM encourages applications from qualified students from groups underrepresented in American medicine. Detailed information may be obtained from the Office of Diversity at (303) 724-4237.

## Regional/Satellite Campuses

Besides the hospitals on the Anschutz campus, students rotate through Denver Health Medical Center, National Jewish Hospital, and multiple hospitals throughout Denver and Colorado.

## Application Process and Requirements 2012–2013

**Primary application service:** AMCAS®
**Earliest filing date:** June 7, 2011
**Latest filing date:** November 1, 2011

**Secondary application required:** Yes
**Sent to:** All applicants
**Contact:** Ashley Ehlers, (303) 724-8025, ashley.ehlers@ucdenver.edu
**Fee:** Yes, $100  **Waiver available:** Yes
**Earliest filing date:** August 1, 2011
**Latest filing date:** December 31, 2011

**MCAT® required:** Yes
**Latest MCAT® considered:** September 2011
**Oldest MCAT® considered:** September 2009

**Early Decision Program:** School does not have EDP
**Applicants notified:** n/a
**EDP available for:** n/a

**Regular acceptance notice —**
**Earliest date:** October 16, 2011
**Latest date:** Until class is full
**Applicant's response to acceptance offer —**
**Maximum time:** Two weeks

**Requests for deferred entrance considered:** Yes

**Deposit to hold place in class:** Yes
**Deposit — In-State Applicants:** $200  **Out-of-State Applicants:** $200
**Deposit due:** Upon acceptance
**Applied to tuition:** Yes
**Deposit refundable:** Yes
**Refundable by:** July 1, 2012

**Estimated number of new entrants:** 160
**EDP:** n/a, **Special Programs:** n/a

**Start month/year:** August 2012

**Interview format:** Two one-on-one academically blind interviews. Regional interviews are not available. Video interviews are not available.

## Preparatory Programs

**Postbaccalaureate Program:** Yes,
By invitation only. Ashley Ehlers, (303) 724-8025, ashley.ehlers@ucdenver.edu

**Summer Program:** No

## 2010–2011 First Year Class

|  | In-State | Out-of-State | International |
|---|---|---|---|
| Applications | 612 | 3,189 | 74 |
| Interviewed | 319 | 258 | 6 |
| Matriculated | 123 | 37 | 0 |

**Total Matriculants: 160**     **Total Enrollment: 621**

## Financial Information

|  | In-State | Out-of-State |
|---|---|---|
| Total Cost of Attendance | $52,024 | $77,595 |
| Tuition and Fees | $29,990 | $55,561 |
| Other (incl. living expenses) | $18,935 | $18,935 |
| Health Insurance (can be waived) | $3,099 | $3,099 |

**Average 2010 Graduate Indebtedness: $150,036**
**% of Enrolled Students Receiving Aid: 95%**

Source: 2009-2010 LCME I-B survey and 2010-2011 AAMC TSF questionnaire

# University of Connecticut School of Medicine

## Farmington, Connecticut

Medical Student Affairs
University of Connecticut
School of Medicine
263 Farmington Avenue, Room AG-062
Farmington, Connecticut 06030-1906

T 860 679 4713    admissions@uchc.edu

**Admissions:** http://medicine.uchc.edu/prospective/admissions/index.html

## General Information

The School of Medicine occupies the University of Connecticut Health Center in Farmington. The Health Center also includes the School of Dental Medicine, Graduate School programs in Biomedical Science and Public Health, the University Hospital and Ambulatory Unit, research buildings, and the Stowe Library. Medical students receive clinical training in Hartford area-affiliated hospitals.

## Mission Statement

The curriculum of the School of Medicine is designed to prepare professional men and women with the ability to practice medicine in an evolving health care system. The primary goal is to develop in all students a fund of knowledge, skills, and attitudes that will enable them to pursue the postgraduate training necessary for their chosen career in medicine.

## Curricular Highlights

**Community Service Requirement:** Required. Numerous opportunities available.

**Research/Thesis Requirement:** Optional. Numerous opportunities available.

The basic science curriculum is based on an organ-systems approach. Normal human biology is presented in the first year of study, followed by the pathophysiology and therapeutic management of disease during the second year. Students learn medical history-taking, physical diagnosis, and other aspects of the physician-patient interaction throughout medical school. Students participate in a weekly longitudinal ambulatory clinical experience during the first three years of medical school, with an option for a fourth year. During the third year, students rotate through major clinical disciplines, while in the fourth year students complete 4 week required rotations in a sub-internship of their choice, critical care, emergency medicine, and radiology (two weeks), a selective experience (8 weeks), and four electives (4 weeks each). The grading system for the basic medical science curriculum is pass-fail. Honors and pass are given for the six core clinical disciplines in the third year, and in the fourth year in the sub-internship/emergency medicine/critical care/radiology blocks. No class rank or class-standing scales are used.

## Selection Factors

The University of Connecticut accepts highly qualified Connecticut residents, with special effort to include those who are disadvantaged. Highly qualified out-of-state residents are considered to achieve a diverse class. The Admissions Committee considers the applicant's interests, achievements, abilities, motivation, and character. GPA and MCAT scores are considered, along with academic program difficulty, academic achievement beyond regular coursework, intellectual growth and development, nonacademic activities, and recommendations. UCSOM policy prohibits discrimination in education, in employment, and in the provision of services on account of race, religion, sex, age, marital status, national origin, ancestry, sexual orientation, disabled veteran status, physical or mental disability, mental retardation, other specifically covered mental disabilities, and criminal records that are not job-related, in accordance with provisions of the Civil Rights Act of 1964, Title IX Education Amendments of 1972, the Rehabilitation Act of 1973, the Americans with Disabilities Act, and other existing federal and state laws and executive orders pertaining to equal rights.

## Information About Diversity Programs

The UCSOM recruits disadvantaged applicants and applicants from groups underrepresented in medicine through the Admissions Office and the Health Careers Opportunity Programs (HCOP) Office. The Admissions Committee reviews applications from these candidates in the same manner as those of all other candidates. Candidates receive a full and careful review, and are selected on a competitive basis. Candidates invited for interview meet with HCOP staff. Summer enrichment programs are available for high school and college students from groups traditionally underrepresented in American medicine. The HCOP Department's telephone number is (860) 679-3483.

## Regional/Satellite Campuses

Students rotate through clinical sites to insure a mix of inpatient and ambulatory experiences. Students complete a Continuity Practice experience with a physician in the community.

## Application Process and Requirements 2012–2013

**Primary application service:** AMCAS®
**Earliest filing date:** June 1, 2011
**Latest filing date:** November 15, 2011

**Secondary application required:** Yes
**Sent to:** All applicants
**URL:** http://medicine.uchc.edu/prospective/firstyear/index.html
**Fee:** Yes, $85    **Waiver available:** Yes
**Earliest filing date:** June 1, 2011
**Latest filing date:** December 31, 2011

**MCAT® required:** Yes
**Latest MCAT® considered:** September 2011
**Oldest MCAT® considered:** September 2008

**Early Decision Program:** School does have EDP
**Applicants notified:** October 1, 2011
**EDP available for:** Both In-State and Out-of-State Applicants

**Regular acceptance notice —**
**Earliest date:** October 15, 2011
**Latest date:** Until class is full
**Applicant's response to acceptance offer —**
**Maximum time:** Two weeks

**Requests for deferred entrance considered:** Yes

**Deposit to hold place in class:** Yes
**Deposit — In-State Applicants:** $100
**Out-of-State:** $100
**Deposit due:** Upon acceptance  **Applied to tuition:** Yes
**Deposit refundable:** Yes  **Refundable by:** May 15, 2012

**Estimated number of new entrants:** 89
**EDP:** 2, **Special Programs:** 10

**Start month/year:** August 2012

**Interview format:** One-on-one and group interview sessions. Regional interviews are not available. Video interviews are not available.

## Preparatory Programs

**Postbaccalaureate Program:** Yes,
http://medicine.uchc.edu/prospective/postbac/index.html,
Dr. Richard Zeff, admissions@uchc.edu

**Summer Program:** Yes, http://medicine.uchc.edu/prospective/enrichment/collegefellow/index.html,
Dr. Richard Zeff, admissions@uchc.edu

## 2010–2011 First Year Class

|  | In-State | Out-of-State | International |
|---|---|---|---|
| Applications | 459 | 2,313 | 317 |
| Interviewed | 269 | 98 | 2 |
| Matriculated | 73 | 16 | 0 |
| **Total Matriculants: 89** | | **Total Enrollment: 352** | |

## Financial Information

|  | In-State | Out-of-State |
|---|---|---|
| Total Cost of Attendance | $54,877 | $79,074 |
| Tuition and Fees | $28,435 | $52,632 |
| Other (incl. living expenses) | $23,822 | $23,822 |
| Health Insurance (can be waived) | $2,620 | $2,620 |

**Average 2010 Graduate Indebtedness: $119,957**
**% of Enrolled Students Receiving Aid: 81%**

*Source: 2009-2010 LCME I-B survey and 2010-2011 AAMC TSF questionnaire*

# Yale University School of Medicine

## New Haven, Connecticut

Richard A. Silverman, Director of Admissions
Yale University School of Medicine
Edward S. Harkness Hall, 367 Cedar Street
New Haven, Connecticut 06510

T 203 785 2696    http://medicine.yale.edu

**Admissions:** http://medicine.yale.edu/education/
admissions

CT

## General Information

The Yale University School of Medicine was established in 1810 as the Medical Institution of Yale College. The present-day Yale-New Haven Medical Center includes the School of Medicine, the School of Nursing, and Yale-New Haven Hospital.

## Mission Statement

The mission of the Yale University School of Medicine is to educate and inspire scholars and future leaders who will advance the practice of medicine and the biomedical sciences.

## Curricular Highlights

**Community Service Requirement:** Optional. Extensive community service opportunities.

**Research/Thesis Requirement:** Required. Original thesis required since 1839.

The Yale System of Medical Education is founded on a belief in the maturity and responsibility of students. Highlights of the program are anonymous examinations, the absence of competitive grades, and a required thesis. The ideal Yale physician is schooled in the current state of knowledge of both medical biology and patient care, with a lifelong commitment to learning. The first two years of the curriculum focus on the basic and clinical sciences. The first year emphasizes normal biological form and function, the second year the study of disease. Throughout both years, a pre-clinical clerkship course provides instruction in history, physical examination, and the art of communicating with patients. The third year is largely devoted to clinical clerkships. In the fourth year, students take electives and a primary care clerkship, and complete their thesis. Required since 1839, the thesis is designed to develop critical thinking, habits of self-education, and application of the scientific method to medicine. Thesis work also gives students an opportunity to work closely with Yale faculty members.

## Selection Factors

The Admissions Committee seeks exceptional students who best suit the educational philosophy of the school. Because of the importance of diversity, applications are encouraged from women and persons from groups underrepresented in medicine. The committee considers each applicant's academic record, MCAT scores, premedical committee evaluations, letters of recommendation, extracurricular and community activities, and personal qualities. In general, the school strives to admit students with the ability to make significant contributions in medicine and a demonstrated capacity for leadership. Interviews are arranged only by invitation of the Admissions Committee. The class that enrolled in 2010 includes graduates of 47 undergraduate colleges. The diversity of the student body is also reflected in a wide variety of academic interests, professional goals, and personal backgrounds. The Yale School of Medicine does not discriminate on the basis of sex, race, color, religion, age, disability, national or ethnic origin, sexual orientation, or gender identity or expression.

## Information About Diversity Programs

Diversity is important in Yale's collaborative learning environment, and applications are encouraged from individuals from groups underrepresented in medicine. Several student organizations sponsor a range of activities throughout the year, all supported by the Office of Multicultural Affairs.

## Regional/Satellite Campuses

Clinical training occurs at Yale-New Haven Hospital and other affiliated hospitals in the region. In addition, there are training sites elsewhere in the United States and abroad. International research and community service opportunities are also available.

## Application Process and Requirements 2012–2013

**Primary application service:** AMCAS®
**Earliest filing date:** June 1, 2011
**Latest filing date:** October 15, 2011

**Secondary application required:** Yes
**Sent to:** All applicants
**URL:** https://bmsweb.med.yale.edu/msa/msa_web.
msa_index
**Fee:** Yes, $85    **Waiver available:** Yes
**Earliest filing date:** June 1, 2011
**Latest filing date:** November 15, 2011

**MCAT® required:** Yes
**Latest MCAT® considered:** September 2011
**Oldest MCAT® considered:** April 2008

**Early Decision Program:** School does have EDP
**Applicants notified:** October 1, 2011
**EDP available for:** Both In-State and Out-of-State Applicants

**Regular acceptance notice —**
**Earliest date:** March 15, 2012
**Latest date:** Until class is full
**Applicant's response to acceptance offer —**
**Maximum time:** Three weeks

**Requests for deferred entrance considered:** Yes

**Deposit to hold place in class:** Yes
**Deposit — In-State Applicants:** $100
**Out-of-State Applicants:** $100
**Deposit due:** With response to acceptance offer
**Applied to tuition:** Yes
**Deposit refundable:** Yes
**Refundable by:** May 15, 2012

**Estimated number of new entrants:** 100
**EDP:** 1, **Special Programs:** n/a

**Start month/year:** August 2012

**Interview format:** One-on-one, open-file interviews. Regional interviews only available if applicant is unable to come to campus. Video interviews are not available.

## Preparatory Programs

**Postbaccalaureate Program:** No

**Summer Program:** Yes, http://info.med.yale.edu/omca/programs/mmep.htm

## 2010–2011 First Year Class

|  | In-State | Out-of-State | International |
|---|---|---|---|
| Applications | 225 | 4,570 | 437 |
| Interviewed | 43 | 699 | 52 |
| Matriculated | 8 | 82 | 10 |

**Total Matriculants: 100**    **Total Enrollment: 382**

## Financial Information

|  | In-State | Out-of-State |
|---|---|---|
| Total Cost of Attendance | $66,540 | $66,540 |
| Tuition and Fees | $46,100 | $46,100 |
| Other (incl. living expenses) | $18,310 | $18,310 |
| Health Insurance (can be waived) | $2,130 | $2,130 |

**Average 2010 Graduate Indebtedness: $124,070**
**% of Enrolled Students Receiving Aid: 88%**

Source: 2009-2010 LCME I-B survey and 2010-2011 AAMC TSF questionnaire

# The George Washington University School of Medicine and Health Sciences

## Washington, District of Columbia

The George Washington University
School of Medicine and Health Sciences
Office of M.D. Admissions
2300 I Street, N.W., Ross Hall 716
Washington, District of Columbia 20037

**T** 202 994 3506   medadmit@gwu.edu

**Admissions:** http://smhs.gwumc.edu/mdprograms/admissions

## General Information

As the 11th oldest medical school in the country just a few blocks from the White House, we are positioned to influence health care locally, nationally, and globally. Adjacent to the School of Medicine in Ross Hall is the GW Hospital with facilities for clinical simulation and standardized patient examinations.

## Mission Statement

With a vision to be a pre-eminent health institution in the Washington area, GW is committed to providing the highest quality of care and health services to the public; excellence and innovation in education; and research that expands the frontiers of science and knowledge.

## Curricular Highlights

**Community Service Requirement:** Required.

**Research/Thesis Requirement:** Optional.

The curriculum contains a course entitled "The Practice of Medicine" (POM). This course spans all four years, allowing students to immediately begin clinical training during the first two years while studying the basic sciences. Each first-year student has a physician mentor. Clinical clerkships begin in the third year, and opportunities for international clinical experiences are available during the fourth year. An Honors/Pass/Conditional/Fail system is used for grading. The Office of Student Opportunities (OSO) is a resource to all students in the School of Medicine and Health Sciences (SMHS) providing a large database of national and international programs for summer study, electives, conferences and other educational opportunities, many of which are funded. The OSO's Track Program supports students in developing a broad perspective and encourages students to pursue paths of leadership within the field through nine tracks of study: community/urban health, emergency management, environmental health, global health, health policy, integrative medicine, medical education leadership, medical humanities, and research.

## Selection Factors

The initial evaluation is based on data in the AMCAS® and GW applications. This evaluation reviews academic performance; MCAT scores; extracurricular, health-related, research, and work experiences; evidence of non-scholastic accomplishments; and examination of personal comments and letters of recommendation. The most promising applicants are invited for interview. The last phase includes the review by the Committee on Admissions of the entire dossier. This phase selects academically prepared students with motivational and personal characteristics the Committee considers important in future physicians.

## Information About Diversity Programs

The School of Medicine is committed to providing an education to students from groups underrepresented in medicine. Applicants are encouraged to meet with students and faculty from groups underrepresented in medicine. There are focused student organizations such as NBLHO and SNMA. Through the DC Health and Academic Prep Program (DCHAPP), SMHS students and medical professionals teach graduating high school seniors about various medical professions as possible career paths. As DC HAPP mentors, SMHS students play an influential role in young students' lives, preparing them for their upcoming college experience and inspiring them to pursue the world of medicine and health.

## Regional/Satellite Campuses

Facilities include the GW Hospital, the teaching services of the Children's National Medical Center, Inova Fairfax Hospital, Holy Cross Hospital, National Naval Medical Center, St. Elizabeth's Hospital, Veterans Administration Hospital, and Washington Hospital Center are also available to students. A variety of ambulatory sites in the DC area are also utilized, including neighborhood clinics that serve underserved patients.

## Application Process and Requirements 2012–2013

**Primary application service:** AMCAS®
**Earliest filing date:** June 1, 2011
**Latest filing date:** December 1, 2011

**Secondary application required:** Yes
**Sent to:** All applicants
**URL:** n/a
**Fee:** Yes, $125   **Waiver available:** Yes
**Earliest filing date:** June 1, 2011
**Latest filing date:** January 1, 2012

**MCAT® required:** Yes
**Latest MCAT® considered:** September 2011
**Oldest MCAT® considered:** April 2009

**Early Decision Program:** School does have EDP
**Applicants notified:** October 1, 2011
**EDP available for:** Both In-States and Out-of-States

**Regular acceptance notice —**
**Earliest date:** October 15, 2011
**Latest date:** Until class is full
**Applicant's response to acceptance offer —**
**Maximum time:** Three Weeks

**Requests for deferred entrance considered:** Yes

**Deposit to hold place in class:** Yes
**Deposit — In-State Applicants:** $100   Out-of-State: $100
**Deposit due:** May 15, 2012
**Applied to tuition:** Yes
**Deposit refundable:** Yes
**Refundable by:** May 15, 2012

**Estimated number of new entrants:** 177
**EDP:** 5, **Special Programs:** 39

**Start month/year:** August 2012

**Interview format:** Two blind interviews with a faculty member and a student. All interviews take place at GW. Video interviews are not available.

### Preparatory Programs

**Postbaccalaureate Program:** No

**Summer Program:** Yes, www.gwumc.edu/dchapp/dchapp.html

## 2010–2011 First Year Class

|  | In-State | Out-of-State | International |
|---|---|---|---|
| Applications | 48 | 13,444 | 516 |
| Interviewed | 47 | 1,098 | 4 |
| Matriculated | 3 | 172 | 2 |

**Total Matriculants: 177**   **Total Enrollment: 719**

## Financial Information

|  | In-State | Out-of-State |
|---|---|---|
| Total Cost of Attendance | $71,100 | $71,100 |
| Tuition and Fees | $49,062 | $49,062 |
| Other (incl. living expenses) | $22,038 | $22,038 |
| Health Insurance (can be waived) | $0 | $0 |

**Average 2010 Graduate Indebtedness: $205,273**
**% of Enrolled Students Receiving Aid: 81%**

Source: 2009-2010 LCME I-B survey and 2010-2011 AAMC TSF questionnaire

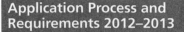

# Georgetown University School of Medicine

## Washington, District of Columbia

Office of Admissions
Georgetown University School
of Medicine, Box 571421
Washington, District of Columbia 20057-1421

T 202 687 1154   medicaladmissions@georgetown.edu

**Admissions:** http://som.georgetown.edu/
prospectivestudents

## General Information

Founded in 1851, Georgetown University School of Medicine has been committed to the pursuit of knowledge in the service of the community. With a tradition of excellence in clinical education, Georgetown seeks to provide its students with a general professional education in medicine that integrates the scientific, clinical, and humanistic disciplines and lays the groundwork for the intellectual and ethical formation of physician-healers, committed to the clinically competent care of, and the well being of their patients.

## Mission Statement

Guided by the Jesuit tradition of 'cura personalis,' caring for the whole person, Georgetown University School of Medicine will educate a diverse student body, in an integrated way, to become knowledgeable, skillful, ethical, and compassionate physicians and biomedical scientists, dedicated to the care of others and the health needs of our society.

## Curricular Highlights

**Community Service Requirement:** Required.

**Research/Thesis Requirement:** Research project required.

Georgetown's curriculum is systems based, emphasizing the body's normal and altered structure and functions reinforced with clinically oriented educational experiences, early introduction to patients, the art of advocacy, and the ethical/cultural dimensions of medicine. Small-group teaching in labs, seminars, and at the bedside begins early in the first year. The third year provides comprehensive clinical training in the care of patients through clerkships in the major medical specialties. The fourth year gives each student substantial responsibility for the management of patients through acting internships, elective study, and research. We have a Mind-Body Medicine Program, a Health Justice Scholars Program, international rotations, and a four-year curriculum in health care ethics. All lectures and powerpoint presentations are recorded. The grading system is Honors, High Pass, Pass, and Fail.

## Selection Factors

The Committee on Admissions selects students on the basis of academic achievement, character, maturity, and motivation. The committee evaluates the applicant's entire academic record, performance on the MCAT, college premedical committee evaluations or letters of recommendation, personal essays, and personal interview. A secondary application and essay are required of all applicants. An applicant may be invited to interview once all credentials have been reviewed by the committee. The personal interview is required and conducted on the medical center campus. The School of Medicine does not discriminate on the basis of race, sex, creed, age, disability, sexual orientation, or national or ethnic origin.

## Information About Diversity Programs

The University was founded on the principle that serious and sustained discourse among people of different faiths, cultures and beliefs promotes intellectual, ethical and spiritual understanding. Consistent with this principle, the School of Medicine strives to ensure that its students become respectful physicians who embrace all dimensions of diversity in a learning environment that understands and includes the varied health care needs and growing diversity of the populations we serve. The School of Medicine has a diverse student body, with students from groups underrepresented in medicine. Inquiries can be addressed to the Office of Admissions.

## Regional/Satellite Campuses

First and Second Year Ambulatory care experiences are within the area. Third and Fourth Year required rotations are divided among seventeen affiliated hospitals, including the University Hospital, MedStar not-for-profit Hospital Network, and other federal and community hospitals in the metro area.

## Application Process and Requirements 2012–2013

**Primary application service:** AMCAS®
**Earliest filing date:** June 1, 2011
**Latest filing date:** October 31, 2011

**Secondary application required:** Yes
**Sent to:** All applicants
**URL:** http://som.georgetown.edu/prospectivestudents
**Fee:** Yes, $130   **Waiver available:** Yes
**Earliest filing date:** June 15, 2011
**Latest filing date:** December 20, 2011

**MCAT® required:** Yes
**Latest MCAT® considered:** September 2011
**Oldest MCAT® considered:** January 2009

**Early Decision Program:** School does not have EDP
**Applicants notified:** n/a
**EDP available for:** n/a

**Regular acceptance notice —**
**Earliest date:** October 16, 2011
**Latest date:** Until class is full
**Applicant's response to acceptance offer —**
**Maximum time:** Three Weeks

**Requests for deferred entrance considered:** Yes

**Deposit to hold place in class:** Yes
**Deposit — In-State Applicants:** $500
**Out-of-State Applicants:** $500
**Deposit due:** June 1, 2012
**Applied to tuition:** Yes
**Deposit refundable:** Yes
**Refundable by:** June 1, 2012

**Estimated number of new entrants:** 196
**EDP:** n/a, **Special Programs:** n/a

**Start month/year:** August 2012

**Interview format:** Interviews are one-on-one, in-person and on-campus only. Regional interviews are not available. Video interviews are not available.

## Preparatory Programs

**Postbaccalaureate Program:** Yes,
http://gems.georgetown.edu

**Summer Program:** Yes, http://gsmi.georgetown.edu

## 2010–2011 First Year Class

|  | In-State | Out-of-State | International |
|---|---|---|---|
| Applications | 40 | 11,027 | 482 |
| Interviewed | 18 | 1,074 | 59 |
| Matriculated | 4 | 188 | 4 |

| **Total Matriculants: 196** | **Total Enrollment: 801** |
|---|---|

## Financial Information

|  | In-State | Out-of-State |
|---|---|---|
| Total Cost of Attendance | $69,835 | $69,835 |
| Tuition and Fees | $47,368 | $47,368 |
| Other (incl. living expenses) | $20,722 | $20,722 |
| Health Insurance (can be waived) | $1,745 | $1,745 |

**Average 2010 Graduate Indebtedness: $194,750**
**% of Enrolled Students Receiving Aid: 89%**

Source: 2009-2010 LCME I-B survey and 2010-2011 AAMC TSF questionnaire

# Howard University College of Medicine

## Washington, District of Columbia

Office of Admissions, Office of the Dean
Howard University College of Medicine,
520 W Street, N.W., Room 2310
Washington, District of Columbia 20059
**T** 202 806 6270    hucmadmissions@howard.edu

**Admissions:** http://medicine.howard.edu/students/
prospective/admissions

## General Information

The Howard University College of Medicine is the oldest and largest historically black medical school in the United States and the 36th oldest of all 133 medical schools in this country. The medical department's primary goal at inception remains the college's goal today: to train students to become competent, compassionate physicians who will provide care in medically underserved communities. The college has more than 4,000 living alumni, including approximately 25 percent of all black practicing physicians in this country. Until 1950, the college contributed nearly half of the black physicians in the United States. The 321-bed Howard University Hospital was completed in 1975. It is the college's primary teaching hospital for medical students and is used for postgraduate training in the various specialties of medicine. Medical students also may serve clerkships at the Children's National Medical Center, INOVA Fairfax Hospital, St. Elizabeth's Hospital, the Washington Veterans Affairs Medical Center, Providence Hospital, and the Washington Hospital Center.

## Mission Statement

Howard University College of Medicine provides students of high academic potential with a medical education of exceptional quality and prepares physicians and other health care professionals to serve the underserved. Particular focus is on the education of disadvantaged students for careers in medicine. Special attention is directed to teaching and research activities that address health care disparities.

## Curricular Highlights

**Community Service Requirement:** Optional.

**Research/Thesis Requirement:** Optional.

An integrated curriculum was implemented in August 2001. Students in the first year complete curriculum blocks in Molecules and Cells, Structure and Function, and Medicine and Society. In year two, pathophysiology, pathology and pharmacology are integrated according to organ system, and the Medicine and Society block is continued. Blocks in Physical Diagnosis and Introduction to Clinical Medicine are also included in year two. The third and fourth years consist of blocks of instruction in a continuum of clerkships and examinations in core clinical disciplines. During the fourth year, opportunity is available for additional clinical or research experience through 24 or 28 weeks of required electives. Pedagogical approaches include learning in small group settings, case-based and team-based learning and opportunities for practical application.

## Selection Factors

There are four major criteria used in the selection of applicants for admission to the College of Medicine: (1) character and discernible motivation for a career in medicine, (2) academic record, (3) results of the MCAT, and (4) letters of recommendation from preprofessional advisors and faculty. Candidates for admission and alternates are selected from among those applicants who satisfy the criteria and who are most likely to serve in communities needing physician services. An invitation for an interview may be extended to an applicant after the Committee on Admissions has made a preliminary examination of the applicant's credentials and has decided that an interview is desirable. Although the total student is evaluated, the Committee on Admissions gives strongest consideration to those who have GPAs of 3.0 and above. There are no residence restrictions. All applicants will be evaluated regardless of the applicants sex, race, religion, national or ethnic origin, age, marital status, or disability. A $100 (refundable) deposit and a $300 (non-refundable) enrollment fee (due with response to acceptance) is required of accepted applicants who have never previously enrolled at Howard University.

## Regional/Satellite Campuses

Student rotations are divided between Howard University Hospital and several hospitals, ambulatory centers, and private physicians' offices in the metropolitan area.

## Application Process and Requirements 2012–2013

**Primary application service:** AMCAS®
**Earliest filing date:** June 1, 2011
**Latest filing date:** December 15, 2011

**Secondary application required:** Yes
**Sent to:** All applicants
**URL:** http://medicine.howard.edu/students/prospective/
admissions/process.htm
**Contact:** Ms. Judith Walk (202) 806-6279,
jwalk@howard.edu
**Fee:** Yes, $75    **Waiver available:** No
**Earliest filing date:** August 15, 2011
**Latest filing date:** January 15, 2012 or thirty days after
receipt of secondary e-mail

**MCAT® required:** Yes
**Latest MCAT® considered:** September 2011
**Oldest MCAT® considered:** August 2009

**Early Decision Program:** School does not have EDP
**Applicants notified:** n/a    **EDP available for:** n/a

**Regular acceptance notice —**
**Earliest date:** October 15, 2011
**Latest date:** Until class is full
**Applicant's response to acceptance offer —**
**Maximum time:** 30 days, until April 15, 2012

**Requests for deferred entrance considered:** Yes

**Deposit to hold place in class:** Yes
**Deposit — In-State Applicants:** $100
**Out-of-State Applicants:** $100
**Deposit due:** With acceptance offer, accompanied by
non-refundable enrollment fee
**Applied to tuition:** Yes    **Deposit refundable:** Yes
**Refundable by:** April 15, 2012

**Estimated number of new entrants:** 110
**EDP:** n/a, **Special Programs:** 5

**Start month/year:** July 2012

**Interview format:** One-on-one interview with
admissions committee member. Regional interviews are
not available. Video interviews are not available.

## Preparatory Programs

**Postbaccalaureate Program:** No

**Summer Program:** Yes, www.smdep.org/progsites/
howard.htm

## 2010–2011 First Year Class

|  | In-State | Out-of-State | International |
|---|---|---|---|
| Applications | 37 | 5,548 | 459 |
| Interviewed | 7 | 302 | 8 |
| Matriculated | 4 | 98 | 8 |

**Total Matriculants: 110    Total Enrollment: 448**

## Financial Information

|  | In-State | Out-of-State |
|---|---|---|
| Total Cost of Attendance | $63,449 | $63,449 |
| Tuition and Fees | $39,606 | $39,606 |
| Other (incl. living expenses) | $23,843 | $23,843 |
| Health Insurance (can be waived) | $0 | $0 |

**Average 2010 Graduate Indebtedness: $165,331**
**% of Enrolled Students Receiving Aid: 95%**

*Source: 2009-2010 LCME I-B survey and 2010-2011 AAMC TSF questionnaire*

# Florida Atlantic University
# Charles E. Schmidt College of Medicine

Boca Raton, Florida

Office of Admissions (BC-71, Room 145)
777 Glades Road
Boca Raton, Florida 33431
**T** 561 297 0440    mdadmissions@fau.edu
Admissions: http://med.fau.edu

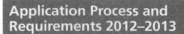
FL

## General Information

Florida Atlantic University served as a regional medical campus for six years before being accredited in 2011 by the Liaison Committee on Medical Education as the new, independent medical school, Florida Atlantic University Charles E. Schmidt College of Medicine. During its years as a regional campus, the College assembled a dedicated faculty and developed the infrastructure necessary for teaching medical students. With the new Integrated Patient Focused Curriculum and partnerships with nine well-established clinical facilities in southeast Florida, the Schmidt College of Medicine provides a comprehensive foundation for the study and practice of medicine. In affiliation with Scripps Florida of The Scripps Research Institute, the College offers an MD/PhD program which provides unique opportunities for those seeking careers combining medicine and research. The College is located on the 850-acre campus of Florida Atlantic University, a public institution, in Boca Raton, Florida, just north of Fort Lauderdale and only a mile from the beaches lining the Atlantic Ocean.

## Mission Statement

The College seeks to produce physicians who can provide the highest quality healthcare to a diverse population and to train physician-scientists who can meet Florida's initiatives in biomedical research.

## Curricular Highlights

**Community Service Requirement:** Required.

**Research/Thesis Requirement:** Optional.

The Integrated Patient Focused Curriculum features an active learning style using problem-based approaches and early patient contact. This begins in the first days of medical school when students visit community health centers and interview patients about their illnesses, treatments, and life changes. The acquisition of clinical skills begins in our Simulation Center and is augmented continuously through patient interactions under the tutelage of community preceptors. The third year features longitudinal integrated clerkships in which students are placed at clinical sites for up to 6 months and become active members of the health care team, learning about the system of care while developing core competencies for residency. The curriculum emphasizes humanistic medicine, professionalism, evidence-based decision making, comprehensive management of chronic diseases, and inter-professional teamwork in addressing each patient's needs.

## Selection Factors

Only United States citizens and permanent residents are accepted. Although residents of Florida are given preference, up to 15% of the class may come from other states. Selection factors include classroom performance, MCAT scores, quality of letters of recommendation, meaningfulness of direct patient contact experiences, diversity of background, volunteerism and community service, and an assessment of personal traits such as maturity, responsibility, integrity, respect for others, altruism and intellectual curiosity in an interview. To join the MD/PhD program, applicants must apply to and be accepted by both the Schmidt College of Medicine and by the Kellogg School of Science and Technology of Scripps Florida. Productive research experiences are essential for selection to the MD/PhD program.

## Information about Diversity Programs

Applicants from groups underrepresented in medicine are encouraged to apply. The Office of Diversity, Cultural and Student Affairs sponsors pipeline programs and works collaboratively with the Office of Medical Education to support the recruitment and retention of qualified minority students.

## Application Process and Requirements 2012–2013

**Primary application service:** AMCAS®
**Earliest filing date:** June 1, 2011
**Latest filing date:** December 15, 2011

**Secondary application required:** Yes
**Sent to:** All applicants who submit a verified AMCAS® application
**Fee:** Yes, $30    **Waiver available:** Yes
**Earliest filing date:** July 1, 2011
**Latest filing date:** January 15, 2012

**MCAT® required:** Yes
**Latest MCAT® considered:** September 2011
**Oldest MCAT® considered:** January 2009

**Early Decision Program:** School does not have EDP
**Applicants notified:** n/a
**EDP available for:** n/a

**Regular acceptance notice —**
**Earliest date:** October 15, 2011
**Latest date:** Until class is full
**Applicant's response to acceptance offer —**
**Maximum time:** Two weeks

**Requests for deferred entrance considered:** Yes

**Deposit to hold place in class:** Yes
**Deposit — In-State Applicants:** $100
**Out-of-State Applicants:** $100
**Deposit due:** After May 15, 2012
**Applied to tuition:** Yes
**Deposit refundable:** No
**Refundable by:** n/a

**Estimated number of new entrants:** 64
**EDP:** n/a, **Special Programs:** n/a

**Start month/year:** August 2012

**Interview format:** Open file. Regional interviews are not available. Video interviews are not available.

### Preparatory Programs
**Postbaccalaureate Program:** No

**Summer Program:** No

## 2010–2011 First Year Class

|  | In-State | Out-of-State | International |
|---|---|---|---|
| Applications | n/r | n/r | n/r |
| Interviewed | n/r | n/r | n/r |
| Matriculated | n/r | n/r | n/r |

**Total Matriculants: n/r    Total Enrollment: n/r**

## Financial Information*

|  | In-State | Out-of-State |
|---|---|---|
| Total Cost of Attendance | $48,515 | $79,669 |
| Tuition and Fees | $26,884 | $58,038 |
| Other (incl. living expenses) | $21,631 | $21,631 |
| Health Insurance (can be waived) | n/r | n/r |

**Average 2010 Graduate Indebtedness: n/r**
**% of Enrolled Students Receiving Aid: n/r**

*Projected figures provided by medical school.

# Florida International University
# Herbert Wertheim College of Medicine
## Miami, Florida

**FL**

Office of Admissions
Florida International University
Herbert Wertheim College of Medicine
11200 S.W. 8th Street – AHC2 660 W2
Miami, Florida 33199
**T** 305 348 0644    med.admissions@fiu.edu
**Admissions:** http://medicine.fiu.edu

## General Information

In August 2009, the College of Medicine welcomed the inaugural class. The four year program, leading to the MD degree, involves in-depth exposure and training in all areas of medical education with specific focus on family and community medicine. Unique to the College is the hands-on experience each student receives in observing and caring for families who have little or no access to medical care. Key in the medical training is the focus on the importance of the doctor-patient relationship in diverse patient populations.

## Mission Statement

The mission of the Florida International University Herbert Wertheim College of Medicine is to lead the next generation of medical education and continually improve the quality of healthcare available to the  community. The College of Medicine will accomplish its mission by training physicians to serve South Florida's diverse population through a patient-centered curriculum instilling cultural competence, providing Florida students greater access to medical education, and fostering research to discover and advance medically relevant knowledge.

## Curricular Highlights

**Community Service Requirement:** Required. An integral part of the mission and curriculum.

**Research/Thesis Requirement:** Required. Research is integrated into the curriculum.

The 4-year course of study leading to the MD degree is based on development of general competencies in medical knowledge, patient-centered care, communication skills, professionalism, system-based medical practice, practice-based learning and quality improvement skills, and socially responsible practices. The educational program is broad and general, preparing students for postgraduate study in their chosen field of medical specialization, licensure, and medical practice. The curriculum is built upon study in five major strands: Human Biology; Human Disease, Illness, and Injury; Clinical Medicine; Professional Development; and Medicine and Society. Course work is multidisciplinary with basic medical and clinical sciences and clinical skills integrated throughout four periods of study. Clinical experiences in primary care and emergency settings begin in the first period of study. Students are engaged with households and communities in a longitudinal service-learning program in collaboration with FIU students from other health professions. Clinical training begins with basic medical conditions in outpatient settings and advances progressively with more complex cases and conditions in hospital settings, culminating in subinternship experiences. Independent scholarship and broad elective opportunities encourage students to explore personal interests and build individualized competencies in preparation for advanced postgraduate study and practice in a specialty area.

## Selection Factors

The Admissions Committee uses AMCAS, a secondary application, letters of recommendation and interview feedback to select applicants who have demonstrated a well-rounded, rigorous academic preparation, character and maturity and who best suit our mission. Applicants must show a strong interest in medicine, a record of personal experiences suggesting medical care exposure, research, altruism, integrity, community service, and leadership with the ability and desire to pursue lifelong learning. Most important are the personal attributes necessary to be a competent compassionate physician. Presently, only US Citizens and permanent residents are considered.

## Information About Diversity Programs

The Herbert Wertheim College of Medicine considers diversity an integral part of the entire academic enterprise. Blending of different life and cultural experiences is of prime importance in the selection of faculty and staff and in the selection of medical students and education of future physicians. HWCOM seeks to foster a broad and diverse community of faculty, staff, and students to enrich the educational environment and expand the knowledge base for our students. The value of this diversity emphasis for HWCOM educational programs and staffing will be realized by the production of culturally competent physicians who can serve South Florida's diverse population. Diversity in HWCOM admissions is multidimensional and holistic, assessing academic background/achievement, personal characteristics, personal attributes, and personal experiences.

## Application Process and Requirements 2012–2013

**Primary application service:** AMCAS®
**Earliest filing date:** June 1, 2011
**Latest filing date:** December 15, 2011

**Secondary application required:** Yes
**Sent to:** All AMCAS® verified applicants
**Contact:** Betty L. Monfort, (305) 348-0644
med.admissions@fiu.edu

**Fee:** Yes, $30  **Waiver available:** Yes (if waived by AMCAS)
**Earliest filing date:** June 1, 2011
**Latest filing date:** January 1, 2012

**MCAT® required:** Yes
**Latest MCAT® considered:** September 2011
**Oldest MCAT® considered:** January 2009

**Early Decision Program:** School does have EDP
**Applicants notified:** October 1, 2011
**EDP available for:** See Website

**Regular acceptance notice —**
**Earliest date:** October 15, 2011
**Latest date:** Varies

**Applicant's response to acceptance offer —**
**Maximum time:** Three Weeks from date of offer

**Requests for deferred entrance considered:** No

**Deposit to hold place in class:** Yes
**Deposit — In-State Applicants:** $100
**Out-of-State Applicants:** $100
**Deposit due:** with offer acceptance
**Applied to tuition:** Yes
**Deposit refundable:** No
**Refundable by:** n/a

**Estimated number of new entrants:** 80
**EDP:** 2, **Special Programs:** n/a

**Start month/year:** August 2012

**Interview format:** Two committee members interview invited applicants. Regional interviews are not available. Video interviews are not available.

## Preparatory Programs

**Postbaccalaureate Program:** No
**Summer Program:** No

## 2010–2011 First Year Class

|  | In-State | Out-of-State | International |
|---|---|---|---|
| Applications | 1,478 | 1,922 | 145 |
| Interviewed | 194 | 85 | 0 |
| Matriculated | 37 | 6 | 0 |
| **Total Matriculants: 43** | | **Total Enrollment: 85** | |

## Financial Information

|  | In-State | Out-of-State |
|---|---|---|
| Total Cost of Attendance | $57,452 | $88,952 |
| Tuition and Fees | $28,791 | $60,291 |
| Other (incl. living expenses) | $26,756 | $26,756 |
| Health Insurance (can be waived) | $1,905 | $1,905 |

**Average 2010 Graduate Indebtedness:** $0
**% of Enrolled Students Receiving Aid:** 100%

*Source: 2009-2010 LCME I-B survey and 2010-2011 AAMC TSF questionnaire*

# Florida State University College of Medicine

## Tallahassee, Florida

Division of Student Affairs and Admissions
Florida State University College of Medicine
1115 West Call Street
P.O. Box 3064300
Tallahassee, Florida 32306-4300

**T** 850 644 7904    medadmissions@med.fsu.edu

**Admissions:** http://med.fsu.edu/
?page=mdAdmissions.home

## General Information

The Florida State University College of Medicine was created in July 2000 by a legislative act to train physicians with a focus on serving medically underserved populations in rural and inner-city areas and the growing geriatric population in the state. The FSU College of Medicine is located in Tallahassee, with regional medical campuses, where students complete third and fourth-year clerkships, in Pensacola, Orlando, Sarasota, Tallahassee, Daytona Beach, and Fort Pierce.

## Mission Statement

The Florida State University College of Medicine will educate and develop exemplary physicians who practice patient-centered health care, discover and advance knowledge, and are responsive to community needs, especially through service to elder, rural, minority, and underserved populations.

## Curricular Highlights

**Community Service Requirement:** Optional.

**Research/Thesis Requirement:** Optional.

The academic program includes instruction in the biopsychosocial sciences and community-based health care. The first and second-year integrated curriculum uses a combination of lecture and case-based and problem-based learning in small-group discussions and simulated standardized-patient interviews. A three-year doctoring course, composed of lecture, small-group discussion, patient encounters, clinical skills instruction, and preceptorships, provides application models to complement years 1, 2, and 3. The third year and part of the fourth year consist of required rotations in internal medicine, surgery, pediatrics, obstetrics-gynecology, family medicine, community medicine, primary care geriatrics, emergency medicine, advanced internal medicine, advanced family medicine, and psychiatry. Students may spend up to 24 weeks in electives designed to provide a foundation on which to develop and fulfill personal interests, broaden clinical knowledge, and prepare for postgraduate medical training.

## Selection Factors

Although scholastic aptitude is necessary to complete studies in medical school, neither high GPAs nor high MCAT scores alone or in combination are adequate to obtain admission. International applicants must have a permanent resident visa. Applicants who have grades and test scores predictive of success in medical school, have demonstrated through their experiences a high degree of motivation for medicine and a strong commitment to the service of others, and have a likelihood of practicing medicine with medically underserved populations will be invited to interview. The committee evaluates all aspects of the applicant's academic record, including trends in scholastic performance.

## Information About Diversity Programs

Because of the mission of the FSU College of Medicine and the educational value of admitting a diverse class, we developed a Master's Bridge Program to provide opportunities for applicants from groups underrepresented in medicine. Applicants from these groups who embody the characteristics valued by the college are selected for the Bridge year, which is used to develop and enhance study, time management, and test-taking skills; psychosocial and basic science backgrounds; and clinical experiences. If these students meet all requirements established for the year, they are admitted to the next year's medical school class. Students may contact the Office of Outreach and Advising at (850) 644-7678 for more information.

## Regional/Satellite Campuses

**Regional Campus Location(s):** Daytona Beach, FL, Fort Pierce, FL, Orlando, FL, Pensacola, FL, Sarasota, FL, Tallahassee, FL, and Jacksonville, FL.

Student rotations in the third year occur at one of the regional campuses. Rural learning opportunities are also available within driving distance of each site.

## Application Process and Requirements 2012–2013

**Primary application service:** AMCAS®
**Earliest filing date:** June 1, 2011
**Latest filing date:** December 1, 2011

**Secondary application required:** Yes
**Sent to:** Screened applicants
**Contact:** (850) 644-7904, medadmissions@med.fsu.edu
**Fee:** No    **Waiver available:** No
**Earliest filing date:** June 1, 2011
**Latest filing date:** December 31, 2011

**MCAT® required:** Yes
**Latest MCAT® considered:** September 2011
**Oldest MCAT® considered:** May 2009

**Early Decision Program:** School does have EDP
**Applicants notified:** October 1, 2011
**EDP available for:** Both In-State and Out-of-State Applicants

**Regular acceptance notice —**
**Earliest date:** October 15, 2011
**Latest date:** Until class is full
**Applicant's response to acceptance offer —**
**Maximum time:** Two weeks

**Requests for deferred entrance considered:** Yes

**Deposit to hold place in class:** No
**Deposit — In-State Applicants:** n/a
**Out-of-State Applicants:** n/a
**Deposit due:** n/a
**Applied to tuition:** n/a
**Deposit refundable:** n/a
**Refundable by:** n/a

**Estimated number of new entrants:** 120
**EDP:** 20, **Special Programs:** 10

**Start month/year:** May 2012

**Interview format:** Two committee members interview invited applicants. Regional interviews are not available. Video interviews are not available.

## Preparatory Programs

**Postbaccalaureate Program:** Yes, http://med.fsu.edu/
index.cfm?page=outreachAdvising.MastersBridge

**Summer Program:** No

## 2010–2011 First Year Class

|  | In-State | Out-of-State | International |
|---|---|---|---|
| Applications | 1,794 | 1,757 | 33 |
| Interviewed | 406 | 12 | 0 |
| Matriculated | 120 | 0 | 0 |

**Total Matriculants: 120    Total Enrollment: 478**

## Financial Information

|  | In-State | Out-of-State |
|---|---|---|
| Total Cost of Attendance | $52,766 | $87,317 |
| Tuition and Fees | $20,341 | $54,892 |
| Other (incl. living expenses) | $31,010 | $31,010 |
| Health Insurance (can be waived) | $1,415 | $1,415 |

**Average 2010 Graduate Indebtedness: $140,883**
**% of Enrolled Students Receiving Aid: 92%**

Source: 2009-2010 LCME I-B survey and 2010-2011 AAMC TSF questionnaire

# University of Central Florida College of Medicine
## Orlando, Florida

MD Program Admissions Office
6850 Lake Nona Blvd
Suite 115
Orlando, FL, 32827

**T** 407 266 1350   mdadmissions@mail.ucf.edu

**Admissions:** www.med.ucf.edu/admissions

## General Information

UCF's College of Medicine enrolled its charter class of 41 students in 2009 and second class of 60 in 2010. The college's vision is to be the nation's premier 21st century college of medicine. Fully integrated into the Central Florida community's health care and medical research infrastructure, the college partners with Orlando Health and Florida Hospital systems, Orlando VA Medical Center and Nemours Children's Hospital to provide students clinical opportunities at more than 17 major facilities. Capitalizing on UCF's strengths in biomedical sciences, modeling and simulation, and optics and photonics, faculty in the college's Burnett School of Biomedical Sciences conduct groundbreaking research in cancer, cardiovascular diseases, neurological diseases and infectious diseases. The Central Florida community has embraced UCF COM's future physicians with their financial contributions and with more than 1,400 local doctors serving as volunteer faculty.

## Mission Statement

The University of Central Florida College of Medicine educates and inspires individuals to be exemplary physicians and scientists, leaders in medicine, scholars in discovery, and adopters of innovative technology to improve the health and well-being of all. Our patient-centered mission is achieved by outstanding medical care and services, groundbreaking research, and leading edge medical and biomedical education in an environment enriched by diversity.

## Curricular Highlights

**Community Service Requirement:** Optional.

**Research/Thesis Requirement:** Required. Basic/clinical science or heath-related topic.

The curriculum is a unique and exciting blend of state-of-the-art technology, virtual patients, clinical and laboratory experiences, research, directed small group sessions, and interactive didactic lectures. The first two years of the curriculum are structured into instructional modules. The first year focuses on how basic science relates to the human body and disease; the second year is an organ system-based approach, applying first-year knowledge to the study of clinical disease, pathological processes, diagnosis, and treatment. Numerous clinical experiences occur throughout the first two years that also includes a Focused Individualized Research Experience module. Third and fourth year curriculum is devoted to clinical experience through core clerkships and electives in our affiliated Orlando Health or Florida Hospital systems facilities.

## Selection Factors

Supplemental applications are available to all qualified U.S. citizens, permanent residents, and asylees upon verification of an AMCAS® application providing that the applicant meets the minimum GPA/MCAT requirements. Applicants chosen for an interview are highly motivated, capable, passionate, academically proven, and possess diverse skills, talents, and life experiences that will benefit the program, community, and fellow classmates.

## Information About Diversity Programs

Increasing diversity and inclusiveness is one of the central goals of UCF. Minorities account for nearly 20 percent of UCF faculty, and an aggressive minority recruitment plan continues to be a priority for the university.

## Application Process and Requirements 2012–2013

**Primary application service:** AMCAS®
**Earliest filing date:** June 1, 2011
**Latest filing date:** December 1, 2011

**Secondary application required:** Yes
**Sent to:** Screened applicants
**URL:** Provided to qualified applicants via e-mail
**Fee:** Yes, $30   **Waiver available:** Yes
**Earliest filing date:** July 1, 2011
**Latest filing date:** January 15, 2012

**MCAT® required:** Yes
**Latest MCAT® considered:** September 2011
**Oldest MCAT® considered:** January 2009

**Early Decision Program:** School does have EDP
**Applicants notified:** October 1, 2011
**EDP available for:** Both In-State and Out-of-State Applicants

**Regular acceptance notice —**
**Earliest date:** October 15, 2011
**Latest date:** Until class is full
**Applicant's response to acceptance offer —**
**Maximum time:** Two weeks

**Requests for deferred entrance considered:** Yes

**Deposit to hold place in class:** No
**Deposit — In-State Applicants:** n/a
**Out-of-State Applicants:** n/a
**Deposit due:** n/a
**Applied to tuition:** n/a
**Deposit refundable:** n/a
**Refundable by:** n/a

**Estimated number of new entrants:** 80
**EDP:** 0, **Special Programs:** n/a

**Start month/year:** August 2012

**Interview format:** Two partially closed faculty interviews. Regional interviews are not available. Video interviews are not available.

## Preparatory Programs
**Postbaccalaureate Program:** No

**Summer Program:** No

## 2010–2011 First Year Class

|  | In-State | Out-of-State | International |
|---|---|---|---|
| Applications | 1,666 | 2,076 | 22 |
| Interviewed | 225 | 88 | 0 |
| Matriculated | 45 | 15 | 0 |

**Total Matriculants: 60**     **Total Enrollment: 100**

## Financial Information

|  | In-State | Out-of-State |
|---|---|---|
| Total Cost of Attendance | $49,380 | $77,080 |
| Tuition and Fees | $24,275 | $51,475 |
| Other (incl. living expenses) | $23,205 | $23,705 |
| Health Insurance (can be waived) | $1,900 | $1,900 |

**Average 2010 Graduate Indebtedness: $0**
**% of Enrolled Students Receiving Aid: 100%**

Source: 2009-2010 LCME I-B survey and 2010-2011 AAMC TSF questionnaire

# University of Florida College of Medicine

Gainesville, Florida

Director, Office of Admissions
P.O. Box 100216, UF Health Sciences Center
University of Florida College of Medicine
Gainesville, Florida 32610-0216

**T** 352 273 7990    med-admissions@ufl.edu

**Admissions:** http://admissions.med.ufl.edu

## General Information

The University of Florida College of Medicine admitted its first class in September 1956. Located in the Health Science Center on the 2,000-acre University of Florida campus, the College of Medicine enjoys strong ties with HSC colleges and other university programs. The UF Health Science Center includes the Shands at UF Hospital including the Cancer Hospital and Critical Care Center that opened in 2009; Stetson Medical Science Building; Communicore; Academic Research Building; Health Professions, Nursing and Pharmacy Building; Cancer and Genetics Research Building; McKnight Brain Institute; Veterans Administration Medical Center; Nanotechnology Center and the Emerging Pathogens Center.

## Mission Statement

The College of Medicine strives to improve health care through consistently excellent leadership in education, clinical care, discovery, and service. We aspire to the following goals: to develop medical professionals who are committed to the highest ideals and standards of the profession and who model an exceptional standard of care for those they treat, lead, and serve; to educate and inspire the next generation of leaders; to provide comprehensive, patient-centered, culturally sensitive, compassionate, and innovative health care of the highest quality to all; to develop and utilize innovative models of interdisciplinary health care delivery; to provide leadership in efforts to promote health, to predict and prevent disease, and to deliver care; to improve our understanding of human health and disease and to translate these discoveries into new solutions; to recruit, develop, and nurture a diverse and academically outstanding community of faculty, students, trainees, and staff; to promote sustained, robust professional and personal growth, productivity, accountability, integrity, and synergy of faculty, students, and staff.

## Curricular Highlights

**Community Service Requirement:** Required. Consistent health care experience preferred.

**Research/Thesis Requirement:** Optional.

The four years are divided into three blocks of time — Preclinical Coursework (2 years), Clinical Clerkships (1 year), and Post-clerkship Electives and Required Courses (1 year). Preclinical coursework provides students with essential basic science and substantial clinical training and experience. The third year is devoted to clinical clerkships. Required clerkships include family medicine, medicine, neurology, pediatrics, psychiatry, obstetrics/gynecology, and surgery. Students spend 10-12 weeks participating in clerkships at UF Health Science Center Jacksonville. During clerkships, students become integral members of the medical team and have direct responsibility for assigned patients. The fourth year includes seven elective periods and three required courses: anesthesiology, emergency medicine, and either senior medicine, community medicine, or pediatrics. An eleventh period is available for accomplishing residency interviews. For students who have already chosen a specialty, fourth-year programs may be designed to provide career choice-related experiences.

## Selection Factors

We appraise applicants on personal attributes, academic record, activities, MCAT, and recommendations. A personal interview is required and is granted at the discretion of the Medical Selection Committee. We do not discriminate on the basis of race, sex, age, disability, creed, or national origin. Florida residents are given preference. Exceptionally well qualified non-residents are considered. We welcome applicants from groups underrepresented in medicine.

## Information About Diversity Programs

The Office of Minority Affairs offers summer research programs. Each year we accept 13 undergraduate and 2 health professions students into this 10 week long program. Students will gain first hand research experience under the guidance of a research faculty mentor.

## Regional/Satellite Campuses

**Regional Campus Location(s):** Jacksonville, FL.

The UF Health Science Center in Jacksonville is our urban campus and includes one of the few Proton Beam facilities in the country. Formal educational affiliations have also been established in Ft. Lauderdale, Miami, Orlando, and Pensacola.

## Application Process and Requirements 2012–2013

**Primary application service:** AMCAS®
**Earliest filing date:** June 1, 2011
**Latest filing date:** December 2, 2011

**Secondary application required:** Yes
**Sent to:** Applicants of interest
**Contact:** Leila Amiri, (352) 273-7990, med-admissions@ufl.edu
**URL:** n/a
**Fee:** Yes, $30    **Waiver available:** No
**Earliest filing date:** July 15, 2011
**Latest filing date:** January 13, 2012

**MCAT® required:** Yes
**Latest MCAT® considered:** September 2011
**Oldest MCAT® considered:** August 2009

**Early Decision Program:** School does not have EDP
**Applicants notified:** n/a
**EDP available for:** n/a

**Regular acceptance notice —**
**Earliest date:** October 17, 2011
**Latest date:** Until class is full
**Applicant's response to acceptance offer —**
**Maximum time:** Two weeks

**Requests for deferred entrance considered:** Yes

**Deposit to hold place in class:** Yes
**Deposit — In-State Applicants:** $100
**Out-of-State Applicants:** $100
**Deposit due:** Two weeks after notice of acceptance
**Applied to tuition:** Yes
**Deposit refundable:** Yes
**Refundable by:** May 15, 2012

**Estimated number of new entrants:** 135
**EDP:** 0, **Special Programs:** 12

**Start month/year:** August 2012

**Interview format:** Two open-file interviews at COM. Regional interviews are not available. Video interview possible under extraordinary circumstances.

## Preparatory Programs

**Postbaccalaureate Program:** No

**Summer Program:** Yes, http://oma.med.ufl.edu/8/summer-research-program/ Office of Minority Affairs, (352) 273-6656

## 2010–2011 First Year Class

|  | In-State | Out-of-State | International |
|---|---|---|---|
| Applications | 1,586 | 999 | 23 |
| Interviewed | 347 | 23 | 0 |
| Matriculated | 125 | 6 | 0 |

**Total Matriculants: 131**    **Total Enrollment: 536**

## Financial Information

|  | In-State | Out-of-State |
|---|---|---|
| Total Cost of Attendance | $49,451 | $78,691 |
| Tuition and Fees | $30,755 | $59,995 |
| Other (incl. living expenses) | $18,696 | $18,696 |
| Health Insurance (can be waived) | $0 | $0 |

**Average 2010 Graduate Indebtedness: $123,992**
**% of Enrolled Students Receiving Aid: 88%**

Source: 2009-2010 LCME I-B survey and 2010-2011 AAMC TSF questionnaire

# University of Miami
# Miller School of Medicine
## Miami, Florida

Office of Admissions
University of Miami Miller School of Medicine
P.O. Box 016159
Miami, Florida 33101

**T** 305 243 3234   med.admissions@miami.edu

**Admissions:** www.miami.edu/medical-admissions

## General Information

The University of Miami Miller School of Medicine is the largest and oldest medical school in the state of Florida. Six hospitals containing nearly 3,000 beds are located on the medical campus and provide a complete spectrum of clinical experiences. Specialty centers at the Miller School of Medicine include The Bascom Palmer Eye Institute and Anne Bates Leach Eye Hospital, the Ambulatory Care Center, the Diabetes Research Institute, the Lois Pope Life Center (which houses The Miami Project to Cure Spinal Cord Paralysis), the Bachelor Children's Research Institute, the Ryder Trauma Center, and the Sylvester Comprehensive Cancer Center.

## Mission Statement

The Miller School of Medicine has four interrelated missions: patient care, teaching, research, and community service.

## Curricular Highlights

**Community Service Requirement:** Optional.

**Research/Thesis Requirement:** Optional.

The curriculum is an integrated program that requires students to be active and responsible learners. It emphasizes faculty and student-led small-group experiences wherein basic science concepts are introduced and assimilated in light of common disease states and clinical relevance. It also includes material not traditionally emphasized: professionalism, humanism and ethics, population medicine, prevention and screening, quality and outcome assessment, medical informatics, geriatrics, alternative medicine, nutrition, medical economics, and end-of-life care. An over-arching theme throughout all four years is the continuous acquisition and refinement of clinical skills through expert teaching and patient encounters, starting in the first weeks of the first year of the curriculum.

## Selection Factors

Secondary applications are sent to all U.S. citizens and permanent residents who submit a verified AMCAS® application. In deciding whether to return secondary materials, applicants are reminded that the last entering class had an average undergraduate cumulative GPA of 3.7 and an average composite MCAT score of 32. Factors assessed by the committee to rate all completed applications include: preparedness to study medicine, diversity of life experiences, meaningfulness of direct patient contact experiences, and quality of letters of recommendation. Applicants with the highest ratings are invited for an interview. Applicants' files are reviewed without regard to race, creed, sex, national origin, age, or handicap.

## Information About Diversity Programs

The school sponsors a special seven-week summer program that provides pre-medical undergraduates with opportunities to gain first-hand knowledge of the requirements of a medical education. Applications and information may be obtained by calling (305) 243-5998.

## Regional/Satellite Campuses

**Regional Campus Location(s):** Palm Beach County Health Department.

The School of Medicine has a regional medical campus in Palm Beach County, Florida. Up to 48 students each year will complete their 3rd and 4th years of medical school for the combined MD-MPH Program. Students at the regional campus gain their clinical training at John F. Kennedy (JFK) Community Hospital and other local hospitals and clinics in conjunction with the Palm Beach County Health Department.

## Application Process and Requirements 2012–2013

**Primary application service:** AMCAS®
**Earliest filing date:** June 1, 2011
**Latest filing date:** December 1, 2011

**Secondary application required:** Yes
**Sent to:** All U.S. citizens and permanent residents
**Contact:** Richard S. Weisman, (305) 243-3234, med.admissions@miami.edu
**Fee:** Yes, $75   **Waiver available:** Yes
**Earliest filing date:** June 15, 2011
**Latest filing date:** January 31, 2012

**MCAT® required:** Yes
**Latest MCAT® considered:** September 2011
**Oldest MCAT® considered:** January 2009

**Early Decision Program:** School does not have EDP
**Applicants notified:** n/a
**EDP available for:** n/a

**Regular acceptance notice —**
**Earliest date:** October 15, 2011
**Latest date:** Until class is full
**Applicant's response to acceptance offer —**
**Maximum time:** Two weeks

**Requests for deferred entrance considered:** Yes

**Deposit to hold place in class:** Yes
**Deposit — In-State Applicants:** $100
**Out-of-State Applicants:** $100
**Deposit due:** After response to acceptance letter
**Applied to tuition:** Yes
**Deposit refundable:** No
**Refundable by:** May 15, 2012

**Estimated number of new entrants:** 198
**EDP:** 0, **Special Programs:** 30

**Start month/year:** August 2012

**Interview format:** Open file, structured, one hour interviews. Regional interviews are not available. Video interviews are not available.

## Preparatory Programs

**Postbaccalaureate Program:** No

**Summer Program:** Yes,
www.miami.edu/medical-admissions
Robert Hernandez, MD, (305) 284-5998

## 2010–2011 First Year Class

|  | In-State | Out-of-State | International |
|---|---|---|---|
| Applications | 1,612 | 3,638 | 33 |
| Interviewed | 272 | 178 | 0 |
| Matriculated | 102 | 47 | 0 |

**Total Matriculants: 149**     **Total Enrollment: 738**

## Financial Information

|  | In-State | Out-of-State |
|---|---|---|
| Total Cost of Attendance | $55,433 | $65,139 |
| Tuition and Fees | $30,113 | $39,319 |
| Other (incl. living expenses) | $23,313 | $23,813 |
| Health Insurance (can be waived) | $2,007 | $2,007 |

**Average 2010 Graduate Indebtedness: $161,505**
**% of Enrolled Students Receiving Aid: 86%**

Source: 2009-2010 LCME I-B survey and 2010-2011 AAMC TSF questionnaire

# University of South Florida College of Medicine

Tampa, Florida

Office of Admissions/MDC-3
University of South Florida College of Medicine
12901 Bruce B. Downs Boulevard
Tampa, Florida 33612-4799

**T** 813 974 2229   md-admissions@health.usf.edu

**Admissions:** www.hsc.usf.edu/nocms/medicine/
mdadmissions

## General Information

USF Health is composed of the College of Medicine (COM), Colleges of Public Health, Pharmacy, Nursing and the School of Physical Therapy and Rehabilitation Science. All offer immersive experiences for interacting with diverse patient populations and building inter-professional relationships at nationally ranked clinical facilities. In our four-year SELECT program, students have the opportunity to complete two years at Tampa and complete their clinical years at Lehigh Valley Health Network (LVHN), one of the most progressive, technologically advanced and highest ranked medical learning facilities in the country.

## Mission Statement

The College of Medicine educates students and professionals of the health and biomedical sciences within a scholarly environment, fostering excellence in the lifelong goals of education, research and compassionate care and providing a training ground for those who harbor a deeply rooted desire to selflessly serve in the medical profession to become medical leaders.

## Curricular Highlights

**Community Service Requirement:** Required. International, national and local opportunities.

**Research/Thesis Requirement:** Optional.

Areas of study include the sciences basic to medicine, the major clinical disciplines, behavioral science, medical ethics, human services and many more. We promote customized, diverse experiences, allowing students the opportunity to be a part of a scholarly concentration in one of ten areas in education, research, public health, health disparities, law and medicine, medical humanities, business and entrepreneurship, gender medicine, health systems engineering or international medicine. The preclinical curriculum years utilize an integrated, systems-based approach and emphasize early clinical experiences from day one. Required clerkships emphasize a patient-centered interdisciplinary approach, and students are given increasing responsibility leading up to graduation. The SELECT program curriculum emphasizes scholarly excellence, leadership experiences, and collaborative training. Students complete their clinical years at LVHN for an expanded network of inter-professional educational experiences.

## Selection Factors

Applicants are selected for interview based on academic achievement, demonstrated motivation to practice medicine, humanism, and leadership. The Admissions Committee uses a holistic process in reviewing all materials including interview evaluations, letters of recommendations, and course load and types of courses taken. Applicants from diverse backgrounds, rural communities, and groups unrepresented in medicine are encouraged to apply. Students are encouraged to complete their applications as soon as possible. The majority of the matriculating class are Florida residents. Highly qualified non-Florida residents are also encouraged to apply particularly for the SELECT program.

## Information About Diversity Programs

The Office of Student Diversity and Enrichment (OSDE) collaborates with Admissions and USF Health to recruit/support a diverse student body. USF Health embraces diversity and fosters academic success. OSDE provides assistance to diversity organizations such as the APAMSA, IHSC, GBLT, LMSA, and SNMA. Visit *http://health.usf.edu/medicine/osde*.

## Regional/Satellite Campuses

**Regional Campus Location(s):** Lehigh Valley Hospital.

Our regional campus is the primary clinical site for the SELECT program. The SELECT program was developed in partnership with LVHN, one of the 100 Most Wired U.S. hospitals that use technology to promote quality and safety. LVHN has a Level I tertiary care referral center for trauma, burns and transplants; a cancer center; primary stroke center; a behavioral health science center; a community hospital; and inner city health centers. LVHN has the second best heart attack survival rate in the nation according to U.S. Centers for Medicare and Medicaid Services "Hospital Compare" data.

## Application Process and Requirements 2012–2013

**Primary application service:** AMCAS®
**Earliest filing date:** June 1, 2011
**Latest filing date:** November 15, 2011

**Secondary application required:** Yes
**Sent to:** All applicants
**URL:** Office of MD Admissions, (813) 974-2229, md-admissions@health.usf.edu
**Fee:** Yes, $30   **Waiver available:** Yes
**Earliest filing date:** June 1, 2011
**Latest filing date:** January 5, 2012

**MCAT® required:** Yes
**Latest MCAT® considered:** September 2011
**Oldest MCAT® considered:** September 2008

**Early Decision Program:** School does have EDP
**Applicants notified:** October 1, 2011
**EDP available for:** Both In-State and Out-of-State Applicants

**Regular acceptance notice —**
**Earliest date:** October 15, 2011
**Latest date:** Until class is full
**Applicant's response to acceptance offer —**
**Maximum time:** Two weeks

**Requests for deferred entrance considered:** Yes

**Deposit to hold place in class:** No. Applicants who are offered acceptance are required to submit a university application and $30.00 application fee.
**Deposit — In-State Applicants:** n/a
**Out-of-State Applicants:** n/a
**Deposit due:** n/a
**Applied to tuition:** n/a
**Deposit refundable:** n/a
**Refundable by:** n/a

**Estimated number of new entrants:** 144
**EDP:** 4, **Special Programs:** 0

**Start month/year:** August 2012

**Interview format:** Open file. Regional interviews are not available. Video interviews are not available

## Preparatory Programs

**Postbaccalaureate Program:** No

**Summer Program:** Yes, http://health.usf.edu/medicine/osde/psep.htm

## 2010–2011 First Year Class

|  | In-State | Out-of-State | International |
|---|---|---|---|
| Applications | 1,846 | 1,157 | 14 |
| Interviewed | 341 | 60 | 0 |
| Matriculated | 108 | 12 | 0 |

**Total Matriculants: 120**   **Total Enrollment: 475**

## Financial Information

|  | In-State | Out-of-State |
|---|---|---|
| Total Cost of Attendance | $50,986 | $76,546 |
| Tuition and Fees | $29,018 | $54,578 |
| Other (incl. living expenses) | $20,428 | $20,428 |
| Health Insurance (can be waived) | $1,540 | $1,540 |

**Average 2010 Graduate Indebtedness: $134,445**
**% of Enrolled Students Receiving Aid: 86%**

Source: 2009-2010 LCME I-B survey and 2010-2011 AAMC TSF questionnaire

# Emory University School of Medicine
## Atlanta, Georgia

Emory University School of Medicine
Office of Admissions
1648 Pierce Drive NE, Suite 231
Atlanta, Georgia 30322-4510

**T** 404 727 5660   medadmiss@emory.edu

**Admissions:** www.med.emory.edu/admissions

## General Information

The Emory University School of Medicine was founded in 1915, resulting from several reorganizations dating from 1854 when the Atlanta Medical College was founded. Student clinical experiences take place in numerous teaching hospitals, which provide more than 3,000 beds and large outpatient clinics. The University has close ties with Grady Memorial Hospital, the Atlanta VA Medical Center, the Centers for Disease Control and Prevention, the Carter Center of Emory University, and other local institutions.

## Mission Statement

We are committed to recruiting and developing a diverse group of students and innovative leaders in biomedical science, public health, medical education, and clinical care. We foster a culture that integrates leading edge basic, translational, and clinical research to further the ability to deliver quality health care, to predict illness and treat the sick, and to promote health of our patients and community.

## Curricular Highlights

**Community Service Requirement:** Optional. Encouraged.

**Research/Thesis Requirement:** Required. 5-month discovery phase.

The new curriculum features a hybrid of lectures, small groups, and enhanced clinical exposure throughout the first 18 months of training. Students begin 12 months of clinical rotations midway through the second year, followed by a 5 month Discovery Phase which allows time for clinical or bench research, international experience, or other academic inquiry. The fourth year is highlighted by a capstone experience which helps further prepare students for entering residency.

## Selection Factors

The Admissions Committee of the School of Medicine seeks a diverse class of students who will ultimately become humane, competent physicians in our community and our world. In addition to the AMCAS® application, all applicants must: (a) present a very high level of scholarship and leadership; (b) demonstrate a strong motivation to practice medicine; (c) have experience in a clinical setting; (d) take the MCAT within four years of the matriculating year; (e) complete the Emory supplemental application, including an application fee; (f) submit the required letter(s) of recommendation; and, (g) appear for a personal interview, if invited. Students from foreign schools must complete all science course requirements at a regionally accredited institution in the U.S. or a similarly accredited institution in Canada. Emory University does not discriminate on the basis of race, sex, color, religion, ethnic or national origin, sexual orientation, gender, gender identity or expression, age, disability, veteran's status, or any factor that is a prohibited consideration under applicable law and prohibits such discrimination by its students, faculty, and staff.

## Information About Diversity Programs

Emory University School of Medicine welcomes applications from students representing minority groups from all areas of the country. Emory is strongly committed to increasing opportunities for minority students, including thorough and individual consideration of each applicant during the admissions process. The Office of Multicultural Medical Student Affairs works in conjunction with the Admissions Committee and the Office of Medical Education and Student Affairs in the recruitment, selection, and retention of qualified minority students.

## Regional/Satellite Campuses

Clinical training for students takes place at numerous Emory affiliated hospitals and outpatient clinics on campus and around the Atlanta metro area.

## Application Process and Requirements 2012–2013

**Primary application service:** AMCAS®
**Earliest filing date:** June 1, 2011
**Latest filing date:** October 15, 2011

**Secondary application required:** Yes
**Sent to:** All verified applicants
**Contact:** Medical School Admissions, (404) 727-5660, medadmiss@emory.edu
**Fee:** Yes, $100   **Waiver available:** Yes
**Earliest filing date:** July 1, 2011
**Latest filing date:** December 1, 2011

**MCAT® required:** Yes
**Latest MCAT® considered:** September 2011
**Oldest MCAT® considered:** January 2008

**Early Decision Program:** School does not have EDP
**Applicants notified:** n/a
**EDP available for:** n/a

**Regular acceptance notice —**
**Earliest date:** October 2011
**Latest date:** Varies
**Applicant's response to acceptance offer —**
**Maximum time:** Two weeks

**Requests for deferred entrance considered:** Yes

**Deposit to hold place in class:** No
**Deposit — In-State Applicants:** n/a
**Out-of-State Applicants:** n/a
**Deposit due:** n/a
**Applied to tuition:** n/a
**Deposit refundable:** n/a
**Refundable by:** n/a

**Estimated number of new entrants:** 138
**EDP:** n/a, **Special Programs:** n/a

**Start month/year:** July 2012

**Interview format:** Group interview and individual interview. Regional interviews are not available. Video interviews are not available

## Preparatory Programs
**Postbaccalaureate Program:** No
**Summer Program:** No

## 2010–2011 First Year Class

|  | In-State | Out-of-State | International |
|---|---|---|---|
| Applications | 604 | 4,887 | 306 |
| Interviewed | 147 | 490 | 28 |
| Matriculated | 47 | 85 | 3 |

**Total Matriculants: 135**   **Total Enrollment: 533**

## Financial Information

|  | In-State | Out-of-State |
|---|---|---|
| Total Cost of Attendance | $75,122 | $75,122 |
| Tuition and Fees | $44,192 | $44,192 |
| Other (incl. living expenses) | $28,783 | $28,783 |
| Health Insurance (can be waived) | $2,147 | $2,147 |

**Average 2010 Graduate Indebtedness: $129,501**
**% of Enrolled Students Receiving Aid: 83%**

*Source: 2009-2010 LCME I-B survey and 2010-2011 AAMC TSF questionnaire*

# Medical College of Georgia at Georgia Health Sciences University

## Augusta, Georgia

Dr. Geoffrey H. Young
Associate Dean for Admissions
Medical College of Georgia
Georgia Health Sciences University
Augusta, Georgia 30912-4760

**T** 706 721 3186    stdadmin@georgiahealth.edu

**Admissions:** www.georgiahealth.edu/careers/medicine.htm

## General Information

The Medical College of Georgia at Georgia Health Sciences University was founded in 1828 and is the nation's 13th oldest medical school. The institution is a separate university under the University System of Georgia. It consists of five schools: medicine, allied health, dentistry, graduate studies, and nursing.

## Mission Statement

Georgia Health Sciences University is committed to a supportive campus climate, necessary services, and leadership and development opportunities, all to educate the whole person and meet the needs of students, faculty, and staff; cultural, ethnic, racial, and gender diversity supported by practices that embody the ideals of an open democratic and global society; technology to advance education; collaborative relationships with other System institutions, state agencies, local schools and technical institutes, and industry, sharing physical, human, and information resources to enhance services available to the citizens of Georgia.

## Curricular Highlights

**Community Service Requirement:** Optional.

**Research/Thesis Requirement:** Optional.

During the pre-clinical years, students acquire the building blocks that underlie medical practice. The modular content of the curriculum is taught in lectures and labs with integrated clinical conferences and small-group activities. The first year of the curriculum is a year long module divided into six systems-based blocks. This module introduces students to Gross Anatomy, Biochemistry, Development, Genetics, Histology, Neuroscience, Physiology, and Psychiatry. The Essentials of Clinical Medicine (ECM) is a two-year sequence emphasizing patient care skills. In year two, the year-long Cellular and Systems Disease States module exposes students to Microbiology, Pathology, and Pharmacology in the context of clinical medicine. Clinical Training: Patient contact begins in year one in the ECM course that extends through year two. Year three consists of required clerkships in Family Medicine, Internal Medicine, Neurology, OB/Gyn, Pediatrics, Psychiatry, and Surgery. During year four, students complete rotations in Emergency Medicine, Critical Care, Ambulatory Medicine, and an acting internship, with the remainder of the year for electives that can include research.

## Selection Factors

Applicants for admission are evaluated on a competitive basis. Information used includes, but is not limited to, the applicant's responsibilities prior to application; activities; shadowing physicians; ethnic, socioeconomic, and cultural background; region of residence with respect to its health professional needs; commitment to practice in an underserved area; references; motivation and potential for serving as a physician; interviews; MCAT performance; and grades. In addition, students must meet specified technical standards to participate effectively in the medical education program and the practice of medicine. Preference is given to Georgia residents. See *www.georgiahealth.edu/SOM/admit/* for more information.

## Information About Diversity Programs

The Medical College of Georgia seeks to encourage applications from qualified students from groups underrepresented in medicine. A summer program is designed for disadvantaged college students who show academic promise and who desire to practice medicine. Students may apply by writing to Kimberly Halbur, EdD, Associate Dean for Diversity Affairs, CB-1843, Georgia Health Sciences University, Augusta, GA 30912-1900.

## Regional/Satellite Campuses

**Regional Campus Location(s):** Athens, GA, Albany, GA, and Savannah, GA.

Core clerkships take place at the MCG Hospitals and Clinics, the Children's Medical Center, and affiliated hospitals and community-based teaching sites throughout Georgia. The Medical College of Georgia at Georgia Health Sciences University in partnership with the University of Georgia created the Medical Partnership Campus in Athens in 2010. The medical partnership campus is a four year curriculum campus.

### GA

### Application Process and Requirements 2012–2013

**Primary application service:** AMCAS®
**Earliest filing date:** June 1, 2011
**Latest filing date:** November 1, 2011

**Secondary application required:** Yes
**Sent to:** All Georgia residents; others are screened
**URL:** Provided by school    **Contact:** (706) 721-3186
**Fee:** No    **Waiver available:** n/a
**Earliest filing date:** June 1, 2011
**Latest filing date:** Two weeks after receipt and must be in the student file by December 1, 2011

**MCAT® required:** Yes
**Latest MCAT® considered:** September 2011
**Oldest MCAT® considered:** January 2009

**Early Decision Program:** School does have EDP
**Applicants notified:** October 1, 2011
**EDP available for:** In-State Applicants only

**Regular acceptance notice —**
**Earliest date:** October 2011
**Latest date:** Until class is full
**Applicant's response to acceptance offer —**
**Maximum time:** Early decision, one week; regular decision, two weeks

**Requests for deferred entrance considered:** Yes

**Deposit to hold place in class:** Yes
**Deposit — In-State Applicants:** $100
**Out-of-State Applicants:** $100
**Deposit due:** With response to acceptance offer, early decision, one week; regular decision, two weeks
**Applied to tuition:** Yes    **Deposit refundable:** Yes
**Refundable by:** May 15, 2012

**Estimated number of new entrants:** 230
**EDP:** 60, **Special Programs:** 6

**Start month/year:** August 2012

**Interview format:** One individual interview with committee member. Regional interviews are not available. Video interviews are not available.

### Preparatory Programs

**Postbaccalaureate Program:** No

**Summer Program:** Yes, www.georgiahealth.edu/careers/specop/, Kimberly Halbur, EdD , (706) 721-2522 KHALBUR@georgiahealth.edu

### 2010–2011 First Year Class

|  | In-State | Out-of-State | International |
|---|---|---|---|
| Applications | 1,049 | 1,034 | 59 |
| Interviewed | 543 | 25 | 0 |
| Matriculated | 228 | 2 | 0 |

**Total Matriculants: 230**    **Total Enrollment: 802**

### Financial Information

|  | In-State | Out-of-State |
|---|---|---|
| Total Cost of Attendance | $48,643 | $66,821 |
| Tuition and Fees | $23,841 | $42,019 |
| Other (incl. living expenses) | $23,261 | $23,261 |
| Health Insurance (can be waived) | $1,541 | $1,541 |

**Average 2010 Graduate Indebtedness: $38,068**
**% of Enrolled Students Receiving Aid: 84%**

Source: 2009-2010 LCME I-B survey and 2010-2011 AAMC TSF questionnaire

# Mercer University School of Medicine
## Macon, Georgia

Office of Admissions and Student Affairs
Mercer University School of Medicine
1550 College Street
Macon, Georgia 31207

**T** 478 301 2524   admissions@med.mercer.edu
**Admissions:** http://medicine.mercer.edu/admissions

## General Information

Mercer University School of Medicine was founded in 1982 to improve health care access to the residents of Georgia. A private institution with strong state support, MUSM has been a leader in educating physicians who practice in the state after their training. MUSM also offers multiple graduate degrees including a Masters in Public Health.

## Mission Statement

The mission of Mercer University School of Medicine (MUSM) is to educate physicians and health professionals to meet the primary care and health care needs of rural and medically underserved areas of Georgia.

## Curricular Highlights

**Community Service Requirement:** Required. Numerous volunteer opportunities are available.

**Research/Thesis Requirement:** Optional.

One of the first schools to adopt an all Problem-Based-Learning curriculum, there are no lectures and students take responsibility for their own learning. This open-ended nature requires and generates maturity and confidence not seen in traditional curricula. Learning must go well beyond the basic facts in that students are called upon to integrate and demonstrate verbally their basic science knowledge base to explain clinical findings. In addition, students are evaluated in areas related to group and interpersonal, problem-solving, information-gathering and evaluation skills. Students interview and examine actual and standardized patients early in the first year. The Community Medicine program provides a continuity experience in the clinical aspects of a community-oriented primary care medical practice during the first, second and fourth years. The third year consists of required clinical rotations in internal medicine, surgery, pediatrics, obstetrics-gynecology, family medicine, and psychiatry. The fourth year includes community medicine and two selectives from acute and critical care and geriatrics.

## Selection Factors

The Admissions Committee only accepts applicants who are legal residents of Georgia. Each applicant must show promise of learning effectively in Mercer's curriculum and strong potential for practice in a medical specialty commensurate with the health care needs of rural and other underserved areas of Georgia. Most counties in Georgia have underserved status by the federal government, and the specialties that are needed include the primary care specialties of Internal Medicine, Pediatrics and Family Medicine, but also Surgery, and Obstetrics and Gynecology. Interviews are by invitation only and are held at both the Macon and Savannah campuses. In making the final decisions for acceptance or rejection, the Admissions Committee considers all criteria, but emphasizes strongly an applicant's demonstrated desire to fulfill the mission of the institution. The committee does not discriminate on the basis of race, sex, creed, national origin, age, or handicap.

## Information About Diversity Programs

MUSM embraces the position that promoting and supporting diversity among the student body is central to the mission of the school. A diverse student body enriches professional education by providing a multiplicity of views and prospective that enhances learning within this highly interactive, student centered curriculum. For additional information and opportunities, please contact *diversity@med.mercer.edu.*

## Regional/Satellite Campuses

**Regional Campus Location(s):** Savannah, GA.

Students may study all four years on either the Macon or Savannah campus with a limited number of spaces for students to complete the first two years in Macon, and the clinical years in Savannah. There are many sites available for the Community Medicine program, and most students are able to return to a location near their home.

## Application Process and Requirements 2012–2013

**Primary application service:** AMCAS®
**Earliest filing date:** June 1, 2011
**Latest filing date:** November 1, 2011

**Secondary application required:** Yes
**Sent to:** Screened applicants
**Contact:** Gail Coleman, (478) 301-2524, admissions@mercer.edu
**Fee:** Yes, $50   **Waiver available:** Yes
**Earliest filing date:** June 2011
**Latest filing date:** January 15, 2012

**MCAT® required:** Yes
**Latest MCAT® considered:** September 2011
**Oldest MCAT® considered:** January 2008

**Early Decision Program:** School does have EDP
**Applicants notified:** October 1, 2011
**EDP available for:** In-States only

**Regular acceptance notice —**
**Earliest date:** November 2011
**Latest date:** Until class is full
**Applicant's response to acceptance offer —**
**Maximum time:** Two weeks

**Requests for deferred entrance considered:** Yes

**Deposit to hold place in class:** Yes
**Deposit — In-State Applicants:** $100
**Out-of-State Applicants:** n/a
**Deposit due:** With response to acceptance offer
**Applied to tuition:** Yes
**Deposit refundable:** Yes
**Refundable by:** May 15, 2012

**Estimated number of new entrants:** 90
**EDP:** 45, **Special Programs:** 4

**Start month/year:** August 2012

**Interview format:** Two, one-hour interviews. Regional interviews are not available. Video interviews are not available

## Preparatory Programs
**Postbaccalaureate Program:** No
**Summer Program:** No

## 2010–2011 First Year Class

|  | In-State | Out-of-State | International |
|---|---|---|---|
| Applications | 835 | 3 | 6 |
| Interviewed | 337 | 0 | 0 |
| Matriculated | 101 | 0 | 0 |

**Total Matriculants: 101**   **Total Enrollment: 341**

## Financial Information

|  | In-State | Out-of-State |
|---|---|---|
| Total Cost of Attendance | $64,060 | n/a |
| Tuition and Fees | $40,060 | n/a |
| Other (incl. living expenses) | $23,621 | n/a |
| Health Insurance (can be waived) | $379 | n/a |

**Average 2010 Graduate Indebtedness: $171,043**
**% of Enrolled Students Receiving Aid: 95%**

Source: 2009-2010 LCME I-B survey and 2010-2011 AAMC TSF questionnaire

# Morehouse School of Medicine

## Atlanta, Georgia

Admissions and Student Affairs
Morehouse School of Medicine
720 Westview Drive, S.W.
Atlanta, Georgia 30310-1495

**T** 404 752 1650 mdadmissions@msm.edu

**Admissions:** www.msm.edu/prospective_students/
admissions.aspx

## General Information

Established in 1975 as the School of Medicine at Morehouse College, Morehouse School of Medicine became independent from its founding institution in 1981. MSM is a member of the Atlanta University Center Consortium Inc.- a consortium of five Historically Black Colleges and Universities. Through our affiliations with Atlanta-based Grady Health System, Children's Healthcare of Atlanta at Hughes Spalding, South Fulton Medical Center and the Atlanta Medical Center, our students and residents are able to experience a broad patient population and engage in the opportunity for the best training experience possible.

## Mission Statement

Morehouse School of Medicine is dedicated to improving the health and well-being of individuals and communities; increasing the diversity of the health professional and scientific workforce; and addressing primary health-care needs through programs in education, research, and service, with emphasis on people of color and the underserved urban and rural populations in Georgia and the nation.

## Curricular Highlights

**Community Service Requirement:** Optional.

**Research/Thesis Requirement:** Optional.

The first two years of the curriculum emphasize an understanding of the principles, concepts, and a major factual background of the basic medical sciences. Exposure to clinical medicine begins in the first year through assignment to a preceptor and increases in the second year with introduction to clinical medicine. Clinical education is continued through core clerkships during the third and fourth years, with 20 weeks of electives in the senior year. Student performance is evaluated primarily by letter grades. Learning resources and other support services are available to all students throughout their four years.

## Selection Factors

Selection of students for admission is made after careful consideration of many factors. These include MCAT scores, academic record, extent of academic improvement, balance and depth of academic program, difficulty of courses taken, and other indicators of maturation of learning ability. Additional factors considered are extracurricular activities, hobbies, the need to work, research projects and experiences, evidence of activities that indicate concurrence with the school's mission, and evidence of pursuing interests and talents in depth. Finally, the committee looks for evidence of those traits of personality and character essential to succeed in medicine: compassion, integrity, motivation, and perseverance. All information available about each applicant is considered without assigning priority to any single factor. Students are admitted on the basis of individual qualifications regardless of sex, age, race, creed, national origin, or handicap. Preferential consideration is given to qualified applicants who are residents of the state of Georgia. Foreign applicants must have a permanent resident visa. Technical standards have been established as a prerequisite for admission and graduation from the MSM. A candidate for the M.D. degree must have aptitude, abilities, and skills in five areas: observation, communication, motor, conceptual integrative and quantitative, as well as behavioral and social attributes. Applicants are not considered for admission who have been dismissed from another medical school for academic or disciplinary reasons. Transfer applications are considered only from students in good standing at an LCME-accredited U.S. or Canadian medical school; transfers from foreign medical schools or osteopathic, veterinary, or dental schools are not accepted. Transfers are accepted into the second year only on a space-available basis. The transfer application deadline is May 1.

## Application Process and Requirements 2012–2013

**Primary application service:** AMCAS®
**Earliest filing date:** June 1, 2011
**Latest filing date:** December 1, 2011

**Secondary application required:** Yes
**Sent to:** All eligible applicants after preliminary screening
**URL:** URL given to invited applicants only
**Fee:** Yes, $50    **Waiver available:** Yes
**Earliest filing date:** July 15, 2011
**Latest filing date:** January 6, 2012

**MCAT® required:** Yes
**Latest MCAT® considered:** December 2011
**Oldest MCAT® considered:** 2009

**Early Decision Program:** School does have EDP
**Applicants notified:** October 1, 2011
**EDP available for:** In-States only

**Regular acceptance notice —**
**Earliest date:** November 2011
**Latest date:** Until class is full
**Applicant's response to acceptance offer —**
**Maximum time:** 14 days

**Requests for deferred entrance considered:** Yes

**Deposit to hold place in class:** Yes
**Deposit —In-State Applicants:** $100
**Out-of-State Applicants:** $100
**Deposit due:** 14 days from acceptance offer
**Applied to tuition:** Yes
**Deposit refundable:** Yes
**Refundable by:** May 15, 2012

**Estimated number of new entrants:** 56
**EDP:** 2, **Special Programs:** n/a

**Start month/year:** July 2012

**Interview format:** One-on-one interview. Regional interviews are not available. Video interviews are not available.

### Preparatory Programs

**Postbaccalaureate Program:** No

**Summer Program:** Yes, www.msm.edu/
educationTraining/degreePrograms/mdProgram/
summerProgram.aspx

## 2010–2011 First Year Class

|  | In-State | Out-of-State | International |
|---|---|---|---|
| Applications | 495 | 3,535 | 22 |
| Interviewed | 80 | 125 | 0 |
| Matriculated | 31 | 26 | 0 |

**Total Matriculants: 57**     **Total Enrollment: 221**

## Financial Information

|  | In-State | Out-of-State |
|---|---|---|
| Total Cost of Attendance | $67,093 | $67,093 |
| Tuition and Fees | $35,887 | $35,887 |
| Other (incl. living expenses) | $28,336 | $28,336 |
| Health Insurance (can be waived) | $2,870 | $2,870 |

**Average 2010 Graduate Indebtedness: $190,191**
**% of Enrolled Students Receiving Aid: 95%**

*Source: 2009-2010 LCME I-B survey and 2010-2011 AAMC TSF questionnaire*

# University of Hawai'i
# John A. Burns School of Medicine
## Honolulu, Hawaii

Office of Student Affairs – Admissions
Medical Education Building
University of Hawai'i, at Manoa
John A. Burns School of Medicine
651 Ilalo Street
Honolulu, Hawaii 96813-5534

**T** 808 692 1000    mnishiki@hawaii.edu

**Admissions:** http://jabsom.hawaii.edu/

## General Information

The University of Hawai'i at Manoa John A. Burns School of Medicine is in the College of Health Sciences and Social Welfare. The School of Medicine is located in Kaka'ako. It also has teaching facilities in affiliated community hospitals and primary care clinics throughout the state.

## Mission Statement

To educate outstanding physicians, scientists, biomedical students, and allied health professionals for Hawai'i and the Pacific, and to conduct both clinical and basic research, education, and community service of specific interest to our region and community. Its student body mirrors the rich diversity of the state's population.

## Curricular Highlights

**Community Service Requirement:** Required. Many students chose to volunteer beyond that.

**Research/Thesis Requirement:** Optional.

The school utilizes a problem-based learning curriculum (PBL), in which basic sciences are learned in the context of the study of health care problems and supplemented by selected lecture and laboratory sessions. Clinical skills and community health activities are prominent, and begin in the first year of the curriculum. Special features include an emphasis on PBL as the primary instructional method in the pre-clinical years; early introduction of clinical training, community service, and research experiences; rural health training opportunities; a longitudinal, interdisciplinary clerkship opportunity in the third-year; and opportunities for training experiences in various communities throughout Hawai'i, the Pacific, and Asia.

## Selection Factors

Applicants are considered without discrimination as to age, sex, race, creed, national origin, religion, or disability. The school admits 64 students to it's first-year class. A priority is to admit applicants with strong ties to the State of Hawaii. Applications go through a screening process. The first screen determines an applicant's ties to the State of Hawaii: legal residence, birthplace, high school graduated, college attended, parent's legal residence, and legacy. Three of the six categories are required to be a resident for application purposes. Applicants who pass the second academic screen will be invited for interviews and asked to submit letters of recommendation. Applicants are responsible for scheduling two one-on-one interviews to be conducted in Hawaii. Acceptance, alternate, and rejection letters are e-mailed in late March.

## Information about Diversity Programs

The student body and faculty are culturally diverse. The school is actively involved in the recruitment, admission, and retention of students from disadvantaged backgrounds who have potential and are interested in pursuing an M.D. degree. Dr. Kalani Brady, Department of Native Hawaiian Health, is the Diversity contact person at the John A. Burns School of Medicine. The Imi Ho'ola Post-Baccalaureate Program is for students from socially, educationally, or economically disadvantaged backgrounds who have demonstrated a strong commitment to serve areas of need in Hawai'i and the U.S.-Affiliated Pacific Islands. For more information, contact Dr. Winona Mesiona Lee, Imi Ho'ola Post-Baccalaureate Program Director (*winonal@hawaii.edu*, (808) 692-1035).

## Regional/Satellite Campuses

Clinical activities of the school's curriculum are conducted in affiliated community hospitals and clinics. There is no university hospital connected to the school of medicine.

## Application Process and Requirements 2012–2013

**Primary application service:** AMCAS®
**Earliest filing date:** June 1, 2011
**Latest filing date:** November 1, 2011

**Secondary application required:** No
**Sent to:** Screened applicants who minimally achieve the required cut-off scores.
**Contact:** Marilyn Nishiki, (808) 692-1000, mnishiki@hawaii.edu
**Fee:** Yes, $50    **Waiver available:** No
**Earliest filing date:** School-specific deadlines
**Latest filing date:** School-specific deadlines

**MCAT® required:** Yes
**Latest MCAT® considered:** September 2011
**Oldest MCAT® considered:** January 2009

**Early Decision Program:** School does have EDP
**Applicants notified:** October 1, 2011
**EDP available for:** In-States only

**Regular acceptance notice —**
**Earliest date:** October 15, 2011
**Latest date:** Until class is full
**Applicant's response to acceptance offer —**
**Maximum time:** Two weeks

**Requests for deferred entrance considered:** Yes

**Deposit to hold place in class:** No. Nonrefundable advanced tuition deposit to be requested in May 15, 2012
**Deposit — In-State Applicants:** n/a
**Out-of-State Applicants:** n/a
**Deposit due:** n/a
**Applied to tuition:** n/a
**Deposit refundable:** n/a    **Refundable by:** n/a

**Estimated number of new entrants:** 64
**EDP:** 1, **Special Programs:** 12

**Start month/year:** July 2012

**Interview format:** Two (2) one-on-one interview. Regional interviews are not available. Video interviews are not available.

## Preparatory Programs

**Postbaccalaureate Program:** Yes, http://jabsom.hawaii.edu, (808) 692-1030

**Summer Program:** No

## 2010–2011 First Year Class

|  | In-State | Out-of-State | International |
|---|---|---|---|
| Applications | 234 | 1,318 | 116 |
| Interviewed | 172 | 71 | 8 |
| Matriculated | 58 | 3 | 3 |

**Total Matriculants: 64**    **Total Enrollment: 257**

## Financial Information

|  | In-State | Out-of-State |
|---|---|---|
| Total Cost of Attendance | $52,947 | $82,131 |
| Tuition and Fees | $27,511 | $56,695 |
| Other (incl. living expenses) | $23,008 | $23,008 |
| Health Insurance (can be waived) | $2,428 | $2,428 |

**Average 2010 Graduate Indebtedness: $80,732**
**% of Enrolled Students Receiving Aid: 85%**

*Source: 2009-2010 LCME I-B survey and 2010-2011 AAMC TSF questionnaire*

# Loyola University Chicago
# Stritch School of Medicine
## Maywood, Illinois

Loyola University Chicago
Stritch School of Medicine Office of Admissions
2160 South First Avenue
Maywood, Illinois 60153

**T** 708 216 3229    SSOM-admissions@lumc.edu

**Admissions:** www.stritch.luc.edu/admissions

## General Information

Loyola University Chicago, founded in 1870 by the Jesuits, is one of the largest Catholic universities in the United States. By 1909, the university had organized several small medical colleges into a new medical school and, in 1948, the school was named in honor of Samuel Cardinal Stritch, Archbishop of Chicago. In 1969 the university opened the Loyola University Medical Center, built on land given by the Veterans Administration, in Maywood, a suburban community located 12 miles west of downtown Chicago. The medical center is home to the Stritch School of Medicine, Loyola University Hospital, Cardinal Bernardin Cancer Center, and Loyola Outpatient Center. Students receive their clinical training at the 561-bed Loyola University Hospital, 250-bed Gottlieb Memorial Hospital and 248-bed Hines Veterans Affairs Hospital, and other affiliated hospitals in the Chicago area.

## Curricular Highlights

**Community Service Requirement:** Optional. Highly desirable.

**Research/Thesis Requirement:** Optional.

Stritch's primary purpose is to train physicians who will care for their patients with skill, respect, and compassion. The personal and intellectual development of each student is promoted through close contact with faculty members and the administration. Students are exposed to a large academic medical center, as well as to VA and community based practices and hospitals, where they learn in an atmosphere of cooperation and mutual assistance. The first year of the curriculum concentrates on the basic principles and processes related to the normal structure, function, and regulation of the human body. In addition, the first year includes instruction in health promotion/disease prevention, and communication skills, medical ethics, and the doctor/patient relationship. The second year focuses on basic science principles related to the mechanisms of human disease, neuroscience, and the therapeutic approach to disease. Additionally, students continue to develop their knowledge about human behavioral science, physical examination skills, basic clinical skills, evidence-based clinical decision-making, and professionalism, medical ethics and the social and community context of healthcare. Students have early clinical experiences through a physician mentor program in ambulatory settings and the peer mentor program. The third and fourth years are organized into clinical clerkships which include up to 34 weeks of elective time during the fourth year as well as exposure to learning seminars offering topics such as business, professional and justice in health care, disaster preparedness, end of life, global health, and religion and healthcare. Vertical learning modules permit a student to master targeted concepts and applications longitudinally within a variety of courses and clerkships in the curriculum. Special curricular features include an emphasis on bioethics and professionalism and intensive training in patient history-taking, physical examination, and communication skills using the Clinical Skills and Human Simulation Centers, which combine the latest in educational technology.

## Selection Factors

A bachelor's degree and the MCAT taken no later than September of the year of application, are required. Any undergraduate major is acceptable. Applicants must be U.S. citizens or hold a permanent resident visa at the time of application. As a rule, applicants are limited to applying no more than twice. Applicants enrolled in advanced degree programs must expect to complete their degrees prior to matriculation. Applicants who present academic credentials that indicate they are capable of succeeding in the rigorous medical education program will be evaluated for evidence of the personal qualifications they can bring to the medical profession. Essential characteristics include an interest in learning, integrity, compassion, and the ability to assume responsibility. Of particular concern will be an applicant's exploration of the field of medicine and the nature of the motivation to enter this profession. Early submission of the AMCAS® application and prompt return of all supporting material will enhance an applicant's chance of being offered a place in the class. Loyola University does not discriminate on the basis of race, religion, national origin, sex, age, or disability.

## Information about Diversity Programs

The Summer Enrichment Program (SEP) at Loyola University Chicago Stritch School of Medicine is a six-week experience for pre-medical students. The program's mission is to offer students a variety of educational experiences and service activities to enhance their preparation for a career in medicine. The program targets students who have the potential to enrich the diversity of the medical student community.

## Application Process and Requirements 2012–2013

**Primary application service:** AMCAS®
**Earliest filing date:** June 1, 2011
**Latest filing date:** November 15, 2011

**Secondary application required:** Yes
**Sent to:** Screened applicants
**URL:** n/a
**Fee:** Yes, $75    **Waiver available:** Yes
**Earliest filing date:** June 2011
**Latest filing date:** February 2012

**MCAT® required:** Yes
**Latest MCAT® considered:** September 2011
**Oldest MCAT® considered:** 2008

**Early Decision Program:** School does not have EDP
**Applicants notified:** n/a
**EDP available for:** n/a

**Regular acceptance notice —**
**Earliest date:** October 15, 2011
**Latest date:** Until class is full
**Applicant's response to acceptance offer —**
**Maximum time:** Two weeks

**Requests for deferred entrance considered:** Yes
**Deposit to hold place in class:** No
**Deposit — In-State Applicants:** n/a
**Out-of-State Applicants:** n/a
**Deposit due:** n/a
**Applied to tuition:** n/a
**Deposit refundable:** n/a
**Refundable by:** n/a

**Estimated number of new entrants:** 150
**EDP:** n/a, **Special Programs:** n/a

**Start month/year:** July 2012

**Interview format:** Semi-open file with admission committee members. Regional interviews are not available. Video interviews are not available.

## Preparatory Programs

**Postbaccalaureate Program:** No

**Summer Program:** Yes, www.stritch.luc.edu/node/120, Office of Student Affairs, (708) 216-3220, SEP@lumc.edu

## 2010–2011 First Year Class

| | In-State | Out-of-State | International |
|---|---|---|---|
| Applications | 1,400 | 8,661 | 24 |
| Interviewed | 188 | 378 | 0 |
| Matriculated | 72 | 78 | 0 |

**Total Matriculants: 150**    **Total Enrollment: 583**

## Financial Information

| | In-State | Out-of-State |
|---|---|---|
| Total Cost of Attendance | $63,000 | $63,500 |
| Tuition and Fees | $42,258 | $42,258 |
| Other (incl. living expenses) | $19,002 | $19,502 |
| Health Insurance (can be waived) | $1,740 | $1,740 |

**Average 2010 Graduate Indebtedness: $172,295**
**% of Enrolled Students Receiving Aid: 89%**

*Source: 2009–2010 LCME I-B survey and 2010–2011 AAMC TSF questionnaire*

# Northwestern University
# The Feinberg School of Medicine

## Chicago, Illinois

Office of Admissions
Northwestern University
Feinberg School of Medicine
303 East Chicago Avenue, Morton I-606
Chicago, Illinois 60611-3008

**T** 312 503 8206  med-admissions@northwestern.edu

**Admissions:** www.feinberg.northwestern.edu/
admissions/md/index.html

## General Information

Northwestern University's Feinberg School of Medicine (FSM), founded in 1859, continues to educate today's students at a premier medical school and outstanding hospitals: Northwestern Memorial, Children's Memorial, Prentice Women's, the Rehabilitation Institute of Chicago, and the Jesse Brown VA Medical Center. Students have translational and clinical research options as well as the opportunity to engage the cultural life of Chicago and work with its diverse population.

## Mission Statement

The mission of the Feinberg School of Medicine is to educate physicians and physician-scientists who will excel both scientifically and clinically. We expect our students to take leadership roles in medicine and to serve the people of our increasingly diverse communities.

## Curricular Highlights

**Community Service Requirement:** Optional. Multiple free clinics are available.

**Research/Thesis Requirement:** Optional. This option includes summer and senior selectives.

We strive to provide a student centered environment where adult learners employ their own questions as the starting point for inquiry. The first two years of the curriculum feature an integrated, organ-system based approach to the essential basic sciences. Small group "Problem Based Learning" sessions augment the concepts developed in lectures and laboratory sessions. The psychosocial foundations of medicine are emphasized in "Patient, Physician and Society (PPS)": students develop clinical skills and study the many ways in which medicine interacts with the larger society. Three short blocks are devoted to medical decision-making where students hone their ability to analyze and to manage the information required for effective clinical decision-making. During the third year clerkships, students continue the PPS curriculum by returning to the medical school each month for discussion of topics common to all clerkships. A sub-internship, ICU and ER rotations, and several electives round out the curriculum in the fourth year.

## Selection Factors

The Committee on Admissions looks for evidence of academic excellence, mature motivation for a career in medicine, altruism, and character. A premium is placed on the breadth and depth of academic and life experiences, as well as clinical and research exposure. Applicants should be liberally educated men and women whose studies have gone beyond the conventional premedical courses. We seek a diverse class and do not discriminate on the basis of race, religion, national origin, gender, sexual orientation, age, or disability. The Illinois Medical School Matriculant Criminal History Records Act requires each entering medical student to submit to a criminal history records check prior to matriculation.

## Information about Diversity Programs

FSM strives to admit a student body whose diversity mirrors that of our society. The Office of Minority and Cultural Affairs supports the broad array of student groups involved in community outreach and offers programming in the formal curriculum, lunchtime speakers, dialogue groups and a film series on health disparities and social justice.

## Regional/Satellite Campuses

Students do required clinical rotations in Chicago at Northwestern Hospitals and the Jesse Brown VA. Senior away rotations are available at affiliated institutions in Latin America, Africa, Europe, and Asia.

## Application Process and Requirements 2012–2013

**Primary application service:** AMCAS®
**Earliest filing date:** July 1, 2011
**Latest filing date:** October 15, 2011

**Secondary application required:** Yes
**Sent to:** AMCAS
**URL:** https://medicalapp.northwestern.edu
**Fee:** Yes, $85  **Waiver available:** Yes
**Earliest filing date:** July 1, 2011
**Latest filing date:** Varies

**MCAT® required:** Yes
**Latest MCAT® considered:** September 2011
**Oldest MCAT® considered:** January 2008

**Early Decision Program:** School does not have EDP
**Applicants notified:** n/a
**EDP available for:** n/a

**Regular acceptance notice —**
**Earliest date:** November 2011
**Latest date:** Until class is full
**Applicant's response to acceptance offer —**
**Maximum time:** Two weeks

**Requests for deferred entrance considered:** Yes

**Deposit to hold place in class:** No
**Deposit — In-State Applicants:** n/a
**Out-of-State Applicants:** n/a
**Deposit due:** n/a
**Applied to tuition:** n/a
**Deposit refundable:** n/a
**Refundable by:** n/a

**Estimated number of new entrants:** 170
**EDP:** 0, **Special Programs:** 25

**Start month/year:** August 2012

**Interview format:** Individual and panel interview. Regional interviews are not available. Video interviews are not available.

## Preparatory Programs

**Postbaccalaureate Program:** Yes, www.scs. northwestern.edu/pdp/cpdp/health/premed.cfm

**Summer Program:** No

## 2010–2011 First Year Class

|  | In-State | Out-of-State | International |
|---|---|---|---|
| Applications | 875 | 5,283 | 377 |
| Interviewed | 80 | 639 | 64 |
| Matriculated | 42 | 115 | 13 |

**Total Matriculants: 170**   **Total Enrollment: 685**

## Financial Information

|  | In-State | Out-of-State |
|---|---|---|
| Total Cost of Attendance | $72,038 | $72,038 |
| Tuition and Fees | $44,993 | $44,993 |
| Other (incl. living expenses) | $24,579 | $24,579 |
| Health Insurance (can be waived) | $2,466 | $2,466 |

**Average 2010 Graduate Indebtedness: $149,626**
**% of Enrolled Students Receiving Aid: 78%**

*Source: 2009-2010 LCME I-B survey and 2010-2011 AAMC TSF questionnaire*

# Rosalind Franklin University of Medicine and Science Chicago Medical School

## North Chicago, Illinois

Rosalind Franklin
University of Medicine and Science
Office of Medical School Admissions
3333 Green Bay Road
North Chicago, Illinois 60064

**T** 847 578 3204   cms.admissions@rosalindfranklin.edu

**Admissions:** www.rosalindfranklin.edu/tabid/1629/default.aspx

## General Information

Founded in 1912, The Chicago Medical School has been dedicated to excellence in medical education for nearly a century. The Chicago Medical School has educated thousands of professionals with recognized innovation in health education, excellence in the creation of knowledge and scientific discovery focused on prediction and prevention of disease, outstanding clinical programs, and compassionate community service. Major hospital affiliates include Advocate Christ Medical Center, Advocate Condell Medical Center, Advocate Illinois Masonic, Advocate Lutheran General Hospital, John H. Stroger, Jr., Hospital of Cook County, Mount Sinai Hospital and Medical Center, and the North Chicago Veterans Affairs Medical Center (NCVAMC).

## Mission Statement

The Chicago Medical School educates physicians and scientists dedicated to providing exemplary, compassionate patient care and excellence in scientific discovery within an inter-professional environment.

## Curricular Highlights

**Community Service Requirement:** Required. Interprofessional health care teams.

**Research/Thesis Requirement:** Optional.

The Chicago Medical School's curriculum offers a strong grounding in the sciences basic to medicine along with assuring competency in skills necessary for the practice of medicine. The CMS curriculum features a unique interprofessional approach, with interaction among a broad range of health professional students and practitioners. The curriculum is a mix of lectures, labs, small-group discussions, team-based learning, and opportunities for peer-to-peer learning. The educational information system, Desire to Learn (D2L), provides 24-hour-a-day access to learning materials. Students have early clinical experiences in the state-of-the-art evaluation and education center, as well as opportunities to connect with physician preceptors. The required junior clinical clerkships include medicine, ambulatory care, surgery, family medicine, obstetrics/gynecology, psychiatry, medCore, pediatrics, neurology, and emergency medicine. The senior requirements include four weeks in a medicine or pediatrics subinternship, plus 32 weeks of approved electives (14 of which must be completed at one of the school's primary affiliated sites). The elective period gives students an opportunity, through both intramural and extramural experiences, to explore and strengthen their personal career interests. For information about the curriculum, please visit the following website: *www.rosalindfranklin.edu/dnn/chicagomedicalschool/home/CMS/MedicalCurriculum/tabid/865/Default.aspx.*

## Selection Factors

Students are selected on the basis of various criteria, including scholarship, character, motivation, and educational background. A student's potential for the study and practice of medicine will be evaluated on the basis of academic achievement, MCAT results, appraisals by a preprofessional advisory committee or individual instructors, and a personal interview, if requested by the Student Admissions Committee. To fulfill the mission of The Chicago Medical School, admissions policies are designed to ensure that the selection process matriculates a class made up of individuals capable of meeting the needs of current and future patients. Applicants will be evaluated not only for educational potential, but with the aim of providing diverse educational experience for other members of the class. For information on selection factors, please visit the following website: *www.rosalindfranklin.edu/dnn/administration/Admissions/CMS/AdmissionRequirements/tabid/1703/Default.aspx.*

## Information about Diversity Programs

The school maintains an extensive recruitment and retention program for students from groups underrepresented in medicine.

## Application Process and Requirements 2012–2013

**Primary application service:** AMCAS®
**Earliest filing date:** June 1, 2011
**Latest filing date:** November 1, 2011

**Secondary application required:** Yes
**Sent to:** All applicants
**URL:** n/a
**Fee:** Yes, $100   **Waiver available:** Yes
**Earliest filing date:** July 1, 2011
**Latest filing date:** December 1, 2011

**MCAT® required:** Yes
**Latest MCAT® considered:** September 2011
**Oldest MCAT® considered:** 2009

**Early Decision Program:** School does have EDP
**Applicants notified:** October 1, 2011
**EDP available for:** Both In-State and Out-of-State Applicants

**Regular acceptance notice —**
**Earliest date:** October 15, 2011
**Latest date:** Until class is full
**Applicant's response to acceptance offer —**
**Maximum time:** Two weeks

**Requests for deferred entrance considered:** Yes

**Deposit to hold place in class:** Yes
**Deposit — In-State Applicants:** $100
**Out-of-State Applicants:** $100
**Deposit due:** With response to acceptance offer.
**Applied to tuition:** Yes
**Deposit refundable:** Yes
**Refundable by:** May 15, 2012

**Estimated number of new entrants:** 185
**EDP:** 3, **Special Programs:** n/a

**Start month/year:** August 2012

**Interview format:** Two on-campus interviews with committee members, faculty, staff, and/or fourth-year students. Regional interviews are not available. Video interviews are not available.

## Preparatory Programs

**Postbaccalaureate Program:** No

**Summer Program:** No

## 2010–2011 First Year Class

|  | In-State | Out-of-State | International |
|---|---|---|---|
| Applications | 1,160 | 8,238 | 668 |
| Interviewed | 253 | 377 | 54 |
| Matriculated | 79 | 96 | 15 |

**Total Matriculants: 190**   **Total Enrollment: 759**

## Financial Information

|  | In-State | Out-of-State |
|---|---|---|
| Total Cost of Attendance | $65,764 | $65,764 |
| Tuition and Fees | $46,008 | $46,008 |
| Other (incl. living expenses) | $17,956 | $17,956 |
| Health Insurance (can be waived) | $1,800 | $1,800 |

**2010 Graduate Indebtedness: $185,970**
**% of Enrolled Students Receiving Aid: 92%**

Source: 2009-2010 LCME I-B survey and 2010-2011 AAMC TSF questionnaire

# Rush Medical College of Rush University

## Chicago, Illinois

Rush Medical College of Rush University
Office of Admissions, Suite 524
600 South Paulina Street
Chicago, Illinois 60612

**T** 312 942 6915   RMC_Admissions@rush.edu

**Admissions:** www.rushu.rush.edu/
medcol/admissions.html

## General Information

Rush Medical College, founded in 1837, is the oldest college of Rush University. Through an academic and healthcare network of more than a dozen affiliated hospitals and a neighborhood health center, Rush University Medical Center serves 1.5 to 2 million patients annually. Students train in urban and suburban areas serving patients from a variety of socioeconomic and ethnic backgrounds.

## Mission Statement

Rush educates students as practitioners, scientists and teachers. Our graduates become exceptional practitioners, leaders in health care and researchers who advance medical knowledge. The university integrates patient care, education and research through the practitioner-teacher model. Rush encourages its students to commit themselves to the pursuit of excellence, to dedicate themselves to community service and to embrace the highest intellectual and ethical standards.

## Curricular Highlights

**Community Service Requirement:** Optional.

**Research/Thesis Requirement:** Optional.

Rush provides a comprehensive background in the science of medicine and clinical practice through a four-year curriculum designed to provide educational flexibility. The faculty have created an environment that fosters a commitment to competent and compassionate patient care and to attitudes of inquiry and life-long learning.

*Preclinical Curriculum* — The primary objective of the first year (M1) is to provide students with exposure to the vocabulary and fundamental concepts upon which clinical medicine is based. The M1 curriculum integrates the basic sciences into case-based, organ system blocks, which utilize lecture, laboratory, small group and workshop formats. The second-year (M2) curriculum centers on the causes and effects of disease and therapeutics. Courses utilize a case-based approach integrating basic sciences into the context of clinical medicine. The Physicianship Program is an integrated, multi-disciplinary, longitudinal program that spans the M1 and M2 years and is designed to provide students with a foundation of clinical knowledge, skills, attitudes and behaviors so students are prepared for clinical experiences where physician skills are practiced in the context of patient care.

*Clinical Curriculum* — The third and fourth years provide students with training in clinical skills, diagnosis and patient management in a variety of clinical settings. The third year is comprised of required core clerkships, while the fourth year provides students with the opportunity to pursue areas of special interest. Students have the opportunity to take most of their required clinical rotations at Rush University Medical Center or at the John H. Stroger Jr. Hospital of Cook County.

## Selection Factors

All applicants are invited to complete the supplemental application and submit letters of recommendation. The Committee on Admissions considers both academic and non-academic qualifications of applicants in making decisions. The Committee looks for objective evidence that the applicant will be able to handle the academic demands of the curriculum. In addition, the Committee places strong emphasis on the applicant's humanistic concerns, unique experiences and demonstrated motivation for a career in medicine, including healthcare experience. Academic achievement, letters of recommendation, MCAT performance, healthcare experience and interviews are considered in the final evaluation of all applicants. Only U.S. citizens or permanent residents are considered for admission.

## Information about Diversity Programs

Rush seeks to attract a diverse student body that is representative of the national population and informed about multicultural determinants of health and the socioeconomic problems affecting the delivery of care.

## Application Process and Requirements 2012–2013

**Primary application service:** AMCAS®
**Earliest filing date:** June 1, 2011
**Latest filing date:** November 1, 2011

**Secondary application required:** Yes
**Sent to:** All applicants
**URL:** www.rushsupp.com
**Contact:** RMC_Admissions@rush.edu
**Fee:** Yes, $75   **Waiver available:** Yes
**Earliest filing date:** July 1, 2011
**Latest filing date:** December 31, 2011

**MCAT® required:** Yes
**Latest MCAT® considered:** October 2011
**Oldest MCAT® considered:** January 2009

**Early Decision Program:** School does not have EDP
**Applicants notified:** n/a
**EDP available for:** n/a

**Regular acceptance notice —**
**Earliest date:** November 2011
**Latest date:** Until class is full
**Applicant's response to acceptance offer —**
**Maximum time:** Two weeks after acceptance offer

**Requests for deferred entrance considered:** Yes

**Deposit to hold place in class:** Yes
**Deposit — In-State Applicants:** $100
**Out-of-State Applicants:** $100
**Deposit due:** Two weeks after acceptance offer
**Applied to tuition:** Yes
**Deposit refundable:** Yes
**Refundable by:** May 15, 2012

**Estimated number of new entrants:** 128
**EDP:** n/a, **Special Programs:** n/a

**Start month/year:** August/September 2012

**Interview format:** Two individual interviews with faculty. Regional interviews are not available. Video interviews are not available.

## Preparatory Programs

**Postbaccalaureate Program:** No
**Summer Program:** No

## 2010–2011 First Year Class

|  | In-State | Out-of-State | International |
|---|---|---|---|
| Applications | 1,375 | 5,089 | 28 |
| Interviewed | 231 | 125 | 0 |
| Matriculated | 100 | 36 | 0 |

**Total Matriculants: 136**   **Total Enrollment: 543**

## Financial Information

|  | In-State | Out-of-State |
|---|---|---|
| Total Cost of Attendance | $66,875 | $66,875 |
| Tuition and Fees | $46,272 | $46,272 |
| Other (incl. living expenses) | $20,603 | $20,603 |
| Health Insurance (can be waived) | $0 | $0 |

**Average 2010 Graduate Indebtedness: $165,437**
**% of Enrolled Students Receiving Aid: 89%**

Source: 2009-2010 LCME I-B survey and 2010-2011 AAMC TSF questionnaire

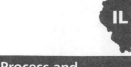

# Southern Illinois University School of Medicine

## Springfield, Illinois

Office of Admissions
Southern Illinois University
School of Medicine, P.O. Box 19624
Springfield, Illinois 62794-9624
**T** 217 545 6013    admissions@siumed.edu

**Admissions:** www.siumed.edu/studentaffairs/admissions

### General Information

Southern Illinois University School of Medicine was established in 1969 and graduated its first class in 1975. Students spend the first 12 months of the program at the medical education facilities on the Carbondale campus and the remaining three years at the Medical Center in Springfield.

### Mission Statement

The mission of the SIU School of Medicine is to assist the people of central and southern Illinois in meeting their health care needs through education, patient care, research and service to the community.

### Curricular Highlights

**Community Service Requirement:** Optional. Highly recommended.

**Research/Thesis Requirement:** Optional.

The overall focus of the first two years of the curriculum is on case-based, student-directed learning in a small-group setting supported by lectures/resource sessions. Close integration of basic science and clinical information takes place throughout the four-year course of study. Clinical training begins in the first year with real and simulated patients. An increased emphasis on issues such as community health care and the psychosocial issues of medicine continues SIU School of Medicine's emphasis on caring while curing and treating patients as people rather than medical conditions. The third year consists of a series of multidisciplinary clinical rotations, with emphasis on both hospital-based and ambulatory practice. The fourth year comprises a series of electives designed to help students with final preparations for residency. The grading system is honors/pass/fail.

### Selection Factors

Applications for the M.D. program are accepted from Illinois residents who are U.S. citizens or possess a permanent resident visa. Completion of a minimum of 90 semester hours of undergraduate work in an accredited degree-granting college or university is required. Applicants with an international education are advised to have completed at least 60 semester hours of coursework in the United States. The M.D.-J.D. program is open to non-Illinois residents. All applicants are expected to have a strong foundation in the natural sciences, social sciences, and humanities; and they must demonstrate facility in writing and speaking the English language. Preference is given to those with sufficient recent academic activity to demonstrate the potential for successful completion of the rigorous educational program and to those who demonstrate the necessary noncognitive characteristics of a successful medical student and physician. Applicants are invited for interviews according to their strengths in academics, extracurricular activities, employment and volunteer experiences, and area of residence, with preference given to central and southern Illinois residents. The School of Medicine does not discriminate on the basis of race, religion, age, sex, handicap, or national or ethnic origin in administration of its education policies, admissions policies, scholarship and loan programs, or other school-administered programs.

### Information about Diversity Programs

An active effort is made to recruit qualified applicants from diverse backgrounds. For more information, contact the Office of Diversity at 217-545-7334. The School of Medicine also sponsors the Medical/Dental Education Preparatory Program (MEDPREP), a non-degree granting program in Carbondale for disadvantaged undergraduate or postbaccalaureate students, as well as underrepresented, rural, or low-income students (*www.siumed.edu/medprep/*).

### Regional/Satellite Campuses

Students receive training in affiliated clinical locations throughout central and southern Illinois.

## Application Process and Requirements 2012–2013

**Primary application service:** AMCAS®
**Earliest filing date:** June 2011
**Latest filing date:** November 15, 2011

**Secondary application required:** Yes
**Sent to:** Selected applicants
**Contact:** Evan Wilson, (217)-545-6013, admissions@siumed.edu
**Fee:** Yes, $50    **Waiver available:** Yes
**Earliest filing date:** July 2011
**Latest filing date:** February 1, 2012

**MCAT® required:** Yes
**Latest MCAT® considered:** September 2011
**Oldest MCAT® considered:** January 2009

**Early Decision Program:** School does not have EDP
**Applicants notified:** n/a
**EDP available for:** n/a

**Regular acceptance notice —**
**Earliest date:** October 15, 2011
**Latest date:** Until class is full

**Applicant's response to acceptance offer —**
**Maximum time:** Two weeks

**Requests for deferred entrance considered:** Yes

**Deposit to hold place in class:** Yes
**Deposit — In-State Applicants:** $100
**Out-of-State Applicants:** $100
**Deposit due:** With receipt of acceptance offer
**Applied to tuition:** Yes
**Deposit refundable:** Yes
**Refundable by:** May 15, 2012

**Estimated number of new entrants:** 72
**EDP:** n/a, **Special Programs:** 2

**Start month/year:** August 2012

**Interview format:** M.D. two one-on-one interviews; M.D./J.D. three one-on-one interviews. Regional interviews are not available. Video interviews are not available.

### Preparatory Programs

**Postbaccalaureate Program:** Yes, www.siumed.edu/medprep/

**Summer Program:** No

## 2010–2011 First Year Class

|  | In-State | Out-of-State | International |
|---|---|---|---|
| Applications | 1,059 | 95 | 3 |
| Interviewed | 309 | 1 | 0 |
| Matriculated | 72 | 0 | 0 |

**Total Matriculants: 72**    **Total Enrollment: 291**

## Financial Information

|  | In-State | Out-of-State |
|---|---|---|
| Total Cost of Attendance | $43,914 | $94,286 |
| Tuition and Fees | $27,920 | $78,292 |
| Other (incl. living expenses) | $15,398 | $15,398 |
| Health Insurance (can be waived) | $596 | $596 |

**Average 2010 Graduate Indebtedness: $142,208**
**% of Enrolled Students Receiving Aid: 91%**

Source: 2009-2010 LCME I-B survey and 2010-2011 AAMC TSF questionnaire

# University of Chicago Division of the Biological Sciences, The Pritzker School of Medicine

## Chicago, Illinois

Office of Admissions, University of Chicago
Pritzker School of Medicine
924 E. 57th Street, BSLC 104W
Chicago, Illinois 60637-5416

**T** 773 702 1937

pritzkeradmissions@bsd.uchicago.edu

**Admissions:** http://pritzker.uchicago.edu/admissions/

## General Information

The Pritzker School of Medicine is unique among medical schools in that it is a part of the academic Division of the Biological Sciences. As an integral part of a world-class university, it offers medical students opportunities for interdisciplinary learning, clinical training, and research in a setting where recognized experts from all disciplines contribute to the development of physicians-in-training.

## Mission Statement

At the University of Chicago, in an atmosphere of interdisciplinary scholarship and discovery, the Pritzker School of Medicine is dedicated to inspiring diverse students of exceptional promise to become leaders and innovators in science and medicine for the betterment of humanity.

## Curricular Highlights

**Community Service Requirement:** Optional. Students have an impressive record of service.

**Research/Thesis Requirement:** Optional. Research is encouraged and supported.

The basic competencies which underlie the curriculum at Pritzker are grouped into four areas: the scientific basis of medicine; the scientific basis of diagnosis, prevention, and treatment of disease; interpersonal communication and teaching; and professional growth and development. Significant programs are devoted to helping students excel in these educational objectives. The library provides a comprehensive set of on-line medical and scientific materials with off-site access by students and faculty. This compliments a Web-based curriculum that includes multimedia presentations and searchable text. A Clinical Performance Center uses standardized patients and videotaped performance to educate students in taking a history, performing a physical examination, and clinical decision-making. The clinical biennium consists of eight clinical clerkships and electives taught entirely by full-time clinical faculty and by selected residents who are trained in the humanistic teaching of medical students. Students are required to complete a mentored scholarly project by the time of graduation in one of five tracks (Scientific Discovery; Medical Education; Quality and Safety; Community Health; Global Health).

## Selection Factors

A supplementary application is made available to everyone who submits an AMCAS® application to the Pritzker School of Medicine. The Committee on Admissions reviews an application once the supplementary application is returned and the required letters of evaluation are received. About 600 applicants are invited to interview on the university campus from August through January. Offers of admission are extended on a rolling basis from October through April. Offers of admission are made solely on the basis of ability, achievement, motivation, and humanistic qualities. Outstanding personal characteristics and a strong career commitment are as important as excellence in academics.

## Information about Diversity Programs

Pritzker is particularly interested in providing a diverse educational experience for its students. Medical students from groups underrepresented in medicine who have attended Pritzker often assume strong leadership roles, both within their class and at the national level. Clinical training occurs primarily at the University of Chicago Medical Center, which attracts patients from the surrounding Chicago metropolitan area and throughout the nation. This rich central experience is broadened by clinical opportunities in affiliated hospitals.

## Application Process and Requirements 2012–2013

**Primary application service:** AMCAS
**Earliest filing date:** June 1, 2011
**Latest filing date:** October 15, 2011

**Secondary application required:** Yes
**Sent to:** All applicants
**Contact:** Sylvia Robertson, (773) 702-1937,
pritzkeradmissions@bsd.uchicago.edu
**Fee:** Yes, $75   **Waiver available:** Yes
**Earliest filing date:** July 1, 2011
**Latest filing date:** December 1, 2011

**MCAT® required:** Yes
**Latest MCAT® considered:** September 2011
**Oldest MCAT® considered:** December 2008

**Early Decision Program:** School does have EDP
**Applicants notified:** October 1, 2011
**EDP available for:** Both In-State and Out-of-State Applicants

**Regular acceptance notice —**
**Earliest date:** October 15, 2011
**Latest date:** Until class is full

**Applicant's response to acceptance offer —**
**Maximum time:** May 15, 2012

**Requests for deferred entrance considered:** Yes

**Deposit to hold place in class:** No
**Deposit — In-State Applicants:** n/a
**Out-of-State Applicants:** n/a
**Deposit due:** n/a
**Applied to tuition:** n/a
**Deposit refundable:** n/a
**Refundable by:** n/a

**Estimated number of new entrants:** 88
**EDP:** 1, **Special Programs:** n/a

**Start month/year:** August 2012

**Interview format:** Three individual interviews. On-campus interviews strongly recommended. Video interviews are available in extremely unusual situations.

## Preparatory Programs

**Postbaccalaureate Program:** No

**Summer Program:** Yes, http://pritzker.bsd.uchicago. edu/about/diversity/pipeline/psomer.shtml

## 2010–2011 First Year Class

|  | In-State | Out-of-State | International |
|---|---|---|---|
| Applications | 789 | 4,688 | 336 |
| Interviewed | 96 | 518 | 16 |
| Matriculated | 23 | 65 | 0 |

**Total Matriculants: 88**   **Total Enrollment: 400**

## Financial Information

|  | In-State | Out-of-State |
|---|---|---|
| Total Cost of Attendance | $68,588 | $68,588 |
| Tuition and Fees | $41,452 | $41,452 |
| Other (incl. living expenses) | $24,178 | $24,178 |
| Health Insurance (can be waived) | $2,958 | $2,958 |

**Average 2010 Graduate Indebtedness: $143,683**
**% of Enrolled Students Receiving Aid: 94%**

Source: 2009-2010 LCME I-B survey and 2010-2011 AAMC TSF questionnaire

# University of Illinois at Chicago College of Medicine

## Chicago, Illinois

Medical College Admissions
University of Illinois College of Medicine
808 South Wood Street
Room 165 CME M/C 783
Chicago, Illinois 60612-7302

**T** 312 996 5635    medadmit@uic.edu

**Admissions:** www.medicine.uic.edu/admissions

## General Information

Recognized as one of the country's best medical schools, the College of Medicine is also its largest. Our diverse student body of 1,403 students hails from a wide variety of cultural and economic backgrounds. This diversity adds to the rich educational experience that is the College of Medicine. The College's four campuses located in Chicago, Peoria, Rockford, and Urbana take advantage of the state's urban and rural environments and offer numerous opportunities for clinical training and research. Our distinguished faculty contributes to the college's reputation as one of the best school for both undergraduate and graduate medical education. The College's 69 residency programs are highly sought after.

## Mission Statement

To enhance the health of the citizens of Illinois through the education of physicians and biomedical scientists, the advancement of our understanding and knowledge of health and disease, and the provision of health care in a setting of education and research. In pursuit of this mission, the college is committed to the goal of achieving excellence in teaching, research, and service in the science, art, and practice of medicine. This goal is best attained by applying valid educational principles, demonstrating high-quality patient care, and establishing a spirit of inquiry leading to scholarly achievement in basic and clinical research.

## Curricular Highlights

**Community Service Requirement:** Optional. Highly Desirable.

**Research/Thesis Requirement:** Optional. Desirable.

Offers a generalist curriculum whose goal is to graduate physicians who are well grounded in basic and clinical sciences, oriented and competent as beginning general physicians, capable of entering graduate training in either generalist specialties or subspecialties, and able to function in an ever changing health care environment. We offer several special programs that allow students to combine medicine with doctoral degrees, business, clinical and translational science and public health, and independent study options to carry out in-depth studies of topics of their choosing.

## Selection Factors

Selected applicants have the best combination of academic and extracurricular achievement, maturity, integrity, and motivation. Selection of students is based on an individualized evaluation of all available data and a personal interview. We consider the quality of work in all subject areas, breadth of education, and experiences that demonstrate initiative and creativity. The college gives preference to Illinois residents and does not discriminate on the basis of race, creed, sex, religion, national origin, age, disability, or status as a disabled veteran.

## Information about Diversity Programs

**Regional Campus Location(s):** Peoria, IL, Rockford, IL, and Urbana-Champaign, IL.

The College has programs to encourage applicants from medically underserved areas of Illinois, a program for candidates interested in practicing in an urban area, and has staff to provide guidance to students from groups underrepresented in medicine.

## Application Process and Requirements 2012–2013

**Primary application service:** AMCAS®
**Earliest filing date:** June 1, 2011
**Latest filing date:** November 15, 2011

**Secondary application required:** Yes
**Sent to:** University of Illinois College of Medicine – Admissions
**Contact:** Admissions Office, (312) 996-5635, medadmit@uic.edu
**Fee:** Yes, $70    **Waiver available:** Yes
**Earliest filing date:** June 15, 2011
**Latest filing date:** December 1, 2011

**MCAT® required:** Yes
**Latest MCAT® considered:** September 2011
**Oldest MCAT® considered:** 2009

**Early Decision Program:** School does have EDP
**Applicants notified:** October 1, 2011
**EDP available for:** Both In-State and Out-of-State Applicants

**Regular acceptance notice —**
**Earliest date:** October 14, 2011
**Latest date:** Until class is full
**Applicant's response to acceptance offer —**
**Maximum time:** Two weeks

**Requests for deferred entrance considered:** Yes

**Deposit to hold place in class:** Yes
**Deposit — In-State Applicants:** $100
**Out-of-State Applicants:** $100
**Deposit due:** With response to acceptance offer
**Applied to tuition:** Yes    **Deposit refundable:** Yes
**Refundable by:** May 15, 2012

**Estimated number of new entrants:** 300
**EDP:** 5, **Special Programs:** 25

**Start month/year:** August 2012

**Interview format:** Individual or panel. Regional interviews are offered at the regional locations. Video interviews are not available.

## Preparatory Programs

**Postbaccalaureate Program:** www.uic.edu/depts/mcam/uhp/, Dr. Javette Orgain, (312)996-6491, uhpcom@uic.edu

**Summer Program:** www.uic.edu/depts/mcam/uhp/, Dr. Javette Orgain, (312)996-6491, uhpcom@uic.edu

## 2010–2011 First Year Class

|  | In-State | Out-of-State | International |
|---|---|---|---|
| Applications | 1,658 | 6,084 | 63 |
| Interviewed | 563 | 287 | 0 |
| Matriculated | 258 | 64 | 0 |

**Total Matriculants: 322    Total Enrollment: 1,403**

## Financial Information

|  | In-State | Out-of-State |
|---|---|---|
| Total Cost of Attendance | $55,816 | $92,196 |
| Tuition and Fees | $35,032 | $71,412 |
| Other (incl. living expenses) | $19,982 | $19,982 |
| Health Insurance (can be waived) | $802 | $802 |

**Average 2010 Graduate Indebtedness: $177,287**
**% of Enrolled Students Receiving Aid: 93%**

Source: 2009-2010 LCME I-B survey and 2010-2011 AAMC TSF questionnaire

# Indiana University School of Medicine

## Indianapolis, Indiana

Medical School Admissions Office,
Indiana University School of Medicine
1120 South Drive, Fesler Hall 213
Indianapolis, Indiana 46202-5113

T 317 274 3772    inmedadm@iupui.edu

Admissions: www.medicine.iu.edu/
body.cfm?id=166

IN

## General Information

Indiana University School of Medicine, founded in 1903, is the sole institution responsible for providing medical education in the state of Indiana and operates the Indiana Statewide Medical Education System. In addition to its responsibilities in teaching, patient care, and service, Indiana University School of Medicine is a major academic research center. In conducting its medical educational programs, Indiana University School of Medicine utilizes six teaching hospitals on or near the medical center campus, as well as other affiliated hospitals in Indianapolis and throughout the state.

## Mission Statement

The goal of the Indiana University School of Medicine is the education of physicians, scientists, and other health professionals in an intellectually rich environment with research as its scientific base. In education, we are committed to imparting a fundamental understanding of both clinical practice and the basic scientific knowledge upon which it rests, to provide a firm foundation for lifelong learning. In research, we are committed to the advancement of knowledge. In patient care, we are committed to the highest standards of medical practice in an atmosphere of respect and empathy for our patients. Education, research, and delivery of health care are inseparable components of our mission. Excellence can only be achieved when all components are of highest quality, well integrated, and mutually supportive.

## Curricular Highlights

**Community Service Requirement:** Optional, *http://medicine.iu.edu/home_body.cfm?id=5316*.

**Research/Thesis Requirement:** Optional.

The School of Medicine's faculty have adopted a competency-based curriculum which equips students with excellent clinical skills balanced by the development of interpersonal and professional skills. The basic medical sciences are presented in the first two years. In addition, an intensive multidisciplinary course, Introduction to Clinical Medicine, spans both years. The faculty utilizes small problem-based learning groups throughout the first two years. A 12-month clinical clerkship program at the Indianapolis medical center and throughout the state occupies the third year. In the fourth year, students complete three clerkships and select seven one-month electives. Arrangements can be made for elective experiences around the country and abroad. Students pursuing the M.D. degree may simultaneously pursue graduate degrees in a variety of disciplines, or elect to participate in the five-year Physician Scholar Program, which incorporates a year of research into the M.D. degree program.

## Selection Factors

Students are offered places in the class on the basis of scholarship, character, personality, references, residence, interview, and performance on the MCAT. In addition, the medical school faculty has specified non-academic criteria (technical standards), which all applicants must meet in order to participate effectively in the medical education program and the practice of medicine. The School of Medicine is state-assisted, and the Admissions Committee shows preference to Indiana residents. Nevertheless, a number of nonresidents are offered acceptances each year (179 for 2008). The applications of nonresidents who have significant ties to the state of Indiana may be given greater consideration. The School of Medicine does not discriminate on the basis of age, color, disability, ethnicity, gender, marital status, national origin, race, religion, sexual orientation, or veteran status.

## Information about Diversity Programs

Information about diversity programs may be found at *www.faculty.medicine.iu.edu/offices/da/*.

## Regional/Satellite Campuses

**Regional Campus Location(s):** Bloomington, IN, Evansville, IN, Fort Wayne, IN, West Lafayette, IN, Muncie, IN, Gary, IN, South Bend, IN, and Terre Haute, IN.

First- and second-year students may be enrolled at host higher education campuses in Bloomington, Evansville, Fort Wayne, Gary, Lafayette, Muncie, South Bend, and Terre Haute, in addition to Indianapolis. The Terre Haute campus offers a four-year Rural Medicine program which was implemented in 2008.

## Application Process and Requirements 2012–2013

**Primary application service:** AMCAS®
**Earliest filing date:** June 1, 2011
**Latest filing date:** December 15, 2011

**Secondary application required:** No
**Contact:** Admissions Office, (317) 274-3772, inmedadm@iupui.edu
**URL:** n/a
**Fee:** Yes, $50    **Waiver available:** No
**Earliest filing date:** n/a
**Latest filing date:** n/a

**MCAT® required:** Yes
**Latest MCAT® considered:** September 2011
**Oldest MCAT® considered:** August 2008

**Early Decision Program:** School does have EDP
**Applicants notified:** October 1, 2011
**EDP available for:** Both In-State and Out-of-State Applicants

**Regular acceptance notice —**
**Earliest date:** October 15, 2011
**Latest date:** Until class is full
**Applicant's response to acceptance offer —**
**Maximum time:** Three weeks

**Requests for deferred entrance considered:** Yes

**Deposit to hold place in class:** No
**Deposit — In-State Applicants:** n/a
**Out-of-State Applicants:** n/a
**Deposit due:** n/a
**Applied to tuition:** n/a
**Deposit refundable:** n/a
**Refundable by:** n/a

**Estimated number of new entrants:** 328
**EDP:** 30, **Special Programs:** n/a

**Start month/year:** August 2012

**Interview format:** Individual interviews. Regional interviews are not available. Video interviews are not available.

## Preparatory Programs

**Postbaccalaureate Program:** Yes, www.msms.iu.edu

**Summer Program:** No

## 2010–2011 First Year Class

|  | In-State | Out-of-State | International |
|---|---|---|---|
| Applications | 675 | 2,703 | 258 |
| Interviewed | 561 | 348 | 22 |
| Matriculated | 269 | 47 | 6 |

**Total Matriculants: 322    Total Enrollment: 1,403**

## Financial Information

|  | In-State | Out-of-State |
|---|---|---|
| Total Cost of Attendance | $56,744 | $70,072 |
| Tuition and Fees | $29,788 | $43,116 |
| Other (incl. living expenses) | $24,156 | $24,156 |
| Health Insurance (can be waived) | $2,800 | $2,800 |

**Average 2010 Graduate Indebtedness: $167,040**
**% of Enrolled Students Receiving Aid: 80%**

*Source: 2009-2010 LCME I-B survey and 2010-2011 AAMC TSF questionnaire*

# University of Iowa Roy J. and Lucille A. Carver College of Medicine

## Iowa City, Iowa

Medical Student Admissions, University of Iowa
Roy J. & Lucille A. Carver College of Medicine
1213 Medical Education and Research Facility
Iowa City, Iowa 52242

**T** 319 335 8052    medical-admissions@uiowa.edu

**Admissions:** www.medicine.uiowa.edu/osac/
admissions

## General Information

The college is part of a major health center serving the state and region. The health sciences campus includes the University of Iowa Hospitals and Clinics; Veterans Affairs Hospital; Hardin Health Sciences Library; Medical Education and Research Facility and basic sciences, dental, nursing, and pharmacy buildings.

## Mission Statement

The Carver College of Medicine has three inextricably linked missions: education, research, and service. The college aspires to be responsive to the needs of society, and in particular the citizens of Iowa, through the excellence of its educational programs in the health professions and biomedical sciences, by the outstanding quality of its research, and through the provision of innovative and comprehensive health care and other services.

## Curricular Highlights

**Community Service Requirement:** Optional.

**Research/Thesis Requirement:** Optional.

Case-based and self-directed learning, clinical correlation, computer-based learning, small-group activities, and vertical integration of material are emphasized in the curriculum. Year 1: investigation of the normal structure and function of the human body. Year 2: investigation of abnormal structure and function. Patient contact, introduction to medical history-taking and physical diagnosis, and coverage of emerging topic areas are presented in Foundations of Clinical Practice, a course that runs the first two years of the curriculum. In the fourth semester, this course provides students with a foundation in clinical medicine that will prepare them to perform in the clinical arena. The two clinical years of the curriculum afford a broad base of training to provide the student with the essential skills and knowledge required to enter residency training. A generalist core is a feature of the clinical years. Ample time for electives is provided.

## Selection Factors

The Admissions Committee selects applicants best qualified for the study and practice of medicine. To be eligible for admission, the applicant must attain at least a 2.5 GPA (based on a 4.0 scale) for all college work undertaken. Factors considered: Overall undergraduate academic record; Science GPA; MCAT Scores; Residence (Preference given to Iowa residents with high scholastic standing. Consideration also given to outstanding non-residents.); Personal characteristics (Evaluated through letters of recommendation, information on the AMCAS® application, interview and information on the supplemental form); On-site personal interview. Applications for transfer are not considered.

## Information about Diversity Programs

The college is committed to the recruitment, selection, and retention of a diverse student body. Financial and academic assistance is provided to disadvantaged students and those from groups underrepresented in American medicine. Financial aid packages are designed on the basis of need, and grant and scholarship assistance are available. The application fee and admission deposit may be waived for financially disadvantaged students upon request. The Office of Cultural Affairs and Diversity Initiatives works closely with other administrative offices and community partners to foster an environment where all members of the UI Health Care community feel welcome. The Office supports the UI Health Care community of students, faculty, post doctoral scholars, staff, residents and fellows in conjunction with the tripartite mission of the academic medical center.

## Regional/Satellite Campuses

**Regional Campus Location(s):** Des Moines, IA.

The College is associated with 6 regional state-wide medical education centers. The major satellite campus is the Des Moines Medical Education Consortium, a cooperative venture of several Des Moines hospitals, where some students complete required clerkships and up to 24 students may fulfill their 3rd year of medical school. Some ambulatory care clerkships are completed with adjunct faculty across the state.

## Application Process and Requirements 2012–2013

**Primary application service:** AMCAS®
**Earliest filing date:** June 1, 2011
**Latest filing date:** November 1, 2011

**Secondary application required:** Yes
**Sent to:** Screened applicants
**URL:** www.medicine.uiowa.edu/osac/admissions
**Fee:** Yes, $60   **Waiver available:** Yes
**Earliest filing date:** July 1, 2011
**Latest filing date:** December 15, 2011

**MCAT® required:** Yes
**Latest MCAT® considered:** September 2011
**Oldest MCAT® considered:** January 2006

**Early Decision Program:** School does not have EDP
**Applicants notified:** n/a
**EDP available for:** n/a

**Regular acceptance notice —**
**Earliest date:** October 15, 2011
**Latest date:** Until class is full

**Applicant's response to acceptance offer —**
**Maximum time:** Two weeks from date of letter

**Requests for deferred entrance considered:** Yes

**Deposit to hold place in class:** Yes
**Deposit In-State Applicants:** $50
**Out-of-State Applicants:** $50
**Deposit due:** March 1, 2012, or within 3 weeks after acceptance offer if after March 1, 2012
**Applied to tuition:** Yes
**Deposit refundable:** Yes
**Refundable by:** June 15, 2012

**Estimated number of new entrants:** 148
**EDP:** 0, **Special Programs:** n/a

**Start month/year:** August 13, 2012
(first day of orientation)

**Interview format:** Candidates interviewed by two faculty members in one room. Regional interviews are not available. Video interviews are not available.

## Preparatory Programs

**Postbaccalaureate Program:** No

**Summer Program:** No

## 2010–2011 First Year Class

|  | In-State | Out-of-State | International |
|---|---|---|---|
| Applications | 334 | 3,072 | 4 |
| Interviewed | 292 | 412 | 0 |
| Matriculated | 99 | 50 | 0 |

**Total Matriculants: 149      Total Enrollment: 587**

## Financial Information

|  | In-State | Out-of-State |
|---|---|---|
| Total Cost of Attendance | $49,215 | $65,029 |
| Tuition and Fees | $30,318 | $46,132 |
| Other (incl. living expenses) | $17,889 | $17,889 |
| Health Insurance (can be waived) | $1,008 | $1,008 |

**Average 2010 Graduate Indebtedness: $125,594**
**% of Enrolled Students Receiving Aid: 95%**

*Source: 2009-2010 LCME I-B survey and 2010-2011 AAMC TSF questionnaire*

# University of Kansas School of Medicine

## Kansas City, Kansas

Associate Dean for Admissions
University of Kansas School of Medicine
Mail Stop 1049, 3901 Rainbow Boulevard
Kansas City, Kansas 66160

**T** 913 588 5245    premedinfo@kumc.edu

**Admissions:** www.kumc.edu/som/prospective
students.html

## General Information

Since the establishment of the University of Kansas School of Medicine in 1905, its students and faculty have built upon a tradition of excellence. Through exceptional medical education, patient care, service, and research, the medical faculty and staff are dedicated to preparing students for the future of medicine by providing the innovative education and training needed to practice in today's ever-changing health care delivery system.

## Mission Statement

The School of Medicine commits to enhance the quality of life and to serve our community through the discovery of knowledge, the education of health professionals, and improving the health of the public.

## Curricular Highlights

**Community Service Requirement:** Optional.

**Research/Thesis Requirement:** Optional.

Program Focus / Emphasis: The interdisciplinary curriculum promotes self-directed, active learning to facilitate students' mastery of the knowledge, skills, attitudes, and behaviors required to become highly competent and compassionate healers. In preparation for lifelong acquisition and synthesis of new discoveries and knowledge, students become critical thinkers who can analyze difficult problems, formulate effective action plans, and provide optimal clinical care. Years one and two consist of 13 sequential modules organized around central themes or organ systems, with didactic instruction and self-directed learning balanced between lectures and small-group activities. Each student uses a tablet computer to access course management, learning, and research systems. Beginning in the first semester, each student is paired with a physician mentor in a longitudinal ambulatory clinical experience. Several summer programs are offered for clinical credit to students who have completed their first year. For core clinical rotations, students rotate through hospitals and community-based clinics located in Kansas City, Salina, Wichita, and select sites throughout the state. Clinical electives may be taken locally, across the country, or at more than 20 approved international locations.

## Selection Factors

Applicants are encouraged to submit their AMCAS® applications by September 1. Qualified Kansas residents receive strong first preference for interview and admission; successful nonresident applicants will have significant Kansas ties and/or add breadth to the class. Academic performance, MCAT scores, application materials, letters of recommendation, impressions gained from interviews, and nonacademic activities are assessed throughout the admissions process. Transfer applications are considered only if a position is available in the third-year class; Kansas residents with a compelling need to transfer receive priority.

## Information about Diversity Programs

The University of Kansas and the School of Medicine believe the intentional creation of a diverse learning environment is essential to achieving their educational missions. Diversity and quality in medical education and health care delivery are ensured through programs that recruit, enroll, and graduate a diverse population of students; train culturally competent physicians; recruit a diverse faculty; institutionalize measures that develop and retain minority academic physicians; and expand research on health care issues affecting disadvantaged and underserved populations.

## Regional/Satellite Campuses

**Regional Campus Location(s):** Wichita, KS, and Salina, KS.

KU School of Medicine has three four-year campuses. The Kansas City campus matriculates 175 students each year; the smaller Salina and Wichita campuses annually matriculate 8 and 28 students, respectively. In addition to the 28 first-year students, approximately one-third of each Kansas City class completes clinical training on the Wichita campus. This premier community-based program is based upon a partnership with four hospitals that offer a total capacity of more than 3,000 licensed beds. Salina students focus on the delivery of health care in rural and secondary care centers. The 353-bed Salina Regional Health Center is the hub of healthcare excellence for north central Kansas.

## Application Process and Requirements 2012–2013

**Primary application service:** AMCAS
**Earliest filing date:** June 1, 2011
**Latest filing date:** October 15, 2011

**Secondary application required:** Yes
**Sent to:** All applicants
**URL:** https://www2.kumc.edu/som/meds/login.aspx
**Fee:** Yes, $50    **Waiver available:** Yes
**Earliest filing date:** July 1, 2011
**Latest filing date:** November 15, 2011

**MCAT® required:** Yes
**Latest MCAT® considered:** September 2011
**Oldest MCAT® considered:** January 2009

**Early Decision Program:** School does have EDP
**Applicants notified:** October 1, 2011
**EDP available for:** Both In-State and Out-of-State Applicants

**Regular acceptance notice —**
**Earliest date:** November 15, 2011
**Latest date:** Varies
**Applicant's response to acceptance offer —**
**Maximum time:** Two weeks

**Requests for deferred entrance considered:** Yes
**Deposit to hold place in class:** Yes
**Deposit — In-State Applicants:** $50
**Out-of-State Applicants:** $50
**Deposit due:** With response to acceptance offer
**Applied to tuition:** Yes
**Deposit refundable:** Yes
**Refundable by:** May 15, 2012

**Estimated number of new entrants:** 191
**EDP:** 45, **Special Programs:** 25

**Start month/year:** July 2012

**Interview format:** Two individual interviews, one open-file with a committee member. Regional interviews are not available. Video interviews are not available.

## Preparatory Programs

**Postbaccalaureate Program:** Yes,
www2.kumc.edu/oced/hcpp.htm

**Summer Program:** Yes,
www2.kumc.edu/oced/hcpp.htm

## 2010–2011 First Year Class

|  | In-State | Out-of-State | International |
|---|---|---|---|
| Applications | 452 | 1,935 | 5 |
| Interviewed | 354 | 118 | 0 |
| Matriculated | 157 | 19 | 0 |

**Total Matriculants: 176**    **Total Enrollment: 720**

## Financial Information

|  | In-State | Out-of-State |
|---|---|---|
| Total Cost of Attendance | $51,201 | $71,621 |
| Tuition and Fees | $27,101 | $47,521 |
| Other (incl. living expenses) | $23,117 | $23,117 |
| Health Insurance (can be waived) | $983 | $983 |

**Average 2010 Graduate Indebtedness: $129,657**
**% of Enrolled Students Receiving Aid: 98%**

*Source: 2009-2010 LCME I-B survey and 2010-2011 AAMC TSF questionnaire*

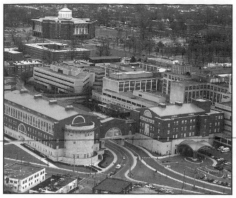

# University of Kentucky College of Medicine
## Lexington, Kentucky

University of Kentucky College of Medicine
Office of Admissions
138 Leader Avenue, Room 118
Lexington, Kentucky 40506-9983

**T** 859 323 6161   kymedap@uky.edu

**Admissions:** www.mc.uky.edu/meded/admissions/index.asp

## General Information

The University of Kentucky College of Medicine admitted its first class in 1960. The College of Medicine is part of the UK Academic Medical Center located on the university campus in Lexington. The medical center comprises six colleges: medicine, nursing, pharmacy, dentistry, health sciences, and public health. The majority of on-site clinical teaching occurs at the University of Kentucky Chandler Hospital, the Veterans Affairs Medical Center, and the Kentucky Clinic. Hospitals in Lexington and across the state hold affiliation agreements with the college for clinical teaching and patient service. Basic science teaching areas for lecture, laboratory, and small-group instruction, and the Medical Center Library, are located in the Willard Medical Sciences Building.

## Mission Statement

Our mission is to develop knowledge, skills and attitudes that promote professionalism, teamwork, life-long learning, empathy, scholarship, cultural sensitivity, and leadership, with the goal of providing excellence in education, health care, and research within the Commonwealth of Kentucky and beyond.

## Curricular Highlights

**Community Service Requirement:** Optional. Interprofessional and underserved exposure recommended.

**Research/Thesis Requirement:** Optional.

The curriculum integrates basic and clinical sciences. Students are taught fundamental problems of human biology, how to recognize causes of these problems, and how to prevent disease and treat patients. Year 1 focuses on normal function of the human body (human structure, cellular structure and function, neurosciences, and human function). First-year students receive early exposure and experience in patient care through the study of interviewing, history-taking, physical exam skills, and clinical decision-making using both standardized and real patients in longitudinal care experiences. In the first two years, students explore principles of prevention and assess the impact of social, ethical, legal, economic, and psychological factors using case study discussions. Year 2 exposes students to abnormal functions of the human body. Coursework is designed to integrate studies of infectious disease, immunology, pathology, pharmacology, and psychiatry. Computer-based instruction and simulation reinforce basic science studies and provide linkages to clinical applications. Clinical students work in both inpatient and outpatient settings and are required to take medical histories, perform physical exams, and monitor laboratory tests. Year 3 includes integrated internal medicine and emergency care clerkships, along with pediatrics, OB/GYN, psychiatry, neurology, family and community medicine, and surgery. Year 4 includes clinical pharmacology, rural medicine experiences, 2 acting internships, and a 4-month elective period. The Rural Physician Leadership Program provides clinical education at rural Kentucky sites.

## Selection Factors

The UKCOM gives preference to qualified applicants who are Kentucky residents. Determination of state residence is made by the University Registrar. Secondary applications are sent to all Kentucky residents and to nonresidents with competitive undergraduate GPAs and MCAT scores. Selected candidates are invited for interviews conducted at the UKCOM. Necessary personal attributes of applicants include time management abilities, interpersonal skills, leadership, and demonstrated service to others. Admission decisions are based upon review of academic and nonacademic factors, including scholastic excellence, MCAT performance, personal attributes, exposure to the profession, premedical recommendations, and admission interviews. Transfers from LCME-accredited schools are rarely considered on a space-available basis. We encourage applications from all academically qualified individuals interested in educational opportunities.

## Information about Diversity Programs

The UKCOM is an equal opportunity university committed to the recruitment and retention of disadvantaged students and students from groups underrepresented in medicine. Interested applicants are encouraged to contact the admissions office.

## Regional/Satellite Campuses

Visit *http://www.mc.uky.edu/meded/rural.asp* to learn more about UKCOM's Rural Physician Leadership Program in Morehead and Western Kentucky.

## Application Process and Requirements 2012–2013

**Primary application service:** AMCAS®
**Earliest filing date:** June 1, 2011
**Latest filing date:** November 1, 2011

**Secondary application required:** Yes
**Sent to:** Screened applicants
**Contact:** Kim Scott, (859) 323-6161, kstahlma@email.uky.edu
**Fee:** Yes, $50   **Waiver available:** Yes
**Earliest filing date:** July 1, 2011
**Latest filing date:** January 15, 2012

**MCAT® required:** Yes
**Latest MCAT® considered:** September 2011
**Oldest MCAT® considered:** January 2009

**Early Decision Program:** School does have EDP
**Applicants notified:** October 1, 2011
**EDP available for:** Both In-State and Out-of-State Applicants

**Regular acceptance notice —**
**Earliest date:** October 15, 2011
**Latest date:** Until class is full
**Applicant's response to acceptance offer —**
**Maximum time:** Two weeks

**Requests for deferred entrance considered:** Yes

**Deposit to hold place in class:** No
**Deposit — In-State Applicants:** n/a
**Out-of-State Applicants:** n/a
**Deposit due:** n/a
**Applied to tuition:** n/a
**Deposit refundable:** n/a
**Refundable by:** n/a

**Estimated number of new entrants:** 123
**EDP:** 20, **Special Programs:** 20

**Start month/year:** August 2012

**Interview format:** Two individual interviews. Regional interviews are not available. Video interviews are not available.

## Preparatory Programs

**Postbaccalaureate Program:** No

**Summer Program:** No

## 2010–2011 First Year Class

|  | In-State | Out-of-State | International |
|---|---|---|---|
| Applications | 427 | 1,419 | 153 |
| Interviewed | 271 | 126 | 13 |
| Matriculated | 81 | 28 | 4 |

**Total Matriculants: 113**    **Total Enrollment: 452**

## Financial Information

|  | In-State | Out-of-State |
|---|---|---|
| Total Cost of Attendance | $57,822 | $82,960 |
| Tuition and Fees | $29,098 | $54,236 |
| Other (incl. living expenses) | $27,712 | $27,712 |
| Health Insurance (can be waived) | $1,012 | $1,012 |

**Average 2010 Graduate Indebtedness: $140,104**
**% of Enrolled Students Receiving Aid: 91%**

*Source: 2009-2010 LCME I-B survey and 2010-2011 AAMC TSF questionnaire*

# University of Louisville School of Medicine

## Louisville, Kentucky

Office of Admissions, School of Medicine
Abell Administration Center
323 East Chestnut, University of Louisville
Louisville, Kentucky 40202-3866

**T** 502 852 5193  medadm@louisville.edu

**Admissions:** www.louisville.edu/medschool/
admissions

### General Information

The School of Medicine was established at the Louisville Medical Institute in 1833 and became affiliated with the University of Louisville in 1846. In 1970 the university became a member of the state system of higher education.

### Mission Statement

The University of Louisville School of Medicine's mission is to excel in the education of physicians and scientists for careers in patient care, service, teaching and research, to bring our fundamental discoveries to the bedside, and to be a vital component in the University's quest to become a premier, nationally recognized metropolitan research university.

### Curricular Highlights

**Community Service Requirement:** Optional.

**Research/Thesis Requirement:** Optional.

The University of Louisville School of Medicine is committed to training humanistically oriented and patient-centered physicians to meet the diverse health care needs of Kentucky's citizens. The curriculum is focused on providing comprehensive exposure to the fundamental aspects of medicine while retaining sufficient flexibility for effective development of each student's individual abilities and interests. The learning environment is structured to maximize individual student success and prepare all students to achieve their specific professional visions. Four goals drive the design, development, implementation and evaluation of our curriculum: Integration of basic and clinical sciences, within courses and clinical rotations; Expanded use of non-lecture teaching and learning modalities, such as directed self-learning, small-group activities, and case-based learning; Expanded use of technology to support teaching and learning, such as course and clerkship Web sites and patient simulations; and Development of course and clerkship learning objectives that support the overall goals and Educational Objectives for the Undergraduate Medical Education Program.

### Selection Factors

The ULSOM is a state institution which gives preference to residents of Kentucky. International applicants are only considered if they have both strong Kentucky ties and a pending permanent residency application. Applicants are selected on the basis of their individual merits without bias concerning sex, race, creed, national origin, age, or handicap. Applicants are chosen on the basis of intellect, integrity, maturity, and interpersonal sensitivity. Consideration is given to the past academic record, college pre-professional committee evaluations/faculty letters of recommendation, extracurricular activities, and personal interviews held at the medical school and the Trover Campus.

### Information about Diversity Programs

Applications from disadvantaged individuals and members of groups underrepresented in medicine are encouraged. Applicants are reviewed by the full Admissions Committee, which accepts students on an individual basis. Selected matriculants have the option to participate in a summer pre-matriculation program offered through the Office of Minority & Rural Affairs.

### Regional/Satellite Campuses

Students rotate at five primary hospital sites; four sites are within walking distance of the Health Science Center campus. Interested candidates may apply for dedicated admission to complete clinical training at the ULSOM Trover Campus in Madisonville, Kentucky.

## Application Process and Requirements 2012–2013

**Primary application service:** AMCAS®
**Earliest filing date:** June 1, 2011
**Latest filing date:** October 15, 2011

**Secondary application required:** Yes
**Sent to:** Screened applicants
**Contact:** medadm@louisville.edu
**Fee:** Yes, $75  **Waiver available:** Yes
**Earliest filing date:** July 1, 2011
**Latest filing date:** December 31, 2011

**MCAT® required:** Yes
**Latest MCAT® considered:** September 2011
**Oldest MCAT® considered:** January 2009

**Early Decision Program:** School does have EDP
**Applicants notified:** October 1, 2011
**EDP available for:** Both In-State and Out-of-State Applicants

**Regular acceptance notice —**
**Earliest date:** October 16, 2011
**Latest date:** Varies
**Applicant's response to acceptance offer —**
**Maximum time:** Two weeks

**Requests for deferred entrance considered:** Yes

**Deposit to hold place in class:** Yes
**Deposit — In-State Applicants:** $100
**Out-of-State Applicants:** $100
**Deposit due:** With acceptance letter
**Applied to tuition:** Yes
**Deposit refundable:** Yes
**Refundable by:** May 15, 2012

**Estimated number of new entrants:** 160
**EDP:** 4, **Special Programs:** 20

**Start month/year:** August 2012

**Interview format:** Academically blind interviews with two committee members. Regional interviews are not available. Video interviews are not available.

### Preparatory Programs

**Postbaccalaureate Program:** Yes, (502) 852-2712, pbpmed@louisville.edu

**Summer Program:** Yes,
http://louisville.edu/medschool/diversity,
Mary Joshua, (502) 852-7159, specprog@louisville.edu

## 2010–2011 First Year Class

|  | In-State | Out-of-State | International |
|---|---|---|---|
| Applications | 404 | 2,238 | 36 |
| Interviewed | 280 | 142 | 2 |
| Matriculated | 120 | 40 | 0 |

**Total Matriculants: 160**     **Total Enrollment: 617**

## Financial Information

|  | In-State | Out-of-State |
|---|---|---|
| Total Cost of Attendance | $48,012 | $63,050 |
| Tuition and Fees | $28,387 | $43,425 |
| Other (incl. living expenses) | $17,879 | $17,879 |
| Health Insurance (can be waived) | $1,746 | $1,746 |

**Average 2010 Graduate Indebtedness: $141,570**
**% of Enrolled Students Receiving Aid: 92%**

*Source: 2009-2010 LCME I-B survey and 2010-2011 AAMC TSF questionnaire*

# Louisiana State University School of Medicine in New Orleans

## New Orleans, Louisiana

Admissions Office, Louisiana State University
School of Medicine in New Orleans
1901 Perdido Street, Box P3-4
New Orleans, Louisiana 70112-1393

**T** 504 568 6262   ms-admissions@lsuhsc.edu

**Admissions:** www.medschool.lsuhsc.edu/admissions

## General Information

LSU School of Medicine in New Orleans was established in 1931 in downtown New Orleans. During the past two decades, several new buildings have been erected, including a state-of-the-art Student Learning Center which includes procedural and simulation labs, a computer lounge, and large and small-group meeting rooms. A new residence facility, Stanislaus Hall, containing a comprehensive fitness center, is among the more recent additions to the campus.

## Mission Statement

The LSUSOM is dedicated to providing the opportunity for an excellent medical education to all Louisiana applicants who are prepared to benefit from its curriculum and instruction. To this end, the Admissions Committee will strive to recruit and admit residents from Louisiana from every geographic, economic, social, and cultural dimension of the state of Louisiana.

## Curricular Highlights

**Community Service Requirement:** Required.

**Research/Thesis Requirement:** Optional.

The first two years of the medical school curriculum emphasize several basic sciences and their relevance to clinical medicine. Clinical experiences begin in the first year in courses such as Science and Practice of Medicine. The second year of medical school utilizes an integrated approach to the teaching of basic science and pre-clinical courses within an environment that fosters an early exposure to patient care. Clerkships begin in the third year where students rotate through the various clinical disciplines. In the fourth year, students are given several months for electives in addition to required rotations in Ambulatory Medicine, Acting Internships, etc. Some of these rotations can be completed at the institutions associated with the LSU School of Medicine throughout the state or at other approved institutions outside the state or country. Computer-assisted instruction is an important component of the curriculum. Entering students are required to purchase laptop computers.

## Selection Factors

Candidates are encouraged to contact the Office of Admissions for a brochure which summarizes the selection process for LSU School of Medicine in New Orleans.

## Information about Diversity Programs

Members of groups underrepresented in medicine are encouraged to apply. The School of Medicine's Office of Community and Minority Health Education actively recruits students from groups underrepresented in medicine and provides counseling for high school and college students. Further information may be obtained by contacting Dr. Edward Helm, Associate Dean for Community and Minority Health Education, at (504) 568-8501.

## Regional/Satellite Campuses

LSU School of Medicine rotates its students among one of several public hospitals, mainly in New Orleans, Baton Rouge, or Lafayette, LA, as well as several private hospitals such as Children's Hospital in the city of New Orleans. The LSU Health Care Services Division has oversight for eight public teaching hospitals in the State of Louisiana in which many LSUSOM medical students, residents and fellows receive training. Several clinics in the metropolitan area and around the state are also similarly used for the training of health care professionals. Beginning in the summer of 2012, LSU School of Medicine will be implementing a three-year accelerated program that will support forty applicants to our medical school who have a definite interest in primary care such as family medicine, internal medicine or pediatrics. The MD degree would be awarded after three years as a medical student. This program will be based at our teaching facilities in Lafayette, Louisiana, and is designed to address the critical shortage of primary care physicians in this country. Applicants who are not residents of the State of Louisiana are welcome to apply for this three-year program.

## Application Process and Requirements 2012–2013

**Primary application service:** AMCAS®
**Earliest filing date:** June 1, 2011
**Latest filing date:** November 30, 2011

**Secondary application required:** Yes
**Sent to:** All applicants
**URL:** www.medschool.lsuhsc.edu/admissions/secondary_application/instructions.aspx
**Fee:** Yes, $50   **Waiver available:** Yes
**Earliest filing date:** June 15, 2011
**Latest filing date:** January 15, 2012

**MCAT® required:** Yes
**Latest MCAT® considered:** September 2011
**Oldest MCAT® considered:** September 2008

**Early Decision Program:** School does have EDP
**Applicants notified:** October 1, 2011
**EDP available for:** Both In-State and Out-of-State Applicants

**Regular acceptance notice —**
**Earliest date:** October 15, 2011
**Latest date:** Varies
**Applicant's response to acceptance offer —**
**Maximum time:** Two weeks

**Requests for deferred entrance considered:** Yes
**Deposit to hold place in class:** Yes
**Deposit — In-State:** $100
**Out-of-State Applicants:** $100
**Deposit due:** Due with acceptance letter
**Applied to tuition:** Yes
**Deposit refundable:** Yes
**Refundable by:** May 15, 2012

**Estimated number of new entrants:** 240
**EDP:** 15, **Special Programs:** 40
**Start month/year:** August 2012

**Interview format:** Three one-on-one interviews. Regional interviews are not available. Video interviews are not available.

## Preparatory Programs

**Postbaccalaureate Program:** No

**Summer Program:** Yes, Dr. Edward Helm, (504) 568-8501, jparke@lsuhsc.edu

## 2010–2011 First Year Class

|  | In-State | Out-of-State | International |
|---|---|---|---|
| Applications | 674 | 445 | 20 |
| Interviewed | 411 | 20 | 0 |
| Matriculated | 181 | 9 | 2 |

**Total Matriculants: 192**    **Total Enrollment: 759**

## Financial Information

|  | In-State | Out-of-State |
|---|---|---|
| Total Cost of Attendance | $38,095 | $53,690 |
| Tuition and Fees | $14,880 | $30,475 |
| Other (incl. living expenses) | $21,578 | $21,578 |
| Health Insurance (can be waived) | $1,637 | $1,637 |

**Average 2010 Graduate Indebtedness: $130,840**
**% of Enrolled Students Receiving Aid: 89%**

*Source: 2009-2010 LCME I-B survey and 2010-2011 AAMC TSF questionnaire*

# Louisiana State University Health Sciences Center School of Medicine in Shreveport

## Shreveport, Louisiana

Office of Student Admissions
Louisiana State University Health Sciences Center
School of Medicine in Shreveport,
1501 Kings Highway
Shreveport, Louisiana 71130

**T** 318 675 5190    shvadm@lsuhsc.edu

**Admissions:** www.admissions.lsuhsc.edu

## General Information

The LSU Health Sciences Center in Shreveport (LSUHSC-S) provides education, research, patient care services, and community outreach. Educating health professionals and scientists at all levels, its major responsibility includes the advancement and dissemination of knowledge in medicine and the basic sciences. It also provides vital public service through its hospital and clinics.

## Mission Statement

LSUHSC-S has a dual mission: to assure the availability of acute and primary health care services to the uninsured, to the underinsured, and to others with problems of access to medical care, and to serve as the principal site for the clinical education of future doctors and other health care professionals.

## Curricular Highlights

**Community Service Requirement:** Optional. Community service is highly desirable.

**Research/Thesis Requirement:** Optional. Desirable, but not required.

The modern curriculum thoroughly integrates medical issues and applications in the first two years, during which the basic sciences are emphasized. Recently, didactic lecture hours were cut dramatically, and small-group, active-learning experiences were dramatically increased. The overall effect was decreased contact hours and increased self-directed learning. All essential basic-science concepts traditionally taught in the first two years are now integrated with clinical examples, clinical cases and standardized patient experiences. The required clerkships occur in the third year, and the fourth year is devoted to electives.

## Selection Factors

Admission is based upon character, motivation, intellectual ability, and achievement as judged by recommendations of premedical advisors, personal interviews with members of the faculty at the School of Medicine, college grades, and MCAT scores. In recent years, the number of applications filed by well-qualified residents of Louisiana has exceeded the number of places available. For this reason, places have not been offered to nonresidents. Determination of state residence is determined by LSU system regulations. Thirty colleges are represented in the 2010 entering class. The School of Medicine in Shreveport does not discriminate in applicant selection on the basis of race, sex, creed, national origin, age, or handicap.

## Information about Diversity Programs

Applications from students from groups underrepresented in medicine are encouraged and will be given every consideration. All students are encouraged to take advantage of the services provided by the Office of Multicultural Affairs. They include a pre-matriculation program, an MCAT preparation course, and a summer research program for high school students, as well as informal counseling for medical students and applicants.

## Regional/Satellite Campuses

The school is affiliated with other local and regional hospitals.

## Application Process and Requirements 2012–2013

**Primary application service:** AMCAS®
**Earliest filing date:** June 1, 2011
**Latest filing date:** November 1, 2011

**Secondary application required:** Yes
**Sent to:** All Louisiana applicants
**URL:** Provided by school
**Contact:** Student Admissions, (318) 675-5190, shvadm@lsuhsc.edu
**Fee:** Yes, $50    **Waiver available:** Yes
**Earliest filing date:** June 1, 2011
**Latest filing date:** December 15, 2011

**MCAT® required:** Yes
**Latest MCAT® considered:** September 2011
**Oldest MCAT® considered:** August 2008

**Early Decision Program:** School does have EDP
**Applicants notified:** October 1, 2011
**EDP available for:** In-States only

**Regular acceptance notice —**
**Earliest date:** October 14, 2011
**Latest date:** Until class is full
**Applicant's response to acceptance offer —**
**Maximum time:** Two weeks

**Requests for deferred entrance considered:** Yes

**Deposit to hold place in class:** Yes
**Deposit — In-State:** $250
**Out-of-State Applicants:** $250
**Deposit due:** May 15, 2012
**Applied to tuition:** Yes
**Deposit refundable:** Yes
**Refundable by:** May 15, 2012

**Estimated number of new entrants:** 118
**EDP:** 15, **Special Programs:** 2

**Start month/year:** July 27, 2012

**Interview format:** Two closed file and one open file, non-stress interviews. Regional interviews are not available. Video interviews are not available.

## Preparatory Programs

**Postbaccalaureate Program:** No

**Summer Program:** Yes,
www.sh.lsuhsc.edu/multicultural/front.htm
Shirley Roberson, (318) 675-5049, srober1@lsuhsc.edu

## 2010–2011 First Year Class

|  | In-State | Out-of-State | International |
|---|---|---|---|
| Applications | 576 | 147 | 4 |
| Interviewed | 260 | 1 | 0 |
| Matriculated | 117 | 1 | 0 |

**Total Matriculants: 118**    **Total Enrollment: 464**

## Financial Information

|  | In-State | Out-of-State |
|---|---|---|
| Total Cost of Attendance | $40,295 | $56,673 |
| Tuition and Fees | $13,159 | $29,537 |
| Other (incl. living expenses) | $25,554 | $25,554 |
| Health Insurance (can be waived) | $1,582 | $1,582 |

**Average 2010 Graduate Indebtedness: $120,847**
**% of Enrolled Students Receiving Aid: 83%**

Source: 2009-2010 LCME I-B survey and 2010-2011 AAMC TSF questionnaire

# Tulane University School of Medicine

## New Orleans, Louisiana

Office of Admissions and Student Affairs
Tulane University School of Medicine
131 S. Robertson Street, Suite 1550, SL-67
New Orleans, Louisiana 70112-2699
**T** 504 988 5187    medsch@tulane.edu

**Admissions:** www.mcl.tulane.edu/admissions

## General Information

Tulane University School of Medicine, a private, nonsectarian institution, was founded in 1834. Today it is one of the eleven colleges comprising Tulane University and is the 15th oldest medical school in the United States.

## Mission Statement

We heal communities through research, education and service.

## Curricular Highlights

**Community Service Requirement:** Required.

**Research/Thesis Requirement:** Optional.

Tulane School of Medicine offers a four-year program leading to the M.D. degree. While the emphasis in the first two years is on the principles of the basic medical sciences, the goal of the first two years is helping students develop clinical problem-solving skills instead of emphasizing the transmission of facts devoid of clinical context. The program in Foundations in Medicine, which spans the first two years, is responsible for instructing students in the complex art and science of the patient-doctor interaction. This objective is accomplished through lectures, small-group discussions, clinical demonstrations, visits to community health facilities, and interactions with both real patients and individuals trained as patient instructors. The third and fourth years provide experience in clinical settings where the emphasis is on patient care and community health. Flexibility is attained throughout the four years by designating approximately one-third of scheduled curriculum time for elective courses and selected advanced studies. The curriculum is under constant review by faculty and students. Tulane offers a wide variety of support systems for medical students, including test-taking skills workshops.

## Selection Factors

In evaluating applicants, the Committee on Admissions relies on such criteria as grade point averages, MCAT scores, faculty appraisals from the applicant's college, special accomplishments and talents, and the substance and level of courses taken in a particular college. Tulane has not established mandatory minimal MCAT or GPA scores, as all components of the application, cognitive and non-cognitive, are taken into account.

## Information about Diversity Programs

Tulane encourages qualified disadvantaged students and students from groups underrepresented in medicine to apply. Special activities available for, but not limited to, students from groups underrepresented in medicine include tutorial and counseling services for students in medical school. The diversity in composition of the members of the Committee on Admissions is reflected in the composition of the medical student body.

## Regional/Satellite Campuses

**Regional Campus Location(s):** Baton Rouge, LA, Portland, LA, and Springfield, LA.

Tulane School of Medicine and Baton Rouge General Medical Center have just created a satellite Tulane Medical School Campus in Baton Rouge. The campus is located at Baton Rouge General's Mid City Hospital. Experienced physicians serve as teachers, mentors, and role models for third and fourth year medical students who choose this campus for it longitudinal ambulatory care experience as well as unique opportunities to participate in rotations in healthcare policy and operations with various state agencies and healthcare organizations. Interdisciplinary education and training occurs with the Baton Rouge General nursing students and students from the University of Louisiana at Monroe College of Pharmacy, also sharing the Baton Rouge General campus.

## Application Process and Requirements 2012–2013

**Primary application service:** AMCAS®
**Earliest filing date:** June 1, 2011
**Latest filing date:** December 15, 2011

**Secondary application required:** Yes
**Sent to:** All applicants
**URL:** www.som.tulane.edu/departments/admissions/
**Fee:** Yes, $125    **Waiver available:** Yes
**Earliest filing date:** June 1, 2011
**Latest filing date:** January 15, 2012

**MCAT® required:** Yes
**Latest MCAT® considered:** August 2011
**Oldest MCAT® considered:** August 2008

**Early Decision Program:** School does have EDP
**Applicants notified:** October 15, 2011
**EDP available for:** Both In-States and Out-of-States

**Regular acceptance notice —**
**Earliest date:** October 15, 2011
**Latest date:** Until class is full
**Applicant's response to acceptance offer —**
**Maximum time:** Two weeks

**Requests for deferred entrance considered:** Yes

**Deposit to hold place in class:** Yes
**Deposit — In-State Applicants:** $100
**Out-of-State Applicants:** $100
**Deposit due:** May 15, 2012
**Applied to tuition:** Yes
**Deposit refundable:** Yes
**Refundable by:** May 15, 2012

**Estimated number of new entrants:** 188
**EDP:** 10, **Special Programs:** n/a

**Start month/year:** August 2012

**Interview format:** Selected applicants are invited for interviews. Regional interviews are not available. Video interviews are not available.

## Preparatory Programs
**Postbaccalaureate Program:** Yes,
www.som.tulane.edu/departments/scb

**Summer Program:** No

## 2010–2011 First Year Class

|  | In-State | Out-of-State | International |
|---|---|---|---|
| Applications | 432 | 9,283 | 323 |
| Interviewed | 43 | 342 | 22 |
| Matriculated | 27 | 155 | 5 |

**Total Matriculants: 187**    **Total Enrollment: 726**

## Financial Information

|  | In-State | Out-of-State |
|---|---|---|
| Total Cost of Attendance | $71,733 | $71,733 |
| Tuition and Fees | $50,959 | $50,959 |
| Other (incl. living expenses) | $19,020 | $19,020 |
| Health Insurance (can be waived) | $1,754 | $1,754 |

**Average 2010 Graduate Indebtedness: $205,463**
**% of Enrolled Students Receiving Aid: 85%**

Source: 2009-2010 LCME I-B survey and 2010-2011 AAMC TSF questionnaire

# Johns Hopkins University School of Medicine

## Baltimore, Maryland

Committee on Admissions
Johns Hopkins University School of Medicine
733 North Broadway, Suite G-49
Baltimore, Maryland 21205

**T** 410 955 3182   somadmiss@jhmi.edu

**Admissions:** www.hopkinsmedicine.org/admissions

## General Information

Johns Hopkins University School of Medicine, founded in 1893, is a private, nondenominational institution which fosters the training of medical practitioners, teachers, and biomedical scientists. The medical center provides library facilities, the Reed Residence Hall, off-campus housing assistance, cafeterias, recreational sports in the Cooley Center, and performing arts programs. Preclinical courses are given in the adjacent basic science complex. Medical care facilities such as the Johns Hopkins Hospital and the Outpatient Center provide an extensive and diverse patient base for the teaching of all clinical subjects. Students also attend educational programs conducted at community hospitals in Baltimore and pursue elective experiences at other medical schools in the U.S. and foreign countries.

## Mission Statement

The Johns Hopkins University School of Medicine is dedicated to preparing students to practice compassionate medicine of the highest standards and to contributing to the advancement of medical knowledge.

## Curricular Highlights

**Community Service Requirement:** Optional.

**Research/Thesis Requirement:** Encouraged. Exceptional research opportunities are available.

The curriculum provides sound foundations in basic sciences and clinical medicine while retaining the flexibility required for students to identify and develop diverse career interests. In lieu of letter grades, the grading system the first two years is pass/fail. Third and fourth year students' grades are honors, high pass, pass or fail. The M.D. program includes the integration of basic sciences and clinical experiences and the expanded use of case-based, small-group learning sessions. Students learn the medical interview and basic physical examination in the first months of medical school, and working with community physicians practices through years 1 and 2. For more information, see www.hopkinsmedicine.org. First year includes integrated coverage of introductory basic sciences, neuroscience, epidemiology, and introduction to clinical medicine. Second-year includes the study of advanced basic sciences, behavioral sciences, clinical skills, and beginning clerkships. In the third and fourth-years, with the assistance of faculty advisors, students develop individualized programs incorporating required clerkships in major clinical areas and electives. Students may use electives for specialized clerkships, research, and public health experiences.

## Selection Factors

A Bachelor's degree is required in addition to proven academic competence, strong communications skills, previous achievements and activities help the Committee on Admissions to evaluate applicants' suitability for medicine. Two of the required Humanities courses must have been writing intensive courses. Applicants who have unusual talents, strong humanistic qualities, demonstrated leadership, and significant experience requiring teamwork skills, and creative abilities, are sought. There are no residency requirements and international students are encouraged to apply. Passage of TOEFL is required for all students whose undergraduate instruction was conducted in a language other than English. Students matriculating at Hopkins are required to undergo a criminal background check. Due to space limitations, Hopkins does not admit transfer students. JHU complies with federal and state laws prohibiting discrimination.

## Information about Diversity Programs

Johns Hopkins is committed to enrolling a diverse student population with a passion for improving health locally and on a global scale. Hopkins has an excellent record of enrolling high quality students from disadvantaged backgrounds and/or are underrepresented in medicine. Contact the assistant dean for student affairs for more information.

## Regional/Satellite Campuses

In addition to the Johns Hopkins Hospital, students may also serve their clinical rotations at the Bayview Medical Center, located three miles from the main medical campus.

## Application Process and Requirements 2012–2013

**Primary application service:** AMCAS®
**Earliest filing date:** July 1, 2011
**Latest filing date:** October 17, 2011

**Secondary application required:** Yes
**Sent to:** All applicants
**URL:** www.hopkinsmedicine.org/admissions
**Fee:** Yes, $80   **Waiver available:** Yes
**Earliest filing date:** July 1, 2011
**Latest filing date:** December 1, 2011

**MCAT® required:** Yes
**Latest MCAT® considered:** September 2011
**Oldest MCAT® considered:** September 2008

**Early Decision Program:** School does not have EDP
**Applicants notified:** n/a
**EDP available for:** n/a
**Regular acceptance notice —**
**Earliest date:** October 17, 2011
**Latest date:** Varies
**Applicant's response to acceptance offer —**
**Maximum time:** Three weeks

**Requests for deferred entrance considered:** Yes

**Deposit to hold place in class:** No
**Deposit — In-State Applicants:** n/a
**Out-of-State Applicants:** n/a
**Deposit due:** n/a
**Applied to tuition:** n/a
**Deposit refundable:** n/a
**Refundable by:** n/a

**Estimated number of new entrants:** 120
**EDP:** n/a, **Special Programs:** n/a

**Start month/year:** August 2012

**Interview format:** Interviews are one-one-one. Regional interview available in limited areas. Video interviews are not available.

## Preparatory Programs

**Postbaccalaureate Program:** Yes, www.jhu.edu/postbac/

**Summer Program:** No

## 2010–2011 First Year Class

|  | In-State | Out-of-State | International |
|---|---|---|---|
| Applications | 377 | 5,059 | 305 |
| Interviewed | 89 | 613 | 26 |
| Matriculated | 17 | 101 | 2 |

**Total Matriculants: 120**     **Total Enrollment: 463**

## Financial Information

|  | In-State | Out-of-State |
|---|---|---|
| Total Cost of Attendance | $63,840 | $63,840 |
| Tuition and Fees | $42,782 | $42,782 |
| Other (incl. living expenses) | $17,986 | $17,986 |
| Health Insurance (can be waived) | $3,072 | $3,072 |

**Average 2010 Graduate Indebtedness: $102,376**
**% of Enrolled Students Receiving Aid: 81%**

Source: 2009-2010 LCME I-B survey and 2010-2011 AAMC TSF questionnaire

# Uniformed Services University of the Health Sciences F. Edward Hébert School of Medicine

## Bethesda, Maryland

Admissions Office, Room A-1041
Uniformed Services University of the Health Sciences
F. Edward Hébert School of Medicine
4301 Jones Bridge Road
Bethesda, Maryland 20814-4799

**T** 301 295 3101   admissions@usuhs.mil

**Admissions:** www.usuhs.mil/admissions.html

## General Information

Created by public law in 1972, the Uniformed Services University of the Health Sciences (USUHS) was founded to prepare young men and women for careers as health care professionals in the uniformed services. The school's charter is to provide a comprehensive education in medicine and to select individuals who demonstrate potential for and commitment to careers as medical officers in the uniformed services.

## Mission Statement

USUHS is the nation's federal health sciences university and is committed to excellence in military medicine and public health during peace and war. Our mission is to provide the nation with health professionals dedicated to career service in the Department of Defense and the United States Public Health Service with scientists who serve the common good.

## Curricular Highlights

**Community Service Requirement:** Optional.

**Research/Thesis Requirement:** Optional.

The school has a four-year program culminating in the doctor of medicine degree. Basic science instruction predominates the initial two academic years, with the final two years devoted to clinical education. Basic science instruction is correlated both interdisciplinarily and clinically. The integration between the clinical and basic sciences is progressive and proceeds with involvement in patient care activities early in the curriculum, starting with the first semester of the first year. The curriculum also includes basic military orientation and concentration on unique aspects of military medicine. A conventional letter grading system is used.

## Selection Factors

The school employs a three-stage, progressive selection process. The first stage consists of the submission of an AMCAS® application; the second, the submission of supplementary materials; and the third, personal interviews, which are conducted on campus. Advancement in the process is competitive, based on candidates' personal and intellectual characteristics. The Admissions Committee does not discriminate on the basis of sex, race, religion, marital status or national origin.

## Information about Diversity Programs

The Office of Recruitment and Admissions is instrumental in the recruitment and retention of a student body that mirrors the diversity of our nation. We provide a welcoming environment to all students by encouraging expression of their diverse ethnic, cultural, economic, and experiential backgrounds. Competitive applicants from groups underrepresented in medicine are encouraged to apply. The application/admissions processes are the same for all students. The staff supports all students during the four years of medical school, recognizing that each student's unique circumstances may require various levels of support and encouragement. The learning environment is enhanced by four key student-sponsored groups: Women in Medicine and Science, the Asian Pacific American Medical Student Association, the Latino Medical Student Association, and the Student National Medical Association. Faculty support is provided by the Office of Recruitment and Admissions to advance the community outreach efforts of these student groups.

## Application Process and Requirements 2012–2013

**Primary application service:** AMCAS®
**Earliest filing date:** June 1, 2011
**Latest filing date:** November 15, 2011

**Secondary application required:** Yes
**Sent to:** All applicants
**Contact:** (301) 295-3101, admissions@usuhs.mil
**Fee:** No   **Waiver available:** n/a
**Earliest filing date:** June 1, 2011
**Latest filing date:** December 15, 2011

**MCAT® required:** Yes
**Latest MCAT® considered:** September 2011
**Oldest MCAT® considered:** January 2009

**Early Decision Program:** School does not have EDP
**Applicants notified:** n/a
**EDP available for:** n/a

**Regular acceptance notice —**
**Earliest date:** October 16, 2011
**Latest date:** Until class is full
**Applicant's response to acceptance offer —**
**Maximum time:** Two weeks

**Requests for deferred entrance considered:** Yes

**Deposit to hold place in class:** No
**Deposit — In-State Applicants:** n/a
**Out-of-State Applicants:** n/a
**Deposit due:** n/a
**Applied to tuition:** n/a
**Deposit refundable:** n/a
**Refundable by:** n/a

**Estimated number of new entrants:** 171
**EDP:** 0, **Special Programs:** n/a

**Start month/year:** June 2012

**Interview format:** Two thirty-minute interviews with medical corps officers. Regional interviews are not available. Video interviews are not available.

## Preparatory Programs

**Postbaccalaureate Program:** No

**Summer Program:** No

## 2010–2011 First Year Class

|  | In-State | Out-of-State | International |
|---|---|---|---|
| Applications | 159 | 2,236 | 3 |
| Interviewed | 50 | 544 | 0 |
| Matriculated | 23 | 146 | 0 |

**Total Matriculants: 169**   **Total Enrollment: 675**

## Financial Information

|  | In-State | Out-of-State |
|---|---|---|
| Total Cost of Attendance | $0 | $0 |
| Tuition and Fees | $0 | $0 |
| Other (incl. living expenses) | $0 | $0 |
| Health Insurance (can be waived) | $0 | $0 |

**Average 2010 Graduate Indebtedness: $0**
**% of Enrolled Students Receiving Aid: 0%**

Source: 2009-2010 LCME I-B survey and 2010-2011 AAMC TSF questionnaire

# University of Maryland School of Medicine
## Baltimore, Maryland

Committee on Admissions, Suite 190
University of Maryland School of Medicine
685 West Baltimore Street
Baltimore, Maryland 21201-1559

T 410 706 7478    admissions@som.umaryland.edu

**Admissions:** www.medschool.umaryland.edu/admissions

## General Information

Organized in 1807, The University of Maryland School of Medicine is the nation's oldest public medical college. The first class was graduated in 1810. The medical school was among the first to erect its own hospital for clinical instruction.

## Mission Statement

The University of Maryland School of Medicine is dedicated to providing excellence in biomedical education, basic and clinical research, quality patient care, and service to improve the health of the citizens of Maryland and beyond. The School is committed to the education and training of medical, M.D./Ph.D., graduate, physical therapy, and medical research technology students. The school will recruit and develop faculty to serve as exemplary role models for our students.

## Curricular Highlights

**Community Service Requirement:** Required; Part of Introduction to Clinical Medicine.

**Research/Thesis Requirement:** Optional.

During the first two years of medical school the basic sciences are integrated and taught as systems, using interdisciplinary teaching by both basic and clinical science faculty. Mornings include lecture and small group sessions; afternoons are devoted to independent study. Curricular materials are available online and laptop computers are required. "Introduction to Clinical Medicine" begins early in the first year and continues through year two, offering instruction in clinical diagnosis, intimate human behavior, problem-based learning, biomedical ethics and dynamics of ambulatory care. Clinical clerkships during the last two years include a month in family medicine and an emphasis on ambulatory teaching in other disciplines and two months of subinternship.

## Selection Factors

Applications are accepted from citizens and permanent residents of the U.S. and citizens of Canada. All AMCAS® applicants are invited to submit a Stage II application. Selection of students is based on careful appraisal of character, motivation for medicine, academic achievement, MCAT scores, letters of reference, extracurricular activities and interviews. The University does not discriminate on the basis of race, creed, sex, gender, national origin, age or handicap.

## Information about Diversity Programs

The School of Medicine values diversity very highly in the educational process and is committed to the recruitment and retention of talented students from underrepresented and disadvantaged backgrounds. A major focus of our recruitment efforts is to provide information on admissions requirements and preparation for medical school, the selection process, and educational and research opportunities at the School of Medicine. There are no fixed quotas for any group and the admissions procedures are the same for all applicants. Information can be obtained from Ms. Raushanah Kareem, in the Office of Admissions.

## Regional/Satellite Campuses

Students complete most of their junior year clinical clerkships at the University of Maryland Medical System and Baltimore Veterans Affairs Medical Center, but do rotate through several of our affiliated community hospitals for selected rotations. During the fourth year of medical school our students will see patients during their ambulatory months at physician's offices in underserved areas of Baltimore City, Western and Southern Maryland and the Eastern Shore.

## Application Process and Requirements 2012–2013

**Primary application service:** AMCAS®
**Earliest filing date:** June 1, 2011
**Latest filing date:** November 1, 2011

**Secondary application required:** Yes
**Sent to:** All applicants
**Contact:** Ms. Towanda Sykes, (410) 706-7478, tsykes@som.umaryland.edu
**Fee:** Yes, $70    **Waiver available:** No
**Earliest filing date:** July 15, 2011
**Latest filing date:** December 15, 2011

**MCAT® required:** Yes
**Latest MCAT® considered:** September 2011
**Oldest MCAT® considered:** January 2008

**Early Decision Program:** School does have EDP
**Applicants notified:** October 1, 2011
**EDP available for:** Both In-State and Out-of-State Applicants

**Regular acceptance notice —**
**Earliest date:** October 15, 2011
**Latest date:** Until class is full
**Applicant's response to acceptance offer —**
**Maximum time:** Three weeks

**Requests for deferred entrance considered:** Yes

**Deposit to hold place in class:** No
**Deposit — In-State Applicants:** n/a
**Out-of-State Applicants:** n/a
**Deposit due:** n/a
**Applied to tuition:** n/a
**Deposit refundable:** n/a
**Refundable by:** n/a

**Estimated number of new entrants:** 160
**EDP:** 5, **Special Programs:** 6

**Start month/year:** August 2012

**Interview format:** Two, one-on-one interviews with faculty or student. Regional interviews are not available. Video interviews are not available.

## Preparatory Programs

**Postbaccalaureate Program:** No

**Summer Program:** Yes, Dr. Sandra Dolan, (410) 706-7669, sdolan@dc.umaryland.edu

## 2010–2011 First Year Class

|  | In-State | Out-of-State | International |
|---|---|---|---|
| Applications | 837 | 3,877 | 211 |
| Interviewed | 319 | 214 | 11 |
| Matriculated | 125 | 35 | 0 |

**Total Matriculants: 160**    **Total Enrollment: 642**

## Financial Information

|  | In-State | Out-of-State |
|---|---|---|
| Total Cost of Attendance | $57,254 | $79,701 |
| Tuition and Fees | $27,952 | $49,199 |
| Other (incl. living expenses) | $26,836 | $28,036 |
| Health Insurance (can be waived) | $2,466 | $2,466 |

**Average 2010 Graduate Indebtedness: $145,594**
**% of Enrolled Students Receiving Aid: 89%**

*Source: 2009-2010 LCME I-B survey and 2010-2011 AAMC TSF questionnaire*

# Boston University School of Medicine

## Boston, Massachusetts

Admissions Office, Building L, Room 124
Boston University School of Medicine
72 East Concord Street
Boston, Massachusetts 02118

**T** 617 638 4630 medadms@bu.edu

**Admissions:** www.bumc.bu.edu/admissions/

## General Information

The New England Female Medical College, founded in 1848, was the first medical college for women in the world. In 1873 the college became the Boston University School of Medicine, the first coeducational medical school in the U.S. The current health sciences campus includes the Schools of Medicine, Dental Medicine, and Public Health, as well as the hospital, Boston Medical Center, the Division of Graduate Medical Sciences, and extensive research facilities.

## Mission Statement

Boston University School of Medicine is dedicated to the educational, intellectual, professional, and personal development of a diverse group of exceptional students, trainees, and faculty who are deeply committed to the study and to the practice of medicine, to biomedical research, and to the health of the public. We, as a community, place great value on excellence, integrity, service, social justice, collegiality, equality of opportunity, and interdisciplinary collaboration.

## Curricular Highlights

**Community Service Requirement:** Optional. Many students and faculty participate.

**Research/Thesis Requirement:** Optional. Thesis may be required for dual degree programs.

BUSM offers a flexible, integrated program of critical inquiry and rigorous study in the biological, social, and behavioral sciences. The early focus is on normal structure and function, unified by Integrated Problems, a clinically focused seminar. Introduction to Clinical Medicine has students interviewing and evaluating patients from the first week. The foundational sciences are linked with applications in clinical practice, emphasizing multidisciplinary, team-based learning. The second-year focus shifts to pathophysiology, with an integrated, multidisciplinary format led by a multidisciplinary faculty. The core clinical training of the third year includes all major disciplines, with ambulatory and inpatient experience in generalist and subspecialty venues. There are also clinical electives. The fourth year includes advanced clerkships and is largely elective. Research opportunities are available in basic science and clinical disciplines, and many students choose electives in international health. Any academic year may be spread over two calendar years and students may switch into several dual degree programs.

## Selection Factors

Applicants are selected by a comprehensive, holistic review process that incorporates the academic record, recommendations, research experience, and involvement in community service, as well as qualities of personality, character, resilience, and life experience. Personal interviews are required and are offered at the discretion of the Committee on Admissions.

## Information about Diversity Programs

BUSM is committed to diversity among faculty and students. Programs for the recruitment and support of students from groups underrepresented in medicine are managed by the Office of Admissions and the Office of Diversity and Multicultural Affairs. All applications are submitted to the Office of Admissions.

## Regional/Satellite Campuses

Basic science programs are all on-campus. Clinical training is largely on-campus, but each student has some off-campus rotations, ensuring that all students experience different venues and styles of practice. All clinical training is directly supervised by BUSM faculty.

## Application Process and Requirements 2012–2013

**Primary application service:** AMCAS®
**Earliest filing date:** June 1, 2011
**Latest filing date:** November 1, 2011

**Secondary application required:** Yes
**Sent to:** All applicants
**URL:** Provided after receipt of initial application
**Contact:** Office of Admissions, (617) 638-4630, medadms@bu.edu
**Fee:** Yes, $110    **Waiver available:** Yes
**Earliest filing date:** June 1, 2011
**Latest filing date:** January 2, 2012

**MCAT® required:** Yes
**Latest MCAT® considered:** September 2011
**Oldest MCAT® considered:** 2008

**Early Decision Program:** School does have EDP
**Applicants notified:** October 1, 2011
**EDP available for:** Both In-State and Out-of-State Applicants

**Regular acceptance notice —**
**Earliest date:** Early January 2012
**Latest date:** Until class is full
**Applicant's response to acceptance offer —**
**Maximum time:** Two weeks

**Requests for deferred entrance considered:** No

**Deposit to hold place in class:** Yes
**Deposit — In-State Applicants:** $500
**Out-of-State Applicants:** $500
**Deposit due:** May 15, 2012
**Applied to tuition:** Yes    **Deposit refundable:** Yes
**Refundable prior to:** May 15, 2012

**Estimated number of new entrants:** 130
**EDP:** 2, **Special Programs:** 45

**Start month/year:** August 2012

**Interview format:** On-campus interview required. Regional interviews are not available. Video interviews are not available.

## Preparatory Programs

**Postbaccalaureate Program:** Yes,
www.bu.edu/met/adult_college_programs/boston_university_metropolitan_college_undergraduate_programs/college_certificate/

**Summer Program:** No

## 2010–2011 First Year Class

|  | In-State | Out-of-State | International |
|---|---|---|---|
| Applications | 781 | 9,829 | 620 |
| Interviewed | 146 | 977 | 40 |
| Matriculated | 39 | 136 | 3 |

**Total Matriculants: 178**    **Total Enrollment: 729**

## Financial Information

|  | In-State | Out-of-State |
|---|---|---|
| Total Cost of Attendance | $71,987 | $71,987 |
| Tuition and Fees | $48,716 | $48,716 |
| Other (incl. living expenses) | $20,853 | $20,853 |
| Health Insurance (can be waived) | $2,418 | $2,418 |

**Average 2010 Graduate Indebtedness: $166,192**
**% of Enrolled Students Receiving Aid: 83%**

*Source: 2009-2010 LCME I-B survey and 2010-2011 AAMC TSF questionnaire*

# Harvard Medical School
## Boston, Massachusetts

Office of the Committee on Admissions
Harvard Medical School
25 Shattuck Street
306 Gordon Hall
Boston, Massachusetts 02115-6092

**T** 617 432 1550   admissions_office@hms.harvard.edu

**Admissions:** http://hms.harvard.edu/admissions/

## General Information

A leader in medical education since its inception in 1782, Harvard Medical School forms the center of one of the nation's premier locations for medical training, research and practice. The school is affiliated with a number of different hospitals and clinical sites, has eight basic and two social science departments and over 11,000 affiliated faculty, including more than 6,000 full and part-time faculty instructors.

## Mission Statement

The mission of Harvard Medical School is to create and nurture a diverse community of the best people committed to leadership in alleviating human suffering caused by disease.

## Curricular Highlights

**Community Service Requirement:** Optional.

**Research/Thesis Requirement:** Required. Scholarly project required for NP; thesis required for HST.

The New Pathway Program (NP) is a problem-based curriculum that emphasizes small-group tutorials and self-directed learning, complemented by laboratories and lectures. The NP Program enrolls 135 students each year. A second M.D. pathway is the Harvard-M.I.T. Division of Health Sciences and Technology Program (HST). This collaboration between the Harvard Medical School and the Massachusetts Institute of Technology is designed for students with a strong interest and background in quantitative science. Courses in the first two years are taught at both HMS and MIT by faculty drawn from both institutions. HST enrolls 30 students per year. Both Programs participate in a Principal Clinical Experience rotating through the departments in a large affiliated teaching hospital, followed in year four by clerkships in other affiliated institutions. Basic science and clinical content are interwoven throughout the four years in both programs.

## Selection Factors

Academic excellence is expected. Committee members consider the entire application, including the essay, extracurricular activities, life experiences, research, community work, and the comments contained in letters of recommendation. Harvard Medical School looks for evidence of integrity, maturity, humanitarian concerns, leadership potential, and an aptitude for working with people. The 2010 entering class came from 74 different undergraduate institutions, including representatives from 30 U.S. States, the District of Columbia, Puerto Rico, Guam, and citizens of 10 other countries. Harvard Medical School does not accept applications for advanced standing or transfer.

## Information about Diversity Programs

Harvard Medical School is committed to the enrollment of a diverse body of talented students who will reflect the character of the people whose health needs the medical profession must serve. HMS's commitment to a diverse student population is reflected not only in the variety of institutions from which students are accepted, but also in the ethnic and economic backgrounds of the student body. For over 30 years, HMS has had one of the highest minority student enrollment and graduation rates of any United States medical school. The HMS Office of Recruitment and Multicultural Affairs provides support services to individuals from groups under-represented in medicine.

## Application Process and Requirements 2012–2013

**Primary application service:** AMCAS®
**Earliest filing date:** June 1, 2011
**Latest filing date:** October 15, 2011

**Secondary application required:** Yes
**Sent to:** All applicants
**URL:** Sent via e-mail after verification of AMCAS® application.
**Contact:** Admissions Office, (617) 432-1550, admissions_office@hms.harvard.edu
**Fee:** Yes, $85   **Waiver available:** Yes
**Earliest filing date:** July 1, 2011
**Latest filing date:** November 1, 2011

**MCAT® required:** Yes
**Latest MCAT® considered:** September 2011
**Oldest MCAT® considered:** January 2008

**Early Decision Program:** School does not have EDP
**Applicants notified:** n/a
**EDP available for:** n/a

**Regular acceptance notice —**
**Earliest date:** March 12, 2012
**Latest date:** Varies
**Applicant's response to acceptance offer —**
**Maximum time:** Three weeks

**Requests for deferred entrance considered:** Yes

**Deposit to hold place in class:** No
**Deposit — In-State Applicants:** n/a
**Out-of-State Applicants:** n/a
**Deposit due:** n/a
**Applied to tuition:** n/a
**Deposit refundable:** n/a
**Refundable prior to:** n/a

**Estimated number of new entrants:** 165

**EDP:** n/a, **Special Programs:** n/a

**Start month/year:** August 2012

**Interview format:** On-campus only; scheduled selectively. Regional interviews are not available. Video interviews are not available.

## Preparatory Programs
**Postbaccalaureate Program:** No
**Summer Program:** No

## 2010–2011 First Year Class

|  | In-State | Out-of-State | International |
|---|---|---|---|
| Applications | 457 | 5,355 | 416 |
| Interviewed | 80 | 828 | 51 |
| Matriculated | 15 | 141 | 9 |

**Total Matriculants: 165**      **Total Enrollment: 705**

## Financial Information

|  | In-State | Out-of-State |
|---|---|---|
| Total Cost of Attendance | $70,000 | $70,000 |
| Tuition and Fees | $46,729 | $46,729 |
| Other (incl. living expenses) | $21,483 | $21,483 |
| Health Insurance (can be waived) | $1,788 | $1,788 |

**Average 2010 Graduate Indebtedness: $106,159**
**% of Enrolled Students Receiving Aid: 85%**

*Source: 2009-2010 LCME I-B survey and 2010-2011 AAMC TSF questionnaire*

# Tufts University School of Medicine
## Boston, Massachusetts

Office of Admissions
Tufts University School of Medicine
136 Harrison Avenue
Boston, Massachusetts 02111
**T** 617 636 6571  med-admissions@tufts.edu

**Admissions:** www.tufts.edu/med/admissions

**MA**

## General Information

Tufts University School of Medicine was established in 1893. The close association of the School with 30-plus hospitals affords diversified facilities for outstanding clinical experiences.

## Mission Statement

The mission of Tufts University School of Medicine is to promote human health. We will fulfill our mission by emphasizing rigorous fundamentals while stimulating innovation as we: educate, in a dynamic learning environment, physicians, scientists, and public health professionals to become leaders in their fields; contribute to the advancement of the sciences basic to medicine through discovery, research, scholarship, and communication, and join with our partner institutions to provide the best care to our patients and communities.

## Curricular Highlights

**Community Service Requirement:** Required. 50 hours of Community Service prior to graduation.

**Research/Thesis Requirement:** Optional.

We combine a rigorous academic foundation with innovative teaching in a spirit of collegiality and cooperation. We have an integrated program that blends basic science with clinical practice that is divided amongst traditional lectures and small classroom settings, often in a Problem-based Learning format. The curriculum emphasizes the basic skills needed by a generalist physician and includes expanded topics such as evidence-based medicine, information mastery, team building skills and cultural competency, in addition to integrated topics such as nutrition, gerontology, health care economics, and ethics.

## Selection Factors

The selection of candidates for admission to the first year is based not only on performance in the required premedical courses, but also on the applicant's entire academic record and extracurricular experiences. Letters of recommendation and additional information supplied by the applicant are reviewed for indications of promise and fitness for a medical career. Personal interviews are a prerequisite for admission and are granted only by invitation of the Admissions Committee. Preference is given to U.S. citizens and permanent residents who will receive a bachelor's degree from an U.S. college or university prior to matriculation. Tufts accepts transfers from other U.S. LCME-accredited medical schools into the third-year class in years when vacancies have been created by attrition. The number of seats available has traditionally been extremely limited.

## Information about Diversity Programs

Diversity and inclusion are central to the educational mission of Tufts University. We foster excellence in our research, teaching and scholarship and encourage and support engaged and active citizenship that underscores a desire to make the world a better place. To do this we value a learning community of women and men of different races, ethnicities, religions, geographic origins, socioeconomic backgrounds, sexual orientations, gender identity and expression, ages, personal characteristics, and interests where differences are understood and respected.

## Regional/Satellite Campuses

Most of the school's clinical affiliates are located in the metropolitan Boston area. Many students participate in rotations that are located outside of Boston, including Baystate Medical Center (the western campus of TUSM) in Springfield, Massachusetts, and Maine Medical Center in Portland.

## Application Process and Requirements 2012–2013

**Primary application service:** AMCAS®
**Earliest filing date:** June 1, 2011
**Latest filing date:** November 1, 2011

**Secondary application required:** Yes
**Sent to:** All applicants
**URL:** www.tufts.edu/med/admissions/ md/howtoapply/secondary.html
**Fee:** Yes, $105    **Waiver available:** Yes
**Earliest filing date:** June 1, 2011
**Latest filing date:** January 15, 2012

**MCAT® required:** Yes
**Latest MCAT® considered:** September 2011
**Oldest MCAT® considered:** January 2007

**Early Decision Program:** School does have EDP
**Applicants notified:** October 1, 2011
**EDP available for:** Both In-State and Out-of-State Applicants

**Regular acceptance notice —**
**Earliest date:** October 15, 2011
**Latest date:** Until class is full
**Applicant's response to acceptance offer —**
**Maximum time:** Two weeks

**Requests for deferred entrance considered:** Yes

**Deposit to hold place in class:** Yes
**Deposit — In-State Applicants:** $100
**Out-of-State Applicants:** $100
**Deposit due:** With response to acceptance offer
**Applied to tuition:** Yes
**Deposit refundable:** Yes
**Refundable by:** May 15, 2012

**Estimated number of new entrants:** 200
**EDP:** 2, **Special Programs:** 20

**Start month/year:** August 2012

**Interview format:** On-campus interviews conducted September–March. Regional interviews are not available. Video interviews are not available.

### Preparatory Programs

**Postbaccalaureate Program:** Yes,
www.tufts.edu/med/education/mbs/index.html

**Summer Program:** Yes, Colleen Romain,
(617) 636-6534, colleen.romain@tufts.edu

## 2010–2011 First Year Class

|  | In-State | Out-of-State | International |
|---|---|---|---|
| Applications | 801 | 7,830 | 293 |
| Interviewed | 219 | 867 | 5 |
| Matriculated | 53 | 147 | 0 |

**Total Matriculants: 200**    **Total Enrollment: 773**

## Financial Information

|  | In-State | Out-of-State |
|---|---|---|
| Total Cost of Attendance | $76,961 | $76,961 |
| Tuition and Fees | $52,992 | $52,992 |
| Other (incl. living expenses) | $20,762 | $20,762 |
| Health Insurance (can be waived) | $3,207 | $3,207 |

**Average 2010 Graduate Indebtedness: $202,845**
**% of Enrolled Students Receiving Aid: 78%**

*Source: 2009-2010 LCME I-B survey and 2010-2011 AAMC TSF questionnaire*

# University of Massachusetts Medical School

## Worcester, Massachusetts

University of Massachusetts Medical School
Office of Admissions
55 Lake Avenue, North, Room S1-112
Worcester, Massachusetts 01655

**T** 508 856 2323   admissions@umassmed.edu

**Admissions:** www.umassmed.edu/som/admissions

### General Information

UMMS is committed to training physicians in a wide range of medical disciplines and emphasizes training for practice in general medicine and the primary care specialties in the public sector and in underserved areas of Massachusetts. This mission has since been expanded to include graduate education in the biomedical sciences and nursing, graduate medical education, and continuing medical education for health professionals. The school's clinical partner is UMass Memorial Medical Center, consisting of two acute care hospitals with a total of 761 beds. Clinical education is also conducted at a number of affiliated community hospitals and health centers in the region.

### Mission Statement

The mission of the University of Massachusetts Medical School is to serve the people of the Commonwealth through excellence in health sciences education, clinical care, research, and public service.

### Curricular Highlights

**Community Service Requirement:** Required. Community Health Clerkships.

**Research/Thesis Requirement:** Optional. Research through dedicated programs.

The Learner-centered Integrated Curriculum (LInC) incorporates innovations in teaching and learning as well as new national standards for medical education. The UMMS educational program prepares students for their future medical careers regardless of specialty choice, while maintaining our founding commitment to prepare students for training in the primary care disciplines. Our curriculum emphasizes early patient care exposure; strong clinical skills development; clinical problem solving and professionalism; student activism in community service; diverse opportunities for research; and promotion of life-long learning skills. Learning communities, which bring together small groups of students and faculty across class years for formal and informal teaching and mentoring, are a featured highlight of our comprehensive curriculum redesign. Educational methods promote interactive learning, with hands-on practice under the close observation of faculty. Our nationally recognized Standardized Patient Program and Simulation Center provide opportunities for ongoing practice, improvement and mastery of essential clinical skills.

### Selection Factors

Current policy limits admission to the M.D. program to students who are Massachusetts residents. Residents and non-residents of Massachusetts are eligible for admission to the joint M.D./Ph.D. program through the Graduate School of Biomedical Sciences and the Medical School. All applicants must be U.S. citizens or have permanent resident status. The admissions committee bases its evaluation of applicants on academic ability and achievement, MCAT scores, and such factors as extracurricular achievement, maturity, motivation, and character as these are reflected in letters of recommendation from preprofessional advisory committees and other persons. Interviews are arranged by invitation only. Applicants are selected on the basis of their individual merits without regard to race, sex, creed, national origin, age, or disability. UMMS has a set of technical standards for admission and promotion, which are available upon request. Two semesters of biology or zoology are required.

### Information about Diversity Programs

For additional information, please contact the Vice Provost for School Services at (508) 856-2444.

### Regional/Satellite Campuses

Student rotations are divided among multiple campuses of UMass Memorial Health Care: University, Memorial, and Hahnemann Campuses and Clinton, Marlborough, Wing Memorial, and HealthAlliance Hospitals. The school is also affiliated with other suburban medical centers, such as the Berkshire Medical Center, Milford-Whitinsville Regional Hospital, St. Elizabeth's Hospital in Brighton, St. Vincent Hospital at Worcester Medical Center, and the Day Kimball Hospital in Connecticut. Students are required to have their own transportation.

## Application Process and Requirements 2012–2013

**Primary application service:** AMCAS®
**Earliest filing date:** June 1, 2011
**Latest filing date:** November 1, 2011

**Secondary application required:** Yes
**Sent to:** All verified applicants
**Contact:** Admissions Office, (508) 856-2323, admissions@umassmed.edul
**Fee:** Yes, $75   **Waiver available:** Yes
**Earliest filing date:** After verified application received
**Latest filing date:** Must be completed by December 15, 2011

**MCAT® required:** Yes
**Latest MCAT® considered:** September 2011
**Oldest MCAT® considered:** January 2008

**Early Decision Program:** School does have EDP
**Applicants notified:** October 1, 2011
**EDP available for:** In-States only

**Regular acceptance notice —**
**Earliest date:** October 15, 2011
**Latest date:** Until class is full

**Applicant's response to acceptance offer —**
**Maximum time:** Two weeks

**Requests for deferred entrance considered:** Yes

**Deposit to hold place in class:** Yes
**Deposit — In-State Applicants:** $100
**Out-of-State Applicants:** $100
**Deposit due:** With response to acceptance offer
**Applied to tuition:** Yes
**Deposit refundable:** Yes

**Refundable by:** May 15, 2012

**Estimated number of new entrants:** 125

**EDP:** 10, **Special Programs:** n/a

**Start month/year:** August 2012

**Interview format:** Students meet one-on-one with two interviewers. Off-campus interviews are available. Video interviews are not available.

### Preparatory Programs
**Postbaccalaureate Program:** No

**Summer Program:** Yes, www.umassmed.edu/summer

## 2010–2011 First Year Class

| | In-State | Out-of-State | International |
|---|---|---|---|
| Applications | 832 | 108 | 4 |
| Interviewed | 535 | 36 | 0 |
| Matriculated | 120 | 5 | 0 |

**Total Matriculants: 125**   **Total Enrollment: 487**

## Financial Information

| | In-State | Out-of-State |
|---|---|---|
| Total Cost of Attendance | $45,772 | n/a |
| Tuition and Fees | $15,738 | n/a |
| Other (incl. living expenses) | $25,628 | n/a |
| Health Insurance (can be waived) | $4,406 | n/a |

**Average 2010 Graduate Indebtedness: $121,119**
**% of Enrolled Students Receiving Aid: 94%**

*Source: 2009-2010 LCME I-B survey and 2010-2011 AAMC TSF questionnaire*

# Michigan State University
# College of Human Medicine

## East Lansing, Michigan

College of Human Medicine
Office of Admissions
A239 Life Science
Michigan State University
East Lansing, Michigan 48824-1317

**T** 517 353 9620   MDadmissions@msu.edu

**Admissions:** http://MDadmissions.msu.edu

## General Information

The College of Human Medicine (CHM), founded in response to Michigan's need for primary care physicians, has expanded in mission and size to meet growing needs. Students begin at either the MSU campus in East Lansing or at the Grand Rapids campus. After two preclinical years of basic science and clinical skills, students enter clinical years at a community campus.

## Mission Statement

The College of Human Medicine at Michigan State University is committed to educating exemplary physicians and scholars, discovering and disseminating new knowledge, and providing service at home and abroad. We enhance our communities by providing outstanding primary and specialty care, promoting the dignity and inclusion of all people, and responding to the needs of the medically underserved.

## Curricular Highlights

**Community Service Requirement:** Required. Numerous service opportunities available.

**Research/Thesis Requirement:** Optional. Research available.

The curriculum integrates basic biological, behavioral, and social sciences using a developmental approach to learning; early teaching of clinical skills, and clinical training utilizing a community-integrated approach. Grading is on a modified pass/no pass system; clinical honors performance is recognized. Block I is a 2½ semester experience in which fundamental medical science is presented in a structured, discipline-based format. It also comprises basic clinical skills, mentor groups, longitudinal patient exposure, opportunities for independent and supplementary learning experiences, and a clinical correlations course that integrates basic science and medicine. Block II presents a clinical problem-based format with emphasis on small-group learning and use of a clinical context for basic science concepts, clinical skills training, and special topics seminars over two semesters. Block III includes 60 weeks of required clerkships, including family medicine, and 20 weeks of elective clerkships. Students may complete elective clerkships in other locations, including third world countries. The Leadership in Medicine for the Underserved/Vulnerable Program, with an international component, and the Rural Physician Program are offered.

## Selection Factors

CHM seeks a class that is academically competent, reflective of the rural and urban character of Michigan, and representative of a wide spectrum of personalities, backgrounds, and talents. Disadvantaged and minority students are encouraged to apply. Ability to pay is not a factor. Selection criteria is multifactorial and includes year-to-year and cumulative GPA (including postbac and graduate); best MCAT performance; fit with the school's mission; relevant clinical and community service; assessment of motivation; ability to communicate and problem solve; maturity and suitability for the MSU program; state of residence, and potential to contribute to the overall quality of the entering class. CHM considers U.S. and Canadian citizens and applicants with U.S. permanent resident status.

## Information about Diversity Programs

The Advanced Baccalaureate Learning Experience (ABLE) is a 13-month, enriched academic experience offered to an invited group of disadvantaged students who have applied for admission to CHM. Students who successfully complete the ABLE program are offered regular admission to CHM's entering class.

## Regional/Satellite Campuses

**Regional Campus Location(s):** Flint, MI, Grand Rapids, MI, Kalamazoo, MI, Lansing, MI, Marquette, MI, Midland/Saginaw, MI, Traverse City, MI.

Clinical campuses (Flint, Grand Rapids, Kalamazoo, Lansing, Marquette, Midland/Saginaw Regional, and Traverse City) comprise full-time, part-time, and volunteer faculty in the clinical disciplines. Students are connected to a wide array of health care resources in the community that allow for hands-on learning, exposure to diverse patient problems, research, and experience in varied medical practice settings.

## Application Process and Requirements 2012–2013

**Primary application service:** AMCAS®
**Earliest filing date:** June 1, 2011
**Latest filing date:** November 1, 2011

**Secondary application required:** Yes
**Sent to:** All applicants with fee paid
**URL:** URL provided upon receipt of $80 Secondary Application fee.
**Fee:** Yes, $80   **Waiver available:** Yes
**Earliest filing date:** July 2011
**Latest filing date:** November 15, 2011 or within two weeks of paying fee after November 1.

**MCAT® required:** Yes
**Latest MCAT® considered:** September 2011
**Oldest MCAT® considered:** April 2008

**Early Decision Program:** School does have EDP
**Applicants notified:** October 1, 2011
**EDP available for:** Both In-State and Out-of-State Applicants

**Regular acceptance notice —**
**Earliest date:** October 15, 2011
**Latest date:** Varies
**Applicant's response to acceptance offer —**
**Maximum time:** Two weeks

**Requests for deferred entrance considered:** Yes

**Deposit to hold place in class:** Yes
**Deposit — In-State Applicants:** $100
**Out-of-State Applicants:** $100
**Deposit due:** With response to acceptance offer
**Applied to tuition:** Yes
**Deposit refundable:** Yes
**Refundable by:** May 15, 2012

**Estimated number of new entrants:** 170
**EDP:** 5, **Special Programs:** 25

**Start month/year:** August 2012

**Interview format:** Individual 30-minute interviews with one faculty and one student. Regional interviews are being considered. Video interviews are not available.

## Preparatory Programs

**Postbaccalaureate Program:** No

**Summer Program:** Yes, Dr. Wanda Lipscomb, (517) 353-7140, chmstudentaffairs@chm.msu.edu

## 2010–2011 First Year Class

|  | In-State | Out-of-State | International |
|---|---|---|---|
| Applications | 1,341 | 4,296 | 342 |
| Interviewed | 349 | 145 | 5 |
| Matriculated | 157 | 43 | 0 |

**Total Matriculants: 200     Total Enrollment: 692**

## Financial Information

|  | In-State | Out-of-State |
|---|---|---|
| Total Cost of Attendance | $53,137 | $82,681 |
| Tuition and Fees | $25,811 | $55,355 |
| Other (incl. living expenses) | $25,936 | $25,936 |
| Health Insurance (can be waived) | $1,390 | $1,390 |

**Average 2010 Graduate Indebtedness: $173,043**
**% of Enrolled Students Receiving Aid: 94%**

Source: 2009-2010 LCME I-B survey and 2010-2011 AAMC TSF questionnaire

# Oakland University William Beaumont School of Medicine

## Rochester, Michigan

216 O'Dowd Hall
2200 North Squirrel Road
Rochester, Michigan 48309
**T** 248 370 2769    medadmit@oakland.edu
**Admissions:** www.oakland.edu/medicine/admissions

## General Information

Oakland University and William Beaumont Hospitals have partnered to form the Oakland University William Beaumont School of Medicine (OUWB). Oakland, a vibrant research university, has a longstanding commitment to strong biomedical and health education programs. Beaumont's three hospital system includes campuses in Royal Oak, Troy and Grosse Point. The Royal Oak campus is a major academic referral center with Level 1 trauma status. Ninety-one medical and surgical specialties are represented on the Beaumont medical staff of more than 3,100 physicians.

## Mission Statement

The Oakland University William Beaumont School of Medicine is a collaborative, diverse, inclusive, and technologically advanced learning community, dedicated to enabling students to become skillful, ethical, and compassionate physicians, inquisitive scientists who are invested in the scholarship of discovery, and dynamic and effective medical educators. Our mission is accomplished through a student-centered approach to biomedical education, a patient-centered approach to the delivery of health care, and a focus on highly original research that includes the biomedical sciences and extends beyond the laboratory to all disciplines that impact the health of patients and their communities.

## Curricular Highlights

**Community Service Requirement:** Optional.

**Research/Thesis Requirement:** Required.

The School of Medicine curriculum offers a fresh approach to an organ system-based, highly integrated program using a combination of educational strategies including large and small groups, team-based learning, and simulation. Students will participate in small, faculty-guided mentoring teams, emphasizing communication, reflection, and academic and career guidance. A strong biomedical sciences foundation, focusing on the acquisition of scientific competencies that can be applied in clinical settings, is delivered by master educators. Dedicated courses in Medical Humanities-Bioethics, Promotion and Maintenance of Health, and the Art and Practice of Medicine include patient experiences and are synchronized with organ-based modules throughout the first two years. The third year focuses on concentrated experiences in clinical medicine. Monthly class-wide assemblies during the third year allow students to reinforce basic science concepts, refine history and physical examination skills, integrate multidisciplinary knowledge, and engage in professionalism and bioethics discussions in the context of their clinical experiences. In the fourth year, students continue to build clinical competencies as well as participate in electives.

## Selection Factors

Students seeking admission must demonstrate that they have acquired a broad education that extends beyond the basic sciences to include the social sciences, history, and the arts. The school seeks to admit applicants with personal and professional integrity, the potential for professional medical competence, the ability to deliver compassionate care, a passion for lifelong learning, intellectual curiosity, educational excellence, ethical conduct, open-mindedness, a service orientation to others, and an understanding that medicine is both art and science.

## Information about Diversity Programs

The School of Medicine is committed to broadening diversity among well-prepared applicants for medical school admissions. The Associate Dean for Academic Affairs, Faculty Development and Diversity leads initiatives to enhance diversity in the pool of qualified applicants by heightening awareness of underrepresented populations about opportunities in medicine and by creating partnerships with community agencies that can identify diverse students for pre-medical education.

## Application Process and Requirements 2012–2013

**Primary application service:** AMCAS®
**Earliest filing date:** June 1, 2011
**Latest filing date:** November 15, 2011

**Secondary application required:** Yes
**Sent to:** Screened applicants
**URL:** n/a
**Contact:** Admissions, (248) 370-2769, medadmit@oakland.edu
**Fee:** Yes, $75    **Waiver available:** Yes
**Earliest filing date:** July 1, 2011
**Latest filing date:** December 31, 2011

**MCAT® required:** Yes
**Latest MCAT® considered:** September 2011
**Oldest MCAT® considered:** September 2008

**Early Decision Program:** School does not have EDP
**Applicants notified:** n/a
**EDP available for:** n/a

**Regular acceptance notice —**
**Earliest date:** October 16, 2011
**Latest date:** Until class is full
**Applicant's response to acceptance offer —**
**Maximum time:** Two weeks

**Requests for deferred entrance considered:** Yes

**Deposit to hold place in class:** Yes
**Deposit — In-State Applicants:** $100
**Out-of-State Applicants:** $100
**Deposit due:** With response to acceptance offer
**Applied to tuition:** Yes
**Deposit refundable:** Yes
**Refundable by:** May 15, 2012

**Estimated number of new entrants:** 75
**EDP:** n/a, special programs: n/a

**Start month/year:** August 6, 2012

**Interview format:** Individual on-campus interviews. Regional interviews are not available. Video interviews are not available.

## Preparatory Programs
**Postbaccalaureate Program:** No

**Summer Program:** No

## 2010–2011 First Year Class

|  | In-State | Out-of-State | International |
|---|---|---|---|
| Applications | n/a | n/a | n/a |
| Interviewed | n/a | n/a | n/a |
| Matriculated | n/a | n/a | n/a |

**Total Matriculants: n/a**    **Total Enrollment: n/a**

## Financial Information*

|  | In-State | Out-of-State |
|---|---|---|
| Total Cost of Attendance | $67,065 | $67,065 |
| Tuition and Fees | $42,760 | $42,760 |
| Other (incl. living expenses) | $24,305 | $24,305 |
| Health Insurance (can be waived) | n/a | n/a |

**Average 2010 Graduate Indebtedness: n/r**
**% of Enrolled Students Receiving Aid: n/r**

*Projected figures provided by medical school.*

# University of Michigan Medical School

## Ann Arbor, Michigan

Office of Admissions
4303 Medical Science Building I
1301 Catherine Street
University of Michigan Medical School
Ann Arbor, Michigan 48109-5624

T 734 764 6317   umichmedadmiss@umich.edu

**Admissions:** www.med.umich.edu/medschool/
admissions

## General Information

The University of Michigan Medical School enjoys a long, distinguished history as part of the world-renowned University of Michigan, which includes many other highly ranked schools in Law, Business, Public Health, Nursing, Dentistry, Social Work and Pharmacy. The University of Michigan has the largest single-site Health System in the world, providing unique opportunities for innovation and collaboration.

## Mission Statement

The University of Michigan Medical School seeks to educate students, physicians and biomedical scholars and to provide a spectrum of comprehensive knowledge, research, patient care and service of the highest quality to the people of the state of Michigan and beyond.

## Curricular Highlights

**Community Service Requirement:** Optional.

**Research/Thesis Requirement:** Optional.

The first year Patients and Populations course acquaints medical students with genetics, principles of disease, epidemiology, and evidence-based medicine. The material is structured within Normal Organ Systems sequences and Microbiology, Infectious Disease and Anatomy courses. Clinical skills are taught in focused 1-2 week modules throughout the first and second years. Training begins with the medical interview, history taking and physical examination skills. In the Family Centered Experience, pairs of first and second year students are assigned to a family in the community. These families will serve as resources for students to understand how health changes, chronic conditions and serious illnesses affect patients and their families. The second year curriculum features Abnormal Organ Systems sequences. Clinical skills modules will continue with expectations for mastery of more advanced physical examination, history taking and communication skills. Clinical training in the third year includes 7 required rotations and opportunities for career exploratory electives. Fourth year requirements include a subinternship, an ICU experience and Advanced Medical Therapeutics. In the subinternship, students are assigned their own patient case-load with nearly the same level of responsibility as a resident. The fourth year includes eight weeks of vacation and interviewing time as well as 12 weeks of electives. This provides opportunities for off-campus and international rotations which are common components of the medical school's Global Reach program. All courses in the first and second years are graded pass/fail. In subsequent years, grades of honors, high pass, pass or fail are awarded.

## Selection Factors

The Admissions Committee is committed to individually assessing each applicant's potential as a physician. Information used in the assessment includes the application, letters of recommendation, personal statements, coursework, interviews and personal communication from those acquainted with the individual. Each applicant will be assessed on essential skills, intelligence, and personal attributes (academic excellence, competency, dedication to medicine, altruism, integrity and communication skills) and on their unique potential to contribute to the educational experience at Michigan and to the profession of medicine.

## Information about Diversity Programs

The University of Michigan Medical School is committed to training a diverse cohort of physicians who are capable of caring for an increasingly diverse patient population. Medical students are active in organizations such as LANAMA (Latino/a American/Native American Medical Association) and BMA (Black Medical Association). Students are involved in diversity and cultural competency programs, in the Health System's Multi-Cultural Community Health Alliance and as Health Disparities Scholars.

## Regional/Satellite Campuses

With three hospitals, approximately 40 health centers and 120 outpatient clinics, the world-class U-M Health System offers an ideal environment for patient care. Additional training sites are available across Michigan, the U.S. and internationally.

## Application Process and Requirements 2012–2013

**Primary application service:** AMCAS®
**Earliest filing date:** June 1, 2011
**Latest filing date:** September 30, 2011

**Secondary application required:** Yes
**Sent to:** Screened applicants and all applicants who are residents of Michigan.
**URL:** Sent electronically upon receipt of AMCAS application.
**Fee:** Yes, $85   **Waiver available:** Yes
**Earliest filing date:** July 1, 2011
**Latest filing date:** October 31, 2011

**MCAT® required:** Yes
**Latest MCAT® considered:** September 2011
**Oldest MCAT® considered:** January 2009

**Early Decision Program:** School does not have EDP
**Applicants notified:** n/a
**EDP available for:** n/a

**Regular acceptance notice —**
**Earliest date:** October 15, 2011
**Latest date:** Until class is full
**Applicant's response to acceptance offer —**
**Maximum time:** May 15, 2012

**Requests for deferred entrance considered:** Yes

**Deposit to hold place in class:** No
**Deposit — In-State Applicants:** n/a
**Out-of-State Applicants:** n/a
**Deposit due:** n/a
**Applied to tuition:** n/a
**Deposit refundable:** n/a
**Refundable by:** n/a

**Estimated number of new entrants:** 170
**EDP:** n/a, **Special Programs:** n/a

**Start month/year:** August 2012

**Interview format:** Three open-file, one-on-one interviews. Regional interviews are not available. Video interviews are not available.

### Preparatory Programs

**Postbaccalaureate Program:** No

**Summer Program:** No

## 2010–2011 First Year Class

| | In-State | Out-of-State | International |
|---|---|---|---|
| Applications | 983 | 4,142 | 52 |
| Interviewed | 185 | 516 | 0 |
| Matriculated | 87 | 83 | 0 |

**Total Matriculants: 170**   **Total Enrollment: 670**

## Financial Information

| | In-State | Out-of-State |
|---|---|---|
| Total Cost of Attendance | $51,245 | $68,683 |
| Tuition and Fees | $28,118 | $44,856 |
| Other (incl. living expenses) | $21,127 | $21,827 |
| Health Insurance (can be waived) | $2,000 | $2,000 |

**Average 2010 Graduate Indebtedness: $123,170**
**% of Enrolled Students Receiving Aid: 93%**

*Source: 2009-2010 LCME I-B survey and 2010-2011 AAMC TSF questionnaire*

# Wayne State University School of Medicine

## Detroit, Michigan

Richard J. Mazurek M.D.
Medical Education Commons
Office of Admissions
320 E. Canfield, Suite 322
Detroit, Michigan 48201

**T** 313 577 1466   admissions@med.wayne.edu

**Admissions:** www.med.wayne.edu/admissions

## General Information

Founded in 1868, the Wayne State University School of Medicine is the largest single-campus medical school in the nation with more than 1,000 medical students. In addition to undergraduate medical education, the school offers masters degree, Ph.D. and M.D.-Ph.D. programs in 14 areas of basic science to about 400 students annually.

## Mission Statement

The mission of the Wayne State University School of Medicine is to provide the Michigan community with medical and biotechnical resources, in the form of scientific knowledge and trained professionals, so as to improve the overall health of the community.

## Curricular Highlights

**Community Service Requirement:** Optional. A co-curricular program is available.

**Research/Thesis Requirement:** Optional.

The curriculum employs a combination of traditional and newer approaches to the teaching of medical students. Year 1 begins with an introductory Clinical Medicine course which runs through all four years including: human sexuality, medical interviewing, physical diagnosis, public health and prevention, and evidence-based medicine. Year 1 is organized around the disciplines of structure (anatomy, histology, and embryology) and function (biochemistry, physiology, genetics, and nutrition), and ends with an integrated neuroscience course. Second year is a completely integrated year focusing on pathophysiology, including immunology/micro-biology and pharmacology. Year 3 is a series of clinical clerkships including medicine, surgery, pediatrics, family medicine, psychiatry, neurology, and obstetrics/gynecology. During Year 3 all students have a six-month Continuity clerkship. Year 4 is predominately an elective year with only three required one month rotations: emergency medicine, a sub-internship, and an ambulatory block month. The School of Medicine uses traditional lectures, small group and panel discussions, computer-assisted instruction, and multimedia in its teaching program. Standardized patients are used for student practice and assessment in the new Richard J. Mazurek, M.D. Medical Education Commons.

## Selection Factors

Consideration is given to the entire record, GPA, MCAT scores, recommendations, and interview results, as these reflect the applicant's personality, maturity, character, and suitability for medicine. Additionally, the committee regards health care experience as desirable. Following an initial screening process, individuals with competitive applications are selected to complete a secondary application. As a state-supported school, the institution must give preference to Michigan residents; however, out-of-state applicants are encouraged to apply. Applicants whose educational backgrounds include academic work outside the United States must have completed two years of coursework at a U.S. or Canadian college, including the prerequisite courses. Interviews are required, but scheduled only with those applicants who are given serious consideration. Students are urged to apply by November 1.

## Information about Diversity Programs

The Diversity Office sponsors programs for students at the high school, undergraduate, and post-baccalaureate educational levels. The programs are designed to develop and support interest in medical careers for students from diverse backgrounds. A one-year post-baccalaureate program for Michigan residents from disadvantaged backgrounds is offered for qualified medical school applicants. The program offers enrichment in the areas of science knowledge, academic skills, and personal and professional development. Students who complete the post-baccalaureate program successfully are admitted to medical school. For additional information, call (313) 577-1598.

## Application Process and Requirements 2012–2013

**Primary application service:** AMCAS®
**Earliest filing date:** June 1, 2011
**Latest filing date:** December 15, 2011

**Secondary application required:** Yes
**Sent to:** Screened applicants
**Contact:** Dawn Yargeau, (313) 577-1466, admissions@med.wayne.edu
**Fee:** Yes, $50   **Waiver available:** Yes
**Earliest filing date:** July 15, 2011
**Latest filing date:** March 15, 2012

**MCAT® required:** Yes
**Latest MCAT® considered:** September 2011
**Oldest MCAT® considered:** September 2008

**Early Decision Program:** School does have EDP
**Applicants notified:** October 1, 2011
**EDP available for:** Both In-State and Out-of-State Applicants

**Regular acceptance notice —**
**Earliest date:** October 20, 2011
**Latest date:** Varies
**Applicant's response to acceptance offer —**
**Maximum time:** Three weeks

**Requests for deferred entrance considered:** Yes

**Deposit to hold place in class:** Yes
**Deposit — In-State Applicants:** $50
**Out-of-State Applicants:** $50
**Deposit due:** With response to acceptance offer
**Applied to tuition:** Yes
**Deposit refundable:** No   **Refundable by:** n/a

**Estimated number of new entrants:** 290
**EDP:** 3, **Special Programs:** 19

**Start month/year:** August 2012

**Interview format:** One-on-one with an Admission Committee member. Regional interviews are not available. Video interviews are not available.

## Preparatory Programs

**Postbaccalaureate Program:** Yes, Dr. Edna Jackson-Gray, (313) 577-1598, egray@med.wayne.edu

**Summer Program:** Yes, Dr. Edna Jackson-Gray, (313) 577-1598, egray@med.wayne.edu

## 2010–2011 First Year Class

|  | In-State | Out-of-State | International |
|---|---|---|---|
| Applications | 1,392 | 1,924 | 454 |
| Interviewed | 591 | 261 | 116 |
| Matriculated | 226 | 49 | 15 |

**Total Matriculants: 290   Total Enrollment: 1,226**

## Financial Information

|  | In-State | Out-of-State |
|---|---|---|
| Total Cost of Attendance | $54,228 | $85,410 |
| Tuition and Fees | $30,350 | $61,225 |
| Other (incl. living expenses) | $21,955 | $22,262 |
| Health Insurance (can be waived) | $1,923 | $1,923 |

**Average 2010 Graduate Indebtedness: $162,175**
**% of Enrolled Students Receiving Aid: 86%**

Source: 2009-2010 LCME I-B survey and 2010-2011 AAMC TSF questionnaire

# Mayo Medical School
## Rochester, Minnesota

Mayo Medical School
200 First Street, SW
Rochester, Minnesota 55905

**T** 507 284 2316   medschoolAdmissions@mayo.edu

**Admissions:** www.mayo.edu/mms/
md-admissions.html

## General Information

Mayo Medical School is an integral part of Mayo Clinic, the world's largest group practice of medicine. Resources of MMS include a diverse patient population of more than 500,000 registrants annually, four hospitals with facilities for clinical and basic research, primary care facilities including a network of clinics, hospitals and other healthcare facilities serving more than 70 communities in the surrounding region and states.

## Mission Statement

Mayo Medical School will use the patient-centered focus and strengths of Mayo Clinic to educate physicians to serve society by assuming leadership roles in medical practice, education, and research.

## Curricular Highlights

**Community Service Requirement:** Required. Student run free clinic.

**Research/Thesis Requirement:** Required. Mandatory research experience in Year III.

The innovative patient-based curriculum is characterized by extensive early patient interaction and creative integration of sciences in all segments of the curriculum. In the first two years, courses occur in blocks and contain a clinical component with experiences related to topics covered in the classroom. Themes of basic science, clinical experiences, improving the public's health and pharmacology are woven throughout the curriculum. First and second year selectives engage students in career exploration, research and service learning. Year three is devoted to developing skills in the basic clinical clerkships, moving beyond acquiring information to the level of synthesis and diagnosis. One quarter of the third year is an opportunity to explore scientific investigation, as every student completes a research endeavor under the mentorship of a Mayo investigator. Over 80 percent of students publish and/or present their research while in medical school. Year three also includes a didactic block to revisit basic science principles. Year four includes a sub-internship, emergency medicine and electives in pediatrics, surgery and medicine. Integrated into the fourth-year curriculum is a didactic experience in preventive medicine, biomedical ethics, palliative medicine, clinical pharmacology and a social medicine rotation. The remainder of the fourth year is fully elective.

## Selection Factors

Mayo Medical School is dedicated to enrolling students with superior academic credentials who possess leadership characteristics and have a profound desire to commit their lives to service. An evaluation of the entire AMCAS® application, including the academic record, MCAT scores, research, healthcare exploration, and service experiences, is considered in the initial review. For selected candidates three letters of recommendation will be requested. If the applicant qualifies, an onsite interview is granted. Appointment notification occurs approximately every four weeks throughout the admissions cycle. Appointments continue to be offered to fill the class up to the time of matriculation. All matriculates must have completed prerequisite courses and must possess a baccalaureate degree granted from an accredited United States or Canadian college or university; the final two years of coursework must be completed at this school. Mayo Medical School actively seeks to matriculate a diverse class of students. Mayo Medical School does not accept transfer students.

## Information About Diversity Programs

Mayo Medical School has a rich tradition of matriculating students from a broad spectrum of diversity. A stated goal of the school is to enroll students from backgrounds that are underrepresented in medicine. In partnership with the Office for Diversity, Mayo Medical School actively seeks to recruit, matriculate, and successfully graduate a diverse class of students. Mayo does not discriminate on the basis of race, sex, creed, national origin, age, or disability in its educational programs or activities.

## Regional/Satellite Campuses

In addition to the Mayo Clinic in Rochester, Minnesota, rotations can be completed at Mayo Clinic campuses in Arizona and Florida.

## Application Process and Requirements 2012–2013

**Primary application service:** AMCAS®
**Earliest filing date:** June 1, 2011
**Latest filing date:** October 15, 2011

**Secondary application required:** No
**Sent to:** n/a
**URL:** n/a
**Fee:** Yes, $100   **Waiver available:** Yes
**Earliest filing date:** n/a
**Latest filing date:** n/a

**MCAT® required:** Yes
**Latest MCAT® considered:** September 2011
**Oldest MCAT® considered:** 2009

**Early Decision Program:** School does not have EDP
**Applicants notified:** n/a
**EDP available for:** n/a

**Regular acceptance notice —**
**Earliest date:** October 15, 2011
**Latest date:** Until class is full
**Applicant's response to acceptance offer —**
**Maximum time:** Two weeks

**Requests for deferred entrance considered:** Yes

**Deposit to hold place in class:** Yes
**Deposit — In-State Applicants:** $100
**Out-of-State Applicants:** $100
**Deposit due:** With response to acceptance offer
**Applied to tuition:** No
**Deposit refundable:** Yes

**Refundable by:** Refundable upon matriculation

**Estimated number of new entrants:** 50
**EDP:** n/a, **Special Programs:** n/a

**Start month/year:** July 2012

**Interview format:** Two one-on-one interviews with Admissions Committee members, between September and December 2011. Regional interviews are not available. Video interviews are not available.

## Preparatory Programs
**Postbaccalaureate Program:** No

**Summer Program:** Yes, www.mayo.edu/mms prospective-students.html, Marcy Landswerk, (507) 284-2316, landswerk.marcy@mayo.edu

## 2010–2011 First Year Class

|  | In-State | Out-of-State | International |
|---|---|---|---|
| Applications | 399 | 3,378 | 215 |
| Interviewed | 48 | 301 | 16 |
| Matriculated | 16 | 32 | 3 |

**Total Matriculants: 51**     **Total Enrollment: 188**

## Financial Information

|  | In-State | Out-of-State |
|---|---|---|
| Total Cost of Attendance | $63,888 | $63,888 |
| Tuition and Fees | $32,620 | $32,620 |
| Other (incl. living expenses) | $31,268 | $31,268 |
| Health Insurance (can be waived) | $0 | $0 |

**Average 2010 Graduate Indebtedness: $58,432**
**% of Enrolled Students Receiving Aid: 100%**

*Source: 2009-2010 LCME I-B survey and 2010-2011 AAMC TSF questionnaire*

# University of Minnesota Medical School

## Minneapolis, Minnesota

University of Minnesota Medical School
MMC 293, 420 Delaware Street SE
G254 Mayo Memorial Building
Minneapolis, Minnesota 55455

Duluth
**T** 218 726 8511    medadmis@d.umn.edu

Twin Cities
**T** 612 625 7977    meded@umn.edu

**Admissions:** www.med.umn.edu/medical-school-students

### General Information

Founded in 1888, the University of Minnesota Medical School is located on the Twin Cities campus of the University. A two-year rural track is located on the Duluth campus. The medical school is a unit of the U of M Academic Health Center.

### Mission Statement

Committed to innovation and diversity, the Medical School educates physicians, scientists, and health professionals; generates knowledge and treatments; and cares for patients and communities with compassion and respect. We value excellence, inclusiveness, collaboration and discovery.

### Curricular Highlights

**Community Service Requirement:** Optional.

**Research/Thesis Requirement:** Optional.

In the Medical School curricula, progress is based on competency achievement, not time. This innovative program offers integrated instruction in scientific foundations of medicine and clinical sciences. An emphasis on critical thinking and self-directed learning is built into courses, reinforced by Foundations of Critical Thinking cases that span the curriculum. Early clinical exposure includes direct patient care focusing on understanding health care processes. Significant flexibility in the structure and scheduling of the 3rd year and beyond allows students to pursue a wide range of clinical/ academic interests. Each student has an advisor throughout medical school to ensure mastery of required competencies. The Twin Cities campus offers a Medical Scientist Training Program and other combined degrees, while Duluth has a mission focused on preparing students for family practice in rural Minnesota and Native American communities.

### Selection Factors

Legal residents of Minnesota are given preference for admission, but qualified out-of-state applicants are also encouraged to apply. Commitment to improving the human condition, unassailable professional conduct, outstanding interpersonal skills, dedication to lifelong learning and cultural sensitivity are evaluated. The medical school seeks to matriculate a diverse student body. Applicant qualifications are evaluated through recommendation letters, post-secondary experiences, undergraduate education, responses to the supplemental application, and on-site interviews. In addition, the medical school's Duluth campus seeks persons with traits that indicate a high potential for becoming a family physician in rural Minnesota or American Indian communities. Transfer students are rarely accepted into Year 3 on the Twin Cities campus. Students accepted to the Twin Cities and Duluth campuses enter a class of 170 and 60 students, respectively. The University of Minnesota Medical School does not discriminate on the basis of race, gender, creed, sexual orientation, disability, or national origin.

### Information about Diversity Programs

Minnesota is committed to the recruitment and education of students from groups underrepresented in medicine. For more information, contact the Office of Minority Affairs and Diversity (Twin Cities, (612) 625-1494), or the Center of American Indian and Minority Health. CAIMH is headquartered in Duluth ((218) 726-7235) and also has a Twin Cities office.

### Regional/Satellite Campuses

**Regional Campus Location(s):** Duluth, MN.

The two-year program at the Medical School's Duluth campus was established to increase the number of family practice physicians with a commitment to serve in rural Minnesota or American Indian communities. Students transition to the Twin Cities for years 3 and 4 with the opportunity to complete some rotations in Duluth as well as participate in RPAP. For more information: Susan Christensen ((218) 726-8511; *medadmis@d.umn.edu*).

## Application Process and Requirements 2012–2013

**Primary application service:** AMCAS®
**Earliest filing date:** June 1, 2011
**Latest filing date:** November 15, 2011
**Secondary application required:** Yes
**Sent to:** All qualified applicants
**URL:** n/a
**Fee:** Yes, $75    **Waiver available:** Yes
**Earliest filing date:** June 1, 2011
**Latest filing date:** January 31, 2012

**MCAT® required:** Yes
**Latest MCAT® considered:** September 2011
**Oldest MCAT® considered:** January 2008

**Early Decision Program:** School does have EDP
**Applicants notified:** October 1, 2011
**EDP available for:** Both In-State and Out-of-State Applicants

**Regular acceptance notice —**
**Earliest date:** October 15, 2011
**Latest date:** Until class is full
**Applicant's response to acceptance offer —**
**Maximum time:** Two weeks

**Requests for deferred entrance considered:** Yes

**Deposit to hold place in class:** Yes
**Deposit — In-State Applicants:** $100
**Out-of-State Applicants:** $100
**Deposit due:** With response to acceptance offer
**Applied to tuition:** Yes
**Deposit refundable:** Yes
**Refundable by:** May 15, 2012

**Estimated number of new entrants:** 230
**EDP:** 20, **Special Programs:** 5

**Start month/year:** August 2012

**Interview format:** Individual interviews are conducted. Regional interviews are not available. Video interviews are not available.

### Preparatory Programs

**Postbaccalaureate Program:** No

**Summer Program:** Yes, www.caimh.org

## 2010–2011 First Year Class

|  | In-State | Out-of-State | International |
|---|---|---|---|
| Applications | 800 | 2,764 | 286 |
| Interviewed | 443 | 308 | 13 |
| Matriculated | 195 | 30 | 4 |

**Total Matriculants: 229**        **Total Enrollment: 985**

## Financial Information

|  | In-State | Out-of-State |
|---|---|---|
| Total Cost of Attendance | $58,042 | $67,312 |
| Tuition and Fees | $35,988 | $45,258 |
| Other (incl. living expenses) | $19,406 | $19,406 |
| Health Insurance (can be waived) | $2,648 | $2,648 |

**Average 2010 Graduate Indebtedness: $154,646**
**% of Enrolled Students Receiving Aid: 95%**

Source: 2009-2010 LCME I-B survey and 2010-2011 AAMC TSF questionnaire

# University of Mississippi School of Medicine

## Jackson, Mississippi

Associate Dean for Admissions
University of Mississippi School of Medicine
2500 North State Street
Jackson, Mississippi 39216-4505

**T** 601 984 5010   AdmitMD@umc.edu

**Admissions:** http://som.umc.edu/admissions.html

## General Information

The School of Medicine, created by a special act of the Board of Trustees in June 1903, operated as a two-year school in Oxford until 1955, when it expanded to four years and moved to the new University of Mississippi Medical Center in Jackson. The Medical Center now houses the Schools of Medicine, Nursing, Health Related Professions, Dentistry, Graduate Studies in Health Sciences, and the 722-bed University Hospitals and Health System.

## Mission Statement

The primary mission of the University of Mississippi School of Medicine is to offer an accredited program of medical education that will provide well-trained physicians, in numbers consistent with the health care needs of the state, who are responsive to the health problems of the people and committed to medical education as a continuum that must prevail throughout professional life.

## Curricular Highlights

**Community Service Requirement:** Optional. Medical students staff the Jackson Free Clinic.

**Research/Thesis Requirement:** Optional.

During the two preclinical years, students learn the sciences basic to the study of medicine and participate in laboratory exercises, small-group discussion, computer-assisted learning, and independent study. The preclinical curriculum integrates and sequences course content and provides earlier clinical experience for students. The third year involves full-time clinical study as students rotate through the major clinical disciplines and participate in the team care of patients in the University Hospitals and Clinics, Veterans Affairs Medical Center, and various community settings. The fourth year consists of eight required calendar month blocks that may be taken at any time during the eleven months available from July through May. Fourth-year clinical clerkships provide greater depth of study in core areas of medicine, as well as in a student's anticipated medical specialty. Opportunities exist for advanced study and research in basic science departments and for electives at other institutions in this country or abroad.

## Selection Factors

The Admissions Committee selects applicants on a competitive basis without regard to age, sex, sexual orientation, race, creed, national origin, marital status, handicap, or veteran status. Strong preference is given to legal residents of Mississippi; in recent years, non-residents have not been admitted. Interviews are arranged at the discretion of the Admissions Committee; major considerations are undergraduate BCPM GPA and MCAT scores. Interviews are used to assess non-cognitive variables and communication skills. Experiences listed on an AMCAS® application document nonacademic and professional attributes, and premedical faculty evaluations reveal an applicant's approach to academic study and professionalism. For details, see *http://som.umc.edu/admissions.html#EvalApps*. Mississippi residents enrolled in other medical schools accredited by the Liaison Committee on Medical Education may be considered for advanced standing transfer.

## Information about Diversity Programs

The Division of Multicultural Affairs (DMA; *http://mca.umc.edu/*) supports the Medical Center's efforts to train a diverse health-care workforce for the state of Mississippi. The Division's overarching mission is to foster an environment that recognizes the benefits of diversity and inclusiveness through academic preparation, instruction, community outreach, and professional development. It also seeks to disseminate valuable resources and research on cultural competency, quality and equity in health care to the Medical Center community. The DMA offers pipeline programs for middle school (STEP), upper school (EXCEL) and undergraduate (MEDCORP) students, a health careers development program for undergraduate students, a summer pre-matriculation program for accepted applicants, and a clinical elective for fourth year medical students.

## Regional/Satellite Campuses

The Jackson Medical Mall, one mile from the campus, houses the hospital's teaching clinics, offices for the Jackson Heart Study and the Medical Center's Cancer Institute. Originally the city's first shopping mall, the Jackson Medical Mall is recognized as a national model of urban revitalization.

## Application Process and Requirements 2012–2013

**Primary application service:** AMCAS®
**Earliest filing date:** June 1, 2011
**Latest filing date:** October 15, 2011

**Secondary application required:** Yes
**Sent to:** URL and password provided after receipt of AMCAS® application.
**URL:** http://som.umc.edu/Amcas/Menu.ctrl?action=Display
**Fee:** Yes, $50   **Waiver available:** Yes
**Earliest filing date:** June 1, 2011
**Latest filing date:** December 1, 2011

**MCAT® required:** Yes
**Latest MCAT® considered:** September 2011
**Oldest MCAT® considered:** April 2008

**Early Decision Program:** School does have EDP
**Applicants notified:** Not later than October 1, 2011
**EDP available for:** In-States only

**Regular acceptance notice —**
**Earliest date:** October 16, 2011
**Latest date:** Until class is full
**Applicant's response to acceptance offer —**
**Maximum time:** Two weeks; but multiple acceptances may be held until May 15

**Requests for deferred entrance considered:** Yes

**Deposit to hold place in class:** No
**Deposit — In-State Applicants:** n/a
**Out-of-State Applicants:** n/a
**Deposit due:** n/a
**Applied to tuition:** n/a
**Deposit refundable:** n/a   **Refundable by:** n/a

**Estimated number of new entrants:** 135
**EDP:** 10, **Special Programs:** 20

**Start month/year:** August 7, 2012

**Interview format:** Three semi-structured, one-on-one interviews. Regional interviews are not available. Video interviews are not available.

### Preparatory Programs

**Postbaccalaureate Program:** Yes, http://som.umc.edu/admissions.html#PPP

**Summer Program:** Yes, http://mca.umc.edu/StudentPrograms.html

## 2010–2011 First Year Class

|  | In-State | Out-of-State | International |
|---|---|---|---|
| Applications | 308 | 2 | 0 |
| Interviewed | 229 | 0 | 0 |
| Matriculated | 135 | 0 | 0 |

**Total Matriculants: 135**   **Total Enrollment: 484**

## Financial Information

|  | In-State | Out-of-State |
|---|---|---|
| Total Cost of Attendance | $42,488 | n/a |
| Tuition and Fees | $15,649 | n/a |
| Other (incl. living expenses) | $24,931 | n/a |
| Health Insurance (can be waived) | $1,908 | n/a |

**Average 2010 Graduate Indebtedness: $112,814**
**% of Enrolled Students Receiving Aid: 92%**

*Source: 2009-2010 LCME I-B survey and 2010-2011 AAMC TSF questionnaire*

# Saint Louis University School of Medicine

## St. Louis, Missouri

Saint Louis University School of Medicine
Office of Admissions
1402 S. Grand Blvd. C130
St. Louis, Missouri 63104

**T** 314 977 9875   slumd@slu.edu

**Admissions:** http://medschool.slu.edu/admissions

## General Information

Established in 1836, Saint Louis University School of Medicine has the distinction of awarding the first M.D. degree west of the Mississippi River. The school has pioneered in geriatric medicine, organ transplantation, chronic disease prevention, cardiovascular disease, neurosciences, and immunology and vaccine research, among others. We train physicians and biomedical scientists, conduct medical research, and provide health services on a local, national, and international level.

## Mission Statement

Beyond the important objective of training physicians who are scholars of human biology, the School of Medicine strives to graduate physicians who manifest in their personal and professional lives an appreciation of humanistic medicine. We regard humanistic medicine as a constellation of ethical and professional attitudes, which affect the physician's interactions with patients, colleagues, and society. Among these attitudes are concern for the sanctity of human life; commitment to dignity and respect in the provision of medical care to all patients; devotion to social justice, especially regarding inequities in the availability of health care; humility and awareness of medicine's limitations in the care of the sick; appreciation of the role of non-medical factors in a patient's state of well-being or illness; and mature, well-balanced professional behavior that derives from comfortable relationships with members of the human family and one's Creator.

## Curricular Highlights

**Community Service Requirement:** Optional. Distinction in Community Service.

**Research/Thesis Requirement:** Optional. Distinction in Research.

The M.D. curriculum provides coordination and integration of the basic and clinical sciences across all four years. Additionally, it follows established principles of adult learning and so is a hybrid of lectures, small group activities, early clinical activities, self-directed learning and problem solving exercises. The first two years of the curriculum are devoted to the study of the fundamental sciences basic to medicine. In year two, a series of integrated modules that are organ-based are coupled with the acquisition of fundamental clinical skills required to begin the clinical clerkships; these are taught in the Applied Clinical Skills; Patient, Physician and Society and Bedside Diagnosis course series. Years three and four concentrate on the further development and refinement of essential clinical skills, while also providing ongoing integration of the basic sciences into clinical practice. Grading is pass-fail for the first two years and honors, near-honors, pass/fail for the clinical years.

## Selection Factors

The school encourages applications from persons who have demonstrated a high level of academic achievement and who manifest in their personal lives those human qualities that are required for a career of service to society.

## Information about Diversity Programs

We are committed to promoting diversity in classrooms and clinics to allow all students to understand and learn from each other about the practice of medicine in a diverse environment. The Office of Multicultural Affairs assists students from diverse backgrounds to be successful as they pursue their studies to become a physician.

## Regional/Satellite Campuses

Major teaching affiliations include: Saint Louis University Hospital, Cardinal Glennon Children's Medical Center, St. Elizabeth's Hospital, St. John's Mercy Medical Center, St. Mary's Hospital, DesPeres Hospital, forrest Park Hospital and the St. Louis Veterans Affairs Hospitals.

## Application Process and Requirements 2012–2013

**Primary application service:** AMCAS®
**Earliest filing date:** June 1, 2011
**Latest filing date:** December 15, 2011
**Secondary application required:** Yes
**Sent to:** All applicants
**URL:** www.oasprod3.com/schools/slusom
**Fee:** Yes, $100   **Waiver available:** Yes
**Earliest filing date:** June 1, 2011
**Latest filing date:** February 15, 2012

**MCAT® required:** Yes
**Latest MCAT® considered:** September 2011
**Oldest MCAT® considered:** April 2008

**Early Decision Program:** School does have EDP
**Applicants notified:** October 1, 2011
**EDP available for:** Both In-States and Out-of-States

**Regular acceptance notice —**
**Earliest date:** October 15, 2011
**Latest date:** Until class is full
**Applicant's response to acceptance offer —**
**Maximum time:** Two weeks

**Requests for deferred entrance considered:** Yes

**Deposit to hold place in class:** Yes
**Deposit — In-State Applicants:** $100
**Out-of-State Applicants:** $100
**Deposit due:** With response to acceptance offer
**Applied to tuition:** Yes
**Deposit refundable:** Yes
**Refundable by:** May 15, 2012

**Estimated number of new entrants:** 175
**EDP:** 2, **Special Programs:** 30

**Start month/year:** August 2012

**Interview format:** A single one-on-one interview. Some regional interviews may be offered. Video interviews are not available.

## Preparatory Programs

**Postbaccalaureate Program:** Yes,
http://medschool.slu.edu/anatomy/caps/

**Summer Program:** No

## 2010–2011 First Year Class

|  | In-State | Out-of-State | International |
|---|---|---|---|
| Applications | 397 | 5,578 | 260 |
| Interviewed | 119 | 862 | 78 |
| Matriculated | 37 | 131 | 9 |

**Total Matriculants: 177**   **Total Enrollment: 736**

## Financial Information

|  | In-State | Out-of-State |
|---|---|---|
| Total Cost of Attendance | $68,492 | $68,492 |
| Tuition and Fees | $46,185 | $46,185 |
| Other (incl. living expenses) | $20,099 | $20,099 |
| Health Insurance (can be waived) | $2,208 | $2,208 |

**Average 2010 Graduate Indebtedness: $185,802**
**% of Enrolled Students Receiving Aid: 89%**

*Source: 2009-2010 LCME I-B survey and 2010-2011 AAMC TSF questionnaire*

# University of Missouri
# Columbia School of Medicine
## Columbia, Missouri

Alison Martin, M.Ed., Director of Admissions
Office of Medical Education,
MA215 Medical Science Building
University of Missouri School of Medicine
One Hospital Drive, Columbia, Missouri 65212

**T** 573 882 9219   MizzouMed@missouri.edu

**Admissions:** http://som.missouri.edu/admit.shtml/

## General Information

The University of Missouri School of Medicine has improved health, education and research in Missouri for more than 160 years. MU physicians treat patients from every county in the state, and MU is a primary provider of training for all physicians in Missouri. The School of Medicine's more than 650 faculty physicians and scientists educate approximately 1,000 medical students, residents, fellows and other students seeking advanced degrees. Their research is focused on potentially lifesaving discoveries that address the most prevalent health problems.

## Mission Statement

The mission of MU School of Medicine is to educate physicians to provide effective patient-centered care for the people of Missouri and beyond. Patient-centered care reflects a respect for individual patient's values, preferences, and expressed needs. This care is grounded in the best available evidence and conserves limited resources, and it depends on shared decision-making and active patient participation. Our graduates' care will be marked by compassion, empathy, and patient advocacy. Our graduates also will be: honest, with high ethical standards; knowledgeable in biomedical sciences, evidence-based practice, and societal and cultural issues; critical-thinkers and problem-solvers; able to communicate with patients and other health-care team members; committed to improving quality and safety; and committed to lifelong learning and professional formation.

## Curricular Highlights

**Community Service Requirement:** Optional.

**Research/Thesis Requirement:** Optional.

In 1993, The University of Missouri School of Medicine implemented a curriculum that substantially reduced lectures in favor of problem-based learning. The curriculum emphasizes problem solving, self-directed learning and early clinical experiences rather than memorization. The first and second years each consist of four 10-week blocks. The third year is made up of seven core clerkships. The fourth year consists of advanced clinical selectives, advanced biomedical selectives and general electives.

## Selection Factors

The Admissions Committee conducts required on-campus personal interviews. Strong preference is given to Missouri residents. Exceptional residents of other states may also be admitted. Non-Missouri residents are evaluated on an individual basis, and may be asked to provide evidence of Missouri ties, diversity, and/or exceptional academics. Selection for interview is based upon academic performance; personal qualities such as motivation, social concern, and integrity; and tested motivation for medicine. Early Decision Program applicants must be Missouri residents with 3.75 cumulative GPA and MCAT sum of 30 with no individual section score below 9. The School of Medicine does not discriminate on the basis of race, sex, creed, national origin, age, handicap, religion, or status as a Vietnam-era veteran in admission or access to or treatment or employment in its programs and activities.

## Information about Diversity Programs

The University of Missouri is committed to the recruitment and education of disadvantaged and nontraditional applicants and applicants from groups underrepresented in medicine. The School of Medicine sponsors summer programs targeting rural and disadvantaged high school students, although students from across Missouri may participate.

## Regional/Satellite Campuses

Students may choose to complete elective clinical rotations in and around Columbia, or off-site in Missouri or across the country. Students may participate in the Rural Track Program, which offers rural sites for both clerkship and elective experiences.

## Application Process and Requirements 2012–2013

**Primary application service:** AMCAS®
**Earliest filing date:** June 1, 2011
**Latest filing date:** November 1, 2011

**Secondary application required:** Yes
**Sent to:** All Missouri residents and screened Out-of-state applicants
**URL:** n/a
**Contact:** Alison Martin, M.Ed., (573) 882-9219 MizzouMed@health.missouri.edu
**Fee:** Yes, $75   **Waiver available:** Yes
**Earliest filing date:** July 1, 2011
**Latest filing date:** January 15, 2012

**MCAT® required:** Yes
**Latest MCAT® considered:** September 2011
**Oldest MCAT® considered:** 2008

**Early Decision Program:** School does have EDP
**Applicants notified:** October 1, 2011
**EDP available for:** In-States only

**Regular acceptance notice —**
**Earliest date:** October 1, 2011
**Latest date:** Until class is full
**Applicant's response to acceptance offer —**
**Maximum time:** 30 days

**Requests for deferred entrance considered:** Yes

**Deposit to hold place in class:** Yes
**Deposit — In-State Applicants:** $100
**Out-of-State Applicants:** $100
**Deposit due:** Within 30 days of acceptance offer until July, after which less time is given.
**Applied to tuition:** Yes
**Deposit refundable:** Yes
**Refundable by:** May 15, 2012

**Estimated number of new entrants:** 104
**EDP:** 2, **Special Programs:** 25

**Start month/year:** July 2012

**Interview format:** Two open file, one-on-one interviews by Admissions Committee members are required. Regional interviews are not available. Video interviews are not available.

## Preparatory Programs

**Postbaccalaureate Program:** No

**Summer Program:** No

## 2010–2011 First Year Class

|  | In-State | Out-of-State | International |
|---|---|---|---|
| Applications | 443 | 1,132 | 16 |
| Interviewed | 236 | 127 | 0 |
| Matriculated | 88 | 16 | 0 |

**Total Matriculants:** 104    **Total Enrollment:** 387

## Financial Information

|  | In-State | Out-of-State |
|---|---|---|
| Total Cost of Attendance | $47,124 | $70,636 |
| Tuition and Fees | $25,968 | $49,480 |
| Other (incl. living expenses) | $18,910 | $18,910 |
| Health Insurance (can be waived) | $2,246 | $2,246 |

**Average 2010 Graduate Indebtedness: $136,197**
**% of Enrolled Students Receiving Aid: 96%**

Source: 2009-2010 LCME I-B survey and 2010-2011 AAMC TSF questionnaire

# University of Missouri — Kansas City School of Medicine

## Kansas City, Missouri

Council on Selection
University of Missouri — Kansas City
School of Medicine
2411 Holmes, Kansas City, Missouri 64108-2792

**T** 816 235 1870 medicine@umkc.edu

**Admissions:** www.umkc.edu/admissions/

## General Information

The Board of Curators of the University of Missouri authorized the establishment of a medical school at the University of Missouri-Kansas City in 1969. Located on the 135-acre Hospital Hill campus, the medical school is located near the Schools of Pharmacy, Nursing and Dentistry, as well as the university and affiliated community hospitals.

## Mission Statement

The mission of the University of Missouri-Kansas City School of Medicine is to prepare graduates so that they are able to enter and complete graduate programs in medical education, qualify for medical licensure, provide competent medical care, and have the educational background necessary for lifelong learning in order to address the health care needs of our state and nation.

## Curricular Highlights

**Community Service Requirement:** Optional.

**Research/Thesis Requirement:** Optional.

The School of Medicine, with the College of Arts and Sciences and the School of Biological Sciences, offers a year-round program leading to baccalaureate and M.D. degrees in six calendar years. The program is designed primarily for high school seniors entering college. To receive the baccalaureate degree, the student must complete 120 semester hours of credit. Under the guidance of a clinician-scholar called a docent, small groups of first and second-year students are introduced to medicine in community hospitals where they can observe patients and their care. During the first two years of the program, the student is occupied predominantly with arts and sciences coursework, with about one-fourth of the time being devoted to introduction to medicine courses. During the last four years of the curriculum, the student, with guidance from a docent and education team coordinator, plans a program for meeting the curricular requirements. Two months of Years 4 through 6 are spent with the docent on an inpatient internal medicine rotation. The remaining months of each year are spent in a number of other required and elective course offerings in the basic and clinical sciences and the humanities and social sciences. Students spend two academic terms in arts and sciences coursework during the last four years of the program. Basic, clinical, and behavioral science information is presented and emphasized throughout the program. The academic program provides the medical student with a realistic working knowledge of community health problems and resources.

## Selection Factors

Selection criteria include: (1) the applicant's academic potential as evaluated by quality and rigor of high school coursework, high school grade point average, and scores on the ACT/SAT. In the 2010 2011 entering class, the average ACT score fell at the 95th percentile, and the average grade point average was a 3.85; (2) the applicant's individual potential for medicine as evaluated by personal qualities, including maturity, leadership, reliability, motivation for medicine, range of interests, interpersonal skills, compassion, and job/volunteer experience. After the Council on Selection carefully reviews all applicants, those who appear to be well qualified are invited for interviews. If invited, the applicant is notified by e-mail and is required to be present at the scheduled date and time of the interview. Students are considered on the basis of their individual qualifications without regard to race, creed, sex, or national origin. Interview statistics for BA/MD are reflected in the Acceptance & Matriculation Chart. The program also accepts a small number of students who have earned, at minimum, a Bachelor's degree. Designated MD-Only, they are required to take the MCAT and, if admitted, pursue the last four years of the program. Promoting third-Year BA/MD students and MDO students are listed in the Acceptance & Matriculation Chart as "Matriculants." The school also accepts transfers. The admissions deadlines for BA/MD, MD-Only and transfer students can be found on the school website.

## Information about Diversity Programs

The School of Medicine believes that a vibrant and diverse institutional climate is essential in providing medical education that promotes the effective delivery of health care in diverse communities. A diverse learning environment includes people with various racial and ethnic origins, socioeconomic backgrounds, rural and urban communities, geographic origins, and academic backgrounds. The Office of Diversity and Community Partnership promotes policies, initiatives and resources that create an environment of success for all, including students underrepresented in medicine.

## Application Process and Requirements 2012–2013

**Primary application service:** School specific
**Earliest filing date:** August 1, 2011
**Latest filing date:** November 1, 2011

**Secondary application required:** Yes
**Sent to:** All applicants
**URL:** n/a
**Fee:** Yes, $35   **Waiver available:** No
**Earliest filing date:** n/a
**Latest filing date:** n/a

**MCAT® required:** Yes, for M.D. only
**Latest MCAT® considered:** June 2011
**Oldest MCAT® considered:** 2007

**Early Decision Program:** School does not have EDP
**Applicants notified:** n/a
**EDP available for:** n/a

**Regular acceptance notice —**
**Earliest date:** April 1, 2012
**Latest date:** Varies
**Applicant's response to acceptance offer —**
**Maximum time:** 30 days

**Requests for deferred entrance considered:** No

**Deposit to hold place in class:** Yes
**Deposit — In-State Applicants:** $100
**Out-of-State Applicants:** $100
**Deposit due:** With response to acceptance offer
**Applied to tuition:** Yes
**Deposit refundable:** Yes
**Refundable by:** May 15, 2012

**Estimated number of new entrants:** 100
**EDP:** n/a, **Special Programs:** 100

**Start month/year:** August 2012 (B.A./M.D. only)

**Interview format:** Two thirty-minute interviews. Regional interviews are not available. Video interviews are not available.

## Preparatory Programs

**Postbaccalaureate Program:** No

**Summer Program:** No

## 2010–2011 First Year Class

|  | In-State | Out-of-State | International |
|---|---|---|---|
| Applications | 256 | 464 | 0 |
| Interviewed | 115 | 125 | 0 |
| Matriculated | 53 | 48 | 0 |

**Total Matriculants: 101     Total Enrollment: 617**

## Financial Information

|  | In-State | Out-of-State |
|---|---|---|
| Total Cost of Attendance | $58,091 | $85,560 |
| Tuition and Fees | $30,150 | $57,619 |
| Other (incl. living expenses) | $27,941 | $27,941 |
| Health Insurance (can be waived) | $0 | $0 |

**Average 2010 Graduate Indebtedness: $145,181**
**% of Enrolled Students Receiving Aid: 84%**

Source: 2009–2010 LCME I-B survey and 2010-2011 AAMC TSF questionnaire

# Washington University School of Medicine

## St. Louis, Missouri

Office of Admissions
Washington University in St. Louis School of Medicine
660 South Euclid Avenue, #8107
St. Louis, Missouri 63110

**T** 314 362 6858   wumscoa@wustl.edu

**Admissions:** http://medadmissions.wustl.edu

### General Information

Dedicated solely to medical education and located at the heart of the 230-acre Washington University Medical Center, the Farrell Learning and Teaching Center provides a state-of-the-art facility in which to learn the compassionate delivery of scientific medicine. This facility complements the outstanding clinical resources at Barnes-Jewish Hospital, and at St. Louis Children's Hospital, two of the top academic hospitals in the country. Learning among the most talented classmates in the country and in world class facilities, medical students at Washington University enjoy a supportive and non-competitive environment where opportunities for discovery, learning and self-fulfillment abound.

### Mission Statement

The mission of Washington University is to promote learning by students and faculty. Teaching, the transmission of knowledge, is central to our mission, as is research, the creation of new knowledge. Our goals are: to foster excellence in our teaching, research, scholarship, and service; to prepare students with attitudes, skills, and habits of lifelong learning and with leadership skills, enabling them to be useful members of a global society; and to be an exemplary institution in our home community, St. Louis, as well as in the nation and the world.

### Curricular Highlights

**Community Service Requirement:** Optional.

**Research/Thesis Requirement:** Optional.

The curriculum provides a state-of-the-art foundation in the science and the art of medicine. Instruction is by lecture and small-group interactive sessions, and includes problem-based exercises, self-directed learning using computers, simulation and other resources led by faculty facilitators. Medical humanities and ethics are integrated into all four years of medical training, with emphasis given to the sociological and cultural aspects of adapting medical care to patient's needs. Patient contact begins in the first semester of the first year and the fourth year is all electives. There are abundant opportunities in basic and clinical research. A five-year M.A. and M.D. degree program is available for students desiring one or two years of research training, while a Medical Scientist Training Program leads to both M.D. and Ph.D. degrees. A pass/fail grading system is used in the first year.

### Selection Factors

A good doctor must be compassionate and understanding, as well as a good scientist. To this end, the School of Medicine selects students who, in addition to possessing keen minds, demonstrate sensitivity and a commitment to serve others. Hence, students are selected on the basis of character, attitude, interest, intellectual ability, motivation, maturity, and achievement as indicated by superior academic and extracurricular accomplishments. Policies and programs are nondiscriminatory, and full consideration is given to all applicants without regard to sex, age, race, handicap, sexual preference, creed, or national or ethnic origin. Students from groups underrepresented in medicine are encouraged to apply. Selected applicants are invited to interview, which is required for acceptance.

### Information about Diversity Programs

Washington University is committed to the recruitment, selection, education, and graduation of students from groups underrepresented in medicine. Students are supported by an active chapter of the Student National Medical Association and a network of faculty from diverse groups.

## Application Process and Requirements 2012–2013

**Primary application service:** AMCAS®
**Earliest filing date:** June 1, 2011
**Latest filing date:** December 1, 2011

**Secondary application required:** Yes
**Sent to:** All applicants
**URL:** http://wumsapply.wustl.edu
**Fee:** Yes, $65   **Waiver available:** Yes
**Earliest filing date:** June 15, 2011
**Latest filing date:** December 31, 2011

**MCAT® required:** Yes
**Latest MCAT® considered:** September 2011
**Oldest MCAT® considered:** September 2008

**Early Decision Program:** School does not have EDP
**Applicants notified:** n/a
**EDP available for:** n/a

**Regular acceptance notice —**
**Earliest date:** November 1, 2011
**Latest date:** Until class is full
**Applicant's response to acceptance offer —**
**Maximum time:** Two weeks

**Requests for deferred entrance considered:** Yes

**Deposit to hold place in class:** Yes
**Deposit — In-State Applicants:** $100
**Out-of-State Applicants:** $100
**Deposit due:** With response to acceptance offer
**Applied to tuition:** Yes
**Deposit refundable:** Yes
**Refundable by:** May 15, 2012

**Estimated number of new entrants:** 120
**EDP:** n/a, **Special Programs:** 20

**Start month/year:** August 2012

**Interview format:** Open, unstructured, one-on-one. Regional interviews are not available. Video interviews are not available.

### Preparatory Programs

**Postbaccalaureate Program:** Yes,
http://ucollege.wustl.edu/programs/special-programs
Elizabeth Fogt, Director of Post-Baccalaureate Premedical Studies Program , (314) 935-6778,
efogt@artsci.wustl.edu

**Summer Program:** No

## 2010–2011 First Year Class

|  | In-State | Out-of-State | International |
|---|---|---|---|
| Applications | 164 | 3,409 | 230 |
| Interviewed | 51 | 1,060 | 60 |
| Matriculated | 8 | 110 | 3 |

**Total Matriculants: 121**     **Total Enrollment: 604**

## Financial Information

|  | In-State | Out-of-State |
|---|---|---|
| Total Cost of Attendance | $65,625 | $65,625 |
| Tuition and Fees | $48,800 | $48,800 |
| Other (incl. living expenses) | $16,825 | $16,825 |
| Health Insurance (can be waived) | $0 | $0 |

**Average 2010 Graduate Indebtedness: $111,058**
**% of Enrolled Students Receiving Aid: 88%**

*Source: 2009-2010 LCME I-B survey and 2010-2011 AAMC TSF questionnaire*

# Creighton University School of Medicine

## Omaha, Nebraska

Creighton University School of Medicine
Office of Medical Admissions
2500 California Plaza
Omaha, Nebraska 68178

**T** 402 280 2799   medadmissions@creighton.edu

**Admissions:** www.medschool.creighton.edu/
medicine/oma/index.php

## General Information

Creighton University School of Medicine, a Jesuit, Catholic institution opened in 1892. The School of Medicine expanded its first year class in 2010 to 152 in order to meet society's need for caring competent physicians. Students complete their first two years of study of basic sciences and clinical skills at the Omaha campus. Afterward students complete their hospital-based clinical instruction either in Omaha or at the Phoenix, AZ campus where training is centered at Saint Joseph's Hospital and Medical Center, a member of Catholic Healthcare West.

## Mission Statement

In the Jesuit, Catholic tradition of Creighton University, the mission of the School of Medicine is to improve the human condition through excellence in educating students, physicians and the public, advancing knowledge, and providing comprehensive patient care. Vision Statement: We will be a School of Medicine respected by our peers for excellence in teaching, research, and clinical care. We will be distinguished for preparing graduates who achieve excellence in their chosen fields and who demonstrate extraordinary compassion and commitment to the service of others.

## Curricular Highlights

**Community Service Requirement:** Optional. Opportunities: ILAC, Magis Clinic, Project CURA.

**Research/Thesis Requirement:** Optional.

The curriculum integrates basic and clinical science in all four years. Year one combines strong basic science content with the fundamentals of physical diagnosis and interviewing techniques. Year two is organized around a series of organ system-based courses and clinical skills training, including longitudinal clinics. Year three is comprised of core clerkships in a variety of inpatient and ambulatory settings. In year four, clinical training continues in critical care, surgery, and primary care and students explore their interests through electives. Ethical and societal issues are prominent in the curriculum in each year. Research can be planned between years one and two. Instructional methodology uses lectures, case-based small-group sessions and computer-assisted instruction. All lectures are podcast. Students are graded against curriculum standards on an honors/satisfactory/unsatisfactory system, to encourage teamwork.

## Selection Factors

The qualities of intellectual ability and curiosity, emotional maturity, honesty, proper motivation, proven scholastic ability, significant service to humanity, physician shadowing, and documented medical experience are of highest importance. Both the AMCAS® and Creighton secondary applications are required of all applicants. A formal interview on campus is conducted prior to acceptance. No restrictions are placed on applicants due to race, religion, sex, national or ethnic origin, age, disability, veteran status, or state of residence. Creighton values diversity in its medical classes. Applicants who complete their pre-professional education at Creighton are given preference.

## Information about Diversity Programs

Qualified candidates from populations underrepresented in medicine are encouraged to apply. Creighton's Office of Health Sciences-Multicultural and Community Affairs has several active programs to increase diversity and provide appropriate support services. The office administers several diversity programs, including pipeline and premedical postbaccalaureate programs.

## Regional/Satellite Campuses

Clinical instruction is divided between two clinical campuses-the Omaha, NE campus and the Phoenix, AZ campus. Students attending the Omaha campus will rotate through Creighton University Medical Center, Omaha VAMC, Children's Hospital, and Alegent Health Facilities. Students attending the Phoenix campus will complete their clinical instruction at St. Joseph's Hospital and Medical Center.

## Application Process and Requirements 2012–2013

**Primary application service:** AMCAS®
**Earliest filing date:** June 1, 2011
**Latest filing date:** November 1, 2011

**Secondary application required:** Yes
**Sent to:** All applicants
**URL:** http://medschool.creighton.edu/medicine/oma/index.php
**Fee:** Yes, $95   **Waiver available:** Yes
**Earliest filing date:** July 1, 2011
**Latest filing date:** January 15, 2012

**MCAT® required:** Yes
**Latest MCAT® considered:** September 2011
**Oldest MCAT® considered:** January 2009

**Early Decision Program:** School does have EDP
**Applicants notified:** October 1, 2011
**EDP available for:** Both In-State and Out-of-State Applicants

**Regular acceptance notice —**
**Earliest date:** October 15, 2011
**Latest date:** Until class is full
**Applicant's response to acceptance offer —**
**Maximum time:** 14 days

**Requests for deferred entrance considered:** Yes

**Deposit to hold place in class:** Yes
**Deposit — In-State Applicants:** $100
**Out-of-State Applicants:** $100
**Deposit due:** With response to acceptance offer
**Applied to tuition:** Yes   **Deposit refundable:** Yes
**Refundable by:** May 15, 2012

**Estimated number of new entrants:** 152
**EDP:** 1, **Special Programs:** 7

**Start month/year:** August 2012

**Interview format:** Two open-file one-on-one interviews with a faculty representative and a medical student. Regional interviews are not available. Video interviews are not available.

## Preparatory Programs

**Postbaccalaureate Program:** Yes, www.creighton.edu/health/hsmaca/premedicalpost-bacprogram/index.php, (402) 280-2799, postbac.appl@creighton.edu

**Summer Program:** No

## 2010–2011 First Year Class

|  | In-State | Out-of-State | International |
|---|---|---|---|
| Applications | 185 | 5,571 | 123 |
| Interviewed | 61 | 600 | 1 |
| Matriculated | 23 | 127 | 0 |

**Total Matriculants: 150**   **Total Enrollment: 525**

## Financial Information

|  | In-State | Out-of-State |
|---|---|---|
| Total Cost of Attendance | $69,159 | $69,159 |
| Tuition and Fees | $48,284 | $48,284 |
| Other (incl. living expenses) | $18,855 | $18,855 |
| Health Insurance (can be waived) | $2,020 | $2,020 |

**Average 2010 Graduate Indebtedness: $206,426**
**% of Enrolled Students Receiving Aid: 95%**

*Source: 2009-2010 LCME I-B survey and 2010-2011 AAMC TSF questionnaire*

# University of Nebraska College of Medicine

## Omaha, Nebraska

Office of Admissions and Student Affairs
University of Nebraska Medical Center
College of Medicine
985527 Nebraska Medical Center
Omaha, Nebraska 68198-5527

**T** 402 559 2259    grrogers@unmc.edu

**Admissions:** www.unmc.edu/com/admissions.htm

## General Information

The University of Nebraska Medical Center is a major health resource for the State of Nebraska and surrounding areas. Several integrated units fulfill the mission of UNMC: The Colleges of Medicine, Nursing, Pharmacy, Dentistry, Allied Health, the Office of Graduate Studies and Research, Meyer Rehabilitation Institute, Eppley Institute for Research in Cancer and Allied Diseases, Nebraska Medical Center, and UNMC Physicians. These facilities are supplemented by direct teaching affiliations with the Veterans Affairs Medical Center and eight community hospitals.

## Mission Statement

The mission of the University of Nebraska Medical Center is to improve the health of Nebraska through premier educational programs, innovative research, the highest quality patient care, and outreach to underserved populations.

## Curricular Highlights

**Community Service Requirement:** Required.

**Research/Thesis Requirement:** Optional.

The College of Medicine enjoys a distinguished record of excellence in medical education. Our goal is for students to acquire the knowledge, skills, experience, and new pattern of behavior that is required in today's rapidly changing health care system, which emphasizes customer satisfaction, efficiency, preventive medicine, teamwork and a spirit of collaboration between health professionals.

## Selection Factors

Selection is based on a total assessment of each candidate's motivation, interests, character, academic record, personal interview, MCAT, and general fitness and promise for a career in medicine. Admission is based on individual qualifications without regard to age, sex, sexual preference, race, national origin, handicap, or religious or political beliefs. Strong preference is given to residents of Nebraska.

## Information about Diversity Programs

UNMC is committed to increasing the number of physicians from groups currently underrepresented in the medical profession. Information is available through the Office of Student Equity and Multicultural Affairs at (402) 559-4437.

## Regional/Satellite Campuses

The Nebraska Medical Center is the primary teaching hospital for the College of Medicine.

## Application Process and Requirements 2012–2013

**Primary application service:** AMCAS®
**Earliest filing date:** June 1, 2011
**Latest filing date:** November 1, 2011

**Secondary application required:** Yes
**Sent to:** All applicants
**URL:** http://net.unmc.edu/apply
**Contact:** Jackie O'Hara, (402) 559-2259
johara@unmc.edu
**Fee:** Yes, $70    **Waiver available:** Yes
Earliest filing date: June 1, 2011
**Latest filing date:** January 15, 2012

**MCAT® required:** Yes
**Latest MCAT® considered:** September 2011
**Oldest MCAT® considered:** January 2009

**Early Decision Program:** School does have EDP
**Applicants notified:** October 1, 2011
**EDP available for:** Both In-State and Out-of-State Applicants

**Regular acceptance notice —**
**Earliest date:** December 2011
**Latest date:** Until class is full
**Applicant's response to acceptance offer —**
**Maximum time:** Two weeks

**Requests for deferred entrance considered:** No

**Deposit to hold place in class:** Yes
**Deposit — In-State Applicants:** $100
**Out-of-State Applicants:** $100
**Deposit due:** With response to acceptance offer
**Applied to tuition:** Yes
**Deposit refundable:** No
**Refundable by:** n/a

**Estimated number of new entrants:** 130
**EDP:** 35, **Special Programs:** n/a

**Start month/year:** August 2012

**Interview format:** By invitation only. Regional interviews are not available. Video interviews are not available.

## Preparatory Programs

**Postbaccalaureate Program:** No

**Summer Program:** Yes, www.unmc.edu/smdep/, Carly Crim, (800) 701-9665, smdep@unmc.edu

## 2010–2011 First Year Class

|  | In-State | Out-of-State | International |
|---|---|---|---|
| Applications | 282 | 1,152 | 12 |
| Interviewed | 213 | 144 | 0 |
| Matriculated | 109 | 18 | 0 |

**Total Matriculants: 127**    **Total Enrollment: 492**

## Financial Information

|  | In-State | Out-of-State |
|---|---|---|
| Total Cost of Attendance | $46,525 | $81,081 |
| Tuition and Fees | $27,016 | $61,572 |
| Other (incl. living expenses) | $18,449 | $18,449 |
| Health Insurance (can be waived) | $1,060 | $1,060 |

**Average 2010 Graduate Indebtedness: $119,999**
**% of Enrolled Students Receiving Aid: 98%**

*Source: 2009–2010 LCME I-B survey and 2010–2011 AAMC TSF questionnaire*

NV

# University of Nevada School of Medicine

## Reno, Nevada

Office of Admissions and Student Affairs
University of Nevada School of Medicine
Mail Stop 0357
Reno, Nevada 89557-0357

**T** 775 784 4604    asa@med.unr.edu

**Admissions:** www.medicine.nevada.edu/dept/
asa/default.asp

## General Information

The University of Nevada School of Medicine is a state-supported, community based, university-integrated school which relies heavily on community physicians as teachers and community health facilities for the majority of its clinical education. The school is dedicated to selecting individuals with diverse backgrounds to study comprehensive health care delivery while considering the needs of the individual, the family and the community.

## Mission Statement

To provide educational opportunities for Nevadans, to improve the quality of healthcare for citizens of Nevada, to create new biomedical knowledge through education, research, patient care and community service, and to provide continuing medical education.

## Curricular Highlights

**Community Service Requirement:** Optional.

**Research/Thesis Requirement:** Optional.

The first two years of the program are concentrated in classrooms and laboratories on the Reno campus. The curriculum emphasizes the biomedical and behavioral sciences basic to medicine. Basic science disciplines are integrated with each other and with clinical problems to promote the learning of problem-solving skills. Early clinical training is provided for students to learn patient interviewing, doctor-patient relationship skills, and the basics of physical examination and diagnosis. Throughout the first and second years, students spend time with a physician to observe medical practice in office and clinic settings. Opportunities to participate in basic and clinical science research throughout the curriculum are available. The third and fourth years emphasize a balance of ambulatory and inpatient medical education designed to better prepare students for residency. Third and fourth year students study clinical medicine in Reno, Las Vegas, and rural Nevada.

## Selection Factors

Candidates are evaluated on the basis of academic performance; results of the MCAT; the nature and depth of scholarly, extracurricular, and health care-related activities during college years (excellence and balance of the natural sciences, social sciences, and humanities); academic letters of evaluation; and the personal interview. A small number of nonresident applicants from Alaska, Idaho, Montana, or Wyoming or residents of northern California counties bordering Nevada (medical catchment area) are considered. Applicants from other western states should contact the office of admissions for updated eligibility information. Applicants are required to be U.S. citizens or have a permanent resident visa. Only those students who are currently enrolled and in good academic standing at LCME-accredited medical schools and have a strong residential tie to Nevada are considered for transfer to the second and third years. The number of positions available for transfer is strictly limited by attrition and compatibility to the school's curriculum. Only U.S. citizens are considered. Transfer applications from students attending foreign medical schools are not considered. Completion of a criminal background check is required of all accepted applicants. The fee for this background check is up to $51.25. Applicants who were denied admission to the University of Nevada School of Medicine during their initial applications are not eligible for transfer from other institutions.

## Information about Diversity Programs

The School of Medicine is committed to the recruitment, selection, and retention of individuals who are members of groups traditionally underrepresented in American medicine. Residents of the state of Nevada and individuals who meet the nonresident criteria and who are from such backgrounds are encouraged to apply. The University of Nevada, Reno, does not discriminate on the basis of race, ethnicity, color, religion, sex, age, creed, national origin, veteran status, physical or mental disability, and, in accordance with university policy, sexual orientation, in any program or activity it operates.

## Regional/Satellite Campuses

The University of Nevada School of Medicine is a state-wide institution with varied clinical sites including a Level I trauma center and numerous research and rural clinical opportunities. The University of Nevada School of Medicine has three campuses: Reno, Las Vegas, and Elko.

## Application Process and Requirements 2012–2013

**Primary application service:** AMCAS®
**Earliest filing date:** June 1, 2011
**Latest filing date:** November 1, 2011

**Secondary application required:** Yes
**Sent to:** Screened applicants
**Contact:** Patricia Romney, (775) 784-6063, promney@medicine.nevada.edu
**Fee:** Yes, $45    **Waiver available:** Yes
**Earliest filing date:** September 1, 2011
**Latest filing date:** December 1, 2011

**MCAT® required:** Yes
**Latest MCAT® considered:** September 2011
**Oldest MCAT® considered:** 2008

**Early Decision Program:** School does have EDP
**Applicants notified:** October 1, 2011
**EDP available for:** Both In-State and Out-of-State Applicants

**Regular acceptance notice —**
**Earliest date:** January 15, 2012
**Latest date:** Varies
**Applicant's response to acceptance offer —**
**Maximum time:** Two weeks

**Requests for deferred entrance considered:** Yes

**Deposit to hold place in class:** No
**Deposit — In-State Applicants:** n/a
**Out-of-State Applicants:** n/a
**Deposit due:** n/a
**Applied to tuition:** n/a
**Deposit refundable:** n/a
**Refundable by:** n/a

**Estimated number of new entrants:** 62
**EDP:** 5, **Special Programs:** 11

**Start month/year:** August 2012

**Interview format:** Interviews are blind and semi-structured. Applicants are interviewed in Reno and Las Vegas. Video interviews are not available.

## Preparatory Programs

**Postbaccalaureate Program:** No

**Summer Program:** No

## 2010–2011 First Year Class

|  | In-State | Out-of-State | International |
|---|---|---|---|
| Applications | 186 | 1,155 | 12 |
| Interviewed | 180 | 40 | 0 |
| Matriculated | 54 | 8 | 0 |

**Total Matriculants: 62**    **Total Enrollment: 246**

## Financial Information

|  | In-State | Out-of-State |
|---|---|---|
| Total Cost of Attendance | $42,468 | $64,920 |
| Tuition and Fees | $15,711 | $38,163 |
| Other (incl. living expenses) | $24,181 | $24,181 |
| Health Insurance (can be waived) | $2,576 | $2,576 |

**Average 2010 Graduate Indebtedness: $110,301**
**% of Enrolled Students Receiving Aid: 90%**

*Source: 2009-2010 LCME I-B survey and 2010-2011 AAMC TSF questionnaire*

# Dartmouth Medical School

## Hanover, New Hampshire

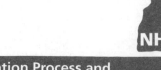

Dartmouth Medical School
Office of Admissions
3 Rope Ferry Road
Hanover, New Hampshire 03755-1404

**T** 603 650 1505   dms.admissions@dartmouth.edu

**Admissions:** http://dms.dartmouth.edu/admissions/

## General Information

Dartmouth Medical School (DMS), the fourth oldest U.S. medical school, is a partner of Dartmouth-Hitchcock Medical Center (DHMC). The 6,000 employees of DHMC serve a patient population of 1.6 million. DHMC includes Mary Hitchcock Memorial Hospital, Dartmouth-Hitchcock Clinic, and the Veterans Affairs Hospital in White River Junction, Vermont. Other facilities contributing to the integration of advanced research and quality care within DHMC include the Norris Cotton Cancer Center (a National Cancer Institute Comprehensive Cancer Center), Children's Hospital at Dartmouth, and the Borwell Research Building. DHMC is a major force for medical treatment and discovery and is the site of numerous clinical trials. Additional teaching sites span nationally and internationally from the New England states to Tanzania. A faculty of approximately 2,000 affords ample opportunity for individual instruction. The President of Dartmouth is Dr. Jim Yong Kim, the Dean of DMS is Dr. Wiley (Chip) Souba, and the Associate Dean for Student Affairs is Dr. Ann Davis.

## Mission Statement

The mission of Dartmouth Medical School is to improve health - locally, nationally, and globally. We do this by educating the leading physicians and scientists of tomorrow, generating new knowledge through research, and empowering all members of our community.

## Curricular Highlights

**Community Service Requirement:** Optional. Many students join in community-service projects.

**Research/Thesis Requirement:** Optional.

The DMS curriculum integrates basic and clinical sciences throughout medical school. Its hallmarks are longitudinal experiences in the basic and clinical sciences, early introduction to patient care, small-group instruction, close relationships with faculty, and opportunities for independent learning. DMS uses various pedagogies, including problem-based learning, lectures, and small elective courses. Year One includes On Doctoring, a course that pairs students with faculty practitioners in the clinical environment. The Scientific Basis of Medicine, an interdisciplinary pathophysiology course combined with an introduction to the mechanisms of disease and the principles of clinical medicine, is a feature of Year Two. Six seven-week clerkships, elective time, and opportunities to practice in diverse settings shape the third year. The fourth year includes two required clerkships, a sub-internship, and four short courses, but students largely spend this year refining their interests through electives.

## Selection Factors

The admissions committee carefully reviews the entire application with attention to personal, scholastic, and scientific qualifications. DMS does not employ numeric cutoffs or inflexible criteria. Selected applicants interview in Hanover from September to March. Dartmouth does not discriminate on the basis of race, color, religion, sex, age, sexual orientation, gender identity or expression, national origin, disability, military or veteran status in access to its programs and activities, and in conditions of admission and employment (hiring, promotion, discharge, pay, fringe benefits).

## Information about Diversity Programs

DMS seeks to enroll a talented and diverse class of students from various racial, ethnic, cultural, religious, and socio-economic backgrounds. Susan M. Pepin, M.D. is the Chief of Diversity.

## Regional/Satellite Campuses

DMS provides a variety of clinical training opportunities; students gain exposure to various patient populations, healthcare delivery systems, and management models. Locations such as Bethel, AK; Tuba City, AZ; Orange, CA; San Francisco, CA; Dar es Salaam, Tanzania; and every New England state except for Massachusetts are only some of the possibilities. Students may also study at the internationally known Dartmouth Institute for Health Policy and Clinical Practice.

## Application Process and Requirements 2012–2013

**Primary application service:** AMCAS®
**Earliest filing date:** June 1, 2011
**Latest filing date:** November 1, 2011

**Secondary application required:** Yes
**Sent to:** All applicants
**URL:** http://dms.dartmouth.edu/admissions/instrs_to_applicants.shtml
**Contact:** Office of Admissions, (603) 650-1505, dms.admissions@dartmouth.edu
**Fee:** Yes, $130   **Waiver available:** Yes
**Earliest filing date:** June 1, 2011
**Latest filing date:** January 2, 2012

**MCAT® required:** No
**Latest MCAT® considered:** 2011
**Oldest MCAT® considered:** 2009

**Early Decision Program:** School does not have EDP
**Applicants notified:** n/a
**EDP available for:** n/a

**Regular acceptance notice —**
**Earliest date:** October 15, 2011
**Latest date:** Until class is full
**Applicant's response to acceptance offer —**
**Maximum time:** Two weeks

**Requests for deferred entrance considered:** Yes

**Deposit to hold place in class:** No
**Deposit — In-State Applicants:** n/a
**Out-of-State Applicants:** n/a
**Deposit due:** n/a
**Applied to tuition:** n/a
**Deposit refundable:** n/a
**Refundable by:** n/a

**Estimated number of new entrants:** 89
**EDP:** n/a, **Special Programs:** n/a

**Start month/year:** August 2012

**Interview format:** Two half-hour interviews. Regional interviews are not available. Video interviews are not available.

### Preparatory Programs

**Postbaccalaureate Program:** No

**Summer Program:** Yes, Kalindi Trietley, (603) 650-6535, Kalindi.E.Trietley@Dartmouth.edu

## 2010–2011 First Year Class

|  | In-State | Out-of-State | International |
|---|---|---|---|
| Applications | 72 | 4,568 | 532 |
| Interviewed | 30 | 608 | 26 |
| Matriculated | 9 | 66 | 15 |

**Total Matriculants: 90**   **Total Enrollment: 343**

## Financial Information

|  | In-State | Out-of-State |
|---|---|---|
| Total Cost of Attendance | $64,640 | $64,640 |
| Tuition and Fees | $46,775 | $46,775 |
| Other (incl. living expenses) | $15,805 | $15,805 |
| Health Insurance (can be waived) | $2,060 | $2,060 |

**Average 2010 Graduate Indebtedness: $120,613**
**% of Enrolled Students Receiving Aid: 88%**

*Source: 2009-2010 LCME I-B survey and 2010-2011 AAMC TSF questionnaire*

# University of Medicine and Dentistry of New Jersey — New Jersey Medical School

## Newark, New Jersey

Director of Admissions
UMDNJ — New Jersey Medical School
185 South Orange Avenue C-653
Newark, New Jersey 07103

**T** 973 972 4631   njmsadmiss@umdnj.edu

**Admissions:** http://njms.umdnj.edu/admissions/index.cfm

## General Information

New Jersey Medical School (NJMS), formerly Seton Hall College of Medicine and Dentistry, is the state's oldest academic medical institution. More than 600 faculty and 1,300 volunteer faculty in our 20 academic departments play a critical role in transforming our students into qualified clinicians who will meet and exceed the healthcare needs of New Jersey and the nation. Clinical instruction is carried out at the University Hospital, Hackensack University Medical Center, Veterans Affairs Medical Center, St. Barnabus Medical Center, Newark Beth Israel Medical Center, Morristown Memorial Hospital, Overlook Hospital, Mountainside Hospital and Kessler Institute for Rehabilitation.

## Mission Statement

To educate students, physicians, and scientists to meet society's current and future healthcare needs through patient-centered education; pioneering research; innovative clinical, rehabilitative and preventive care; and collaborative community outreach.

## Curricular Highlights

**Community Service Requirement:** Optional.

**Research/Thesis Requirement:** Optional.

Years 1 and 2 are graded as pass/fail and integrate the basic sciences with early clinical exposure. The basic sciences are taught utilizing various teaching modalities, including lectures, laboratories, team-based learning (TBL) and the expanded use of case-based small group learning sessions. Students will engage in a comprehensive introduction to the field of medicine through a course called the "Physician's Core." This will provide them access to the Clinical Skills Training Center during the first two years, which features 12 simulated patient examination rooms equipped to monitor mock patient encounters with standardized patients. Years 3 and 4 are devoted to providing in-depth exposure to clinical medicine. In Year 3, students rotate through the major disciplines in medicine (internal medicine, surgery, family medicine, pediatrics, psychiatry/neurology and obstetrics-gynecology) and in Year 4, students will assume a higher degree of autonomy and responsibility as they rotate through acting internships, as well as emergency medicine, physical medicine and rehabilitation and public health clerkships. Students are also able to select from a wide range of electives, not only at NJMS and throughout the U.S. but internationally as well.

## Selection Factors

Applicants are selected on the basis of academic excellence, leadership qualities, demonstrated compassion for others and broad extracurricular experiences. Related factors such as passion, perseverance, special aptitudes and stamina are also considered. Intense competition tends to favor those with stronger credentials. Although some preference is given to residents of NJ, out-of-state residents are encouraged to apply.

## Information about Diversity Programs

NJMS is committed to the recruitment of a diverse student body as well as enhancing the cultural competency of medical students in order to improve access to care for underserved populations. Several programs have been established to support these goals. Information may be obtained by contacting the Office of Special Programs at (973) 972-3762.

## Application Process and Requirements 2012–2013

**Primary application service:** AMCAS®
**Earliest filing date:** June 1, 2011
**Latest filing date:** December 1, 2011

**Secondary application required:** Yes
**Sent to:** All applicants
**URL:** https://njmsintra.umdnj.edu/nonmbm/education/admissions/supplementalApp.cfm
**Contact:** njmsadmiss@umdnj.edu
**Fee:** Yes, $80   **Waiver available:** Yes
**Earliest filing date:** July 1, 2011
**Latest filing date:** December 15, 2011

**MCAT® required:** Yes
**Latest MCAT® considered:** September 2011
**Oldest MCAT® considered:** n/a

**Early Decision Program:** School does have EDP
**Applicants notified:** October 1, 2011
**EDP available for:** Both In-States and Out-of-States

**Regular acceptance notice —**
**Earliest date:** October 15, 2011
**Latest date:** Until class is full
**Applicant's response to acceptance offer —**
**Maximum time:** Two weeks
**Requests for deferred entrance considered:** Yes

**Deposit to hold place in class:** Yes
**Deposit — In-State Applicants:** $100
**Out-of-State Applicants:** $100
**Deposit due:** Within two weeks of acceptance
**Applied to tuition:** Yes
**Deposit refundable:** Yes
**Refundable by:** May 15, 2012

**Estimated number of new entrants:** 170
**EDP:** 20, **Special Programs:** 25

**Start month/year:** August 2012

**Interview format:** One-to-one, non-stress interview with faculty. Optional student interview also available. Video interviews are not available.

## Preparatory Programs

**Postbaccalaureate Program:** No

**Summer Program:** Yes, http://njms.umdnj.edu/education/special_programs/index.cfm, (973) 972-3762

## 2010–2011 First Year Class

|  | In-State | Out-of-State | International |
|---|---|---|---|
| Applications | 1,189 | 2,179 | 34 |
| Interviewed | 569 | 61 | 0 |
| Matriculated | 174 | 4 | 0 |

**Total Matriculants: 178**   **Total Enrollment: 754**

## Financial Information

|  | In-State | Out-of-State |
|---|---|---|
| Total Cost of Attendance | $60,149 | $78,858 |
| Tuition and Fees | $32,013 | $50,722 |
| Other (incl. living expenses) | $25,895 | $25,895 |
| Health Insurance (can be waived) | $2,241 | $2,241 |

**Average 2010 Graduate Indebtedness: $142,062**
**% of Enrolled Students Receiving Aid: 84%**

*Source: 2009-2010 LCME I-B survey and 2010-2011 AAMC TSF questionnaire*

# University of Medicine and Dentistry of New Jersey — Robert Wood Johnson Medical School

## Piscataway, New Jersey

Associate Dean for Admissions
University of Medicine and Dentistry of New Jersey
Robert Wood Johnson Medical School
675 Hoes Lane
Piscataway, New Jersey 08854-5635

**T** 732 235 4576    rwjapadm@umdnj.edu

**Admissions:** http://rwjms.umdnj.edu/education/admissions

### General Information

Robert Wood Johnson Medical School, formerly known as Rutgers Medical School, has campuses in Piscataway and New Brunswick. A full complement of clinical training facilities including Robert Wood Johnson University Hospital, Bristol Myers Squibb Children's Hospital, and numerous ambulatory sites, and a full complement of research institutes including the Child Health Institute, The Cancer Institute of NJ and the Environmental and Health Sciences Institute, provide outstanding educational experiences. The medical school encompasses 22 basic science and clinical departments and more than 2,500 full-time and volunteer faculty members.

### Mission Statement

The medical school is dedicated to the pursuit of excellence in education, research, health care delivery and the promotion of community health. Excellence is achieved through the work of a scholarly and creative faculty and a high-achieving and diverse student body.

### Curricular Highlights

**Community Service Requirement:** Optional. Distinction in Service to the Community.

**Research/Thesis Requirement:** Optional. Distinction in Research or Distinction in Medical Education.

A systems-based M1 and M2 curriculum integrates relevant content from multiple disciplines applied in the context of real clinical problems with weekly capstone exercises. Learner-centered teaching strategies develop skills for life-long study and critical thinking. The preclerkship pass/fail curriculum introduces patient care and service learning via the learning communities of the Patient Centered Medicine course. There is ample elective time in the M3 year, which is graded on a 5-point scale. In the M4 year students rotate in emergency medicine, neurology critical care, a sub-internship, outpatient subspecialties and 20 weeks of electives. A longitudinal primary care experience and an independent project round out the clinical curriculum. The Clinical Skills Center begins assessments in M1, runs clerkship OSCEs and an end of M3 year summative clinical assessment. The Student Scholar year allows personalization of the undergraduate program in activities such as research, community service or global health. There are a number of dual degree options including a program in Clinical and Translational research, MD/MPH, MD/MBA and Distinction programs. The MD/PhD is a tri-institutional program with Princeton University and Rutgers University.

### Selection Factors

Preference is given to NJ residents. OOS applicants are encouraged to apply. Admission is determined on the basis of academics, MCAT, preprofessional evaluations, character, motivation, and interview. We believe that a diverse student body contributes to the educational program of all students. Selection and recruitment is based on a holistic review of each applicant's experiences, personal qualities and potential to enhance the learning environment. Applications from members of groups underrepresented in medicine are encouraged. Interviews are by invitation. Multiple Mini Interview format is used.

### Information about Diversity Programs

RWJMS is committed to the education of physicians from groups underrepresented in medicine. Diversity is viewed broadly. Applications from in-state and out-of-state candidates are welcome. Numerous support services are available for disadvantaged students, including a pre-matriculation summer program.

### Regional/Satellite Campuses

**Regional Campus Location(s):** Camden, NJ.

The regional campus is closed to new students.

## Application Process and Requirements 2012–2013

**Primary application service:** AMCAS®
**Earliest filing date:** June 1, 2011
**Latest filing date:** December 1, 2011

**Secondary application required:** Yes
**Sent to:** rwjsecondary@umdnj.edu
**URL:** n/a
**Contact:** Marilyn Wagensellar, (732) 235-4587, wagensma@umdnj.edu
**Fee:** Yes, $80    **Waiver available:** Yes
**Earliest filing date:** June 1, 2011
**Latest filing date:** February 1, 2012

**MCAT® required:** Yes
**Latest MCAT® considered:** September 2011
**Oldest MCAT® considered:** September 2008

**Early Decision Program:** School does not have EDP
**Applicants notified:** n/a
**EDP available for:** n/a

**Regular acceptance notice —**
**Earliest date:** December 15, 2011
**Latest date:** Until class is full
**Applicant's response to acceptance offer —**
**Maximum time:** Two weeks

**Requests for deferred entrance considered:** Yes

**Deposit to hold place in class:** Yes
**Deposit — In-State Applicants:** $50
**Out-of-State Applicants:** $50
**Deposit due:** With response to acceptance offer
**Applied to tuition:** Yes
**Deposit refundable:** Yes
**Refundable by:** May 15, 2012

**Estimated number of new entrants:** 110
**EDP:** n/a, **Special Programs:** 10

**Start month/year:** August 2012

**Interview format:** Multiple mini interviews. Video interviews are not available.

### Preparatory Programs

**Postbaccalaureate Program:** No

**Summer Program:** Yes, Sonia Garcia Laumbach, (732) 235-4060, sgarcia@umdnj.edu

## 2010–2011 First Year Class

|  | In-State | Out-of-State | International |
|---|---|---|---|
| Applications | 1,162 | 2,084 | 31 |
| Interviewed | 404 | 52 | 0 |
| Matriculated | 109 | 4 | 0 |

**Total Matriculants: 113**    **Total Enrollment: 685**

## Financial Information

|  | In-State | Out-of-State |
|---|---|---|
| Total Cost of Attendance | $61,756 | $80,465 |
| Tuition and Fees | $32,391 | $51,100 |
| Other (incl. living expenses) | $27,124 | $27,124 |
| Health Insurance (can be waived) | $2,241 | $2,241 |

**Average 2010 Graduate Indebtedness: $130,461**
**% of Enrolled Students Receiving Aid: 81%**

Source: 2009-2010 LCME I-B survey and 2010-2011 AAMC TSF questionnaire

# University of New Mexico School of Medicine

## Albuquerque, New Mexico

University of New Mexico Health Sciences Center
School of Medicine, Office of Admissions,
MSC09 5085, Health Sciences Library and
Informatics Center, Room 125
Albuquerque, New Mexico 87131-0001

**T** 505 272 4766   somadmissions@salud.unm.edu

**Admissions:** http://hsc.unm.edu/som/admissions

## General Information

The University of New Mexico enrolled its first 24 medical students in September of 1964. The School of Medicine is both a professional and graduate school where students may earn an M.D. degree, a Ph.D. degree, a combined M.D./Ph.D. degree, a combined M.D./M.P.H., or B.S. or M.S. degrees in several allied health science fields. Medical education at the resident and postgraduate levels is offered through the University's teaching hospital and various state-of-the-art facilities.

## Mission Statement

The mission of the University of New Mexico is to educate students, scientists, physicians and other health professionals in the art and science of medicine through the transmission of biomedical knowledge acquired from research and patient care. We aspire to improve the health of all New Mexicans by being a model of excellence in education while working to reduce disparities among medically underrepresented populations and communities.

## Curricular Highlights

**Community Service Requirement:** Required. A community research project is required.

**Research/Thesis Requirement:** Required. A research project and report is required.

The School of Medicine utilizes a hybrid curriculum, which incorporates the integration of basic sciences and clinical medicine with problem-based and student-centered learning techniques. Early clinical skills are coupled with medical education taught from three perspectives: biologic, population and behavioral, and these perspectives are continued throughout the clinical years. Medical students are exposed to patient care during the first year of education, and finish that year with a 9 week, in-depth Practical Immersion Experience (PIE) in a professional setting in one of New Mexico's communities. The goals of the curriculum are to graduate physicians who are enthusiastic and responsible for their continued learning; have the ability to define problems, formulate questions, and carry out scholarly inquiry, are skilled in self and peer assessment; and have a broad perspective on the importance of human biology, behavior, environment, culture, and social setting in the health of individuals and populations. Student assessment is competency-based and values mastery of knowledge, critical appraisal, interpersonal and clinical skills, and peer and self-assessment.

## Selection Factors

In general, only those applicants with ties to the state of New Mexico, Native Americans who reside on reservations contiguous with the State of New Mexico, and residents of WICHE states (Montana and Wyoming) will receive consideration for admission. Selection is based upon many factors, including scholastic achievement, performance on the MCAT, personal statement, interviews, and letters of recommendation.

## Information about Diversity Programs

Our mission is to promote ethnic, racial, socio-economic, gender, and geographic diversity in the Health Sciences, and to create opportunities to address the health disparities that affect all New Mexicans. Strategies to achieve this mission include creating programs that increase college awareness and identifying, recruiting, and supporting students, residents, and faculty from these diverse backgrounds.

## Regional/Satellite Campuses

**Regional Campus Location(s):** Rio Rancho, NM.

The new UNM Sandoval Regional Medical Center located in Rio Rancho is scheduled to open in Spring 2012. This brand new facility will include an emergency room, inpatient/outpatient medical and surgical services, diagnostic imaging and testing and a dozen other key clinical services.

## Application Process and Requirements 2012–2013

**Primary application service:** AMCAS®
**Earliest filing date:** June 1, 2011
**Latest filing date:** November 15, 2011

**Secondary application required:** Yes
**Sent to:** Screened applicants
**URL:** http://hsc.unm.edu/som/admissions
**Fee:** Yes, $75   **Waiver available:** Yes
**Earliest filing date:** August 1, 2011
**Latest filing date:** February 1, 2012

**MCAT® required:** Yes
**Latest MCAT® considered:** September 2011
**Oldest MCAT® considered:** August 2007

**Early Decision Program:** School does have EDP
**Applicants notified:** October 1, 2011
**EDP available for:** Both In-State and Out-of-State Applicants

**Regular acceptance notice —**
**Earliest date:** March 15, 2012
**Latest date:** Until class is full
**Applicant's response to acceptance offer —**
**Maximum time:** Two weeks

**Requests for deferred entrance considered:** Yes

**Deposit to hold place in class:** Yes
**Deposit — In-State Applicants:** $100
**Out-of-State Applicants:** $100
**Deposit due:** May 15, 2012
**Applied to tuition:** Yes
**Deposit refundable:** Yes
**Refundable by:** May 15, 2012

**Estimated number of new entrants:** 100
**EDP:** 6, **Special Programs:** 7

**Start month/year:** July 2012

**Interview format:** Two one-on-one interviews by committee members. Video interviews are not available.

## Preparatory Programs

**Postbaccalaureate Program:** Yes,
http://hsc.unm.edu/SOM/UME/OARS/index.shtml
Steven Mitchell, (505) 925-4441,
smmitchell@salud.unm.edu

**Summer Program:** No

## 2010–2011 First Year Class

|  | In-State | Out-of-State | International |
|---|---|---|---|
| Applications | 228 | 451 | 9 |
| Interviewed | 207 | 18 | 0 |
| Matriculated | 92 | 1 | 1 |

**Total Matriculants: 94**     **Total Enrollment: 344**

## Financial Information

|  | In-State | Out-of-State |
|---|---|---|
| Total Cost of Attendance | $41,807 | $72,034 |
| Tuition and Fees | $19,498 | $49,725 |
| Other (incl. living expenses) | $20,882 | $20,882 |
| Health Insurance (can be waived) | $1,427 | $1,427 |

**Average 2010 Graduate Indebtedness: $123,667**
**% of Enrolled Students Receiving Aid: 93%**

Source: 2009-2010 LCME I-8 survey and 2010-2011 AAMC TSF questionnaire

# Albany Medical College
## Albany, New York

Office of Admissions, Mail Code 3
Albany Medical College
47 New Scotland Avenue
Albany New York 12208

**T** 518-262-5521    admissions@mail.amc.edu

**Admissions:** www.amc.edu/academic/
Undergraduate_Admissions/

## General Information

Founded in 1839, Albany Medical College is one of the oldest medical schools in the country and one of the largest teaching hospitals in New York State. The college is coeducational, nondenominational, and privately supported. The college and the 650-bed Albany Medical Center Hospital comprise Albany Medical Center. Patient care, from primary to tertiary, is provided for over 2.5 million residents of eastern New York and western New England.

## Mission Statement

The mission of the Albany Medical College is to: educate medical students, physicians, bio-medical scientists, and other health professionals from demograhically diverse backgrounds to meet future primary and specialty health care needs; foster biomedical research that leads to scientific advances and improvement of public health; and provide a broad range of patient services.

## Curricular Highlights

**Community Service Requirement:** Required.

**Research/Thesis Requirement:** Optional. M.D. with Distinction in Service, M.D. with Distinction in Research, M.D. with Distinction in Health Systems Analysis, M.D. with Distinction in Bioethics.

Basic and clinical sciences are integrated into themes stressing normal function in Year 1 and pathological processes in Year 2. There are also five longitudinal themes integrated throughout the curriculum: clinical skills, ethical and health systems issues, evidence-based medicine, nutrition, and informatics. In every theme, learning focuses on clinical presentations. Beginning in Year 1, students learn to interview and examine both real and standardized patients. Clinical skills competence is highlighted throughout the four years. Basic science knowledge is reinforced during years 3 and 4. Primary care is emphasized throughout the four years. Year 3 clerkships focus on care in ambulatory settings. Year 4 required rotations concentrate on care in hospital-based settings, preparing students for residency and practice. The remainder of fourth year includes electives chosen by the students and a required course in learning how to teach.

## Selection Factors

In selecting students, emphasis is placed upon integrity, character, academic achievement, motivation, emotional stability, and social and intellectual suitability. The college is committed to the belief that educational opportunities should be available to all eligible persons without regard to race, creed, age, gender, religion, marital status, handicap, national origin, or sexual orientation. Admission is not restricted to state residents. The committee evaluates applications based on a number of factors in addition to MCAT scores and GPAs. Invitations for interview are made at the discretion of the committee. Preapplication inquiries or questions concerning the status of applications are always welcome.

## Information About Diversity Programs

We believe that Albany Medical College's mission is enriched by a community of people with diverse backgrounds. Recognition and respect of all differences that exist is crucial to the development of core professional attributes in our students, to the continued nurturing of such attributes among our faculty, staff and workforce. To that end we seek to recruit students who will bring a diversity of thought, experience and backgrounds to our community. Please call the Office of Admissions at (518) 262-5521 for more information.

## Regional/Satellite Campuses

The medical college is affiliated with other hospitals in New York State. Clinical departments utilize a network of community physicians to serve the ambulatory care educational needs of students. The college, which is combined with Albany Medical Center Hospital on its campus, is also affiliated with the Veterans Administration Hospital, community hospitals, and private and community clinics in surrounding counties.

## Application Process and Requirements 2012–2013

**Primary application service:** AMCAS®
**Earliest filing date:** June 1, 2011
**Latest filing date:** November 1, 2011

**Secondary application required:** Yes
**Sent to:** All applicants
**Fee:** Yes, $105.00    **Waiver available:** Yes
**Earliest filing date:** June 2011
**Latest filing date:** December 15, 2011

**MCAT® required:** No
**Latest MCAT® considered:** September 2011
**Oldest MCAT® considered:** 2008

**Early Decision Program:** School does not have EDP
**Applicants notified:** n/a
**EDP available for:** n/a

**Regular acceptance notice —**
**Earliest date:** October 15, 2011
**Latest date:** Until class is full
**Applicant's response to acceptance offer —**
**Maximum time:** Two weeks

**Requests for deferred entrance considered:** Yes

**Deposit to hold place in class:** Yes
**Deposit — In-State Applicants:** $100
**Out-of-State Applicants:** $100
**Deposit due:** With response to acceptance offer
**Applied to Tuition:** Yes
**Deposit Refundable:** Yes
**Refundable by:** May 15, 2012

**Estimated number of new entrants:** 140
**EDP:** n/a, **Special Programs:** n/a

**Start month/year:** August 2012

**Interview format:** Individual interviews by Admissions Committee. Regional interviews are not available. Video interviews are not available.

## Preparatory Programs

**Postbaccalaureate Program:** No

**Summer Program:** No

## 2010–2011 First Year Class

|  | In-State | Out-of-State | International |
|---|---|---|---|
| Applications | 1,598 | 5,907 | 460 |
| Interviewed | 180 | 450 | 0 |
| Matriculated | 55 | 80 | 2 |

**Total Matriculants: 137**    **Total Enrollment: 571**

## Financial Information

|  | In-State | Out-of-State |
|---|---|---|
| Total Cost of Attendance | $74,598 | $75,298 |
| Tuition and Fees | $48,241 | $48,241 |
| Other (incl. living expenses) | $23,326 | $24,026 |
| Health Insurance (can be waived) | $3,031 | $3,031 |

**Average 2010 Graduate Indebtedness: $175,152**
**% of Enrolled Students Receiving Aid: 85%**

*Source: 2009-2010 LCME I-B survey and 2010-2011 AAMC TSF questionnaire*

# Albert Einstein College of Medicine of Yeshiva University

## Bronx, New York

Office of Admissions
Albert Einstein College of Medicine of Yeshiva U
Jack and Pearl Resnick Campus
1300 Morris Park Avenue
Bronx New York 10461

T 718-430-2106  admissions@aecom.yu.edu

**Admissions:** www.aecom.yu.edu/home/admissions

## General Information

There are many facilities devoted to biomedical research and teaching, including a new building for genetic and translational research, and a new Clinical Skills Facility. Clinical education takes place in acute care hospitals, long-term care and skilled nursing facilities, hospices, and neighborhood health centers that serve a diverse population of patients in and around the NY metropolitan area.

## Mission Statement

Einstein combines scientific excellence with a social mission to improve health through engagement in local, national, and global communities. Einstein's dynamic curriculum unites the biomedical sciences and hands-on clinical training with the flexibility to pursue research and meet the healthcare needs of underserved populations in the Bronx, the New York metropolitan area, and beyond. Einstein attracts a diverse student body and provides a collegial and collaborative environment that fosters our students' growth as future clinicians, educators, physician scientists, and leaders in the field.

## Curricular Highlights

**Community Service Requirement:** Optional.

**Research/Thesis Requirement:** Required.

Years 1 and 2 consist of interdisciplinary courses with self-directed case-based learning in small groups, and the "Introduction to Clinical Medicine" course in which students see patients three weeks after matriculation. Year 3 consists of clerkship rotations. Year 4 provides experience in ambulatory care, neurology and a hospital-based subinternship. 4th year electives include overseas exchange programs, global health fellowships, and research. Many students do a tuition-free/fellowship supported fifth year to conduct year-long projects. Performance is graded as Pass/Fail in Years 1 and 2, and Honors, High Pass, Pass, and detailed narrative reports in Years 3 and 4.

## Selection Factors

In addition to the usual selection factors, attention is paid to community service, potential for professional achievement, motivation, and evidence of other personal qualities deemed essential for the study and practice of medicine. Einstein seeks traditional and non-traditional applicants who add diversity to the class and bring various perspectives to the study and practice of medicine. (Non-discrimination statement at: *www.einstein.yu.edu/admissions/page.aspx?id=568&ekmensel=15074e 5e_1106_1108_btnlink*).

## Information About Diversity Programs

The College of Medicine welcomes applications from students who are from groups underrepresented in medicine and/or who are economically disadvantaged. The College's Office of Diversity Enhancement provides opportunities for students to participate in special programs for high school and college students. Individual counseling is provided to students in need of long-term assistance to assure retention. The Office offers a summer research program to college students. Information on a summer research program can be obtained at (718) 430-3091.

## Regional/Satellite Campuses

The medical school is affiliated with six hospital centers. It is also affiliated with three mental health facilities and four long-term care facilities. Through its extensive affiliation network, Einstein runs one of the largest post-graduate medical training programs in the United States, offering some 150 residency programs to more than 2,500 physicians in training.

## Application Process and Requirements 2012–2013

**Primary application service:** AMCAS®
**Earliest filing date:** June 1, 2011
**Latest filing date:** November 1, 2011

**Secondary application required:** Yes
**Sent to:** All applicants
**Contact:** Office of Admissions, (718) 430-2106, admissions@einstein.yu.edu
**Fee:** Yes, $120.00    **Waiver available:** Yes
**Earliest filing date:** July 1, 2011
**Latest filing date:** February 15, 2012

**MCAT® required:** No
**Latest MCAT® considered:** September 2011
**Oldest MCAT® considered:** April 2008

**Early Decision Program:** School does have EDP
**Applicants notified:** October 1, 2012
**EDP available for:** Both In-State and Out-of-State Applicants

**Regular acceptance notice —**
**Earliest date:** January 15, 2012
**Latest date:** Until class is full
**Applicant's response to acceptance offer —**
**Maximum time:** Two weeks until May 1, 2012; one week thereafter

**Requests for deferred entrance considered:** Yes

**Deposit to hold place in class:** Yes
**Deposit — In-State Applicants:** $100
**Out-of-State Applicants:** $100
**Deposit due:** April 1, 2012
**Applied to tuition:** Yes
**Refundable:** Yes
**Refundable by:** June 1, 2012

**Estimated number of new entrants:** 183
**EDP:** 5, **Special Programs:** 3

**Start month/year:** August 2012

**Interview format:** One interview with a faculty member only. Regional interviews are not available. Video interviews are not available.

## Preparatory Programs

**Postbaccalaureate Program:** No

**Summer Program:** Yes, www.einstein.yu.edu/phd/index.asp?surp

## 2010–2011 First Year Class

|  | In-State | Out-of-State | International |
|---|---|---|---|
| Applications | 1,537 | 5,296 | 504 |
| Interviewed | 442 | 944 | 49 |
| Matriculated | 86 | 94 | 3 |

**Total Matriculants: 183**    **Total Enrollment: 780**

## Financial Information

|  | In-State | Out-of-State |
|---|---|---|
| Total Cost of Attendance | $66,251 | $66,251 |
| Tuition and Fees | $42,863 | $42,863 |
| Other (incl. living expenses) | $19,920 | $19,920 |
| Health Insurance (can be waived) | $3,468 | $3,468 |

**Average 2010 Graduate Indebtedness: $141,488**
**% of Enrolled Students Receiving Aid: 90%**

*Source: 2009-2010 LCME I-B survey and 2010-2011 AAMC TSF questionnaire*

# Columbia University
# College of Physicians and Surgeons

New York, New York

Columbia University
College of Physicians and Surgeons
Admissions Office, Room 1-416
630 West 168th Street
New York, New York 10032

**T** 212 305 3595  psadmissions@columbia.edu

**Admissions:** www.cumc.columbia.edu/dept/
ps/admissions

## General Information

The College of Physicians and Surgeons originated in 1767 as the Medical Faculty of King's College and was the first school to award an earned doctor of medicine degree in the American colonies. The college is part of the Columbia University Medical Center. Clinical teaching is provided at CUMC; Roosevelt-St. Luke's Hospital Center and Harlem Hospital Center in Manhattan; Bassett Hospital in Cooperstown, NY; and Stamford Hospital in Connecticut.

## Mission Statement

The mission of Columbia is to produce physicians who excel in both the science and art of medicine, and who will become leaders in their fields. It seeks to do this by providing an atmosphere that is collegial rather than competitive, and by offering students opportunities to express their interests in a wide variety of humanistic as well as scientific activities.

## Curricular Highlights

**Community Service Requirement:** Optional.

**Research/Thesis Requirement:** Required.

In the fall of 2009, P&S implemented a new curriculum. Hallmarks of the new curriculum include: emphasis on collaboration and teamwork; cultivation of a commitment to life-long inquiry; a self-directed, faculty mentored, in-depth scholarly project in an area of special interest to the student; and a longitudinal approach to content that will teach basic science, professionalism, public health and clinical medicine throughout the four years. The preclinical component of the curriculum is now eighteen months long, integrating basic and clinical sciences with progressive clinical skills building and patient responsibilities during the first semester. The major clinical year, divided into twelve week long blocks, will offer instruction in all areas of clinical medicine. Between blocks students will return to the campus for inter-sessions focused on topics relevant during clinical training. After the major clinical year students will have an additional fourteen months to explore their individual interests.

## Selection Factors

We seek applicants who have shown the greatest evidence of excellence and leadership potential in the science and art of medicine. Beyond academic ability, medicine also demands integrity, the ability to relate easily to others, and concern for their welfare. The school evaluates by several means: letters of recommendation, participation in extracurricular and summer activities, breadth of interests and undergraduate education, and the personal interview. Each year, some applicants are accepted who display extraordinary promise with regard to either the science or the art of medicine, even though they do not meet, in optimal measure, all of the criteria described above. CUMC seeks diversity of background among its applicants, geographical and otherwise; no preference is given to state of residence. Admission is possible for all qualified applicants regardless of sex, race, age, religion, sexual orientation, national origin, or handicap.

## Information about Diversity Programs

The College has a strong commitment to increase the numbers of medical students from groups underrepresented in medicine. There is a highly diverse student body and faculty. For additional information, call (212) 305-4157.

## Regional/Satellite Campuses

**Regional Campus Location(s):** Cooperstown, NY.

Students may train at some–or all–of P&S's affiliated hospitals in rural and urban settings. Columbia's Bassett track provides the first year and a half training in parallel with New York based students, and the next two and a half at a campus located in Cooperstown, NY. This program features education in an integrated health care system serving an extensive rural community.

## Application Process and Requirements 2012–2013

**Primary application service:** AMCAS®
**Earliest filing date:** June 1, 2011
**Latest filing date:** October 15, 2011

**Secondary application required:** Yes
**Sent to:** All applicants
**URL:** https://app.applyyourself.com/?id=COL-MED
**Fee:** Yes, $85  **Waiver available:** Yes
**Earliest filing date:** June 15, 2011
**Latest filing date:** November 15, 2011

**MCAT® required:** Yes
**Latest MCAT® considered:** September 2011
**Oldest MCAT® considered:** September 2009

**Early Decision Program:** School does not have EDP
**Applicants notified:** n/a
**EDP available for:** n/a

**Regular acceptance notice —**
**Earliest date:** March 1, 2012
**Latest date:** Varies
**Applicant's response to acceptance offer —**
**Maximum time:** Three weeks

**Requests for deferred entrance considered:** Yes

**Deposit to hold place in class:** No
**Deposit — In-State Applicants:** n/a
**Out-of-State Applicants:** n/a
**Deposit due:** n/a

**Estimated number of new entrants:** 153
**EDP:** n/a, **Special Programs:** 10

**Start month/year:** August 2012

**Interview format:** Monday through Friday, September through February. Regional interviews are not available. Video interviews are not available.

## Preparatory Programs

**Postbaccalaureate Program:** Yes,
www.columbia.edu/cu/gs/postbacc, (212) 854-2881,
pmaofficers@columbia.edu

**Summer Program:** Yes,
www.oda-ps.cumc.columbia.edu

## 2010–2011 First Year Class

|  | In-State | Out-of-State | International |
|---|---|---|---|
| Applications | 1109 | 5463 | 498 |
| Interviewed | 200 | 1053 | 51 |
| Matriculated | 38 | 120 | 8 |

**Total Matriculants: 166**     **Total Enrollment: 638**

## Financial Information

|  | In-State | Out-of-State |
|---|---|---|
| Total Cost of Attendance | $71,742 | $71,742 |
| Tuition and Fees | $47,862 | $47,862 |
| Other (incl. living expenses) | $20,780 | $20,780 |
| Health Insurance (can be waived) | $3,100 | $3,100 |

**Average 2010 Graduate Indebtedness: $117,544**
**% of Enrolled Students Receiving Aid: 84%**

Source: 2009-2010 LCME I-B survey and 2010-2011 AAMC TSF questionnaire

# Hofstra North Shore — LIJ School of Medicine at Hofstra University

Hempstead, New York

Hofstra University, Hempstead, New York 11549
**T** 516-463-7516   medicine@hofstra.edu
**Admissions:** http://medicine.hofstra.edu/admission/index.html

## General Information

Hofstra North Shore-LIJ School of Medicine at Hofstra University is ready to be a national leader in medical education. The goal of the educational program is to train physicians who earn the confidence of their patients and colleagues because of their scientifically anchored, team-based patient care; ability to make medical decisions despite uncertainty and with attention to the non-medical factors that affect health; and commitments to continual inquiry and learning, both critical skills in our discovery-filled world. The combination of the University's rich academic resources and growing national reputation with the exceptional clinical facilities of the Health System, now the second largest, non-profit, secular, integrated healthcare system in the United States, provides students with access to the continuum of healthcare delivery and to one of the most diverse patient populations in the country. Our 48,000 square foot Medical Education Center offers a full service café, 16 flexible learning areas, a 108-seat lecture hall, a dedicated medical education library, and a structure lab all equipped with the latest state-of-the-art technological tools. The Patient Safety Institute, part of our 45,000 square foot Center for Learning and Innovation, features a human simulation lab that includes PC-based interactive, virtual reality technology, digitally-enhanced mannequins. The Bioskills Education Center — a 6,200-square-foot state of-the-art training facility — brings the most advanced video and endoscopic surgical technologies to medical students, physicians and other healthcare professionals in support of their training, continuing medical education and research.

## Mission Statement

The School of Medicine, in a culture of community, scholarship, and innovation, is dedicated to inspiring diverse and promising students to lead and transform medicine for the betterment of humanity.

## Curricular Highlights

**Community Service Requirement:** Optional.

**Research/Thesis Requirement:** Optional.

The educational program is innovative and stresses translation of knowledge and understanding into action. Its goal is early transformation of students from medical bystanders and passive recipients of information into active participants and learners in meaningful patient encounters. Science and clinical medicine are wrapped together throughout all four year of the curriculum in an interactive format that emphasizes critical evaluation and application of basic and clinical scientific information to socially contextualized patient care, as well as direct assessment of the developmental growth of each student throughout the program. The first course, From the Person to the Professional: Challenges, Privileges and Responsibilities, is constructed upon the framework of the New York State Department of Health's Emergency Medical Technician's curriculum, which has been intentionally reshaped beyond its traditional learning methods to include more advanced scientific and clinical concepts and suit it well to its opening role in the curriculum.

## Selection Factors

Selection criteria include academic credentials; personal traits including character, motivation, capacity for work, experiences in the health sciences, human services, or community; career objectives; and the individual's ability to make a positive contribution to society, the profession, the discipline and the school. Specifically, the Admissions Committee considers, among other criteria: personal statement describing his/her personal, educational and social backgrounds; response to personal challenges; character traits including honesty, integrity, leadership, team work, empathy, maturity, emotional stability, creativity and self-direction; ability to communicate; perseverance through adversity; academic performance and GPA; rigor of undergraduate study, honors and awards, MCAT scores; extracurricular activities including community service, leadership roles and unique accomplishments; capacity to contribute diversity to the educational environment; employment and research experience; and a demonstrated commitment to a future career in medicine.

## Information about Diversity Programs

The School of Medicine's dedication to ensuring diversity among its student body is consistent with the university's commitment to developing a diverse and inclusive campus. Diversity is a central core value and consistent with the School of Medicine's mission statement. It is in the best interest of the community, as well as the educational environment of the School of Medicine, for the Admissions Committee to strive to select a class whose members represent a broad range of diverse experiences, backgrounds and interests.

## Application Process and Requirements 2012–2013

**Primary application service:** AMCAS®
**Earliest filing date:** July 1, 2011
**Latest filing date:** December 1, 2011

**Secondary application required:** Yes
**Sent to:** Applicants with a verified AMCAS® application
Contact: Office of Admissions, (516) 463-7516, medicine@Hofstra.edu
**Fee:** Yes, $100   **Waiver available:** Yes
**Earliest filing date:** July 2011
**Latest filing date:** December 31, 2011

**MCAT® required:** Yes
**Latest MCAT® considered:** September 2011
**Oldest MCAT® considered:** December 2008

**Early Decision Program:** School does not have EDP
**Applicants notified:** n/a
**EDP available for:** n/a

**Regular acceptance notice —**
**Earliest date:** Janurary 2012
**Latest date:** Until class is full
**Applicant's response to acceptance offer —**
**Maximum time:** Two weeks

**Requests for deferred entrance considered:** Yes

**Deposit to hold place in class:** Yes
**Deposit — In-State Applicants:** $100
**Out-of-State Applicants:** $100
**Deposit due:** Two weeks after acceptance
**Applied to tuition:** Yes
**Deposit refundable:** Yes
**Refundable by:** May 15, 2012

**Estimated number of new entrants:** 60
**EDP:** n/a, **Special Programs:** n/a

**Start month/year:** August 2012

**Interview format:** Two one-on-one interviews with members of our faculty. Regional interviews are not available. Video interviews are not available.

## Preparatory Programs

**Postbaccalaureate Program:** No

**Summer Program:** No

## 2010–2011 First Year Class

|  | In-State | Out-of-State | International |
| --- | --- | --- | --- |
| Applications | n/a | n/a | n/a |
| Interviewed | n/a | n/a | n/a |
| Matriculated | n/a | n/a | n/a |

**Total Matriculants: n/r**     **Total Enrollment: n/r**

## Financial Information*

|  | In-State | Out-of-State |
| --- | --- | --- |
| Total Cost of Attendance | $68,695 | $68,695 |
| Tuition and Fees | $43,500 | $43,500 |
| Other (incl. living expenses) | $21,255 | $21,255 |
| Health Insurance (can be waived) | $3,940 | $3,940 |

**Average 2010 Graduate Indebtedness: n/r**
**% of Enrolled Students Receiving Aid: n/r**
*Projected figures provided by medical school.*

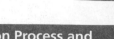

# Mount Sinai School of Medicine of New York University

New York, New York

Office of Admissions,
Mount Sinai School of Medicine
Annenberg Building, Room 5-04
One Gustave L. Levy Place – Box 1002
New York, New York 10029-6574

**T** 212 241 6696   admissions@mssm.edu

**Admissions:** www.mssm.edu/education/medical-education/programs/md-program/admissions

## General Information

The Mount Sinai Medical Center encompasses both The Mount Sinai Hospital and Mount Sinai School of Medicine. Established in 1968, Mount Sinai School of Medicine is one of few medical schools embedded in a hospital in the United States. It has more than 3,400 faculty in 32 departments and 15 institutes, and ranks among the top 20 medical schools in National Institute of Health funding. The school received the 2009 Spencer Foreman Award for Outstanding Community Service from the Association of American Medical Colleges.

## Mission Statement

The school is committed to serving science and society through outstanding research, education, patient care, and community service. We strive to develop new approaches to teaching, translate scientific discoveries into improvements in patient care, and identify new ways to enhance the health and educational opportunities of the communities we serve.

## Curricular Highlights

**Community Service Requirement:** Optional.

**Research/Thesis Requirement:** Optional.

Mount Sinai School of Medicine's curriculum is designed to teach a core knowledge of the biological basis of health and disease, skills in critical thinking, life-long learning skills, professional and humanistic attitudes, a scientific approach to medicine, and an appreciation of the physician's obligations to society and the community. The curriculum emphasizes the interdisciplinary nature of the basic and clinical sciences; it utilizes lectures and small group, case-based seminars, laboratory exercises and early clinical and longitudinal experiences. Courses are graded pass/fail during the first two years, and honors/high pass/pass/fail in the last two years.

## Selection Factors

Excellence in scholarship, personal maturity, integrity, intellectual creativity, and motivation for medicine are important factors. The interview, recommendations, and MCAT scores are criteria for evaluation. All applicants are considered, regardless of race, sex, color, creed, age, national origin, handicap, veteran status, marital status, or sexual orientation.

## Information about Diversity Programs

Strongly motivated students from groups underrepresented in medicine are actively sought and encouraged to apply. A pre-entrance summer enrichment program is available for students who are accepted to the first-year class. Tutorial assistance is available for all students. The school's Center for Multicultural and Community Affairs provides leadership and coordination for minority affairs activities, multicultural diversity program activities, a variety of enrichment programs, and advisory and career counseling services.

## Regional/Satellite Campuses

The main teaching site is the Mount Sinai Hospital, located on the main campus. Students also rotate to inpatient and ambulatory sites within a teaching consortium, among the largest in the country, which consists of outstanding public and private institutions in New York City and the suburbs of New Jersey.

## Application Process and Requirements 2012–2013

**Primary application service:** AMCAS®
**Earliest filing date:** June 1, 2011
**Latest filing date:** October 15, 2011

**Secondary application required:** Yes
**Sent to:** All applicants
**Contact:** (212) 241-6996, admissions@mssm.edu
**Fee:** Yes, $105   **Waiver available:** Yes
**Earliest filing date:** July 1, 2011
**Latest filing date:** December 1, 2011

**MCAT® required:** Yes
**Latest MCAT® considered:** September 2011
**Oldest MCAT® considered:** January 2009

**Early Decision Program:** School does not have EDP
**Applicants notified:** n/a
**EDP available for:** n/a

**Regular acceptance notice —**
**Earliest date:** November 1, 2011
**Latest date:** Until class is full
**Applicant's response to acceptance offer —**
**Maximum time:** Two weeks

**Requests for deferred entrance considered:** Yes

**Deposit to hold place in class:** No
**Deposit — In-State Applicants:** n/a
**Out-of-State Applicants:** n/a
**Deposit due:** n/a

**Estimated number of new entrants:** 128
**EDP:** 1, **Special Programs:** 12

**Start month/year:** August 15, 2012

**Interview format:** Two thirty-minute interviews
Regional interviews are not available. Video interviews are not available.

## Preparatory Programs

**Postbaccalaureate Program:** No

**Summer Program:** Yes,
grads@mssm.edu, (212) 241-6546

## 2010–2011 First Year Class

|  | In-State | Out-of-State | International |
|---|---|---|---|
| Applications | 1,403 | 4,524 | 379 |
| Interviewed | 195 | 552 | 36 |
| Matriculated | 41 | 94 | 6 |

**Total Matriculants: 141**    **Total Enrollment: 588**

## Financial Information

|  | In-State | Out-of-State |
|---|---|---|
| Total Cost of Attendance | $61,107 | $61,107 |
| Tuition and Fees | $39,726 | $39,726 |
| Other (incl. living expenses) | $18,225 | $18,225 |
| Health Insurance (can be waived) | $3,156 | $3,156 |

**Average 2010 Graduate Indebtedness: $124,846**
**% of Enrolled Students Receiving Aid: 72%**

Source: 2009-2010 LCME I-B survey and 2010-2011 AAMC TSF questionnaire

# New York Medical College
## Valhalla, New York

Office of Admissions
Administration Building
New York Medical College
Valhalla, New York 10595

**T** 914 594 4507    mdadmit@nymc.edu

**Admissions:** www.nymc.edu/admit/medical/info/index.asp

## General Information

Founded in 1860, New York Medical College is located in suburban Westchester County, 25 miles from New York City. The university educates students for careers in medicine, biomedical science, and the health professions through its School of Medicine, Graduate School of Basic Medical Sciences, and School of Public Health.

## Mission Statement

New York Medical College is a health sciences university whose purpose is to educate physicians, scientists, public health specialists, and other healthcare professionals, and to conduct biomedical and population-based research. Through its faculty and affiliated clinical partners, the College provides service to its community in an atmosphere of excellence, scholarship and professionalism. New York Medical College believes that the rich diversity of its student body and faculty is important to its mission of educating outstanding health care professionals for the multicultural world of the 21st century.

## Curricular Highlights

**Community Service Requirement:** Optional.

**Research/Thesis Requirement:** Optional.

NYMC's goal is to provide a general professional education that prepares students for all career options in medicine. There is emphasis on critical thinking, evidence-based decision making, and cultural humility throughout the curriculum. Clinical exposure begins in the first year with a longitudinal assignment to a primary care physician where students focus on communication skills, history-taking, and preventive medicine. In addition to traditional lectures and laboratory exercises, basic science courses utilize self directed study, small group discussion, computer assisted instruction, and problem-based learning. Clerkships in seven disciplines at a wide variety of hospitals and community-based clinical settings comprise the third year. In the required fourth year sub-internships, students are expected to function at the level of a beginning resident in required rotations and electives at medical institutions around the country and the world. Highlights of the curriculum include an optional Summer Research Fellowship Program between the first and second years; exposure to medical informatics; an integrated curriculum in biomedical ethics; rigorous sub-internships in Medicine or Pediatrics; palliative care components in the medicine clerkship; and a required fourth year rotation in Geriatric Medicine or Chronic Care Pediatrics.

## Selection Factors

The Admissions Committee selects students after considering factors of intellect, character, and personality pointing toward their ability to become informed and caring physicians. A history of academic excellence is essential. Undergraduate major is not a factor in selection. Clear evidence of a strong motivation toward medicine and a sense of dedication to the service of others is encouraged. Qualities of character and personality are evaluated from letters of evaluation, personal statements, and the interview. The school does not deny admission to any applicant on the basis of any legally prohibited discrimination involving, but not limited to, such factors as race, color, creed, religion, national or ethnic origin, age, sex, sexual orientation, or disability.

## Information about Diversity Programs

New York Medical College seeks to admit a diverse class, including diversity of gender, race, ethnicity, cultural and economic background, and life experience. A diverse student body provides a valuable educational experience that prepares medical students for the real world of medical practice in a multicultural society.

## Regional/Satellite Campuses

New York Medical College's wide range of affiliated hospitals, including large urban medical centers, small suburban hospitals, and technologically advanced regional tertiary care facilities, provide extensive resources and educational opportunities.

## Application Process and Requirements 2012–2013

**Primary application service:** AMCAS®
**Earliest filing date:** June 1, 2011
**Latest filing date:** December 15, 2011

**Secondary application required:** Yes
**Sent to:** All applicants
**URL:** www.nymc.edu/medadmission/Instructions.html
**Fee:** Yes, $105    **Waiver available:** Yes
**Earliest filing date:** July 1, 2011
**Latest filing date:** January 31, 2012

**MCAT® required:** Yes
**Latest MCAT® considered:** September 2011
**Oldest MCAT® considered:** April 2009

**Early Decision Program:** School does have EDP
**Applicants notified:** October 1, 2011
**EDP available for:** Both In-State and Out-of-State Applicants

**Regular acceptance notice —**
**Earliest date:** November 15, 2011
**Latest date:** Until class is full
**Applicant's response to acceptance offer —**
**Maximum time:** Two weeks

**Requests for deferred entrance considered:** Yes

**Deposit to hold place in class:** Yes
**Deposit — In-State Applicants:** $100
**Out-of-State Applicants:** $100
**Deposit due:** By May 15, 2012
**Applied to tuition:** Yes
**Deposit refundable:** Yes
**Refundable by:** May 15, 2012

**Estimated number of new entrants:** 190
**EDP:** 2, **Special Programs:** n/a

**Start month/year:** August 2012

**Interview format:** One-on-one blind and minimally structured interviews. Regional interviews are not available. Video interviews are not available.

### Preparatory Programs

**Postbaccalaureate Program:** Yes, www.nymc.edu/gsbms/interdisciplinary.asp

**Summer Program:** No

## 2010–2011 First Year Class

|  | In-State | Out-of-State | International |
|---|---|---|---|
| Applications | 1,878 | 8,935 | 531 |
| Interviewed | 381 | 1,027 | 30 |
| Matriculated | 66 | 124 | 4 |

**Total Matriculants: 194**    **Total Enrollment: 790**

## Financial Information

|  | In-State | Out-of-State |
|---|---|---|
| Total Cost of Attendance | $70,248 | $70,248 |
| Tuition and Fees | $46,406 | $46,406 |
| Other (incl. living expenses) | $20,066 | $20,066 |
| Health Insurance (can be waived) | $3,776 | $3,776 |

**Average 2010 Graduate Indebtedness: $181,055**
**% of Enrolled Students Receiving Aid: 86%**

*Source: 2009-2010 LCME I-B survey and 2010-2011 AAMC TSF questionnaire*

# New York University
# School of Medicine
## New York, New York

New York University School of Medicine
Office of Admissions
550 First Avenue
New York, New York 10016

**T** 212 263 5290  admissions@nyumc.org

**Admissions:** http://admissions.med.nyu.edu/

## General Information

Founded in 1841, NYU School of Medicine is one of the nation's preeminent academic institutions. For over 150 years, NYU has trained thousands of physician-scientists who have enriched countless lives and helped shape medical history. Through scientific research, medical education, and patient care, NYU continues its deep, abiding commitment to improve the human condition. NYU is among the nation's leaders in consistently producing physician graduates who go on to become full-time members of medical school faculties. Students train at Bellevue, the nation's first hospital. NYU is a "private university in the public service." The School of Medicine combines the best of modern biomedical science with a rich tradition of caring for all populations at the highest level of human achievement.

## Mission Statement

NYU has a threefold mission: the education and training of physicians and scientists, the search for new knowledge, and the care of the sick. The three are inseparable. Medicine can be handed on to succeeding generations only by long training in the scientific method of investigation and by the actual care of patients. Progress in medicine, which is medical research, must look constantly to the school for its investigators, and to the patient for its problems, whereas the whole future of medical care rests upon a continuing supply of physicians and upon the promise of new discovery. The purpose, then, can only be achieved by endeavor in all three directions — medical education, research, and patient care — and they must be carried on simultaneously, for they are wholly dependent upon each other, not only for inspiration, but also for their very means of success.

## Curricular Highlights

**Community Service Requirement:** Optional. Most students participate in community service.

**Research/Thesis Requirement:** Optional. M.D. with honors given upon completion.

The aim of NYU's new Curriculum for the 21st Century (C21) is to create physician-scholars who have been taught, trained, and mentored within an innovative and comprehensive four-stage patient-centered, disease-focused environment. From groundwork human biology through medical major or concentration, the education process is based on a spiral curriculum, or pillars, where learning wraps around and builds upon specific content areas of medicine. The educational experience encompasses a formal required curriculum supplemented by electives, selectives and enrichment experiences, and a program of academic and career mentoring. This curriculum provides flexibility that will allow students to choose areas of concentration and customize their educational experience. NYU's teaching hospitals provide the diversity of patient population that allows students an extraordinary opportunity to develop adaptability, cultural-awareness, and excellence in their communication, diagnostic, and interpersonal skills. At every stage, the curriculum is enhanced and supported by cutting-edge medical and informational technology.

## Selection Factors

Applicants are considered from several viewpoints: excellence in coursework, trends in college progress, the MCAT, premedical committee evaluation, and the interview. Volunteer activities, independent research, and accomplishments in the humanities and liberal arts fields are also strongly considered. Only international applicants who hold a permanent resident visa will be considered for admission.

## Information about Diversity Programs

The School of Medicine is committed to admitting a diverse class. The Office of Diversity Affairs and Advisory Council has established programs and services to meet the academic, educational, personal, and cultural needs of students from groups underrepresented in medicine. See: *http://diversity.med. nyu.edu/*.

## Application Process and Requirements 2012–2013

**Primary application service:** AMCAS®
**Earliest filing date:** June 1, 2011
**Latest filing date:** October 15, 2011

**Secondary application required:** Yes
**Sent to:** All applicants
**URL:** http://admissions.med.nyu.edu/how-apply
**Fee:** Yes, $100   **Waiver available:** Yes
**Earliest filing date:** July 1, 2011
**Latest filing date:** December 1, 2011

**MCAT® required:** Yes
**Latest MCAT® considered:** September 2011
**Oldest MCAT® considered:** January 2009

**Early Decision Program:** School does not have EDP
**Applicants notified:** n/a
**EDP available for:** n/a

**Regular acceptance notice —**
**Earliest date:** November 15, 2011
**Latest date:** Until class is full
**Applicant's response to acceptance offer —**
**Maximum time:** Two weeks

**Requests for deferred entrance considered:** Yes

**Deposit to hold place in class:** Yes
**Deposit — In-State Applicants:** $100
**Out-of-State Applicants:** $100
**Deposit due:** With response to acceptance offer
**Applied to tuition:** Yes
**Deposit refundable:** Yes
**Refundable by:** May 15, 2012

**Estimated number of new entrants:** 166
**EDP:** 0, **Special Programs:** n/a

**Start month/year:** August 2012

**Interview format:** One-on-one interview with a faculty member. Regional interviews are not available. Video interviews are not available.

## Preparatory Programs

**Postbaccalaureate Program:** Yes,
www.nyu.edu/cas/prehealth/postbacc/index.html

**Summer Program:** Yes,
www.med.nyu.edu/sackler/programs/summer.html

## 2010–2011 First Year Class

|  | In-State | Out-of-State | International |
|---|---|---|---|
| Applications | 1,382 | 5,594 | 265 |
| Interviewed | 212 | 720 | 24 |
| Matriculated | 47 | 115 | 0 |

**Total Matriculants: 162    Total Enrollment: 736**

## Financial Information

|  | In-State | Out-of-State |
|---|---|---|
| Total Cost of Attendance | $68,929 | $68,929 |
| Tuition and Fees | $46,778 | $46,778 |
| Other (incl. living expenses) | $17,800 | $17,800 |
| Health Insurance (can be waived) | $4,351 | $4,351 |

**Average 2010 Graduate Indebtedness: $176,194**
**% of Enrolled Students Receiving Aid: 81%**

*Source: 2009-2010 LCME I-B survey and 2010-2011 AAMC TSF questionnaire*

# State University of New York Downstate Medical Center College of Medicine

## New York, New York

Admissions Office, State University of New York
Downstate Medical Center
450 Clarkson Avenue — Box 60
Brooklyn, New York 11203-2098
**T** 718 270 2446    admissions@downstate.edu
**Admissions:** http://sls.downstate.edu/admissions/
medicine/index.html

## General Information
Current information about the college, curriculum, and admissions is available on the Web site at *www.downstate.edu.*

## Mission Statement
To provide high quality education for the next generation of health professionals. Integral to our concept of professional education are both a commitment to confront the health problems of urban communities and a responsibility to advance the state of knowledge and practice in the health disciplines through basic and applied clinical research.

## Curricular Highlights
**Community Service Requirement:** Strongly recommended.

**Research/Thesis Requirement:** Optional.

Beginning with the class entering in 2012, SUNY Downstate will launch an innovative, new curriculum that will prepare our graduates to practice medicine in a changing medical and social environment. The competency based curriculum will feature the three principles of Integration, Collaboration, and Relevance. Biomedical and clinical science will be integrated throughout the four years of the curriculum. This new curriculum takes advantage of the latest knowledge about how adults learn and is designed to inspire students to develop life-long learning skills essential to being an excellent physician. It fosters the team-based approach that is an essential element of medicine today. Other features include early clinical exposure starting in the first year, a longitudinal patient experience, starting clinical clerkships earlier to allow more time for medical specialty career exploration, as well as a robust advanced clinical year (senior year) to best prepare our graduates for residency.

## Selection Factors
The Committee on Admissions considers the total qualifications of each applicant without regard to sex, sexual orientation, race, color, creed, religion, national origin, age, marital status, or disability. Decisions are based on multiple factors, including, but not limited to, prior academic performance; completion of required courses for admission; potential for academic success, including performance on the MCAT; communication skills, interpersonal skills, experiences in a healthcare setting, motivation for medicine, and evidence of altruism.

## Information about Diversity Programs
SUNY Downstate is committed to the enrollment of students from groups underrepresented in medicine. The Office of Minority Affairs directs several programs to furnish information and support to students from underrepresented and disadvantaged backgrounds. Entering students from groups underrepresented in medicine may be matched with a faculty mentor. The Daniel Hale Williams Society also provides peer support for underrepresented students. Contact the Office of Minority Affairs at *oma@downstate.edu.*

## Application Process and Requirements 2012–2013

**Primary application service:** AMCAS®
**Earliest filing date:** June 1, 2011
**Latest filing date:** December 15, 2011

**Secondary application required:** Yes
**Sent to:** All applicants – download from website
**URL:** http://sls.downstate.edu/admissions/
medicine/programs/procedures/index.html
**Fee:** Yes, $80   **Waiver available:** Yes
**Earliest filing date:** June 1, 2011
**Latest filing date:** February 1, 2012

**MCAT® required:** Yes
**Latest MCAT® considered:** September 2011
**Oldest MCAT® considered:** August 2009

**Early Decision Program:** School does have EDP
**Applicants notified:** October 1, 2011
**EDP available for:** Both In-State and Out-of-State Applicants

**Regular acceptance notice —**
**Earliest date:** October 15, 2011
**Latest date:** Until class is full
**Applicant's response to acceptance offer —**
**Maximum time:** Two weeks

**Requests for deferred entrance considered:** Yes

**Deposit to hold place in class:** Yes
**Deposit — In-State Applicants:** $100
**Out-of-State Applicants:** $100
**Deposit due:** Between May 1-15, 2012
**Applied to tuition:** Yes
**Deposit refundable:** Yes
**Refundable by:** May 15, 2012

**Estimated number of new entrants:** 185
**EDP:** 5, **Special Programs:** 10

**Start month/year:** August 2012

**Interview format:** One-on-one, about one hour in length. Regional interviews are not available. Video interviews are not available.

### Preparatory Programs
**Postbaccalaureate Program:** No

**Summer Program:** n/a

## 2010–2011 First Year Class

|  | In-State | Out-of-State | International |
|---|---|---|---|
| Applications | 2,268 | 2,998 | 85 |
| Interviewed | 726 | 418 | 0 |
| Matriculated | 140 | 43 | 0 |

| **Total Matriculants: 183** | **Total Enrollment: 789** |
|---|---|

## Financial Information

|  | In-State | Out-of-State |
|---|---|---|
| Total Cost of Attendance | $49,174 | $73,094 |
| Tuition and Fees | $25,422 | $49,342 |
| Other (incl. living expenses) | $20,320 | $20,320 |
| Health Insurance (can be waived) | $3,432 | $3,432 |

**Average 2010 Graduate Indebtedness: $125,265**
**% of Enrolled Students Receiving Aid: 91%**

*Source: 2009-2010 LCME I-B survey and 2010-2011 AAMC TSF questionnaire*

# State University of New York
# Upstate Medical Center
# College of Medicine
## Syracuse, New York

Admissions Office
SUNY Upstate Medical University
766 Irving Avenue.
Syracuse, New York 13210

**T** 315 464 4570   admiss@upstate.edu

**Admissions:** www.upstate.edu/com/admissions/

## General Information

The College of Medicine was established in 1834 as the Geneva Medical College. The college was transferred to the State University of New York (SUNY) system in 1950. In 1999, its name changed to SUNY Upstate Medical University to best reflect the college's academic mission in medical care, research, and education.

## Mission Statement

The main mission of SUNY Upstate is the education of health professionals and to conduct biomedical research. Upstate's clinical faculty and health care professionals commit themselves to education and patient care, demonstrating excellence and compassion. In pursuing its mission, Upstate provides its faculty, staff, students, and volunteers an environment of mutual trust and respect, with opportunities to grow personally and professionally, and to make a positive difference in the lives of others.

## Curricular Highlights

**Community Service Requirement:** Optional.

**Research/Thesis Requirement:** Optional.

The curriculum integrates the basic and clinical sciences and provides clinical exposure in the first semester. All courses are aligned by organ systems. The curriculum also addresses the humanistic aspects of medicine, including its ethical, legal, and social implications. During the third year, the students apply the principles of basic science to clinical problem-solving. Clerkships in subspecialty services are required. A research track is available, in which students spend the first two summers and elective time on a research project. Another interesting opportunity is the Rural Medical Education Program, which places students in rural communities for nine consecutive months of clinical and didactic education during the 3rd and 4th year. A modified pass/fail grading system is used.

## Selection Factors

The Admissions Committee takes an applicant's total qualifications into consideration for the study and practice of medicine. Major factors in the selection of applicants include: review of college records, MCAT scores, letters of recommendation from premedical advisory committees, personal interview, communication skills, character, and motivation.

## Information about Diversity Programs

Upstate is committed to making student enrollment reflective of the diverse New York State population. Disadvantaged students and students from groups underrepresented in medicine are actively sought. A summer Human Anatomy program is available for all students. For more information, please contact the Office of Admissions.

## Regional/Satellite Campuses

**Regional Campus Location(s):** Binghamton, NY.

At the beginning of the third year, one quarter of the class moves from SUNY Upstate's main campus in Syracuse to the Binghamton Campus. The Binghamton Campus is located 70 miles south of Syracuse. There, clinical training occurs in a community-based setting similar to the environment in which most physicians practice.

## Application Process and Requirements 2012–2013

**Primary application service:** AMCAS®
**Earliest filing date:** June 1, 2011
**Latest filing date:** October 15, 2011

**Secondary application required:** Yes
**Sent to:** All verified AMCAS® applicants.
**URL:** n/a
**Fee:** Yes, $100   **Waiver available:** Yes
**Earliest filing date:** Upon receipt of verified AMCAS® application.
**Latest filing date:** December 1, 2011

**MCAT® required:** Yes
**Latest MCAT® considered:** September 2011
**Oldest MCAT® considered:** September 2008

**Early Decision Program:** School does have EDP
**Applicants notified:** October 1, 2011
**EDP available for:** Both In-State and Out-of-State Applicants

**Regular acceptance notice —**
**Earliest date:** October 15, 2011
**Latest date:** Until class is full
**Applicant's response to acceptance offer —**
**Maximum time:** Two weeks

**Requests for deferred entrance considered:** Yes

**Deposit to hold place in class:** Yes
**Deposit — In-State Applicants:** $100
**Out-of-State Applicants:** $100
**Deposit due:** With response to acceptance offer
**Applied to tuition:** Yes
**Refundable:** Yes
**Refundable by:** May 15, 2012

**Estimated number of new entrants:** 160
**EDP:** 2, **Special Programs:** 15

**Start month/year:** August 2012

**Interview format:** On campus with two individual interviewers. Regional interviews are not available. Video interviews are not available.

## Preparatory Programs
**Postbaccalaureate Program:** No

**Summer Program:** Yes,
Jennifer Welch, (315) 464-4570, admiss@upstate.edu

## 2010–2011 First Year Class

|  | In-State | Out-of-State | International |
|---|---|---|---|
| Applications | 1,941 | 2,523 | 439 |
| Interviewed | 570 | 157 | 19 |
| Matriculated | 131 | 22 | 8 |

**Total Matriculants: 161**      **Total Enrollment: 680**

## Financial Information

|  | In-State | Out-of-State |
|---|---|---|
| Total Cost of Attendance | $46,970 | $70,890 |
| Tuition and Fees | $26,190 | $50,110 |
| Other (incl. living expenses) | $17,542 | $17,542 |
| Health Insurance (can be waived) | $3,238 | $3,238 |

**Average 2010 Graduate Indebtedness: $139,600**
**% of Enrolled Students Receiving Aid: 82%**

Source: 2009-2010 LCME I-B survey and 2010-2011 AAMC TSF questionnaire

# Stony Brook University School of Medicine

## Stony Brook, New York

Committee on Admissions
Level 4 Health Sciences Center
Stony Brook University School of Medicine
Stony Brook, New York 11794-8434

**T** 631 444 2113   somadmissions@stonybrook.edu

**Admissions:** www.stonybrookmedicalcenter.org/
som/admissions

## General Information

Stony Brook University's School of Medicine accepted its first class in 1971. It is part of the Stony Brook University Medical Center, which includes the 540-bed University Hospital.

## Mission Statement

The School of Medicine strives to improve the quality of health care by demonstrating national leadership in education, research, patient care, and community service. The School of Medicine prepares its students for careers in medical practice or research through its state-of-the-art curriculum and clinical and research opportunities.

## Curricular Highlights

**Community Service Requirement:** Optional.

**Research/Thesis Requirement:** Optional.

The curriculum of the School of Medicine provides the opportunity for extensive training in the basic medical sciences and teaching in the clinical disciplines of medicine. The curriculum requires the acquisition and utilization of a variety of skills in basic and clinical sciences. The official grading system is honors/pass/fail. The first two years are devoted to basic sciences and the integrated Foundations of Medicine course. The Foundations course teaches medical ethics, patient assessment skills, preventive medicine, human behavior, and nutrition. The second year focuses on an organ system-based pathophysiology and therapeutics course. Third year students complete core clerkships in medicine, pediatrics, family medicine, obstetrics-gynecology, psychiatry, ambulatory medicine and surgery. One month of elective time is available. Fourth year students are offered selectives and electives. Core clerkships are completed at University Hospital or one of five teaching affiliates. Electives can be completed at other sites.

## Selection Factors

Grades, MCAT scores, letters of evaluation, and extracurricular and work experiences are carefully examined. Motivational and personal characteristics as indicated in the application and a personal interview are also a major part of the admissions assessment. There is no discrimination in the admissions process on the basis of race, color, sex, age, ethnicity, religion, national origin, sexual orientation, disability, marital status, or veterans' status. The school attempts to enroll a class representative of a variety of backgrounds and academic interests. Stony Brook hopes to attract a significant representation of persons from groups that have historically been underrepresented in medicine. The School of Medicine adheres to the AAMC definition of underrepresented in medicine: "Underrepresented in medicine means those racial and ethnic populations that are underrepresented in the medical profession relative to their numbers in the general population." Premedical coursework must be completed at an American college or university. While residents of New York constitute the majority of the applicants and entrants, out-of-state applicants are given due consideration. Required supporting documentation includes official transcripts of all college work and official letters of evaluation. Personal interviews will be arranged at the initiative of the school for candidates who appear to be serious contenders for admission. Stony Brook does not utilize a "cut-off" in grades or MCAT scores in making admission decisions. The school is committed to giving all applicants the individualized attention that they merit.

## Information about Diversity Programs

Stony Brook is committed to admitting a diverse class each year. The school makes a concerted effort to enroll qualified students from groups underrepresented in medicine.

## Application Process and Requirements 2012–2013

**Primary application service:** AMCAS®
**Earliest filing date:** June 1, 2011
**Latest filing date:** December 15, 2011

**Secondary application required:** Yes
**Sent to:** All applicants
**URL:** ww.stonybrookmedicalcenter.org/som/admissions
**Fee:** Yes, $100    **Waiver available:** Yes
**Earliest filing date:** July 1, 2011
**Latest filing date:** December 30, 2011

**MCAT® required:** Yes
**Latest MCAT® considered:** September 2011
**Oldest MCAT® considered:** 2007

**Early Decision Program:** School does have EDP
**Applicants notified:** October 1, 2011
**EDP available for:** Both In-State and Out-of-State Applicants

**Regular acceptance notice —**
**Earliest date:** October 15, 2011
**Latest date:** Until class is full

**Applicant's response to acceptance offer —**
**Maximum time:** 15 days, unless otherwise specified

**Requests for deferred entrance considered:** Yes

**Deposit to hold place in class:** Yes
**Deposit — In-State Applicants:** $100
**Out-of-State Applicants:** $100 **Deposit due:** With response to acceptance offer
**Applied to tuition:** Yes
**Refundable:** Yes
**Refundable by:** May 15, 2012

**Estimated number of new entrants:** 124
**EDP:** 2, **Special Programs:** 8

**Start month/year:** August 2012

**Interview format:** Two individual interviews with admission committee members. Regional interviews are not available. Video interviews are not available.

## Preparatory Programs

**Postbaccalaureate Program:** Yes, www.amsny.org/site/content/diversity/post-baccalaureate-programs

**Summer Program:** No

## 2010–2011 First Year Class

|  | In-State | Out-of-State | International |
|---|---|---|---|
| Applications | 2,162 | 1,896 | 168 |
| Interviewed | 500 | 167 | 0 |
| Matriculated | 95 | 29 | 0 |

**Total Matriculants: 124**    **Total Enrollment: 506**

## Financial Information

|  | In-State | Out-of-State |
|---|---|---|
| Total Cost of Attendance | $48,255 | $72,175 |
| Tuition and Fees | $26,159 | $50,079 |
| Other (incl. living expenses) | $20,910 | $20,910 |
| Health Insurance (can be waived) | $1,186 | $1,186 |

**Average 2010 Graduate Indebtedness: $122,783**
**% of Enrolled Students Receiving Aid: 85%**

Source: 2009-2010 LCME I-B survey and 2010-2011 AAMC TSF questionnaire

# University at Buffalo School of Medicine and Biomedical Sciences

Buffalo, New York

Office of Medical Admissions
University at Buffalo
131 Biomedical Education Building
Buffalo, New York 14214-3013

**T** 716 829 3466    jjrosso@buffalo.edu

**Admissions:** www.smbs.buffalo.edu/ome/ome_admission.htm

## General Information

The School of Medicine was founded in 1846 by Millard Fillmore and a group of physicians. In 1962, the University of Buffalo joined the State University of New York (SUNY) system. The University at Buffalo has the most comprehensive campus in the SUNY system and was honored in 1989 with election to the Association of American Universities. The clinical education program is conducted in cooperation with nine area hospitals.

## Mission Statement

To provide well-trained physicians and other health care professionals who will attend to the health needs of citizens. To offer a source of continuing education to the community of health care providers. To provide a center of research and scholarship that will advance and promote health-related services. As a public institution, the mission places particular emphasis on diversity, inclusion, and the special needs of New York State, such as minority recruitment and retention, and the underserved urban and rural health populations.

## Curricular Highlights

**Community Service Requirement:** Optional.

**Research/Thesis Requirement:** Optional.

The curriculum emphasizes the relevance of medical education to the practice of medicine and the relevance of basic science to clinical practice. It introduces patient contact and patient-centered learning in the first year of medical school, and it increases ambulatory care experiences in the clinical years. The first two years contain an integrated curriculum that includes the Introduction to Clinical Medicine course continuum, which prepares students in the knowledge, skills, and attitudes required for third-year clinical clerkships and provides the foundation for a medical career. Ethics, the doctor-patient relationship, principles of health promotion, disease prevention, and promotion of self-learning and inquiry are emphasized, in addition to extensive education in the skills basic to medical practice and patient care. The clinical years include required clerkships and electives. There is ample time for additional electives during the senior year.

## Selection Factors

The Admissions Committee seeks to identify and select students who display favorable qualities deemed important for the pursuit of a career in medicine. In making its assessments and determinations, the committee relies on information contained in the application and in documents submitted in support of the applicant. Based on careful screening, applicants are invited to appear for an interview. Reapplications are treated no differently than initial applications. Rejected applicants should seek the advice and counsel of their premedical advisor. Students are accepted without regard to race, sex, creed, national origin, age, sexual preference, or handicap. All applicants will receive the "Technical Standards of the Medical School Curriculum" with the secondary application. Some preference is given to qualified residents of New York State. Competitive out-of-state applicants are encouraged to apply.

## Information about Diversity Programs

The Summer Enrichment and Support Program helps facilitate students' retention in medical school. It is designed for admitted first-year educationally and socioeconomically disadvantaged students. Tutorial and counseling services are available throughout the summer and academic year.

## Regional/Satellite Campuses

Student rotations are divided among nine teaching hospitals and several clinics in the metro Buffalo area. The medical school is also affiliated with ambulatory care centers in outlying suburban areas.

## Application Process and Requirements 2012–2013

**Primary application service:** AMCAS®
**Earliest filing date:** June 1, 2011
**Latest filing date:** November 15, 2011

**Secondary application required:** Yes
**Sent to:** All applicants
**Contact:** James J. Rosso, (716) 829-3466, jjrosso@buffalo.edu
**Fee:** Yes, $65    **Waiver available:** Yes
**Earliest filing date:** June 1, 2011
**Latest filing date:** December 15, 2011

**MCAT® required:** Yes
**Latest MCAT® considered:** September 2011
**Oldest MCAT® considered:** January 2008

**Early Decision Program:** School does have EDP
**Applicants notified:** October 1, 2011
**EDP available for:** Both In-State and Out-of-State Applicants

**Regular acceptance notice —**
**Earliest date:** October 15, 2011
**Latest date:** Until class is full
**Applicant's response to acceptance offer —**
**Maximum time:** Two weeks
**Requests for deferred entrance considered:** Yes

**Deposit to hold place in class:** Yes
**Deposit — In-State Applicants:** $100
**Out-of-State Applicants:** $100
**Deposit due:** With response to acceptance offer
**Applied to tuition:** Yes
**Refundable:** Yes
**Refundable by:** May 15, 2012

**Estimated number of new entrants:** 140
**EDP:** 3, **Special Programs:** 4

**Start month/year:** August 2012

**Interview format:** Two, one-on-one interviews. Regional interviews are not available. Video interviews are not available.

## Preparatory Programs

**Postbaccalaureate Program:** Yes

**Summer Program:** No

## 2010–2011 First Year Class

|  | In-State | Out-of-State | International |
|---|---|---|---|
| Applications | 1,854 | 2,397 | 78 |
| Interviewed | 429 | 216 | 0 |
| Matriculated | 105 | 39 | 0 |

**Total Matriculants: 144        Total Enrollment: 575**

## Financial Information

|  | In-State | Out-of-State |
|---|---|---|
| Total Cost of Attendance | $49,010 | $66,850 |
| Tuition and Fees | $24,427 | $42,267 |
| Other (incl. living expenses) | $22,703 | $22,703 |
| Health Insurance (can be waived) | $1,880 | $1,880 |

**Average 2010 Graduate Indebtedness: $130,531**
**% of Enrolled Students Receiving Aid: 84%**

Source: 2009-2010 LCME I-B survey and 2010-2011 AAMC TSF questionnaire

# University of Rochester
# School of Medicine and Dentistry
## Rochester, New York

Director of Admissions, University of Rochester
School of Medicine and Dentistry
601 Elmwood Avenue, Box 601A
Rochester, New York 14642

**T** 585 275 4539   mdadmish@urmc.rochester.edu

**Admissions:** www.urmc.rochester.edu/education/
md/admissions

## General Information

The School of Medicine and Dentistry is an academic division of the University of Rochester, a privately endowed institution founded in 1850. The Medical Center includes the School of Medicine and Dentistry, School of Nursing, Eastman Dental Center, James P. Wilmot Cancer Center, Strong Memorial Hospital, Golisano Children's Hospital at Strong and Highland Hospital.

## Mission Statement

The University of Rochester Medical Center is dedicated to training future physicians/scientists/ humanists who excel and become leaders in their professions. Rochester is committed to health improvement through leadership, innovation, education and research that leads to enhanced patient care. As home of the biopsychosocial model, Rochester combines evidence-based medical science with the relationship-centered art of medicine. Our student body is diverse and reflects the diversity of the patient population that characterizes America. The School is committed to respect for the individual, and values community involvement and collegiality, both within the medical profession and across all health professions.

## Curricular Highlights

**Community Service Requirement:** Required. Community Health Improvement Clerkship.

**Research/Thesis Requirement:** Optional. Graduate with "Distinction in Research" honors.

Rochester's Double Helix Curriculum is a hybrid PBL curriculum that captures the integrated strands of basic science and clinical medicine as they are woven throughout the four-year curriculum. Our focus is not merely on the transfer of information, but the transformation of the learner in a culture providing that ingenious combination of support and challenge, which leads to education. Courses are interdisciplinary and clinical exposure begins during the first week of school with an introduction to clinical medicine and the start of the ambulatory Primary Care Clerkship during the first spring semester. The School provides a supportive, challenging environment designed to foster collaboration rather than competition. Emphasis is placed on active student-centered learning and curriculum management based on competencies, learning objectives, and outcomes. All courses except the required clinical clerkships are graded Pass/Fail. Clerkships are graded Honors/High Pass/Pass/Fail.

## Selection Factors

Evaluation of applicants includes a careful examination of the entire academic record, letters of recommendation, and the candidate's personal statement. Demonstrated excellence in a demanding academic program is expected and evidence of intrinsic intellectual drive and curiosity is highly valued. Attention is given to achievements that demonstrate breadth and commitment in areas of research, community outreach, and clinical experience. Students interested in academic medicine, serving the underserved, and global medicine are especially encouraged to apply.

## Information about Diversity Programs

The Center for Advocacy, Community Health, Education and Diversity represents a serious commitment on the part of the School of Medicine and Dentistry to meet the urgent need for diverse physicians in all aspects of the medical profession. Rochester believes that a diverse class enriches the educational environment for all of its students. The office also coordinates numerous academic and cultural events for the education of all students.

## Regional/Satellite Campuses

Students also rotate through community and private ambulatory clinics.

## Application Process and Requirements 2012–2013

**Primary application service:** AMCAS®
**Earliest filing date:** June 1, 2011
**Latest filing date:** October 15, 2011

**Secondary application required:** Yes
**Sent to:** All applicants
**URL:** www.urmc.rochester.edu/education/md/
admissions/
**Fee:** Yes, $85   **Waiver available:** Yes, (AMCAS® FAP)
**Earliest filing date:** June 29, 2011
**Latest filing date:** November 15, 2011

**MCAT® required:** Yes
**Latest MCAT® considered:** September 2011
**Oldest MCAT® considered:** March 2008

**Early Decision Program:** School does not have EDP
**Applicants notified:** n/a
**EDP available for:** n/a

**Regular acceptance notice —**
**Earliest date:** October 16, 2011
**Latest date:** Until class is full
**Applicant's response to acceptance offer —**
**Maximum time:** Two weeks

**Requests for deferred entrance considered:** Yes

**Deposit to hold place in class:** Yes
**Deposit — In-State Applicants:** $100
**Out-of-State Applicants:** $100
**Deposit due:** With response to acceptance offer
**Applied to tuition:** Yes
**Refundable:** Yes
**Refundable by:** May 15, 2012

**Estimated number of new entrants:** 104
**EDP:** 0, **Special Programs:** 20

**Start month/year:** August 2012

**Interview format:** Two interviews. Regional interviews are not available. Video interviews are not available.

## Preparatory Programs

**Postbaccalaureate Program:** Yes, www.rochester.edu/
College/premed/

**Summer Program:** Yes,
www.urmc.rochester.edu/education/md/undergraduate-
programs/college-students.cfm

## 2010–2011 First Year Class

|  | In-State | Out-of-State | International |
|---|---|---|---|
| Applications | 1,256 | 3,647 | 6 |
| Interviewed | 191 | 424 | 0 |
| Matriculated | 43 | 61 | 0 |

**Total Matriculants: 104**   **Total Enrollment: 418**

## Financial Information

|  | In-State | Out-of-State |
|---|---|---|
| Total Cost of Attendance | $61,304 | $61,304 |
| Tuition and Fees | $42,970 | $42,970 |
| Other (incl. living expenses) | $16,000 | $16,000 |
| Health Insurance (can be waived) | $2,334 | $2,334 |

**Average 2010 Graduate Indebtedness: $131,289**
**% of Enrolled Students Receiving Aid: 90%**

Source: 2009-2010 LCME I-B survey and 2010-2011 AAMC TSF questionnaire

# Weill Cornell Medical College
## New York, New York

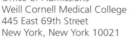

Office of Admissions
Weill Cornell Medical College
445 East 69th Street
New York, New York 10021

**T** 212 746 1067   wcmc-admissions@med.cornell.edu

**Admissions:** www.med.cornell.edu/education/
admissions

### General Information

Founded in 1898 as Cornell University Medical College, the school is now known as Weill Cornell Medical College. The medical school campus embraces New York-Presbyterian Hospital, Memorial Sloan-Kettering Cancer Center, Rockefeller University, and the Hospital for Special Surgery. In addition, students train in clinical care throughout our affiliated network, including public, private, research, tertiary care, and community hospitals as well as primary care sites.

### Mission Statement

WCMC is committed to excellence in research, teaching, patient care, and the advancement of the art and science of medicine. To this end, our mission is to provide the finest education possible for medical students, to provide superior continuing medical education for the lifelong education of physicians throughout their careers, to conduct research at the cutting edge of knowledge, to improve the health care of the nation and world both now and for further generations, and to provide the highest level of clinical care for the communities we serve.

### Curricular Highlights

**Community Service Requirement:** Optional. Special degree program: M.D. with Honors in Service.

**Research/Thesis Requirement:** Optional. Special degree program: M.D. with Honors in Research.

The first two years center on Problem-Based Learning (PBL), in which students learn by actively solving problems with the faculty in small group seminars. Lectures, anatomic dissection, experimental laboratories and journal clubs augment the learning experience. Basic science courses are integrated and multidisciplinary. Students begin to work with patients immediately during the three-year sequence Medicine, Patients, and Society, which focuses on clinical skills, the doctor-patient relationship, health care systems, ethics, and end-of-life care. The core clinical clerkships include Medicine, Neurology, Obstetrics and Gynecology, Pediatrics, Primary Care, Psychiatry, Public Health, and Surgery. Year 4 provides the major time block for electives in clinical medicine, research, and international health experiences, as well as a return to advanced biomedical science.

### Selection Factors

WCMC considers each applicant on an individual basis and welcomes those with backgrounds in the basic sciences, social sciences, and liberal arts. We encourage applicants to sample a broad range of academic disciplines and to explore one or more areas in depth. Participation in other activities should demonstrate commitment and initiative. We encourage applicants to explore medicine via research, clinical work, and volunteer service. We seek students who demonstrate emotional maturity, personal depth, commitment to others' well-being, and ethical and moral integrity. We seek to build a diverse class and emphasize diversity in all its dimensions, including race, ethnicity, educational and socio-economic background, personal experiences, and fields of interest. Typically a third of our entering students majored in liberal arts, and a quarter are 25 years of age or older.

### Information about Diversity Programs

Cornell University has been deeply committed to diversity from its very founding, and the Medical College upholds this principle. WMC's educational mission is dedicated to the inclusion of students from diverse ethnic, racial, social, economic, and educational backgrounds. Special summer research programs are available for college undergraduates who have a major interest in the medical problems of the underserved. Further information is available at *www.med.cornell.education/student/min_aff. html*.

### Regional/Satellite Campuses

Students rotate throughout New York City at public, private, community, research, and tertiary care hospitals, as well as primary care sites. Rural rotations are also available.

## Application Process and Requirements 2012–2013

**Primary application service:** AMCAS®
**Earliest filing date:** June 2011
**Latest filing date:** October 15, 2011

**Secondary application required:** Yes
**Sent to:** All applicants
**URL:** Sent to verified applicants only.
**Contact:** Office of Admissions, (212) 746-1067, wcmc-admissions@med.cornell.edu
**Fee:** Yes, $75   **Waiver available:** Yes
**Earliest filing date:** First transmission of verified AMCAS® applications.
**Latest filing date:** November 15, 2011

**MCAT® required:** Yes
**Latest MCAT® considered:** September 2011
**Oldest MCAT® considered:** September 2008

**Early Decision Program:** School does have EDP
**Applicants notified:** October 1
**EDP available for:** Both In-State and Out-of-State Applicants

**Regular acceptance notice —**
**Earliest date:** December 2011
**Latest date:** Until class is full
**Applicant's response to acceptance offer —**
**Maximum time:** Two weeks
**Requests for deferred entrance considered:** Yes

**Deposit to hold place in class:** Yes
**Deposit — In-State Applicants:** $100
**Out-of-State Applicants:** $100
**Deposit due:** May 15, 2012   **Applied to tuition:** Yes
**Refundable:** Yes   **Refundable by:** May 15, 2012

**Estimated number of new entrants:** 101
**EDP:** 1, **Special Programs:** 3

**Start month/year:** August 2012

**Interview format:** Two individual interviews with admissions committee members. No regional interviews. Video interviews are not available.

### Preparatory Programs
**Postbaccalaureate Program:** No

**Summer Program:** Yes, www.med.cornell.edu/
education/student/min_sum_pro.html,
Elizabeth Wilson-Anstey, (212) 746-1058,
eaanstey@med.cornell.edu

### 2010–2011 First Year Class

|  | In-State | Out-of-State | International |
|---|---|---|---|
| Applications | 1,133 | 4,136 | 296 |
| Interviewed | 140 | 637 | 16 |
| Matriculated | 26 | 73 | 2 |

**Total Matriculants:** 101   **Total Enrollment:** 396

### Financial Information

|  | In-State | Out-of-State |
|---|---|---|
| Total Cost of Attendance | $71,441 | $71,441 |
| Tuition and Fees | $47,848 | $47,848 |
| Other (incl. living expenses) | $19,474 | $19,474 |
| Health Insurance (can be waived) | $4,119 | $4,119 |

**Average 2010 Graduate Indebtedness: $139,996**
**% of Enrolled Students Receiving Aid: 78%**

*Source: 2009-2010 LCME I-B survey and 2010-2011 AAMC TSF questionnaire*

# The Brody School of Medicine at East Carolina University

## Greenville, North Carolina

Associate Dean
Office of Admissions
The Brody School of Medicine
at East Carolina University
Greenville, North Carolina  27834

**T** 252-744-2202   somadmissions@ecu.edu

**Admissions:** www.ecu.edu/bsomadmissions

## General Information

In 1972, East Carolina University enrolled students in the First-Year Program in Medical Education. The Board of Governors and the State General Assembly authorized the expansion to a degree-granting School of Medicine in 1975, and the first class was enrolled in August 1977. The school's educational facilities are located in the nine-story Brody Medical Sciences Building on the 100-acre Health Sciences Center campus.

## Mission Statement

Our mission is threefold: educating primary care physicians, making medical care more readily available to the people of eastern North Carolina, and providing opportunities for minority and disadvantaged students.

## Curricular Highlights

**Community Service Requirement:** Optional.

**Research/Thesis Requirement:** Optional.

The first year of the four-year curriculum is devoted to the study of the body through courses in anatomy, biochemistry, physiology, microbiology/immunology, nuerosciences, and genetics. Courses in clinical skills, the psychosocial basis of medicine, ethical and social issues in medicine, and a primary care preceptorship are also presented. The second-year curriculum is directed toward clinical medicine, with courses including microbiology, pharmacology, pathology, psychiatry (including human sexuality and lifestyle abuse), ethical and social issues, clinical skills, and a primary care preceptorship. The third year is composed of eight required clerkships in family medicine, internal medicine, obstetrics and gynecology, pediatrics, psychiatry, surgery, cardiovascular science, and a two-week clinical elective. The fourth year is composed of 36 weeks of clinical and basic science electives, which must include blocks in primary care, intensive care, and other specific areas. Student performance is evaluated by letter grade, and promotion to the next year's class is recommended to the dean by the Promotions Committee of the respective year.

## Selection Factors

Factors considered in the selection process encompass the social, personal, and intellectual development of each applicant. All available application data are evaluated: MCAT scores; academic performance; comments contained in letters of reference/recommendation; and (for invited applicants) the results of two personal interviews, conducted only at the medical school campus, with two members of the Admissions Committee. The Brody School of Medicine at East Carolina University seeks competent students of diverse personalities and backgrounds, and all applicants are evaluated without discrimination based on race, religion, sex, color, national origin, age, or disability. Very strong preference is given to qualified residents of North Carolina. In conjunction with the undergraduate Honors College, the Brody School of Medicine offers an Early Assurance Program for highly qualified high school seniors. Selected scholars enroll in the University and are assured of a spot in the medical school class after receiving their baccalaureate degree (provided certain academic standards are maintained). Qualified North Carolina residents from schools with similar medical curricula may be considered for transfer into the second or third-year classes, but advanced standing positions are dependent on the very limited number of seats that become available through attrition. Interested students should send letters describing their circumstances to the Office of Admissions for further information.

## Information about Diversity Programs

Persons from groups underrepresented in medicine who hold residence in North Carolina are encouraged to apply. There is diverse membership on the Admissions Committee, and the Academic Support and Enrichment Services Office offers a wide range of services to students desiring assistance or guidance.

## Application Process and Requirements 2012–2013

**Primary application service:** AMCAS®
**Earliest filing date:** June 1, 2011
**Latest filing date:** November 15, 2011

**Secondary application required:** Yes
**Sent to:** All North Carolina applicants
**URL:** somadmissions@ecu.edu
**Fee:** Yes, $60   **Waiver available:** Yes
**Earliest filing date:** July 1, 2011
**Latest filing date:** November 15, 2011 or 2 weeks after receipt of AMCAS®

**MCAT® required:** Yes
**Latest MCAT® considered:** September 2011
**Oldest MCAT® considered:** April 2008

**Early Decision Program:** School does have EDP
**Applicants notified:** October 1, 2011
**EDP available for:** In-State Applicants only

**Regular acceptance notice —**
**Earliest date:** October 15, 2011
**Latest date:** Varies
**Applicant's response to acceptance offer —**
**Maximum time:** Three weeks

**Requests for deferred entrance considered:** No

**Deposit to hold place in class:** Yes
**Deposit — In-State Applicants:** $100
**Out-of-State Applicants:** $100
**Deposit due:** May 15, 2012
**Applied to tuition:** Yes
**Refundable:** Yes
**Refundable by:** May 15, 2012

**Estimated number of new entrants:** 78
**EDP:** 6, **Special Programs:** 0

**Start month/year:** August 2012

**Interview format:** Two individual interviews with admissions committee members. No regional interviews. Video interviews are not available.

## Preparatory Programs

**Postbaccalaureate Program:** No

**Summer Program:** Yes, www.ecu.edu/cs-dhs/ascc/SPFD.cfm

## 2010–2011 First Year Class

|  | In-State | Out-of-State | International |
|---|---|---|---|
| Applications | 914 | 2 | 2 |
| Interviewed | 506 | 0 | 0 |
| Matriculated | 78 | 0 | 0 |

**Total Matriculants: 78**   **Total Enrollment: 305**

## Financial Information

|  | In-State | Out-of-State |
|---|---|---|
| Total Cost of Attendance | $30,639 | $56,574 |
| Tuition and Fees | $11,554 | $37,489 |
| Other (incl. living expenses) | $18,257 | $18,257 |
| Health Insurance (can be waived) | $828 | $828 |

**Average 2010 Graduate Indebtedness: $92,416**
**% of Enrolled Students Receiving Aid: 88%**

Source: 2009-2010 LCME I-B survey and 2010-2011 AAMC TSF questionnaire

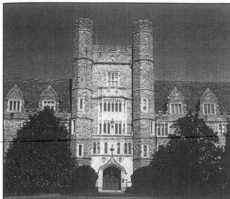

# Duke University School of Medicine

## Durham, North Carolina

Committee on Admissions
Duke University School of Medicine
DUMC 3710
Durham, North Carolina 27710

**T** 919 684 2985    medadm@mc.duke.edu

**Admissions:** http://dukemed.duke.edu

## General Information

Duke University Health System is a world-class health care network dedicated to outstanding patient care, innovative medical education and biomedical research.

## Mission Statement

DukeMed is a community of scholars devoted to understanding the causes, prevention and treatment of human disease. Our missions are to train scholars and leaders across a broad spectrum of careers in medicine. These missions are undertaken by students from diverse communities committed to the highest of academic goals: the generation, conservation, and dissemination of knowledge leading to the prevention and eradication of human disease throughout the world through innovative curricula and broadly-based clinical training, unparalleled resources in education, clinical care, and basic science and clinical research.

## Curricular Highlights

**Community Service Requirement:** Optional.

**Research/Thesis Requirement:** Required.

Required to complete the third year of medical school. The curriculum stimulates rapid expansion of medical knowledge. First-year students study basic science principles alongside the first of two-years' introduction to clinical medicine. The second year is the clinical clerkship year. The third and fourth years are elective including half basic science/half clinical coursework with opportunities for mentored research. Students also elect from a number of dual-degree programs which begin during the third year. The fourth year is an advanced clinical clerkship year to prepare for postgraduate study. The MST Program provides MD/Ph.D degrees over a six-to-seven-year period. It is expected that candidates for this combined degree plan will have careers in academic medicine.

## Selection Factors

Selection is based on evidence of outstanding academic and experiential preparation, including but not limited to outstanding curricular/extracurricular achievement, evidence of leadership, participation in volunteer/community service activities, excellent oral and written communications skills, supportive letters of recommendations from teachers/advisors and individuals with whom the candidates have worked in community service activities, competitive MCAT scores, exposure to and/or participation in scholarly research and the applicant's interview evaluation. Successful students have high GPAs/strong performance on the MCATs, demonstrated leadership on campus and in their respective communities and a demonstrated commitment to service. Duke Med does not discriminate on the basis of sex, race, religion, sexual orientation, creed, age, handicap, or national origin.

## Information about Diversity Programs

The Multicultural Resource Center is a resource-intensive repository providing opportunities for diverse learning experiences for all students and targeted pipeline programs for women, URM/disadvantaged, and students interested in careers in healthcare and biomedical research beginning as early as elementary school through undergraduate and graduate education. MRC integrates cross-cultural issues in medicine to the medical school curriculum and within the entirety of the medical school.

## Regional/Satellite Campuses

Students are based throughout the Duke Health System at Duke University Hospital, the VA Hospital, Durham Regional Hospital, Lennox Baker Children's Hospital, Duke Children's Hospital, and more than 70 outpatient clinics located in Durham, Raleigh, Chapel Hill and surrounding communities.

## Application Process and Requirements 2012–2013

**Primary application service:** AMCAS®
**Earliest filing date:** June 1, 2011
**Latest filing date:** October 15, 2011

**Secondary application required:** Yes
**Sent to:** All applicants
**URL:** http://dukemed.duke.edu
**Fee:** Yes, $85    **Waiver available:** Yes
**Earliest filing date:** Once AMCAS® has verified application.
**Latest filing date:** November 1, 2011

**MCAT® required:** Yes
**Latest MCAT® considered:** September 2011
**Oldest MCAT® considered:** August 2008

**Early Decision Program:** School does not have EDP
**Applicants notified:** n/a
**EDP available for:** n/a

**Regular acceptance notice —**
**Earliest date:** March 1, 2012
**Latest date:** Until class is full
**Applicant's response to acceptance offer —**
**Maximum time:** Two weeks

**Requests for deferred entrance considered:** Yes

**Deposit to hold place in class:** Yes
**Deposit — In-State Applicants:** $100
**Out-of-State Applicants:** $100
**Deposit due:** May 15, 2012
**Applied to tuition:** Yes
**Refundable:** Yes
**Refundable by:** May 15, 2012

**Estimated number of new entrants:** 100
**EDP:** n/a, **Special Programs:** n/a

**Start month/year:** August 1, 2012

**Interview format:** Multiple Mini Interviews. Regional interviews are not available. Video interviews are not available.

## Preparatory Programs

**Postbaccalaureate Program:** No

**Summer Program:** Yes, www.smdep.org
Maureen Cullins, (919) 684-5882 mcullins@duke.edu

## 2010–2011 First Year Class

|  | In-State | Out-of-State | International |
|---|---|---|---|
| Applications | 396 | 4,159 | 277 |
| Interviewed | 110 | 900 | 37 |
| Matriculated | 12 | 84 | 4 |

**Total Matriculants: 100**    **Total Enrollment: 408**

## Financial Information

|  | In-State | Out-of-State |
|---|---|---|
| Total Cost of Attendance | $73,435 | $73,435 |
| Tuition and Fees | $47,977 | $47,977 |
| Other (incl. living expenses) | $23,800 | $23,800 |
| Health Insurance (can be waived) | $1,658 | $1,658 |

**Average 2010 Graduate Indebtedness: $120,202**
**% of Enrolled Students Receiving Aid: 91%**

Source: 2009-2010 LCME I-B survey and 2010-2011 AAMC TSF questionnaire

# University of North Carolina at Chapel Hill School of Medicine

## Chapel Hill, North Carolina

Office of Admissions
CB #9500 1001 Bondurant Hall, First Floor
University of North Carolina at Chapel Hill
School of Medicine
Chapel Hill, North Carolina 27599-9500

**T** 919 962 8331
Admis_UNC-SOM@listserv.med.unc.edu

**Admissions:** www.med.unc.edu/admit

## General Information

The School of Medicine was established on February 12, 1879.

## Mission Statement

Our mission is to improve the health of North Carolinians and others whom we serve. We will accomplish this by achieving excellence and providing leadership in the interrelated areas of patient care, education, and research.

## Curricular Highlights

**Community Service Requirement:** Optional.

**Research/Thesis Requirement:** Optional.

The curriculum offers an education that reflects our mission. The first year presents courses in basic biomedical science. Presentation is through lectures, problem and case based small-group sessions, and electronic resource materials. Introduction to the profession of medicine begins in the first week of the first year through Introduction to Clinical Medicine (ICM). ICM provides a two-year continuum of weekly small-group seminars and experience with simulated and real patients. A second weekly first year seminar, Medicine and Society, focuses on health care issues. The second year presents the pathophysiology of disease in organ-based courses. Clinical skills development continues through the second year of ICM, and issues in social aspects of health care are presented through selectives offered by the Department of Social Medicine. The third and fourth year present a two-year continuum of instruction in clinical medicine. Core clinical rotations, which are primarily completed in the third year, include internal medicine, surgery, family medicine, obstetrics and gynecology, pediatrics, neurology, and psychiatry. Some rotations are at AHEC sites. The advanced clinical curriculum of the fourth year builds more independence and increased responsibility. Students are assisted in choosing post graduate training through counseling and a broad choice of electives. Students may conduct research with faculty mentorship support by school or grant funding, or through selection to the Distinguished Medical Scholars or Doris Duke programs (a year of funded study and research). Students may pursue interests in rural and community medicine, public policy, or public health through Social Medicine selectives, fourth year Advanced Practice Selectives, and projects. The grading system is honors/pass/fail.

## Selection Factors

The Committee on Admissions evaluates the qualifications of all applicants to select those with the greatest potential for accomplishment in one of the many careers open to medical graduates. Preference is given to North Carolina residents. The University of North Carolina at Chapel Hill is open to all people of all races, is committed to equality of educational opportunity, and does not discriminate against applicants, students, or employees based on race, color, gender, national origin, age, religion, creed, disability, veteran's status, sexual orientation, gender identity, or gender expression. The Equal Opportunity/ADA Office has primary responsibility for administering this policy. Moreover, the University actively seeks to promote diversity by recruiting and enrolling disadvantaged students and underrepresented groups. In making its final selections from the group of qualified applicants, the committee considers evidence of each candidate's motivation, maturity, leadership, integrity, and a variety of other personal qualifications and accomplishments in addition to the scholastic record. All information available about each applicant is considered without assigning priority to any single factor. No special admission tracks or quotas are applied among applicants. Undergraduate major is not an important consideration, but excellence in the chosen field is expected. Re-applications are compared to those applications previously submitted.

## Information about Diversity Programs

The Medical Education Development Program is a nationally recognized pipeline program that acquaints disadvantaged students with medical and dental school curricula and faculty. *http://www.med.unc.edu/medprogram*.

## Regional/Satellite Campuses

**Regional Campus Location(s):** Asheville, NC, and Charlotte, NC.

Students can self-nominate to spend their third and fourth years at our Asheville campus, where a small number are chosen to participate in a longitudinal curriculum with a focus on rural medicine. About a dozen students spend their entire third year in a traditional block-style curriculum on our Charlotte campus, where the focus is medicine in an urban environment.

## Application Process and Requirements 2012–2013

**Primary application service:** AMCAS®
**Earliest filing date:** June 1, 2011
**Latest filing date:** November 15, 2011

**Secondary application required:** Yes
**Sent to:** Screened applicants
**URL:** n/a
**Fee:** Yes, $68    **Waiver available:** Yes
**Earliest filing date:** June 1, 2011
**Latest filing date:** January 1, 2012

**MCAT® required:** Yes
**Latest MCAT® considered:** September 2011
**Oldest MCAT® considered:** September 2007

**Early Decision Program:** School does not have EDP
**Applicants notified:** n/a
**EDP available for:** n/a

**Regular acceptance notice —**
**Earliest date:** October 15, 2011
**Latest date:** Until class is full
**Applicant's response to acceptance offer —**
**Maximum time:** Three weeks

**Requests for deferred entrance considered:** Yes

**Deposit to hold place in class:** Yes
**Deposit — In-State Applicants:** $100
**Out-of-State Applicants:** $100
**Deposit due:** With response to acceptance offer
**Applied to tuition:** Yes
**Refundable:** Yes
**Refundable by:** May 15, 2012

**Estimated number of new entrants:** 170
**EDP:** 0, **Special Programs:** 0

**Start month/year:** August 2012

**Interview format:** One-on-one, open file. Regional interviews are not available. Video interviews are not available.

## Preparatory Programs

**Postbaccalaureate Program:** No

**Summer Program:** No

## 2010–2011 First Year Class

|  | In-State | Out-of-State | International |
|---|---|---|---|
| Applications | 937 | 3,554 | 138 |
| Interviewed | 517 | 122 | 38 |
| Matriculated | 140 | 20 | 0 |

**Total Matriculants: 160**    **Total Enrollment: 753**

## Financial Information

|  | In-State | Out-of-State |
|---|---|---|
| Total Cost of Attendance | $43,922 | $63,720 |
| Tuition and Fees | $14,448 | $38,846 |
| Other (incl. living expenses) | $28,750 | $24,150 |
| Health Insurance (can be waived) | $724 | $724 |

**Average 2010 Graduate Indebtedness: $86,967**
**% of Enrolled Students Receiving Aid: 90%**
*Source: 2009-2010 LCME I-B survey and 2010-2011 AAMC TSF questionnaire*

# Wake Forest University School of Medicine

## Winston-Salem, North Carolina

Office of Medical School Admissions
Wake Forest University School of Medicine
Medical Center Boulevard
Winston-Salem, North Carolina 27157-1090

**T** 336 716 4264    medadmit@wfubmc.edu

**Admissions:** www.wfubmc.edu/MDProgram/
admissions

## General Information

The School of Medicine was established in 1902 at Wake Forest, North Carolina, and, of the existing 166 medical schools, it was one of 11 that required college preparation. Patient care, research, education, and community service remain the fourfold mission of the school as part of Wake Forest University. The name of the medical school was changed from The Bowman Gray School of Medicine to Wake Forest University School of Medicine, the Bowman Gray Campus, in 1997. The main teaching hospital of the medical school is the 880-bed North Carolina Baptist Hospital. Affiliated institutions include the 896-bed Forsyth Memorial Hospital, the Downtown Health Plaza of Baptist Hospital, and Northwest Area Health Education Center.

## Mission Statement

The Medical Center is committed to serving society by providing a superior education; by rendering exemplary and efficient patient care; by fostering the discovery and application of new knowledge through research; and to improve the health and well-being of the nation.

## Curricular Highlights

**Community Service Requirement:** Optional.

**Research/Thesis Requirement:** Optional.

WFUSM provides excellence in teaching in a collegial atmosphere. The curriculum, is organized to meet the seven goals of the undergraduate medical education program: self-directed learning and life-long learning skills, core biomedical science knowledge, clinical skills, problem-solving/clinical-reasoning skills, interviewing and communication skills, information management skills, and professional attitudes and behavior. Students study the basic and clinical sciences in an integrated fashion throughout the four-year curriculum utilizing small-group case centered learning, lectures, and labs which are closely integrated through the computer network. Early community-based clinical experience, as well as a focus on population health, are hallmarks of the curriculum. Professionalism issues are addressed longitudinally across the curriculum in formats designed to provide students with a clear understanding of the role and responsibilities of physicians within society. Information technology is integrated into the curriculum.

## Selection Factors

Candidates are selected on the basis of the quality of their academic records, MCAT scores, and general qualifications. There are no restrictions because of race, creed, sex, religion, age, physical disadvantages, marital status, or national origin. The Committee on Admissions (CoA) and/or the Associate Dean for Admissions evaluate each application. Secondary applications are selectively sent and all other applicants are notified of their status. Applicants with completed secondaries are considered for interviews at the medical school. The School of Medicine is not able to accept transfer students at this time.

## Information about Diversity Programs

The Office of Student Services/Diversity and Development Initiatives actively recruits students from groups underrepresented in medicine and has developed programs for academic enrichment, academic reinforcement, tutorial, and counseling services for enrolled students. Address inquiries to the Office of Diversity and Development Initiatives.

## Application Process and Requirements 2012–2013

**Primary application service:** AMCAS®
**Earliest filing date:** June 1, 2011
**Latest filing date:** November 1, 2011

**Secondary application required:** Yes
**Sent to:** Screened applicants
**Contact:** medadmit@wfubmc.edu
**Fee:** Yes, $65    **Waiver available:** Yes
**Earliest filing date:** July 15, 2011
**Latest filing date:** January 15, 2012

**MCAT® required:** Yes
**Latest MCAT® considered:** September 2011
**Oldest MCAT® considered:** September 2008

**Early Decision Program:** School does have EDP
**Applicants notified:** October 1, 2011
**EDP available for:** Both In-State and Out-of-State Applicants

**Regular acceptance notice —**
**Earliest date:** October 15, 2011
**Latest date:** Until class is full
**Applicant's response to acceptance offer —**
**Maximum time:** Two weeks

**Requests for deferred entrance considered:** Yes

**Deposit to hold place in class:** Yes
**Deposit — In-State Applicants:** $100
**Out-of-State Applicants:** $100
**Deposit due:** With response to acceptance offer
**Applied to tuition:** Yes
**Refundable:** Yes
**Refundable by:** May 1, 2012

**Estimated number of new entrants:** 120
**EDP:** 2, **Special Programs:** 10

**Start month/year:** July 2012

**Interview format:** Three individual 20-minute interviews with faculty. Regional interviews are not available. Video interviews are not available.

### Preparatory Programs

**Postbaccalaureate Program:** Yes,
www.wfubmc.edu/school/Diversity/postbaccalaureate-Premedical-Program.htm

**Summer Program:** No

## 2010–2011 First Year Class

|  | In-State | Out-of-State | International |
|---|---|---|---|
| Applications | 762 | 6,324 | 303 |
| Interviewed | 180 | 364 | 0 |
| Matriculated | 52 | 68 | 0 |

**Total Matriculants: 120**    **Total Enrollment: 480**

## Financial Information

|  | In-State | Out-of-State |
|---|---|---|
| Total Cost of Attendance | $61,356 | $61,356 |
| Tuition and Fees | $40,575 | $40,575 |
| Other (incl. living expenses) | $18,297 | $18,297 |
| Health Insurance (can be waived) | $2,484 | $2,484 |

**Average 2010 Graduate Indebtedness: $159,559**
**% of Enrolled Students Receiving Aid: 91%**

*Source: 2009-2010 LCME I-B survey and 2010-2011 AAMC TSF questionnaire*

# University of North Dakota School of Medicine and Health Sciences

## Grand Forks, North Dakota

Secretary, Committee on Admissions
University of North Dakota
School of Medicine and Health Sciences
501 North Columbia Road, Stop 9037
Grand Forks, North Dakota 58202-9037

**T** 701 777 4221   judy.heit@med.und.edu

**Admissions:** http://smhs.med.und/education/admissions.cfm

## General Information

The School of Medicine was established in 1905 as a basic science public medical school. In 1973, legislative action created an expanded curriculum and, in 1981, a full four-year medical education program was instituted in the state. The school is university-based and community-integrated.

## Mission Statement

The mission of the University of North Dakota School of Medicine and Health Sciences is to educate and prepare physicians, medical scientists, and other health professionals for service to North Dakota and the nation, and to advance medical and biomedical knowledge through research.

## Curricular Highlights

**Community Service Requirement:** Optional. A variety of activities is available.

**Research/Thesis Requirement:** Required during third year.

The School of Medicine's renewed curriculum was initiated during the 1998-99 academic year. Utilizing a "patient-centered learning" (PCL) approach, the number of lecture hours was reduced significantly, and greater emphasis was placed on small-group teaching and learning, active student participation, and early clinical experience. The curriculum is integrated across disciplines, consisting of four 10-week blocks of instruction during each of the first two years. Students either complete six 8-week clerkships in year 3 or they participate in the ROME (Rural Opportunities in Medical Education) Program, completing 7 months of clinical experience in a rural community. The school emphasizes the training of primary care physicians, but also offers a M.D.-Ph.D. program.

## Selection Factors

A student must maintain a GPA of 3.0 or better to be considered for admission. Selection is based upon the scholastic record, letters of recommendation, MCAT scores, and a personal interview. Interviews are conducted only at the medical school. In addition to high academic achievement, selection is based on a number of factors, including the demonstration of motivation and commitment to a medical career, empathy, compassion in interpersonal relationships, problem-solving, and the ability to work well in small groups. Qualified North Dakota residents are given preference in admission. The only exceptions include a limited number of Minnesota residents or admission through WICHE participation. Only persons who are U.S. citizens or legal permanent residents of the United States are eligible for consideration for admission. The school participates in the Professional Student Exchange Program administered by WICHE, under which legal residents of western states without a medical school may receive preference in admission. WICHE students who are certified and supported by their home state pay resident tuition. The school does not utilize AMCAS. Applications are ranked based on a combination of state of residency, grade-point average, and MCAT scores. The school is unable to accept transfer students from other medical schools except in very unique circumstances.

## Information about Diversity Programs

The INMED (Indians into Medicine) Program is a recruitment and retention program for American Indian students. It is a federally funded program that provides educational opportunities for fully qualified enrolled members of U.S. recognized tribes. State residency is not a consideration for admission through the INMED Program.

## Regional/Satellite Campuses

**Regional Campus Location(s):** Minot, ND, Bismarck, ND, and Fargo, ND.

## Application Process and Requirements 2012–2013

**Primary application service:** School specific
**Earliest filing date:** July 1, 2011
**Latest filing date:** November 1, 2011

**Secondary application required:** No
**Sent to:** All qualified applicants
**URL:** www.med.und.nodak.edu/
**Fee:** Yes, $50   **Waiver available:** Yes
**Earliest filing date:** July 1, 2011
**Latest filing date:** November 1, 2011

**MCAT® required:** Yes
**Latest MCAT® considered:** September 2011
**Oldest MCAT® considered:** June 2008

**Early Decision Program:** School does not have EDP
**Applicants notified:** n/a
**EDP available for:** n/a

**Regular acceptance notice —**
**Earliest date:** January 15, 2012
**Latest date:** Until class is full
**Applicant's response to acceptance offer —**
**Maximum time:** Four weeks

**Requests for deferred entrance considered:** Yes

**Deposit to hold place in class:** Yes
**Deposit — In-State Applicants:** $100
**Out-of-State Applicants:** $100
**Deposit due:** With response to acceptance offer
**Applied to tuition:** Yes
**Refundable:** Yes
**Refundable by:** May 15, 2012

**Estimated number of new entrants:** 62
**EDP:** n/a, **Special Programs:** n/a

**Start month/year:** August 2012

**Interview format:** M.D. and Ph.D. faculty and medical students conduct one-hour interview. Video interviews are not available.

### Preparatory Programs

**Postbaccalaureate Program:** No

**Summer Program:** Yes, INMED Program
www.med.und.edu/inmed/, (701) 777-3039, eugene.delorme@med.und.edu

## 2010–2011 First Year Class

| | In-State | Out-of-State | International |
|---|---|---|---|
| Applications | 125 | 193 | 0 |
| Interviewed | 109 | 42 | 0 |
| Matriculated | 48 | 14 | 0 |

**Total Matriculants: 62**    **Total Enrollment: 241**

## Financial Information

| | In-State | Out-of-State |
|---|---|---|
| Total Cost of Attendance | $45,415 | $65,940 |
| Tuition and Fees | $25,726 | $46,251 |
| Other (incl. living expenses) | $19,689 | $19,689 |
| Health Insurance (can be waived) | $0 | $0 |

**Average 2010 Graduate Indebtedness: $162,169**
**% of Enrolled Students Receiving Aid: 97%**

Source: 2009-2010 LCME I-B survey and 2010-2011 AAMC TSF questionnaire

# Case Western Reserve University School of Medicine

## Cleveland, Ohio

Office of Admissions, T-308
Case Western Reserve University
School of Medicine
10900 Euclid Avenue
Cleveland, Ohio 44106-4920

T 216 368 3450    casemed-admissions@case.edu

**Admissions:** http://casemed.case.edu/admissions

## General Information

Since 1843, the Case Western Reserve University School of Medicine has been at the forefront of medical education and research. CWRU SOM is one of the nation's leaders in NIH funding. Current educational innovations include curricular reform within the University Track and partnership since 2002 with the Cleveland Clinic in the Cleveland Clinic Lerner College of Medicine (College Track), a distinct program to train physician-investigators.

## Mission Statement

To advance the health of humankind through research, service and education.

## Curricular Highlights

**Community Service Requirement:** Optional. Medical and non-medical community activities are strongly encouraged.

**Research/Thesis Requirement:** Required. University track 16 weeks; College track 2 summers plus 1 year.

Case Western School of Medicine offers two types of MD tracks, a Medical Scientist Training program (MSTP), and several dual-degree and masters programs. To apply, applicants choose CWRU School of Medicine on AMCAS. Applicants may then choose to apply to one or more MD tracks on our secondary application. Separate interviews are required for each track. The University Track(UT), a 4-year MD program designed to train physician-scholars, is based on four tenets: clinical mastery, research, leadership, and civic professionalism. The innovative curriculum integrates basic sciences, clinical medicine, and population health, focusing on the care of individual patients within social and environmental contexts. Students are introduced to basic sciences in a learner-centered environment which emphasizes small group and team-based learning in a pass-fail system. Learning is interactive with faculty and students as partners. Independent learning and scholarship are emphasized. Material is organized in system-based blocks, with basic science and clinical integration throughout the four years. Early clinical experiences include rotating apprenticeships and a longitudinal outpatient preceptorship. A required, mentored research thesis is supported by the Office of Medical Student Research. Advising occurs in small groups by the Office of Student Affairs. The 5-year College Track (CT) admits 32 students, each of whom will graduate with an MD with Special Qualifications in Biomedical Research. A student-centered approach fosters critical thinking and scientific inquiry. Basic sciences are taught in small groups using problem-based learning, interactive seminars, journal clubs, and labs; there are no formal lectures and no grades. Early clinical experiences include a longitudinal outpatient preceptorship throughout the first two years. A core research curriculum offers basic/translational and clinical research in the summers, with a year long project in year 3 or 4. A master's level thesis is required. Students document their progress using a portfolio that details skills and expertise they achieve. A physician adviser ensures students' mastery of required competencies. A college level biochemistry course and research experience is required of all applicants to the College Track. Neither program utilizes traditional grading nor class rank.

## Selection Factors

The School of Medicine seeks a diverse student body. Students are selected without regard to age, nationality, race, religion, sex, sexual orientation, or state of residence. All candidates must have demonstrated exceptional academic strength and personal achievements. Written statements and letters of recommendation are also important. Transfer students are not accepted.

## Information about Diversity Programs

The Office of Multicultural Affairs offers academic and personal support for all underrepresented medical students and recruits students for all programs in the School of Medicine. It sponsors a rigorous, six-week, summer premed/predental program for college freshmen and sophomores and has an NIH-funded summer research program for undergraduate and medical students. The office supports the Case Western Student National Medical Association chapter and the Minority Graduate Student Organization.

## Application Process and Requirements 2012–2013

**Primary application service:** AMCAS®
**Earliest filing date:** June 1, 2011
**Latest filing date:** November 1, 2011

**Secondary application required:** Yes
**Sent to:** All applicants
**URL:** https://iapply.case.edu/
**Fee:** Yes, $85    **Waiver available:** Yes
**Earliest filing date:** Mid-July 2011
**Latest filing date:** December 15, 2011

**MCAT® required:** Yes
**Latest MCAT® considered:** September 2011
**Oldest MCAT® considered:** June 2008

**Early Decision Program:** School does not have EDP
**Applicants notified:** n/a
**EDP available for:** n/a

**Regular acceptance notice —**
**Earliest date:** October 15, 2011
**Latest date:** Until class is full
**Applicant's response to acceptance offer —**
**Maximum time:** Four weeks
**Requests for deferred entrance considered:** Yes

**Deposit to hold place in class:** No
**Deposit — In-State Applicants:** n/a
**Out-of-State Applicants:** n/a
**Deposit due:** n/a
**Applied to tuition:** n/a
**Refundable:** n/a
**Refundable by:** n/a

**Estimated number of new entrants:** 199
**EDP:** n/a, **Special Programs:** 7
**Start month/year:** July 2012

**Interview format:** UT: one faculty and one student interview. CT: two faculty and one student interview. Regional interviews are not available. Video interviews are not available.

## Preparatory Programs

**Postbaccalaureate Program:** No

**Summer Program:** Yes, www.smdep.org
Joseph T. Williams, (216) 368-1914
joseph.williams@case.edu

## 2010–2011 First Year Class

|  | In-State | Out-of-State | International |
|---|---|---|---|
| Applications | 722 | 4,670 | 442 |
| Interviewed | 182 | 1053 | 124 |
| Matriculated | 32 | 157 | 10 |

**Total Matriculants: 199**    **Total Enrollment: 823**

## Financial Information

|  | In-State | Out-of-State |
|---|---|---|
| Total Cost of Attendance | $72,380 | $72,380 |
| Tuition and Fees | $47,770 | $47,770 |
| Other (incl. living expenses) | $23,290 | $23,290 |
| Health Insurance (can be waived) | $1,320 | $1,320 |

**Average 2010 Graduate Indebtedness: $142,981**
**% of Enrolled Students Receiving Aid: 76%**

*Source: 2009-2010 LCME I-B survey and 2010-2011 AAMC TSF questionnaire*

# Northeastern Ohio Universities College of Medicine

## Rootstown, Ohio

OH

Office of Enrollment Services
Northeastern Ohio Universities
College of Medicine
P.O. Box 95
Rootstown, Ohio 44272-0095

T 330 325 6270   admission@neoucom.edu

**Admissions:** www.neoucom.edu/audience/applicants

## General Information

NEOUCOM is a state (public) medical school consisting of a basic medical sciences campus in Rootstown, a consortium of four major public universities and 20 community hospitals with more than 6,500 teaching beds in the greater Akron, Canton, and Youngstown areas. The clinical faculty numbers more than 1,800.

## Mission Statement

The mission of the Northeastern Ohio Universities College of Medicine is to effectively and efficiently develop, implement, and administer the educational programs that graduate competent, caring health professions, with strong communication skills, character, and commitment to the community.

## Curricular Highlights

**Community Service Requirement:** Required. All student organizations are required to do so.

**Research/Thesis Requirement:** Optional.

The integrated curriculum is offered in five steps. This Longitudinal curriculum includes the biomedical, behavioral, social, community and population health, clinical sciences, and humanities to provide an understanding of the interplay of these in patient care. The first year curriculum focuses on professionalism, doctor-patient relationships, human anatomy, biochemistry, molecular pathology, genetics, physiology, microbiology, immunology and pharmacology of infectious diseases. The second year curriculum instruction is centered on organ systems pathophysiology, including integrated education in Internal Medicine, Pathology, Pharmacology and Radiology; with an emphasis on applying knowledge to the clinical settings. The third year curriculum focuses on core clinical clerkships in family medicine, internal medicine, obstetrics/gynecology, pediatrics, psychiatry and surgery and an exploratory experience. The fourth year curriculum focuses on clinical electives and Clinical Epilogue and Capstone, focusing on professionalism, humanities, social science disciplines and provides vital skills needed as residents and interns.

## Selection Factors

Applicants must demonstrate strong academic preparation as measured by GPAs and MCAT scores, and show motivation for the practice of medicine. Interviews are by invitation only. Admission preference is given to Ohio residents. All applicants are considered; no formulas are used for selection. Only those who complete the secondary application are given consideration. Early submission of application material is strongly encouraged, particularly through the Early Decision Program (EDP).

## Information about Diversity Programs

NEOUCOM believes that diversity is a value that is central to its educational, research, service and health care missions. The Admissions Committee conducts a holistic review of all qualified applicants, striving to bring together a diverse student body constituted by academically gifted, highly motivated, resilient students who share a deep commitment to the values and goals of our profession and the College.

## Regional/Satellite Campuses

Rotations are completed among 20 associated hospitals, eight of which are major teaching facilities.

## Application Process and Requirements 2012–2013

**Primary application service:** AMCAS®
**Earliest filing date:** June 1, 2011
**Latest filing date:** December 1, 2011

**Secondary application required:** Yes
**Sent to:** All applicants
**URL:** www.neoucom.edu/audience/applicants
**Fee:** Yes, $85   **Waiver available:** Yes
**Earliest filing date:** July 1, 2011
**Latest filing date:** November 1, 2011

**MCAT® required:** Yes
**Latest MCAT® considered:** December 2011
**Oldest MCAT® considered:** June 2009

**Early Decision Program:** School does have EDP
**Applicants notified:** October 1, 2011
**EDP available for:** Both In-State and Out-of-State Applicants

**Regular acceptance notice —**
**Earliest date:** October 1, 2011
**Latest date:** Until class is full
**Applicant's response to acceptance offer —**
**Maximum time:** Two weeks

**Requests for deferred entrance considered:** Yes

**Deposit to hold place in class:** Yes
**Deposit — In-State Applicants:** $100
**Out-of-State Applicants:** $100
**Deposit due:** Two weeks after offer of acceptance
**Applied to tuition:** Yes
**Refundable:** No
**Refundable by:** May 15, 2012

**Estimated number of new entrants:** 30
**EDP:** 5, **Special Programs:** 80

**Start month/year:** August 2012

**Interview format:** 30-minute interview by two faculty. Regional interviews are not available. Video interviews are not available.

## Preparatory Programs

**Postbaccalaureate Program:** No

**Summer Program:** No

## 2010–2011 First Year Class

|  | In-State | Out-of-State | International |
|---|---|---|---|
| Applications | 885 | 997 | 19 |
| Interviewed | 83 | 4 | 0 |
| Matriculated | 109 | 5 | 0 |

**Total Matriculants: 114**   **Total Enrollment: 492**

## Financial Information

|  | In-State | Out-of-State |
|---|---|---|
| Total Cost of Attendance | $56,015 | $85,487 |
| Tuition and Fees | $31,483 | $60,955 |
| Other (incl. living expenses) | $22,900 | $22,900 |
| Health Insurance (can be waived) | $1,632 | $1,632 |

**Average 2010 Graduate Indebtedness: $155,684**
**% of Enrolled Students Receiving Aid: 86%**

Source: 2009-2010 LCME I-B survey and 2010-2011 AAMC TSF questionnaire

# The Ohio State University College of Medicine

## Columbus, Ohio

Admissions Office, The Ohio State University
College of Medicine
I55D Meiling Hall, 370 West 9th Avenue
Columbus, Ohio 43210-1238

T 614 292 7137    medicine@osu.edu

**Admissions:** http://medicine.osu.edu/students/
admissions/Pages/index.aspx

## General Information

Since 1914 The Ohio State University College of Medicine has blended traditional medical education, innovative learning opportunities, and a strong reputation in the preparation of students for primary care and specialized residencies, encouraging research interests and a strong emphasis on a personalized approach to patient care.

## Mission Statement

The Ohio State University College of Medicine seeks to recruit self-directed learners who are driven to become empathetic physicians providing evidence-based, compassionate medical care. The Admissions Committee will assemble a class that displays diversity in background and thought, strong intellect, and the potential to improve people's lives through innovation in research, education and community service.

## Curricular Highlights

**Community Service Requirement:** Required. Clinical Assessment and Problem Solving component.

**Research/Thesis Requirement:** Optional.

Initial ten-week gross anatomy and embryology course, followed by choice of two preclinical pathways. Integrated Pathway features body systems-oriented content that fuses basic and clinical sciences using methods of student-centered active learning, small-group case-based discussion, and lectures. Independent Study Pathway students use highly structured objectives, resource guides, Web and computer-based materials to read, review, and learn on their own. Clinical experiences begin in the first year with the Clinical Assessment and Problem Solving course. Additionally, standardized patients help students build clinical proficiency in the state-of-the-art clinical skills center. Third-year clerkships include family medicine, internal medicine, obstetrics and gynecology, pediatrics, psychiatry, neurology, surgery and one elective. A clinical skills immersion experience ensures all students have an in-depth understanding of a core set of procedurally based clinical skills. Fourth-year selectives focus on caring for patients at various stages of illness and wellness: undifferentiated patient; patient with chronic care needs; and a sub-internship. In the fourth year, students also have 4 months of elective rotations and 3 months of vacation.

## Selection Factors

Completed applications are subjected to a holistic review process to ensure that excellent candidates who do not fit the general profile are not overlooked. Factors considered include clinical experiences, community service and leadership activities, research experience, recommendations, suitability for the study of medicine, and extracurricular activities.

## Information about Diversity Programs

The Admissions Committee considers diversity to be a desirable characteristic in the student body. Students whose previous educational and economic deprivation warrants special consideration are carefully evaluated and offered special help in the acquisition of additional resources. The Medpath Medical Careers Pathway is a postbaccalaureate program aimed at developing the academic knowledge base and skills of students enhancing their preparation for medical school.

## Regional/Satellite Campuses

Clinical rotations occur within the Medical Center, at community hospitals within Columbus and Ohio, in rural settings in Ohio, and at locations outside of Ohio. About 35 percent of the fourth-year class gains exposure to international health care with the assistance of the College of Medicine Office of Global Health.

## Application Process and Requirements 2012–2013

**Primary application service:** AMCAS®
**Earliest filing date:** June 1, 2011
**Latest filing date:** November 1, 2011

**Secondary application required:** Yes
**Sent to:** All applicants
**Contact:** Admissions Office, (614) 292-7137, medicine@osu.edu
**Fee:** Yes, $80    **Waiver available:** Yes
**Earliest filing date:** June 1, 2011
**Latest filing date:** January 1, 2012

**MCAT® required:** Yes
**Latest MCAT® considered:** September 2011
**Oldest MCAT® considered:** 2008

**Early Decision Program:** School does have EDP
**Applicants notified:** October 1, 2011
**EDP available for:** Both In-State and Out-of-State Applicants

**Regular acceptance notice —**
**Earliest date:** October 15, 2011
**Latest date:** Varies
**Applicant's response to acceptance offer —**
**Maximum time:** Two weeks

**Requests for deferred entrance considered:** Yes

**Deposit to hold place in class:** No
**Deposit — In-State Applicants:** n/a
**Out-of-State Applicants:** n/a
**Deposit due:** n/a    **Applied to tuition:** n/a
**Refundable:** n/a    **Refundable by:** n/a

**Estimated number of new entrants:** 220
**EDP:** 10, **Special Programs:** 15

**Start month/year:** August 2012

**Interview format:** Open-file conversation; one faculty interview and one student interview. Regional interviews are not available. Video interviews are not available.

## Preparatory Programs

**Postbaccalaureate Program:** Yes, http://medicine.osu.edu/students/diversity/Programs/medpath/Pages/index.aspx, Nikki Radcliffe, (614) 292-3161, nikki.radcliffe@osumc.edu

**Summer Program:** Yes, Nikki Radcliffe, (614) 292-3161, nikki.radcliffe@osumc.edu

## 2010–2011 First Year Class

|  | In-State | Out-of-State | International |
|---|---|---|---|
| Applications | 1,080 | 3,144 | 13 |
| Interviewed | 324 | 556 | 0 |
| Matriculated | 131 | 89 | 0 |

**Total Matriculants: 220**    **Total Enrollment: 863**

## Financial Information

|  | In-State | Out-of-State |
|---|---|---|
| Total Cost of Attendance | $53,881 | $69,931 |
| Tuition and Fees | $30,948 | $46,998 |
| Other (incl. living expenses) | $21,123 | $21,123 |
| Health Insurance (can be waived) | $1,810 | $1,810 |

**Average 2010 Graduate Indebtedness: $150,143**
**% of Enrolled Students Receiving Aid: 94%**

Source: 2009-2010 LCME I-B survey and 2010-2011 AAMC TSF questionnaire

# University of Cincinnati College of Medicine

## Cincinnati, Ohio

Office of Student Affairs/Admissions
University of Cincinnati College of Medicine
P.O. Box 670552
Cincinnati, Ohio 45267-0552
**T** 513 558 7314   comadmis@ucmail.uc.edu
**Admissions:** www.medonestop.uc.edu

**OH**

## General Information

The UCCOM provides both outstanding re-search facilities and superb clinical and teaching experiences. Graduates, ranked as highly competitive by national residency program directors, choose careers in a broad range of specialty areas. Extensive research opportunities are available. UCCOM is ranked in the top third among all public medical schools in NIH, research funding.

## Mission Statement

The mission of the University of Cincinnati College of Medicine is to improve the health of the public by educating physicians and scientists and by producing new knowledge.

## Curricular Highlights

**Community Service Requirement:** Optional.

**Research/Thesis Requirement:** Optional.

UCCOM provides a stimulating learning environment, creating the undifferentiated MD ready to excel in residency training and provide excellent patient care. Using an integrated curricular approach including lab, small-group discussion, and team-based learning and lectures, the first two years provide students with the scientific, clinical and humanistic principles of medicine. Years 1 and 2 focus on the normal structure, function and development of the human body and emphasizes the basis and mechanisms of human disease. During Year 3, students rotate through six core clerkships. Students also begin exploring career options by participating in three specialty clerkships of their choosing. In Year 4, students hone their clinical skills during their Acting Internship and required Neuroscience selectives. Students can also choose from over 100 elective offerings.

## Selection Factors

After AMCAS, secondary applications and letters of recommendations are received, completed applicants are evaluated for interviews. The UCCOM website list provides applicants with admissions status information. The College utilizes the Multiple Mini Interview and the interview day consists of a description of the College and student services and includes: a presentation about the admissions process, curriculum, student services, financial aid; lunch; and tour. Acceptance offers are based on characteristics and qualities. Postbaccalaureate and graduate coursework will be considered. Personal characteristics include demonstrated motivation, maturity, coping skills, interpersonal skills, sensitivity and tolerance toward others and communication and critical-thinking skills. Students are admitted regardless of age, religion, gender, sexual orientation, race, color or national origin.

## Information about Diversity Programs

UCCOM Office of Diversity and Community Affairs works to increase diversity of the medical student body, residency training programs and faculty through regional and national recruitment efforts of underrepresented groups. The Office retention activities include mentoring, connections with community physicians, academic and psychological support and career development. Community partners support many of the office activities. Student groups are active in many community efforts that work to prevent health care disparities.

## Application Process and Requirements 2012–2013

**Primary application service:** AMCAS®
**Earliest filing date:** June 1, 2011
**Latest filing date:** November 15, 2011

**Secondary application required:** Yes
**Sent to:** All applicants
**URL:** www.MedOneStop.uc.edu
**Fee:** Yes, $25   **Waiver available:** Yes
**Earliest filing date:** July 15, 2011
**Latest filing date:** December 15, 2011

**MCAT® required:** Yes
**Latest MCAT® considered:** September 2011
**Oldest MCAT® considered:** April 2009

**Early Decision Program:** School does have EDP
**Applicants notified:** October 1, 2011
**EDP available for:** Both In-State and Out-of-State Applicants

**Regular acceptance notice —**
**Earliest date:** October 15, 2011   **Latest date:** Varies
**Applicant's response to acceptance offer —**
**Maximum time:** Two weeks

**Requests for deferred entrance considered:** Yes

**Deposit to hold place in class:** No
**Deposit — In-State Applicants:** n/a
**Out-of-State Applicants:** n/a
**Deposit due:** n/a   **Applied to tuition:** n/a
**Refundable:** n/a   **Refundable by:** n/a

**Estimated number of new entrants:** 170
**EDP:** 10, **Special Programs:** 18

**Start month/year:** August 2012

**Interview format:** Multiple Mini Interview with a series of six to eight short interviews, one interview at a time, focused on the discussion of common scenarios. Regional interviews are not available. Video interviews are not available.

## Preparatory Programs

**Postbaccalaureate Program:** Yes,
www.mcp.uc.edu, Jeannie Cummins , (513) 558-3102,
jeannie.cummins@uc.edu

**Summer Program:** Yes,
www.mcd.uc.edu/admissions/summerenrich.cfm
Lathel Bryant, (513) 558-0693, lathel.bryant@uc.edu

### 2010–2011 First Year Class

|  | In-State | Out-of-State | International |
|---|---|---|---|
| Applications | 1,117 | 2,800 | 27 |
| Interviewed | 358 | 274 | 0 |
| Matriculated | 108 | 62 | 0 |

**Total Matriculants: 170**   **Total Enrollment: 641**

### Financial Information

|  | In-State | Out-of-State |
|---|---|---|
| Total Cost of Attendance | $52,607 | $69,358 |
| Tuition and Fees | $30,855 | $47,406 |
| Other (incl. living expenses) | $20,303 | $20,503 |
| Health Insurance (can be waived) | $1,449 | $1,449 |

**Average 2010 Graduate Indebtedness: $157,398**
**% of Enrolled Students Receiving Aid: 86%**

Source: 2009-2010 LCME I-B survey and 2010-2011 AAMC TSF questionnaire

# The University of Toledo College of Medicine
**(Formerly Medical University of Ohio)**

## Toledo, Ohio

Admissions Office
3000 Arlington Avenue, Mail Stop 1043
Toledo, Ohio 43614

**T** 419 383 4229    medadmissions@utoledo.edu

**Admissions:** www.utoledo.edu/med/md/admissions/index.html

## General Information

The Medical University of Ohio and the University of Toledo merged on July 1, 2006, thus creating the third largest university in Ohio, which is now known as The University of Toledo. The health and research colleges located on the Health Science Campus include the College of Medicine, the College of Nursing, and the College of Pharmacy along with The University of Toledo Medical Center.

## Mission Statement

The mission of The University of Toledo College of Medicine is to improve the human condition. We do this by providing a world-class education for the next generation of physicians and scientists, by creating new knowledge that is translated into cutting-edge clinical practice, and by providing the highest level of professionalism and compassion as we deliver university quality health care.

## Curricular Highlights

**Community Service Requirement:** Optional.

**Research/Thesis Requirement:** Optional.

The preclinical basic science content is integrated into the following interdisciplinary instructional units: Cellular and Molecular Biology, Human Structure and Development, Neurosciences/Behavioral Science, Immunity and Infection, and Organ Systems. All students participate in a Clinical Decision Making course, which spans the first two years. The third year of the curriculum is devoted to mandatory clerkships in internal medicine, surgery, pediatrics, obstetrics and gynecology, psychiatry, family medicine, and neurology as well as a 4-week elective. The fourth year of elective clerkships consists of 44 weeks, including a basic science elective requirement and a required acting internship. A broad spectrum of clinical research and public health electives are also available. Most components of the curriculum are evaluated on an Honors, High Pass, Pass, Fail system.

## Selection Factors

Interviews are by invitation only. Re-applicants are not penalized. Preference is given to Ohio residents.

## Information about Diversity Programs

The University of Toledo is committed to increasing opportunities for individuals under represented in medicine and those from economically disadvantaged backgrounds. The Admissions Office works in cooperation with the Office of Faculty and Student Diversity, and the Office of Student Affairs and other campus departments in the recruitment, selection, and retention of qualified students.

## Regional/Satellite Campuses

The clinical clerkships are completed at The University of Toledo Medical Center on the Health Science Campus, as well as at several other area teaching hospitals, including Mercy St. Vincent Medical Center, Mercy Children's Hospital, The Toledo Hospital, Toledo Children's Hospital, Flower Hospital, and St. Luke's Hospital. All students complete a minimum of 8 weeks of clerkships in a rural Area Health Education Center. Opportunities are also available for students to do their required clerkships at Riverside Methodist Hospital in Columbus, Ohio, St. Joseph's and St. Mary's Health System in Southern Michigan and at Henry Ford Health System in Detroit, Michigan. In the fourth-year, students are able to complete several months of elective rotations at other approved institutions.

## Application Process and Requirements 2012–2013

**Primary application service:** AMCAS®
**Earliest filing date:** June 1, 2011
**Latest filing date:** November 1, 2011

**Secondary application required:** Yes
**Sent to:** Screened applicants
**URL:** http://hsc.utoledo.edu/med/md/admissions/secondary.html
**Fee:** Yes, $80    **Waiver available:** Yes
**Earliest filing date:** June 15, 2011
**Latest filing date:** January 1, 2012

**MCAT® required:** Yes
**Latest MCAT® considered:** September 2011
**Oldest MCAT® considered:** September 2009

**Early Decision Program:** School does have EDP
**Applicants notified:** October 1, 2011
**EDP available for:** In-State Applicants only

**Regular acceptance notice —**
**Earliest date:** October 15, 2011
**Latest date:** Until class is full
**Applicant's response to acceptance offer —**
**Maximum time:** Two weeks

**Requests for deferred entrance considered:** Yes

**Deposit to hold place in class:** No
**Deposit — In-State Applicants:** n/a
**Out-of-State Applicants:** n/a
**Deposit due:** n/a
**Applied to tuition:** n/a
**Refundable:** n/a
**Refundable by:** n/a

**Estimated number of new entrants:** 175
**EDP:** 3, **Special Programs:** 16

**Start month/year:** August 2012

**Interview format:** Two, one-on-one interviews with faculty. Regional interviews are not available. Video interviews are not available.

## Preparatory Programs

**Postbaccalaureate Program:** Yes, www.utoledo.edu/graduate/prospectivestudents/programs/hsc/medicine/medicalsciences.htm

**Summer Program:** Yes, www.hsc.utoledo.edu/ med/md/admissions/srp.html

## 2010–2011 First Year Class

|  | In-State | Out-of-State | International |
|---|---|---|---|
| Applications | 1,055 | 3,167 | 19 |
| Interviewed | 308 | 237 | 0 |
| Matriculated | 116 | 59 | 0 |

**Total Matriculants: 175**    **Total Enrollment: 690**

## Financial Information

|  | In-State | Out-of-State |
|---|---|---|
| Total Cost of Attendance | $47,896 | $69,100 |
| Tuition and Fees | $29,352 | $59,556 |
| Other (incl. living expenses) | $16,271 | $7,271 |
| Health Insurance (can be waived) | $2,273 | $2,273 |

**Average 2010 Graduate Indebtedness: $158,613**
**% of Enrolled Students Receiving Aid: 92%**

*Source: 2009-2010 LCME I-B survey and 2010-2011 AAMC TSF questionnaire*

# Wright State University School of Medicine

## Dayton, Ohio

Office of Student Affairs/Admissions
Wright State University
Boonshoft School of Medicine
P.O. Box 1751
Dayton, Ohio 45401-1751

**T** 937 775 2934   som_saa@wright.edu

**Admissions:** www.med.wright.edu/admiss

## General Information

The Boonshoft School of Medicine is a community-based medical school. Clinical facilities include seven major teaching hospitals with over 3,500 patient beds. A faculty of over 1,200 provides students with opportunities for individualized attention. The School emphasizes research, generalist training, community service, patient focused care, cultural competence, cultural diversity, health promotion, disease prevention, and the provision of care to underserved populations.

## Mission Statement

The mission of the School is to educate culturally diverse students to become excellent physicians by focusing on generalist training that is integrated, supported, and strengthened by specialists and researchers. The faculty values patient-focused care, community service, research, and have passion for improving health in our communities. These goals and objectives are achieved through: opportunities to learn in clinical settings beginning in the first month; integration of basic and clinical science throughout four years; instruction in community-based, inpatient and outpatient settings; utilization of diverse learning strategies; interaction with faculty in an atmosphere that fosters teamwork, camaraderie, and collegiality; and diversity in the student body and patient population, reflecting many ethnic, racial, social, age, lifestyle, and gender differences.

## Curricular Highlights

**Community Service Requirement:** Required. Students complete 60 hours.

**Research/Thesis Requirement:** Optional.

In the first interdisciplinary year, structure, function, cells, tissues, principles of disease, and social and ethical issues are taught. Throughout the first two years, students are instructed in medical history-taking, physical examination, and catastrophic illnesses. Each year includes a two-week clinical elective. In the second organ systems-based year, evidence-based decision making, pathobiology, therapeutics, and eight organ systems are taught. The year concludes with USMLE preparation and time for study. In the third year, students learn through six core clerkships. The fourth year includes two clerkships, six electives (some may be done away), and time for USMLE study and residency interviewing.

## Selection Factors

The School seeks a student body of diverse social, ethnic, and educational backgrounds. Applicants are admitted solely on the basis of individual qualifications without regard to race, religion, gender, sexual orientation, disability, veteran status, national origin, age, or ancestry. Dedication to human concerns, compassion, intellectual capacity, and maturity are of greater importance than specific areas of preprofessional preparation. The School also values evidence of motivation, altruism, leadership, and communication skills. Also considered are one's academic record, MCAT performance, letters of recommendation, history of service, and the results of a personal interview (by invitation). Non-residents of Ohio are strongly encouraged to apply.

## Information about Diversity Programs

The School and its faculty have a stated policy of providing educational opportunities to disadvantaged applicants and applicants from groups underrepresented in medicine. The admissions process gives careful consideration to all applicants. A pre-matriculation program, mentoring, big brother/big sister program, tutoring, USMLE preparation, and assistance in critical thinking and learning are available.

## Regional/Satellite Campuses

The School partners with area hospitals, clinics, and other health care providers. Students spend time in federal hospitals, private hospitals, a children's hospital, neighborhood clinics, nursing homes, and private physician offices. Approximately 360 full time clinical faculty are located in affiliated health care institutions. Many of the School's outreach programs have received national recognition.

---

## Application Process and Requirements 2012–2013

**Primary application service:** AMCAS®
**Earliest filing date:** June 1, 2011
**Latest filing date:** October 15, 2011

**Secondary application required:** Yes
**Sent to:** All applicants
**URL:** www.med.wright.edu/admiss/start.html
**Fee:** Yes, $55   **Waiver available:** Yes
**Earliest filing date:** July 1, 2011
**Latest filing date:** December 31, 2011

**MCAT® required:** Yes
**Latest MCAT® considered:** September 2011
**Oldest MCAT® considered:** September 2008

**Early Decision Program:** School does have EDP
**Applicants notified:** October 1, 2011
**EDP available for:** In-States only

**Regular acceptance notice —**
**Earliest date:** October 15, 2011
**Latest date:** Until class is full
**Applicant's response to acceptance offer —**
**Maximum time:** Two weeks for return of Committal Form

**Requests for deferred entrance considered:** Yes

**Deposit to hold place in class:** No
**Deposit — In-State Applicants:** n/a
**Out-of-State Applicants:** n/a
**Deposit due:** n/a
**Applied to tuition:** n/a
**Refundable:** n/a
**Refundable by:** n/a

**Estimated number of new entrants:** 105
**EDP:** 5, **Special Programs:** 12

**Start month/year:** Early August or Late July 2012

**Interview format:** Two one-on-one interviews, each lasting 30-40 minutes. Regional interviews are not available. Video interviews are not available.

### Preparatory Programs
**Postbaccalaureate Program:** No

**Summer Program:** No

### 2010–2011 First Year Class

|  | In-State | Out-of-State | International |
|---|---|---|---|
| Applications | 1,018 | 1,683 | 17 |
| Interviewed | 328 | 136 | 0 |
| Matriculated | 77 | 24 | 0 |

**Total Matriculants: 101**   **Total Enrollment: 428**

### Financial Information

|  | In-State | Out-of-State |
|---|---|---|
| Total Cost of Attendance | $52,934 | $67,934 |
| Tuition and Fees | $30,188 | $45,188 |
| Other (incl. living expenses) | $20,252 | $20,252 |
| Health Insurance (can be waived) | $2,494 | $2,494 |

**Average 2010 Graduate Indebtedness: $163,930**
**% of Enrolled Students Receiving Aid: 93%**

Source: 2009-2010 LCME I-B survey and 2010-2011 AAMC TSF questionnaire

# University of Oklahoma College of Medicine

## Oklahoma City, Oklahoma

Dotty Shaw Killam
University of Oklahoma College of Medicine
P.O. Box 26901
Oklahoma City, Oklahoma 73126
**T** 405 271 2331    AdminMed@ouhsc.edu

**Admissions:** www.oumedicine.com/body.cfm?id=655

## General Information

The University of Oklahoma College of Medicine offers students a quality education with added advantages. Access to modern patient care facilities and research are provided at a reasonable cost, with a proven record of choice residency placement. Students gain experience in a variety of clinical settings. The college is part of a modern health sciences complex that serves as the state's principal education and research facility for physicians, dentists, nurses, biomedical scientists, pharmacists, public health administrators, and allied health professionals.

## Mission Statement

The University of Oklahoma provides our students the best educational experience through excellence in teaching, research and creative activity, and service to the state and society. New facilities and technology — plus an internationally prominent faculty — will undoubtedly make the University of Oklahoma Health Sciences Center and the College of Medicine one of the next century's regional leaders in education, research, and patient care. OU Medicine believes that caring for our patients with honesty and integrity is essential. We strive for teamwork, effective communication, respect and continual improvement in education and research.

## Curricular Highlights

**Community Service Requirement:** Optional. The Community Health Alliance serves 11 clinics.

**Research/Thesis Requirement:** Optional.

Our program focuses on the development of the physician-patient relationship with attendant experiences for acquiring scientific knowledge, problem-solving skills, and professional behaviors. A significant feature of the curriculum is early exposure to clinical skills through a series of courses that integrate the basic and clinical sciences. A new Clinical Skills Education and Testing Center provides students with opportunities to learn and practice a variety of clinical skills. The online Hippocrates system is also a valuable educational tool for students. Several summer research opportunities are available. There is a growing opportunity for students to study abroad through our International Studies Program.

## Selection Factors

Acceptance into the College of Medicine is based on GPA, MCAT scores, letters of recommendation, and personal interviews conducted on campus by members of the Admissions Board. Review of applicants is holistic. Non-residents can represent up to 25% of the student body. The University of Oklahoma College of Medicine does not discriminate on the basis of race, sex, creed, national origin, age, or handicap.

## Information about Diversity Programs

The University of Oklahoma has a strong commitment to identify, recruit, and educate qualified students from groups underrepresented in medicine. Applications are strongly encouraged from these groups, as well as from any candidate with a disadvantaged background.

## Regional/Satellite Campuses

**Regional Campus Location(s):** Tulsa, OK.

The College of Medicine's primary campus is in Oklahoma City, with a clinical campus in Tulsa.

## Application Process and Requirements 2012–2013

**Primary application service:** AMCAS®
**Earliest filing date:** June 1, 2011
**Latest filing date:** October 15, 2011

**Secondary application required:** Yes
**Sent to:** All applicants
**URL:** https://app.applyyourself.com/?id=UOK-MED
**Fee:** Yes, $65    **Waiver available:** No
**Earliest filing date:** June 1, 2011
**Latest filing date:** November 1, 2011

**MCAT® required:** Yes
**Latest MCAT® considered:** September 2011
**Oldest MCAT® considered:** January 2008

**Early Decision Program:** School does not have EDP
**Applicants notified:** n/a
**EDP available for:** n/a

**Regular acceptance notice —**
**Earliest date:** November 1, 2011
**Latest date:** Until class is full
**Applicant's response to acceptance offer —**
**Maximum time:** Two weeks

**Requests for deferred entrance considered:** Yes

**Deposit to hold place in class:** Yes
**Deposit — In-State Applicants:** $100
**Out-of-State Applicants:** $100
**Deposit due:** Within two weeks with response to acceptance offer
**Applied to tuition:** Yes
**Refundable:** Yes
**Refundable by:** May 15, 2012

**Estimated number of new entrants:** 165
**EDP:** n/a, **Special Programs:** n/a

**Start month/year:** August 2012

**Interview format:** Held October through February. Regional interviews are not available. Video interviews are not available.

## Preparatory Programs

**Postbaccalaureate Program:** No

**Summer Program:** No

## 2010–2011 First Year Class

|  | In-State | Out-of-State | International |
|---|---|---|---|
| Applications | 378 | 1,114 | 9 |
| Interviewed | 263 | 54 | 0 |
| Matriculated | 146 | 19 | 0 |

**Total Matriculants: 165    Total Enrollment: 659**

## Financial Information

|  | In-State | Out-of-State |
|---|---|---|
| Total Cost of Attendance | $49,917 | $75,543 |
| Tuition and Fees | $22,112 | $47,738 |
| Other (incl. living expenses) | $26,105 | $26,105 |
| Health Insurance (can be waived) | $1,700 | $1,700 |

**Average 2010 Graduate Indebtedness: $146,942**
**% of Enrolled Students Receiving Aid: 93%**

*Source: 2009-2010 LCME I-B survey and 2010-2011 AAMC TSF questionnaire*

# Oregon Health & Science University School of Medicine

## Portland, Oregon

Oregon Health & Science University
Office of Education and Student Affairs, L102
3181 S.W. Sam Jackson Park Road
Portland, Oregon 97239-3098

**T** 503 494 2998

**Admissions:** www.ohsu.edu/xd/education/schools/
school-of-medicine/academic-programs/md-program/
admissions/index.cfm

## General Information

Oregon Health & Science University (OHSU) occupies a 101-acre site overlooking the city of Portland. Campus physical facilities include basic science, research, and laboratory buildings, two hospital units with a capacity of 509 beds, and outpatient clinics.

## Mission Statement

The mission of the School of Medicine is to enhance human health through programs of excellence in education, research, health care, and public service to the larger community including underserved populations. In achieving these goals, the OHSU School of Medicine seeks to establish an educational environment that challenges students to strive for academic excellence and fosters development of compassion, humanism, professionalism, and cultural competence in the care of patients from their first days in the classroom to their final rotation in the hospitals and clinics. A priority throughout OHSU is to enable each student to fulfill his or her potential as a human being and as a health care professional while effectively meeting the health-related needs of the multiple communities he or she will serve.

## Curricular Highlights

**Community Service Requirement:** Optional. Community service activities are encouraged.

**Research/Thesis Requirement:** Optional.

The 1st and 2nd year integrated curriculum is devoted to the sciences basic to medicine, focusing on the normal structure and function of the body and continuing with the study of the pathophysiological basis of disease and its treatment. An early clinical experience is afforded through the Principles of Clinical Medicine course, which teaches fundamental knowledge and skills in interviewing and physical diagnosis through a continuity clinical preceptorship. Third year clinical clerkships are completed at OHSU Hospital and Clinics and affiliated hospitals in the Portland area. OHSU offers regional clinical experiences throughout Oregon.

## Selection Factors

The Admissions Committee seeks students who have demonstrated academic excellence and readiness for the profession of medicine and who will contribute to the diversity necessary to enhance the medical education of all students. Applicants are selected on the basis of demonstrated motivation for medicine, humanistic attitudes, and a realistic understanding of the role of the physician in providing excellent health care to all communities in need of care. Attention is paid to achievements that demonstrate applicants' breadth of interests and experiences, commitment to others, leadership among their peers, and ability to contribute diverse and innovative perspectives to problem-solving in medicine and health care. Evaluation of applicants includes the academic record as demonstration of scholarship; the MCAT; recommendations from undergraduate or graduate school faculty, employers, and those familiar with applicants' health care, volunteer, and community service experiences; and the interviews. Preference is given to residents of Oregon, WICHE-certified residents of Montana and Wyoming, MD/PhD and MD/MPH candidates, and non-resident applicants with superior achievements in academics and other related experiences. The School of Medicine Admissions Committee fully recognizes the importance of diversity in its student body and in the physician workforce in the provision of effective health care delivery. Accordingly, the OHSU School of Medicine strongly encourages applications from persons from all socioeconomic, racial, ethnic, religious, and educational backgrounds and from persons from groups underrepresented in medicine. The committee adheres to a policy of equal opportunity and non-discrimination on the basis of sex, age, race, ethnic origin, religion, disability, military service, sexual orientation, or any other status protected by law.

## Information about Diversity Programs

Information may be obtained by contacting Leslie Garcia, MPA, Asst. Vice Provost, Diversity, Center for Diversity & Multicultural Affairs, (503) 494-5657 or email garcial@ohsu.edu. Web site is www.ohsu.edu/xd/education/student-services/education-diversity/.

## Regional/Satellite Campuses

**Regional Campus Location(s):** Eugene, OR, and Bend, OR.

Third and fourth year students may participate in required and elective clinical experiences in Eugene and Bend, Oregon. Additionally, third year students have the opportunity to complete a clerkship in a rural Oregon community.

## Application Process and Requirements 2012–2013

**Primary application service:** AMCAS®
**Earliest filing date:** June 1, 2011
**Latest filing date:** October 15, 2011

**Secondary application required:** Yes
**Sent to:** All applicants
**URL:** Sent via e-mail after verification of AMCAS® application.
**Fee:** Yes, $100   **Waiver available:** Yes
**Earliest filing date:** July 1, 2011
**Latest filing date:** February 1, 2012

**MCAT® required:** Yes
**Latest MCAT® considered:** September 2011
**Oldest MCAT® considered:** 2009

**Early Decision Program:** School does not have EDP
**Applicants notified:** n/a
**EDP available for:** n/a

**Regular acceptance notice —**
**Earliest date:** October 15, 2011
**Latest date:** Until class is full
**Applicant's response to acceptance offer —**
**Maximum time:** Two weeks

**Requests for deferred entrance considered:** No

**Deposit to hold place in class:** No
**Deposit — In-State Applicants:** n/a
**Out-of-State Applicants:** n/a
**Deposit due:** n/a
**Applied to tuition:** n/a
**Refundable:** n/a
**Refundable by:** n/a

**Estimated number of new entrants:** 120
**EDP:** n/a, **Special Programs:** n/a

**Start month/year:** August 2012

**Interview format:** Multiple interviews on OHSU campus. Regional interviews are not available. Video interviews are not available.

### Preparatory Programs

**Postbaccalaureate Program:** No

**Summer Program:** No

## 2010–2011 First Year Class

|  | In-State | Out-of-State | International |
|---|---|---|---|
| Applications | 400 | 4,079 | 22 |
| Interviewed | 217 | 297 | 0 |
| Matriculated | 95 | 29 | 0 |

**Total Matriculants: 124**   **Total Enrollment: 508**

## Financial Information

|  | In-State | Out-of-State |
|---|---|---|
| Total Cost of Attendance | $59,303 | $72,984 |
| Tuition and Fees | $36,099 | $49,780 |
| Other (incl. living expenses) | $18,619 | $18,619 |
| Health Insurance (can be waived) | $4,585 | $4,585 |

**Average 2010 Graduate Indebtedness: $180,703**
**% of Enrolled Students Receiving Aid: 96%**

Source: 2009-2010 LCME I-B survey and 2010-2011 AAMC TSF questionnaire

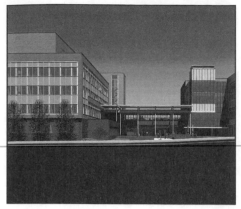

# The Commonwealth Medical College

## Scranton, Pennsylvania

The Commonwealth Medical College
P.O. Box 766, Scranton, Pennsylvania 18501
**T** 570 504 9068 admissions@tcmedc.org
**Admissions:** www.thecommonwealthmedical.com
/admissions

## General Information

The Commonwealth Medical College (TCMC) is a regional, community-based, independent medical school committed to creating patient-centered physicians who will possess the skills needed for 21st century medical practice. TCMC is distinguished by its innovative curriculum including an emphasis on team and case-based learning, an early exposure to community-based clinical settings, the use of medical simulation, and longitudinally integrated clinical clerkships. TCMC has a distributive model of education with three clinical campuses in the Scranton, Wilkes-Barre and Williamsport areas which span both urban and rural settings. In these regions, TCMC partners with community hospitals, residency programs and physicians to provide students an exceptional and diverse clinical experience. At the start of the first year curriculum students are assigned a multi-generational family to follow through the end of their medical school career. Working with their physician mentor, the student will experience the health care system through this family many of whom will have chronic illnesses and challenges with access to care. Students also engage in a community public health project, emphasizing TCMCs commitment to promoting social responsibility and community engagement.

## Mission Statement

The Commonwealth Medical College will educate aspiring physicians and scientists to serve society using a community-based, patient-centered, interprofessional and evidence-based model of education that is committed to inclusion, promotes discovery and utilizes innovative techniques.

## Curricular Highlights

**Community Service Requirement:** Required.

**Research/Thesis Requirement:** Optional.

The pre-clinical curriculum creates an atmosphere of active learning that is less than 20% lecture based, emphasizing individual, small group, and case based learning. Clinical experiences are integrated into the first two years and the third year offers a longitudinal clerkship model that integrates all core specialty objectives over the entire year in order to increase retention of knowledge, create student-centered experiences, encourage continuity with patients, and enhance student satisfaction. The curriculum was designed around the characteristics that make a physician successful, including the ability to: acquire new scientific information and adapt practice patterns to reflect this information; communicate effectively with patients and members of the health care team; work as a member of a an interprofessional team; build long term relationships with patients; improve the health of communities through population-based research and service; incorporate quality improvement and patient safety into their practices; use technology to enhance patient and physician decision making and patient safety and satisfaction.

## Selection Factors

We are looking for students with a strong sense of social responsibility, who desire a sophisticated community-based practice caring for their patients, while improving the health of the community.

## Information about Diversity Programs

The Social Justice and Diversity Department (SJ&D) works with faculty, students and staff to ensure TCMC's core mission and commitment to inclusion permeates our academic and work environment. The Dean allocates yearly scholarships to support students who add to the diversity and SJ&D provides a pre-matriculate Summer Research Internship program to qualified disadvantaged and minority students. TCMC strives to recruit and retain a diverse student-body to enrich the classroom experience and promote service in medically underserved areas in the region.

## Regional/Satellite Campuses

Students complete the majority of the first two years in Scranton, but they integrate into one of three communities with three one-week rotations in each of the first two years, and complete the third and fourth year in their region. The three regional campuses are centered around the Scranton, Wilkes-Barre and Williamsport areas. All campuses include urban and rural regions, and expose students to abundant and diverse clinical experiences.

## Application Process and Requirements 2012–2013

**Primary application service:** AMCAS®
**Earliest filing date:** June 1, 2011
**Latest filing date:** December 15, 2011

**Secondary application required:** Yes
**Sent to:** Secondary application will be sent to all applicants upon receipt of verified AMCAS® application.
**Contact:** Admissions Office, (570) 504-9068, admissions@tcmedc.org
**Fee:** Yes, $100    **Waiver available:** Yes
**Earliest filing date:** August 1, 2011
**Latest filing date:** January 15, 2012

**MCAT® required:** Yes
**Latest MCAT® considered:** September 2011
**Oldest MCAT® considered:** September 2009

**Early Decision Program:** School does not have EDP
**Applicants notified:** n/a
**EDP available for:** n/a

**Regular acceptance notice —**
**Earliest date:** October 15, 2011
**Latest date:** Until class is full
**Applicant's response to acceptance offer —**
**Maximum time:** Two weeks

**Requests for deferred entrance considered:** Yes

**Deposit to hold place in class:** Yes
**Deposit — In-State Applicants:** $100
**Out-of-State Applicants:** $100
**Deposit due:** With response to acceptance offer
**Applied to tuition:** Yes
**Refundable:** Yes    **Refundable by:** May 15, 2012

**Estimated number of new entrants:** 100
**EDP:** n/a, **Special Programs:** n/a

**Start month/year:** August 2012

**Interview format:** Interviews are with both a clinical and basic science faculty member in a conversational format. Regional interviews are not available. Video interviews are not available.

## Preparatory Programs

**Postbaccalaureate Program:** Yes,
www.thecommonwealthmedical.com/mbs
MBS Program, (570) 504-9068, mbs@tcmedc.org

**Summer Program:** No

## 2010–2011 First Year Class

|  | In-State | Out-of-State | International |
|---|---|---|---|
| Applications | 675 | 2,256 | 46 |
| Interviewed | 267 | 270 | 0 |
| Matriculated | 46 | 19 | 0 |

**Total Matriculants: 65**    **Total Enrollment: 129**

## Financial Information

|  | In-State | Out-of-State |
|---|---|---|
| Total Cost of Attendance | $64,172 | $69,422 |
| Tuition and Fees | $38,650 | $43,900 |
| Other (incl. living expenses) | $22,066 | $22,066 |
| Health Insurance (can be waived) | $3,456 | $3,456 |

**Average 2010 Graduate Indebtedness: n/a**
**% of Enrolled Students Receiving Aid: 100%**

*Source: 2009-2010 LCME I-B survey and 2010-2011 AAMC TSF questionnaire*

# Drexel University
# College of Medicine
## Philadelphia, Pennsylvania

Admissions Office
Drexel University College of Medicine
2900 Queen Lane
Philadelphia, Pennsylvania 19129
**T** 215 991 8202   medadmis@drexel.edu
**Admissions:** www.drexelmed.edu/Home/
Admissions/MDProgram.aspx

PA

## Application Process and Requirements 2012–2013

**Primary application service:** AMCAS®
**Earliest filing date:** June 1, 2011
**Latest filing date:** December 1, 2011

**Secondary application required:** Yes
**Sent to:** All applicants
**URL:** http://webcampus.drexelmed.edu/admissions/MyApplication
**Fee:** Yes, $75   **Waiver available:** Yes
**Earliest filing date:** July 2011
**Latest filing date:** January 1, 2012

**MCAT® required:** Yes
**Latest MCAT® considered:** September 2011
**Oldest MCAT® considered:** April 2009

**Early Decision Program:** School does have EDP
**Applicants notified:** October 1, 2011
**EDP available for:** Both In-State and Out-of-State Applicants

**Regular acceptance notice —**
**Earliest date:** October 15, 2011
**Latest date:** Until class is full
**Applicant's response to acceptance offer —**
**Maximum time:** 21 days

**Requests for deferred entrance considered:** Yes

**Deposit to hold place in class:** Yes
**Deposit — In-State Applicants:** $100
**Out-of-State Applicants:** $100
**Deposit due:** 21 days from acceptance offer
**Applied to tuition:** Yes
**Refundable:** Yes
**Refundable by:** May 15, 2012

**Estimated number of new entrants:** 260
**EDP:** n/a, **Special Programs:** 70

**Start month/year:** August 2012

**Interview format:** One faculty open-file, one student closed-file. Regional interviews are not available. Video interviews are not available.

## Preparatory Programs
**Postbaccalaureate Program:** Yes,
www.drexelmed.edu/Home/AcademicPrograms/ProfessionalStudiesintheHealthSciences/Admissions.aspx

**Summer Program:** No

## General Information
Drexel University College of Medicine was formed when two historic Philadelphia medical schools joined their rich histories and resources. The Medical College of Pennsylvania (MCP) was founded in 1850 as the first medical school for women. Hahnemann University, a private nondenominational institution, was founded in 1848. Drexel offers a medical education rich in history and diversity, while providing the foundational curriculum and learning environment necessary for the scientific, technological, and ethical decisions required of physicians in the 21st century.

## Mission Statement
Drexel University College of Medicine delivers innovative biomedical education in an environment that embraces inquiry and collaboration, founded on excellence in patient care, and based on a culture of, and respect for diversity. These principles are built upon the College's legacy of a firm commitment to meeting the healthcare needs of the communities in which we live and work.

## Curricular Highlights
**Community Service Requirement:** Required. 16 hours required in year one.

**Research/Thesis Requirement:** Optional. Though optional, many students conduct research.

Medical students are trained to consider each patient in a comprehensive, integrated manner, taking into account more factors than the presenting physiological condition. The school is dedicated to preparing "physician healers," who practice the art, science, and skill of medicine. Drexel offers a choice between two innovative curricula for the first two years. Interdisciplinary Foundations of Medicine (IFM) integrates basic science courses and presents them through symptom-based modules. Learning in IFM is faculty-driven; students learn in lectures, labs, and small groups. Learning in the Program for Integrated Learning (PIL), a problem-based curriculum, is student-driven, supervised and facilitated by faculty. Students learn in small groups, labs, and resource sessions by focusing on case studies. Both options stress problem-solving, lifelong learning, and the coordinated training of basic science with clinical medicine. Both include the introduction of clinical skills training very early in the first year. The Pathway Program in the fourth year includes a balance of required and elective clinical experiences selected with the pathway advisors to be consistent with general medical training and the student's ultimate career goals.

## Selection Factors
Drexel seeks highly qualified, motivated students who demonstrate the desire, intelligence, integrity, and emotional maturity to become excellent physicians. We encourage nontraditional applicants and are committed to a diverse student body. We seek students who have a firm grasp of the biological and physical sciences as well as broad educational experiences in other areas. Students who demonstrate a commitment to community service are strongly considered. All students must be able to meet the technical standards of the medical school. Applicants must be U.S. citizens or permanent residents. All aspects of an applicant's file are considered, including grades, MCATs, experiences, letters and essay. Interviews with a faculty member and student are important to an applicant's review at committee.

## Information about Diversity Programs
Applications are actively encouraged from groups underrepresented in medicine. Applications from women, those who come from Pennsylvania, and students interested in a career as a generalist physician are also encouraged.

## Regional/Satellite Campuses
**Regional Campus Location(s):** Pittsburgh, PA, and Long Branch, PA.

Students have the opportunity for clinical training in our extensive, integrated network of clinical campuses.

## 2010–2011 First Year Class

|  | In-State | Out-of-State | International |
|---|---|---|---|
| Applications | 1,130 | 11,415 | 39 |
| Interviewed | 441 | 915 | 0 |
| Matriculated | 96 | 164 | 0 |

**Total Matriculants: 260   Total Enrollment: 1,082**

## Financial Information

|  | In-State | Out-of-State |
|---|---|---|
| Total Cost of Attendance | $72,413 | $72,413 |
| Tuition and Fees | $46,985 | $46,985 |
| Other (incl. living expenses) | $21,450 | $21,450 |
| Health Insurance (can be waived) | $3,978 | $3,978 |

**Average 2010 Graduate Indebtedness: $205,502**
**% of Enrolled Students Receiving Aid: 89%**

*Source: 2009-2010 LCME I-B survey and 2010-2011 AAMC TSF questionnaire*

# Jefferson Medical College of Thomas Jefferson University

## Philadelphia, Pennsylvania

**PA**

Office of Admissions
Jefferson Medical College
of Thomas Jefferson University
1015 Walnut Street, Suite 110
Philadelphia, Pennsylvania 19107-5099

**T** 215 955 6983    jmc.admissions@jefferson.edu

**Admissions:** www.jefferson.edu/jmc/admissions

## General Information

As one of the oldest institutions of higher education in the nation, Thomas Jefferson University has, since its founding as the Jefferson Medical College in 1824, emphasized the attainment of clinical excellence in its educational programs. A recent significant expansion of the research programs has created a balanced institutional mission and has enhanced the clinical instruction at Thomas Jefferson University Hospital and its 17 affiliated hospitals.

## Mission Statement

Jefferson's teaching mission centers on the education of outstanding individuals to become physicians well-prepared for medical practice in any specialty area. Our goal is to recruit and educate a diverse student body, and to provide each individual with the educational foundations essential to becoming a knowledgeable, skillful, ethical, and compassionate physician. We aspire to ensure that our students and faculty are respectful, collaborative healthcare professionals who embrace all dimensions of diversity in an environment that promotes understanding of the health care needs of the populations we serve. As has been our legacy since 1824, we are proud to be training future leaders in medicine and in the related biomedical sciences.

## Curricular Highlights

**Community Service Requirement:** Required.

**Research/Thesis Requirement:** Optional.

The curriculum is designed to enable each student to achieve competence in biomedical and social sciences, clinical and research skills, and in the professional values, attitudes, and behaviors requisite for residency training and beyond. The tradition of providing a clinically balanced medical education, encouraged by the faculty, is that students support and cooperate with each other. In the first year, students focus on the function of human organism in its physical and psychosocial context. Clinical coursework focuses on the doctor-patient relationship, medical interviewing and history-taking, human development, behavioral science principles, and core clinical skills and reasoning. In addition to increasing emphasis on the study of clinical skills, the curriculum shifts in the second year to the study of pathophysioiogy and disease. The curriculum includes small-group sessions focusing on problem-solving, evidence-based medicine, and service-based learning. The clinical program consists of two 42-week phases. Phase I covers required clerkships and six weeks of selectives. Advanced basic science, emergency medicine/advanced clinical skills, in- and outpatient subinternships, four weeks of medicine and 20 weeks of elective time, are included in Phase II.

## Selection Factors

Jefferson, in accordance with local, state, and federal law, is committed to providing equal educational and employment opportunities for all persons, without regard to race, color, national and ethnic origin, religion, sexual orientation, age, handicap, or veteran status. Jefferson complies with all relevant ordinances and state and federal statutes in the administration of its educational and employment policies and is an affirmative action employer. The selection of students is made after careful consideration of many factors, including the academic record, letters of recommendation, MCAT scores and interview results regarding the applicant's personal qualities, motivation, interpersonal skills, and achievement in nonacademic areas. Jefferson Medical College traditionally has given special consideration to the offspring of alumni and faculty, groups underrepresented in medicine, and applicants to Jefferson's special programs. International applicants must have a baccalaureate degree from an accredited U.S. or Canadian college or university.

## Information about Diversity Programs

Applications from qualified students from groups underrepresented in medicine are encouraged.

## Application Process and Requirements 2012–2013

**Primary application service:** AMCAS®
**Earliest filing date:** June 1, 2011
**Latest filing date:** November 15, 2011

**Secondary application required:** Yes
**Sent to:** All applicants
**URL:** www.jefferson.edu/jmc/admissions/appforms.cfm
**Fee:** Yes, $80    **Waiver available:** Yes
**Earliest filing date:** June 1, 2011
**Latest filing date:** January 16, 2012

**MCAT® required:** Yes
**Latest MCAT® considered:** September 2011
**Oldest MCAT® considered:** September 2008

**Early Decision Program:** School does have EDP
**Applicants notified:** September 30, 2011
**EDP available for:** Both In-State and Out-of-State Applicants

**Regular acceptance notice —**
**Earliest date:** October 17, 2011
**Latest date:** Until class is full
**Applicant's response to acceptance offer —**
**Maximum time:** Three weeks

**Requests for deferred entrance considered:** Yes

**Deposit to hold place in class:** Yes
**Deposit — In-State Applicants:** $100
**Out-of-State Applicants:** $100
**Deposit due:** at time of acceptance
**Applied to tuition:** Yes
**Refundable:** Yes
**Refundable by:** May 15, 2012

**Estimated number of new entrants:** 260
**EDP:** 5, **Special Programs:** 40

**Start month/year:** August 2012

**Interview format:** One-on-one, open file (faculty) and closed file (student). Regional interview available on campus only. Video interviews are not available.

## Preparatory Programs

**Postbaccalaureate Program:** No

**Summer Program:** No

## 2010–2011 First Year Class

|  | In-State | Out-of-State | International |
|---|---|---|---|
| Applications | 1,080 | 8,143 | 538 |
| Interviewed | 236 | 542 | 24 |
| Matriculated | 113 | 140 | 7 |

**Total Matriculants: 260    Total Enrollment:1,035**

## Financial Information

|  | In-State | Out-of-State |
|---|---|---|
| Total Cost of Attendance | $70,696 | $70,696 |
| Tuition and Fees | $46,628 | $46,628 |
| Other (incl. living expenses) | $20,505 | $20,505 |
| Health Insurance (can be waived) | $3,563 | $3,563 |

**Average 2010 Graduate Indebtedness: $167,509**
**% of Enrolled Students Receiving Aid: 85%**

Source: 2009-2010 LCME I-B survey and 2010-2011 AAMC TSF questionnaire

# Pennsylvania State University College of Medicine

## Hershey, Pennsylvania

Pennsylvania State University College of Medicine
Office of Medical Student Affairs, H060
500 University Drive
P.O. Box 850
Hershey, Pennsylvania 17033

T 717-531-8755 studentadmissions@hmc.psu.edu

**Admissions:** www.pennstatehershey.org/college

## General Information

Penn State's Milton S. Hershey Medical Center opened its doors to the first class of medical students in 1967 and became the first medical school in the nation to establish a Department of Humanities, introducing humanistic disciplines into the required medical curriculum. The College of Medicine was also the first to start an independent Department of Family and Community Medicine. From its beginning, medical education and patient care have been guided by the institution's commitment to provide humane, compassionate, and expert care.

## Mission Statement

Penn State College of Medicine is dedicated to the education of physicians and scientists in all of the disciplines of medicine and biomedical investigation for careers in practice, teaching, and research. Necessary to this educational mission are the provision of outstanding medical care and services and the enhancement of new knowledge through clinical and basic biomedical research.

## Curricular Highlights

**Community Service Requirement:** Optional. *www.pennstatehershey.org/college*

**Research/Thesis Requirement:** Required. *www.pennstatehershey.org/msr*

A single integrated curriculum for years one and two combines elements of traditional medical teaching and case-based learning. The first-year curriculum and courses are interdisciplinary, combining case-based, student-centered learning with strategic lectures, laboratories, and small-group discussions. The second-year curriculum is more heavily oriented to case-based learning in an organ system approach to human health, pathophysiology, and disease. Year three includes a sequence of required core clinical clerkships in internal medicine, general surgery, pediatrics, obstetrics and gynecology, psychiatry, family and community medicine, and primary care, supplemented by selectives. In addition, there are four week-long sessions in Advanced Clinical Diagnostics and Therapeutics, Communications and Professionalism, and Improving Healthcare. Year four consists of four elective rotations and four required advanced experiences. The College of Medicine offers a wide variety of both clinical and research electives. Students may select outpatient clinical rotations at teaching hospitals or in university-affiliated physicians' offices located in a variety of rural and metropolitan communities nationwide and abroad. All students participate in an individualized research program.

## Selection Factors

Applicants must show evidence of strong undergraduate achievement and outstanding personal characteristics. Each application is holistically reviewed. A decision is reached after thorough evaluation of the applicant's academic record, letters of recommendation, extracurricular activities, unique characteristics and accomplishments, personal qualities, MCAT scores, service to their communities and on-campus interviews. Since the practice of medicine requires a lifelong devotion to self-education, emphasis is placed on the excellence of the individual scholar no matter what the student's previous area of study.

## Information about Diversity Programs

Diversity is a core value of the Penn State College of Medicine. Students from groups underrepresented in medicine are strongly encouraged to apply. Faculty, staff and students actively participate in the recruitment of students from underrepresented minorities.

## Regional/Satellite Campuses

**Regional Campus Location(s):** State College, PA.

The College of Medicine has forged a large number of collaborations that provide extensive opportunities for medical students. Students rotate at defined institutions that meet the College of Medicine's high standards of educational quality.

## Application Process and Requirements 2012–2013

**Primary application service:** AMCAS®
**Earliest filing date:** June 1, 2011
**Latest filing date:** November 15, 2011

**Secondary application required:** Yes
**Sent to:** All applicants
**Contact:** Office of Medical Student Admissions, (717) 531-8755, studentadmissions@hmc.psu.edu
**Fee:** Yes, $75    **Waiver available:** Yes
**Earliest filing date:** Based on e-mail invitation
**Latest filing date:** January 15, 2012

**MCAT® required:** Yes
**Latest MCAT® considered:** September 2011
**Oldest MCAT® considered:** 2009

**Early Decision Program:** School does have EDP
**Applicants notified:** October 1, 2011
**EDP available for:** Both In-State and Out-of-State Applicants

**Regular acceptance notice —**
**Earliest date:** October 16, 2011
**Latest date:** Until class is full
**Applicant's response to acceptance offer —**
**Maximum time:** Two weeks

**Requests for deferred entrance considered:** Yes
**Deposit to hold place in class:** Yes
**Deposit — In-State Applicants:** $100
**Out-of-State Applicants:** $100
**Deposit due:** May 15, 2012
**Applied to tuition:** Yes
**Refundable:** Yes
**Refundable by:** May 15, 2012

**Estimated number of new entrants:** 145
**EDP:** n/a, **Special Programs:** n/a

**Start month/year:** August 2012

**Interview format:** Interviews occur on campus by individual invitation. Regional interviews are not available. Video interviews are not available.

## Preparatory Programs

**Postbaccalaureate Program:** No

**Summer Program:** No

## 2010–2011 First Year Class

|  | In-State | Out-of-State | International |
|---|---|---|---|
| Applications | 1,057 | 6,045 | 460 |
| Interviewed | 288 | 534 | 54 |
| Matriculated | 72 | 70 | 3 |

**Total Matriculants: 145    Total Enrollment: 584**

## Financial Information

|  | In-State | Out-of-State |
|---|---|---|
| Total Cost of Attendance | $54,296 | $65,782 |
| Tuition and Fees | $37,842 | $49,328 |
| Other (incl. living expenses) | $15,010 | $15,010 |
| Health Insurance (can be waived) | $1,444 | $1,444 |

**Average 2010 Graduate Indebtedness: $183,509**
**% of Enrolled Students Receiving Aid: 92%**

*Source: 2009-2010 LCME I-B survey and 2010-2011 AAMC TSF questionnaire*

# Temple University School of Medicine
## Philadelphia, Pennsylvania

Office of Admissions
Temple University School of Medicine
3500 N. Broad Street, Suite 124
Philadelphia, Pennsylvania 19140

**T** 215 707 3656   medadmissions@temple.edu
**Admissions:** www.temple.edu/medicine/admissions

## General Information

A 480,000 square foot 11-story medical school building opened in 2009. This state of the art teaching and collaborative research space has transformed the medical school campus and allowed its continued growth as one of the nation's premier urban academic medical centers.

## Mission Statement

A center of humanistic medicine, Temple University School of Medicine (TUSM) is known for its culture of service, diversity and collaboration. TUSM has three major interrelated missions: 1) provide excellent learner-centered education to a diverse body of medical and graduate students, instilling in them an ethic of human service and lifelong learning; 2) engage in research that advances medical science and clinical care; and 3) provide state-of-the-art health care.

## Curricular Highlights

**Community Service Requirement:** Optional.

**Research/Thesis Requirement:** Optional.

Temple has a competency-based, Integrated Curriculum (IC), providing integration among basic science disciplines and between basic science and clinical disciplines. The IC provides students with the opportunities to learn and practice the basic knowledge, clinical skills, and attitudes/behaviors essential to the practice of medicine. The IC is divided into a number of interdisciplinary blocks, each organized according to body or organ systems, and taught by faculty from several basic science and clinical academic departments. The clerkships in years 3 and 4 will provide exposure to a unique variety of clinical experiences, both inpatient and ambulatory. The curriculum incorporates state-of-the-art teaching technologies, including patient simulation, and fosters critical thinking skills with team teaching case-based workshops. Service learning activities play a prominent role in the clinical components of years 1 and 2. International opportunities recognize the importance of the globalization of health care.

## Selection Factors

An individualized holistic review of each completed application includes a variety of objective and subjective factors. The academic record, the college attended, MCAT scores, recommendations, extracurricular activities, work experience, medically related experience, and community service activities are all taken into account when selecting candidates for interview. While not required, many students have participated in research activities. Approximately half of the matriculants are Pennsylvania residents, but non-residents with a particular interest in Temple and strong credentials are encouraged to apply. Students in the 2010 entering class attended 91 different schools.

## Information about Diversity Programs

The School of Medicine is committed to diversity in the faculty and student body. The Recruitment, Admissions, & Retention (RAR) program provides exceptional resources for professional academic guidance and counseling for applicants and students who are from disadvantaged backgrounds or groups underrepresented in medicine.

## Regional/Satellite Campuses

**Regional Campus Location(s):** Danville, PA, Bethlehem, PA, and Pittsburgh, PA.

In addition to the clinical experience and instruction provided at Temple University Hospital, clinical and regional campuses have been established throughout the Commonwealth. Sites include the Geisinger Health System in Danville, the St. Luke's Hospital and Health System in Bethlehem and the West Penn Allegheny Health System in Pittsburgh. Applicants rank their regional or clinical campus preferences on the supplemental application. Students accepted to one of the clinical campuses will complete the first and second year of medical school in Philadelphia and the third and fourth year required rotations in Danville, Pittsburgh or the Philadelphia region. Students can also select our newly established regional campus, The Medical School of Temple University/ St. Luke's Hospital and Health Network. Students at the new St. Luke's Regional Campus will complete the first year in Philadelphia, followed by years two, three, and four at St. Luke's Hospital in Bethlehem. Year two of the program includes clinically-related integrated basic science classroom study in a small group setting, and years three and four include clinical rotations at the St. Luke's Hospital-Bethelehem Campus.

## Application Process and Requirements 2012–2013

**Primary application service:** AMCAS®
**Earliest filing date:** June 1, 2011
**Latest filing date:** December 15, 2011

**Secondary application required:** Yes
**Sent to:** U.S. citizens, permanent residents or applicants who have refugee/asylee status.
**URL:** Sent when verified AMCAS® application is received
**Fee:** Yes, $75   **Waiver available:** Yes
**Earliest filing date:** July 1, 2011
**Latest filing date:** January 15, 2012

**MCAT® required:** Yes
**Latest MCAT® considered:** September 2011
**Oldest MCAT® considered:** January 2009

**Early Decision Program:** School does have EDP
**Applicants notified:** October 1, 2011
**EDP available for:** Both In-State and Out-of-State Applicants

**Regular acceptance notice —**
**Earliest date:** October 15, 2011
**Latest date:** Varies
**Applicant's response to acceptance offer —**
**Maximum time:** Two weeks

**Requests for deferred entrance considered:** Yes

**Deposit to hold place in class:** Yes
**Deposit — In-State Applicants:** $100
**Out-of-State Applicants:** $100
**Deposit due:** Within two weeks of acceptance offer
**Applied to tuition:** Yes
**Refundable:** Yes
**Refundable by:** May 15, 2012

**Estimated number of new entrants:** 210
**EDP:** 5, **Special Programs:** 30

**Start month/year:** August 2012

**Interview format:** Applicants have an interview with a faculty member and a student. Regional interviews are available only for applicants to St. Luke's. Video interviews are not available.

## Preparatory Programs

**Postbaccalaureate Program:** Yes,
www.temple.edu/medicine/postbac

**Summer Program:** Yes,
www.temple.edu/medicine/rar

## 2010–2011 First Year Class

|  | In-State | Out-of-State | International |
|---|---|---|---|
| Applications | 1,144 | 8,316 | 46 |
| Interviewed | 311 | 676 | 0 |
| Matriculated | 99 | 79 | 0 |

**Total Matriculants: 178**     **Total Enrollment: 750**

## Financial Information

|  | In-State | Out-of-State |
|---|---|---|
| Total Cost of Attendance | $68,567 | $78,296 |
| Tuition and Fees | $44,368 | $54,182 |
| Other (incl. living expenses) | $20,924 | $20,839 |
| Health Insurance (can be waived) | $3,275 | $3,275 |

**Average 2010 Graduate Indebtedness: $200,052**
**% of Enrolled Students Receiving Aid: 92%**

Source: 2009-2010 LCME I-B survey and 2010-2011 AAMC TSF questionnaire

# University of Pennsylvania School of Medicine

## Philadelphia, Pennsylvania

Office of Admissions and Financial Aid
Suite 100, Edward J. Stemmler Hall
University of Pennsylvania School of Medicine
3450 Hamilton Walk
Philadelphia, Pennsylvania 19104-6056

**T** 215 898 8001 admiss@mail.med.upenn.edu

**Admissions:** www.med.upenn.edu/admiss

## General Information

The School of Medicine, the first in the United States is a private, nondenominational school on the urban campus of the University of Pennsylvania. There is broad interaction and collaboration between disciplines and organizations in the University and the School of Medicine. This one university concept enrolls medical students as members of the university as well as the School of Medicine community.

## Mission Statement

Our mission is to create the future of medicine through: Patient Care and Service Excellence, Educational Pre-eminence, New Knowledge and Innovation, and National and International Leadership.

## Curricular Highlights

**Community Service Requirement: Required.** Three-year patient-centered experience.

**Research/Thesis Requirement: Required.** Three month scholarly pursuit and/or dual degree.

The four-year curriculum has three themes: Science of Medicine, Technology and Practice of Medicine, and Professionalism and Humanism. Module 1 (four months) provides the foundation of basic sciences and is divided into four blocks: Developmental and Molecular Biology; Cell Physiology and Metabolism: Human Body, Structure, and Function; and Host Defenses and Responses. Grades are pass/fail. Module 2 (40 weeks) integrates basic science across organ systems and ends in December of Year 2. Topics are organized by: Normal Development, Normal Processes, Abnormal Processes, Therapeutics and Disease Management, Epidemiology/Evidenced-based Medicine, Prevention, and Nutrition. Grades are honors/pass/fail. Module 3, Technology and Practice of Medicine, runs on two afternoons per week, concurrent with modules 1 and 2 and promotes competency in epidemiology and biostatistics, decision-making, health care economics, population-based medicine, patient safety, quality assurance, geriatrics, and cultural competency. Grades are honors, pass/fail. Module 4, (clinical clerkships), runs from January of Year 2 through December of Year 3 and is composed of 48 weeks of required clinical clerkships divided into four three-month cross-disciplinary experiences. Basic science concepts are reinforced weekly in didactic sessions. Grades in module 4 are Honors, High Pass, Pass, Fail. Module 5 (16 months) begins in January of Year 3 and continues until graduation. It provides students flexibility in their elective/selective and scholarly pursuit experiences and exposure to upper level electives and mentors prior to residency selection. Grades are honors/high pass/ pass/fail. Module 6, Professionalism and Humanism, runs concurrently throughout the curriculum and covers bioethics, multiculturalism, spirituality, research ethics, and confidentiality. Grades are pass/fail. The curriculum is an active learning experience which emphasizes teamwork and small group interaction as well as technology. The design of the curriculum and its flexibility permits dual degrees, certificates, opportunities for global health experiences, research and fellowship programs and an opportunity to customize and personalize your educational experience. Detailed curriculum information can be found at *www.med.upenn.edu/admiss/curriculum.*

## Selection Factors

Selection factors include academic excellence, out-of-classroom activities, and life experience, as well as community service, research, letters of recommendation, and leadership potential. Personal qualities of maturity, integrity, the ability to work with others, and humanistic interests are sought. The entering class of 2010 has representation from 62 undergraduate colleges. Applicants from all states are welcome, but some preference is given to PA residents. Penn does not discriminate on the basis of race, sex, sexual orientation, age, religion, national or ethnic origin, or physical handicap. There is no transfer admission program.

## Information about Diversity Programs

Penn values and encourages diversity of all kinds throughout its student body, housestaff, faculty and health system. The Penn community is one of openness and inclusion while retaining its focus on the recruitment of groups underrepresented in medicine. The cultural competency curriculum, plethora of community outreach programs, and the development of pipeline programs with colleges and high schools are important in meeting our commitment to diversity.

## Application Process and Requirements 2012–2013

**Primary application service:** AMCAS®
**Earliest filing date:** June 1, 2011
**Latest filing date:** October 15, 2011

**Secondary application required:** Yes
**Sent to:** All applicants
**URL:** n/a
**Fee:** Yes, $80  **Waiver available:** Yes
**Earliest filing date:** July 1, 2011
**Latest filing date:** November 15, 2011, 12 a.m. EST

**MCAT® required:** Yes
**Latest MCAT® considered:** September 2011
**Oldest MCAT® considered:** September 2008

**Early Decision Program:** School does have EDP
**Applicants notified:** October 1, 2011
**EDP available for:** Both In-State and Out-of-State Applicants

**Regular acceptance notice —**
**Earliest date:** March 15, 2012
**Latest date:** Until class is full
**Applicant's response to acceptance offer —**
**Maximum time:** Two weeks

**Requests for deferred entrance considered:** Yes

**Deposit to hold place in class:** Yes
**Deposit — In-State Applicants:** $100
**Out-of-State Applicants:** $100
**Deposit due:** May 15, 2012, 5 p.m. EST
**Applied to tuition:** Yes
**Refundable:** Yes
**Refundable by:** May 15, 2012, 5 p.m. EST

**Estimated number of new entrants:** 160
**EDP:** 3, **Special Programs:** 10

**Start month/year:** August 2012

**Interview format:** Two individual interviews/faculty and student. Regional interviews are not available. Video interviews are not available.

## Preparatory Programs

**Postbaccalaureate Program:** Yes,
www.sas.upenn.edu/lps/postbac/

**Summer Program:** Yes,
www.med.upenn.edu/bgs/applicants_other.shtml

## 2010–2011 First Year Class

|  | In-State | Out-of-State | International |
|---|---|---|---|
| Applications | 660 | 5,411 | 303 |
| Interviewed | 119 | 733 | 8 |
| Matriculated | 34 | 127 | 1 |

**Total Matriculants: 162**   **Total Enrollment: 746**

## Financial Information

|  | In-State | Out-of-State |
|---|---|---|
| Total Cost of Attendance | $69,362 | $69,362 |
| Tuition and Fees | $47,196 | $47,196 |
| Other (incl. living expenses) | $19,466 | $19,466 |
| Health Insurance (can be waived) | $2,700 | $2,700 |

**Average 2010 Graduate Indebtedness: $119,800**
**% of Enrolled Students Receiving Aid: 87%**

Source: 2009-2010 LCME I-B survey and 2010-2011 AAMC TSF questionnaire

# University of Pittsburgh School of Medicine

Pittsburgh, Pennsylvania

Office of Admissions and Financial Aid
3550 Terrace Street, 518 Scaife Hal
University of Pittsburgh School of Medicine
Pittsburgh, Pennsylvania 15261

**T** 412 648 9891   admissions@medschool.pitt.edu

**Admissions:** www.medadmissions.pitt.edu

## General Information

The University of Pittsburgh School of Medicine excels in research, curricular development and clinical care with over 2000 full time faculty and a core group of master educators. The University of Pittsburgh and affiliates are ranked 5th in NIH funding. The students rotate through multiple top hospitals drawing from diverse patient populations.

## Mission Statement

Our mission is to improve the health and well-being of individuals and populations through cutting-edge biomedical research, innovative educational programs in medicine and biomedical science and leadership in academic medicine with the highest professional and ethical standards, in a culture of diversity and inclusiveness.

## Curricular Highlights

**Community Service Requirement:** Optional. Participation in multiple activities possible.

**Research/Thesis Requirement:** Required. Completion of a longitudinal scholarly project.

The focus of the curriculum is on teaching patient centered care that is evidence based. The students are encouraged to develop habits of self-education through problem-based and small group learning, literature review, and computer-assisted education. The curriculum is organized into blocks. Students see patients in the first week of school and throughout their entire four years. Training in patient interviewing and examination continues throughout the first and second years until the clerkships begin at the end of the second year. All students do rotations in family medicine, internal medicine, obstetrics-gynecology, pediatrics, psychiatry/neurology, surgery, anesthesia, surgical subspecialties and ambulatory care. Students chose from multiple electives during the third and fourth years. All students complete a longitudinal mentored scholarly project. An honors/pass/fail system is used for grading the first two years.

## Selection Factors

Applicants are chosen on the basis of intellect, integrity, maturity, creativity and strong interpersonal skills. The academic record; MCAT scores; essays; evaluations of college preprofessional committees; letters of recommendation, preferably from faculty members with whom the student has interacted in scholarly pursuits; extracurricular activities, in particular those showing service and medical exposure, are all important in the decision to admit. On campus interviews by both a current medical student and faculty member are required and are weighed heavily in the final decision. All applicants are considered without regard to race, color, religion, ethnicity, national origin, age, sex, sexual orientation, marital, veteran, or handicap status.

## Information about Diversity Programs

The School of Medicine is committed to maintaining a broadly diverse student body/community. We believe such diversity is invaluable in a curriculum heavily based on small group and interactive learning. The school hosts a premedical summer enrichment program organized by the Diversity Office, as well as a Prologue to Medicine Program for all those admitted students who might benefit from such a program. Following admission, a broad range of support services are available to ensure retention. Specific information on the services provided to applicants from groups underrepresented in medicine can be obtained by contacting the Office of Student Affairs and Diversity Programs at (412) 648-8987.

## Regional/Satellite Campuses

The core of the health care system is located in the Oakland, Shadyside and Lawrenceville neighborhoods of Pittsburgh. Students can engage in international experiences in Cyprus, Ireland, Italy, Qatar, and the United Kingdom. Altoona Regional Health System provides experience in rural medicine.

## Application Process and Requirements 2012–2013

**Primary application service:** AMCAS®
**Earliest filing date:** June 1, 2011
**Latest filing date:** November 1, 2011

**Secondary application required:** Yes
**Sent to:** All applicants
**URL:** https://admissions.medschool.pitt.edu
**Fee:** Yes, $85   **Waiver available:** Yes
**Earliest filing date:** July 1, 2011
**Latest filing date:** December 1, 2011

**MCAT® required:** Yes
**Latest MCAT® considered:** September 2011
**Oldest MCAT® considered:** 2008

**Early Decision Program:** School does have EDP
**Applicants notified:** October 1, 2011
**EDP available for:** Both In-State and Out-of-State Applicants

**Regular acceptance notice —**
**Earliest date:** November 15, 2011
**Latest date:** Until class is full
**Applicant's response to acceptance offer —**
**Maximum time:** Two weeks

**Requests for deferred entrance considered:** Yes

**Deposit to hold place in class:** Yes
**Deposit — In-State Applicants:** $100
**Out-of-State Applicants:** $100
**Deposit due:** May 16-25, 2012
**Applied to tuition:** Yes
**Refundable:** No
**Refundable by:** n/a

**Estimated number of new entrants:** 148
**EDP:** 2, **Special Programs:** 10

**Start month/year:** August 2012

**Interview format:** An on-site faculty interview and student interview are required. Regional interviews are not available. Video interviews are not available.

### Preparatory Programs

**Postbaccalaureate Program:** No

**Summer Program:** Yes, www.medschool.pitt.edu/future/future_03_office.asp

## 2010–2011 First Year Class

|  | In-State | Out-of-State | International |
|---|---|---|---|
| Applications | 809 | 4,470 | 13 |
| Interviewed | 156 | 846 | 0 |
| Matriculated | 39 | 109 | 0 |

**Total Matriculants: 148**    **Total Enrollment: 602**

## Financial Information

|  | In-State | Out-of-State |
|---|---|---|
| Total Cost of Attendance | $60,567 | $63,789 |
| Tuition and Fees | $39,555 | $42,777 |
| Other (incl. living expenses) | $18,012 | $18,012 |
| Health Insurance (can be waived) | $3,000 | $3,000 |

**Average 2010 Graduate Indebtedness: $143,075**
**% of Enrolled Students Receiving Aid: 92%**

*Source: 2009-2010 LCME I-B survey and 2010-2011 AAMC TSF questionnaire*

# Ponce School of Medicine
## Ponce, Puerto Rico

Admissions Office
Ponce School of Medicine and Health Sciences
P.O. Box 7004
Ponce, Puerto Rico 00732

**T** 787 840 2575 x 2142   admissions@psm.edu

**Admissions:** www.psm.edu/Student_Affairs/
Admissions/about_department.htm

## General Information

The Ponce School of Medicine and Health Sciences (formerly the Catholic University of Puerto Rico School of Medicine) has been under the governance of the Board of Trustees of the Ponce Medical School Foundation, Inc. since July 1, 1980. It is a free standing school. The Basic Sciences are offered in the main campus. Is affiliated with a number of hospitals and health care facilities. The Institution also owns an Outpatient Clinic located in its main campus and six Behavioral Health Centers at different sites such as Mayaguez, Aguadilla, Coamo, Guayama, Orocovis and Ponce. The affiliation network provides over 2,000 beds and several ambulatory facilities available for clinical teaching and training. Clinical training is offered at the following major facilities: Damas Hospital, a private institution with 356 beds; La Playa Diagnostic Center, which serves as the main training area for community and family practice; Metropolitan Dr. Pila Hospital, with 160 beds; St. Luke's Hospital, with 550 beds; all of these are in Ponce and La Concepcion Hospital, with 188 beds, located in San German; and Dr. Tito Mattei Metropolitan Hospital in Yauco, with 140 beds.

## Mission Statement

The mission of Ponce School of Medicine and Health Sciences is to provide high quality education, research and health services in medicine, biological sciences, clinical psychology, public health, and other health care fields, to the population we serve, through an innovative health sciences curriculum, while preparing students to be ethical practitioners and scientist.

## Curricular Highlights

**Community Service Requirement:** Optional.

**Research/Thesis Requirement:** Optional.

Our academic goal focuses both on scientific medicine and on meeting effectively the primary health care needs of the people in the Commonwealth of Puerto Rico, particularly the southern region of the island. The holistic concept of patient is enforced through a variety of teaching experiences that relate social, environmental, emotional, and cultural factors to medical disorders. During the first two years, the basic medical sciences are thoroughly emphasized. The correlation between the basic and clinical sciences is achieved in a multidisciplinary program. Throughout the four-year program great emphasis is placed on the student's contact with patients and their families as a complement to the student's academic-hospital experience. Every academic semester contains, in addition to the regular curriculum, a series of supplementary seminars dealing with the ethical and social components of medical practice. A problem-based learning program has been introduced in clinical correlation sessions in the first year of medical studies and in the pathophysiology course, where it is presented as a student-centered integrative exercise. Subject-oriented small group discussions are included in basic sciences courses. The curriculum provides students with an early experience in family and community health needs. The program seeks to develop well-balanced, mature general practitioners, equally well qualified in the professional and ethical aspects of medicine. Students' work is graded according to an Honor/Pass/Fail system.

## Selection Factors

Selection of applicants is made by the Admissions Committee on the basis of academic achievement, MCAT scores, recommendation letters, and personal interviews. Interviews are used to determine the motivation and character of the applicants. Only those who pass the preliminary screening are interviewed. Careful consideration is given to all applicants regardless of national or ethnic background, religious affiliation, sex or sexual orientation, or handicap (we comply with ADA). Residents of Puerto Rico are given preference, although a limited number of applicants who live in the United States are accepted. Candidates who are not proficiently fluent in both English and Spanish are not encouraged to apply. Teaching is given in both languages and our patient population only speak Spanish. The 2010 entering class composition is of 79% students from Puerto Rico, and 21% from continental USA.

## Information about Diversity Programs

PSMHS is committed to the recruitment and retention of the best qualified students regardless of being disadvantaged or underrepresented, as long as they meet all the requisites established by the Institution.

## Application Process and Requirements 2012–2013

**Primary application service:** AMCAS®
**Earliest filing date:** June 1, 2011
**Latest filing date:** December 15, 2011

**Secondary application required:** No
**Sent to:** n/a
**URL:** n/a
**Fee:** Yes, $100   **Waiver available:** No
**Earliest filing date:** September 1, 2011
**Latest filing date:** n/a

**MCAT® required:** Yes
**Latest MCAT® considered:** September 2011
**Oldest MCAT® considered:** January 2009

**Early Decision Program:** School does have EDP
**Applicants notified:** October 1, 2011
**EDP available for:** Both In-State and Out-of-State Applicants

**Regular acceptance notice —**
**Earliest date:** December 2011
**Latest date:** Until class is full
**Applicant's response to acceptance offer —**
**Maximum time:** Twenty days

**Requests for deferred entrance considered:** No

**Deposit to hold place in class:** Yes
**Deposit — In-State Applicants:** $100
**Out-of-State Applicants:** $100
**Deposit due:** With response to acceptance offer
**Applied to tuition:** Yes
**Refundable:** Yes
**Refundable by:** April 15, 2012

**Estimated number of new entrants:** 66
**EDP:** 3, **Special Programs:** n/a

**Start month/year:** July 2012

**Interview format:** Interviews are individually or in groups. Regional interviews are not available. Video interviews are not available.

## Preparatory Programs

**Postbaccalaureate Program:** No

**Summer Program:** No

## 2010–2011 First Year Class

|  | In-State | Out-of-State | International |
|---|---|---|---|
| Applications | 409 | 814 | 24 |
| Interviewed | 178 | 40 | 0 |
| Matriculated | 52 | 14 | 0 |

**Total Matriculants: 66**    **Total Enrollment: 66**

## Financial Information

|  | In-State | Out-of-State |
|---|---|---|
| Total Cost of Attendance | $49,616 | $63,291 |
| Tuition and Fees | $24,554 | $35,625 |
| Other (incl. living expenses) | $23,760 | $26,364 |
| Health Insurance (can be waived) | $1,302 | $1,302 |

**Average 2010 Graduate Indebtedness: $166,952**
**% of Enrolled Students Receiving Aid: 77%**

*Source: 2009-2010 LCME I-B survey and 2010-2011 AAMC TSF questionnaire*

# San Juan Bautista School of Medicine
## Caguas, Puerto Rico

Admissions Office
P.O. Box 4968
Caguas, Puerto Rico 00726-4968

**T** 787 743 3038  x 236
admissions@sanjuanbautista.edu

**Admissions:** www.sanjuanbautista.edu/
Admissions.aspx

## General Information

The School of Medicine was founded in 1978 in San Juan, Puerto Rico, as a not-for-profit corporation, incorporated under the laws of the Commonwealth of Puerto Rico. It is located in Caguas, Puerto Rico, one of the most important urban centers. It is authorized by the Puerto Rico Council on Higher Education to offer studies leading to the M.D. degree. The MSCHE granted accreditation to the School in 2004. The LCME granted accreditation to the academic program on 2007. As of June 30, 2010, the School of Medicine has graduated a total of 1,035 medical doctors who have been successfully integrated in their communities as competent and caring health providers, both in Puerto Rico and abroad.

## Mission Statement

Vision: Our endeavor is to excel, as a private academic health center, in the preparation of primary care physicians and other allied health professionals focusing on community-based humanistic medicine. Respect, honesty, compassion, and empathy are attributes that should characterize the SJBSM alumni.  Mission: The San Juan Bautista School of Medicine is a non-profit private institution founded in 1978.  It is located in the east-central region of Puerto Rico. The Medical School's mission is to teach and train students as primary care physicians, and other allied health professionals, which can provide holistic diagnosis and treatment to communities in need of health care services.  Its major purpose is to provide an opportunity for an excellent medical education to students who wish to study on the Island. The Institution is committed to providing high quality medical education, services and research that will foster students' comprehensive development so that they can become capable, competent, skilled and honest professionals. The SJBSM students will be prepared and qualified to go beyond the challenges brought forth by new knowledge and technology in the fields of health services, medical education, and allied health professions in accordance with accrediting agencies emphasizing the integration of science and medical education.

## Curricular Highlights

**Community Service Requirement:** Required. 155 hours required during the first three years.

**Research/Thesis Requirement:** Required. Research project required for graduation.

SJBSM had defined its curriculum within a student-centered approach, highlighting the values, attitudes, and social responsibility of the practice of medicine. It facilitates active learning and integration, offering early exposure to clinical scenarios and technological experiences in the learning process and using diverse assessment methodologies. The curriculum is structured in five emphases: medical knowledge, clinical skills, research and information literacy, professionalism and community awareness. These emphases are incorporated throughout the four years. The preclinical courses are offered in a system-based approach during the first two years. The third year is devoted to core clinical clerkships, both inpatient and outpatient scenarios, including a research clerkship. The fourth year reinforces the practice of medicine with core and electives sub-internships.

## Selection Factors

The Admissions office evaluates all applications, taking into consideration academic and personal qualifications. The analysis includes academic achievement, premedical studies required for admission to the program, and MCAT scores. The motivations to study medicine, leadership qualities, ability to relate to other people and deal with problems, and participation in community/scientific activities, are also taken into consideration by the Admissions Committee. Qualified applicants are required to appear for an interview.

## Information about Diversity Programs

The School of Medicine is committed to diversity in the faculty and the student body. Its goal is to recruit, admit and graduate students that comply with all the requirements. The office of Diversity Affairs has programs to assist to help meeting the objectives of all student body.

## Regional/Satellite Campuses

The School of Medicine has established several collaborations that provide opportunities for its students. Students rotate at hospitals and ambulatory health care systems that met the School's high standards of educational quality.

## Application Process and Requirements 2012–2013

**Primary application service:** AMCAS®
**Earliest filing date:** June 1, 2011
**Latest filing date:** December 15, 2011

**Secondary application required:** No
**Sent to:** n/a
**URL:** www.sanjuanbautista.edu/Admissions.aspx
Jaymi Sanchez-Cruz, (787) 743-3038 x236
admissions@sanjuanbautista.edu
**Fee:** Yes, $100   **Waiver available:** No
**Earliest filing date:** n/a
**Latest filing date:** n/a

**MCAT® required:** Yes
**Latest MCAT® considered:** December 2011
**Oldest MCAT® considered:** December 2008

**Early Decision Program:** School does have EDP
**Applicants notified:** October 1, 2011
**EDP available for:** Both In-State and Out-of-State Applicants

**Regular acceptance notice —**
**Earliest date:** January 2012
**Latest date:** Until class is full
**Applicant's response to acceptance offer —**
**Maximum time:** Two weeks

**Requests for deferred entrance considered:** No

**Deposit to hold place in class:** Yes
**Deposit — In-State Applicants:** $100
**Out-of-State Applicants:** $100
**Deposit due:** Two weeks
**Applied to tuition:** Yes
**Refundable:** Yes
**Refundable by:** May 15, 2012

**Estimated number of new entrants:** 60
**EDP:** 3, **Special Programs:** 0

**Start month/year:** July 2012

**Interview format:** Interviews occur individually or in groups on campus. Regional interviews are not available. Video interviews are not available.

## Preparatory Programs
**Postbaccalaureate Program:** Yes

**Summer Program:** No

## 2010–2011 First Year Class

|  | In-State | Out-of-State | International |
|---|---|---|---|
| Applications | 318 | 568 | 24 |
| Interviewed | 101 | 77 | 0 |
| Matriculated | 49 | 16 | 0 |

**Total Matriculants: 65**      **Total Enrollment: 272**

## Financial Information

|  | In-State | Out-of-State |
|---|---|---|
| Total Cost of Attendance | $54,066 | $57,066 |
| Tuition and Fees | $19,295 | $22,295 |
| Other (incl. living expenses) | $33,185 | $33,185 |
| Health Insurance (can be waived) | $1,586 | $1,586 |

**Average 2010 Graduate Indebtedness: $82,087**
**% of Enrolled Students Receiving Aid: 95%**

*Source: 2009-2010 LCME I-B survey and 2010-2011 AAMC TSF questionnaire*

# Universidad Central del Caribe
# School of Medicine

Bayamón, Puerto Rico

Office of Admissions
Universidad Central del Caribe
School of Medicine,
P.O. Box 60-327
Bayamon, Puerto Rico 00960-6032

**T** 787 798 3001   icordero@uccaribe.edu
edlopez@uccaribe.edu

**Admissions:** www.uccaribe.edu

PR

## General Information

The UCC-SOM was founded in 1976 as a nonprofit private institution chartered under the laws of the Commonwealth of Puerto Rico. The basic sciences building, library, animal house, and central administration was inaugurated in 1990 adjacent to Dr. Ramon Ruiz Arnau University Hospital, which serves as the principal teaching hospital. The school facilities are located in a 56-acre academic health center in the city of Bayamon.

## Mission Statement

The mission of the UCC-SOM is to form competent diverse health professionals with an excellent academic preparation within a humanistic and holistic framework. Our guiding principle is to ensure that our graduates possess a strong sense of professionalism and commitment to their social duties and to service to Puerto Rico and Hispanic communities in the mainland.

## Curricular Highlights

**Community Service Requirement:** Optional.

**Research/Thesis Requirement:** Optional.

The medical curriculum is organized in two years of preclinical and two years of clinical experiences. A longitudinal curriculum in bioethics and humanities in medicine characterizes the medical education program. Clinical correlations are included in the basic science courses. Exposure to real and standardized patients is provided beginning with the first year. Introduction to clinical medicine has as its foundation the biopsychosocial model. A problem-based course is structured around prevalent problems encountered in primary care. The third-year learning experience revolves around required clerkships in internal medicine, pediatrics, obstetrics-gynecology, general surgery, and family medicine. The latter takes place in the ambulatory setting. Also, during the third year, students enroll in the surgical subspecialties and psychiatry clerkships. Eighteen weeks of electives are provided in the fourth year, plus three months in required courses in neurology, ambulatory medicine, selected topics, and bioethics and humanities in medicine. Individual student evaluation in all requisite basic science and clinical science courses is based on letter grade and Pass/Fail systems. Student evaluation in all elective courses is based on an Honors/Pass/Fail system.

## Selection Factors

The selection of candidates for admission is made exclusively by the Admissions Committee. The admission process does not discriminate against any individual on the basis of sex, age, race, religion, economic status, political ideology, or national origin. Applicants must demonstrate proficiency in both Spanish and English. Lectures may be in either language. Spanish is the predominant language of the institution. Major factors considered in the selection of candidates for admission include undergraduate academic record, overall GPA and science GPA, performance in all areas of the MCAT, community services, research and others experiences, results of a personal interview, and letters of recommendation. A personal interview is required prior to consideration for admission. All interviews are arranged by the Office of Admissions and are conducted at the medical school facilities in Bayamon. Rejected applicants are given the opportunity to reapply for admission.

## Regional/Satellite Campuses

Island Student rotations are divided between the University Hospital and a rich network of clinical settings in the Island.

## Application Process and Requirements 2012–2013

**Primary application service:** AMCAS®
**Earliest filing date:** June 1, 2011
**Latest filing date:** December 15, 2011

**Secondary application required:** No
**Sent to:** Several documents must be submitted.
Irma L. Cordero, (787) 798-3001 x 2403,
irma.cordero@uccaribe.edu
**Fee:** Yes, $100   **Waiver available:** No
**Earliest filing date:** n/a
**Latest filing date:** n/a

**MCAT® required:** Yes
**Latest MCAT® considered:** September 2011
**Oldest MCAT® considered:** January 2008

**Early Decision Program:** School does not have EDP
**Applicants notified:** n/a
**EDP available for:** n/a

**Regular acceptance notice —**
**Earliest date:** January 2012
**Latest date:** Until class is full
**Applicant's response to acceptance offer —**
**Maximum time:** Two weeks

**Requests for deferred entrance considered:** No

**Deposit to hold place in class:** Yes
**Deposit — In-State Applicants:** $100
**Out-of-State Applicants:** $100
**Deposit due:** 15 days after notification
**Applied to tuition:** No
**Refundable:** No
**Refundable by:** n/a

**Estimated number of new entrants:** 65
**EDP:** n/a, **Special Programs:** n/a

**Start month/year:** August 2012

**Interview format:** Group interviews. Video interviews are not available.

## Preparatory Programs
**Postbaccalaureate Program:** Yes,
Edllian Lopez, (787) 798-3001 x 2404,
edllian.lopez@uccaribe.edu

**Summer Program:** No

## 2010–2011 First Year Class

|  | In-State | Out-of-State | International |
|---|---|---|---|
| Applications | 396 | 561 | 25 |
| Interviewed | 139 | 30 | 1 |
| Matriculated | 53 | 11 | 1 |

**Total Matriculants: 65**     **Total Enrollment: 252**

## Financial Information

|  | In-State | Out-of-State |
|---|---|---|
| Total Cost of Attendance | $50,005 | $57,575 |
| Tuition and Fees | $25,185 | $32,755 |
| Other (incl. living expenses) | $23,078 | $23,078 |
| Health Insurance (can be waived) | $1,742 | $1,742 |

**Average 2010 Graduate Indebtedness: $43,744**
**% of Enrolled Students Receiving Aid: 87%**

Source: 2009-2010 LCME I-B survey and 2010-2011 AAMC TSF questionnaire

# University of Puerto Rico School of Medicine

## San Juan, Puerto Rico

Central Admissions Office
School of Medicine, Medical Sciences Campus
University of Puerto Rico, P.O. Box 365067
San Juan, Puerto Rico 00936-5067

**T** 787 758 2525 x5215    margarita.rivera4@upr.edu

**Admissions:** www.md.rcm.upr.edu

## General Information

The UPR-SOM was established in 1949. The affiliated hospitals of the P.R. Medical Center and the Hospital Consortium, which include the main health care facilities in other cities, serve the medical school for teaching purposes. On the Medical Sciences Campus, the School of Medicine works in close relation with the School of Dentistry, the College of Allied Health Professions, the Faculty of Biosocial Sciences and Graduate School of Public Health, the School of Nursing, and the School of Pharmacy in an interdisciplinary team approach. Its location, adjacent to the University District Hospital, permits integration of basic and clinical departments and an improved utilization of all Medical Sciences Campus resources.

## Mission Statement

The mission of the UPR-SOM is to transmit, enrich, and increase knowledge in the medical sciences through teaching, research, and clinical service. The school is committed to achieve the ideals of personal and academic excellence through the interdisciplinary model for providing education and health services, especially at the primary level. The school will provide an academic and institutional environment conducive to the personal and professional development of both students and faculty.

## Curricular Highlights

**Community Service Requirement:** Optional.

**Research/Thesis Requirement:** Optional.

The new curriculum is four academic years in length. The first two years include the fundamentals of biological, behavioral, and clinical sciences and are mostly handled by the basic sciences departments. Part of the sophomore year is dedicated to pathophysiology, physical diagnosis, and basic clerkship, which are offered by a multidisciplinary faculty. Small-group sessions utilizing the problem-based learning approach are introduced at the beginning of the medical studies. Human behavior, environmental factors, and public health concepts are integrated into the curriculum. The third and fourth years are dedicated to required clinical experiences and elective courses. Through the Hispanic Center of Excellence, the curriculum has been focused on community-oriented primary care exposure. Support services, counseling, tutorials, and other services are provided to students to assist in retention. Students are graded on a letter grade system during all four years.

## Selection Factors

Since the UPR-SOM is a state-supported institution, preference will be given to qualified applicants who are legal residents of Puerto Rico. Foreign national applicants with an established residence in P.R. will be considered only if, at the time of application, they are either U.S. citizens or have been granted a permanent resident visa in the United States. In selecting students, the Admissions Committee considers the candidate's academic performance, MCAT scores, recommendations of instructors, attitudinal and other personality factors assessed in personal interviews, extracurricular activities, and any other pertinent information. Personal interviews are conducted only by invitation from the Admissions Committee for those students with high numerical ranks according to the admission formula. The admission formula gives equal weight to academic indices and MCAT scores, with somewhat less weight given to ratings derived from evaluations by premedical committees and interviewers. Rejected applicants are given the opportunity to reapply for admission. Applicants, without exception, must submit all application material and supporting documents by December 1 of the year preceding the school year for which they request admission. The UPR-SOM has the policy of giving equal opportunity for education and training in the practice of the health professions without regard to race, creed, sex, national origin, age, or handicap.

## Application Process and Requirements 2012–2013

**Primary application service:** AMCAS®
**Earliest filing date:** June 1, 2011
**Latest filing date:** December 1, 2011

**Secondary application required:** Yes
**Sent to:** All applicants
**Fee:** Yes, $20    **Waiver available:** No
**Earliest filing date:** August 15, 2011
**Latest filing date:** December 1, 2011

**MCAT® required:** Yes
**Latest MCAT® considered:** September 2011
**Oldest MCAT® considered:** September 2008

**Early Decision Program:** School does not have EDP
**Applicants notified:** n/a
**EDP available for:** n/a

**Regular acceptance notice —**
**Earliest date:** December 2010
**Latest date:** Varies
**Applicant's response to acceptance offer —**
**Maximum time:** Two weeks

**Requests for deferred entrance considered:** No

**Deposit to hold place in class:** Yes
**Deposit — In-State Applicants:** $100
**Out-of-State Applicants:** $100
Deposit due: With response to acceptance offer
**Applied to tuition:** Yes
**Refundable:** No
**Refundable by:** n/a

**Estimated number of new entrants:** 110
**EDP:** n/a, **Special Programs:** n/a

**Start month/year:** August 2012

**Interview format:** Regional interviews are not available. Video interviews are not available.

## Preparatory Programs

**Postbaccalaureate Program:** No

**Summer Program:** No

## 2010–2011 First Year Class

|  | In-State | Out-of-State | International |
|---|---|---|---|
| Applications | 370 | 539 | 10 |
| Interviewed | 164 | 0 | 0 |
| Matriculated | 108 | 2 | 0 |

**Total Matriculants: 110**    **Total Enrollment: 445**

## Financial Information

|  | In-State | Out-of-State |
|---|---|---|
| Total Cost of Attendance | $36,617 | $45,873 |
| Tuition and Fees | $11,978 | $21,234 |
| Other (incl. living expenses) | $24,639 | $24,639 |
| Health Insurance (can be waived) | $0 | $0 |

**Average 2010 Graduate Indebtedness: $66,090**
**% of Enrolled Students Receiving Aid: 78%**

*Source: 2009-2010 LCME I-B survey and 2010-2011 AAMC TSF questionnaire*

# The Warren Alpert Medical School of Brown University

## Providence, Rhode Island

Office of Admissions
Alpert Medical School
97 Waterman Street, Box G-A213
Providence, Rhode Island 02912-9706

**T** 401 863 214   MedSchool_Admissions@brown.edu

**Admissions:** http://med.brown.edu/admissions

## General Information

The MD Class of 2015 matriculated into a new medical education building a short distance from the main campus. The new facility allows for eventual enrollment of 120 students per class while providing for the social, technological and educational needs of the next generation of physician scientists. The medical school and its seven affiliated hospitals receive $170 million annually in research funding. Brown is home to the state's only Master of Public Health degree program and to ten public health research centers. Entry into Alpert Medical School is possible through four admission routes.

## Mission Statement

Our mission is to educate physicians in the scientific, ethical, and humanistic dimensions of medicine and to advance our ability to diagnose, treat, and prevent human illness.

## Curricular Highlights

**Community Service Requirement:** Optional.

**Research/Thesis Requirement:** Optional.

Semester I: core basic sciences (semester-long, integrated medical sciences courses and Doctoring, (group sessions on core clinical skills plus community-based clinical skills teaching with physician mentors). Semesters II-IV: systems-based (integrated physiology, pathophysiology, pathology, pharmacology, etc.); and integrated Doctoring. Students in the third and fourth years are required to complete 44 weeks of clinical clerkships (internal medicine, surgery, psychiatry, obstetrics and gynecology, pediatrics, family medicine), an advanced clinical clerkship, an ambulatory longitudinal clerkship and electives.

## Selection Factors

Selection criteria are academic achievement, faculty evaluations, and evidence of maturity, leadership, integrity, and compassion. Eligible candidates generally must present a minimum cumulative grade point average of 3.00 (4.00 scale) in undergraduate courses. Premedical requirements must be completed at an accredited US or Canadian institution of higher learning. Applicants must complete baccalaureate degree requirements before matriculation. Brown University adheres to a policy of equal opportunity in medical education and considers applicants without regard to sex, race, religion, age, disability, status as a veteran, national or ethnic origin, sexual orientation, or gender identity.

## Information about Diversity Programs

Alpert Medical School invites applications from members of ethnic and racial groups underrepresented in medicine. The objective of the Office of Minority Medical Affairs (OMMA) is the recruitment, retention, and graduation of students from groups underrepresented in medicine. The OMMA provides academic and personal counseling, workshops, information on scholarship awards, and a program linking students from groups underrepresented in medicine with alumni/ae from such groups.

## Regional/Satellite Campuses

Clinical training in all four years occurs in a variety of settings, from the affiliated hospitals to diverse community-based sites.

## Application Process and Requirements 2012–2013

**Primary application service:** AMCAS®
**Earliest filing date:** June 1, 2011
**Latest filing date:** November 1, 2011

**Secondary application required:** Yes
**Sent to:** All verified AMCAS® applicants
**URL:** http://bms.brown.edu/admissions/applications
**Fee:** Yes, $100   **Waiver available:** Yes
**Earliest filing date:** June 15, 2011
**Latest filing date:** December 31, 2011

**MCAT® required:** Yes
**Latest MCAT® considered:** September 2011
**Oldest MCAT® considered:** September 2007

**Early Decision Program:** School does not have EDP
**Applicants notified:** n/a
EDP available for: n/a

**Regular acceptance notice —**
**Earliest date:** November 2011
**Latest date:** Until class is full
**Applicant's response to acceptance offer —**
**Maximum time:** Three weeks

**Requests for deferred entrance considered:** Yes

**Deposit to hold place in class:** No
**Deposit — In-State Applicants:** n/a
**Out-of-State Applicants:** n/a
**Deposit due:** n/a
**Applied to tuition:** n/a
**Refundable:** n/a
**Refundable by:** n/a

**Estimated number of new entrants:** 65
**EDP:** n/a, **Special Programs:** 55

**Start month/year:** August 2012

**Interview format:** Group session and two individual meetings. All interviews are at Alpert Medical School. Video interviews are not available.

## Preparatory Programs

**Postbaccalaureate Program:** No

**Summer Program:** No

## 2010–2011 First Year Class

|  | In-State | Out-of-State | International |
|---|---|---|---|
| Applications | 91 | 4,994 | 362 |
| Interviewed | 11 | 250 | 3 |
| Matriculated | 8 | 88 | 1 |

**Total Matriculants: 97**    **Total Enrollment: 416**
*Includes PMLE Program Data*

## Financial Information

|  | In-State | Out-of-State |
|---|---|---|
| Total Cost of Attendance | $63,520 | $63,520 |
| Tuition and Fees | $43,838 | $43,838 |
| Other (incl. living expenses) | $17,334 | $17,334 |
| Health Insurance (can be waived) | $2,348 | $2,348 |

**Average 2010 Graduate Indebtedness: $138,551**
**% of Enrolled Students Receiving Aid: 78%**

*Source: 2009-2010 LCME I-B survey and 2010-2011 AAMC TSF questionnaire*

# Medical University of South Carolina College of Medicine

Charleston, South Carolina

College of Medicine Dean's Office
Medical University of South Carolina
96 Jonathan Lucas Street, Suite 601
P.O. Box 250617
Charleston, South Carolina 29425

**T** 843 792 3283    taylorwl@musc.edu

**Admissions:** www.musc.edu/es/

## General Information

The College of Medicine at MUSC was founded in Charleston in 1824 and is the South's oldest medical school. MUSC's Medical Center is comprised of four separate hospitals (the University Hospital, Ashley River Tower, the Institute of Psychiatry, and the Children's Hospital.) There are centers for specialized care (Heart Center, Transplantation Center, Hollings Cancer Center, Digestive Diseases Center, and Storm Eye Institute). The adjacent VA Hospital, with consortium/community hospitals in Greenville, Spartanburg, Columbia, and Florence, supply additional facilities for clinical teaching.

## Mission Statement

The COM is committed to maintaining an educational environment for all students which prepares them for a career of excellence in the practice of medicine and service. It ensures optimal opportunities for all students, faculty, and administration, including all backgrounds and levels of diversity, to achieve full potential.

## Curricular Highlights

**Community Service Requirement:** Optional.

**Research/Thesis Requirement:** Optional.

The goal of the COM is to produce caring and competent physicians capable of choosing any postgraduate career. The curriculum in the first 2 years integrates basic science concepts with problem solving strategies and clinical skills. Students take histories and physicals and are introduced to the role of the physician in society. Emphasis is placed on small-group instruction and independent, self-directed learning. The 3rd year consists of clerkships in medicine, obstetrics/gynecology, pediatrics, family medicine, surgery, and psychiatry. Selectives in multiple disciplines are also provided for students to gain exposure to major specialty areas. The development of clinical, interpersonal, and professional competence is emphasized. In the 4th year, students are required to have additional training in surgery and internal medicine, complete an externship, and take up to five elective rotations in a wide variety of subspecialties.

## Selection Factors

Selection is based on the total evaluation of a student. Screening for interviews is based on the cumulative GPA and best total MCAT score. Although SC residency is a primary admission consideration, nonresidents with excellent credentials are considered, especially those with close SC ties. Noncognitive traits and accomplishments are evaluated during interviews. Interpersonal skills, motivation, judgment, and compassion are assessed; as well as the quality of recommendations, leadership, and volunteer/clinical/work experiences. Applicants with unique qualities or experiences important for diversity may be considered for added value. Early Decision is offered for applicants with a gpa of 3.5 or above and MCAT scores of 27 or higher. Foreign students must have a permanent resident visa to be considered for the regular MD program.

## Information about Diversity Programs

Students from groups underrepresented in medicine are encouraged to apply; an active recruitment program is in place. PREP is an individually tailored undergraduate course of study prescribed for a few underprepared, but promising SC students who seek admission through AMCAS. The curriculum at the College of Charleston spans two semesters and is full time. No separate application is required. Students considered are those who apply through AMCAS® and are denied admission. Students are selected annually; stipends are provided. A Summer Institute, devoted to underrepresented or rural students, focuses on MCAT/test-taking skills. The COM and the Center for Academic Excellence provide counseling and support services for Summer Institute students.

## Application Process and Requirements 2012–2013

**Primary application service:** AMCAS®
**Earliest filing date:** June 1, 2011
**Latest filing date:** December 1, 2011

**Secondary application required:** Yes
**Sent to:** All applicants
**URL:** www.musc.edu/em/admissions/apply.html
**Fee:** Yes, $85    **Waiver available:** No
**Earliest filing date:** July 15, 2011
**Latest filing date:** January 15, 2012

**MCAT® required:** Yes
**Latest MCAT® considered:** September 2011
**Oldest MCAT® considered:** August 2009

**Early Decision Program:** School does have EDP
**Applicants notified:** October 1, 2011
**EDP available for:** Both In-State and Out-of-State Applicants

**Regular acceptance notice —**
**Earliest date:** November 1, 2011
**Latest date:** Until class is full
**Applicant's response to acceptance offer —**
**Maximum time:** Four weeks

**Requests for deferred entrance considered:** Yes

**Deposit to hold place in class:** Yes
**Deposit — In-State Applicants:** $485
**Out-of-State Applicants:** $485
**Deposit due:** Within four weeks of response to acceptance offer
**Applied to tuition:** No
**Refundable:** Yes
**Refundable by:** May 15, 2012

**Estimated number of new entrants:** 165
**EDP:** 30, **Special Programs:** 3

**Start month/year:** August 2012

**Interview format:** Three one-on-one interviews are required. Regional physicians assist with interviews. Video interviews are not available.

## Preparatory Programs

**Postbaccalaureate Program:** No

**Summer Program:** No

## 2010–2011 First Year Class

|  | In-State | Out-of-State | International |
| --- | --- | --- | --- |
| Applications | 522 | 2,078 | 53 |
| Interviewed | 358 | 71 | 0 |
| Matriculated | 141 | 22 | 2 |

**Total Matriculants: 165**    **Total Enrollment: 697**

## Financial Information

|  | In-State | Out-of-State |
| --- | --- | --- |
| Total Cost of Attendance | $56,911 | $81,643 |
| Tuition and Fees | $33,304 | $58,036 |
| Other (incl. living expenses) | $22,380 | $22,380 |
| Health Insurance (can be waived) | $1,227 | $1,227 |

**Average 2010 Graduate Indebtedness: $162,738**
**% of Enrolled Students Receiving Aid: 90%**

*Source: 2009-2010 LCME I-B survey and 2010-2011 AAMC TSF questionnaire*

# University of South Carolina School of Medicine

## Columbia, South Carolina

Office of Admissions
University of South Carolina School of Medicine
Columbia, South Carolina 29208

**T** 803 216 3625    jeanette.ford@uscmed.sc.edu

**Admissions:** http://admissions.med.sc.edu

## General Information

The University of South Carolina SOM was established in 1977 and is located in the state's capital, Columbia. The school offers a wide range of educational and professional opportunities to its students, featuring a small class size, a nationally recognized Senior Mentor Program, and a state-of-the-art ultrasound curriculum. The school works closely with its three major teaching hospitals to provide students with a wide range of clinical experiences.

## Mission Statement

Established as "A Promise in Practice" the mission of the University of South Carolina SOM is to improve the health of the people of the state of South Carolina through the development and implementation of programs for medical education, research, and the delivery of health care.

## Curricular Highlights

**Community Service Requirement:** Required. Required of all second year students.

**Research/Thesis Requirement:** Optional.

The SOM offers a program of study designed to provide education and training in the art and science of medicine and to prepare students for a wide variety of medical career choices. Each of the first two years consists of two academic semesters housing both basic science and clinically relevant coursework. The correlation between basic and clinical science information in the first two years is emphasized by means of an interdisciplinary, four-semester Introduction to Clinical Medicine course continuum, during which students are exposed to patients in various inpatient, outpatient, community, and rural settings. Third year students rotate through required clinical clerkships in medicine, surgery, pediatrics, obstetrics-gynecology, family medicine, neurology, and psychiatry, plus 2 two-week electives. The fourth year is devoted to advanced clinical work, including 20 weeks each of required and elective rotations, during which students have the opportunity to strengthen their clinical skills and pursue individual academic interests and career goals in preparation for the lifelong study of medicine. An integrated ultrasound curriculum (iUSC) has been introduced in both the basic science and clinical years and is one of the six vertical curricula at the SOM.

## Selection Factors

The selection process involves the comparative evaluation and review of all available application data, including MCAT scores, undergraduate academic performance, letters of evaluation, and the results of personal interviews with Admissions Committee members. The opportunity for admission is greatest for legal residents of South Carolina. Applications are only accepted from permanent residents or U.S. citizens. The ultimate selection of a student is based upon a total and comparative appraisal of the applicant's suitability for the successful practice of medicine. The AMCAS® application is used for preliminary screening. After this initial review, the Admissions Committee may extend an invitation for personal interviews. Each applicant is evaluated on the basis of individual qualifications without regard to age, race, creed, national origin, sex, or disability.

## Information about Diversity Programs

The SOM actively recruits and encourages applications from members of groups underrepresented in the medical profession. The diverse, representative membership of the Admissions Committee assures a thorough, sensitive review of each applicant. For more information, contact Dr. Carol McMahon, the assistant dean for minority affairs at (803) 216-3607.

## Regional/Satellite Campuses

**Regional Campus Location(s):** Greenville, SC.

Students have the option of completing core clinical training in the third and fourth years at the Greenville Hospital System University Medical Center (GHSUMC), the largest comprehensive medical care facility in upstate South Carolina with 642 beds and just under 35,000 admissions per year. On average 35 students in each of the third and fourth years complete clinical training at the regional campus in Greenville.

## Application Process and Requirements 2012–2013

**Primary application service:** AMCAS®
**Earliest filing date:** June 1, 2011
**Latest filing date:** December 1, 2011

**Secondary application required:** Yes
**Sent to:** All applicants
**Contact:** Ms. Shelley Streeter, (803) 216-3625, shelley.streeter@uscmed.sc.edu
**Fee:** Yes, $95    **Waiver available:** Yes
**Earliest filing date:** June 1, 2011
**Latest filing date:** January 15, 2012

**MCAT® required:** Yes
**Latest MCAT® considered:** September 2011
**Oldest MCAT® considered:** 2006

**Early Decision Program:** School does have EDP
**Applicants notified:** October 1, 2011
**EDP available for:** In-States only

**Regular acceptance notice —**
**Earliest date:** October 15, 2011
**Latest date:** Until class is full
**Applicant's response to acceptance offer —**
**Maximum time:** Two weeks

**Requests for deferred entrance considered:** Yes

**Deposit to hold place in class:** Yes
**Deposit — In-State Applicants:** $250
**Out-of-State Applicants:** $250
**Deposit due:** Within four weeks of response to acceptance offer
**Applied to tuition:** Yes    **Refundable:** Yes
**Refundable by:** May 15, 2012 with written request

**Estimated number of new entrants:** 95
**EDP:** 5, **Special Programs:** n/a

**Start month/year:** August 2012

**Interview format:** Two 30-minute interviews. Regional interviews are available in Greenville, South Carolina. Video interviews are not available.

## Preparatory Programs

**Postbaccalaureate Program:** Yes, www.med.sc.edu/Post.Baccalaureate.Certificates.asp, Dr. Chandrashekhar Patel, (803) 733-3274 Chandrashekhar.patel@uscmed.sc.edu

**Summer Program:** No

## 2010–2011 First Year Class

|  | In-State | Out-of-State | International |
|---|---|---|---|
| Applications | 447 | 2,169 | 31 |
| Interviewed | 338 | 77 | 0 |
| Matriculated | 71 | 19 | 0 |

**Total Matriculants: 90**    **Total Enrollment: 337**

## Financial Information

|  | In-State | Out-of-State |
|---|---|---|
| Total Cost of Attendance | $55,366 | $92,580 |
| Tuition and Fees | $30,998 | $68,212 |
| Other (incl. living expenses) | $23,135 | $23,135 |
| Health Insurance (can be waived) | $1,233 | $1,233 |

**Average 2010 Graduate Indebtedness: $140,407**
**% of Enrolled Students Receiving Aid: 96%**

Source: 2009-2010 LCME I-B survey and 2010-2011 AAMC TSF questionnaire

# University of South Dakota
# Sanford School of Medicine
Vermillion, South Dakota

SD

Medical School Admissions
Sanford School of Medicine
University of South Dakota
414 East Clark Street
Vermillion, South Dakota 57069

T 605 677 6886   md@usd.edu

**Admissions:** www.usd.edu/medical-school/medical-doctor-program/index.cfm

## General Information

The School of Medicine was established in 1907 as a 2-year school, and in 1974 became a 4-year, MD program graduating its first class in 1977. Years 1-2 are based in Vermillion, years 3-4 are in either Sioux Falls, Yankton or Rapid City. In 2005, the name was changed to Sanford School of Medicine of the University of South Dakota.

## Mission Statement

The mission of the Sanford School of Medicine of the University of South Dakota School is to provide the opportunity for South Dakota residents to receive a quality, broad-based medical education with an emphasis on family medicine. The curriculum is to be established to encourage graduates to serve people living in medically underserved areas of South Dakota and to require excellence in the basic sciences and in all clinical disciplines. (Complete mission statement on website.)

## Curricular Highlights

**Community Service Requirement:** Required. A community based, cultural diversity program.

**Research/Thesis Requirement:** Optional.

Years 1-2 are subject based with clinical experiences included. To cap year 2, students spend 4 weeks with a primary care MD in a rural community. For year 3 in Sioux Falls or Rapid City, the clerkships in family medicine, internal medicine, pediatrics, ob/gyn, psychiatry, neurology, and surgery are hospital based. For Yankton, year 3 is an ambulatory-based program, with students rotating through all six clerkships throughout the year. Year 4 has rural family medicine, emergency medicine, surgical subspecialties and a sub-internship plus 22 weeks of electives; many take 4-8 weeks outside the state. Grading is A-B-C-D-F.

## Selection Factors

Applicants are chosen on the basis of intellect, character, and motivation. Their academic achievements as indicated by scholastic records and MCAT scores, and personal characteristics including integrity, work ethic, commitment to service, and other indicators of professional development are evaluated. Applicants invited to interview must meet in person with at least two committee members. Interviews are conducted at the office or clinic of the interviewer or at the Vermillion campus. Top priority for supplemental applications and interviews is given to legal residents of South Dakota, with invitation of selected non-residents with very strong ties to South Dakota. An Alumni Student Scholars Program offers up to 4 future/provisional acceptances to South Dakota high school seniors who meet strict criteria. Applications for transfer are only considered for Years 2 or 3 and only from students currently in good standing at an LCME-accredited medical school. Transfers are limited, with priority given to South Dakota residents.

## Information about Diversity Programs

The Sanford School of Medicine is committed to training a diverse group of students to meet the needs of the diverse population of the state. Applicants may contact the Director of Diversity Affairs for information about diversity enhancement programs.

## Regional/Satellite Campuses

**Regional Campus Location(s):** Yankton, SD, and Rapid City, SD.

Besides the 4 major campuses, students have options to rotate through many training sites around the state.

## Application Process and Requirements 2012–2013

**Primary application service:** AMCAS®
**Earliest filing date:** June 1, 2011
**Latest filing date:** November 15, 2011

**Secondary application required:** Yes
**Sent to:** Most South Dakota residents and selected non-residents with strong ties to South Dakota
**Contact:** Jill Christopherson (605) 677-6886 Jill.Christopherson@usd.edu
**Fee:** Yes, $35   **Waiver available:** No
**Earliest filing date:** July 1, 2011
**Latest filing date:** Two weeks after offer of Secondary Application

**MCAT® required:** Yes
**Latest MCAT® considered:** September 2011
**Oldest MCAT® considered:** January 2009

**Early Decision Program:** School does not have EDP
**Applicants notified:** n/a
**EDP available for:** n/a

**Regular acceptance notice —**
**Earliest date:** November 15, 2011
**Latest date:** Until class is full
**Applicant's response to acceptance offer —**
**Maximum time:** Two weeks after offer

**Requests for deferred entrance considered:** Yes

**Deposit to hold place in class:** Yes
**Deposit — In-State Applicants:** $100
**Out-of-State Applicants:** $100
**Deposit due:** With response to acceptance offer
**Applied to tuition:** Yes
**Refundable:** Yes
**Refundable by:** June 1, 2012

**Estimated number of new entrants:** 48
**EDP:** n/a, **Special Programs:** 6

**Start month/year:** August 1, 2012

**Interview format:** Open file, two individual face-to-face interviews. Regional interviews are not available. Video interviews are not available.

## Preparatory Programs
**Postbaccalaureate Program:** No

**Summer Program:** No

## 2010–2011 First Year Class

|  | In-State | Out-of-State | International |
|---|---|---|---|
| Applications | 118 | 332 | 5 |
| Interviewed | 108 | 45 | 0 |
| Matriculated | 44 | 10 | 0 |

**Total Matriculants: 54**     **Total Enrollment: 217**

## Financial Information

|  | In-State | Out-of-State |
|---|---|---|
| Total Cost of Attendance | $47,279 | $71,405 |
| Tuition and Fees | $23,011 | $47,137 |
| Other (incl. living expenses) | $20,404 | $20,404 |
| Health Insurance (can be waived) | $3,864 | $3,864 |

**Average 2010 Graduate Indebtedness: $129,741**
**% of Enrolled Students Receiving Aid: 98%**

*Source: 2009-2010 LCME I-B survey and 2010-2011 AAMC TSF questionnaire*

# East Tennessee State University
# James H. Quillen
# College of Medicine

Johnson City, Tennessee

Assistant Dean for Admissions and Records
East Tennessee State University
James H. Quillen College of Medicine
P.O. Box 70580,
Johnson City, Tennessee 37614-1708

T 423 439 2033    sacom@etsu.edu

**Admissions:** www.etsu.edu/com/sa/admissions/default.aspx

**TN**

## General Information

Opening in 1978, ETSU's Quillen College of Medicine has established itself as a national leader in primary care and rural medicine. Quillen students enjoy an exceptional success rate in the national residency match, and over 50 percent of graduates choose a career in primary care. Quillen's Community Partnerships Program and the Rural Primary Care Track continues to garner national recognition. A collegial atmosphere is encouraged at all levels and student involvement is valued. The medical campus is located on the grounds of the VA Medical Center pictured above and boasts one of the most technologically advanced patient simulation programs in the nation. The school is located in Tennessee's fourth largest metropolitan area (population 1.2 million) and is part of the state's fourth largest university (enrollment 16,000). It is supported by modern and convenient medical centers and clinics throughout the Tri-Cities area, as well as by hospitals and clinics located in small, rural communities such as Rogersville, Sevierville and Mountain City. The school enrolls one class of 72 new students in August of each year.

## Mission Statement

The primary mission of Quillen College of Medicine is to prepare and educate excellent physicians, especially those with an interest in primary care, to practice in underserved rural communities. The college is also committed to excellence in biomedical research and is dedicated to the improvement of health care in Northeast Tennessee and the surrounding Appalachian Region.

## Curricular Highlights

**Community Service Requirement:** Optional.

**Research/Thesis Requirement:** Optional.

The Quillen College of Medicine enjoys a dynamic and ever-changing curriculum. Student input is a key component in curricular change, along with the rapidly changing body of knowledge and the needs of the profession. The curriculum includes a mix of traditional, systems-based, and case-based learning, as well as a wide range of educational experiences, patient populations, and hospitals. The highly diversified faculty considers students as colleagues. Patient contact comes early in the curriculum and continues throughout. Flexibility is allowed for students to decelerate a portion of the curriculum for elective courses, including research and advanced clinical studies or the combined MD/MPH program. The goals of the curriculum are to prepare students to be well grounded in the science and art of medicine, capable practitioners of their profession, and self-directed, lifelong learners.

## Selection Factors

To be admitted, an applicant must be a U.S. or Canadian citizen or possess a U.S. permanent resident visa. Admission is based upon a competitive selection process involving those applicants who meet the minimum requirements for admission. The Admissions Committee selects students who give the promise of being not merely satisfactory medical students, but also capable, responsible, professional physicians of high ethical standards. The Admissions Committee screens applicants on the basis of academic achievement, MCAT scores, letters of recommendation, pertinent extracurricular research and work experiences, and evidence of non-scholastic accomplishments. After a general screening, the Admissions Committee may request supplementary information and a personal interview with the applicant. Interviews are held only on the campus and are at the applicant's expense. Admission preferences are for residents of the state of Tennessee who are U.S. citizens, veterans of U.S. military service, and recipients of baccalaureate degrees prior to enrollment. Marginally qualified non-residents should not apply.

## Information about Diversity Programs

The College of Medicine actively seeks applicants of both sexes and members of groups underrepresented in medicine. African-American matriculants may be eligible for financial awards from the state of Tennessee. Support services are available to matriculants to assist in the timely completion of the medical curriculum. ETSU values diversity and does not discriminate on the basis of race, sex, creed, national origin, age, or disability. The university is an equal opportunity/affirmative action employer.

## Application Process and Requirements 2012–2013

**Primary application service:** AMCAS®
**Earliest filing date:** June 1, 2011
**Latest filing date:** November 15, 2011

**Secondary application required:** Yes
**Sent to:** Selected applicants
**URL:** n/a
**Fee:** Yes, $50    **Waiver available:** Yes
**Earliest filing date:** June 1, 2011
**Latest filing date:** Twenty-one days from request

**MCAT® required:** Yes
**Latest MCAT® considered:** September 2011
**Oldest MCAT® considered:** January 2009

**Early Decision Program:** School does have EDP
**Applicants notified:** October 1, 2011
**EDP available for:** Both In-State and Out-of-State Applicants

**Regular acceptance notice —
Earliest date:** October 15, 2011
**Latest date:** Until class is full
**Applicant's response to acceptance offer —
Maximum time:** Two weeks

**Requests for deferred entrance considered:** Yes
**Deposit to hold place in class:** Yes
**Deposit    In-State Applicants:** $100
**Out-of-State Applicants:** $100
**Deposit due:** With response to acceptance offer
**Applied to tuition:** Yes
**Refundable:** Yes
**Refundable by:** May 15, 2012

**Estimated number of new entrants:** 72
**EDP:** 3, **Special Programs:** n/a

**Start month/year:** August 2012

**Interview format:** Two, unstructured, one-on-one with admissions committee members. Regional interviews are not available. Video interviews are not available.

**Preparatory Programs**
**Postbaccalaureate Program:** No
**Summer Program:** No

## 2010–2011 First Year Class

|  | In-State | Out-of-State | International |
|---|---|---|---|
| Applications | 564 | 1,012 | 40 |
| Interviewed | 209 | 58 | 0 |
| Matriculated | 63 | 8 | 0 |

**Total Matriculants: 71**    **Total Enrollment: 258**

## Financial Information

|  | In-State | Out-of-State |
|---|---|---|
| Total Cost of Attendance | $45,852 | $71,748 |
| Tuition and Fees | $26,567 | $52,463 |
| Other (incl. living expenses) | $18,003 | $18,003 |
| Health Insurance (can be waived) | $1,282 | $1,282 |

**Average 2010 Graduate Indebtedness: $132,337**
**% of Enrolled Students Receiving Aid: 93%**

*Source: 2009-2010 LCME I-B survey and 2010-2011 AAMC TSF questionnaire*

# Meharry Medical College
# School of Medicine
## Nashville, Tennessee

Director, Admissions and Recruitment
Meharry Medical College
1005 Dr. D. B. Todd Boulevard
Nashville, Tennessee 37208

**T** 615 327 6223   admissions@mmc.edu

**Admissions:** www.mmc.edu/admissions/index.html

## General Information

In 1876, Meharry Medical College was founded and established as the Meharry Medical Department of Central Tennessee College by the Freedmen's Aid Society of the Methodist Episcopal Church. Meharry's inception was part of the society's continuing effort to educate freed slaves and to provide health care services for the poor and underserved. Today, the School of Medicine continues to provide excellent educational opportunities to promising students from groups underrepresented in medicine. Clinical teaching facilities include the Metropolitan Nashville General Hospital; Blanchfield Army Hospital; Veterans Affairs Tennessee Valley Health Care System, Nashville Campus and the Alvin C. York Murfreesboro Campus; Vanderbilt's Monroe Carrell Children's Hospital; and a number of affiliated hospitals and clinics. The provision of primary care, particularly in medically underserved areas, is a special emphasis, as is health disparities research.

## Mission Statement

Meharry Medical College exists to improve the health and health care of minority and underserved communities by offering excellent education and training programs in the health sciences placing special emphasis on providing opportunities to people of color and individuals from disadvantaged backgrounds, regardless of race or ethnicity; delivering high quality health services; and conducting research that fosters the elimination of health disparities.

## Curricular Highlights

**Community Service Requirement:** Optional.

**Research/Thesis Requirement:** Required. Encouraged in areas of health disparities.

The school has an integrated curriculum for the freshman year in which instruction is organized into modules that include basic, clinical, and social sciences. The modules include Principles and Practice Of Medicine, Molecular Cell Biology, Genetics, Gross Anatomy, and Embryology; also included are Integrated Neuroscience, Immunology, Principles of Infectious Disease, and Foundations in Human Disease and Treatment. The sophomore year is organized around a series of organ systems. The clinical years consist of the following blocks: family medicine, psychiatry, obstetrics and gynecology, pediatrics, internal medicine, surgery, an ambulatory rotation served in an urban or rural underserved area, internal medicine subinternship, capstone, and radiology, as well as guided electives.

## Selection Factors

Applicants are selected on a competitive basis with regard to cognitive and non-cognitive skills that denote probable success in medical school. Performance in the basic science prerequisite subjects and MCAT scores form the basis for screening for the interview process in which the non-cognitive aspects of the applicant are assessed. While special empathy is held for minority and disadvantaged applicants of all origins, Meharry Medical College seeks to attract a wide demographic, cultural, and educational population to reflect the caliber of social interchange in which the eventual practice of medicine will occur. Meharry Medical College does not discriminate on the basis of race, sex, creed, national origin, age, or handicap.

## Information about Diversity Programs

For over 130 years, Meharry has produced a large percentage of the minority health professionals in the United States and abroad.

## Application Process and Requirements 2012–2013

**Primary application service:** AMCAS®
**Earliest filing date:** June 1, 2011
**Latest filing date:** December 15, 2011

**Secondary application required:** Yes
**Sent to:** All applicants do not receive the secondary application; they are prescreened.
**Contact:** Deborah Davis, (615) 327-6223, ddavis@mmc.edu
**Fee:** Yes, $65   **Waiver available:** Yes
**Earliest filing date:** August 1, 2011
**Latest filing date:** January 15, 2012

**MCAT® required:** Yes
**Latest MCAT® considered:** September 2011
**Oldest MCAT® considered:** April 2009

**Early Decision Program:** School does have EDP
**Applicants notified:** October 1, 2011
**EDP available for:** Both In-State and Out-of-State Applicants

**Regular acceptance notice —**
**Earliest date:** November 1, 2011
**Latest date:** Until class is full
**Applicant's response to acceptance offer —**
**Maximum time:** Three weeks

**Requests for deferred entrance considered:** Yes

**Deposit to hold place in class:** Yes
**Deposit —In-State Applicants:** $300
**Out-of-State Applicants:** $300
**Deposit due:** With response to acceptance offer
**Applied to tuition:** Yes   **Refundable:** Yes
**Refundable by:** $200 refundable prior to April 15, 2012

**Estimated number of new entrants:** 83
**EDP:** 2, **Special Programs:** 20

**Start month/year:** June 2012

**Interview format:** One-two 30-minute interviews. Regional interviews are seldom available. Video interviews are not available.

## Preparatory Programs

**Postbaccalaureate Program:** Yes, by invitation only (20 places)

**Summer Program:** Yes, Pre-Baccalaureate program, Sharon Turner-Friley, (615) 327-5966, sfriley@mmc.edu

## 2010–2011 First Year Class

|  | In-State | Out-of-State | International |
|---|---|---|---|
| Applications | 239 | 4,234 | 187 |
| Interviewed | 86 | 422 | 9 |
| Matriculated | 13 | 90 | 2 |

| **Total Matriculants: 105** | **Total Enrollment: 431** |
|---|---|

## Financial Information

|  | In-State | Out-of-State |
|---|---|---|
| Total Cost of Attendance | $71,957 | $71,957 |
| Tuition and Fees | $38,894 | $38,894 |
| Other (incl. living expenses) | $30,465 | $30,465 |
| Health Insurance (can be waived) | $2,598 | $2,598 |

**Average 2010 Graduate Indebtedness: $195,795**
**% of Enrolled Students Receiving Aid: 95%**

Source: 2009-2010 LCME I-B survey and 2010-2011 AAMC TSF questionnaire

# University of Tennessee Health Science Center College of Medicine

## Memphis, Tennessee

University of Tennessee,
Health Science Center College of Medicine
910 Madison Avenue, Suite 500
Memphis, Tennessee 38163
**T** 901 448 5559   nstrother@uthsc.edu
**Admissions:** www.uthsc.edu/Medicine/Admissions

## General Information

The UTHSC College of Medicine traces its origin to 1851 as the Medical Department of the University of Nashville. Today, the college utilizes over 20 facilities statewide for its training programs, including the Boston-Baskin Cancer Group, Campbell Orthopedic Clinic, LeBonheur Children's Medical Center, Methodist University Hospital, Memphis Mental Health Institute, Regional Medical Center, Semmes-Murphy Clinic, St. Jude Children's Research Hospital, UT Medical Group, VA Medical Center, Baptist Hospital-Memphis, St. Francis Hospital, UT Knoxville Medical Center, Erlanger Medical Center-Chattanooga, Baptist Hospital-Nashville, and Family Practice Center-Jackson.

## Mission Statement

The Faculty of the College of Medicine is committed to educating physicians whose primary responsibilities will be evaluating, treating and preventing disease. The educational program is designed to prepare students to become knowledgeable, skillful, and compassionate physicians. Students embrace the study of medicine as a lifelong process and the physician's deep commitment to high moral and ethical standards regarding patients, colleagues, and society.

## Curricular Highlights

**Community Service Requirement:** Required. Community service project.

**Research/Thesis Requirement:** Optional.

A revised curriculum will begin in August 2011. Year 1 will describe structure and function (both gross and molecular/cellular levels), diagnostic and pharmacologic principles, and features common to multiple diseases. Year 2 will use an organ/systems based approach to integrate physiology, pathophysiology, pathology, neuroscience, pharmacology, and infectious disease. The Principles of Clinical Medicine course will run throughout the first two years to ensure clinical relevance in the basic sciences and to expose students to the practice of medicine. Year 3 clerkships will focus on patient problem solving with an increasing level of responsibility. Year 4 will consist of six 4-week clerkships and four 4-week electives.

## Selection Factors

The criteria the Committee on Admissions uses in the selection process are the academic record, MCAT scores, preprofessional evaluations, and personal interviews. Personal interviews by members of the committee provide candidates with an opportunity to review their curricular and extracurricular activities. More important, the interviewers gain insight into the character of the applicants and how they have formulated their plans for the study and practice of medicine. Applicants must be citizens or permanent residents of the U.S. at the time of application. Applications are considered from residents of Tennessee and its contiguous states (Mississippi, Arkansas, Missouri, Kentucky, Virginia, North Carolina, Georgia, and Alabama). Children of UT alumni may also be considered, regardless of their state of residence. Since priority is given to qualified Tennesseans, non-residents must possess superior qualifications to be offered admission. Only 10% of the entering class may be non-residents. Upon initial review of the AMCAS® application, a secondary application will be sent to applicants considered competitive for further review. Advanced standing applications will be considered for Year 3 only. Applicants for transfer must be residents of Tennessee, be attending LCME-accredited schools, have successfully completed the basic science curriculum, and have passed USMLE Step 1. Applicants must also provide evidence of circumstances necessitating a transfer. Deadline for transfer applications is April 1.

## Information about Diversity Programs

The College of Medicine actively encourages applications from members of groups underrepresented in medicine. The Committee on Admissions evaluates both academic and non-academic factors in the selection process, with consideration given to the unique backgrounds and challenges of these applicants. Among American medical schools, the college is a leader in the admission, matriculation, and graduation of students from groups underrepresented in medicine.

## Regional/Satellite Campuses

**Regional Campus Location(s):** Chattanooga, TN, and Knoxville, TN.

Rotations are available at all three campuses: Memphis, Knoxville and Chattanooga.

## Application Process and Requirements 2012–2013

**Primary application service:** AMCAS®
**Earliest filing date:** June 1, 2011
**Latest filing date:** November 15, 2011

**Secondary application required:** Yes
**Sent to:** Screened applicants
**Contact:** Nelson Strother, (901) 448-5561, nstrother@uthsc.edu
**Fee:** No   **Waiver available:** n/a
**Earliest filing date:** July 2011
**Latest filing date:** February 2012

**MCAT® required:** Yes
**Latest MCAT® considered:** September 2011
**Oldest MCAT® considered:** August 2006

**Early Decision Program:** School does not have EDP
**Applicants notified:** n/a
**EDP available for:** n/a

**Regular acceptance notice —**
**Earliest date:** October 15, 2011
**Latest date:** Varies
**Applicant's response to acceptance offer —**
**Maximum time:** Two weeks

**Requests for deferred entrance considered:** Yes

**Deposit to hold place in class:** No
**Deposit — In-State Applicants:** n/a
**Out-of-State Applicants:** n/a
**Deposit due:** n/a
**Applied to tuition:** n/a
**Refundable:** n/a
**Refundable by:** n/a

**Estimated number of new entrants:** 165
**EDP:** 0, **Special Programs:** n/a

**Start month/year:** August 2012

**Interview format:** Two individual interviews with admissions committee members. May have 1 in Memphis and 1 regional. Video interviews are not available.

## Preparatory Programs

**Postbaccalaureate Program:** No

**Summer Program:** Yes, www.uthsc.edu/TIP

## 2010–2011 First Year Class

|  | In-State | Out-of-State | International |
|---|---|---|---|
| Applications | 634 | 734 | 3 |
| Interviewed | 456 | 63 | 0 |
| Matriculated | 154 | 11 | 0 |

**Total Matriculants: 165**      **Total Enrollment: 638**

## Financial Information

|  | In-State | Out-of-State |
|---|---|---|
| Total Cost of Attendance | $52,654 | $74,190 |
| Tuition and Fees | $23,225 | $44,761 |
| Other (incl. living expenses) | $28,440 | $28,440 |
| Health Insurance (can be waived) | $989 | $989 |

**Average 2010 Graduate Indebtedness: $118,863**
**% of Enrolled Students Receiving Aid: 91%**

Source: 2009-2010 LCME I-B survey and 2010-2011 AAMC TSF questionnaire

# Vanderbilt University School of Medicine
## Nashville, Tennessee

Office of Medical School Admissions
215 Light Hall
Vanderbilt University School of Medicine
Nashville, Tennessee 37232-0685

**T** 615 322 2145   pat.sagen@vanderbilt.edu

**Admissions:** www.mc.vanderbilt.edu/
medschool/admissions

## General Information

VUSM is a private medical school located on the campus of Vanderbilt University. The Vanderbilt University Medical Center and affiliated hospitals provide a total of over 900 beds for diversified, comprehensive clinical experience. These hospitals share common goals of education, research, patient care, and community service.

## Mission Statement

VUSM seeks to matriculate a diverse group of academically exceptional students whose attributes and accomplishments suggest that they will be future leaders and/or scholars in medicine to begin the process of lifelong learning in the science and practice of medicine.

## Curricular Highlights

**Community Service Requirement:** Optional.

**Research/Thesis Requirement:** Required.

Medical education at Vanderbilt is oriented toward promoting the intellectual development of students and equipping them with the disciplined approach, knowledge, and skills required of both a physician and scientist. The curriculum provides the student with a fundamental knowledge of basic medical principles, but flexibility is stressed. Changes in curriculum content and teaching methods continually evolve from Vanderbilt's focus upon new ways to assist students in their preparation for a lifetime of learning. The curriculum offers a productive blend of required and elective courses throughout all four years of the program. The Emphasis Program, whose primary goal is to develop leadership potential, is scheduled for the first two years of the curriculum, including eight weeks during the intervening summer. Areas of focus include: laboratory-based research, patient-oriented research, healthcare research, community health initiatives, international medicine, biomedical informatics, medical education, law and medicine, and medical humanities.

## Selection Factors

Applicants are invited without regard to race, sex, religion, national origin, sexual orientation, or state of residence. Applicants must possess sufficient intellectual ability, emotional stability, and sensory and motor functions to meet the academic requirements of the school of medicine without fundamental alteration in the nature of this program. Applications are reviewed in two stages. The initial review is made from material provided through AMCAS. Competitive strength of credentials reflecting preparation for medical studies, motivation, personal qualities, and educational background are evaluated by the Admissions Committee and determine the recipients of secondary applications and invitations to interview. There is a holistic review of academic performance and non-academic factors (patient care experience, research experience, extracurricular involvement, leadership roles, sports activities, relationship to the medical school, and applicants from underserved populations). Interviews are held at Vanderbilt.

AP credit, CLEP credit, and PASS/FAIL credit are not accepted for any required courses. In lieu of required courses with AP credit, higher level coursework should be taken. Vanderbilt undergraduates with at least a 3.5 GPA are eligible to apply for the binding Early Acceptance Program during the spring of the sophomore year. Those accepted are encouraged to broaden their curricular experiences. Acceptance for transfer is limited to third year with places made available by attrition only.

## Information about Diversity Programs

Matriculation of a diverse student body is a central goal of VUSM. Diversity is defined in the broadest sense (gender, race, ethnicity, sexual preference, socio-economic background, geographic origin).

## Regional/Satellite Campuses

Student rotations are divided between Vanderbilt Hospital and the Nashville VA Hospital. Clinical opportunities also exist at Meharry Medical School as part of a formal collaboration.

## Application Process and Requirements 2012–2013

**Primary application service:** AMCAS®
**Earliest filing date:** June 1, 2011
**Latest filing date:** November 15, 2011

**Secondary application required:** Yes
**Sent to:** Screened applicants invited to interview
**URL:** www.mc.vanderbilt.edu/medschool/admissions
**Fee:** Yes, $50   **Waiver available:** Yes
**Earliest filing date:** August 1, 2011
**Latest filing date:** December 31, 2011

**MCAT® required:** Yes
**Latest MCAT® considered:** September 2011
**Oldest MCAT® considered:** April 2008

**Early Decision Program:** School does not have EDP
**Applicants notified:** n/a
**EDP available for:** n/a

**Regular acceptance notice —**
**Earliest date:** October 16, 2011
**Latest date:** Until class is full
**Applicant's response to acceptance offer —**
**Maximum time:** Two weeks

**Requests for deferred entrance considered:** Yes

**Deposit to hold place in class:** No
**Deposit — In-State Applicants:** n/a
**Out-of-State Applicants:** n/a
**Deposit due:** n/a
**Applied to tuition:** n/a
**Refundable:** n/a
**Refundable by:** n/a

**Estimated number of new entrants:** 105
**EDP:** n/a, **Special Programs:** 10

**Start month/year:** July 2012

**Interview format:** Individual interview with faculty member. Regional interviews are not available. Video interviews are not available.

### Preparatory Programs
**Postbaccalaureate Program:** No

**Summer Program:** Yes,
https://medschool.mc. vanderbilt.edu/summer_academy/

## 2010–2011 First Year Class

|              | In-State | Out-of-State | International |
|--------------|----------|--------------|--------------|
| Applications | 328      | 4,726        | 343          |
| Interviewed  | 57       | 919          | 60           |
| Matriculated | 9        | 84           | 12           |

**Total Matriculants: 105**   **Total Enrollment: 436**

## Financial Information

|                                        | In-State | Out-of-State |
|----------------------------------------|----------|--------------|
| Total Cost of Attendance               | $66,420  | $66,420      |
| Tuition and Fees                       | $40,911  | $40,911      |
| Other (incl. living expenses)          | $23,367  | $23,367      |
| Health Insurance (can be waived)       | $2,142   | $2,142       |

**Average 2010 Graduate Indebtedness: $113,449**
**% of Enrolled Students Receiving Aid: 98%**

*Source: 2009-2010 LCME I-B survey and 2010-2011 AAMC TSF questionnaire*

# Baylor College of Medicine
## Houston, Texas

Office of Admissions
Baylor College of Medicine
One Baylor Plaza, MS BCM 110
Houston, Texas 77030

**T** 713 798 4842   admissions@bcm.edu

**Admissions:** www.bcm.edu/admissions

## General Information

Baylor College of Medicine (BCM) is a private, nonsectarian institution governed by an independent Board of Trustees composed of community leaders. BCM is the academic center around which the 1000-acre Texas Medical Center was developed. The Baylor faculty currently is composed of 1,854 full-time members and 1,395 voluntary members. Facilities include teaching and research buildings and eight affiliated teaching hospitals (including private, county, and Veterans Affairs hospitals).

## Mission Statement

The mission of BCM is to promote health for all people through education, research, and public service. The College pursues this mission by sustaining excellence in educating medical and graduate students, primary care and specialty physicians, biomedical scientists and allied health professionals; by advancing basic and clinical biomedical research; by fostering public awareness of health and the prevention of disease; and by promoting patient care of the highest standard.

## Curricular Highlights

**Community Service Requirement:** Optional. Service projects available.

**Research/Thesis Requirement:** Optional. Scholarly project.

The educational program is structured to prepare graduates to pursue careers as primary care physicians, specialists, research scientists, academic physicians, or physicians involved in public health policy. The integration of basic and clinical sciences includes direct patient-care experiences early in the first year and a focus on core basic science topics prior to graduation. This integration also includes special courses featuring integrated problem-solving and clinical skills training that encourages application of content learned in lectures and labs. The BCM curriculum is unique in that the basic sciences are taught in slightly less than one and a half years, giving students more time to take advantage of a wealth of clinical experiences. During the clinical curriculum, students have flexibility in organizing their schedules to complete 56 weeks of required clinical clerkships, four weeks of selectives, and 20 weeks of elective experiences. All students will be encouraged to develop and execute, with faculty mentorship, a scholarly project of their choice during their medical education. Interested students are given the opportunity to do research or to apply for a combined M.D./Ph.D. program. Students with an interest in ethics, care for the underserved, medical management (business), research, international health, or geriatrics may participate in tracks designed for the specific topic. There are several joint degree programs: a 5 year M.D./M.B.A. program with a health care focus with the Jones School of Management at Rice University; a six year M.D./J.D. program with the University of Houston Law Center and a 5 year M.D./M.P.H. with The University of Texas School of Public Health.

## Selection Factors

All applicants offered places in the class are interviewed at BCM. All available information is utilized in the selection process. Attention is paid to course selections and the academic challenge imposed by the student's curriculum. Intellectual ability and academic achievement alone are not sufficient to support the development of the ideal physician. To work effectively in a profession dependent upon interpersonal relationships, physicians should possess those traits of personality and character which permit them to communicate effectively with warmth and compassion. Written requests for deferred matriculation from accepted students will be reviewed on an individual basis. BCM does not discriminate on the basis of race, sex, marital status, creed, national origin, age, or disability.

## Information about Diversity Programs

BCM encourages applications from members of groups underrepresented in medicine. Students from these groups comprise a substantial portion of the student body; they also serve as Admissions Committee members.

## Application Process and Requirements 2012–2013

**Primary application service:** AMCAS®
**Earliest filing date:** June 1, 2011
**Latest filing date:** November 1, 2011

**Secondary application required:** Yes
**Sent to:** All applicants
**URL:** www.bcm.edu/admissions/?PMID=1776
**Fee:** Yes, $100   **Waiver available:** Yes
**Earliest filing date:** July 1, 2011
**Latest filing date:** December 1, 2011

**MCAT® required:** Yes
**Latest MCAT® considered:** September 2011
**Oldest MCAT® considered:** July 2007

**Early Decision Program:** School does have EDP
**Applicants notified:** October 1, 2011
**EDP available for:** Both In-State and Out-of-State Applicants

**Regular acceptance notice —**
**Earliest date:** October 15, 2011
**Latest date:** Until class is full
**Applicant's response to acceptance offer —**
**Maximum time:** n/a

**Requests for deferred entrance considered:** Yes

**Deposit to hold place in class:** Yes
**Deposit — In-State Applicants:** $300
**Out-of-State Applicants:** $300
**Deposit due:** May 15, 2012
**Applied to tuition:** Yes
**Refundable:** No
**Refundable by:** n/a

**Estimated number of new entrants:** 190
**EDP:** 5, **Special Programs:** 40

**Start month/year:** July 2012

**Interview format:** Interview format: Currently under review. Regional interviews are not available. Video interviews are not available.

## Preparatory Programs

**Postbaccalaureate Program:** No

**Summer Program:** No

## 2010–2011 First Year Class

|  | In-State | Out-of-State | International |
|---|---|---|---|
| Applications | 1,446 | 3,052 | 187 |
| Interviewed | 533 | 348 | 0 |
| Matriculated | 133 | 51 | 1 |

**Total Matriculants: 185**   **Total Enrollment: 725**

## Financial Information

|  | In-State | Out-of-State |
|---|---|---|
| Total Cost of Attendance | $42,341 | $55,441 |
| Tuition and Fees | $15,668 | $28,768 |
| Other (incl. living expenses) | $24,165 | $24,165 |
| Health Insurance (can be waived) | $2,508 | $2,508 |

**Average 2010 Graduate Indebtedness: $90,789**
**% of Enrolled Students Receiving Aid: 82%**

*Source: 2009-2010 LCME I-B survey and 2010-2011 AAMC TSF questionnaire*

# Paul L. Foster School of Medicine at Texas Tech University Health Sciences Center at El Paso

## El Paso, Texas

Paul L. Foster School of Medicine at Texas Tech
University Health Sciences Center at El Paso
5001 El Paso Drive
El Paso, Texas 79905

**T** 915 783 1250    fostersom.admissions@ttuhsc.edu

**Admissions:** www.ttuhsc.edu/fostersom/admissions/

## General Information

Our unique setting provides exposure not only to traditional medicine, but also to international, bi-cultural and border health care issues. El Paso is a vibrant city where the mild climate provides year round cultural, intellectual, social and recreational opportunities. Once on campus students enjoy our state-of-the-art educational, research, and clinical facilities. The new Medical Education Building is 125,000 square feet of auditoriums, classrooms, laboratories, group meeting rooms, a clinical skills/simulation center, fitness room, lounge areas and a library. The Medical Sciences Building houses leading research currently conducted in chronic kidney disease, breast carcinogenesis and infectious disease. Plans for research focus on health disparities and diseases that affect the region and are based in rapidly growing research Centers of Excellence in Infectious Diseases, Neurosciences, Obesity and Diabetes, and Cancer. The University Medical Center (UMC) of El Paso, our main teaching hospital, is located on campus and is the only Level 1 Trauma Center in the region. The UMC is currently undergoing significant growth as construction of a new children's hospital is underway with plans to open in 2012. In addition, students are also trained throughout the El Paso community at other clinical training facilities which include El Paso Psychiatric Center, William Beaumont Army Medical Center, Texas Tech University Health Sciences Center ambulatory clinics and off-campus community sites.

## Mission Statement

The school's mission is to provide exceptional opportunities for students, trainees, and physicians; to advance knowledge through innovative scholarship and research in medicine with a focus on international health and health care disparities; and to provide exemplary patient care and service to the entire El Paso community and beyond.

## Curricular Highlights

**Community Service Requirement:** Required. In Society, Community and the Individual course.

**Research/Thesis Requirement:** Required. Completion of a research project is required.

The Paul L. Foster School of Medicine is committed to excellence in medical education founded on modern scientific principles, strong ethical values and sensitivity to our community needs. Our integrated curriculum, which received a commendation from the Liaison Committee on Medical Education for its clinical orientation, teaches the basic sciences with relevance to clinical presentations assigned to organ-system based units. Clinical presentations are the ways in which a patient presents to a physician. Students learn the anatomy, biochemistry, physiology and other basic science concepts and content needed to understand specific clinical presentations. Guided instruction by discipline experts through lecture, small group and laboratory exercises is utilized to establish this relevance. This approach has demonstrated enhanced knowledge comprehension, improved retention and promoted the development of diagnostic reasoning skills like those used by experienced physicians. The first two years of the curriculum consists of four major courses; Scientific Principles of Medicine (organ-system units), Medical Skills, Master's Colloquium, and Society, Community and the Individual (SCI). The grading system is pass/fail. Preparation for the United States Medical Licensing Examinations includes cumulative unit exams and periodic use of the Comprehensive Basic Sciences Exam. In an effort to support our medical students along the way, each class is divided into learning communities called colleges, where College Masters monitor student performance on a weekly basis. All students engage in a language immersion course in conversational and medical Spanish. Application of skills and knowledge learned is applied early, as students are exposed to patient care within a month of arriving on campus. The third and fourth year of the curriculum provide richly diverse and varied patient care experiences in major specialties and subspecialties.

## Selection Factors

Candidates who are considered to be competitive for admission, based on criteria established by the school, will be invited to interview. These criteria include scores from the MCAT; academic performance as reflected by the science and overall GPA; rigor of the undergraduate curriculum, extracurricular activities (medical and non-medical) and employment and their impact on performance and maturation; recommendations from premedical advisors or faculty; socioeconomic and disadvantaged background; personal statement and its reflection of communication skills, personal qualities, leadership, maturity, determination, and motivation for a career in medicine; and regional origin. The interview evaluates the applicant's interest and knowledge of the health care field and motivation for a medical career; personal characteristics; and problem solving skills.

## Application Process and Requirements 2012–2013

**Primary application service:** TMDSAS
**Earliest filing date:** May 2, 2011
**Latest filing date:** October 1, 2011

**Secondary application required:** No
**Sent to:** n/a
**URL:** n/a
**Fee:** n/a    **Waiver available:** n/a
**Earliest filing date:** n/a
**Latest filing date:** n/a

**MCAT® required:** Yes
**Latest MCAT® considered:** September 2011
**Oldest MCAT® considered:** 2007

**Early Decision Program:** School does not have EDP
**Applicants notified:** n/a
**EDP available for:** n/a

**Regular acceptance notice —**
**Earliest date:** November 15, 2011
**Latest date:** Until class is full
**Applicant's response to acceptance offer —**
**Maximum time:** Two weeks

**Requests for deferred entrance considered:** Yes

**Deposit to hold place in class:** Yes
**Deposit — In-State Applicants:** $100
**Out-of-State Applicants:** $100
**Deposit due:** May 15, 2012
**Applied to tuition:** No
**Refundable:** Yes
**Refundable by:** May 15, 2012

**Estimated number of new entrants:** 80
**EDP:** n/a, **Special Programs:** n/a

**Start month/year:** July 2012

**Interview format:** Two individual 30-minute interviews. Regional interviews are not available. Video interviews are not available.

## Preparatory Programs
**Postbaccalaureate Program:** No

**Summer Program:** No

## 2010–2011 First Year Class

|  | In-State | Out-of-State | International |
|---|---|---|---|
| Applications | 2,171 | 291 | 70 |
| Interviewed | 365 | 13 | 0 |
| Matriculated | 57 | 2 | 1 |

**Total Matriculants: 60**    **Total Enrollment: 98**

## Financial Information

|  | In-State | Out-of-State |
|---|---|---|
| Total Cost of Attendance | $41,986 | $55,086 |
| Tuition and Fees | $14,470 | $27,570 |
| Other (incl. living expenses) | $26,616 | $26,616 |
| Health Insurance (can be waived) | $900 | $900 |

**Average 2010 Graduate Indebtedness: n/a**
**% of Enrolled Students Receiving Aid: 100%**

Source: 2009-2010 LCME I-B survey and 2010-2011 AAMC TSF questionnaire

# Texas A&M University System Health Science Center College of Medicine

## College Station, Texas

Office of Admissions
The Texas A&M Health Science Center
College of Medicine
8447 State Highway 47
Bryan, Texas 77807-3260

T 979 436 0237  admissions@medicine.tamhsc.edu

**Admissions:** http://medicine.tamhsc.edu/admissions/index.htm

## General Information

Established in 1973, the College of Medicine is part of The Texas A&M Health Science Center, a public health sciences university. The college's first class of 32 began in 1977. In 1999, the College of Medicine joined the newly created Texas A&M Health Science Center and to date, more than 1,400 physicians have received their medical training here. The College of Medicine utilizes approximately 1300 basic and clinical science faculty in instructional programs in Bryan-College Station, Temple, Round Rock, Dallas, and Corpus Christi.

## Mission Statement

The College of Medicine is dedicated to the education of humane and highly skilled physicians and to the development of knowledge in the biomedical and clinical sciences. In order to improve the quality and efficacy of medical care through its programs of medical education and research, the College of Medicine maintains a personalized educational experience for medical students. The College's overarching goals are building signature research and clinical programs and reaffirming its land grant heritage of community outreach and service.

## Curricular Highlights

**Community Service Requirement:** Optional.

**Research/Thesis Requirement:** Optional.

The College of Medicine implemented a new integrative curriculum in 2009-2010. The focus of the new medical curriculum is an enhanced level of integration of material that is taught to students in the first two years. Students in the curriculum do not take separate courses in the traditional basic sciences. Rather this material is appropriately organized into integrated blocks of instruction of 3 to 10 weeks in duration depending on the theme of the block and structured into phases of instruction. During the third and fourth years of medical school or Phases III and IV of the curriculum, students receive clinical training in several different patient care venues, ranging from Bryan-College Station, Corpus Christi and Austin, Texas to Dallas, Round Rock and Temple, Texas. The curriculum allows for a highly personalized medical education experience from the very onset.

## Selection Factors

Intellectual capacity, record of academic achievement and performance on the MCAT are important selection criteria. Equally important are interpersonal and communication skills, maturity, motivation, and demonstrated compassion. Careful consideration is given to other factors such as community service, disadvantaged circumstances, socioeconomic background, race/ethnicity, research, primary care interest, service in a rural/underserved area, and/or support by college faculty. Knowledge of and experiences in the medical profession are given serious consideration. Admission is open to qualified individuals regardless of race, color, religion, gender, age, national origin, or disability. Applicants are invited for personal interviews based upon their competitiveness in the review process.

## Information about Diversity Programs

The college believes that diversity enhances its ability to provide care and to serve communities across a broad range of racial and ethnic groups. As part of its commitment to this effort, the college administers several programs for students who are disadvantaged or from groups underrepresented in medicine. The Joint Admissions Medical Program is open to economically disadvantaged students, and the Partnership for Primary Care Program is open to students from rural/underserved communities in Texas. Also, the adjustment and retention of minority students is facilitated through the college's chapter of the Student National Medical Association (SNMA).

## Regional/Satellite Campuses

**Regional Campus Location(s):** Bryan/College Station, TX, Dallas, TX, Round Rock, TX and Temple, TX.

In addition to traditional clerkships and ambulatory care experiences in Austin, College Station, Corpus Christi, Fort Hood, Temple, and Waco, the college recently opened teaching and clinical facilities on new campuses in Round Rock, Bryan and Dallas, Texas.

## Application Process and Requirements 2012–2013

**Primary application service:** TMDSAS
**Earliest filing date:** May 1, 2011
**Latest filing date:** October 1, 2011

**Secondary application required:** Yes
**Sent to:** All applicants
**URL:** http://medicine.tamhsc.edu/admissions/index.htm
**Fee:** Yes, $60  **Waiver available:** Yes
**Earliest filing date:** May 1, 2011
**Latest filing date:** October 1, 2011

**MCAT® required:** Yes
**Latest MCAT® considered:** September 2011
**Oldest MCAT® considered:** August 2007

**Early Decision Program:** School does not have EDP
**Applicants notified:** n/a
**EDP available for:** n/a

**Regular acceptance notice —**
**Earliest date:** November 15, 2011 for Texas residents; October 15, 2011 for non-residents
**Latest date:** Until class is full
**Applicant's response to acceptance offer —**
**Maximum time:** Two weeks

**Requests for deferred entrance considered:** Yes

**Deposit to hold place in class:** No
**Deposit — In-State Applicants:** n/a
**Out-of-State Applicants:** n/a
**Deposit due:** n/a
**Applied to tuition:** n/a
**Refundable:** n/a
**Refundable by:** n/a

**Estimated number of new entrants:** 170
**EDP:** n/a, **Special Programs:** 13

**Start month/year:** July 2012

**Interview format:** Two individual 30-minute interviews. Regional interviews are not available. Video interviews are available.

## Preparatory Programs

**Postbaccalaureate Program:** No

**Summer Program:** Yes, www.utsystem.edu/jamp/

## 2010–2011 First Year Class

|  | In-State | Out-of-State | International |
|---|---|---|---|
| Applications | 2,608 | 484 | 114 |
| Interviewed | 723 | 44 | 0 |
| Matriculated | 136 | 9 | 5 |

**Total Matriculants: 150**   **Total Enrollment: 534**

## Financial Information

|  | In-State | Out-of-State |
|---|---|---|
| Total Cost of Attendance | $38,780 | $51,880 |
| Tuition and Fees | $13,582 | $26,682 |
| Other (incl. living expenses) | $23,418 | $23,418 |
| Health Insurance (can be waived) | $1,780 | $1,780 |

**Average 2010 Graduate Indebtedness: $95,156**
**% of Enrolled Students Receiving Aid: 87%**

Source: 2009-2010 LCME I-B survey and 2010-2011 AAMC TSF questionnaire

# Texas Tech University Health Sciences Center School of Medicine

## Lubbock, Texas

Texas Tech University Health Sciences Center
School of Medicine
Office of Admissions, Room 2B116
3601 4th Street
Lubbock, Texas 79430

**T** 806 743 2297   somadm@ttuhsc.edu

**Admissions:** www.ttuhsc.edu/som/admissions

## General Information

The TTUHSC School of Medicine was established in 1969. All medical students spend the first two years at the Lubbock campus; third and fourth year students receive their clinical training in Lubbock, Amarillo, or Midland/Odessa (Permian Basin). Affiliations with teaching hospitals provide over 2,900 beds for clinical teaching. The medical school has 394 full-time and 46 part-time faculty members and more than 902 volunteer clinical faculty members. Agreements have been developed with three area universities to provide early acceptance of qualified students into TTUHSC School of Medicine. Applicants must be academically talented. Following satisfactory interview, the Admissions Committee recommends acceptance of the applicant. Applicants who continue to maintain the required GPA are guaranteed admission to Texas Tech School of Medicine in the fall following graduation. The MCAT is waived for these applicants.

## Mission Statement

TTUHSC School of Medicine provides the highest standard of excellence in higher education, while pursuing continuous quality improvement. The school is committed to health care delivery for its 135,000 square mile service area. At the same time and as part of improvement of health care, its efforts include support of meaningful academic research for the betterment of future health care.

## Curricular Highlights

**Community Service Requirement:** Optional.

**Research/Thesis Requirement:** Required. Completion of a research project is required.

The new four-year curriculum provides a broad innovative integration of basic and clinical care, with emphasis on developing the student's analytical problem-solving skills. The first two years blend core concepts of basic sciences with early clinical experience. Introduction to patience care sbookills begins in the first month. The second year now follows an overall systems approach, again aligned with supervised patient care experiences. Teaching formats include small group discussions, PBL, and team learning. Summer preceptorships are also available. The third and fourth years include clerkships in family medicine, internal medicine, neurology, obstetric-gynecology, pediatrics, psychiatry, and surgery. The fourth year combines required and elective rotations. Research opportunities include summer preceptorships, a Research Honors Program, and an integrated M.D.–Ph.D. program. Joint degree programs in the M.B.A./ M.D. and J.D./M.D. are also offered. Students are graded using a categorical grading system: Honors, High Pass, Pass, Marginal Pass and Fail.

## Selection Factors

Applications are invited from qualified Texas residents and service area counties of New Mexico and Oklahoma. Only U.S. citizens or applicants with permanent resident visas are considered. Application forms and procedural information may be obtained from the Texas Medical and Dental Schools Application Service (*www.utsystem.edu/tmdsas*). A secondary application to TTUHSC School of Medicine is also required. The Admissions Committee carefully reviews all applications. Evidence of high intellectual ability and a record of strong academic achievement are essential for success in the study of medicine. Qualities such as compassion, motivation, the ability to communicate with people, maturity, and personal integrity are also important. There is no discrimination on the basis of race, sex, creed, national origin, age, or disability. It is the goal of the institution to recruit a diverse medical class exhibiting the qualities promising academic success and to meet the needs of an increasingly diverse population. Personal interviews are offered to those candidates deemed competitive for admission. Interviews are conducted on the Lubbock campus.

## Information about Diversity Programs

In an effort to recruit a highly qualified and diverse student body, which reflects the demographics of the West Texas region, race/ethnicity as well as a socioeconomically disadvantaged background, is among the many factors considered in the admission process.

## Regional/Satellite Campuses

**Regional Campus Location(s):** Amarillo, TX, and Odessa, TX.

All students spend the first two years of medical school on the Lubbock campus. The in-depth clinical training for medical students is divided among three campuses: Lubbock, Amarillo, or Midland/Odessa (Permian Basin).

## Application Process and Requirements 2012–2013

**Primary application service:** TMDSAS
**Earliest filing date:** May 1, 2011
**Latest filing date:** October 1, 2011

**Secondary application required:** Yes
**Sent to:** Required of all applicants
**URL:** https://www.ttuhsc.edu/som/admissions/secondaryapp/default.asp
**Fee:** Yes, $50   **Waiver available:** No
**Earliest filing date:** May 1, 2011
**Latest filing date:** October 1, 2011

**MCAT® required:** Yes
**Latest MCAT® considered:** September 2011
**Oldest MCAT® considered:** September 2006

**Early Decision Program:** School does have EDP
**Applicants notified:** October 1, 2011
**EDP available for:** In-States only

**Regular acceptance notice —**
**Earliest date:** November 15, 2011
**Latest date:** Until class is full
**Applicant's response to acceptance offer —**
**Maximum time:** Two weeks

**Requests for deferred entrance considered:** Yes

**Deposit to hold place in class:** Yes
**Deposit — In-State Applicants:** $100
**Out-of-State Applicants:** $100 **Deposit due:** May 15, 2012
**Applied to tuition:** No
**Refundable:** Yes
**Refundable by:** May 15

**Estimated number of new entrants:** 144
**EDP:** 8, **Special Programs:** 18

**Start month/year:** August 2012

**Interview format:** Two individual thirty-minute interviews. Regional interviews are not available. Video interviews are not available.

## Preparatory Programs

**Postbaccalaureate Program:** No

**Summer Program:** No

## 2010–2011 First Year Class

|  | In-State | Out-of-State | International |
|---|---|---|---|
| Applications | 2,522 | 381 | 87 |
| Interviewed | 663 | 46 | 0 |
| Matriculated | 134 | 10 | 0 |

**Total Matriculants: 144      Total Enrollment: 583**

## Financial Information

|  | In-State | Out-of-State |
|---|---|---|
| Total Cost of Attendance | $41,358 | $54,458 |
| Tuition and Fees | $14,471 | $27,571 |
| Other (incl. living expenses) | $25,987 | $25,987 |
| Health Insurance (can be waived) | $900 | $900 |

**Average 2010 Graduate Indebtedness: $124,466**
**% of Enrolled Students Receiving Aid: 93%**

*Source: 2009-2010 LCME I-B survey and 2010-2011 AAMC TSF questionnaire*

# University of Texas Medical Branch at Galveston
## Galveston, Texas

Office of Student Affairs and Admissions
University of Texas Medical Branch
301 University Boulevard
Galveston, Texas 77555-0817

**T** 409 772 6958    tsilva@utmb.edu

**Admissions:** www.utmb.edu/somstudentaffairs

## General Information

The University of Texas Medical Branch (UTMB Health), established in 1891, is a state-owned academic health center with 4 hospitals, 475 teaching beds, and 123 specialty and subspecialty clinics directed by UTMB Health's administration. It is comprised of 4 schools (Medicine, Graduate School of Biomedical Sciences, Nursing, and Health Professions) and three institutes (Translational Sciences, Medical Humanities, and Human Infections and Immunity).

## Mission Statement

The mission of UTMB Health is to provide scholarly teaching, innovative scientific investigation, and state-of-the-art patient care in a learning environment to better the health of society. UTMB Health's education programs enable the state's talented individuals to become outstanding practitioners, teachers and investigators in the health care sciences. Its comprehensive primary, specialty and subspecialty clinics support the educational mission of the SOM, which is committed to the healthcare of all Texans through the delivery of state-of-the-art preventive, diagnostic and treatment services.

## Curricular Highlights

**Community Service Requirement:** Optional.

**Research/Thesis Requirement:** Optional.

The Integrated Medical Curriculum (IMC) is a four-year program that emphasizes continuous integration of the basic medical sciences with clinical medicine, early clinical skills, clinical experiences, and professionalism. In this student-centered curriculum, which utilizes small-group problem-based learning, computer-assisted instruction, lectures, and labs, the basic medical sciences are learned in clinical contexts. Its organ system-based approach and clinical science contexts promote basic science integration across disciplines. The third and fourth years of the IMC are centered on ambulatory and inpatient experiences in emergency medicine, family medicine, internal medicine, neurology, obstetrics and gynecology, pediatrics, psychiatry, and surgery. A unique feature of the third-year curriculum is an elective month, which allows students to expand their experience in a primary care field or explore potential career interests in a medical specialty. The fourth year also includes an acting internship, community-based ambulatory medicine, and a scholarly project in which a basic science or medical humanities topic is explored in depth. UTMB Health employs a grading system of Honors, High Pass, Pass, and Fail for required core courses and Pass/Fail for elective courses.

## Selection Factors

UTMB Health includes race and ethnicity in the broad range of criteria which is used for student admission and academic scholarship awards. All available information is utilized in the selection process such as intellect, achievement, character, interpersonal skills, and motivation. All candidates are evaluated individually and holistically; consideration is given to the total academic record, the results of aptitude and achievement tests, college preprofessional committee evaluations, the personal statement and interview.

## Information about Diversity Programs

UTMB Health is committed to increasing the number of low socio-economic and disadvantaged students in medicine. Each applicant is reviewed holistically and individually by experienced members of the Admissions Committee with particular emphasis on the applicant's potential. Both cognitive and noncognitive factors are considered. Following admission, a broad range of support services are available to assist students in completing the medical curriculum. UTMB Health does not discriminate on the basis of race, sex, creed, national origin, age, sexual orientation, religion, or handicap.

## Regional/Satellite Campuses

**Regional Campus Location(s):** Austin, TX.

A limited number of clerkship positions are available for third and fourth year students to spend their entire years in Austin, Houston or Corpus Christi, Texas. However, all third and fourth year students can choose to do a portion of their clerkships at these additional training sites.

## Application Process and Requirements 2012–2013

**Primary application service:** TMDSAS
**Earliest filing date:** May 1, 2011
**Latest filing date:** October 1, 2011

**Secondary application required:** No
**Sent to:** n/a
**URL:** n/a
**Fee:** No    **Waiver available:** No
**Earliest filing date:** n/a
**Latest filing date:** n/a

**MCAT® required:** Yes
**Latest MCAT® considered:** September 2011
**Oldest MCAT® considered:** January 2006

**Early Decision Program:** School does not have EDP
**Applicants notified:** n/a
**EDP available for:** n/a

**Regular acceptance notice —**
**Earliest date:** November 15, 2011
**Latest date:** Until class is full
**Applicant's response to acceptance offer —**
**Maximum time:** Varies; two weeks from the date of offer.

**Requests for deferred entrance considered:** Yes

**Deposit to hold place in class:** No
**Deposit — In-State Applicants:** n/a
**Out-of-State Applicants:** n/a
**Deposit due:** n/a
**Applied to tuition:** n/a
**Refundable:** n/a
**Refundable by:** n/a

**Estimated number of new entrants:** 230
**EDP:** n/a, **Special Programs:** 20

**Start month/year:** August 2012

**Interview format:** Two interviews, presentation, student panel, and a tour. No phone interviews. Regional interviews are not available. Video interviews are not available.

## Preparatory Programs

**Postbaccalaureate Program:** No

**Summer Program:** Yes,
www.utmb.edu/somstudentaffairs/specialprograms,
Lisa Cain, Ph.D., (409) 772-1212, ldcain@utmb.edu

## 2010–2011 First Year Class

|  | In-State | Out-of-State | International |
|---|---|---|---|
| Applications | 2,834 | 547 | 122 |
| Interviewed | 857 | 79 | 0 |
| Matriculated | 215 | 7 | 7 |

**Total Matriculants: 229**    **Total Enrollment: 923**

## Financial Information

|  | In-State | Out-of-State |
|---|---|---|
| Total Cost of Attendance | $39,662 | $52,762 |
| Tuition and Fees | $14,875 | $27,975 |
| Other (incl. living expenses) | $24,787 | $24,787 |
| Health Insurance (can be waived) | n/a | n/a |

**Average 2010 Graduate Indebtedness: $129,379**
**% of Enrolled Students Receiving Aid: 84%**

*Source: 2009-2010 LCME I-B survey and 2010-2011 AAMC TSF questionnaire*

# University of Texas Medical School at Houston
## Houston, Texas

Office of Admissions—Room G.300
University of Texas Medical School at Houston
6431 Fannin, MSB G.300
Houston, Texas 77030

**T** 713 500 5116   ms.admissions@uth.tmc.edu

**Admissions:** http://med.uth.tmc.edu/
administration/admissions/

## General Information

UT-Houston Medical School is located in the Texas Medical Center in Houston. Memorial Hermann Hospital, a 650-bed general medical and surgical hospital, and Level I trauma center, is the school's primary teaching hospital. Other major teaching hospitals include the U. of Texas M.D. Anderson Cancer Center, the LBJ Hospital, the Harris County Psychiatric Center, Texas Heart Institute, St. Luke's Episcopal Hospital, Methodist Hospital and others.

## Mission Statement

The mission of the University of Texas Medical School at Houston is to provide the highest quality of education and training of future physicians for the state of Texas and to conduct the highest caliber of research in the biomedical and health sciences.

## Curricular Highlights

**Community Service Requirement:** Optional. Unlimited opportunities.

**Research/Thesis Requirement:** Optional. Unlimited opportunities.

The first two academic years are divided into four semesters, with three months of vacation between the first and second years. The initial four semesters are devoted to preparing the student for clerkship experiences in the clinical years. During the first two years the student becomes familiar with the basic and applied biomedical sciences. The student progresses from a study of the morphology of the human body and the fundamentals of molecular and cellular biology to that of the normal and abnormal structure and function of the various organ systems. Taking a history and conducting a physical examination are emphasized. After completion of this sequence, the student progresses through a series of clinical clerkships in the major disciplines for the next 12 months. In the fourth year, there are four required months and five to seven months of electives. Medical jurisprudence and technical skills are taught. In consultation with faculty, each student devises an educational sequence that relates specifically to ultimate career goals and postgraduate educational plans.

## Selection Factors

Applicants are selected with an emphasis on motivation and potential for service, especially in the state of Texas. Emphasis is given to students who have a broad education as well as academic achievement. A command of the English language with the ability to write and speak well is essential. The applicant's academic record is evaluated with special attention to the subjects taken and the demonstration of a broad-based comprehensive educational experience regardless of undergraduate institution. Significant attention is given to humanitarian endeavors, achievement in a nonacademic field of activity, and the applicant's specific interest in The University of Texas Medical School at Houston. Admission decisions are made in light of the school's mission, with preference given to Texas residents and those who will practice in underserved areas in the state and in needed specialties. Veteran status is also considered. The University of Texas Medical School at Houston does not discriminate on the basis of race, sex, creed, national origin, age, or handicap. For more information, go to *med.uth.tmc.edu*.

## Information about Diversity Programs

The UTH Office of Cultural and Institutional Diversity offers workshops and individual consultations to enhance skills such as writing, oral presentation, and time management. Diagnostic testing is available to assist students enhance their academic performance. Active student organizations and professional organizations in the Houston community support minority students.

## Regional/Satellite Campuses

Student rotations are completed at several hospitals and clinics in the Texas Medical Center and nearby.

## Application Process and Requirements 2012–2013

**Primary application service:** TMDSAS
**Earliest filing date:** May 1, 2011
**Latest filing date:** October 1, 2011

**Secondary application required:** No
**Sent to:** n/a
**URL:** n/a
**Fee:** No   **Waiver available:** No
**Earliest filing date:** n/a
**Latest filing date:** n/a

**MCAT® required:** Yes
**Latest MCAT® considered:** September 2011
**Oldest MCAT® considered:** August 2006

**Early Decision Program:** School does not have EDP
**Applicants notified:** n/a
**EDP available for:** n/a

**Regular acceptance notice —**
**Earliest date:** October 15 – November 15
**Latest date:** Until class is full
**Applicant's response to acceptance offer —**
**Maximum time:** Two weeks

**Requests for deferred entrance considered:** No

**Deposit to hold place in class:** No
**Deposit — In-State Applicants:** n/a
**Out-of-State Applicants:** n/a
**Deposit due:** n/a
**Applied to tuition:** n/a
**Refundable:** n/a
**Refundable by:** n/a

**Estimated number of new entrants:** 230
**EDP:** n/a, **Special Programs:** n/a

**Start month/year:** August 2012

**Interview format:** Personal interview with two faculty members. Regional interviews are not available. Video interviews are not available.

## Preparatory Programs
**Postbaccalaureate Program:** No

**Summer Program:** Yes,
http://med.uth.tmc.edu/administration/edu_programs/
ep/pre-entry_program.htm

## 2010–2011 First Year Class

|  | In-State | Out-of-State | International |
|---|---|---|---|
| Applications | 2,913 | 667 | 124 |
| Interviewed | 947 | 114 | 2 |
| Matriculated | 219 | 11 | 0 |

**Total Matriculants: 230**     **Total Enrollment: 953**

## Financial Information

|  | In-State | Out-of-State |
|---|---|---|
| Total Cost of Attendance | $32,949 | $46,049 |
| Tuition and Fees | $12,509 | $25,609 |
| Other (incl. living expenses) | $19,340 | $19,340 |
| Health Insurance (can be waived) | $1,100 | $1,100 |

**Average 2010 Graduate Indebtedness: $115,769**
**% of Enrolled Students Receiving Aid: 79%**

*Source: 2009-2010 LCME I-B survey and 2010-2011 AAMC TSF questionnaire*

# University of Texas School of Medicine at San Antonio

## San Antonio, Texas

Medical School Admissions, Office of the Dean
University of Texas School of Medicine at San Antonio
7703 Floyd Curl Drive, San Antonio, Texas 78229-3900

**T** 210 567 6080   medadmissions@uthscsa.edu

**Admissions:** http://som.uthscsa.edu/admissions/

## General Information

The University of Texas School of Medicine at San Antonio is located at the South Texas Medical Center in NW San Antonio. Clinical instruction is carried out at the University Hospital, University Health Center, Audie Murphy Veterans Hospital, Santa Rosa Children's Hospital, and affiliated hospitals including Wilford Hall USAF Hospital and Brooke Army Hospital.

## Mission Statement

The mission of the School of Medicine is to serve the needs of the citizens of Texas by providing medical education and training to medical students and physicians at all career levels and fostering an environment of life-long learning that is flexible and emphasizes professionalism, with special commitment to the preparation of physicians in both the art and science of medical practice; conducting biomedical and other health-related research, with particular attention to translational research; delivering exemplary health care; and providing a responsive resource in health-related affairs for the nation and the state, with particular emphasis on South Texas.

## Curricular Highlights

**Community Service Requirement:** Optional.

**Research/Thesis Requirement:** Optional.

The four-year curriculum offers an integrated program with more clinical exposure in the first two years. There is total integration of material organized within organ system modules, so that in any given module the instruction begins with the normal function/structure of the organ system and transitions into the diseases/disorders covering among other topics, anatomy, physiology, pathophysiology, pharmacology, patient communication, physical examination, epidemiology, and prevention. The second year ends in March and the third year clinical clerkships begin in June. The third year encompasses extensive clinical training in six major areas: family medicine, internal medicine, obstetrics and gynecology, pediatrics, psychiatry and surgery, with time available for few electives. The fourth year has eight weeks of required clinical rotations, eighteen weeks of elective rotations and five weeks of capstone course. Ten weeks are available for vacation. A letter grading system is used for all four years.

## Selection Factors

Ranking of applicants considers GPA, MCAT section scores, evaluation by premedical advisors, and judgment by the Committee on Admissions of the candidate's nonacademic achievements and personal qualifications, such as responsibility, integrity, maturity, and motivation, socioeconomic history, positions of leadership held, communication skills, and clinical/volunteer experiences. No person shall be excluded from participation in, denied the benefits of, or subject to discrimination under any program or activity sponsored or conducted by the University of Texas System on the basis of age, race, national origin, religion, or sex. Three hundred thirty five acceptances were offered to obtain a class of 221 first-year students.

## Information about Diversity Programs

Diversity of the student body is a compelling interest of the University of Texas School of Medicine at San Antonio. With this in mind, race and ethnicity is among the factors considered for acceptance of students. The School of Medicine is the state's leader in number of both Hispanic medical students and Hispanic faculty.

## Regional/Satellite Campuses

**Regional Campus Location(s):** Harlingen, TX, and Laredo, TX.

The Regional Academic Health Center (RAHC) located in Harlingen, Texas, is a second clinical education campus providing third year clerkship experiences at hospitals and clinics throughout the Lower Rio Grande Valley. Fourth year students participate in the didactic and externship opportunities identical to those available at the San Antonio campus. Starting with the 2012 entry year, applicants will indicate their preference to accomplish their clinical education at the Harlingen RAHC through the Texas Medical and Dental Schools Application Service (TMDSAS) match. Thirty students will be accepted through this process whereby education in the basic sciences is completed in San Antonio, and education in the clinical sciences completed at the RAHC-affiliated hospitals and clinics in Harlingen.

## Application Process and Requirements 2012–2013

**Primary application service:** TMDSAS
**Earliest filing date:** May 1, 2011
**Latest filing date:** October 1, 2011

**Secondary application required:** No
**Sent to:** n/a
**URL:** n/a
**Fee:** n/a   **Waiver available:** n/a
**Earliest filing date:** n/a
**Latest filing date:** n/a

**MCAT® required:** Yes
**Latest MCAT® considered:** September 2011
**Oldest MCAT® considered:** 2008

**Early Decision Program:** School does not have EDP
**Applicants notified:** n/a
**EDP available for:** n/a

**Regular acceptance notice —**
**Earliest date:** October 15, 2011 (Out-of-State)
November 15, 2011 (In-State)
**Latest date:** Until class is full
**Applicant's response to acceptance offer —**
**Maximum time:** Two weeks

**Requests for deferred entrance considered:** Yes

**Deposit to hold place in class:** No
**Deposit — In-State Applicants:** n/a
**Out-of-State Applicants:** n/a
**Deposit due:** n/a
**Applied to tuition:** n/a
**Refundable:** n/a
**Refundable by:** n/a

**Estimated number of new entrants:** 220
**EDP:** 0, **Special Programs:** 12

**Start month/year:** July 23, 2012

**Interview format:** Two 30-minute interviews; interviewers have only personal essays and a short bio sketch. Regional interviews are not available. Video interviews are not available.

## Preparatory Programs

**Postbaccalaureate Program:** No

**Summer Program:** No

## 2010–2011 First Year Class

|  | In-State | Out-of-State | International |
|---|---|---|---|
| Applications | 2,835 | 604 | 95 |
| Interviewed | 870 | 119 | 0 |
| Matriculated | 200 | 17 | 3 |

**Total Matriculants: 220**      **Total Enrollment: 901**

## Financial Information

|  | In-State | Out-of-State |
|---|---|---|
| Total Cost of Attendance | $40,651 | $53,751 |
| Tuition and Fees | $15,813 | $28,913 |
| Other (incl. living expenses) | $24,838 | $24,838 |
| Health Insurance (can be waived) | n/a | n/a |

**Average 2010 Graduate Indebtedness: $132,007**
**% of Enrolled Students Receiving Aid: 88%**

*Source: 2009-2010 LCME I-B survey and 2010-2011 AAMC TSF questionnaire*

# University of Texas Southwestern Medical Center at Dallas Southwestern Medical School

## Dallas, Texas

The University of Texas
Southwestern Medical Center at Dallas
5323 Harry Hines Boulevard
Dallas, Texas 75390-9162

**T** 214 648 5617   admissions@utsouthwestern.edu

**Admissions:** www.utswmedadmissions.org

### General Information
Founded in 1943, UT Southwestern is a multifaceted academic health science center nationally recognized for its excellence in educating physicians, biomedical scientists, and other health care professionals.

### Mission Statement
UT Southwestern is dedicated to educating physicians who are thoroughly grounded in the scientific basis of modern medicine, who are inspired to maintain lifelong medical scholarship, and who care for patients in a responsible and compassionate manner. UT Southwestern's mission emphasizes the importance of training primary care physicians, educating doctors who will practice in underserved areas of Texas, and preparing physician-scientists who seek careers in academic medicine and research.

### Curricular Highlights
**Community Service Requirement:** Optional.

**Research/Thesis Requirement:** Optional.

UT Southwestern offers a four-year curriculum based on departmental as well as interdisciplinary teaching. The purpose of the first two years is to provide a strong background in the basic sciences and an introduction to clinical medicine. The first-year curriculum is designed to begin the study of the normal human body and its processes at the molecular and cellular levels. The second year is an organ system-based curriculum that integrates pharmacology, microbiology, pathology, and clinical medicine. Contact with patients begins early in the first year with history-taking and physical examination, as well as visits to outpatient clinics. The third and fourth years provide intense clinical experiences involving the student in direct inpatient and outpatient care in a variety of clinical settings. Specific information about the UT Southwestern medical curriculum is available at *http://medschool.swmed.edu/*.

### Selection Factors
The following factors are considered in evaluating each applicant's acceptability: MCAT scores; undergraduate GPA; rigor of the undergraduate curriculum; letters of recommendation; research experience; extracurricular activities; socioeconomic background; time spent in outside employment; personal integrity and compassion for others; race/ethnicity; the ability to communicate in English; other personal qualities and individual factors such as leadership, social/family support, self-appraisal, maturity/coping skills, and determination; and motivation for a career in medicine. Additionally, applicants are evaluated with regard to the mission of Southwestern Medical School. State law requires at least 90 percent of the class be residents of Texas. Therefore, the minimum credentials for non-residents are more stringent than are those for Texas residents. Early application is strongly advised. A personal on-campus interview is required; interviews are held on Saturdays between early September and early January.

### Information about Diversity Programs
The Admissions Committee at UT Southwestern Medical School recognizes the need for increased numbers of physicians from groups underrepresented in medicine and encourages applications from Texas residents who are members of these groups. UT Southwestern uses race/ethnicity as one of the criteria for evaluating applicants in an effort to provide a diverse educational environment.

### Regional/Satellite Campuses
Clinical training takes place at university sites and affiliated hospitals and clinics throughout the North Texas area, including Parkland Memorial Hospital, Children's Medical Center Dallas, the Dallas VA Medical Center, University Hospital, and University Hospital-Zale Lipshy.

## Application Process and Requirements 2012–2013

**Primary application service:** TMDSAS
**Earliest filing date:** May 1, 2011
**Latest filing date:** October 1, 2011

**Secondary application required:** Yes
**Sent to:** All applicants
**URL:** https://sws004.swmed.edu/mdsuppapp/home.asp
**Fee:** No   **Waiver available:** n/a
**Earliest filing date:** May 1, 2011
**Latest filing date:** October 1, 2011

**MCAT® required:** Yes
**Latest MCAT® considered:** September 2011
**Oldest MCAT® considered:** September 2007

**Early Decision Program:** School does not have EDP
**Applicants notified:** n/a
**EDP available for:** n/a

**Regular acceptance notice —**
**Earliest date:** November 15, 2011
**Latest date:** Varies
**Applicant's response to acceptance offer —**
**Maximum time:** Three weeks

**Requests for deferred entrance considered:** Yes

**Deposit to hold place in class:** No
**Deposit — In-State Applicants:** n/a
**Out-of-State Applicants:** n/a
**Deposit due:** n/a
**Applied to tuition:** n/a
**Refundable:** n/a
**Refundable by:** n/a

**Estimated number of new entrants:** 230
**EDP:** n/a, **Special Programs:** n/a

**Start month/year:** August 2012

**Interview format:** Two 25-minute faculty interviews. Regional interviews are not available. Video interviews are not available.

### Preparatory Programs
**Postbaccalaureate Program:** No

**Summer Program:** No

## 2010–2011 First Year Class

|              | In-State | Out-of-State | International |
|--------------|----------|--------------|--------------|
| Applications | 2,672    | 676          | 137          |
| Interviewed  | 730      | 96           | 6            |
| Matriculated | 199      | 26           | 5            |

**Total Matriculants: 230**   **Total Enrollment: 926**

## Financial Information

|                                        | In-State | Out-of-State |
|----------------------------------------|----------|--------------|
| Total Cost of Attendance               | $40,779  | $53,879      |
| Tuition and Fees                       | $15,640  | $28,740      |
| Other (incl. living expenses)          | $24,039  | $24,039      |
| Health Insurance (can be waived)       | $1,100   | $1,100       |

**Average 2010 Graduate Indebtedness: $110,629**
**% of Enrolled Students Receiving Aid: 86%**

*Source: 2009-2010 LCME I-B survey and 2010-2011 AAMC TSF questionnaire*

# University of Utah
# School of Medicine
## Salt Lake City, Utah

Office of Admissions
University of Utah School of Medicine
30 North 1900 East Room 1C029
Salt Lake City, Utah 84132-2101

**T** 801 581 7498  deans.admissions@hsc.utah.edu

**Admissions:** http://medicine.utah.edu/admissions/

## General Information

A minimum of 75% of positions are offered to Utah residents. The school contracts with the State of Idaho to accept eight Idaho residents each year. Nonresident applicants must have significant ties to Utah or be specifically recognized as a member of a population group underrepresented in the physician workforce. (Africans and African Americans, American Indians, Alaska Natives, Chamorros, Polynesians including Native Hawaiians, Tongans, Samoans, Filipinos, Tahitians, Maoris, Fijians, Niueans, Palauans; Chicanos/as and Latinos/as including Puerto Ricans, Mexican Americans, Central Americans and South Americans), or apply to the MD/PhD program. MD/PhD applicants must be U.S. citizens or U.S. permanent residents. Application may be made for three consecutive years. Applicants who have been dismissed from, or on probation or under suspension at another medical school will not be considered. Transfers are considered on rare occasions and must meet specific criteria. The school does not discriminate with respect to applicants' age, color, gender, sexual orientation, race, national origin, religion, status as a person with a disability, or status as a veteran or a disabled veteran. The University of Utah provides reasonable accommodation to known disabilities of applicants.

## Mission Statement

The School of Medicine has three major missions: education, research, and clinical service. The three missions are closely interrelated. Each supports and, in turn, benefits from the others. All are considered to be of equal importance.

## Curricular Highlights

**Community Service Requirement:** Optional.

**Research/Thesis Requirement:** Research required. Thesis optional.

The educational mission of the medical school at the University of Utah is to prepare all medical students to be well versed in scientific fundamentals, be technically proficient, and be medically, socially and culturally responsive to the needs of their patients. The curriculum at the University of Utah will serve to optimize patient care by preparing medical students to become competent, compassionate and conscientious physicians who, as lifelong learners, are able to effectively respond to the ever-changing demands of a complex system of healthcare.

## Selection Factors

Minimum acceptable GPA for science, non-science and overall is 3.0. Average GPA for entering freshmen is 3.6. Minimum acceptable score for each section of the MCAT is 7. The school considers MCATs taken within 3 years of application. The highest scores in each area will be used. The average score for entering freshmen is 30. Letters of Recommendation: 3 Academic letters - Letters must be from professors who taught you in a classroom setting (labs not allowed) and assigned you a grade. At least 1 letter must be from a science professor. 3 Supervisor letters (direct supervisor)Community Service, Clinical Experience, Research-must be in a scholarly or scientific hypothesis investigation. There are specific criteria for each of the following requirements. Extracurricular, Community/Volunteer Service, Leadership, Research, Physician Shadowing, and Patient Exposure. Detailed information may be obtained by visiting our website.

## Information about Diversity Programs

The mission of the Office of Inclusion and Outreach (OIO)is to extend an open invitation to all embracing and supporting all values for the enrichment of the entire Utah community. With medical student volunteers, we organize and run twenty different outreach programs for multiple age groups from pre-K to 12th grade.

## Regional/Satellite Campuses

Rotations are performed at University, Intermountain Healthcare hospitals including Primary Children's Medical Center and the Veterans Affairs (VA) hospital.

## Application Process and Requirements 2012–2013

**Primary application service:** AMCAS®
**Earliest filing date:** June 1, 2011
**Latest filing date:** November 1, 2011

**Secondary application required:** Yes
**Sent to:** Screened applicants
**E-mail:** deans.admissions@hsc.utah.edu
**Fee:** Yes, $100  **Waiver available:** Yes
**Earliest filing date:** August 2011
**Latest filing date:** January 2012

**MCAT® required:** Yes
**Latest MCAT® considered:** September 2011
**Oldest MCAT® considered:** January 2009

**Early Decision Program:** School does not have EDP
**Applicants notified:** n/a
**EDP available for:** n/a

**Regular acceptance notice —**
**Earliest date:** October 15, 2011
**Latest date:** Until class is full
**Applicant's response to acceptance offer —**
**Maximum time:** Two weeks

**Requests for deferred entrance considered:** Yes

**Deposit to hold place in class:** Yes
**Deposit — In-State Applicants:** $100
**Out of State Applicants:** $100
**Deposit due:** With response to acceptance offer
**Applied to tuition:** Yes
**Refundable:** Yes
**Refundable by:** May 15, 2012

**Estimated number of new entrants:** 82
**EDP:** 0, **Special Programs:** n/a

**Start month/year:** August 2012

**Interview format:** Each applicant will have two interviews. Regional interviews are not available. Video interviews are not available.

## Preparatory Programs
**Postbaccalaureate Program:** No

**Summer Program:** No

## 2010–2011 First Year Class

|  | In-State | Out-of-State | International |
|---|---|---|---|
| Applications | 393 | 799 | 15 |
| Interviewed | 275 | 145 | 8 |
| Matriculated | 60 | 21 | 1 |

**Total Matriculants: 82**　　**Total Enrollment: 373**

## Financial Information

|  | In-State | Out-of-State |
|---|---|---|
| Total Cost of Attendance | $48,875 | $72,683 |
| Tuition and Fees | $27,509 | $51,317 |
| Other (incl. living expenses) | $21,366 | $21,366 |
| Health Insurance (can be waived) | $0 | $0 |

**Average 2010 Graduate Indebtedness: $147,988**
**% of Enrolled Students Receiving Aid: 96%**

Source: 2009-2010 LCME I-B survey and 2010-2011 AAMC TSF questionnaire

# University of Vermont
# College of Medicine

Burlington, Vermont

The University of Vermont
College of Medicine
Office of Admissions,
The Courtyard at Given
89 Beaumont Avenue
Burlington, Vermont 05405

**T** 802 656 2154   medadmissions@uvm.edu

**Admissions:** www.med.uvm.edu/Admissions

## General Information

The University of Vermont College of Medicine, located in Burlington, Vermont, was established in 1822 as the seventh medical school in the U.S. The College is located on the main campus of the University of Vermont and is adjacent to teaching hospital partner Fletcher Allen Health Care, which provides primary, secondary and tertiary health care services to over 1 million people in the region. A spacious Medical Education Center and Ambulatory Care Center opened in 2005 to support the College's 450 medical students and 275 residents, who also train at over 30 patient care sites and 100 outreach clinics throughout the region. A new 7500 square foot clinical simulation laboratory opens in 2011.

## Mission Statement

Our missions are to educate new generations of physicians and scientists, to advance medical knowledge through research, to render compassionate and effective care, and to collaborate and engage with the communities we serve.

## Curricular Highlights

**Community Service Requirement:** Required.

**Research/Thesis Requirement:** Optional.

The Vermont Integrated Curriculum (VIC) progresses from the study of Foundations of Medicine, both clinical and basic science, to applications in Clinical Clerkship, to senior scholarship and supervised patient management in Advanced Integration. Areas of focus include progressive skill development, health care systems, preventive care, and a greater understanding of applied sciences, particularly genetics, ethics and epidemiology. The VIC also places emphasis on professionalism, cultural competency, scholarly research, teaching skills, and community service.

## Selection Factors

The Committee on Admissions seeks a diverse student body. We look for evidence of excellence accompanied by genuine concern for the welfare of others. Effective interpersonal skills are important, and successful applicants often have a history of service to the community. Selection is based upon a past pattern of academic performance plus an assessment of the applicant's fitness for the study and practice of medicine in terms of aptitude, interests, experience, motivation, leadership abilities, and maturity. Letters of recommendation and a personal interview are required and form an important part of the application process. Students from groups underrepresented in medicine are encouraged to apply. The University of Vermont does not discriminate on the basis of race, color, sex, sexual orientation, religion, age, handicap, national origin, or Vietnam veteran status.

## Information about Diversity Programs

The College of Medicine strongly encourages applications from those who have the potential to increase the overall diversity of the class based on a variety of factors such as economic hardship, first generation college graduates, race, and cultural background.

## Regional/Satellite Campuses

Students gain clinical experience from the first day of medical school, with our teaching hospital partner Fletcher Allen Health Care, located adjacent to the medical school, and at clinics throughout the region. In addition, clinical sites for training include Danbury Hospital in Danbury, CT; St. Mary's Medical Center in West Palm Beach, FL; Eastern Maine Medical Center in Bangor, ME and Central Maine Medical Center in Lewiston, ME.

## Application Process and Requirements 2012–2013

**Primary application service:** AMCAS®
**Earliest filing date:** June 1, 2011
**Latest filing date:** November 1, 2011

**Secondary application required:** Yes
**Sent to:** All applicants
**Contact:** Admissions Office, (802) 656-2154, medadmissions@uvm.edu
**Fee:** Yes, $95   **Waiver available:** Yes
**Earliest filing date:** June 15, 2011
**Latest filing date:** December 23, 2011

**MCAT® required:** Yes
**Latest MCAT® considered:** September 2011
**Oldest MCAT® considered:** January 2008

**Early Decision Program:** School does have EDP
**Applicants notified:** September 30, 2011
**EDP available for:** Both In-State and Out-of-State Applicants

Regular acceptance notice —
Earliest date: October 16, 2011
**Latest date:** Until class is full
**Applicant's response to acceptance offer —
Maximum time:** Two weeks

**Requests for deferred entrance considered:** Yes

**Deposit to hold place in class:** Yes
**Deposit — In-State Applicants:** $100
**Out-of-State Applicants:** $100
**Deposit due:** With response to acceptance offer
**Applied to tuition:** Yes
**Refundable:** Yes
**Refundable by:** May 15, 2012

**Estimated number of new entrants:** 114
**EDP:** 5, **Special Programs:** n/a

**Start month/year:** August 2012

**Interview format:** Campus interview with admissions committee member. Regional interviews are not available. Video interviews are not available.

## Preparatory Programs

**Postbaccalaureate Program:** Yes
http://learn.uvm.edu/?Page=postbac.html

**Summer Program:** No

## 2010–2011 First Year Class

|  | In-State | Out-of-State | International |
|---|---|---|---|
| Applications | 72 | 5,406 | 38 |
| Interviewed | 61 | 606 | 0 |
| Matriculated | 28 | 83 | 0 |

**Total Matriculants: 111**        **Total Enrollment: 452**

## Financial Information

|  | In-State | Out-of-State |
|---|---|---|
| Total Cost of Attendance | $50,887 | $72,862 |
| Tuition and Fees | $30,317 | $51,657 |
| Other (incl. living expenses) | $18,916 | $19,551 |
| Health Insurance (can be waived) | $1,654 | $1,654 |

**Average 2010 Graduate Indebtedness: $164,292**
**% of Enrolled Students Receiving Aid: 90%**

Source: 2009-2010 LCME I-B survey and 2010-2011 AAMC TSF questionnaire

# Eastern Virginia Medical School
## Norfolk, Virginia

Office of Admissions
Eastern Virginia Medical School
700 W. Olney Road
Norfolk, Virginia 23507-1607

**T** 757 446 5812    mclendm@evms.edu

**Admissions:** www.evms.edu/md-programs/
md-programs-home.html

## General Information

Established in 1973 to enhance the quality and diversity of health care throughout the Hampton Roads region, the mission of EVMS is deeply rooted in the education and training of primary care physicians, arming them with the requisite scientific, academic, and humanistic skills most relevant to today's practice of medicine. EVMS provides health care for more than one quarter of Virginia's population as well as neighboring regions of North Carolina.

## Mission Statement

EVMS is a public institution dedicated to medical and health education, biomedical research, and the enhancement of health care in the Commonwealth of Virginia.

## Curricular Highlights

**Community Service Requirement:** Optional.

**Research/Thesis Requirement:** Optional.

The first two years focus on clinical medicine through two vehicles: the Theresa A. Thomas Professional Skills Teaching and Assessment Center and a Longitudinal Mentorship with a generalist physician in community practice. Careful coordination between basic sciences and generalist disciplines permits an integrated curriculum. Weekly small-group sessions introduce students to clinical problem-solving. This early introduction to clinical medicine teaches medical history-taking and physical examination along with the application of basic science knowledge to patient care. Third-year clinical clerkships focus on ambulatory care in community-based sites in balance with inpatient care experiences. In addition to the required clerkships are rotations in substance abuse, geriatrics, and surgical subspecialties. For those interested in generalist medicine, electives are offered in special populations and rural health care, and an elective honors track in generalist medicine. Elective opportunities are available for those interested in research or subspecialty care. Students are graded as Honors, High Pass, Pass, or Fail.

## Selection Factors

EVMS does not discriminate on the basis of sex, race, creed, age, national origin, marital status, or handicap. A supplementary application packet is sent to those applicants receiving a favorable initial screening of their completed AMCAS® application. The Admissions Committee considers the entire academic record, including science and overall GPA, MCAT scores, exposure to the medical field, maturity, character, and motivation. The application fee will be waived if a fee waiver is granted by AMCAS. Preference is given to legal residents of Virginia. EVMS seeks persons with personal and background traits that indicate a high potential for becoming a primary care physician. Applicants who have completed one or more years in a medical school accredited by the LCME can be considered for transfer into the second or third year only to fill vacancies that may arise with the withdrawal of previously enrolled students. All transfers must meet the requirements stated for general admission.

## Information about Diversity Programs

EVMS is committed to producing a diverse physician workforce to meet the health care needs of the region. Applicants from rural or other underserved regions and those who have been disadvantaged or underrepresented for economic, racial, or social reasons, and who possess the motivation and aptitude required for the study of medicine are strongly encouraged to apply.

## Regional/Satellite Campuses

EVMS partners with 33 local area hospitals, including Sentara Norfolk General Hospital, the Children's Hospital of the King's Daughters, the U.S. Naval Medical Center in Portsmouth, and the Veterans Affairs Hospital in Hampton.

## Application Process and Requirements 2012–2013

**Primary application service:** AMCAS®
**Earliest filing date:** June 1, 2011
**Latest filing date:** November 15, 2011

**Secondary application required:** Yes
**Sent to:** Screened applicants
**URL:** www.evms.edu/apply-home/md-admissions-application-home.html
**Fee:** Yes, $100    **Waiver available:** Yes
**Earliest filing date:** July 2011
**Latest filing date:** January 2012

**MCAT® required:** Yes
**Latest MCAT® considered:** September 2011
**Oldest MCAT® considered:** December 2009

**Early Decision Program:** School does have EDP
**Applicants notified:** October 1, 2011
**EDP available for:** Both In-State and Out-of-State Applicants

**Regular acceptance notice —**
**Earliest date:** October 15, 2011
**Latest date:** Until class is full
**Applicant's response to acceptance offer —**
**Maximum time:** Two weeks

**Requests for deferred entrance considered:** Yes

**Deposit to hold place in class:** Yes
**Deposit — In-State Applicants:** $100
**Out-of-State Applicants:** $100
**Deposit due:** With response to acceptance offer
**Applied to tuition:** Yes
**Refundable:** Yes
**Refundable by:** May 15, 2012

**Estimated number of new entrants:** 130
**EDP:** 2, **Special Programs:** n/a

**Start month/year:** August 2012

**Interview format:** Panel interviews. Regional interviews are not available. Video interviews are not available.

**Preparatory Programs**
**Postbaccalaureate Program:** Yes,
www.evms.edu/evms-school-of-health-professions/ms-in-biomedical-sciences-medical-masters.html

**Summer Program:** No

## 2010–2011 First Year Class

|  | In-State | Out-of-State | International |
|---|---|---|---|
| Applications | 816 | 3,848 | 294 |
| Interviewed | 370 | 298 | 22 |
| Matriculated | 67 | 47 | 4 |

**Total Matriculants: 118**    **Total Enrollment: 469**

## Financial Information

|  | In-State | Out-of-State |
|---|---|---|
| Total Cost of Attendance | $48,825 | $74,263 |
| Tuition and Fees | $29,196 | $54,634 |
| Other (incl. living expenses) | $16,972 | $16,972 |
| Health Insurance (can be waived) | $2,657 | $2,657 |

**Average 2010 Graduate Indebtedness: $163,020**
**% of Enrolled Students Receiving Aid: 89%**

Source: 2009-2010 LCME I-B survey and 2010-2011 AAMC TSF questionnaire

# University of Virginia School of Medicine

## Charlottesville, Virginia

Medical School Admissions Office
P.O. Box 800725
University of Virginia School of Medicine
Charlottesville, Virginia 22908

T 434 924 5571   medsch-adm@virginia.edu

**Admissions:** www.medicine.virginia.edu/education/
medical-students/admissions

### General Information

The University of Virginia School of Medicine was opened for instruction in 1825, making it one of the oldest medical schools in the South. Both the School of Medicine and the University of Virginia Medical Center are located on the grounds of the University of Virginia in Charlottesville.

### Mission Statement

Our mission is to educate students to fulfill the need for practitioners and scientists; to provide cost-effective, high-quality patient care at primary, secondary, and tertiary levels; to produce new knowledge required to advance health by conducting research; and to provide public service as needed by citizens or by public jurisdictions.

### Curricular Highlights

**Community Service Requirement:** Required. Yes, including one semester community placement.

**Research/Thesis Requirement:** Optional. A thesis is required for Generalist Scholars only.

Our curriculum integrates scientific knowledge, clinical care, and research throughout the entire four years of medical school. The Claude Moore Medical Education Building, finished in 2010, was created for the "Next Generation" Cells to Society Curriculum. The building integrates small group learning and individual instruction with state of the art educational spaces, including the "Learning Studio" which uses technology to enable active learning. The systems-based curriculum is integrated and uses clinical cases for problem solving. A Clinical Performance Education Center has 14,000 square feet devoted to 4 mock spaces (an ER, ICU, OR and L&D suite), as well as 20 patient rooms. State of the art stimulators, standardized patients, and other technologies, allow for experiential learning and complement real patient experience. Students have 2-3 afternoons a week for elective activities or productive self study and a largely elective post clerkship period for student directed advanced clinical learning or research. 26 weeks of electives and 12 weeks of selectives in the fourth year allow students the opportunity to pursue their own interests and needs, including clinical experience, graduate courses, and research activities.

### Selection Factors

All applicants must have completed at least 90 semester hours of course work in a U.S. or Canadian accredited college or university. The Committee on Admissions does not discriminate on the basis of race, sex, gender identity, sexual orientation, creed, national origin, age, or disability. Grades, MCAT scores, healthcare and volunteer experience, letters of recommendation, and the interview influence committee decisions.

### Information about Diversity Programs

The University of Virginia encourages applications from qualified applicants from groups that are underrepresented in medicine. Systems in place to facilitate preparation and success of students include: (1) a six-week summer enrichment program; (2) extensive tutorial and other academic support programs upon admission; and (3) need-based and merit-based financial assistance. For more information, please contact Dr. M. Norman Oliver, Associate Dean for Diversity, at *mno3p@virginia.edu.*

### Regional/Satellite Campuses

**Regional Campus Location(s):** Roanoke, VA.

In their 3rd year clerkships, students will spend about one third of their time away from the University to experience other clinical sites. These include the Roanoke Memorial Hospital in Roanoke, VA, the Salem Veterans Affairs Hospital, and the INOVA Fairfax Hospital in Fairfax, VA. Students will be there in small groups; housing and meals are provided for these off site locations.

## Application Process and Requirements 2012–2013

**Primary application service:** AMCAS®
**Earliest filing date:** June 1, 2011
**Latest filing date:** November 1, 2011

**Secondary application required:** Yes
**Sent to:** All applicants
**Contact:** Eileen K. Oswald, M.S., (434) 924-5571, eko2v@virginia.edu
**Fee:** Yes, $80   **Waiver available:** Yes
**Earliest filing date:** June 1, 2011
**Latest filing date:** January 3, 2012

**MCAT® required:** Yes
**Latest MCAT® considered:** September 2011
**Oldest MCAT® considered:** April 2009

**Early Decision Program:** School does not have EDP
**Applicants notified:** n/a
**EDP available for:** n/a

**Regular acceptance notice —**
**Earliest date:** October 16, 2011
**Latest date:** Until class is full
**Applicant's response to acceptance offer —**
**Maximum time:** Three weeks

**Requests for deferred entrance considered:** Yes

**Deposit to hold place in class:** No
**Deposit — In-State Applicants:** n/a
**Out-of-State Applicants:** n/a
**Deposit due:** n/a
**Applied to tuition:** n/a
**Refundable:** n/a
**Refundable by:** n/a

**Estimated number of new entrants:** 156
**EDP:** n/a, **Special Programs:** n/a

**Start month/year:** August 2012

**Interview format:** Two one-on-one, half-hour interviews. Regional interviews are not available. Video interviews are not available.

### Preparatory Programs
**Postbaccalaureate Program:** Yes, www.scps.virginia.edu/postbac/

**Summer Program:** Yes, www.healthsystem.virginia.edu/internet/academic-support/maap1-a.cfm

### 2010–2011 First Year Class

|  | In-State | Out-of-State | International |
|---|---|---|---|
| Applications | 729 | 3,392 | 165 |
| Interviewed | 144 | 368 | 22 |
| Matriculated | 71 | 76 | 6 |

**Total Matriculants: 153**   **Total Enrollment: 581**

### Financial Information

|  | In-State | Out-of-State |
|---|---|---|
| Total Cost of Attendance | $58,438 | $69,432 |
| Tuition and Fees | $37,880 | $48,874 |
| Other (incl. living expenses) | $18,407 | $18,407 |
| Health Insurance (can be waived) | $2,151 | $2,151 |

**Average 2010 Graduate Indebtedness: $132,525**
**% of Enrolled Students Receiving Aid: 89%**

Source: 2009-2010 LCME I-B survey and 2010-2011 AAMC TSF questionnaire

# Virginia Commonwealth University School of Medicine

## Richmond, Virginia

Virginia Commonwealth University
School of Medicine
P.O. Box 980565
Richmond, Virginia 23298-0565

T 804 828 9629   somumc@vcu.edu

**Admissions:** www.medschool.vcu.edu/admissions/md/index.html

## General Information

The School of Medicine, which has been in continuous operation since 1838, is the founding institution of Virginia Commonwealth University. The vitality of VCU's clinical, educational, and research programs is reflected in the caliber of its faculty, the success of its patient care programs, and the level of research funding.

## Mission Statement

The mission of the School of Medicine is to provide eminent education to physicians and scientists, and to improve the quality of health care for humanity. Through the use of innovative, scholarly activity and a diverse educational context, the School seeks to create new knowledge, and to provide and continuously improve systems of medical and science education. Furthermore, it is our mission to develop more effective health care methods to address the needs of the diverse populations we serve, and to provide distinguished leadership in the advancement of medicine and science.

## Curricular Highlights

**Community Service Requirement:** Required. M1 students are required to complete 20 hours.

**Research/Thesis Requirement:** Optional.

The first year is spent studying normal structure and function in a traditional discipline format. The second year emphasizes the pathogenesis of disease and its manifestations and is taught in an organ system manner. Pathogenesis, pathology, pharmacology, and the major manifestations and principles of management are discussed in each of the major body systems. In the longitudinal clinical experience for first- and second-year students, students spend two afternoons per month in a small group learning the fundamentals of clinical medicine. This is supplemented by a clinical experience in the office of a primary care physician two afternoons per month. The clinical experience is integrated with the basic sciences in a way that enhances and enriches students' learning. There is a computer lab with over 40 workstations and a full array of commercial and in-house, faculty-developed educational software. Third-year rotations are at the University and Veterans Affairs Hospitals, with ambulatory care rotations at non-university primary care sites. A select number of students will complete the third and fourth years at the Inova campus in Northern Virginia. The fourth year is primarily elective time with two required rotations.

## Selection Factors

Applicants are selected on the basis of their potential as prospective physicians as well as students of medicine. Attributes of character, personality factors, academic skills, and exposure to medicine are considered along with academic performance, GPA, MCAT scores, letters of recommendation, and personal interviews at the School of Medicine.

## Information about Diversity Programs

The office of Student Outreach Programs endeavors to provide support for the school's diverse population. Student Outreach's objectives are to recruit and retain students from disadvantaged or non-traditional backgrounds to an environment conducive for exchange of ideas where students learn from faculty and peers. The main goal of the program is to provide medical school graduates that will best meet the healthcare needs of the state and nation.

## Regional/Satellite Campuses

**Regional Campus Location(s):** Fairfax, VA.

There is a regional campus at Inova Hospital, Fairfax, VA, which is used for third- and fourth-year training.

## Application Process and Requirements 2012–2013

**Primary application service:** AMCAS®
**Earliest filing date:** June 1, 2011
**Latest filing date:** October 15, 2011

**Secondary application required:** Yes
**Sent to:** Screened applicants
**Contact:** Shenia Tyler, (804) 828-9629, shenia.tyler@vcu.edu
**Fee:** Yes, $80   **Waiver available:** Yes
**Earliest filing date:** June 1, 2011
**Latest filing date:** January 30, 2012

**MCAT® required:** Yes
**Latest MCAT® considered:** September 2011
**Oldest MCAT® considered:** January 2009

**Early Decision Program:** School does have EDP
**Applicants notified:** October 1, 2011
**EDP available for:** Both In-State and Out-of-State Applicants

**Regular acceptance notice —**
**Earliest date:** October 16, 2011
**Latest date:** Until class is full
**Applicant's response to acceptance offer —**
**Maximum time:** Two weeks

**Requests for deferred entrance considered:** Yes
**Deposit to hold place in class:** Yes
**Deposit — In-State Applicants:** $100
**Out-of-State Applicants:** $100
**Deposit due:** With response to acceptance offer
**Applied to tuition:** Yes
**Refundable:** Yes
**Refundable by:** May 15, 2012

**Estimated number of new entrants:** 200
**EDP:** 1, **Special Programs:** 22

**Start month/year:** August 2012

**Interview format:** Single, one-on-one interview
Regional interviews are not available. Video interviews are not available.

## Preparatory Programs

**Postbaccalaureate Program:** Yes, www.medschool.vcu.edu/graduate/premed_cert/index.html

**Summer Program:** Yes, www.healthdisparities.vcu.edu

## 2010–2011 First Year Class

|  | In-State | Out-of-State | International |
| --- | --- | --- | --- |
| Applications | 877 | 5,339 | 136 |
| Interviewed | 421 | 450 | 0 |
| Matriculated | 103 | 94 | 3 |

**Total Matriculants: 200**    **Total Enrollment: 769**

## Financial Information

|  | In-State | Out-of-State |
| --- | --- | --- |
| Total Cost of Attendance | $54,103 | $68,566 |
| Tuition and Fees | $29,185 | $43,648 |
| Other (incl. living expenses) | $22,730 | $22,730 |
| Health Insurance (can be waived) | $2,188 | $2,188 |

**Average 2010 Graduate Indebtedness: $150,022**
**% of Enrolled Students Receiving Aid: 91%**

Source: 2009-2010 LCME I-B survey and 2010-2011 AAMC TSF questionnaire

# Virginia Tech Carilion School of Medicine

Roanoke, Virginia

2 Riverside Circle
Suite M140
Roanoke, Virginia 24016

**T** 540 526 2500
vtcadmissions2012@carilionclinic.org

**Admissions:** http://vtc.vt.edu/education/admissions/index.html

VA

## General Information

The Virginia Tech Carilion School of Medicine and Research Institute (VTC) is a public-private partnership formed by Virginia Tech and Carilion Clinic. The Virginia Tech Carilion School of Medicine is a private four-year medical school offering the doctor of medicine (M.D.) degree. Utilizing an innovative patient-centered curriculum, VTC addresses the increasing need for physicians who translate research from the bench to the bedside and into the community. The curriculum provides an exemplary education in basic sciences and clinical sciences and skills, but transcends the traditional medical education model by providing a solid foundation in, and opportunities to explore, the disciplines of research and interprofessionalism. Our small class size of 42 students allows for individualized attention and participation by each student which will in turn foster an intense and rewarding educational experience. We envision that VTC students will be highly sought after by residency programs and will become physician thought leaders in their chosen field of medicine.

## Mission Statement

VTC's mission is to develop physician thought leaders through inquiry, research and discovery, using an innovative curriculum based on adult learning methods in a patient-centered context. Our graduates will be physicians with outstanding clinical skills and significantly enhanced research capabilities who will remain life-long learners. The VTC physician will have an understanding of the importance of interprofessionalism to enable them to function more effectively as part of a modern healthcare team.

## Curricular Highlights

**Community Service Requirement:** Required. An inter-professional service learning project.

**Research/Thesis Requirement:** Required. A research manuscript of publishable quality.

The VTC interprofessionalism program involves VTC students in a collaborate project with students from other health professions on a service learning project in the community in the first year. For their required research project, each VTC student must complete a hypothesis-driven scholarly project guided by a mentoring team, provide a written document suitable for publication, and present their work in an appropriate venue in order to graduate.

## Selection Factors

VTC offers a four-year M.D. degree and admits both Virginia state and out-of-state residents. Applicants must be U.S. citizens or U.S. permanent residents. VTC is committed to attracting a diverse body of learners who will likely achieve academic success in the rigorous academic setting of medical school, while experiencing further growth in other important aspects of professionalism. Our admissions process identifies candidates with evidence of leadership, scholarship, and motivation for a career in medicine as evidenced by superior academic credentials. VTC seeks individuals whose accomplishments reveal originality and a capacity for independent, critical thinking. Those who are interested in a life-long career of inquiry, including the practice of evidence-based medicine, clinical and basic science research, and scholarship, are encouraged to apply.

## Information about Diversity Programs

VTC is committed to matriculating a diverse body of exceptional individuals who reflect the people whose health needs the medical profession must serve. VTC's commitment to diversity will be shown in the ethnic, cultural and socio-economic backgrounds of the student body.

## Application Process and Requirements 2012–2013

**Primary application service:** AMCAS®
**Earliest filing date:** June 2011
**Latest filing date:** December 1, 2011

**Secondary application required:** Yes
**Sent to:** Screened applicants
**URL:** Invitation only
**Fee:** Yes, $50    **Waiver available:** Yes
**Earliest filing date:** July 1, 2011
**Latest filing date:** January 15, 2012

**MCAT® required:** Yes
**Latest MCAT® considered:** September 2011
**Oldest MCAT® considered:** September 2008

**Early Decision Program:** School does not have EDP
**Applicants notified:** n/a
**EDP available for:** n/a

**Regular acceptance notice —**
**Earliest date:** October 15, 2011
**Latest date:** Until class is full
**Applicant's response to acceptance offer —**
**Maximum time:** Two weeks

**Requests for deferred entrance considered:** Yes

**Deposit to hold place in class:** Yes
**Deposit — In-State Applicants:** $100
**Out-of-State Applicants:** $100
**Deposit due:** With response to acceptance offer
**Applied to tuition:** Yes
**Refundable:** Yes
**Refundable by:** May 15, 2012

**Estimated number of new entrants:** 42
**EDP:** n/a, **Special Programs:** n/a

**Start month/year:** August 2012

**Interview format:** On-campus Multiple Mini-Interview (MMI) with a series of ten raters. Regional interviews are not available. Video interviews are not available.

## Preparatory Programs
**Postbaccalaureate Program:** No

**Summer Program:** No

## 2010–2011 First Year Class

|  | In-State | Out-of-State | International |
|---|---|---|---|
| Applications | 520 | 1,105 | 29 |
| Interviewed | 83 | 135 | 0 |
| Matriculated | 14 | 28 | 0 |

**Total Matriculants: 42**    **Total Enrollment: 42**

## Financial Information

|  | In-State | Out-of-State |
|---|---|---|
| Total Cost of Attendance | $62,630 | $62,630 |
| Tuition and Fees | $40,450 | $40,450 |
| Other (incl. living expenses) | $19,780 | $19,780 |
| Health Insurance (can be waived) | $2,400 | $2,400 |

**Average 2010 Graduate Indebtedness: n/a**
**% of Enrolled Students Receiving Aid: n/a**

*Source: 2009-2010 LCME I-B survey and 2010-2011 AAMC TSF questionnaire*

# University of Washington School of Medicine

Seattle, Washington

Office of Admissions
Health Sciences Center A-300
Box 356340, University of Washington
Seattle, Washington 98195-6340

T 206 543 7212   askuwsom@uw.edu

**Admissions:** www.uwmedicine.org/admissions

## General Information

Ranked as the top medical school training primary care physicians for 17 years, and first among public medical schools in federal research funding, the UWSOM is dedicated to improving the health of the public by advancing medical knowledge, providing outstanding primary and specialty care to people of the region, and preparing tomorrow's physicians and scientists. The top-ranked programs in family medicine and rural health are enhanced by clinical faculty who provide community-based medical education in the states of Washington, Wyoming, Alaska, Montana, and Idaho. The UWSOM is committed to building and sustaining a diverse academic community and to assuring that access to education and training is open to all segments of society.

## Mission Statement

Our missions are: meeting the health-care needs of our region, especially by recognizing the importance of primary care and providing service to underserved populations, advancing knowledge, and assuming leadership in the biomedical sciences and academic medicine.

## Curricular Highlights

**Community Service Requirement:** Optional.

**Research/Thesis Requirement:** Required. Independent Investigative Inquiry is required.

First two years of the curriculum integrate basic sciences and clinical medicine. Patient contact begins in the first year. The College system consists of faculty mentors who each guide 24 students for 4 years in acquiring fundamental clinical skills. Problem based learning, observed standardized clinical examinations, and capstone courses provide transitions from 2nd to 3rd year and from 4th year to residency. Opportunities are provided for a longitudinal interdisciplinary clerkship and for required and elective rotations in the WWAMI region and internationally. There is ample time for electives ranging from rural experiences to bench research. Certification can be earned in Indian Health, Global Health, Hispanic Health and Underserved Pathways. Students selected for TRUST will be specially trained to practice in underserved settings.

## Selection Factors

Selection is based on motivation, maturity, integrity, and the academic record. Demonstrated humanitarian qualities, community service, communication skills, knowledge of issues in health care delivery, ability to think analytically, and intellectual curiosity are also considered. At least 40 hours of MD shadowing is expected. Preference is given to residents of the WWAMI states; less than 5% of the class is from outside the WWAMI region. Applicants with an interest in research may apply for the MD/PhD program regardless of residency. Competitive candidates are asked to send additional materials. Criminal background check is required. Only U.S. citizens or permanent residents are considered. Candidates may apply up to 3 times.

## Information about Diversity Programs

UWSOM is committed to creating an inclusive and diverse learning environment for all students and training culturally competent physicians to care for the region's increasingly diverse population. We welcome applicants from groups underrepresented in medicine and those committed to working with the underserved. The Office of Multicultural Affairs supports student activities that promote inclusion, equity and diversity in all forms.

## Regional/Satellite Campuses

**Regional Campus Location(s):** Anchorage, AK, Bozeman, MT, Laramie, WY, Moscow, ID, Pullman, WA, and Spokane, WA.

## Application Process and Requirements 2012–2013

**Primary application service:** AMCAS®
**Earliest filing date:** June 1, 2011
**Latest filing date:** November 1, 2011

**Secondary application required:** Yes
**Sent to:** Screened applicants
**URL:** www.somas.washington.edu/uwappstatus.htm
**Contact:** (206) 543-7212, uwsomapp@uw.edu
**Fee:** Yes, $35   **Waiver available:** Yes
**Earliest filing date:** July 15, 2011
**Latest filing date:** January 13, 2012

**MCAT® required:** Yes
**Latest MCAT® considered:** September 2011
**Oldest MCAT® considered:** January 2009

**Early Decision Program:** School does not have EDP
**Applicants notified:** n/a
**EDP available for:** n/a

**Regular acceptance notice —**
**Earliest date:** November 1, 2011
**Latest date:** Until class is full
**Applicant's response to acceptance offer —**
**Maximum time:** Two weeks

**Requests for deferred entrance considered:** Yes

**Deposit to hold place in class:** No
**Deposit — In-State Applicants:** n/a
**Out-of-State Applicants:** n/a
**Deposit due:** n/a
**Applied to tuition:** n/a
**Refundable:** n/a
**Refundable by:** n/a

**Estimated number of new entrants:** 216
**EDP:** n/a, **Special Programs:** n/a

**Start month/year:** August 2012

**Interview format:** A three-member panel interviews each applicant. Limited regional interviews are available. Video interviews are not available.

### Preparatory Programs

**Postbaccalaureate Program:** No

**Summer Program:** Yes,
http://depts.washington.edu/omca/leadership/SMDEP.html,
Pam Racansky, (206) 685-2489, racansky@uw.edu

## 2010–2011 First Year Class

|  | In-State* | Out-of-State* | International |
|---|---|---|---|
| Applications | 1,048 | 3,387 | 24 |
| Interviewed | 621 | 79 | 0 |
| Matriculated | 198 | 18 | 0 |

**Total Matriculants: 216**     **Total Enrollment: 925**

*Residents of WA, WY, AK, MT, and ID are considered as "in-state" residents.*

## Financial Information

|  | In-State | Out-of-State |
|---|---|---|
| Total Cost of Attendance | $43,189 | $72,169 |
| Tuition and Fees | $23,049 | $52,029 |
| Other (incl. living expenses) | $20,140 | $20,140 |
| Health Insurance (can be waived) | $0 | $0 |

**Average 2010 Graduate Indebtedness: $131,166**
**% of Enrolled Students Receiving Aid: 92%**

*Source: 2009-2010 LCME I-B survey and 2010-2011 AAMC TSF questionnaire*

# Marshall University
# Joan C. Edwards School of Medicine
## Huntington, West Virginia

Admissions Office, Marshall University
Joan C. Edwards School of Medicine
1600 Medical Center Drive
Huntington, West Virginia 25701-3655
**T** 800 544 8514    warren@marshall.edu
**Admissions:** http://musom.marshall.edu/admissions

## General Information

The Marshall University School of Medicine was granted full accreditation and graduated its first class in 1981. The School of Medicine is a community-based program which provides learning opportunities in varied settings: a state-of-the-art ambulatory care center, the Veterans Affairs Medical Center, rural clinics, highly specialized tertiary-care hospitals, offices of private physicians and others. Educational opportunities are further enhanced by the Edwards Comprehensive Cancer Center, the Robert C. Byrd Biotechnology Science Center and the Byrd Clinical Center.

## Mission Statement

Long before it became trendy to do so, the Marshall University School of Medicine was addressing two problems that have now taken on national prominence. The first problem is the need for better health care in rural areas; the second is the need to develop physicians who will practice on the front lines of medicine through primary-care specialties such as family practice, pediatrics and general internal medicine: about two-thirds of its graduates enter these specialties.

## Curricular Highlights

**Community Service Requirement:** Optional. Can graduate with distinction in Community Service.

**Research/Thesis Requirement:** Optional.

Both the year one and year two curriculum are now integrated into a systems-based format. Students begin in their first semester to integrate basic science with clinical medicine. The integrated curriculum involves topics such as: Core Principles, Infectious Agents & Antimicrobials, Neoplasia & Hematology, Nervous System, Cardiovascular System, Pulmonary System & ENT, Gastrointestinal System, Renal & Endocrine Systems, Musculoskeletal, Genitourinary, Dermatology, Toxicology and Eye. Throughout both years students have direct patient contact through the Mentorship Program giving them a natural framework to integrate their growing knowledge of the traditional sciences basic to medicine. During both years students learn the foundational principles of patient care including the skills of history taking and the physical exam. Topics such as preventative medicine, ethics, professionalism, and biostatistics and epidemiology are woven throughout the curriculum. During the third and fourth years, students rotate through clerkships at participating community hospitals and other locations in the clinical fields of medicine, surgery, pediatrics, psychiatry/neurology, family practice, obstetrics-gynecology and emergency medicine. Two months of rural health care at approved sites are required of all students. Twenty-two weeks are devoted to electives in the senior year. A letter grading system (A,B,C,F) is utilized.

## Selection Factors

There is no discrimination because of race, gender, religion, age, handicap, sexual orientation, or national origin. Qualified members of groups who are underrepresented in medicine are encouraged to apply. Applicants are evaluated on the basis of their academic records, MCAT scores, recommendations from instructors, and personal qualifications as judged through interviews. A minimum MCAT score of 24 is required for an interview. Interviews are arranged only by invitation of the Admissions Committee. As a state-assisted institution, the School of Medicine gives preference in selection of students to West Virginia residents. A number of positions will be available to well-qualified nonresidents from states contiguous to West Virginia or to nonresidents who have strong ties to West Virginia. Other nonresidents are not considered. Only applicants who are U.S. citizens or who have permanent resident visas are eligible for admission.

## Information About Diversity Programs

Hisham Keblawi, M.D., (*hkeblawi@marshall.edu*), Institutional Diversity Affairs Officer and Marie Veitia, Ph.D., (*veitia@marshall.edu*), Individual Institutional Diversity Affairs Officer.

## Application Process and Requirements 2012–2013

**Primary application service:** AMCAS®
**Earliest filing date:** June 1, 2011
**Latest filing date:** November 1, 2011

**Secondary application required:** Yes
**Sent to:** State residents and those from states bordering West Virginia
**Contact:** Cynthia A. Warren, (800) 544-8514, warren@marshall.edu
**Fee:** Yes, $75 (In-State), $100 (Out-of-State)
**Waiver available:** Yes
**Earliest filing date:** July 15, 2011
**Latest filing date:** December 31, 2011

**MCAT® required:** Yes
**Latest MCAT® considered:** September 2011
**Oldest MCAT® considered:** January 2009

**Early Decision Program:** School does not have EDP
**Applicants notified:** n/a
**EDP available for:** n/a

**Regular acceptance notice —**
**Earliest date:** October 15, 2011
**Latest date:** Until class is full
**Applicant's response to acceptance offer —**
**Maximum time:** Two weeks

**Requests for deferred entrance considered:** Yes

**Deposit to hold place in class:** No
**Deposit — In-State Applicants:** n/a
**Out-of-State Applicants:** n/a
**Deposit due:** n/a
**Applied to tuition:** n/a
**Refundable:** n/a
**Refundable by:** n/a

**Estimated number of new entrants:** 75
**EDP:** n/a, **Special Programs:** n/a

**Start month/year:** August 2012

**Interview format:** Two one-on-one interviews. Regional interviews are not available. Video interviews are not available.

## Preparatory Programs
**Postbaccalaureate Program:** No

**Summer Program:** No

## 2010–2011 First Year Class

|  | In-State | Out-of-State | International |
|---|---|---|---|
| Applications | 186 | 1159 | 3 |
| Interviewed | 105 | 94 | 0 |
| Matriculated | 48 | 27 | 0 |

**Total Matriculants: 75**    **Total Enrollment: 301**

## Financial Information

|  | In-State | Out-of-State |
|---|---|---|
| Total Cost of Attendance | $46,811 | $73,601 |
| Tuition and Fees | $ 8,536 | $45,326 |
| Other (incl. living expenses) | $24,771 | $24,771 |
| Health Insurance (can be waived) | $3,504 | $3,504 |

**Average 2010 Graduate Indebtedness: $156,170**
**% of Enrolled Students Receiving Aid: 91%**

*Source: 2009-2010 LCME I-B survey and 2010-2011 AAMC TSF questionnaire*

# West Virginia University School of Medicine

## Morgantown, West Virginia

Office of Student Services
West Virginia University School of Medicine
Health Sciences Center, P.O. Box 9111
Morgantown, West Virginia 26506-9111

**T** 304 293 2408    medadmissions@hsc.wvu.edu

**Admissions:** www.hsc.wvu.edu/som/students/
aboutSoM/admissionProcess/index.asp

## General Information

WVU School of Medicine is a public institution located within the Robert C. Byrd Health Sciences Center. There are three campuses: Morgantown, the main campus, serves north and central WV with primary and tertiary care; Charleston serves as a regional referral center for southern WV; and Eastern provides care to a nine county area in eastern WV near MD and VA. *www.hsc.wvu.edu/som*.

## Mission Statement

The mission of the West Virginia University School of Medicine is to improve the health of West Virginians through the education of health professionals, through basic/clinical scientific research and research in rural health care delivery, through the provision of continuing professional education, and through participation in the provision of direct and supportive health care.

## Curricular Highlights

**Community Service Requirement:** Required. 100 hours.

**Research/Thesis Requirement:** Optional.

WVU's education provides a strong foundation for any medical specialty. The basic medical sciences are covered in the MS1 and MS2 years in lecture and problem-based learning formats with computer-based testing. The Physical Diagnosis course encompasses MS1 and MS2 years. Summer experiences are available. The required MS3 clerkships are medicine, surgery, pediatrics, family medicine, OB-GYN, and psychiatry-neurology. The MS4 year consists of 50% required and 50% elective rotations. Two months of community rotations are required. International travel scholarships are available.

## Selection Factors

WV residents are given strong preference. There are available spaces for well-qualified non-residents, especially with strong WV ties. Admission is based upon scholarship, MCAT scores, personal qualifications noted on application and interview, recommendations, community service, medical experiences and leadership. We do not discriminate on the basis of race, gender, creed, national origin, age, or disability. Campus assignments for MS3 and MS4 years are made upon admission.

## Information about Diversity Programs

Health Careers Opportunity Program is available for the disadvantaged or underrepresented *www.cahcon.org/*.

## Regional/Satellite Campuses

**Regional Campus Location(s):** Charleston, Martinsburg

Three campuses: Morgantown (*www.hsc.wvu.edu/som*) Years 1-4; Charleston (*www.hsc.wvu.edu/charleston*)Yr 3-4; Eastern (*www.hsc.wvu.edu/eastern*) Years 3-4.

## Application Process and Requirements 2012–2013

**Primary application service:** AMCAS®
**Earliest filing date:** June 1, 2011
**Latest filing date:** November 1, 2011

**Secondary application required:** Yes
**Sent to:** Sent to select applicants by secure e-mail
**Contact:** Beth Ann McCormick, 1-800-543-5650, medadmissions@hsc.wvu.edu
**Fee:** Yes, $100    **Waiver available:** Yes
**Earliest filing date:** July 15, 2011
**Latest filing date:** January 1, 2012

**MCAT® required:** Yes
**Latest MCAT® considered:** September 2011
**Oldest MCAT® considered:** January 2010

**Early Decision Program:** School does have EDP
**Applicants notified:** October 1, 2011
**EDP available for:** Both In-State and Out-of-State Applicants

**Regular acceptance notice —**
**Earliest date:** October 15, 2011
**Latest date:** Until class is full
**Applicant's response to acceptance offer —**
**Maximum time:** Two weeks

**Requests for deferred entrance considered:** Yes

**Deposit to hold place in class:** Yes
**Deposit — In-State Applicants:** $100
**Out-of-State Applicants:** $100
**Deposit due:** With response to acceptance offer
**Applied to tuition:** Yes
**Refundable:** Yes
**Refundable by:** May 15, 2012

**Estimated number of new entrants:** 110
**EDP:** 15, **Special Programs:** 4

**Start month/year:** August 13, 2012

**Interview format:** Campus tour and lunch with medical students. Interview with 1-2 Admissions Committee members. Regional tours can be arranged. Video interviews are not available.

## Preparatory Programs

**Postbaccalaureate Program:** No

**Summer Program:** No

## 2010–2011 First Year Class

|  | In-State | Out-of-State | International |
|---|---|---|---|
| Applications | 196 | 2,341 | 41 |
| Interviewed | 126 | 262 | 0 |
| Matriculated | 64 | 40 | 0 |

**Total Matriculants: 104**    **Total Enrollment: 424**

## Financial Information

|  | In-State | Out-of-State |
|---|---|---|
| Total Cost of Attendance | $36,929 | $62,691 |
| Tuition and Fees | $22,796 | $48,558 |
| Other (incl. living expenses) | $13,139 | $13,139 |
| Health Insurance (can be waived) | $994 | $994 |

**Average 2010 Graduate Indebtedness: $152,400**
**% of Enrolled Students Receiving Aid: 94%**

*Source: 2009-2010 LCME I-B survey and 2010-2011 AAMC TSF questionnaire*

# Medical College of Wisconsin
## Milwaukee, Wisconsin

WI

Office of Admissions
Medical College of Wisconsin
8701 Watertown Plank Road
Milwaukee, Wisconsin 53226
**T** 414 955 8246    medschool@mcw.edu
**Admissions:** www.mcw.edu/medicalschool

## General Information

The Medical College of Wisconsin became a private, free-standing school of medicine in 1967. Located on the Milwaukee Regional Medical Campus, maintaining strong relationships and educational programs with institutions statewide. Major affiliated teaching hospitals include Froedtert Hospital, Children's Hospital of Wisconsin and the VA Medical Center.

## Mission Statement

To be a national leader in the education and development of the next generation of physicians and scientists, to discover and translate new knowledge in the biomedical sciences, to provide "cutting edge" interdisciplinary and compassionate clinical care of the highest quality and to improve the health of the communities we serve.

## Curricular Highlights

**Community Service Requirement:** Optional.

**Research/Thesis Requirement:** Optional.

The curriculum provides a foundation for a career in any discipline of medicine and is evolving to enhance flexibility, individuality and early clinical exposure. Students gain exposure to basic science and clinical experiences during required courses/modules, the Clinical Continuum or the Longitudinal Experience to Advance Patient Care during the first two years. Required clinical clerkships and an optional elective experience occur in the third year while fourth year students complete both medically- and surgically oriented sub-internships, ambulatory medicine, an Integrated Selective and five one-month electives in the fourth year. Students can pursue their own interests in medicine in one of five pathways (Clinician Educator, Global Health, Master Clinician, Physician Scientist or Urban and Community Health). Joint degree programs or Honors in Research are available to interested students.

## Selection Factors

Student selection is based on a careful analysis of the suitability for the medical profession. Academic achievement and MCAT scores are carefully evaluated. Subjective factors include the personal statement, experiences, recommendations and interviews. Interviews are integral, done only at the college and required before acceptance. Applications are reviewed on a rolling basis by date of completion. Interviews are conducted and offers are also made on a rolling basis until the class is filled. Candidates are encouraged to complete the application in a timely fashion. The Medical College of Wisconsin does not discriminate on the basis of race, gender, creed, disability, age, national origin or sexual orientation.

## Information about Diversity Programs

The college encourages applications from students of diverse backgrounds. In addition to academic credentials, letters of recommendation, and personal interviews, a student's motivation and educational background are carefully considered. The Office of Academic Affairs/Diversity offers various programs to assist students, demonstrating the college's commitment to their recruitment, retention and graduation.

## Regional/Satellite Campuses

The Milwaukee Regional Medical Campus provides students with the opportunity to complete all of their clinical clerkships and rotations at this location.

## Application Process and Requirements 2012–2013

**Primary application service:** AMCAS®
**Earliest filing date:** June 1, 2011
**Latest filing date:** November 1, 2011

**Secondary application required:** Yes
**Sent to:** All applicants
**Contact:** Michael Istwan, (414) 955-8246, mistwan@mcw.edu
**Fee:** Yes, $70    **Waiver available:** Yes
**Earliest filing date:** July 1, 2011
**Latest filing date:** January 31, 2012

**MCAT® required:** Yes
**Latest MCAT® considered:** September 2011
**Oldest MCAT® considered:** September 2009

**Early Decision Program:** School does have EDP
**Applicants notified:** October 1, 2011
**EDP available for:** Both In-State and Out-of-State Applicants

**Regular acceptance notice —**
**Earliest date:** October 15, 2011
**Latest date:** Until class is full
**Applicant's response to acceptance offer —**
**Maximum time:** One month

**Requests for deferred entrance considered:** Yes

**Deposit to hold place in class:** Yes
**Deposit — In-State Applicants:** $100
**Out-of-State Applicants:** $100
**Deposit due:** One month after acceptance
**Applied to tuition:** Yes
**Refundable:** Yes
**Refundable by:** May 15, 2012

**Estimated number of new entrants:** 204
**EDP:** 5, **Special Programs:** n/a

**Start month/year:** August 2012

**Interview format:** Two, thirty-minute interviews. Regional interviews are not available. Video interviews are not available.

## Preparatory Programs
**Postbaccalaureate Program:** No

**Summer Program:** No

## 2010–2011 First Year Class

|  | In-State | Out-of-State | International |
|---|---|---|---|
| Applications | 631 | 5,405 | 219 |
| Interviewed | 178 | 516 | 5 |
| Matriculated | 69 | 135 | 0 |

**Total Matriculants: 204**    **Total Enrollment: 820**

## Financial Information

|  | In-State | Out-of-State |
|---|---|---|
| Total Cost of Attendance | $54,711 | $54,711 |
| Tuition and Fees | $41,381 | $41,381 |
| Other (incl. living expenses) | $13,330 | $13,330 |
| Health Insurance (can be waived) | $0 | $0 |

**Average 2010 Graduate Indebtedness: $153,228**
**% of Enrolled Students Receiving Aid: 96%**

Source: 2009-2010 LCME I-B survey and 2010-2011 AAMC TSF questionnaire

# University of Wisconsin
# School of Medicine and Public Health
## Madison, Wisconsin

MD Admissions Office
2130 Health Sciences Learning Center
University of Wisconsin
School of Medicine and Public Health
750 Highland Avenue
Madison, Wisconsin 53705-2221

T 608 265-6344    medadmissons@med.wisc.edu

**Admissions:** www.med.wisc.edu/education/md/
admissions/main/102

## General Information

The University of Wisconsin has over 100 years of tradition in the education of health professionals and the expansion of the boundaries of science through research. The University of Wisconsin has had a four-year program in medicine since 1924. In 2005 the name was changed to the School of Medicine and Public Health to reflect the new vanguard uniting public health with medical education. National surveys consistently rank the UW Hospital and Clinics among the finest academic medical centers in the United States. Our classrooms extend beyond the modern Health Sciences Learning Center and Clinical Science Center (UW Hospital and Clinics) to experiential opportunities in the Madison community, in many urban and rural parts of Wisconsin, and with underserved populations in the United States and abroad.

## Mission Statement

The University of Wisconsin School of Medicine and Public Health's mission is to advance health without compromise through service, scholarship, science and social responsibility. Our vision is to be a national leader in healthcare, advancing the well-being of the people of Wisconsin and beyond. Our values include excellence, innovation, compassion, integrity, respect and accountability.

## Curricular Highlights

**Community Service Requirement:** Optional.

**Research/Thesis Requirement:** Optional.

The curriculum introduces students to the generalist practice of medicine by exposing them to community-based settings in the first and second years. There is a focus on active learning; case-based problem-solving; interdisciplinary teaching by basic science and clinical faculty throughout the first and second years; a four-year curriculum that prepares students for either a primary care or specialty career; diverse clinical clerkship experiences around the state, including inner-city and rural sites; and a six-week one-on-one preceptorship with an experienced clinician in Year 4. The senior year provides elective opportunities for study at other institutions and abroad. Opportunities for research are available to medical students in individually arranged programs.

## Selection Factors

The Admissions Committee seeks students with diverse backgrounds and interests. Breadth and depth of academic and nonacademic interests and experiences, ability to communicate with others, motivation for medicine, service to others, personal characteristics, and intellectual ability are some of the factors considered. Preference is given to residents of Wisconsin. Non-resident applicants compete for relatively few places. Secondary applications and interview invitations are sent to selected applicants.

## Information about Diversity Programs

The University of Wisconsin School of Medicine and Public Health is committed to increasing the number of physicians from groups underrepresented in medicine and those showing evidence of socioeconomically and educationally-disadvantaged backgrounds. Applications are encouraged from persons with socioeconomic disadvantages and from members of groups underrepresented in medicine.

## Regional/Satellite Campuses

**Regional Campus Location(s):** La Crosse, Marshfield, and Milwaukee.
The typical UW medical student spends at least 16 weeks at clinical sites outside Madison and throughout the state of Wisconsin. Other locations are LaCrosse, Marshfield, Green Bay, and Milwaukee teaching hospitals, and community clinics in other cities.

## Application Process and Requirements 2012–2013

**Primary application service:** AMCAS®
**Earliest filing date:** June 1, 2011
**Latest filing date:** November 1, 2011

**Secondary application required:** Yes
**Sent to:** Selected applicants
**URL:** Invitation only
**Fee:** Yes, $56    **Waiver available:** Yes
**Earliest filing date:** August 16, 2011
**Latest filing date:** December 1, 2011

**MCAT® required:** Yes
**Latest MCAT® considered:** September 2011
**Oldest MCAT® considered:** April 2008

**Early Decision Program:** School does have EDP
**Applicants notified:** October 1, 2011
**EDP available for:** In-States only

**Regular acceptance notice —**
**Earliest date:** October 15, 2011
**Latest date:** Until class is full
**Applicant's response to acceptance offer —**
**Maximum time:** Two weeks

**Requests for deferred entrance considered:** Yes

**Deposit to hold place in class:** No
**Deposit — In-State Applicants:** n/a
**Out-of-State Applicants:** n/a
**Deposit due:** n/a
**Applied to tuition:** n/a
**Refundable:** n/a
**Refundable by:** n/a

**Estimated number of new entrants:** 175
**EDP:** 0, **Special Programs:** 20

**Start month/year:** August 2012

**Interview format:** Selected applicants are invited to interview. Regional interviews are not available. Video interviews are not available.

## Preparatory Programs
**Postbaccalaureate Program:** No
**Summer Program:** No

## 2010–2011 First Year Class

|  | In-State | Out-of-State | International |
|---|---|---|---|
| Applications | 670 | 2,846 | 11 |
| Interviewed | 343 | 140 | 0 |
| Matriculated | 129 | 42 | 0 |

**Total Matriculants: 171**    **Total Enrollment: 652**

## Financial Information

|  | In-State | Out-of-State |
|---|---|---|
| Total Cost of Attendance | $44,196 | $54,933 |
| Tuition and Fees | $24,021 | $34,758 |
| Other (incl. living expenses) | $17,970 | $17,970 |
| Health Insurance (can be waived) | $2,205 | $2,205 |

**Average 2010 Graduate Indebtedness: $135,111**
**% of Enrolled Students Receiving Aid: 88%**

Source: 2009-2010 LCME I-B survey and 2010-2011 AAMC TSF questionnaire

# Chapter 15:

## Information About Canadian Medical Schools
Accredited by the LCME and by the CACMS

*The 17 medical schools in Canada are members of the Association of Faculties of Medicine of Canada (www.afmc.ca) and affiliate members of the AAMC. They participate in the activities of both associations. Canadian medical schools are accredited jointly by the Liaison Committee on Medical Education (www.lcme.org, LCME) and the Committee on Accreditation of Canadian Medical Schools (www.afmc.ca/index-e.php, CACMS). All are M.D. degree granting schools with high- quality educational programs.*

*Admission policies and procedures of Canadian schools are similar in many respects to those followed in U.S. schools; thus, many of the suggestions for applicants in chapters 1 through 9 will also apply. Schools vary with respect to the emphasis placed on selection factors, and applicants are encouraged to refer to the individual school entries for additional details.*

*Fifteen Canadian medical schools offer four-year educational programs; two, McMaster and Calgary, are three-year programs. Some students at the Université de Montréal are admitted into a one-year preparatory program prior to beginning the M.D. curriculum. McGill University's five-year M.D. program includes an initial year that must be completed by graduates of the province of Quebec's Collège d'en-seignement général et professionnel (CÉGEP).*

### Selection Criteria

As reflected in the individual school entries in this chapter, Canadian medical schools vary with respect to the number of years of undergraduate instruction required of applicants. Medical schools also vary with respect to recommended content during premedical undergraduate education. Table 15-A shows that physics, inorganic and organic chemistry, biology, biochemistry, humanities, and English are the most common subjects required in undergraduate education by the Canadian medical schools.

### Language of Instruction

Three Canadian medical schools—Laval, Montréal and Sherbrooke, all located in the province of Quebec—require students to be fluent in French as all instruction is in that language. Instruction in the other 14 schools is in English, and the University of Ottawa offers the M.D. curriculum in both French and English.

## Table 15-A

Subjects Required by Two or More Canadian Medical Schools, 2010–2011 Entering Class

| Required Subject | # of Schools |
|---|---|
| Biochemistry | 6 |
| Biology | 7 |
| Calculus | 2 |
| College English | 4 |
| College Mathematics | 3 |
| Humanities | 3 |
| Inorganic Chemistry | 7 |
| Organic Chemistry | 8 |
| Physics | 6 |
| Social Sciences | 2 |

NOTE: n=17. Figures based on data provided fall 2010. Four of the 17 medical schools (Dalhousie, Northern Ontario, McMaster, and Western Ontario) did not indicate specific course requirements and are not included in the tabulations.

In Canada, universities fall under provincial jurisdiction and the majority of places in each faculty of medicine are allocated to permanent residents of the province in which the university is located.

Not all faculties of medicine accept applications from international students. Conversely, some faculties of medicine may reserve positions for international students, possibly as part of agreements with foreign governments and institutions. Statistics compiled by the Association of Faculties of Medicine of Canada (www.afmc.ca) show that most medical schools admit international students. In 2008–09, 189 U.S. students applied to the 16 Canadian medical schools that supplied data and recorded a 4.2 percent success rate. In the same year, 299 non-U.S. international students applied to the 16 Canadian medical schools that supplied data and recorded a 9.4 percent success rate. The success rate for Canadian applicants to the same schools was 24.3 percent. Additional information about Canadian medical schools can be found in the *Association of Faculties of Medicine of Canada publication, Admission Requirements of Canadian Faculties of Medicine* (2011) *www.afmc.ca/publications-admission-e.php.*

Positions filled by international students in Canadian medical schools are not necessarily subsidized by provincial/territorial governments. As such, international students, including U.S. students, may pay higher tuition and fees compared to those of Canadian residents.

### Academic Record/Suitability

Although an excellent academic record is a very important factor in gaining admission to a Canadian medical school, great deal of effort is expended in assessing applicants' suitability for a medical career based on other factors. Personal suitability is assessed in a variety of ways by the schools; applicants who can demonstrate that they possess the qualities considered important in the practice of medicine may sometimes be admitted even if their academic record is not outstanding. Alternately, applicants with outstanding records who do not possess these qualities may not gain a place in medical school.

Most applicants to Canadian medical schools are interviewed prior to acceptance, so the interview information in Chapter 7 will be useful.

### Medical College Admission Test (MCAT®)

Eleven Canadian medical schools require applicants to take the MCAT®: Alberta, British Columbia, Calgary, Dalhousie, Manitoba, McMaster, Memorial, Queen's, Saskatchewan, Toronto, and Western Ontario.

### Other Considerations

Canadian faculties of medicine do not discriminate on the basis of race, religion, or gender in admitting new students. The admission of Aboriginal students (First Nations, Inuit, Métis) is encouraged at Canadian medical schools and most allocate positions specifically for Aboriginal applicants including Laval, Sherbrooke, Montréal, McGill, Ottawa, Queen's, McMaster, Western Ontario, Northern Ontario School of Medicine, Saskatchewan, Alberta, and British Columbia.

The number of female applicants has leveled off in recent years, with correspondingly consistent  proportions of women in schools' entering classes. Women comprised 57 percent of the 2008–09 applicant pool, and the success rate for women was slightly higher than that for men. The 2008 entering classes at the 16 Canadian medical schools reporting data about male and female matriculants included 58 percent women and 42 percent men. Overall, 24 percent of applicants received at least one offer of admission.

## Expenses/Financial Aid

Tuition and student fees for Canadian and non-Canadian students in the 2010 entering class are provided in Table 15-B and in individual school entries. Expenses vary from school to school and from student to student. Tuition at several Canadian schools is slightly higher for the first year than for successive years. Some financial aid information is provided in the individual school entries. Eligible Canadian students may apply for a Canadian Student Loan, or they may apply to the Department of Education in their province for a provincial student loan.

## Table 15-B

Tuition and Student Fees for 2010–2011 First-Year Students at Canadian Medical Schools (in Canadian Dollars)

| Categories of Students | Range | Average |
|---|---|---|
| In-Province | $3,954-$21,568 | $13,276* |
| Canada, Out-of-Province | $7,393–$21,568 | $14,791* |
| Visa | $21,986–$52,560 | $32,034* |

NOTE: Figures based on data provided fall 2008

* Average In-Province data were derived from all 17 Canadian schools. Average Out-of-Province data were derived from all 17 Canadian schools reporting. Average visa data were derived from 7 schools that accept foreign students.

Source: Association of Faculties of Medicine of Canada

# University of Alberta
# Faculty of Medicine and Dentistry
## Edmonton, Alberta

1-002 Katz Center for Pharmacy & Health Research
University of Alberta
Faculty of Medicine & Dentistry
Edmonton, Alberta Canada T6G 2E1

**T** 780 492 6350   admission@med.ualberta.ca

**Admissions:** www.med.ualberta.ca/
education/ume/

## General Information

The Faculty of Medicine and Dentistry at the University of Alberta in Edmonton has a storied history of success in world-class research, education and patient care. Established in 1913, it is now home to 20 departments, seven divisions, and many research groups, centers and institutions. The Faculty of Medicine & Dentistry has access to world-class facilities for research, patient care and education. The majority of pre-clinical education is conducted on the University campus in proximity to the University of Alberta Hospital (UAH). During clinical education years, students train at a number of other major health-care facilities in the area. The Faculty and campus have experienced tremendous growth over the past decade. Medical students are educated in new top-of-the-line laboratories, classrooms, and educational resource centers.

## Mission Statement

The Faculty of Medicine and Dentistry is dedicated to the improvement of health through excellence and leadership in our educational programs, in fundamental and applied research, and in the prevention and treatment of illness. Central to our mission is the preparation of physicians to provide the highest quality of health care to the people of Alberta and beyond, and the advancement of knowledge and its application through research. The Faculty is committed to a tradition of excellence by national and international standards in our programs.

## Curricular Highlights

**Community Service Requirement:** Required. Rural Family Medicine training.

**Research/Thesis Requirement:** Optional.

The objectives of our medical education program leading to the M.D. degree are achieved through a four-year program. Years 1 and 2 are the pre-clinical years in which the material is presented in a series of system-based course blocks. Each block presents the material in a reasoned progression from basic information to clinical application. There are two separate, but coordinated courses, dealing with the social /sociological and public/health aspects of medicine, which are scheduled throughout this period. Years 3 and 4 are the clinical years. Third year is 52 weeks duration and includes the Link Course followed by clinical rotations, electives and holidays (4 weeks). A new innovative 34 week Longitudinal Integrated Clerkship is an available option. Fourth year commences immediately after the end of third year and is composed of further clinical studies, rotations and electives plus holidays (3 weeks). It ends with a Review course and exams. Throughout the program, emphasis is on self-education; much instruction is on a small-group basis. A graduate training program leading to eligibility for specialist qualifications by the Royal College of Physicians and Surgeons of Canada is offered in most clinical specialties.

## Selection Factors

The Admissions Committee selects applicants without discrimination to gender, race, religion, or age. Selection factors include undergraduate academic achievement, MCAT, personal activities, letters of reference, and interview. Preference is given to Alberta residents. The University of Alberta does not accept applications from international students. For more information on the admission requirements and selection process visit: *www.med.ualberta.ca/Education/UME/admissions.*

## Information about Diversity Programs

Of the positions available, 5 are over quota for aboriginal applicants and 10 are over quota for rural applicants.

## Regional/Satellite Campuses

The majority of pre-clinical education is conducted on the University campus in proximity to the University of Alberta Hospital. During clinical education years, students train at a number of other major health-care facilities located within and around Edmonton.

## Application Process and Requirements 2012–2013

**Primary application service:** AMCAS®
**Earliest filing date:** July 2, 2011
**Latest filing date:** November 1, 2011

**Secondary application required:** Yes
**Sent to:** All applicants
**URL:** n/a
**Fee:** No   **Waiver available:** n/a
**Earliest filing date:** July 2, 2011
**Latest filing date:** November 1, 2011

**MCAT® required:** Yes
**Latest MCAT® considered:** September 2011
**Oldest MCAT® considered:** November 2006

**Early Decision Program:** School does have EDP
**Applicants notified:** May 15, 2012
**EDP available for:** Both In-Province and Out-of-Province

**Regular acceptance notice —**
**Earliest date:** May 15, 2012
**Latest date:** Until class is full
**Applicant's response to acceptance offer —**
**Maximum time:** Five business days

**Requests for deferred entrance considered:** No

**Deposit to hold place in class:** Yes
**Deposit — In-Province:** $1,000
**Out-of-Province:** $1,000
**Deposit due:** With response to acceptance offer
**Applied to tuition:** Yes
**Deposit refundable:** No
**Refundable by:** n/a

**Estimated number of new entrants:** 167
**EDP:** n/a, special program: n/a

**Start month/year:** August 2012

**Interview format:** Multiple mini-interviews (MMI). No regional interviews are available. Video interviews are not available.

## Preparatory Programs
**Postbaccalaureate Program:** No
**Summer Program:** No

## 2010–2011 First Year Class

|  | In-Province | Out-of-Province | International |
|---|---|---|---|
| Applications | 693 | 541 | 0 |
| Interviewed | 409 | 65 | 0 |
| Matriculated | 155 | 12 | 0 |

**Total Matriculants: 167     Total Enrollment: 654**

## Financial Information

|  | In-Province | Out-of-Province |
|---|---|---|
| Total Cost of Attendance | n/r | n/r |
| Tuition and Fees | $12,756 | $12,756 |
| Other (incl. living expenses) | n/r | n/r |
| Health Insurance (can be waived) | n/r | n/r |

**Average 2010 Graduate Indebtedness:** n/r
**% of Enrolled Students Receiving Aid:** n/r

# University of Calgary Faculty of Medicine

Calgary, Alberta

Office of Admissions
University of Calgary, Faculty of Medicine
3330 Hospital Drive, N.W.
Calgary, Alberta   Canada T2N 4N1

**T** 403 220 4262   ucmedapp@ucalgary.ca
**Admissions:** www.medicine.ucalgary.ca

## General Information

The Faculty of Medicine at the University of Calgary accepted its first students in September 1970. In 1972, the Faculty of Medicine moved into its permanent facilities in the Calgary Health Sciences Center. The center has been designed to complement the objectives of the faculty's integrated teaching program.

## Mission Statement

We wish to be a medical school which is: responsive to community and societal needs; determined to shape the future of society; rooted in basic research and discovery; committed to excellence and pursuit of excellence and to continuous improvement in all endeavors; and committed to innovation and creativity.

## Curricular Highlights

**Community Service Requirement:** Optional. Strongly recommended.

**Research/Thesis Requirement:** Optional.

The curriculum is based on clinical presentations of the way patients present to physicians. One hundred twenty clinical presentations have been defined, ranging from simple to complex, and they are grouped by body system and human development. The clinical presentation curriculum teaches the basic science and clinical knowledge pertinent to each clinical presentation and provides an approach to the solution of the clinical problems. The Introductory Clinical Skills of Communication and Physical Examination commence in the first weeks of the curriculum. The curriculum maintains an active learning environment with more than 25 percent of scheduled instructional activities spent in small-group, case-based learning sessions. Students have the opportunity to reinforce in a clinical setting what they have learned in the body systems as they progress through each of the systems. The curriculum also focuses on the relevance of the family and the community in health and disease. The school employs a pass/fail grading system. Each academic year lasts about 11 months. At the end of the three years, students will be granted the M.D. degree. The school's philosophy is to produce generalist physicians who can proceed to further training in specialty, family medicine, or research.

## Selection Factors

The Admissions Committee selects applicants without discrimination to gender, race, religion, or age, and attempts to apply five criteria: undergraduate academic achievement, employment history, extracurricular activities, letters of recommendation, and the MCAT. Final applicants will be required to attend an interview at the University of Calgary at their own expense. Final applicants will also be required to write an on-site essay on a topic assigned by the Admissions Committee. Preference is given to Alberta residents. The University of Calgary does not accept applications from individual international students. Presently, seats for international students are limited to those students who come from institutions/countries with whom the Faculty of Medicine has a formal, contractual agreement. Rejected applicants are given the opportunity to reapply for admission. Applicants who have been asked to withdraw or who have been suspended or expelled from any medical school will not usually be considered.

## Regional/Satellite Campuses

Students have clinical experiences on-site at the Foothills Medical Center, as well as at two other general hospitals and the children's hospital in Calgary. During the final year, they may rotate through hospitals in smaller centers in the province, in addition to doing electives outside of Alberta.

## Application Process and Requirements 2012–2013

**Primary application service:** School specific
**Earliest filing date:** July 15, 2011
**Latest filing date:** October 15, 2011

**Secondary application required:** No
**Sent to:** n/a
**URL:** n/a
**Fee:** No   **Waiver available:** n/a
**Earliest filing date:** n/a
**Latest filing date:** n/a

**MCAT® required:** Yes
**Latest MCAT® considered:** September 2011
**Oldest MCAT® considered:** April 1999

**Early Decision Program:** School does not have EDP
**Applicants notified:** n/a
**EDP available for:** n/a

**Regular acceptance notice —**
**Earliest date:** May 15, 2011
**Latest date:** Until class is full
**Applicant's response to acceptance offer —**
**Maximum time:** Two weeks. Less for offers to applicants on the waitlist.

**Requests for deferred entrance considered:** Yes

**Deposit to hold place in class:** Yes
**Deposit — In-of-Province:** $500
**Out-of-Province:** $500
**Deposit due:** With response to acceptance offer
**Applied to tuition:** Yes
**Deposit refundable:** No
**Refundable by:** n/a

**Estimated number of new entrants:** 180
**EDP:** n/a, special program: n/a

**Start month/year:** August 2012

**Interview format:** A series of short standardized interviews. No regional interviews are available. Video interviews are not available.

## Preparatory Programs

**Postbaccalaureate Program:** No

**Summer Program:** No

## 2010–2011 First Year Class

|  | In-Province | Out-of-Province | International |
|---|---|---|---|
| Applications | 950 | 900 | 0 |
| Interviewed | 440 | 120 | 0 |
| Matriculated | 152 | 28 | 0 |

**Total Matriculants: 180**     **Total Enrollment: 495**

## Financial Information

|  | In-Province | Out-of-Province |
|---|---|---|
| Total Cost of Attendance | $35,000 | $86,000 |
| Tuition and Fees | $14,000 | $65,000 |
| Other (incl. living expenses) | $21,000 | $21,000 |
| Health Insurance (can be waived) | $193 | $193 |

**Average 2010 Graduate Indebtedness: $100,000**
**% of Enrolled Students Receiving Aid: 90%**

# University of British Columbia
# Faculty of Medicine

Vancouver, British Columbia

MD Undergraduate Program
Faculty of Medicine, Dean's Office
University of British Columbia
317-2194 Health Sciences Mall
Vancouver, British Columbia  Canada V6T 1Z3

**T** 604 875 8298   **F** 604 822 6061

www.med.ubc.ca/home.htm

**Contact:** Denis Hughes, Director, Admissions

**Admissions:** www.med.ubc.ca/admissionsmd
**E-mail:** admissions.md@ubc.ca

## General Information

The MD Undergraduate Program at the University British Columbia is one of the largest in North America with 256 positions. Currently, the program is distributed across three sites (Vancouver, Victoria and Prince George) and a fourth site with 32 positions is set to open in Kelowna this year. The mode of learning in the first two years is small group and problem-based. This is supplemented by lectures, laboratories, clinical skills courses and independent study. Media technology plays a large role in supporting the distributed program and learning at the individual sites.

## Mission Statement

The MD Undergraduate Program recruits, admits, educates, and supports students who will graduate with defined and demonstrated personal qualities, competencies, knowledge, and behaviors rooted in the vision, missions, and values of UBC and its Faculty of Medicine, and in an ethical context of social responsibility for the health needs of British Columbians.

## Curricular Highlights

**Community Service Requirement:** Optional.

**Research/Thesis Requirement:** Optional.

The program is built on principles of student self-directed learning, integration of biomedical and social sciences, early clinical contact, information management, professional development, and social responsibility. See the UBC Web site for information at *www.med.ubc.ca/education/md_ugrad/ Schedule_Courses.htm.*

## Selection Factors

The selection of candidates for admission to UBC's medical school is governed by guidelines established by the Senate of UBC, and is the responsibility of the Faculty of Medicine Admissions Selection Committee. See the Web site for selection criteria at *www.med.ubc.ca/education/md_ugrad/ MD_Undergraduate_Admissions/Selection.htm.* The UBC Faculty of Medicine's Associate Dean of Admissions oversees the selection process to ensure that all applicants are given careful consideration without regard to age, gender, sexual orientation, race, ancestry, color, place of origin, family status, physical or mental disability, political belief, religion, or marital or economic status.

## Information about Diversity Programs

The UBC Faculty of Medicine is committed to increasing opportunities for Aboriginal (Status or Non-Status Indians, Treaty, First Nations, Metis, or Inuit) applicants through the Aboriginal Admissions Subcommittee. Contact James Andrew, Aboriginal Programs Coordinator, for more information at *james.andrew@ubc.ca* or (604) 875-4111, x 68946. Applicants with disabilities are considered in accordance with UBC's policy on Academic Accommodation for Students with Disabilities. The Northern Medical Program provides an opportunity to complete undergraduate training in a northern regional center and may be of particular interest to those applicants who come from, or are interested in, rural, remote, or northern communities.

## Regional/Satellite Campuses

The Island Medical Program (IMP) at the University of Victoria, the Northern Medical Program (NMP) at the University of Northern British Columbia, the Southern Medical Program (SMP) at the University of British Columbia–Okanagan, in September 2011, and the UBC-based Vancouver Fraser Medical Program (VFMP).

## Application Process and Requirements 2012–2013

**Primary application service:** AMCAS®
**Earliest filing date:** June 1, 2011
**Latest filing date:** August 15, 2011

**Secondary application required:** Yes
**Sent to:** Applicable applicants
**URL:** n.a
**Contact:** Admissions Office, (604) 875-8298, admissions.md@ubc.ca
**Fee:** No   **Waiver available:** n/a
**Earliest filing date:** n/a
**Latest filing date:** n/a

**MCAT® required:** Yes
**Latest MCAT® considered:** August 2011
**Oldest MCAT® considered:** June 2007

**Early Decision Program:** School does not have EDP
**Applicants notified:** n/a
**EDP available for:** n/a

**Regular acceptance notice —**
**Earliest date:** Mid-May 2012
**Latest date:** Until class is full
**Applicant's response to acceptance offer —**
**Maximum time:** Varies

**Requests for deferred entrance considered:** Yes

**Deposit to hold place in class:** Yes
**Deposit — In-Province:** $1,000
**Out-of-Province:** $1,000
**Deposit due:** With response to acceptance offer (electronic)
**Applied to tuition:** Yes   **Deposit refundable:** No
**Refundable by:** n/a

**Estimated number of new entrants:** 288
**EDP:** n/a, special program: n/a

**Start month/year:** Late August 2012

**Interview format:** Applicants are presented with a series of scenarios designed to evaluate non-academic qualities. No regional interviews are available. Video interviews are not available.

## Preparatory Programs

**Postbaccalaureate Program:** Yes , www.med.ubc.ca/education/md_postgrad.htm

**Summer Program:** No

## 2010–2011 First Year Class

|  | In-Province | Out-of-Province | International |
|---|---|---|---|
| Applications | 1,316 | 477 | 0 |
| Interviewed | 601 | 57 | 0 |
| Matriculated | 244 | 12 | 0 |

**Total Matriculants: 256    Total Enrollment: 1,024**

## Financial Information

|  | In-Province | Out-of-Province |
|---|---|---|
| Total Cost of Attendance | n/r | n/r |
| Tuition and Fees | $15,457 | n/r |
| Other (incl. living expenses) | $12,000 | n/r |
| Health Insurance (can be waived) | n/r | n/r |

**Average 2010 Graduate Indebtedness: n/r**
**% of Enrolled Students Receiving Aid: n/r**

# University of Manitoba Faculty of Medicine
## Winnipeg, Manitoba

Chair, Admissions Committee
Faculty of Medicine, University of Manitoba
260-727 McDermot Avenue
Winnipeg, Manitoba  Canada  R3E 3P5

**T** 204 789 3499    registrar_med@umanitoba.ca

**Admissions:** www.umanitoba.ca/faculties/medicine/
admissions/index.html

## General Information

The Faculty of Medicine has recently celebrated its 125th anniversary, and in so doing marked many generations of contribution to education, research and clinical service as Western Canada's first medical school. The Faculty is now an integral part of an academic health sciences network associated with the Winnipeg Regional Health Authority, and the research enterprise not only within the province, but with established national and international initiatives. There are great opportunities for all medical learners to achieve their learning objectives in diverse environments, to explore opportunities in research, and to attain the skills and professional attributes for future practice and lifelong learning.

## Mission Statement

The Mission of Undergraduate Medical Education is to provide an environment which will assist students to become competent, caring, ethical physicians with the ability to think critically. This experience will prepare students to choose wisely their area of training, to successfully continue their education, and subsequently to meet responsibilities to their patients and society.

## Curricular Highlights

**Community Service Requirement:** Optional.

**Research/Thesis Requirement:** Optional.

Medical education at the University of Manitoba is founded on the CanMeds-Family Medicine competency framework, and the learning objectives are based on the seven roles identified in the framework. Two years of foundational science, population and public health principles and clinical sciences are followed by two years of progressive responsibility for patient care and management in core rotations and elective opportunities. Further details regarding the curriculum can be accessed at: *http://umanitoba.ca/faculties/medicine/education/undergraduate/program_overview.html.*

## Selection Factors

The selection of candidates for admission is governed by policies and processes approved by the University Senate, and is the responsibility of the Faculty of Medicine Admissions Committee as overseen by the Associate Dean, Students. All students must be Canadian citizens or permanent residents of Canada, and preference is given to residents of Manitoba and applicants of Aboriginal ancestry. An applicant's composite score is determined based upon: adjusted grade point, MCAT; and the score from a Multiple Mini Interview. The composite score may be modified based upon rural attributes and/or advanced education beyond a masters degree. See the Applicant Information Bulletin for more details: *www.umanitoba.ca/faculties/medicine/admissions.*

## Information on Diversity Programs

The University of Manitoba and the Faculty of Medicine are committed to promoting and supporting diversity at all levels in our working and learning environment and to meeting the needs of the diverse body of students, faculty, staff and the communities we serve. Diversity in the health professions workforce strengthens our capacity to provide care and to address disparities in health status and access to health care education and services. The Faculty of Medicine is committed to: recruiting a diverse learner population and a diverse faculty; creating a diverse learning environment with an inclusive curriculum; and creating a diverse research enterprise focusing on underserviced areas and global public health. Admissions policies place specific emphasis on candidates of Aboriginal ancestry, individuals with connections to rural communities, and applicants with disabilities who can manifest the requisite skills and abilities with or without reasonable accommodation.

## Application Process and Requirements 2012–2013

**Primary application service:** School specific
**Earliest filing date:** August 15, 2011
**Latest filing date:** October 7, 2011

**Secondary application required:** Yes
**Sent to:** All applicants
**URL:** www.umanitoba.ca/medicine/admissions
**Fee:** Yes, $95    **Waiver available:** No
**Earliest filing date:** August 15, 2011
**Latest filing date:** October 7, 2011

**MCAT® required:** Yes
**Latest MCAT® considered:** September 2011
**Oldest MCAT® considered:** April 2008

**Early Decision Program:** School does not have EDP
**Applicants notified:** n/a
**EDP available for:** n/a

**Regular acceptance notice —**
**Earliest date:** May 15, 2012
**Latest date:** Until class is full
**Applicant's response to acceptance offer —**
**Maximum time:** Two weeks or as specified in the offer.

**Requests for deferred entrance considered:** Yes

**Deposit to hold place in class:** Yes
**Deposit — In-Province:** $500  **Out-of-Province:** $500
**Deposit due:** With response to acceptance offer.
**Applied to tuition:** Yes
**Deposit refundable:** No
**Refundable by:** n/a

**Estimated number of new entrants:** 110
**EDP:** n/a, special program: n/a

**Start month/year:** August 2012

**Interview format:** Multiple mini-interviews (MMI). No regional interviews are available. Video interviews are not available.

## Preparatory Programs

**Postbaccalaureate Program:** No

**Summer Program:** Yes, www.umanitoba.ca/faculties/ medicine/student_affairs/summerearlyexposure.html.

## 2010–2011 First Year Class

|  | In-Province | Out-of-Province | International |
|---|---|---|---|
| Applications | 286 | 436 | 0 |
| Interviewed | 247 | 50 | 0 |
| Matriculated | 103 | 7 | 0 |

**Total Matriculants: 110**    **Total Enrollment: 424**

## Financial Information

|  | In-Province | Out-of-Province |
|---|---|---|
| Total Cost of Attendance | $4,000 | $4,000 |
| Tuition and Fees | $8,500 | $8,500 |
| Other (incl. living expenses) | n/r | n/r |
| Health Insurance (can be waived) | n/r | n/r |

**Average 2010 Graduate Indebtedness: n/r**
**% of Enrolled Students Receiving Aid: n/r**

# Memorial University of Newfoundland
# Faculty of Medicine

## St. John's, Newfoundland

Memorial University of Newfoundland
Faculty of Medicine
St. John's, Newfoundland/Labrador
Canada A1B 3V6

**T** 709 777 6615  munmed@mun.ca

**Admissions:** www.med.mun.ca/admissions

## General Information

Memorial is the only university in the province of Newfoundland. The university was established as Memorial College in 1925 and incorporated as a university in 1949. In 1959, campus buildings were erected on a 1,000-acre site. There are some 12,000 undergraduates and a faculty of about 1,000 (including visiting professors) working on the campus, which is situated on the periphery of St. John's. The medical school is fully accredited by the Committee on Accreditation of Canadian Medical Schools (CACMS) of the Association of Canadian Medical Colleges and the Canadian Medical Association and the Liaison Committee on Medical Education (LCME) of the Association of American Medical Colleges and the American Medical Association. Thus, the medical school is equivalent in every respect to other medical schools in Canada and the United States. Approved teaching programs for interns and residents are under the direction of the medical school. Research work is being conducted both in the hospitals and in the Health Sciences Center.

## Mission Statement

Our purpose is to enhance the health of people by educating physicians and health scientists, by conducting research in clinical and basic medical sciences and applied health sciences, and by promoting the skills and attitudes of lifelong learning.

## Curricular Highlights

**Community Service Requirement:** Optional.

**Research/Thesis Requirement:** Optional.

The curriculum, the physical structure, and the administrative organization of the school were planned to allow for maximum cooperation among the various basic science and clinical disciplines. The M.D. degree is granted upon completion of the fourth year. Canadian students take the LMCC (Medical Council of Canada) Examinations and U.S. students take the USMLE (United States Medical Licensing Examination) Step 1 and Step 2. During the first year of the medical program, students take introductory courses in cell structure and functions, biochemistry, physiology, molecular genetics, pharmacology, microbiology, anatomy, behavioral science, ethics, interviewing skills, and community medicine. In the second half of the first year and the second year, teaching has a systems approach; material from anatomy, physiology, pathology, and clinical medicine is presented in an integrated manner. The third year is a structured clinical clerkship that includes eight weeks of electives, and the fourth year is made up of electives and selectives. Rotations for Rural Medicine take place in the first, third, and fourth years. A pass/fail system is used for grading. Medical students may apply through the Offices of Undergraduate Medical Education and Research/ Graduate Studies for the M.D./Ph.D. program.

## Selection Factors

The school admits students on the basis of residency priority as follows: bona fide residents of Newfoundland and Labrador, of New Brunswick, of Prince Edward Island, of Yukon Territory, other Canadian provinces, and non-Canadians. In every case, a high academic standard is required. Age by itself is not used as a basis for selection or rejection. However, both age and length of time away from full-time academic studies may be taken into consideration. Normally, the medical school does not accept transfer students from other medical schools. In rare circumstances, a transfer applicant may be considered if there is space available.

## Information about Diversity Programs

For entry in 2011, there will be two positions available for Newfoundland and Labrador aboriginal students. Also, the Admissions Committee will take into consideration the background of all applicants in making its decisions.

## Application Process and Requirements 2012–2013

**Primary application service:** School specific
**Earliest filing date:** July 1, 2011
**Latest filing date:** October 17, 2011

**Secondary application required:** No
**Sent to:** n/a
**URL:** n/a
**Fee:** No    **Waiver available:** n/a
**Earliest filing date:** n/a
**Latest filing date:** n/a

**MCAT® required:** Yes
**Latest MCAT® considered:** September 2011
**Oldest MCAT® considered:** September 2006

**Early Decision Program:** School does not have EDP
**Applicants notified:** n/a
**EDP available for:** n/a

**Regular acceptance notice —**
**Earliest date:** March 1, 2012
**Latest date:** Until class is full
**Applicant's response to acceptance offer —**
**Maximum time:** Two weeks

**Requests for deferred entrance considered:** Yes

**Deposit to hold place in class:** Yes
**Deposit — In-Province:** $200  **Out-of-Province:** $200
**Deposit due:** With response to acceptance offer.
**Applied to tuition:** Yes
**Deposit refundable:** No
**Refundable by:** n/a

**Estimated number of new entrants:** 64
**EDP:** n/a, special program: n/a

**Start month/year:** September 2012

**Interview format:** One-hour interview with two interviewers. No regional interviews are available. Video interviews are not available.

## Preparatory Programs

**Postbaccalaureate Program:** No

**Summer Program:** Yes, MedQuest, (709) 777-6690, mdray@mun.ca.

## 2010–2011 First Year Class

|  | In-Province | Out-of-Province | International |
|---|---|---|---|
| Applications | 189 | 425 | 11 |
| Interviewed | 146 | 96 | 4 |
| Matriculated | 48 | 16 | 0 |

**Total Matriculants: 64**      **Total Enrollment: 263**

## Financial Information

|  | In-Province | Out-of-Province |
|---|---|---|
| Total Cost of Attendance | $27,500 | $51,400 |
| Tuition and Fees | $6,250 | $30,000 |
| Other (incl. living expenses) | $21,000 | $20,790 |
| Health Insurance (can be waived) | $162 | $610 |

**Average 2010 Graduate Indebtedness: $100,000**
**% of Enrolled Students Receiving Aid: 75%**

# Dalhousie University Faculty of Medicine

## Halifax, Nova Scotia

Admissions and Student Affairs
Room C-124, Lower Level
Clinical Research Center, Dalhousie University
Halifax, Nova Scotia   Canada B3H 4H7

T 902 494 1874   medicine.admissions@dal.ca

**Admissions:** http://admissions.medicine.dal.ca

## General Information

Dalhousie University, a privately endowed institution founded in 1838, established the Faculty of Medicine in 1868. The main responsibility of the Faculty of Medicine is to the three Maritime Provinces of Canada (Nova Scotia, New Brunswick, and Prince Edward Island), which have a population of 1.7 million. The teaching hospitals located in the immediate vicinity of the medical school have a total of 2,300 beds covering inpatient and outpatient services in all branches of medicine.

## Mission Statement

The Faculty of Medicine, Dalhousie University, strives to benefit society through equal commitment to exemplary patient care, education and the discovery and advancement of knowledge. We aim to create and maintain a learning and research environment of national and international stature, enabling our graduates and us to serve the health needs of the Maritime Provinces and Canada.

## Curricular Highlights

**Community Service Requirement**: Optional.

**Research/Thesis Requirement:** Optional.

Dalhousie aims to provide a basic education that would permit a graduate to enter any branch of postgraduate training. Medicine One and Two begin in early September and extend through May. Medicine Three begins in late August/early September and ends the following September. Medicine Four begins in late September and extends until the following May. In the first year, students have extensive patient contact hours, with great emphasis on the development of clinical skills. During the first two years, students work in small groups with a tutor. The curriculum is organized around clinical problems to provide an integrated context for students to learn both basic and clinical science, and to begin the development of clinical reasoning skills. The third and fourth years are predominantly clinical, with third year comprised of 12-week units in the major disciplines. The fourth year is arranged with initial blocks of elective time. Students finish with a unit in Continuing and Preventive Care. Dalhousie offers post-graduate medical trainees university-arranged and university-supervised clinical training which meets national accreditation standards. In all provinces with the exception of Quebec, the basis for licensure for the majority of trainees in a postgraduate training program affiliated with a CACMS/LCME medical school is successful completion of the two-part Medical Council of Canada Qualifying Examination (MCCQE), plus certification by either the College of Family Physicians of Canada or the Royal College of Physicians and Surgeons of Canada.

## Selection Factors

Sources of information and factors considered by the Admissions Committee include academic requirements, ability as judged on university records and on the MCAT, confidential assessments received from referees of the applicant's choice and from any others the committee may wish to consult, interviews (selected applicants only), and place of residence. Detailed comments and explanations on these selection factors may be obtained in the Faculty of Medicine Calendar. Dalhousie does not discriminate on the basis of race, sex, creed, national origin, age, or handicap.

## Regional/Satellite Campuses

The New Brunswick-based program will admit thirty students each year  and the admission requirements are exactly the same as the Dalhousie MD program in Halifax  except that all applicants to the New Brunswick program must meet the residency criteria to be considered a resident of New Brunswick.

## Application Process and Requirements 2012–2013

**Primary application service:** School specific
**Earliest filing date:** July 1, 2011
**Latest filing date:** August 15, 2011

**Secondary application required:** No
**Sent to:** n/a
**URL:** n/a
**Fee:** No   **Waiver available:** n/a
**Earliest filing date:** n/a
**Latest filing date:** n/a

**MCAT® required:** Yes
**Latest MCAT® considered:** August 2011
**Oldest MCAT® considered:** August 2006

**Early Decision Program:** School does not have EDP
**Applicants notified:** n/a
**EDP available for:** n/a

**Regular acceptance notice —**
**Earliest date:** December 15, 2011
**Latest date:** Until class is full
**Applicant's response to acceptance offer —**
**Maximum time:** Two weeks

**Requests for deferred entrance considered:** Yes

**Deposit to hold place in class:** Yes
**Deposit — In-Province:** $1,000
**Out-of-Province:** $1,000
**Deposit due:** With response to acceptance offer.
**Applied to tuition:** Yes
**Deposit refundable:** No
**Refundable by:** n/a

**Estimated number of new entrants:** 108
**EDP:** n/a, special program: n/a

**Start month/year:** September 2012

**Interview format:** Multiple mini-interviews (MMI). No regional interviews are available. Video interviews are not available.

## Preparatory Programs

**Postbaccalaureate Program:** No

**Summer Program:** No

## 2010–2011 First Year Class

|  | In-Province | Out-of-Province | International |
|---|---|---|---|
| Applications | 270 | 364 | 0 |
| Interviewed | 270 | 80 | 0 |
| Matriculated | n/r | n/r | 0 |

**Total Matriculants: n/r**     **Total Enrollment: 410**

## Financial Information

|  | In-Province | Out-of-Province |
|---|---|---|
| Total Cost of Attendance | n/r | n/r |
| Tuition and Fees | n/r | n/r |
| Other (incl. living expenses) | n/r | n/r |
| Health Insurance (can be waived) | n/r | n/r |

**Average 2010 Graduate Indebtedness: n/r**
**% of Enrolled Students Receiving Aid: n/r**

# McMaster University, Michael G. DeGroote School of Medicine

## Hamilton, Ontario

ON

Michael G. DeGroote School of Medicine
McMaster University, MD Admissions, MDCL 3104
1200 Main Street West
Hamilton, Ontario   Canada L8N 3Z5

**T** 905 525 9140 x22235   mdadmit@mcmaster.ca

**Admissions:** www.fhs.mcmaster.ca/mdprog/admissions/admissions.htm

## General Information

The Faculty of Health Sciences at McMaster University offers programs in health sciences education, including undergraduate and post-graduate medical education. The clinical programs use the teaching hospital and extensive ambulatory facilities of the McMaster Division of the Hamilton Health Sciences Corporation, but they also involve clinical teaching units at the major Hamilton hospitals and surrounding community health care centers.

## Mission Statement

"Together, Advancing Health Through Learning and Discovery."

## Curricular Highlights

**Community Service Requirement:** Optional.

**Research/Thesis Requirement:** Optional.

The three-year M.D. program at McMaster uses an approach to learning that will apply throughout a physician's career. The components have been organized in a logical manner, with early exposure to patients. Flexibility is ensured to allow for the variety of backgrounds and career goals. Graduates of McMaster's Medical Program will have developed the knowledge, ability, and attitudes necessary to qualify for further education in any medical career. The goals for students include the following: the development of competency in problem-based learning and problem-solving, the development of personal characteristics and attitudes compatible with effective health care, the development of clinical and communication skills, and the development of the skills to be a lifelong, self-directed learner and self-reflective practitioner. To achieve these objectives, students are introduced to patients within the first Medical Foundation block of the curriculum. They are presented with a series of tutorial cases and questions requiring the understanding of principles and data collection. Much of the students' learning occurs within the small-group tutorial. Faculty members serve as tutors or sources of expert knowledge. The medical program is arranged as a preclerkship sequence of five Medical Foundations followed by clerkship. A Professional Competencies curriculum runs horizontally across the Foundations and into the clerkship. There are elective opportunities, both in block periods and horizontal electives taken concurrently. The clerkship emphasizes the clinical application of concepts learned in the earlier Foundations and consists of experience in inpatient and ambulatory settings. These include internal medicine, family medicine, emergency medicine, surgery, psychiatry, obstetrics-gynecology, anesthesia, and pediatrics. Students will have the opportunity to work in both teaching hospital and community hospital environments.

## Selection Factors

Students and members of the community and faculty are involved in the assessment of applicants. The aim is to select students who not only have the necessary academic standards, but who also display characteristics that are deemed to be important for the study and practice of medicine. These include characteristics that suggest sensitivity to the needs of the community; sensitivity to the emotional, psychological, and physical aspects of patients; the ability to detect and solve problems; the ability to learn independently; the ability to function as a member of a small group; and the ability to plan one's career in a way that reflects the needs of the community. Applicants rating highest in academic achievement and in non-cognitive qualities will be invited to the interview. From these applicants, 203 students will be selected for three campuses.

## Regional/Satellite Campuses

Tutorial and clinical training opportunities exist at McMaster University and in community hospitals throughout Central West Ontario. Satellite campuses are now open in the Waterloo Region (28 students admitted/year) and Niagara region (28 students admitted/year).

## Application Process and Requirements 2012–2013

**Primary application service:** OMCAS
**Earliest filing date:** July 1, 2011
**Latest filing date:** September 15, 2011

**Secondary application required:** Yes
**Sent to:** OMSAS
**URL:** www.ouac.on.ca/omsas
**Fee:** Yes, $210   **Waiver available:** No
**Earliest filing date:** July 1, 2011
**Latest filing date:** September 15, 2011

**MCAT® required:** Yes
**Latest MCAT® considered:** September 2011
**Oldest MCAT® considered:** September 2006

**Early Decision Program:** School does not have EDP
**Applicants notified:** n/a
**EDP available for:** n/a

**Regular acceptance notice —**
**Earliest date:** May 15, 2011
**Latest date:** Until class is full
**Applicant's response to acceptance offer —**
**Maximum time:** Two weeks

**Requests for deferred entrance considered:** Yes

**Deposit to hold place in class:** Yes
**Deposit — In-Province:** $1,000
**Out-of-Province:** $1,000
**Deposit due:** With acceptance offer
**Applied to tuition:** Yes
**Deposit refundable:** No
**Refundable by:** Not refundable once offer is accepted

**Estimated number of new entrants:** 203
**EDP:** n/a special program: n/a

**Start month/year:** Late August 2012

**Interview format:** Multiple mini-interviews (MMI). No regional interviews are available. Video interviews are not available.

## Preparatory Programs

**Postbaccalaureate Program:** No

**Summer Program:** No

## 2010–2011 First Year Class

|  | In-Province | Out-of-Province | International |
|---|---|---|---|
| Applications | 2,979 | 762 | 44 |
| Interviewed | 477 | 48 | 1 |
| Matriculated | 194 | 9 | 1 |

**Total Matriculants: 204**   **Total Enrollment: 553**

## Financial Information

|  | In-Province | Out-of-Province |
|---|---|---|
| Total Cost of Attendance | $24,567 | $112,282 |
| Tuition and Fees | $21,567 | $109,282 |
| Other (incl. living expenses) | n/r | n/r |
| Health Insurance (can be waived) | n/r | n/r |

**Average 2010 Graduate Indebtedness: $120,000**
**% of Enrolled Students Receiving Aid: 70%**

# Queen's University
# Faculty of Health Sciences
## Ottawa, Ontario

Admissions Office
Queen's University
School of Medicine
68 Barrie Street
Kingston Ontario   Canada K7L 3N6

T 613-533-3307     queensmd@queensu.ca

**Admissions:** http://meds.queensu.ca/undergraduate/prospective_students

## General Information

The educational program leading to the MD degree is central to the purpose of the Faculty. It must meet all the requirements for accreditation and prepare graduates for postgraduate training leading to licensure and certification by the College of Family Physicians or the Royal College of Physicians and Surgeons. Its special strengths are related to the opportunities for close, personal interaction between students and faculty members and for students to obtain particularly relevant, extensive, hands-on clinical experience under supervision, especially in ambulatory settings. There is great potential for students to benefit from greater integration of the clinical and basic sciences in the curriculum and from increased collaboration in education among the clinical disciplines.

## Mission Statement

The mission of Queen's Medicine is to advance our tradition of preparing excellent physicians and leaders in health care. We embrace a spirit of inquiry and innovation in education and research.

## Curricular Highlights

**Community Service Requirement:** Optional.

**Research/Thesis Requirement:** Optional.

The educational program leading to the MD degree is central to the purpose of the Faculty. It must meet all the requirements for accreditation and prepare graduates for postgraduate training leading to licensure and certification by the College of Family Physicians or the Royal College of Physicians and Surgeons. Its special strengths are related to the opportunities for close, personal interaction between students and faculty members and for students to obtain particularly relevant, extensive, hands-on clinical experience under supervision, especially in ambulatory settings. There is great potential for students to benefit from greater integration of the clinical and basic sciences in the curriculum and from increased collaboration in education among the clinical disciplines.

## Selection Factors

Students are selected on the basis of a strong academic record and assessment of personal characteristics considered to be most appropriate for the study of medicine at Queen's University and for the subsequent practice of medicine. Candidates meeting the academic requirements are then assessed based on confidential letters of reference, the autobiographic sketch, and the personal interview. The Admissions Committee does not give preference to applicants who have studied in any particular university program nor any particular level of training. Place of residence and location of the university where studies have been undertaken are not criteria in selection. Age, gender, race, and religion are not factors considered in the selection process.

## Information about Diversity Programs

Queen's University is committed to diversity within its student body. To that end, financial assistance options are provided to students of low socio-economic circumstances. Additionally, Queen's accepts men and women from across Canada representing a wide range of backgrounds. As well, Queen's University recognizes the critical shortage of aboriginal physicians in Canada and the need to educate more aboriginal physicians to serve as role models and to address the health care needs of Canada's aboriginal people. To meet this need an alternate process for the assessment of aboriginal candidates has been implemented.

## Regional/Satellite Campuses

Clinical rotations occur in Kingston teaching hospitals and in affiliated regional sites in Southeastern Ontario.

## Application Process and Requirements 2012–2013

**Primary application service:** OMSAS
**Earliest filing date:** July 2011
**Latest filing date:** October 1, 2011

**Secondary application required:** No
**Sent to:** n/a
**URL:** n/a
**Fee:** No   **Waiver available:** n/a
**Earliest filing date:** n/a
**Latest filing date:** n/a

**MCAT® required:** Yes
**Latest MCAT® considered:** September 2011
**Oldest MCAT® considered:** September 2007

**Early Decision Program:** School does not have EDP
**Applicants notified:** n/a
**EDP available for:** n/a

**Regular acceptance notice —**
**Earliest date:** May 5, 2012
**Latest date:** Until class is full
**Applicant's response to acceptance offer —**
**Maximum time:** Two weeks

**Requests for deferred entrance considered:** Yes

**Deposit to hold place in class:** Yes
**Deposit — In-Province:** $1,050
**Out-of-Province:** $1,050
**Deposit due:** With response to a firm acceptance
**Applied to tuition:** Yes
**Deposit refundable:** No
**Refundable by:** n/a

**Estimated number of new entrants:** 100
**EDP:** n/a, special program: n/a

**Start month/year:** September 2012

**Interview format:** Multiple mini-interviews (MMI). No regional interviews are available. Video interviews are not available.

## Preparatory Programs

**Postbaccalaureate Program:** No

**Summer Program:** No

## 2010–2011 First Year Class

|  | In-Province | Out-of-Province | International |
|---|---|---|---|
| Applications | 3,300 | n/a | n/a |
| Interviewed | 700 | n/a | n/a |
| Matriculated | 100 | n/a | n/a |

**Total Matriculants: 100     Total Enrollment: 400**

## Financial Information

|  | In-Province | Out-of-Province |
|---|---|---|
| Total Cost of Attendance | $160,000 | $160,000 |
| Tuition and Fees | $18,228 | $18,228 |
| Other (incl. living expenses) | $20,000 | $20,000 |
| Health Insurance (can be waived) | n/r | n/r |

**Average 2010 Graduate Indebtedness: n/r**
**% of Enrolled Students Receiving Aid: n/r**

# University of Ottawa
# Faculty of Medicine

Ottawa, Ontario

Admissions, University of Ottawa
Faculty of Medicine
451 Smyth Road
Ottawa, Ontario Canada K1H 8M5
**T** 613 562 5409   admissmd@uottawa.ca
**Admissions:** www.uottawa.ca/prospective

## General Information

The University of Ottawa received its charter from the province of Ontario in 1866. It was founded by the Missionary Oblates of Mary Immaculate, who were its administrators until 1965, when important structural reforms were introduced through an act of the legislative assembly of the province of Ontario. The management, discipline, and control of the university are free from the restrictions and control of any outside body, whether lay or religious. The Faculty of Medicine was established in 1945.

## Mission Statement

We explore, we learn, we care. We develop society's leaders who improve the health of Canadians and communities worldwide. We do this through the integration of education, research, patient care, and technology in an inclusive environment, in both official languages.

## Curricular Highlights

**Community Service Requirement:** Optional.

**Research/Thesis Requirement:** Optional.

Students acquire the knowledge, skills and attitudes they need to recognize, understand and apply effective, efficient strategies for the prevention and management of the most common and most severe health problems. Emphasis is placed on self-learning; principles and facts are learned in a multidisciplinary fashion, in the context of clinical problems. Whole-class lectures and seminars are used to discuss basic concepts, explore new developments and provide overviews of the biomedical sciences fundamental to the practice of medicine. Training occurs in ambulatory, primary, secondary and tertiary settings, and the students function as members of the medical team in collaboration with other health professionals. The training fosters trust and compassion, communication skills, ethical professional conduct and patient advocacy. The program is scheduled over four calendar years and is divided into two sections. Pre-clerkship includes 64 weeks of study of essential biomedical principles and consists of six multidisciplinary units. The second section, of two calendar years duration is the clerkships and includes core rotations in, Internal Medicine, Surgery, Pediatrics, Obstetrics & Gynecology, Psychiatry, Family Medicine, acute care as well as mandatory selective. A period of eighteen weeks is available for elective study in fourth year. All students must also complete a month in a rural setting.

## Selection Factors

Academic excellence, the detailed autobiographical sketch, and interview rating are the main selection factors used. Academics are measured by an assessment of marks and by a comparison of the applicant's academic record with those of the other applicants. No preference is given to one academic program over another. The selection is not made by quota. No candidate will be admitted without an interview. It is highly desirable that the candidate who has a broad exposure to biology and physical sciences also have a broad exposure to the arts, humanities, and social sciences. Sex, race, age, religion, and socioeconomic status play no part in the selection process.

## Information about Diversity Programs

In 2005, the Faculty established a dedicated admissions program for candidates of Aboriginal ancestry as part of its mission to improve access to better health care for Aboriginal peoples and to better serve society's needs.

## Application Process and Requirements 2012–2013

**Primary application service:** AMCAS®
**Earliest filing date:** July 2011
**Latest filing date:** September 15, 2011

**Secondary application required:** No
**Sent to:** n/a
**URL:** n/a
**Fee:** No   **Waiver available:** n/a
**Earliest filing date:** n/a
**Latest filing date:** n/a

**MCAT® required:** No
**Latest MCAT® considered:** n/a
**Oldest MCAT® considered:** n/a

**Early Decision Program:** School does not have EDP
**Applicants notified:** n/a
**EDP available for:** n/a

**Regular acceptance notice —**
**Earliest date:** May 13, 2012
**Latest date:** Until class is full
**Applicant's response to acceptance offer —**
**Maximum time:** Two weeks

**Requests for deferred entrance considered:** Yes

**Deposit to hold place in class:** Yes
**Deposit — In-Province:** $1,000
**Out-of-Province:** n/a
**Deposit due:** With acceptance
**Applied to tuition:** Yes
**Deposit refundable:** No
**Refundable by:** n/a

**Estimated number of new entrants:** 168
**EDP:** n/a, special program: 12

**Start month/year:** September 2012

**Interview format:** Semi-structured, 45-minute interviews. No regional interviews are available. Video interviews are not available.

### Preparatory Programs

**Postbaccalaureate Program:** No

**Summer Program:** No

## 2010–2011 First Year Class

|  | In-Province | Out-of-Province | International |
|---|---|---|---|
| Applications | 2,631 | 1,007 | n/a |
| Interviewed | 573 | n/a | n/a |
| Matriculated | 130 | 34 | n/a |

**Total Matriculants: 164**   **Total Enrollment: 632**

## Financial Information

|  | In-Province | Out-of-Province |
|---|---|---|
| Total Cost of Attendance | n/r | n/r |
| Tuition and Fees | $18,407 | n/r |
| Other (incl. living expenses) | $432 | n/r |
| Health Insurance (can be waived) | $180 | n/r |

**Average 2010 Graduate Indebtedness: n/r**
**% of Enrolled Students Receiving Aid: n/r**

# University of Toronto Faculty of Medicine

## Toronto, Ontario

University of Toronto, Faculty of Medicine
Medical Sciences Building, Room 2135
1 King's College Circle
Toronto, Ontario   Canada M5S 1A8

**T** 416 978 7928    medicine.admiss@utoronto.ca

**Admission:** www.md.utoronto.ca/admissions.htm

### General Information

Founded in 1843 as a school of medicine, the University of Toronto's Faculty of Medicine is an integral component of one of North America's largest health science complexes. The Faculty is part of a network of ten fully affiliated and nineteen partially affiliated teaching hospitals and health-care sites, as well as a myriad of community-based health units. With a catchment population of close to five million people, these offer students access to a broad spectrum of educational experience, and an extraordinary environment for clinical care, research, and education.

### Mission Statement

We prepare future health leaders, contribute to our communities, and improve the health of individuals and populations through the discovery, application and communication of knowledge.

### Curricular Highlights

**Community Service Requirement:** Required. Community placement during a longitudinal course.

**Research/Thesis Requirement:** Optional.

Our M.D. program is four years in length, with curriculum provided on two University of Toronto campuses, one in downtown Toronto and one in Mississauga. The two-year pre-clerkship phase consists of five sequential multidisciplinary block courses. Lectures, seminars and laboratory exercises complement small-group, problem-based learning sessions. Additionally, two half-days per week are spent in community and clinical settings. During the clerkship, learning occurs on the wards and in ambulatory care units of the affiliated teaching hospitals in addition to community hospitals and physician offices. Students complete specific core clinical rotations, as well as 12 weeks in elective rotations. Each core rotation includes community experiences as well as elements of problem-based learning and basic science.

### Selection Factors

Applicants are judged upon both their academic and nonacademic records. A maximum of seven places will be offered to applicants with student visas. Applicants must have completed at least one full-course equivalent in social sciences, humanities, OR a second language, plus at least two full-course equivalents in any life sciences. Successful candidates must be deemed acceptable in all aspects of the admissions process, including cumulative grade point average, MCAT scores, reference letters, nonacademic factors, English proficiency, performance on interview, and any other criteria put forward by the faculty.

### Information About Diversity Programs

The Faculty of Medicine supports mentorship and role modeling for students from under-represented groups through a number of programs. These include summer mentorship programs organized by the Faculty in collaboration with the Association for the Advancement of Blacks in Health Sciences. These programs include both black and Aboriginal students.

### Regional/Satellite Campuses

Our M.D. program is centered on two University of Toronto campuses, one in downtown Toronto and one in Mississauga. Placements in all years of the medical program, including core clerkship placements, are not limited to the major teaching hospital sites and will extend into the Greater Toronto Area (GTA), including Peel, York and Durham regions. All students will be required to travel outside of areas served by local transit or hospital and University shuttle services in order to complete their studies.

## Application Process and Requirements 2012–2013

**Primary application service:** OMSAS
**Earliest filing date:** July 4, 2011
**Latest filing date:** September 15, 2011

**Secondary application required:** No
**Sent to:** n/a
**URL:** n/a
**Fee:** No    **Waiver available:** n/a
**Earliest filing date:** n/a
**Latest filing date:** n/a

**MCAT® required:** Yes
**Latest MCAT® considered:** September 2011
**Oldest MCAT® considered:** September 2006

**Early Decision Program:** School does not have EDP
**Applicants notified:** n/a
**EDP available for:** n/a

**Regular acceptance notice —**
**Earliest date:** May 15, 2012
**Latest date:** Until class is full
**Applicant's response to acceptance offer —**
**Maximum time:** Normally two weeks from date of offer.

**Requests for deferred entrance considered:** No

**Deposit to hold place in class:** Yes
**Deposit — In-Province:** $1,000
**Out-of-Province:** $1,000
**Deposit due:** With response to acceptance of offer.
**Applied to tuition:** Yes
**Deposit refundable:** No
**Refundable by:** n/a

**Estimated number of new entrants:** 259
**EDP:** n/a, special program: n/a

**Start month/year:** August 20, 2012

**Interview format:** Forty-five minute interview with faculty and student. No regional interviews are available. Video interviews are not available.

## Preparatory Programs

**Postbaccalaureate Program:** No

**Summer Program:** No

## 2010–2011 First Year Class

|  | In-Province | Out-of-Province | International |
|---|---|---|---|
| Applications | 3,069 | n/a | 39 |
| Interviewed | 521 | n/a | 3 |
| Matriculated | 248 | n/a | 2 |

**Total Matriculants: 250**       **Total Enrollment: 928**

## Financial Information

|  | Domestic | International |
|---|---|---|
| Total Cost of Attendance | $39,315 | $70,533 |
| Tuition and Fees | $19,833 | $51,051 |
| Other (incl. living expenses) | $19,482 | $19,482 |
| Health Insurance (can be waived) | n/a | n/a |

**Average 2010 Graduate Indebtedness: $88,885**
**% of Enrolled Students Receiving Aid: 82%**

# Northern Ontario School of Medicine
## Thunder Bay and Sudbury, Ontario

**West Campus**
955 Oliver Road, Thunder Bay, ON, P7B 5E1
**T** 807 766 7300

**East Campus**
935 Ramsey Lake Road, Sudbury, ON, P3E 2C6
**T** 705 675 4883

**Admissions:** admissions@nosm.ca

## General Information

The Northern Ontario School of Medicine is the first new medical school in Canada in the 21st century. It is the Faculty of Medicine of Laurentian University, Sudbury, and of Lakehead University, Thunder Bay. With main campuses in Thunder Bay and Sudbury, the school has multiple teaching and research sites distributed across Northern Ontario, including large and small communities.

## Mission Statement

The Northern Ontario School of Medicine (NOSM) is committed to the education of high quality physicians and health professionals, and to international recognition as a leader in distributed, learning-centerd, community-engaged education and research.

## Curricular Highlights

**Community Service Requirement:** Required.

**Research/Thesis Requirement:** Optional.

Grounded in Northern Ontario, our four-year M.D. program provides students with a unique mix of learning opportunities in a diverse range of sites, including Aboriginal and Francophone communities. The curriculum is highly integrated, with students undertaking most learning in small-group, patient-centered Case-Based Learning. The cases present complex real-life scenarios, which present people in their home/family/community context. In addition to small-group learning, students participate in hands-on practical classes, self-directed learning, and clinical education in a range of different health service and community settings. Through the mix of themes and different learning modalities, the program covers core curricula, ensuring that students gain a strong grounding in the basic medical sciences, the humanities, social and behavioral sciences, and clinical medicine.

## Selection Factors

Applications that meet the minimum requirement are assigned a score based on the grade point average, the autobiographic sketch and school submission questions, and context. Context is primarily based on place(s) of residence of one year or more. Advantage is given to those applicants from within Northern Ontario, rural and remote areas in the rest of Canada, and Aboriginal and Francophone applicants. Based on the total application score, the top-ranked candidates are invited to participate in the admission interviews. The final selection for admission is based on a combination of the total application and interview scores. Check our website *www.nosm.ca* for current information.

## Information About Diversity Programs

The aim is to have class profiles which reflect the demographics of the population of Northern Ontario. It is the intention of the Northern Ontario School of Medicine to maximize the recruitment of students who are from Northern Ontario and/or students who have a strong interest in and aptitude for practicing medicine in Northern urban, rural and remote communities. We are also committed to recruiting Aboriginal and Franco-Ontarian students.

## Regional/Satellite Campuses

While the majority of the first two years will be spent in either Thunder Bay or Sudbury, students will spend a month during the first year in an Aboriginal community. In the second year, there will be two placements of six weeks in rural and remote communities throughout Northern Ontario. The majority of third year will be spent in the small urban and large rural communities of Northern Ontario. The Clinical Clerkship in the 4th year is primarily in hospitals of Thunder Bay, Sudbury, and other large urban northern centers.

## Application Process and Requirements 2012–2013

**Primary application service:** School specific
**Earliest filing date:** 2011
**Latest filing date:** October 1, 2011

**Secondary application required:** No
**Sent to:** n/a
**URL:** n/a
**Fee:** No   **Waiver available:** n/a
**Earliest filing date:** n/a
**Latest filing date:** n/a

**MCAT® required:** No
**Latest MCAT® considered:** n/a
**Oldest MCAT® considered:** n/a

**Early Decision Program:** School does not have EDP
**Applicants notified:** n/a
**EDP available for:** n/a

**Regular acceptance notice —**
**Earliest date:** May 15, 2011
**Latest date:** Until class is full
**Applicant's response to acceptance offer —**
**Maximum time:** Two weeks

**Requests for deferred entrance considered:** Yes

**Deposit to hold place in class:** Yes
**Deposit — In-Province:** $1,000
**Out-of-Province:** $1,000
**Deposit due:** Two weeks after offer date
**Applied to tuition:** Yes
**Deposit refundable:** No
**Refundable by:** n/a

**Estimated number of new entrants:** 64
**EDP:** n/a, special program: n/a

**Start month/year:** August 2012

**Interview format:** Multiple mini-interviews (MMI) which take place at both campuses. No regional interviews are available. Video interviews are not available.

## Preparatory Programs

**Postbaccalaureate Program:** No

**Summer Program:** No

## 2010–2011 First Year Class

|  | In-Province | Out-of-Province | International |
|---|---|---|---|
| Applications | 1,748 | 0 | 0 |
| Interviewed | 393 | 0 | 0 |
| Matriculated | 64 | 0 | 0 |

**Total Matriculants: 64**       **Total Enrollment: 64**

## Financial Information

|  | In-Province | Out-of-Province |
|---|---|---|
| Total Cost of Attendance | n/r | n/a |
| Tuition and Fees | $17,920 | n/a |
| Other (incl. living expenses) | n/r | n/a |
| Health Insurance (can be waived) | n/r | n/a |

**Average 2010 Graduate Indebtedness: n/r**
**% of Enrolled Students Receiving Aid: n/r**

# The University of Western Ontario
# Faculty of Medicine and Dentistry
## London, Ontario

Admissions and Student Affairs
Schulich School of Medicine and Dentistry
The University of Western Ontario
London, Ontario   Canada  N6A 5C1

**T** 519 661 3744
admissions.medicine@schulich.uwo.ca

**Admissions:** www.schulich.uwo.ca/admissions/
medicine

## General Information

The Schulich School of Medicine & Dentistry at The University of Western Ontario has a long tradition of excellence, beginning with the founding of the medical school in 1881. Home to more than 1,800 faculty and 2,700 students in medicine, dentistry, medical sciences, graduate and postgraduate training, Western is one of Canada's oldest post-secondary institutions and is committed to providing the best student experience among Canada's leading research-intensive universities.

## Mission Statement

The Schulich School of Medicine & Dentistry provides outstanding education within a research-intensive environment where tomorrow's physicians, dentists, and health researchers learn to be socially responsible leaders in the advancement of human health.

## Curricular Highlights

**Community Service Requirement:** Optional.

**Research/Thesis Requirement:** Optional.

The Doctor of Medicine program is offered from two sites — London and Windsor, Ontario. A section of each year's class will complete all of their academic studies on the campus of the University of Windsor and graduate from The University of Western Ontario. Curriculum and clinical training will be equivalent at both sites. The undergraduate curriculum is patient-centered in content and student-centered in delivery. It is designed to provide students with an opportunity to acquire the knowledge, skills, and attitudes required to advance to postgraduate training leading to clinical practice, research and other medical careers. The format is a blend of lectures, laboratory experience, small-group learning sessions, and supervised clinical experiences.

The curriculum in first and second year provides students with solid grounding in the basic and clinical sciences. System-based courses include: Introduction to Medicine, Blood, Digestive System & Nutrition, Emergency Care, Endocrine & Metabolism, Heart & Circulation, Infection & Immunity, the Musculoskeletal System, Respiration & Airways, Neurosciences, Eye & Ear, Psychiatry & Behavioral Sciences, and Reproductive & Urinary Systems. Students are also introduced to Community Health and have numerous opportunities for community involvement. The Clinical Methods courses span two years with patient contact beginning in the first year. During third year Clerkships, students become active members of clinical care teams in family medicine, medicine, obstetrics and gynecology, pediatrics, psychiatry, and surgery. Under faculty and senior In-Province supervision, clerks are given graded responsibility in the diagnosis, investigation, and management of patients in hospital, clinic, and outpatient settings. All third-year students are required to complete a community Clinical Clerkship in a region outside London or Windsor for a minimum of four weeks through Schulich's Southwestern Ontario Medical Education Network, to ensure students at all levels gain an understanding and experience of the practice of medicine from both a rural/regional and a tertiary care/urban perspective. Fourth-year Clinical Electives are arranged entirely by the student in any area of medicine. After completion of the Clinical Electives, students return in the Winter term for the Transition Period to complete advanced integrative basic and clinical science topics.

## Selection Factors

Admission consideration is based on academic achievement, MCAT scores, and a personal interview score. Only those applicants deemed competitive will be selected for an interview.

## Information About Diversity Programs

Schulich Medicine has designated three seats in each entering class for First Nations, Metis, and Inuit students who provide proof of Indigenous status or ancestral Indigenous origin.

## Regional/Satellite Campuses

Schulich Medicine operates one program at two campuses; The University of Western Ontario and the University of Windsor.

## Application Process and Requirements 2012–2013

**Primary application service:** OMSAS
**Earliest filing date:** July 2011 (via OMSAS)
**Latest filing date:** September, 2011

**Secondary application required:** No
**Sent to:** n/a
**URL:** n/a
**Fee:** No   **Waiver available:** n/a
**Earliest filing date:** n/a
**Latest filing date:** n/a

**MCAT® required:** Yes
**Latest MCAT® considered:** September 2011
**Oldest MCAT® considered:** September 2006

**Early Decision Program:** School does not have EDP
**Applicants notified:** n/a
**EDP available for:** n/a

**Regular acceptance notice —**
**Earliest date:** May 2012
**Latest date:** Until class is full
**Applicant's response to acceptance offer —**
**Maximum time:** Two weeks after offer is made

**Requests for deferred entrance considered:** Yes

**Deposit to hold place in class:** Yes
**Deposit — In-Province:** $1,000
**Out-of-Province:** $1,000
**Deposit due:** As soon as affirmative response is submitted electronically through OMSAS
**Applied to tuition:** Yes
**Deposit refundable:** No
**Refundable by:** n/a

**Estimated number of new entrants:** 171
**EDP:** n/a, special program: n/a

**Start month/year:** September 2012

**Interview format:** One physician, one community person, one senior medical student. No regional interviews are available. Video interviews are not available.

## Preparatory Programs

**Postbaccalaureate Program:** No

**Summer Program:** Yes,
www.meduquestwestern.ca/
Kathy Van Dinther, (519) 661-2111 ext 22147,
kathy.vandinther@schulich.uwo.ca

## 2010–2011 First Year Class

|  | In-Province | Out-of-Province | International |
|---|---|---|---|
| Applications | 1,784 | 588 | n/a |
| Interviewed | 353 | 74 | n/a |
| Matriculated | 161 | 10 | n/a |

**Total Matriculants: 171**   **Total Enrollment: 619**

## Financial Information

|  | In-Province | Out-of-Province |
|---|---|---|
| Total Cost of Attendance | n/r | n/r |
| Tuition and Fees | $18,666 | $18,666 |
| Other (incl. living expenses) | $16,550 | $16,550 |
| Health Insurance (can be waived) | n/r | n/r |

**Average 2010 Graduate Indebtedness: $70,500**
**% of Enrolled Students Receiving Aid: 74%**

# Laval University Faculty of Medicine
## Quebec, Quebec

QC

Admissions Committee
Université Laval
Faculty of Medicine
1050 Avenue de la Médecine
Quebec, Quebec   Canada  G1V 0A6

**T** 418-656-2131 x2492    admission@fmed.ulaval.ca

**Admissions:** www.reg.ulaval.ca/p4.html

## General Information

Université Laval was established by a Royal Charter in 1852, named after Monseigneur de Laval, first bishop of Quebec. For more than 150 years, the medical school has been dedicated to the formation of health professionals through high standard teaching programs and research activities. The clinical teaching is provided through a network of affiliated health institutions. There is a University Health Service for students, as well as vocational guidance and counseling services.

## Mission Statement

The overall goal of the program is to assure a theoretical and clinical formation which prepares students for practicing medicine competently in a contemporary health system, with emphasis on an approach which is scientific, ethical, global, and humanistic.

## Curricular Highlights

**Community Service Requirement:** Optional.

**Research/Thesis Requirement:** Optional.

The curriculum aims to prepare students to undertake any career in medicine. During the first two years, the program provides early introduction to clinical problems and interdepartmental teaching by both basic science and clinical faculty. This part of the curriculum is designed to be flexible and can be spread over three calendar years. The basic clinical clerkships are given in the fourth and fifth years and provide a basic exposure to each major clinical discipline, including family medicine. Both faculty and students monitor the curriculum.

## Selection Factors

Preference is given to applicants from the province of Quebec. Admission requirements for application from Quebec colleges (CEGEP) and universities include a standardized autobiographical note and Multiple Mini Interviews, a subjective structured admission tool with 12 short-interview stations. This test evaluates different personal characteristics of the candidates. A few outstanding French-speaking candidates are admitted from other Canadian provinces and the United States. These candidates are selected on the basis of scholastic achievement, interview, and curriculum vitae. Sex, race, religion, age, and socioeconomic status are not considered in the selection process.

## Information About Diversity Programs

Our School of Medicine, associated with other Quebec medical schools, has a program focused on integrating more aboriginal students with four dedicated seats each year. They are supported all along their medical formation. We facilitate the access of students from certain regional areas and from different socio-economical backgrounds. It has policies which valorizes diversity in the student body and in the staff.

## Regional/Satellite Campuses

Students rotate among several general and specialized hospitals and affiliated ambulatory care centers. Locations are spread throughout the city and in several towns in the eastern and western parts of the province of Quebec.

## Application Process and Requirements 2012–2013

**Primary application service:** AMCAS®
**Earliest filing date:** November 15, 2011
**Latest filing date:** March 1, 2012 (Quebec colleges)
February 1, 2012 (all others)

**Secondary application required:** No
**Sent to:** n/a
**URL:** n/a
**Fee:** No    **Waiver available:** n/a
**Earliest filing date:** n/a
**Latest filing date:** n/a

**MCAT® required:** No
**Latest MCAT® considered:** n/a
**Oldest MCAT® considered:** n/a

**Early Decision Program:** School does not have EDP
**Applicants notified:** n/a
**EDP available for:** n/a

**Regular acceptance notice —**
**Earliest date:** May 7, 2012
**Latest date:** Until class is full
**Applicant's response to acceptance offer —**
**Maximum time:** Ten days after the offer

**Requests for deferred entrance considered:** No

**Deposit to hold place in class:** No
**Deposit — In-Province:** n/a
**Out-of-Province:** n/a
**Deposit due:** n/a
**Applied to tuition:** n/a
**Deposit refundable:** n/a
**Refundable by:** n/a

**Estimated number of new entrants:** 218
**EDP:** 0, special program: 20

**Start month/year:** September 2012

**Interview format:** Multiple mini-interviews (MMI) — 12 OSCE-style stations. No regional interviews are available. Video interviews are not available.

## Preparatory Programs

**Postbaccalaureate Program:** Yes, www.fmed.ulalal.ca
**Summer Program:** No

## 2010–2011 First Year Class

|  | In-Province | Out-of-Province | International |
|---|---|---|---|
| Applications | 1,943 | 72 | 108 |
| Interviewed | 574 | 10 | 4 |
| Matriculated | 221 | 5 | 2 |

**Total Matriculants: 228**      **Total Enrollment: 228**

## Financial Information

|  | In-Province | Out-of-Province |
|---|---|---|
| Total Cost of Attendance | $5,000 | $16,000 |
| Tuition and Fees | $1,800 | $12,000 |
| Other (incl. living expenses) | $15,000 | $15,000 |
| Health Insurance (can be waived) | n/r | $700 |

**Average 2010 Graduate Indebtedness: n/r**
**% of Enrolled Students Receiving Aid: 33%**

# McGill University Faculty of Medicine
## Montréal, Quebec

Office of Admissions, Equity and Diversity
of the Faculty of Medicine
3708 Peel Street
Montréal, Quebec   Canada H3A 1W9
**T** 514 398 3517   admissions.med@mcgill.ca
**Admissions:** www.mcgill.ca/medadmissions/

## General Information
McGill, in the heart of Montreal (Quebec) lies at the foundation, and stands at the avant-garde, of medicine and medical education in Canada, and is one of the country's leading research-intensive universities. With students coming to McGill from about 150 countries, our student body is the most internationally diverse of any medical-doctoral university in Canada.

## Mission Statement
The advancement of learning through teaching, scholarship, and service to society by offering the best education available; carrying out internationally-recognized scholarly activities; and providing service to society in those ways for which we are well-suited by virtue of our academic strengths. You can read more at *www.mcgill.ca/medicine/about/mission/*.

## Curricular Highlights
**Community Service Requirement:** Optional.

**Research/Thesis Requirement:** Optional.

Our curriculum prepares students to meet the highest standards of medical practice and professionalism, cultivating career-long excellence in whole-person care. Graduates function responsibly, in a supervised clinical setting, at the level of "undifferentiated" physicians. Basic sciences and scientific methodology are emphasized as pillars of medical knowledge. Students experience traditional lectures, small group learning, lab- and computer-based teaching. Physicianship & Physician Apprenticeship components give students a longitudinal approach to the art of the profession. Students benefit from a six-month introduction to clinical medicine giving them a strong hands-on approach before entering the clerkships.

## Selection Factors
Pre-selection is based on academic achievement evidenced by undergraduate GPA, MCAT, and science prerequisite GPA. Personal characteristics and accomplishments as evidenced in a personal narrative, C.V. and references are also used in pre-selection. All candidates are reviewed without regard to gender, age, ethnic, religious, linguistic, or socio-cultural/economic backgrounds. In general, successful applicants have an overall undergraduate degree GPA of 3.5+ and an MCAT total of 30+. Interviews are in Multiple Mini-Interview (MMI) format and are by invitation only, on-site (no off-site or teleconference interviews accepted). Final selection is largely based on interview results.

## Information About Diversity Programs
We are committed to pursuing our mission of social accountability, including a diverse student body and equity for under-represented groups, while maintaining a tradition of selecting students most apt for the challenges of medicine in the 21st century. The Faculty welcomes applications from students with diverse backgrounds, including students from underrepresented ethnic, cultural and racial groups as well as from all economic backgrounds. Residents of Quebec who self-identify as belonging to the Inuit, Cree, and Naskapi First Nations cultural groups may apply under the aegis of the special program for First Nations and Inuit applicants.

## Regional/Satellite Campuses
There are no regional or satellite campuses. A one-year regional integrated clerkship in the Gatineau area (near Ottawa, ON) is available.

## Application Process and Requirements 2012–2013

**Primary application service:** School specific
**Earliest filing date:** September 1, 2011
**Latest filing date — In-Province:** January 15, 2012
**Out-of-Province:** November 15, 2011

**Secondary application required:** No
**Sent to:** McGill online application system
**URL:** www.mcgill.ca/medicine/admissions/
**Fee:** Yes, $85   **Waiver available:** No
**Earliest filing date:** n/a
**Latest filing date:** n/a

**MCAT® required:** Yes
**Latest MCAT® considered:** September 2011
**Oldest MCAT® considered:** November 2006

**Early Decision Program:** School does not have EDP
**Applicants notified:** n/a
**EDP available for:** n/a

**Regular acceptance notice —**
**Earliest date:** March 2012
**Latest date:** Until class is full
**Applicant's response to acceptance offer —**
**Maximum time:** Two weeks

**Requests for deferred entrance considered:** Yes

**Deposit to hold place in class:** Yes
**Deposit — In-Province:** $500
**Out-of-Province:** $500
**Deposit due:** With response to acceptance offer
**Applied to tuition:** Yes
**Deposit refundable:** Yes
**Refundable by — In-Province:** May 15, 2012
**Out-of-Province:** June 15, 2012

**Estimated number of new entrants:** 187
**EDP:** n/a, special program: 7

**Start month/year:** Mid-August 2012

**Interview format:** Multiple Mini-Interviews (MMI) on-site. No regional interviews are available. Video interviews are not available.

## Preparatory Programs
**Postbaccalaureate Program:** No

**Summer Program:** No

## 2010–2011 First Year Class

|  | In-Province | Out-of-Province | International |
|---|---|---|---|
| Applications | 890 | 494 | 74 |
| Interviewed | 394 | 30 | 20 |
| Matriculated | 160 | 9 | 4 |

**Total Matriculants: 173**    **Total Enrollment: 701**

## Financial Information

|  | In-Province | International |
|---|---|---|
| Total Cost of Attendance | $30,130 | $53,140 |
| Tuition and Fees | $5,370 | $28,380 |
| Other (incl. living expenses) | n/r | n/r |
| Health Insurance (can be waived) | n/a | $591 |

**Average 2010 Graduate Indebtedness: $17,169**
**% of Enrolled Students Receiving Aid:** n/r

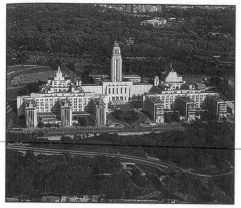

# Université de Montréal
# Faculty of Medicine
Montréal, Quebec

Comité d'admission — études médicales de 1er cycle
Université de Montréal Faculté de médecine
C.P. Box 6128, Succursale Center-Ville
Montréal, Quebec   Canada  H3C 3J7
**T** 514 343 6265    admission-md@umontreal.ca
**Admissions:** www.med.umontreal.ca/etudes/
programme _formation/doctorate_medicine/
admission.html

## General Information

The Faculty of Medicine of the Université de Montréal can be traced back to a school first established in Montreal in 1843 and incorporated in 1845 under the name of École de Médecine et de Chirurgie de Montréal. In 1891 the school merged with the Faculté de Médecine of the Montreal branch of l'Université Laval, which had been founded in 1877. In 1920, by an act of the Quebec legislature, the Montreal branch of l'Université Laval was granted its independence, and the school of medicine became known by its present name. All instruction is in French, and clinical instruction is carried out at 16 affiliated teaching hospitals and research centers.

## Mission Statement

The Faculty of Medicine of the Université de Montréal seeks through its undergraduate medical program to provide medical knowledge, clinical skills and professional attitudes so that students will be able to enter postgraduate training in family medicine or medical specialization, or fields related to research, teaching, or health care management.

## Curricular Highlights

**Community Service Requirement:** Optional.

**Research/Thesis Requirement:** Optional.

In September 1993, a new four-year curriculum came into effect. It consists of two years (70 weeks) of problem-based learning during which students are exposed to biomedical and psychosocial sciences basic to medicine. Courses are inter-disciplinary and system-based. Early introduction to clinical skills takes place in a continuous fashion throughout those two preclinical years. Clinical exposure begins with Year 1 combine with laboratory simulation. Forty-five hours of electives are mandatory during each of the first two years. The third and fourth years consist of an 80-week clerkship. In the new curriculum, formal lecturing is reduced to a minimum and replaced by active methods, especially problem-based learning and small-group discussion. A premedical year devoted to basic biological and behavioral sciences is restricted to students having just graduated from the provincial colleges of general and professional education (CEGEP). Students who have completed one to three years at the university level in others than biomedical fields are also eligible for the premedical year. Residency training in the teaching hospitals is under the responsibility of the Faculty of Medicine. Various courses and symposia are organized by the continuing medical education division.

## Selection Factors

Candidates accepted must be either Canadian citizens or landed immigrants, but due consideration is given to French-speaking applicants from other provinces of Canada. Selection of candidates is competitive and based on a global score derived from scholastic records and interviews. Interviews (Multiple Mini-Interviews), conducted on the site of the medical school, are granted to about one-half of the applicants on the basis of their scholastic records. This interview can be eliminatory. For candidates holding a Ph.D. degree, performance in research may constitute an important selection factor. No consideration is given to race, sex, creed, or age.

## Information About Diversity Programs

Since 2008, a yearly total of four positions are reserved for Quebec aboriginal students (First Nations and Inuit) in the Faculties of Medicine of Quebec.

## Regional/Satellite Campuses

Since 2004, there is a regional campus in the city of Trois-Rivières, located 125 kilometers (75 miles) east of Montreal. Each year, forty students start medical school on the Trois-Rivières campus, most of them at the pre-medical level. The curriculums at the Montréal campus and Trois-Rivières campus are identical. Clinical training is completed at community hospitals in the Mauricie region. A medical student can complete his entire undergraduate instruction at this decentralized rural campus.

## Application Process and Requirements 2012–2013

**Primary application service:** AMCAS®
**Earliest filing date:** December 1, 2011
**Latest filing date:** January 15, 2012 (March 1, 2012 for Quebec CEGEP students)

**Secondary application required:** No
**Sent to:** n/a
**URL:** n/a
**Fee:** n/a   **Waiver available:** n/a
**Earliest filing date:** n/a
**Latest filing date:** n/a

**MCAT® required:** No
**Latest MCAT® considered:** n/a
**Oldest MCAT® considered:** n/a

**Early Decision Program:** School does not have EDP
**Applicants notified:** n/a
**EDP available for:** n/a

**Regular acceptance notice —**
**Earliest date:** May 15, 2012
**Latest date:** Until class is full
**Applicant's response to acceptance offer —**
**Maximum time:** Two weeks or as specified in the offer

**Requests for deferred entrance considered:** No

**Deposit to hold place in class:** Yes
**Deposit — In-Province:** $200
**Out-of-Province:** $200
**Deposit due:** With response to acceptance offer
**Applied to tuition:** Yes
**Deposit refundable:** No
**Refundable by:** n/a

**Estimated number of new entrants:** 290
**EDP:** n/a, special program: n/a

**Start month/year:** August 2012

**Interview format:** Multiple mini-interviews (MMI). Regional interviews are available for Maritimes applicants only. Video interviews are not available.

## Preparatory Programs

**Postbaccalaureate Program:** No

**Summer Program:** No

## 2010–2011 First Year Class

|  | In-Province | Out-of-Province | International |
|---|---|---|---|
| Applications | 2,235 | 32 | 164 |
| Interviewed | 1,028 | 12 | 4 |
| Matriculated | 294 | 3 | 1 |

**Total Matriculants: 298    Total Enrollment: 1,308**

## Financial Information

|  | In-Province | Out-of-Province |
|---|---|---|
| Total Cost of Attendance | n/r | n/r |
| Tuition and Fees | $5,000 | $26,500 |
| Other (incl. living expenses) | $10,000 | $10,000 |
| Health Insurance (can be waived) | n/r | n/r |

**Average 2010 Graduate Indebtedness: n/r**
**% of Enrolled Students Receiving Aid: n/r**

# University of Sherbrooke
# Faculty of Medicine
## Sherbrooke, Quebec

Medical Admission Office,
University of Sherbrooke
Faculty of Medicine and Health Sciences
3001, 12e Avenue Nord
Sherbrooke, Quebec   Canada  J1H 5N4

**T** 819 564 5200   admission-med@usherbrooke.ca

**Admissions:** www.usherbrooke.ca/ doctorat_
medecine

## General Information

The Faculty admitted its first MD students in 1966. Recognized for its educational innovations it is engaged towards responding to the needs of commmunities it serses. The Faculty opened two outside campuses in 2006. Students complete the program either in the central campus in Sherbrooke (145 admissions) or in Moncton (25 admissions), or Saguenay (35 students). Postgraduate programs are available in most clinical disciplines.

## Mission Statement

Improve health and well-being of people and populations through education, research, clinical services, and knowledge transfer.

## Curricular Highlights

**Community Service Requirement:** Optional.

**Research/Thesis Requirement:** No compulsory requirement.

The MD program is system intregrated and small-group problem bascd. Clerkship is offered throughout a network of primary to tertiary health care institutions located in urban, suburban, peripheral, rural and remote areas. Each student must spend at least 1/3 of its clerkship in community-based settings.

## Selection Factors

Cognitive abilities (previous academic records)and non-cognitive abilities (personality test and MMI). Admission groups are candidates from Quebec, New Brunswick, Atlantic and Western canadian provinces, Quebec First Nations and Inuits, Canadian Forces. Applicants must be fluent in both written and spoken French.

## Information about Diversity Programs

Diversity actions: Significant increase in admission (1998: 90; since 2006: more than 200). Numerous admissions groups. Consideration of non-cognitive factors. Special consideration for candidates coming from remote or rural areas: Implementation of outside campuses. Numerous data collected.

## Satellite Campuses/Facilities

Saguenay (150 000 people), a central city of a Quebec peripheral region, at 500 km from Sherbrooke. The main teaching hospital, has more than 500 beds and 3 community hospitals of the region collaborate to the program. Moncton, (150 000 people, 40% french speaking) a central city of the neighbor province of New Brunswick (750 000 people, 33% french speaking). The Georges L. Dumont hospital (250 beds) at Moncton is the main teaching hospital. Three community hospitals distributed in the province collaborate to the program.

## Application Process and Requirements 2012–2013

**Primary application service:** School specific
**Earliest filing date:** November 1, 2011
**Latest filing date:** March 1, 2012 for Quebec college students, January 15, 2012 for all others

**Secondary application required:** Yes
**Sent to:** Bureau de la registraire — Université de Sherbrooke
**URL:** www.usherbrooke.ca/doctorat_medecine/ admission
**Fee:** Yes, $70    **Waiver available:** No
**Earliest filing date:** n/a
**Latest filing date:** n/a

**MCAT® required:** No
**Latest MCAT® considered:** n/a
**Oldest MCAT® considered:** n/a

**Early Decision Program:** School does not have EDP
**Applicants notified:** n/a
**EDP available for:** n/a

**Regular acceptance notice —**
**Earliest date:** May 15, 2012
**Latest date:** Until class is full
**Applicant's response to acceptance offer —**
**Maximum time:** From 10 days to 3 hours at the end of the process.

**Requests for deferred entrance considered:** No

**Deposit to hold place in class:** Yes
**Deposit — In-Province:** $200
**Out-of-Province:** $200
**Deposit due:** With admission
**Applied to tuition:** Yes
**Deposit refundable:** Yes
**Refundable by:** September 15, 2012

**Estimated number of new entrants:** 210
**EDP:** n/a, special program: n/a

**Start month/year:** August 2012

**Interview format:** Multiple mini-interviews (MMI). Regional interviews are available in Moncton. Video interviews are available for international applicants only.

## Preparatory Programs
**Postbaccalaureate Program:** No

**Summer Program:** No

## 2010–2011 First Year Class

|  | In-Province | Out-of-Province | International |
|---|---|---|---|
| Applications | 1,872 | 114 | 67 |
| Interviewed | 814 | 86 | 4 |
| Matriculated | 180 | 31 | 2 |

**Total Matriculants: 213**     **Total Enrollment: 801**

## Financial Information

|  | In-Province | Out-of-Province |
|---|---|---|
| Total Cost of Attendance | $9,600 | $18,900-37,400 |
| Tuition and Fees | $5,000 | $10,500-29,000 |
| Other (incl. living expenses) | $700/month | |

**Average 2010 Graduate Indebtedness: $30,000**
**% of Enrolled Students Receiving Aid: 25%**

# University of Saskatchewan College of Medicine

Saskatoon, Saskatchewan

Admissions
University of Saskatchewan College of Medicine
A204 Health Sciences Building, 107 Wiggins Road
Saskatoon, Saskatchewan   Canada S7N 5E5

**T** 306 966 4030   med.admissions@usask.ca

**Admissions:** www.medicine.usask.ca/admissions

## General Information

The University of Saskatchewan began teaching medical students in a two-year medical sciences program in 1926. The present college was introduced in 1953, with a four-year curriculum leading to the M.D. degree. In 1968, the curriculum changed to five years with a one-year premedical university requirement. The curriculum reverted to a four-year program in 1988 with a minimum two-year premedical requirement. Clinical teaching is based at the Royal University, St. Paul's, and Saskatoon City Hospitals in Saskatoon, and the Plains Health Center and General Hospital in Regina. Students also complete rotations in Saskatchewan Health Regions. The class size is 84 students with future possible expansions to 100 students.

## Mission Statement

The College of Medicine is a departmentalized collegial unit of the University of Saskatchewan. The mission is to improve health through excellence in education, research, and clinical care.

## Curricular Highlights

**Community Service Requirement:** Optional.

**Research/Thesis Requirement:** Optional.

The College of Medicine provides a curriculum leading to the general professional education of the physician; graduates may select careers in family medicine, specialty practice, or research. The current curriculum was launched in the fall of 1997. Phase A (31 weeks) provides students with an overview of the basic science disciplines appropriate to the study of medicine, as well as an introduction to professional skills (including primary clinical skills) within the context of developing the patient-doctor relationship. This phase includes a two-week clinical experience done in one of the Saskatchewan Health Districts. Phase B (33 weeks) enables students to acquire specific knowledge in those subjects bridging the basic and clinical sciences and to enhance basic clinical skills. Phase C (15 weeks), enables learning of the principles and methods in core clinical knowledge and linking courses. Phase D (64 weeks) of clinical clerkships provides an opportunity to apply the knowledge, skills, and attitudes students have acquired to the management of patients. Provision is made for clinical electives. Learning in the basic and clinical sciences has been organized by body systems with a problem-solving emphasis.

## Selection Factors

The Admissions Committee considers academic ability and personal qualities assessed through scholastic records, letters of recommendation, and results of an interview. All eligible candidates are interviewed during a weekend in March.

## Information About Diversity Programs

There is an Aboriginal Access Program for Canadian residents of Aboriginal ancestry. For more information, contact the Admissions office.

## Setting

Our medical school is situated on 755 hectares of land, in the heart of the city of Saskatoon on the scenic bank of the South Saskatchewan River. Much of the original architecture remains from the University's opening in 1909, and greystone buildings ornamented with garrets and turrets are a monument of fine craftsmanship. The University of Saskatchewan has the largest collection of health sciences in Canada.

## Satellite Campuses/Facilities

The University of Saskatchewan College of Medicine has a distributive learning environment in which a number of clinical educational experiences take place in a number of Saskatchewan Health Regions and teaching hospitals. Students will be assigned to a core set of rotations centered either in the Saskatoon Health Region or in the Regina/Qu'Appelle Health Region.

## Application Process and Requirements 2012–2013

**Primary application service:** School specific
**Earliest filing date:** July 1, 2011
**Latest filing date:** October 31, 2011

**Secondary application required:** No
**Sent to:** n/a
**URL:** n/a
**Fee:** No   **Waiver available:** n/a
**Earliest filing date:** n/a
**Latest filing date:** n/a

**MCAT® required:** Yes
**Latest MCAT® considered:** September 2011
**Oldest MCAT® considered:** April 2007

**Early Decision Program:** School does not have EDP
**Applicants notified:** n/a
**EDP available for:** n/a

**Regular acceptance notice —**
**Earliest date:** May 13, 2011
**Latest date:** Until class is full
**Applicant's response to acceptance offer —**
**Maximum time:** Two weeks

**Requests for deferred entrance considered:** Yes

**Deposit to hold place in class:** Yes
**Deposit — In-of-Province:** $500  **Out-of-Province:** $500
**Deposit due:** With response to acceptance offer
**Applied to tuition:** Yes
**Deposit refundable:** No
**Refundable by:** n/a

**Estimated number of new entrants:** 84
**EDP:** n/a; special program: n/a

**Start month/year:** August 2012

**Interview format:** Multiple mini-interviews (MMI). No regional interviews are available. Video interviews are not available.

## Preparatory Programs

**Postbaccalaureate Program:** No

**Summer Program:** No

## 2010–2011 First Year Class

|  | In-Province | Out-of-Province | International |
|---|---|---|---|
| Applications | 370 | 478 | n/a |
| Interviewed | 283 | 56 | n/a |
| Matriculated | 80 | 4 | n/a |

**Total Matriculants: 84**   **Total Enrollment: 325**

## Financial Information

|  | In-Province | Out-of-Province |
|---|---|---|
| Total Cost of Attendance | n/r | n/r |
| Tuition and Fees | $12,973 | n/r |
| Other (incl. living expenses) | n/r | n/r |
| Health Insurance (can be waived) | n/r | n/r |

**Average 2010 Graduate Indebtedness: n/r**
**% of Enrolled Students Receiving Aid: n/r**

## Resources for Other Health Careers

1. **American Academy of Physician Assistants**
   950 North Washington Street
   Alexandria, VA 22314-1552
   (703) 836-2272;  (703) 684-1924
   *www.aapa.org*

2. **American Association of Colleges of Osteopathic Medicine**
   5550 Friendship Boulevard, Suite 310
   Chevy Chase, MD 20815-7231
   (301) 968-4100; *www.aacom.org*

3. **American Association of Colleges of Pharmacy**
   1727 King Street
   Alexandria, VA 22314-2815
   (703) 739-2330; *www.aacp.org*

4. **American Association of Colleges of Podiatric Medicine**
   15850 Crabbs Branch Way, Suite 320
   Rockville, MD 20855-4307
   (800) 922-9266; (301) 948-9760
   info@aacpm.org; *www.aacpm.org*

5. **American Association of Colleges of Nursing**
   One Dupont Circle, N.W., Suite 530
   Washington, D.C. 20036
   (202) 463-6930; (202) 785-8320
   *www.aacn.nche.edu*

6. **American Association of Dental Schools**
   1400 K Street, N.W., Suite 1100
   Washington, D.C. 20005
   (202) 289-7201; *www.adea.org*

7. **Association of American Veterinary Medical Colleges**
   1101 Vermont Avenue, N.W., Suite 301
   Washington, D.C. 20005-3521
   (202) 371-9195; *www.aavmc.org*

8. **Association of Schools and Colleges of Optometry**
   6110 Executive Boulevard, Suite 420
   Rockville, MD 20852
   (301) 231-5944
   *admini@opted.org; www.opted.org*

9. **Association of Schools of Public Health**
   1900 M Street NW, Suite 710
   Washington, DC 20036
   (202) 296-1099
   *info@asph.org; www.asph.org*

10. **ExploreHealthCareers.org**
    American Dental Education Association
    1400 K Street, NW, Suite 1100
    Washington, DC 20005
    (202) 289-7201; (347) 365-9253

## Publications for the Health Professions

1. **Autsin, L., What's Holding You Back? 8 Critical Choices for Women's Success**
$14.00
Basic Books, 2000
*www.perseusbooksgroup.com/basic/book_detail.jsp?isbn=046503263X*

2. **Bickel, J., Women in Medicine: Getting In, Growing & Advancing**
$41.95
Sage, 2000
(805) 499-9774
*www.sagepub.com/books/Book9436?*

3. **Educational Survival Skills Study Guide**
Free
Office of Statewide Health
Planning and Development
Health Professions Career
Opportunity Program
400 R Street, Suite 330
Sacramento, CA 95811-6213
*www.oshpd.ca.gov/HWDD/pdfs/StudySkills.pdf*

4. **Financial Advice and Health Careers Resources Directory for Students**
Free
Office of Statewide Health
Planning and Development
Health Professions Careers
Opportunity Program
400 R Street, Suite 330
Sacramento, CA 95811-6213
*www.oshpd.ca.gov/HWDD/pdfs/FinancialAdvice.pdf*

5. **The Journal for Minority Medical Students**
Free, published quarterly
Spectrum Unlimited
1194A Buckhead Crossing
Woodstock, GA 30189
(770) 852-2671, (504) 433-5040
*http://journalmms.com/*

6. **Kaltreider, Nancy B., Dilemmas of a Double Life, Women Balancing Careers and Relationship**
$49.95
Jason Aronson, Inc., 1997
(800) 462-6420;
*www.rowmanlittlefield.com/Catalog/*

7. **Minorities in Medicine: A Guide for Premedical Students**
Free
Office of Statewide Health Planning
and Development
Health Professions Career
Opportunity Program
400 R Street, Suite 330
Sacramento, CA 95811-6213
*www.oshpd.ca.gov/HWDD/pdfs/MinoritiesMedicine.pdf*

8. **More, E.S., Restoring the Balance: Women Physicians and the Profession of Medicine, 1850–1995.**
$34.00 paperback
Harvard University Press, 2000
*www.hup.harvard.edu*

9. **Need a Lift? College Financial Aid Handbook**
$1.95, available on CD-Rom
The American Legion
P.O. Box 36460
Indianapolis, IN 46236
888-453-4466;
*www.emblem.legion.org*

10. **The Student Guide**
U.S. Department of Education Federal
Student Aid Information Center
P.O. Box 84
Washington, D.C. 20044-0084
(800) 4-FED-AID, (800) 433-3243
*http://studentaid.ed.gov/students/attachments/siteresources/FundingEduBeyondHighSchool_0809.pdf*

11. **Time Management for Students**
Free
Office of Statewide Health
Planning and Development
Health Professions Career
Opportunity Program
400 R Street, Suite 330
Sacramento, CA 95811-6213
*www.oshpd.ca.gov/HWDD/pdfs/TimeManagement.pdf*

12. **Wear, D. (Ed), Women in Medical Education: An Anthology of Experience**
$52.50 hardcover, $29.95 paperback
SUNY Press, 1996
*www.sunypress.edu/details.asp?id=53512*

13. **The Young Scientist: A Career Guide for Underrepresented Science Graduates**
Free, published annually
Spectrum Unlimited
1194A Buckhead Crossing
Woodstock, GA 30189
(770) 852-2671, (504) 433-5040
*http://youngscientistmms.com/*

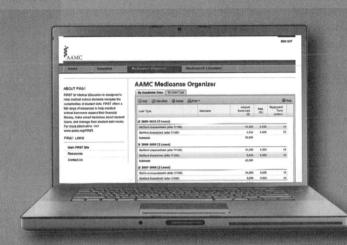

# Official MCAT® Preparation

First Edition
The Official Guide
to the MCAT® Exam

## Step 1: Learn the basics

### The Official Guide to the MCAT® Exam
Full of tips and data to help you plan,
along with 138 unique test items with solutions.
www.aamc.org/officialmcatguide

## Step 2: Get a baseline score

### Free MCAT Practice Test 3
Take a timed test to learn how you might perform
on the actual exam.
www.e-mcat.com

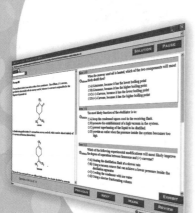

## Step 3: Study & track progress

### Seven additional practice tests
Take more timed tests to track improvements
and to study with real test items.
www.e-mcat.com

MedEdPORTAL
AAMC
Whoever said
"nothing in this world is free"
was wrong!
Why bother?
✔ Download from a bank of 1,000+ high-quality images and Flash animations covering health education.
✔ Experience 75+ virtual patients.
✔ Find study guides, test-taking strategies, clinical cards and self-testing resources.
✔ Discover medical education tutorials, lab guides and videos.
✔ Supplement your education for examinations and visualize difficult concepts.
Enough said. Get into it.
www.mededportal.org
MedEdPORTAL® is a program of the Association of American Medical Colleges
In partnership with the American Dental Education Association